Democracy Redefined

For Irene and Owen Fiss
Role models for a better century

Democracy Redefined

Michel Chiha and the Lebanese Constitution

Chibli Mallat

EDINBURGH
University Press

Edinburgh University Press is one of the leading university presses in the UK. Publishing new research in the arts and humanities, EUP connects people and ideas to inspire creative thinking, open new perspectives and shape the world we live in. For more information, visit www.edinburghuniversitypress.com.

Edinburgh University Press Ltd
13 Infirmary Street, Edinburgh EH1 1LT

Typeset in 11/15 EB Garamond by
Cheshire Typesetting Ltd, Cuddington, Cheshire
Printed and bound in the UK using 100% renewable electricity by
CPI Group (UK) Ltd

A CIP record for this book is available from the British Library

ISBN 978 1 3995 5270 7 (hardback)
ISBN 978 1 3995 5271 4 (webready PDF)
ISBN 978 1 3995 5272 1 (epub)

FONDATION
MICHEL
CHIHA

EU Authorised Representative:
Easy Access System Europe
Mustamäe tee 50, 10621 Tallinn, Estonia
gpsr.requests@easproject.com

MIX
Paper | Supporting responsible forestry
FSC® C013604
FSC www.fsc.org

This book is printed using paper from well-managed forests, recycling and other controlled sources

Contents

Expanded Table of Contents vii
List of Tables xi
Preface xii
Acknowledgements xv
Transliteration xviii
Abbreviations and Chiha-related Primary Sources xix

1 Orientation: Two Centuries of Institutional Communalism in Lebanon 1

PART ONE COMMUNALISM AND THE BIRTH OF ELECTIONS

2 The Birth of Representative Communalism: From Simqaniyya (1697) to the Beirut Consultative Council (1834) 15

3 The Entrenchment of Communalism and the Birth of the Electoral Principle (1840–1920) 42

PART TWO THE LEBANESE CONSTITUTION OF 1926

4 The Constitution of 1926: Reconstructing the Timeline 75

5 The Constitution of 1926: Structure and Inspiration 110

6 Building Constitutional Blocks: The Communitarian Straitjacket 141

7 Building Constitutional Blocks: Modern Constitutionalism 163

PART THREE CHIHA AFTER THE CONSTITUTION

8 The Constitution Undermined 195

9 Chiha's Worldview 222

10 Chiha's Nation 251

PART FOUR CONSTITUTIONALISM AND GROUP REPRESENTATION

11 Lebanese Constitutionalism and the Political-Theological Middle East 277

12 Constitutional Frontiers: The Lebanese Constitution and the World 307

13 Democracy Redefined 330

14 Epilogue 361

General Bibliography 365

Index 383

Expanded Table of Contents

List of Tables xi
Preface xii
Acknowledgements xv
Transliteration xviii
Abbreviations and Chiha-related Primary Sources xix

1 Orientation: Two Centuries of Institutional Communalism in Lebanon 1
A Terminological Detour 2
Synopsis: From Communalism to a New Definition of Democracy 10

PART ONE COMMUNALISM AND THE BIRTH OF ELECTIONS

2 The Birth of Representative Communalism: From Simqaniyya (1697) to the Beirut Consultative Council (1834) 15
A Brief Sketch of Lebanon's Constitutional History 15
Symbolism at Simqaniyya (1697) 17
The Birth of Consultative Councils (Cairo 1829, Damascus 1832, Beirut 1834) 23
The Council's Work in Practice 35

3 The Entrenchment of Communalism and the Birth of the Electoral Principle (1840–1920) 42
The Two Kaïmacams' Councils (1842–1860) 43
The Administrative Council (1861–1920) 49
The rise of the Electoral Principle 52

Elections in the Ottoman Empire 58
Transitioning from Mount Lebanon to Great Lebanon 68

PART TWO THE LEBANESE CONSTITUTION OF 1926

4 **The Constitution of 1926: Reconstructing the Timeline 75**
The Commission Administrative and the Council of Representatives (1920–1925) 75
Enter Michel Chiha 80
Michel Chiha as Drafter of the Lebanese Constitution 85
Constructing the Puzzle of the Constitutional Timeline: Chronology and Dates 87
A Grey Area – Mid-February to Mid-March 90
The March of the Constitutional Draft 93
The Other Drafts 96
Intensification of the Process and the Publication of the Draft 100
The Last Phase: The Debates in the CR and the Adoption of the Constitution 106

5 **The Constitution of 1926: Structure and Inspiration 110**
LEJ(F)ARC: The Lebanese Version of the 'Atlantic Constitution' 110
Outside Influence: Lebanese (Menassa, Trad ...), French (de Jouvenel, Souchier, Duguit ...) 125

6 **Building Constitutional Blocks: The Communitarian Straitjacket 141**
A Lasting Straitjacket 141
Communalism in the Legislative Branch 145
Communalism in the Judiciary, the Cabinet and the Administration 154
Conclusion 161

7 **Building Constitutional Blocks: Modern Constitutionalism 163**
The Nature of the Constitutional Regime 163
The Emergence of a Bicephalous Executive 171
Chiha's Budgetary Concerns 175
Electoral Templates 178
Conclusion 191

PART THREE CHIHA AFTER THE CONSTITUTION

8 The Constitution Undermined **195**
Suspension(s) and Restoration(s) of the Constitution during the Mandate 197
An Overbearing Mandate 206
The Dominance of Executive Power 210
The Abolition of the Senate 214
Budgetary Developments 218

9 Chiha's Worldview **222**
The French Connection 222
Longue Durée 229
'Economics' 239
Human Capital and *Etat-moins* 243
Wider Horizons: Poetry, Palestine, Etc. 246

10 Chiha's Nation **251**
'Associated Religious Minorities' v. 'Nationalism' 251
Chiha's Nationalism 255
Looking for Constitutional Temperaments to Communalism 259
Chiha's 'Positions de Principe' 262
The Swiss Example 270

PART FOUR CONSTITUTIONALISM AND GROUP REPRESENTATION

11 Lebanese Constitutionalism and the Political-Theological Middle East **277**
The Depth of Middle Eastern Constitutionalism 277
Disruptive Elections 280
'Un monstre ingouvernable' 281
A Bullet-like Reading of Contemporary History 283
The Pluses of Communal Constitutionalism 288
Ta'ef 290
Lebanese and Middle Eastern Constitutionalism 294
Constitutional Windows out of Communalism 299

Government–Elections–Parties: A Constitutionally Elusive Triangle 302
The Triangle beyond the Middle East 304

12 Constitutional Frontiers: The Lebanese Constitution and the World 307
On Democracy 308
On Secularism 312
Minority, Community, Group: The Better US Scholarship 315
Back to Lebanon 323

13 Democracy Redefined 330
Subordination 337
Critique 344
Conclusion 360

14 Epilogue 361
Democracy Redefined 363

General Bibliography 365
Index 383

Tables

4.1 A timeline of the Lebanese Constitution 108

5.1 Chiha's first draft and the Lebanese Constitution compared 111

7.1 Population and number of seats; 1925 Council of Representatives/1926 Chamber of Deputies 179

7.2 Communitarian composition of legislative chambers 1922–2025 180

13.1 Democracy in Prévert-style random groups 341

Preface

In early 2022, the Chiha Foundation put at my disposal the archives of Lebanese statesman Michel Chiha (1891–1954), pronounced /Shee-haa/ (with a strong h, transliteration Shīḥā), including the full set of previously unknown constitutional papers. It was with great emotion that I saw, touched and started studying the original version of our Lebanese constitution, almost a hundred years after it was put to paper in his elegant and distinct handwriting. Chiha never published these drafts. I can only surmise that his natural modesty prevailed. He mentioned on the rare occasion having penned the Constitution, almost as a passing thought about a banal matter.

For the oldest constitutions in the world, starting with the 1787 American and the 1791 French Constitutions, preparatory works have been visited time and again, as have more recent constitutions like the German Basic Law of 1949 or the French Constitution of the Fifth Republic. It is more unusual to be the first person graced with access to the founding social contract of his country one hundred years later.

Why did Michel Chiha decide not to publish his constitutional papers, or at least write more extensively on the Constitution's preparatory works? Having now learnt more about his natural modesty both in life and in the style of his writings, I can speculate that he simply did not wish to dwell on his remarkable achievements. It might also be that he was not totally happy with one or the other aspect of the result, for instance that the Lebanese Constitution, despite his own personal penchant for merit over identity, was not able to free the country from the sectarian straitjacket that centuries of communalism imposed on Lebanon. It might also be because Chiha never accepted the overbearing final sections which the French reserved for themselves, to undermine the Constitution at will. There might be other explanations. We will probably never know.

That it took a century in Lebanon to work on the earliest versions of the Constitution was not because of the failure of distinguished jurists and historians. Edmond Rabbath and Antoine Hokayem have published remarkable studies on its genesis, and Ahmad al-Zein extremely useful documentation. But now that the Chiha constitutional papers (CCP) are available, we know a lot more about the genesis of the Lebanese Constitution, including its original drafter and the textual iterations, from the end of December 1925 to its adoption in the early hours of Sunday, 23 May 1926.

Most books have a story behind painstaking progress in research and writing, and some serendipity. I came to know of the first handwritten manuscript at an exhibit of the Chiha Foundation at the Sursock Museum in Beirut during May–June 2001. I remember my surprise at seeing the manuscript in a glass casing. Here it was, the mysterious first draft of the 1926 Constitution which lawyers and historians have been looking for in vain. At last, we had answers to the two most basic questions: the Constitution's first draft was penned by one person, and it was Chiha. And the draft was composed in French, not in Arabic.

The Exhibit was memorialised in an elegant book of text and photographs, edited by Claude Doumet-Serhal and Michèle Hélou-Nahas, *Michel Chiha 1991–1954* (Beirut, Fondation Michel Chiha 2001). The Exhibit coincided with a conference held under the auspices of Samir Khalaf at the American University of Beirut, and I had been asked to present a paper on the trials and tribulations of the Lebanese Constitution. The Conference papers were never published, and my article lingered undisturbed in a file on my laptop.

I was putting some order into my computer in January 2022 when I chanced upon my 2001 draft. The work had generally stood the test of time and deserved to be renewed and completed with the original material. I called upon Claude Asfar, a dear friend and the sometime Secretary-General of the Chiha Foundation. She said that another long-time friend, Isabelle Doumet Skaf, one of Chiha's granddaughters, kept the material. Isabelle, her sister Claude Serhal, a scholar in her own right, and their cousin Michèle Nahas extended an open invitation to visit the archive, and they followed up on my various requests with professionalism and generosity.

The successive versions of the draft and other documents were a unique trove. I did not wish to damage the papers, and I benefited from the technological knowhow of the Dergham imprint in Beirut who scanned them at the request of the Chiha granddaughters. I sought initially to quickly complete the dormant article with the newly accessible material. Chiha's constitutional papers clearly deserved far more extensive treatment. The more I worked on the papers, the larger the manuscript grew away from a simple article.

The book expanded. Its scope became increasingly ambitious, pushing constitutionalism in the Middle East back to the Egyptian conquest of the Levant in the 1830s and bringing out its two central dimensions, the communal recognition in the founding text, and the corresponding slow progress of the electoral system that upholds it. I revisited the Lebanese Constitution through the papers of its main drafter and the perspectives of Chiha's wider worldview. I increasingly became aware that the questions raised by my research forced a novel thinking of democracy, which I draw in the last part of the book.

The book in the reader's hand ushers in a new phase of historical and constitutional scholarship at the threshold of the Lebanese Constitution's second century. As this study ages and is honed, contradicted, and displaced by new readings and further documentation, I can only hope that a few scholars will still use it when the third century of the Lebanese Constitution strikes midnight.

This book is part of a set of two volumes. Each volume stands alone. The second volume, *Michel Chiha's Constitutional Papers*, is a facsimile publication of the CCP, and provides a wealth of original documents for those who live, practise and research the Lebanese Constitution. It is published together with this book by the Chiha Foundation, with a preface and short guide partly based on the present book.

Acknowledgements

Throughout the research, with ups and downs weighing on progress – a persistent constitutional deadlock in Lebanon, an enduring Gaza conflict and a full Lebanese war, as well as my own lawyerly work – I benefited from the hospitality of several institutions which assisted me in various ways. Bilal Orfali facilitated my access to the library of the American University of Beirut, where competent colleagues put at my disposal the minutes of the 1834 Beirut Council, part of the papers of Asad Rustum (a remarkable twentieth century historian whom I cite often in this book), and sundry other sources. For daily papers, Nayla de Freige and Sylvia Chaer gave me unfettered access to the collection of the French daily *L'Orient* in the key first half of 1926. Michel Zaccour put at my disposal the full collection of his namesake grandfather's courageous newspaper *al-Maʿrad*. I was fortunate also to have the published edited collection of *al-Maʿrad* (in two volumes), and of the *al-Ahrar al-Musawwara* presented to me graciously by Ziad Chebib at Dar al-Nahar. Early on, I met a then doctoral student, Pierre-André Hervé, who shared his thoughts on communalism during the Mandate and a rich bibliography on Lebanon. As usual, I am in the debt of long-time colleagues at my law office, Nada Chahine and Samir Doumit.

Serendipity and hospitality were not merely Lebanese. Lebanon's close ties to France and the small Franco-Lebanese world of literati provide a unique vantage perspective. I had met Anne de Jouvenel, the granddaughter of the French High Commissioner who had asked the Lebanese to write their own Constitution in 1925. This was in 2000 in Beirut, on the occasion of her lecture on precious stones hosted by Sélim Mouzannar, my brother-in-law of world fame for the design and manufacturing of highly coveted jewels. Rekindling the brief acquaintance of Anne de Jouvenel in Paris opened up another set of original documents. It took a simple WhatsApp request for her to recognise her grandfather's handwriting in some comment on the Chiha manuscript as it evolved. I also benefited from Anne's knowledge of the archives of the family and the kind disposition of the Fonds Henry de Jouvenel in Corrèze, the French department from which the Jouvenels hail.

Several friends read part or all of this book. I am particularly grateful for the comments of Owen Fiss, Guillaume Tusseau and Percy Kemp for feedback on the chapters on democracy. As the work progressed, I was lucky to be hosted by the School of Law at Sciences-Po. Guillaume Tusseau and Sebastien Pimont added to their hospitality the accolade of distinguished colleagues, who sharpened my starry-eyed vision on the redefinition of democracy by way of constitutionalism in an enjoyable and fruitful seminar. Thanks to Sciences-Po, I met Anne Brigot-Laperrousaz, who contributed qualitatively to my research by unearthing and interpreting some intriguing Parisian 1926 sideroads in the making of the Lebanese Constitution.

I should also mention the kind reception at Edinburgh University Press, where Emma House, Sarah Foyle, Isobel Birks, Eddie Clark, their copy-editor Layla Saleh and the whole capable team looked after the protracted and enriching publication progress. There is a new policy at EUP which allows anonymous readers to divulge their names if they wish to after their reviews have been submitted to the press. I like this policy. It allowed me to discuss with both of them some of their criticism. I found out that they chose Jane Mansbridge and John Borneman as readers. I have not read an anthropologist as versatile and innovative as John Borneman, and I cannot think of a more thoughtful theoretician of democracy in the world of political science than Jane Mansbridge. Jenny graced me in particular with a line-by-line reading and commentary on both style and substance, and a subsequently rich correspondence. Chapter 13 in particular was the subject of a caring and exacting criticism the like of which I had never encountered in my career. As this book goes to press, I am anxious that the several revisions of the chapter over a period of six months still fall short of the standard her criticism deserves. I should also acknowledge the sharp criticism by my son Wajdi of the reworked chapter.

Last and not least, I owe a huge gratitude to Julie Flint, exemplary humanist and journalist extraordinaire of the Middle East, for expressing an interest in this book, correcting its *francicismes* and *arabicismes*, and enriching it with erudition, grace and humour. I would also like to express my debt to Saoud el Mawla, long-time friend and prolific scholar, who translated this book into Arabic. I learned a lot from him as the translation proceeded, and I adjusted the English text in light of inconsistencies and weaknesses which he drew my attention to.

Finally, I should mention that the present book appears simultaneously with a facsimile reproduction of the full set of *Michel Chiha's Constitutional Papers* in a separate volume, published in Beirut by the Chiha Foundation with prefaces and short guides in Arabic, French and English. The reader can draw his own conclusions in the direct light of these fascinating documents and pursue unfathomable depths of constitutional and other scholarship with the primary sources in hand. The two volumes, however, can be read independently.

Transliteration

To prevent a constant interruption of non-English words, I sought to put as many as possible in the footnotes. As in my previous books, I use the Middle East Studies Association's IJMES transliteration for Arabic and Ottoman Turkish, but I made it simpler by removing diacritics, except for the authors and works cited in the bibliography. /i/ and /e/ are often interchangeable in Arabic for /ya'/ and /kasra/, with a slight emphasis on the /ya'/, so the reader will see *mutasarref* and *Mutasarrifiyya*, without a difference in the /kasra/ in the original Arabic. Common names can be written in different ways, Hussen as Hussein or Hussayn, Husayn ... Some words such as qadi (the famed Weberian kadi, judge) or shari'a have now been accepted in the Oxford English Dictionary, and they are not italicised here. In addition, the names of various protagonists are written in the way they wrote it themselves, or in the way they are referred to in Lebanese papers in French at the time. The former president of Lebanon Béchara El-Khoury is one example. A scientific transliteration would have his name transliterated as Bishara al-Khuri, but I prefer to keep the spelling as he chose to write it. Also, since P is an unknown letter in Arabic, I wrote Ibrahim Pasha when the context was mainly Ottoman, and Ibrahim Basha when the setting was Egyptian or Lebanese. I am not fond of capital letters, so the reader will find Council of ministers rather than Council of Ministers, and Constitution or Republic only when they are specifically French, American, or Lebanese.

Abbreviations and Chiha-related Primary Sources

1- Consultative and governing councils and assemblies (Chronological)

Abbreviations

CC for Consultative Council (*majlis al-mashura, majlis al-shura*), 1834–1840.
KC for Kaïmacam Council (*majlis al-qa'immaqamiyya*), 1845–1860.
AC for Administrative Council (*majlis al-idara*) 1861–1920.
CA for Commission Administrative, 1920–1922.
CR for Conseil Représentatif (*al-majlis al-tamhili*), 1922–1926.
CSO for Commission du Statut Organique, 1925–1926.
CD for Chambre des Députés (*majlis al-nuwwab*), 1926-to date.

2- Chiha Constitutional Papers and the Chiha Archive

Abbreviations

CA for Chiha Archive (easily distinguished in context from CA as the Commission Administrative, 1920–1922 mentioned above)
CCP for Michel Chiha's Constitutional Papers. The CA includes the CCP but is much wider.
DOC for Document in the CCP only, so that the reader can consult it easily in the second volume.
MC for Michel Chiha
Ms. for manuscript

Michel Chiha's Archive is large and includes drafts, personal notes, newspapers cuttings, correspondence in French, Arabic and English, and articles published in newspapers and journals. It also includes the full collection of *Les Ebauches*, a magazine which he published when he was a law student in Egypt during the First World War, and the *Eastern Times*, a daily newspaper in English which Chiha published from 1941 to 1947. Both are major undertakings which deserve separate studies on worldviews from Cairo and Beirut at key junctures of history.

I refer in this book to the general Chiha archive as 'Chiha Archive' (CA), in contradistinction with the Chiha Constitutional Papers (CCP). Reference to a document in the Chiha Archive varies, since some are available onsite, and others are not yet fully referenced. Some are in my files and I have kept a copy of all documents cited.

The CCP files are distinct and kept separately. They consist of 29 Documents, referred to in the book as DOC 1 and so on. Each Document bears the title of the title or first words on its front page. They are all in French, except for a few in Arabic, here mentioned as AR next to the document. The key CCP are, with two exceptions, not dated. Some manuscripts and typed texts clearly follow previous versions, but several documents are hard to put in chronological order. I tried my best to reorganise them with a careful examination of the language and by following the logic of the progression of the texts. The sequencing and subdivisions are explained in the course of this book.

List of Chiha's Constitutional Papers

CCP are organised in three parts and in subsets within parts. The DOCs bear the title or first words in the version published in the second volume.

Part A- Primary preparatory works, the Chiha drafts

First set, DOCs 1 to 4

DOC 1- *Titre 1er Dispositions fondamentales* (manuscript, in MC's hand). 85 Arts, 15 pp.

DOC 2- *Titre 1er Dispositions fondamentales* (typed version of DOC 1, with annotations not in MC's hand). 85 Arts, 25 pp.

DOC 3- *Avant-Projet de Constitution pour le Gd-Liban* (typed version of DOC 1 with some annotations not in MC's hand). 85 Arts, 27 pp.

DOC 4- *Constitution du Grand-Liban* (typed version of DOC 1, with annotations in MC's hand). 85 Arts, 25 pp.

Second set, DOCs 5 to 10

DOC 5- *Titre 1er Dispositions fondamentales* (typed version of DOC 1, with annotations in MC's hand). 96 Arts, 25 pp.

DOC 6- *Titre 1er Dispositions fondamentales* (typed version of DOC 5, with annotations in MC's hand, and annotations in de Jouvenel's hand). 96 Arts, 14 pp.

DOC 7- *Titre 1er Dispositions fondamentales* (typed version of DOC 5, with two sets of annotations, one by MC). 96 Arts, 14 pp.

DOC 8- *Titre 1er Dispositions fondamentales* (typed version of DOC 5, with annotations in MC's hand). 96 Arts, 14 pp.

DOC 9- ['Souchier Observations'] *Observations sur le projet de Constitution* (typed), with marginal comments by MC, 6 pp.

DOC 10- *Le Président de la République* [*Duguit Document*]; 'Une constitution viable en dehors du Mandat'. Ms in MC's hand 2 pp.

Third set, DOCs 11 to 15- Consolidated and printed versions

DOC 11- *Titre 1er Dispositions fondamentales* (typed, no annotations, 10 Arts added in separate type colour after Art. 96), 106 Arts., 16 pp.

DOC 12- *CONSTITUTION LIBANAISE – AVANT-PROJET* (printed booklet, no annotations, n.d.). 108 Arts., 10 pp.

DOC 13- *CONSTITUTION LIBANAISE – AVANT-PROJET* (same version as DOC 12, with annotations in MC's hand). 108 Arts., 10 pp.

DOC 14- AR- *Al-bab al-awwal* [First part] (Printed Arabic translation of DOC 11, n.d., with annotations in Arabic). 107 Arts + addendum (*dhayl*) Art.43, 10 pp.

DOC 15- AR *al-dustur al-lubnani* (Lebanese constitution) Beirut: Matba'at al-adab (printed booklet, n.d.). 102 Arts + errata page, 20 pp.

Part B- Secondary preparatory works

First set- Contemporaneous constitutions

DOC 16- File entitled *CONSTITUTIONS DIVERSES* (all printed). It includes the Egyptian Constitution of 1923, as well as the Lithuanian,

Latvian (French Lettonie), Finnish and Romanian Constitutions enacted in the early 1920s.

Second set- Files' covers

DOC 17- *Conseil Représentatif: Projets en cours* (handwritten by MC, one page).

DOC 18- *Dernier Texte: dernières notes* ('Last text last notes', handwritten by MC, one page).

Third set- Partial drafts probably prepared by Chiha

DOC 19- *Ch.IV Du Pouvoir Exécutif* (handwritten in MC's hand). 25 Arts., 5pp (Arts.50 to 75).

DOC 20- *PROJET DE CONSTITUTION LIBANAISE* (typed, also on executive power). 19 Arts, 3 pp.

DOC 21- *PROJET DE CONSTITUTION LIBANAISE* (typed, also on executive power) 29 Arts, 4 pp.

Fourth set- The Menassa letter and constitutional draft

DOC 22- *Monsieur le Député* (typed) + *AVANT PROJET DE CONSTITUTION LIBANAISE* attached (typed). 110 Arts., 11 pp.

Fifth set- The 'Chiha/Trad Drafts'

DOC 23- *CONSTITUTION DE L'ETAT DU GRAND-LIBAN* (typed with annotations not in the hand of MC). 110 Arts, 19 pp.

DOC 24- *Constitution de l'Etat du Grand Liban* (typed, no annotations). 110 Arts, 18 pp.

Sixth set- Another constitutional draft, author unknown

DOC 25- *Titre 1er Disposition générales* (typed, with typed edits). 54 Arts., 21 pp.

Part C- Miscellaneous

DOC 26- AR Dr Ayyub Tabet, *Mashru' al-nazam al-asasi li-dawlat lubnan* (Project of a basic law for the State of Lebanon), Beirut: Matba'at al-misbah 1926 (printed booklet). 74 Arts, 11 pp.

DOC 27- AR *Projet de Sami Bey El Solh* (French words in handwriting not by MC, under official heading *Al-jumhuriyya al-lubnaniyya* (Lebanese Republic official heading) (typed), with Anis Saleh business card 1+ 4 pp.

DOC 28- AR *mashru' qanun* (Draft [electoral] law) (typed with MC annotations on top of page 1) (n.d.). 61 Arts, 11 pp.

DOC 29- AR *'yadayy al-majlis'* ('in the hands of the council'). Typed, 4 pp.

3- Chiha's published books

Michel Chiha did not publish a full monograph in his lifetime, but his (sometimes extensive) lectures and many newspaper articles were assembled by him first, then by his family, in a collection of ten books in French at Editions Le Trident in Beirut. There is sometimes an overlap in the collection; for instance *Liban d'Aujourd'hui* is available as a separate publication but is also included as one of the five lectures/essays in *Visage et Présence du Liban*. Full translations in Arabic and English are also available for some books. Several books in the collection were reprinted by the Chiha Foundation.

With the establishment of a dedicated site, MichelChiha.org, many more lectures, articles and editorials are easily available, and the site is constantly enlarged with new material and translations. Several of his books have been scanned or retyped for the site, and are searchable, but I use here the more enduring pagination of the printed French editions, and mention the date of the chapter or article when available. Chiha commonly uses italics and capital letters for emphasis, and I kept the French quotes and English translations with his original emphasis. A selection of his various articles was published as Michel Chiha, *Anthologie des Ecrits Politiques et Littéraires*, Beirut: Fondation Michel Chiha 2018, 427 p.

When a chapter cites Chiha's books repeatedly, I use the following abbreviations or brief title:

Essais I for *Essais I*, Beirut, Editions du Trident 1950, reprint 1980, 233 pp.

Essais II for *Essais II*, Beirut, Editions du Trident 1953, reprint 1980, 243 pp.

LA for *Liban d'Aujourd'hui*, Beirut, Editions du Trident 1949 (original 1942), 78 pp.

MC for *La Maison des Champs, suivie de Poèmes Inédits*, 2nd edition, Beirut, Imprimerie Catholique 1965, reprint Fondation Chiha 1994, 138 pp. (first edition at Beirut: Editions de la Revue Phénicienne 1934, 96 pp).

Pal for *Palestine*, Beirut, Editions du Trident 1957, reprint Fondation Chiha 1994, 294 pp.

Plain-Chant, Propos Dominicaux, Beirut, Editions du Trident 1954, reprint Fondation Chiha 1994, 356 pp.

Pol Int for *Politique Intérieure*, Beirut, Editions du Trident 1964, reprint 1980, 316 pp.

PEL for *Propos d'Économie Libanaise*, Beirut, Editions du Trident 1965, 348 pp.

VM for *Variations sur la Méditerranée*, Beirut, Editions du Trident 1973, reprint 1994, 247 pp.

VPL for *Visage et Présence du Liban*, Beirut, Editions du Trident 1964, reprint 1984, 247 pp.

1

Orientation: Two Centuries of Institutional Communalism in Lebanon

Ours is one of the longest histories.[1]

A constitution is meant to bring about a functioning system of governance for the citizen, but Lebanese constitutionalism suffers from a taxing communalism known in the language of political science as 'consociationalism'.[2] Consociationalism responds to hard identity edges which prevent a normal majoritarian voting system from operating. Consociational countries challenge the majoritarian principle at the core of democracy. They are prone therefore to systemic blockage, oftentimes descending into civil strife along fixed community lines defined ethnically, religiously, or linguistically. In Lebanon and much of the Middle East, fracture lines are religious, more specifically religious sect-based. The common thread of Middle Eastern consociationalism is the functioning and dysfunctions of government along lines of primordial affiliations defined by the individual's religion, and, more specifically as identity, by his or her religious sect.

The present chapter is designed to help the reader find their intellectual bearings in the hope of making the book more accessible to the non-expert in

[1] 'Notre histoire est parmi les plus longues.' Chiha, 'La leçon du passé', 1 September 1944, Pol Int 60.

[2] Arend Lijphart is the leading author in the field, with consociationalism a concept he developed first in *Democracy in Plural Societies: A Comparative Exploration*, New Haven: Yale University Press 1977 (On Lebanon in particular, 147–57); see also for an overview of the field and summary recommendations his 'Constitutional design for divided societies', *Journal of Democracy*, 15, 2004, 96–109. The concept is criticised for its limitations and 'circularity' by Donald Horowitz, *Ethnic Groups in Conflict*, Berkeley, U. of California Press 1985, esp. at 572–3, 576. Tellingly, consociationalism is more of a political than a legal or constitutional concept.

Lebanese history and/or in political philosophy, the latter an overcharged field of study. The chapter presents a lexical approximation of polysemous words, a synopsis of the book, and a sketch of Lebanese institutional history.

A terminological detour

Sect, community, confession, rite

Sectarian, communal, communitarian and confessional are terms that converge for the purpose of this book on the same concept of a group whose identity, discreteness and cohesion are defined for an individual-in-the-group by religion or religious sect. Membership is usually acquired by birth, with the birth trait generally difficult to change. 'Sectarian' connotes a negative judgment, so I prefer to use 'communal' (sometimes 'communitarian') over the other signifiers, to relate it more neutrally to the wider comparative legal world.[3]

The modern concept of communalism is rendered in Arabic by *ta'ifiyya*, from *ta'ifa* (plural *tawa'ef*), the individual's 'religious sect' in the historical and constitutional context of the Middle East.[4] The word appears already in the sense of group, faction, community about twenty times in the Qur'an.[5] *Ta'ifa* (group, community) has long been polysemous, for instance in '*muluk al-tawa'ef*, the kings of the principalities', when Islamic Spain collapsed in the eleventh century into separate, competing, principalities. In the Ottoman Empire, the dominant use was *millet*, which has its own origins in Arabic as *milla*, plural *milal*. *Milla* appears ten times in the Qur'an, often as *millat ibrahim,* the sect or people of Abraham.[6]

[3] The legal description particular to India is that of a 'communal' legal system, despite common constitutional references to its system being secular. Mathew John, *India's Communal Constitution*, Cambridge CUP 2023. India's description as 'secular' did not appear in the original text of the Constitution (1949) but was included in the 42nd amendment in 1976.

[4] See Azmi Bishara, *Al-Ta'ifa, al-Ta'ifiyya, al-Tawa'ef al-Mutakhayyala* (Sect, sectarianism and imagined sects), Beirut, Arab Center for Research and Policy Studies 2018), 103–8 for the classical concept of *ta'ifa*, which he considers non-religious.

[5] For example, Qur'an, *al-Tawba*, 9:122:'*fa-lawla nafara min kulli firqatin minhum ta'ifatun min al-mu'minin*, why should not a party of every section of them go already forth', in Arberry's translation on corpus.quran.com, a site which provides a useful concordance for *ta'ifa* and other terms discussed in this chapter.

[6] For example, in Qur'an, *al-Baqara*, 2:130 and 2:135.

John Wansbrough's 'sectarian milieu' provides the most sophisticated scholarship on this time-honoured structural characteristic of Middle Eastern societies, a concept which he developed in the formation of the community as Muslim in the three first centuries in relation to, or against, Christianity and Judaism.[7] An early exposition in classical Islam is Shahrastani's (d.1153) *Al-Milal wal-Nihal* (sects and creeds).[8] In French, the prevailing terms are *confessionnel*, *confessionalisme*, but references in the French colonial period in Lebanon also mention *rite*.

The rise of religion and sect as markers of hardening community boundaries hovers over the Middle East with replicas of Lebanese constitutionalism developing everywhere, as religion becomes an ever-sharper marker of identity against the basic egalitarian credo of a constitutional system.[9] The centrality of religions is not limited to the region. Constitutional theory needs to adjust to a persistent challenge which is evident in the Balkans, Africa, South and Southeast Asia, and spills over into established Western democracies with the persistence of minorities defined by their religion or sect.[10] The expansion of religious identification also triggers a revival and hardening of religious-sectarian identities or coincides with their entrenchment in public life.[11]

The challenge is not merely religious or sectarian. The problem of 'minorities' plagues the constitutional systems of majoritarian democracy

[7] Wansbrough's two celebrated books on this emergence are *Qur'anic Studies*, Oxford: Oxford University Press 1977, and *The Sectarian Milieu*, Oxford: Oxford University Press 1978.

[8] Beirut: Dar al-ma'rifa 1992 (a description of the various religious communities in Shahrastani's time). Another common term in the early Islamic period is *jama'a*, group, and *shi'a*, following, the latter eventually morphing into the Muslims who follow 'Ali ibn Abi Taleb, the cousin and son-in-law of the Prophet (hence Shi'ism).

[9] Religious markers in the Middle East are general in Egypt (Muslim-Christian Copts), Sudan (Christian-Muslim), or Israel-Palestine (Jewish-Muslim). More specific sectarian markers characterise Syria ('Alawi-Sunni), Iraq (Shi'i-Sunni), Saudi Arabia (Sunni, Shi'i).

[10] Ireland is the exemplar of religious communalism in contemporary Europe; see for example Thomas Mohr, 'Religious minorities under the constitution of the Irish Free State, 1922–1937', *American Journal of Legal History*, 61, 2021, 235–72. The Irish Constitution of 1922 took Protestant minorities into account in limited form through proportional laws and choice themes such as divorce or censorship. The difference in the Lebanese scope of communal constitutionalism will appear clearly in the present study. Demography is obviously important for both in terms of numbers and historical evolution. In the Ireland of the 1920s, Mohr writes at 242, Protestants formed less than 10 per cent of the population of the 26 counties in the South, then diminished into present insignificance.

[11] The United States is the foremost and best-known example of the political rise of Christian 'fundamentalism', but the phenomenon is attested across the Christian-majority world.

the world over. Even a US constitutional lawyer will recognise the 'discrete and insular minority' as a topos of continued relevance since the celebrated footnote 4 of the US Supreme Court's 1938 *Carolene Products* judgment, where the expression emerged in reference mainly to the historically subordinated Black group in the country.[12] In various intensities and at various rhythms, Lebanization (or Lebanonization) has become a synonym of the threat to democracy and the collapse of societies and states from the deadly pull of minorities that Daniel Moynihan and Robert Fossaert warned against forcefully at the beginning of the 1990s.[13]

The central problem is one of political representation of minorities in all three branches of government, especially in the councils, chambers, and parliaments, which has emerged since the eighteenth century Atlantic revolutions to formally represent 'the people'.[14] While such councils of government – or governing councils – usually belong to the legislative branch under the concept of separation of powers, the representation of minorities also creates quandaries in the executive branch, through cabinet representation and the administration, and in the judiciary, through the composition of the top benches.

In Lebanon, the building of institutions as representative governing councils started timidly during the 1830s, about ten years before the general scholarly understanding of their emergence, in a phenomenon important already at the time as 'Middle Eastern'.[15] In the Middle Eastern legal template, laws are

[12] United States v. Carolene Products Company, 304 U.S. 144 (1938), fn 4. See discussion in Chapter 12. A parallel to the role of the US Supreme Court in judicial recourse can be found in the Privy Council of the Irish State: see Mohr, 'Religious minorities under the constitution of the Irish Free State, 1922–1937, above n.10, 258–63.

[13] Daniel Moynihan, *Pandemonium*, New York: Oxford University Press 1994 (warning against the rising world trend of 'Balkanization'); Robert Fossaert, *Le Monde au 21ème Siècle*, Paris: Fayard 1991, especially 'Tutelle des Etats évanescents', 238–40. On the term Lebanonization and its iterations, William Safire, 'On language; Izationization, *The New York Times*, 21 April 1991.

[14] On the concept of 'the Atlantic Revolution(s)', see Jacques Godechot and Robert Palmer, 'Le problème de l'Atlantique du XVIIIe au XXe siècle', *Relazioni del X Congresso Internazionale di Scienze Storiche, Roma, 1955, vol. 5. Storia Contemporanea*, Florence, Sansoni, 1955, 175–239.

[15] There is a considerable literature on communalism in Lebanon. A master analyst is sociologist Samir Khalaf; see for example his *Civil and Uncivil Violence in Lebanon*, New York, Columbia UP 2002 (on the deeply entrenched communalism since 1820 and the interaction of domestic and international troubles). See also Eduardo Wassim Aboultaif, *Power Sharing in Lebanon-Consociationalism since 1820*, New York, Routledge 2019 (more specifically on consociationalism as a tool for understanding the country's history and persistent political structures). See Mas'ud Daher, *Al-Judhur al-Tarikhiyya lil-Mas'ala al-Ta'ifiyya fi Lubnan 1697–1861* (The historical roots of the communal question in Lebanon 1697–1861), Beirut: Farabi 2nd ed. 2009

a function of a particular societal set-up where religious communities form an essential part of constitutional life and its legal and political expressions.[16]

Nation-State

A constitution attaches by definition to a territory with recognised frontiers widely known since around the Second World War as 'nation-state'. A precise date for the birth of this composite term is elusive. The larger historical context for the rise of the nation-state is provided by Fernand Braudel's masterpiece *La Méditerranée et le Monde Méditerranéen à l'Epoque de Philippe II.*[17] This is the pioneering analysis of a worldwide shift, in the second half of the sixteenth century, from the hitherto dominance of 'empires' to the 'nation-state'. Braudel describes the slow but massive move of the world economy from the Mediterranean to the Atlantic during that period taking place at the same time as the political and cultural prevalence of nation-state over empire, with the battle of Lepanto in 1571 as its symbolic crucible. Lepanto stands in the book as the first symbolic victory of a coalition of nation-states over the Ottoman Empire, heralding the slow retreat of the Ottomans until their ultimate demise in 1918, together with the other remaining empire in the world, the Austro-Hungarian Empire.[18]

It took some four centuries for the term 'nation-state', with a hyphen, to become common. It appears for the first time in English in 1895 with reference

(original 1986) (on social disturbances and their effects on constitutional communalism). The reference book on Lebanese institutional history is Edmond Rabbath, *La Formation Historique du Liban Constitutionnel*, Beirut, Lebanese University Publications, 2nd ed. 1986 (original 1973). A sample of good works, selected in the bibliography under their names, includes books by Ahmad Beydoun, Georges Corm, Theodore Hanf, Isam Khalife, Saoud el Mawla, Antoine Messarra, and Elizabeth Picard. Nary a book on Lebanon (or on the Middle East generally) fails to mention the country's communal set-up.

16 For further context and literature, see my *Introduction to Middle Eastern Law*, Oxford, Oxford University Press, 2007 (hereafter IMEL), 140–80.

17 Paris: Armand Colin, 1966, revised 2nd edition, 2 vols (Original 1949).

18 In international law, the system of nation-states which culminates in its formal establishment in the League of Nations at the end of the First World War is generally called 'the Westphalian system'. The emergence of the intangibility of borders in the Treaty of Westphalia (1648) is doubtful. On the basis of the works of the Abbé de Saint-Pierre (d.1756) and Rousseau (d.1778), I ascribe the birth of the principle of border inviolability to the Treaty of Utrecht (1712–3); see my *Philosophy of Nonviolence: Revolution, Constitutionalism, and Justice beyond the Middle East*, New York: Oxford University Press 2015 (hereinafter PNV), 99–101. Of note is the absence of the word 'nation-state' in both the Covenant of the League of Nations and the Charter of the United Nations.

to 'the Teutons, the architects *par excellence* of the nation-state, a clear recognition of community of country as a prime force in political coalescence.'[19] N-grams in English and French reveal only a timid reference to the name from the end of the nineteenth century to the mid-1940s, with a significant jump in use from the mid-1980s.[20]

There is no exact equivalent in Arabic to the expression 'nation-state' or 'Etat-nation'. In the late twentieth century, it translates as *al-dawla al-qawmiyya*, literally the national state. The word *qawm*, from which *qawmiyya* derives, appears over 300 times in the Qur'an, and is translated generally as 'people'. *Qawmiyya* is an adjective, so *al-dawla al-qawmiyya* is 'the national state.' Nation-state is more accurately translated as *al-dawla al-umma* ('the state nation'), but the term has not gained currency in daily or scholarly use. This is partly because *umma*, which appears in the Qur'an over 60 times in a polysemous context, connotes a larger community, as in community of Muslims (and other religions and 'peoples'). The *umma*'s wide scope stands in contradistinction with that of the narrower *ta'ifa* or *milla*. For a more expressive Arab composite, my preference is for *al-dawla al-wataniyya*, but it has not gained traction despite the fact that *watan* is the closest equivalent to nation in modern parlance.

Constitution, dustur

In most countries of the Arab world, the word used for constitution is *dustur*, plural *dasatir*.[21] *Dustur* in the sense of constitution is a latecomer in the Middle East.

[19] Charles Malcom Platt, 'A Triad of political conceptions: State, sovereign, government', *Political Science Quarterly*, 1895, 292–323, at 294.

[20] Google Ngram viewer, search /nation-state/ conducted 29 December 2024. The word 'nation-state' may have been made current in English by a then influential text where the word is used extensively, Emery Reeves, *Anatomy of Peace*, New York, Harper 1945. In a comment, Jane Mansbridge suggests that nation-state has practically no use until 1989-90-91 and then jumps, and that 'nation state' without the hyphen begins to rise in the late 1950s, but never reached even half the usage of 'nation-state.' Not surprisingly, the German *Nationalstaat* and Italian *Statonazione* appear much earlier, in the mid-nineteenth century as the momentum for the unification of a fissiparous assortment of smaller principalities rises decisively to form a legal entity (State) on the basis of a community defined as 'Nation.' The French Revolution's cry at the battle of Valmy in September 1792, 'Vive la Nation', was noted in a celebrated text of Goethe.

[21] The exception is the Kingdom of Saudi Arabia, which enacted in 1992 a set of three laws (*nizam*, also pronounced *nazam*, plural *anzima*) forming together what can be recognised as a constitution

In classical law, the word *dustur* or *dastur* does not appear as a legal category in the jurists' works. In *Subh al-A'sha,* the early 14th century encyclopedia of chancery documents, one finds *dustur* or *dastur* meant as manual, with *dast* in *kateb al-dast,* the registrar holding the manual, a secretary whose position stands relatively low in the administrative hierarchy.[22] *Dastur* bears several meanings in the larger literature, including register or list (as in army conscript list), as well as the minister as holder of such register.[23] The word *dast* is originally Persian, and its etymology denotes power, authority (for *dast, dst,* in old Persian) and combines with the suffix *ur,* master of.[24] Ibn Khaldun (d.1406) uses the word *dast* in his *Muqaddima* as 'power'.[25] There is no entry on *dustur* in Ibn Manzur's *Lisan al-'arab* (d. 1311) but the later lexicographer Fayruzabadi (d. 1414) defines *dustur* in his *al-Qamus al-Muhit* as 'a copy used by groups who edit it', probably meaning a type of legal manual or *coutumier.*[26] This is taken up in Zabidi (d.1790)'s *Taj al-'Arus,* with a telling addendum anticipating the use during the Ottoman Empire of the word *dustur* as a collection of laws. *Dustur,* Zabidi explains, 'is the name of the copy used by groups like the registers which they edit to collect the laws of the realms and its orders. Arabised from the Persian.'[27]

for the Kingdom: *al-Nizam al-asasi lil-hukm* (Basic law of government;) *Nizam majlis al-shura* (Law of the shura/ consultative council); and *Nizam al-manateq* (Law of the regions). All were decreed by Royal Orders on 27.8.1412/2.3.1992. For a discussion, see my *The Normalization of Saudi Law,* New York: Oxford UP, Chapter 14, 325–36. In 2003, the State of Palestine also issued a basic law, *qanun asasi,* probably saving the name *dustur* for the full international recognition of the country. English texts of all constitutions are available on www.constituteproject.org.

22 Qalqashandi (d. 1418), *Subh al-A'sha fi Sina'at al-Insha,* Cairo: Dar al-kutub al-misriyya, 14 vols, 1914–22. *Subh al-A'sha,* is searchable on the shamela.ws website, Qalqashandi.

23 Minister, *wazir.* For an Internet resource on the word in several classical and modern dictionaries, see the site arabiclexicon.hawramani.com, s.v. *dustur.*

24 Mansur Shaki, *Encyclopedia Iranica,* s.v. *Dastur* (online, entry dated 2011). The classical Arabic equivalent of the holder of any power is *saheb,* for instance the police, *saheb al-shurta. 'wa kal-sayf yatafarra'ila saheb al-harb wa saheb al-shurta wa saheb al-barid* (like the [power of the sword] branches out into the holder/master of war, the master of police, the master of the post)'. Ibn Khaldun, *al-Muqaddima,* Cairo, Matba'at al-taqaddum 1904, 186.

25 *'wa lamma muhiya rasm al-khilafa wa ta'attala dastuha'*, 'when the stamp of the caliphate faded and its power was undermined', id., 181.

26 Fayruzabadi (or Firuzabadi), *Al-Qamus al-Muhit,* Cairo: Dar al-hadith, 2008, entry *dustur,* 542: *'al-nuskha al-ma'mula lil-jama'at allati minha tahriruha, mu'arrab, j[am']: dasatir'.*

27 Zabidi, *Taj al-'Arus,* excerpt from maajim.con/dictionary, s.v. *dustur,* emphasis added in my English translation: *'huwa ism al-nuskha al-ma'mula lil-jama'at kal-dafater allati minha tahriruha wa yujma'fiha qawanin al-mulk wa dawabituh'.*

In the modern period which is generally associated with Napoleon's occupation of Egypt in 1798, the word *dustur* appears in a proto-constitutional Egyptian text in 1824 in combination with *'amal*, mode, operation.[28] 'Mode of operating, *dustur al-'amal*', is the expression which combines in that text the Ottoman/Persian *dustur* and Arabic *'amal*. The combination also appears in the presentation of the first Ottoman Constitution of 1876 by the reformist statesman Midhat Pasha (d.1884).[29] In the Arabic dictionary *Muhit al-Muhit* (or. 1867–70), Butros al-Bustani (d.1883) includes an entry, '*dastar, al-dustur*', meaning list (for army), or register. Bustani explains at the end of the entry that '*dustur* is also the law, the permission and the rule by which work is done'.[30] It is therefore around the 1870s that the word started being associated with codified law.

The Tunisian, Ottoman and Persian founding texts are historical markers of Middle Eastern constitutionalism.[31] It is generally thought that the first constitution in the Middle East emerged in Tunisia in 1861 and was preceded in a Bill of Rights in 1857.[32] The use of the word *dustur* for the Tunisians is retrospective. The 1861 manuscript is entitled *qanun*, not *dustur*.[33] The Ottomans' 1876 Constitution was not called *dustur* either, but *qanun-e asasi*,

[28] The text can be found on the site of the University of Minnesota's Human Rights Library, together with other early Egyptian 'constitutions', at http://hrlibrary.umn.edu/arabic/Egyptian_Constitution. It is a translation from Turkish Ottoman, with *dustur al-'amal* appearing in the list (*la'iha*) attached to an order of the Egyptian Khedive/ruler Muhammad 'Ali (d. 1849) to his top aide, the katkhuda Muhammad beik Laz Ogli (d.1827), at 5. The list includes administrative arrangements for the reunion of the Council appointed by the Khedive. The order is dated 5 Rabi' al-Thani 1240/27 November 1824 (with a typo, 1834 instead of 1824). On the important contribution of Muhammad 'Ali to Middle Eastern 'governing councils' and their charters, see Chapter 3.

[29] Preface of Midhat Pasha, dated 7 dhu al-hujja 1293/ 23 December 1876, Ottoman text included in vol. 4 of *Dustur*, Istanbul: 'Amereh 1294/1878, 3.

[30] '*wal-dustur aydan al-qanun wal-ijaza wal-qa'ida yajri al-'amal bi-mujabiha*', Butros al-Bustani, *Muhit al-Muhit*, vol. 1 (n.p, n.d), s.v. *dustur*, 650.

[31] There is a large literature on the early constitutions in the Middle East. In English, historical scholarship can be found in the works of Bernard Lewis on Turkey and Abbas Amanat on Persia/Iran. Scholarship on constitutional texts and developments includes books by Haider Hammoudi and Zaid al-Ali on Iraq, and by Asghar Schirazi and Said Arjomand on Iran. Details under authors' names in the bibliography. On the Arab and Israeli constitutions and basic laws, see my IMEL, chs 4 to 6, 140–235 and PNV, chs 9 to 11, 133–214, with the references cited.

[32] *'ahd al-aman*, translated in French as Pacte Fondamental. We shall see further in Chapter 2 that the Egyptians had enacted an earlier proto-constitutional set of texts, some applying in Lebanon as early as 1834 during the Egyptian conquest of Palestine, Lebanon and Syria.

[33] Front page of Ms available on Wikipedia (French), s.v. Constitution Tunisienne de 1861.

basic law, and the laws in the era of reform known as the *Tanzimat* were collectively named *dustur*. The 1906 Constitution of Persia was called *qanun-e asasi-ye mashrute*.[34]

It took a while for *dustur* to settle in as the equivalent of 'constitution' in the modern Arab world, where its use became common only in the second and third decades of the twentieth century. A well-known book at the time by Bulos Mas'ad was published in 1909 under the title *Lebanon and the Ottoman Constitution* (using the word *dustur*).[35] Mas'ad discusses the Ottoman constitution/*dustur* as the collection of the Empire's laws, but his book's subtitle is more specific to the 1876 founding text which had just been reinstated by the 1908 Revolution. Around that time is probably when the amalgamation took place between the late nineteenth century *dustur* as collection of rules and laws and the more precise meaning of constitution as a discrete document standing as the written social pact in the nation-state. A public figure and a prominent Ottoman man of letters, Sulaiman al-Bustani, published a book in 1909 just after the restoration of the 1876 Ottoman Constitution, entitled *The Ottoman state before and after the Constitution (dustur)*.[36] Bustani explains that 'the ensemble of the laws and decrees was known in the countries of the

[34] *Mashrute*, also *mashrutiyyye* in common use, derive from *shurut*, clauses, conditions, with both terms meaning conditioned, conditional. The acceptation is that of a limited law in contrast with the absolute and unlimited divine law, as well as a limiting one on the powers of the ruler. See for a discussion of the first Ottoman (1876) and Persian basic laws (1906–7), and their translation in English, Tilman Röder, 'The Separation of powers in Muslim countries', in Rainer Grote and Tilman Röder eds, *Constitutionalism in Islamic Countries*, New York: Oxford UP, 321–72.

[35] Bulos Mas'ad (d.1946), *Lubnan wal-Dustur al-'uthmani* (Lebanon and the Ottoman Constitution), Cairo: Matba'at al-Adab 1909. The subtitle is *Bahth siyasi wa qanuni tarikhi fi mawqef lubnan al-hader iza' al-dawla al-'uthmaniyya qabl al-dustur wa ba'dah* (Political and legal historical study of the postition of Lebanon towards the Ottoman State before and after the [revival in 1908 of the 1876] Constitution). The book argues against the participation of the residents of Mount Lebanon in the elections of the newly established Majlis al-Mab'uthin (Chamber of the Emissaries), the Ottoman Empire's elected lower house.

[36] Sulaiman al-Bustani, *'Ibra wa dhikra aw al-dawla al-'uthmaniyya qabl al-dustur wa ba'dah* (Lesson and recollection, or the Ottoman state before and after the Constitution), Khaled Ziadeh ed., Beirut: Arab Center for Research and Policy Studies 3d ed 2019. Bustani (1856–1925) was a Lebanese encyclopedic scholar famous for his translation of the Iliad into Arabic from the original Greek. He was highly regarded in Istanbul, where he lived for a long time, and was appointed minister of agriculture in the Ottoman government in 1913. He is a relative of Butros a-Bustani, above n.30 and accompanying text, and worked with his sons on various literary projects.

Ottoman state by the name of *dustur* (Code)',[37] and considers the '*dustur*' of 1876 as the fundamental piece of this legislative corpus.

It is the Egyptian Constitution of 1923 which uses *dustur* in its official title for the first time, with lasting effect.[38] The previous 'constitution' of 1882 was still entitled basic law (or list).[39] The 1923 Egyptian *dustur* was soon followed by the Lebanese *dustur* of 1926. Since then, the word has prevailed in the Arab Middle East as the exact equivalent of a constitution in the west. The late use of the word *dustur* in in the Arab states explains why *dustur* is not used for constitution in the countries where the main language is not Arabic.[40]

Synopsis: from communalism to a new definition of democracy

Representative councils come late to the long history of the Middle East, and elections come even later. When are such councils first attested, how were they formed, and what power did they have? And when did the designation of their members give way to an electoral process?

The book tracks these two essential constitutional traits in four parts, with 13 chapters and an epilogue.

Following on the lexical clarification of the present chapter, the first part considers the rise of communally representative councils with religion as explicit marker of membership, and the timid introduction of election as a mode of social choice in the nineteenth century. Chapter 2 shows how the Middle Eastern prototype of such councils emerged in the territories of the Levant occupied by Egypt in the 1830s. The Beirut Council of 1834 is

[37] Id., 35: '*fa-majmu' hadhih al-qawanin wal-nizamat huwa alladhi kana ma'rufan fi bilad al-dawla al-'uthmaniyya bi ism al-dustur (Code).*' Code is in French in the original.

[38] The Syrians used the word *dustur* when the Syrian National Congress adopted the Constitution of 19 July 1920 under the leadership of Emir Faisal, the main leader of the Arab revolt which started in Mecca in 1916. The Syrian *dustur* of 1920 lived a mere few days. The French armies occupied Damascus on 25 July. On the Syrian Constitution of 1920, Elizabeth Thompson, *How the West Stole Democracy from the Arabs: The Syrian Arab Congress of 1920 and the Destruction of Its Historical Liberal-Islamic Alliance*, London: Grove Press UK 2020 (Kindle).

[39] Basic law, *la'iha asasiyya.*

[40] In Turkey, the term was modernised into *anayasa.* Following the collapse of the Ottoman Empire, the 1921 and 1924 constitutions were called *Teşkilāt-ı Esāsiye Kānūnū* (basic legal constitution/formation), and retrospectively referred to as *anayasası.* in Iran, the constitution of 1979 has retained the 1906 wording, *qanūn-e asasi*; in Israel, where there is no formal constitution, the word is *khuka (ḥuka)*, which originates in the Biblical Hebrew for law. Basic laws are *ḥukey ha-yesod.* I am grateful for the Ottoman/Turkish clarification to Soli Ozel, and to Itamar Mann for the Hebrew/Israeli nuance.

one amongst various such councils established in the large territory wrested by Egyptian conquest from long-established Ottoman rule. This chapter also examines the charters of the Damascus and Beirut Consultative Councils as the first constitutional or proto-constitutional documents establishing communal government. In Beirut in particular, where some archival minutes of Consultative Councils meetings survive, the 1834 Council heralds a joint rule under an expressly egalitarian Muslim-Christian representation.

Chapter 3 presents the entrenchment of communal councils in the troubled period 1840–1860, then in the stable peace of the Mutasarrifiyya, a special legal-constitutional status for Mount Lebanon, the core part of what would become Great Lebanon (Grand Liban) in 1920, and Lebanon in 1943. Mount Lebanon was remarkably peaceful under Ottoman rule between 1860 and the end of the First World War. The chapter also tracks the slow introduction of electoral processes for access to limited but tangible executive power.

The second part is based on the archive of the main drafter of the Lebanese Constitution of 1926, Michel Chiha (d.1954). Chapter 4 examines the genesis of the Constitution and the distinct role of Chiha in its drafting. Chapter 5 discusses the structure and central characteristics of the text in light of the Chiha archive. It also addresses French influence and some of the referenced sources to constitutional scholarship at the time. Chapters 6 and 7 continue the discussion in 'the building blocks' of the Constitution. Chapter 6 examines the emergence of communal constitutionalism, which represents the main characteristic of the legal system in Lebanon, in light of the Chiha documents and the debates in the larger Lebanese Council of Representatives formally tasked to write the Constitution by French Mandatory power. Chapter 7 moves to constitutional themes of more general import, such the bicephalous executive, the budget and the electoral system.

The third part examines Chiha's occasional reactions to the iterations of the Constitution and his worldview beyond the constitutional text. Chapter 8 examines some of these reactions to constitutional developments after 1926, during the French Mandate (1920–1943) and after Independence in 1943, and his written legacy through to his death a decade later. Chapter 9 presents Chiha's larger worldview in light of his many writings on history and politics in particular. Chapter 10 examines more closely the tension between communities and nation in Chiha's philosophy.

The fourth part of the book presents the main developments of constitutionalism after Chiha, in Lebanon, in the Middle East, and in the wider comparative world, leading to my redefinition of the concept of democracy. Chapter 11 sets constitutions as social contract within the context of later constitutional developments in Lebanon and pursues Lebanese constitutionalism as the template for persistently deadlocked constitutional governance across the Middle East. Chapter 12 situates the debate over constitutional communalism within the larger problem of democratic representation and participation of minoritarian groups, especially in US constitutional theory. Chapter 13 redefines democracy in light of the investigation carried out in the book, as a constitutional system of governmental representation which necessarily includes members of historically subordinate groups.

The Epilogue, Chapter 14, summarises some of the book's findings.

PART ONE

COMMUNALISM AND THE BIRTH OF ELECTIONS

2

The Birth of Representative Communalism From Simqaniyya (1697) to the Beirut Consultative Council (1834)

> It is a paltry quarrel that which pretends to start a country at some determined historical hour.[1]

A brief sketch of Lebanon's constitutional history

'*Bilad al-Sham*' (the countries of Syria), comprises at its core present-day Syria, Palestine, and Lebanon, and roughly corresponds to 'the Levant, *al-mashreq*'. The region came under Ottoman rule in 1516, when the Egyptian Mamluk rulers were defeated in a series of decisive battles. Ottoman rule over *Bilad al-Sham* ended only in the First World War, with a brief, important constitutional interlude in the 1830s.

In a broad brush, the Ottoman sultans governed the territory covering all of present-day Lebanon in uneven historical periods until 1918. It may be useful for the reader not familiar with Lebanese history to keep the following sequence in mind:[2]

[1] 'C'est une pauvre querelle que celle qui prétend faire partir un pays d'une heure historique déterminée.' 'Horizons', 27 June 1945, Pol Int 85.

[2] For the history of modern Lebanon generally, a good all-rounded introduction is Fawaz Traboulsi, *A History of Modern Lebanon*, London: Pluto Press 2007. In Arabic, Mas'ud Daher, *Tarikh Lubnan al-Ijtima'i al-Mu'asir* (Contemporary Social History of Lebanon), Beirut: Nahar 2022. For a history stretching back to late antiquity, see William Harris, *Lebanon: A History, 600–2011*, New York: Oxford University Press 2012. In French, see for a general book on nineteenth-twentieth century history, Denise Ammoun, *Histoire du Liban Contemporain*, vol. 1, *1860–1943*, Paris: Fayard 2014; vol. 2, *1940–1990*, Paris: Fayard 2005. Earlier standard reference works in English are by Philip Hitti, *Lebanon in History*, London: St Martin's Press 1957, and Kamal Salibi, *Modern History* of *Lebanon*, London: Weidenfeld & Nicolson 1965, and, in Arabic the textbook by Fu'ad Efrem al-Bustani and Asad Rustum, *Tarikh Lubnan al-Mujaz* (Short History of Lebanon), n.p, n.d, 1937.

(a) the Emirate (1516–1831);
(b) a brief but significant Egyptian occupation between 1831 and 1840, with
(c) continued communal troubles over the following two decades (1840–1860), including a significant peasants' 'republican' revolt in 1858, morphing into
(d) large-scale massacres in 1860. These led to renewed military intervention by the Ottomans and by European powers, and the return of peace under Ottoman rule from 1860–1 through the First World War.[3]

To each of these four periods correspond prototype 'governing' councils:

(a) A fleetingly representative council 'chose' the Emir of Mount Lebanon in 1697.
(b) The Egyptian rulers introduced various representative councils in the larger cities, in particular the Damascus Consultative Council ('CC') of 1832 and the Beirut CC of 1834.
(c) As communal strife developed between 1840 and 1860, the region described administratively as Mount Lebanon was divided into two districts with a council each, built on rigid communal representation.
(d) The wide-scale civil war of 1860 following the failure of the 1858 commoners' revolt led to international arrangements providing a long period of stability until 1914, which was regulated constitutionally by one Administrative Council ('AC') under the governorship of an Ottoman non-Lebanese Christian appointee. It is in this period that electoral representation gradually developed for the AC.

At the end of the First World War, France took over Lebanon and Syria in the wake of agreements with Britain to divide the Ottoman Empire between them. The two main periods which followed were:

[3] In the past century, a rich legacy of economic and institutional scholarship of nineteenth century Lebanon is represented in the works of Asad Rustum, Dominique Chevallier, Antoine Kheir, Irena Smilanskaia, and by more recent scholarship penned by Cesar Farah, Edmond Rabbath, Samir Khalaf, and Makram Rabah. Archival work regarding the second half of the nineteenth century in particular was conducted by Hasan Hallaq, Leila Fawaz, Engin Akarli, Jens Hansen, and Ussama Makdisi. See the bibliography for their main works.

(e) The French Mandate (1920–43), which founded Great Lebanon on a much larger territory than Mount Lebanon and saw the adoption of the Lebanese Constitution in 1926 by the Council of Representatives ('CR'), which renamed the country as Lebanon, and more specifically as the 'Lebanese Republic'.

(f) Independent Lebanon after 1943, with significant constitutional amendments in 1990 following the so-called 'Ta'ef agreement' reached the previous year.[4]

Symbolism at Simqaniyya (1697)

The Emirate established in and around Mount Lebanon's core in the wake of Ottoman occupation of the Near East in the early sixteenth century saw the succession of two dynasties, the Maʿn (Maan), from 1544 to 1697, and the Shihab (Chehab), from 1697 to 1840. Their most famous princes were for the Maʿn Fakhreddin II (r.1590–1633), and for the Shihab Bashir II (r. 1788–1840), both reigning intermittently as lords of Mount Lebanon under Ottoman rule, both seeking as much autonomy as they could get from the powers-that-be, mainly Ottoman but also Egyptian in the case of Bashir, and both ultimately failing in securing independent control and forced into exile.[5]

In the search for institutional patterns laying the ground for modern constitutionalism, we have an authoritative reflection by Albert Hourani dating the birth of modern Lebanon at a meeting in 1697 in Simqaniyya, in the

[4] For the period of the French Mandate from 1920 to formal Lebanese independence in 1943, scholarship includes books authored or edited by Henry Laurens, Carla Eddé, Nadine Méouchy, Isam Khalifeh, Hasan Hallaq, Wajih Kawtharani, Masʿud Daher, Antoine Hokayem, Peter Sluglett and Meir Zamir; For the post-Independence period, the May 2001 Chiha conference organised at the American University of Beirut by Samir Khalaf and Carole Hakim, which stands as the origins of the present book, featured some of the most prominent colleagues in their various fields of expertise. Paper contributors were Ahmad Beydoun, Farid al-Khazen, Nawaf Salam, Elisabeth Picard, Adnane al-Amine, Reinoud Leenders, Fawaz Gerges, Volker Perthes, Joseph Maila, Toufic Gaspard, Makram Sader, Kamal Hamdan and the late Samir Kassir, Samir Frangieh, Melhem Chaoul and Fares Sassine. The sessions were chaired by Samir Khalaf, Marwan Hamade, Nadim Shehadi, Michel El-Khoury, and the late Fouad Boutros, Ghassan Tueni, and Michel Eddé. They are all prominent figures with significant contributions as scholars and actors in contemporary Lebanon. See a selection of their works under their authors' names in the bibliography.

[5] Fakhreddin II, also known as Fakhreddin the Great (*al-kabir*), was exiled to Istanbul in 1633 and executed in 1635. Bashir was exiled to Malta in 1840, then to Istanbul, where he died in 1850.

present-day Shuf region about 30km from the coast. This was a delicate period marking the passage of the Emirate from the Ma'n dynasty to the Shihabs:

> If we want a symbolic date for the emergence of Lebanon, it might be 1697, when the family to which Fakhr al-Din belonged became extinct, and some of the lords met in the village of Simqaniyya and chose as their new overlord a member of the family of Shihab, from a southern district.[6]

The event provides a rare instance of a group coming together on a governance decision, namely the appointment of their leader. At the meeting in Simqaniyya in Mount Lebanon, the Druze notables chose the person of Emir Bashir Shihab I to succeed the Ma'n dynasty which lacked an available direct male successor. But what does 'appointment' or 'choice' mean from an institutional perspective?

To ascertain more closely the mechanisms and significance of the event, we have three Lebanese chronicles which mention the meeting, one of them contemporaneous.

The contemporaneous report on the meeting was published much later, in 1890. This was the chronicle of Maronite church history by Patriarch and man of letters Istifan al-Dwaihi (d.1704) who lived at the time of the momentous event. His chronicle for year 1697 reads:

> On the 15th of September [1697] Emir Ahmad ibn Ma'n died. With him ended the just Ma'n dynasty. At the time Fadli Agha al-Hawali was in Deir al-Qamar [about 20 km inland just south of Beirut, then the most important town in Mount Lebanon] on behalf of the governor of Saida Husain Basha.[7] He secured the safe and the furniture of [Ahmad] ibn Ma'n and told the Basha about it. The judge of the city, the mufti, the head of the notables[8] and the scholars of Saida were summoned to go to Deir al-Qamar and took over his estate. He owed sixty purses and another sixty purses to the Sultan. Upon which the notables of the Shuf region, emirs, *muqaddams* [title below emir],

[6] Albert Hourani, 'Political society in Lebanon Massachusetts Institute of Technology: An historical introduction,' Center for International Studies, Cambridge, MA 1985, 10. The southern district in this case was in the Rashayya region in the plain of the Bekaa (al-Biqa').

[7] governor, *wali*.

[8] Head of the notables, *naqib al-ahsraf.*

> and *mashayekh* [sheikhs][9] *chose (ikhtaru)* Emir Bashir Shihab in his place and paid the remainder of his debt which Husain Basha received and informed the Porte about.[10]

At the other end of the available chronicles stands the report of Tannus al-Shidiaq (d.1861), which differs in a choice of words that is telling:

> In 1697, when Emir Ahmad of Maʿn deceased and the Maʿn dynasty ended with him, notables of Mount Lebanon met *to elect (li-yantakhibu)* a ruler over them.[11] The opinions of all the notables agreed on Emir Bashir, son of the Emir of Rashayya [in the Bekaa, about 50 km from the coast] Husain al-Shihabi. This is because he was the son of the sister of the deceased Emir Ahmad. They went to Rashayya to call upon him to rule and he accepted.[12] He put in his place the son of his brother Emir Mansur as ruler [of Rashayya] and went with them to Deir al-Qamar where the people received him with great pomp and *acclaimed* him to rule over Mount Lebanon.[13] At the same time, the judge and mufti of Saida arrived in Deir al-Qamar and released the [deceased Maʿn Emir's] estate by order of Mustafa Basha the ruler of Saida.[14]

Between the contemporaneous chronicle of Dwaihi c. 1700 and the one by Shidiaq c. 1860, a long time, stands an intermediary chronicle. This was *Ghurar al-hisan fi akhbar abna' al-zaman* by Haydar Shihab (d.1835).[15] His chronicle is the most detailed and thoughtful.[16] It is too long to translate here,

[9] The three formal social rankings of the Druze community leadership at the time.

[10] Istifan al-Dwaihi, *Tarikh al-Ta'ifa al-Maruniyya* (History of the Maronite community), Beirut: Catholic Press 1890, 257. Emphasis added. Note *ikhtaru*, chose, selected.

[11] Notables of Mount Lebanon, *akaber jabal lubnan*; elect, *yantakhibu*; ruler, *wali*.

[12] Call upon him to rule, *daʿawhu lil-wilaya*.

[13] Acclaimed him to rule over Mount Lebanon, *bayaʿuh al-wilaya ʿala jabal lubnan*. Emphasis added on acclaimed, *bayaʿuh*, from the traditional concept of the Caliph's *bayʿa*.

[14] Tannus al-Shidiaq (d.1861), *Akhbar al-Aʿyan fi Jabal Lubnan* (History of notables in Mount Lebanon), Fuad Efrem al-Bustani ed., Beirut: Manshurat al-jamiʿa al-lubnaniyya 1969 (Original 1855), Year 1697, vol. 1, 311. Estate, legacy, *al-matrukat*.

[15] Haydar Shihab, *Lubnan fi ʿahd al-umara' al-shihabiyyin* (Lebanon during the rule of the Shihabs), Fuad Efrem al-Bustani and Asad Rustom eds, Beirut: Imprimerie Catholique, 1933, 3–5. The book includes Books 2 and 3 of the *Ghurar*, which chronicle the modern period. The first book is not included, as the editors found it of little interest because of Haydar Shihab's coverage of Muslim history just repeating the classical Arab chronicles.

[16] Id., chronicle over three pages, at 3–5. A *petite histoire* riddle is that none of the chronicles mentions Simqaniyya by name. The first instance of 'the plain of Simqaniyya (*marj simqaniyya*)' in Arabic appears in a 1916 contribution to Lebanese history ('*Lamha fi tarikh Lubnan*, Note

but it includes descriptions of protagonists, local and regional intrigues, and a more sophisticated set of explanations than in the other local accounts. It also includes a twist in the narrative on the sole surviving son of Emir Fakhreddin II, Husain.

Fakhreddin II's rule over most of present Lebanon and his threat of expanding into Syria had been thwarted in 1633 and his nuclear family, including his wives, brothers and sons, all killed by 1635. The weakened rule of the Maan continued haltingly with Fakhreddin's nephew Mulhim (d.1658), then Mulhim's son, Ahmad, with whom the male descendance ended in 1697, the year of Simqaniyya.

Fate saved one of Fakhreddin's sons, Husain. When Husain was one year of age in 1622, our chronicler relates, he drew the attention of Khalil Pasha (then an admiral before becoming Minister for the Marine) upon a mission to Beirut. His father delivered the *miri* (the 'Emir's tax') to Khalil through him; whether it was at the time or a few years later is not clear.[17] Khalil liked Husain and when Fakhreddin was arrested and taken to Istanbul for execution two years later, he spared Husain the cauldron of violence accompanying the

on the history of Lebanon') by Bulos Nujaym (d.1931). For a collection of chapters under the title *Lubnan, Mabahith 'ilmiyya wa Ijtima'iyya* (Lebanon, scientific and social studies), see Fuad Efrem al-Bustani ed, Beirut: Manshurat al-jami'a al-lubnaniyya 1969 (Originally commissioned and published in 1916 by Isma'il Haqqi Bey, the last Ottoman governor (*mutasarrif*) of Mount Lebanon), vol. 2, 340. It is the same Nujaym (under the pseudonym of M. Jouplain), who had written one of the early books in defence of the autonomy of Mount Lebanon, *La Question du Liban*. This was his thesis in the Department of Law at the Sorbonne in 1908 (Paris: Rousseau Press). On p. 123 he writes: 'The Porte ... respected the Lebanese constitution (*respecta la constitution libanaise*) and agreed, in return for an annual tax, to the election (*élection*) of a new Grand-Emir by the lords of the Mountain (*seigneurs de la Montagne*). The lords met in a solemn assembly *in the plain of Somkânia*, between Deir-el-Kamar et Mokhtara.' (Emphasis added) This is the first instance I could find in published records where Simqaniyya is mentioned by name. The chronicles which Jouplain cites in the footnote (Dweihi, our first chronicle), Shidiaq (our third chronicle) and Shihab (our second chronicle), do not mention Sumqaniyya by name. Still, the name is too specific for Jouplain to have invented it. It may have appeared in the manuscript version of Haydar Shihab which Jouplain had access to, and which he cites in the footnote as '*Histoire manuscrite des Chehab*, de l'émir Haydar Chehab'.

17 Shihab, *Lubnan fi 'ahd al-Shihabiyyin* (Lebanon during the rule of the Shihabs), above n.14 at 4, is not too clear about dates, but the author writes that Husain the youngest son of Fakhreddin was one-year old in 1622, and it is probable that the *miri* tax was delivered to Khalil to give to the Porte when he was still a boy, which would have been a few years later, maybe on a special visit to Istanbul. When Fakhreddin was arrested and taken to Istanbul, Husain would have been eleven.

demise of his father. Husain remained in Istanbul and grew up at the Ottoman court. Ḥe took over official functions and 'lived for a long time'.[18]

Husain's courtly life must have made Mount Lebanon distant and generally alien to him. The surviving son of Fakhreddin was seventy-five when the last Lebanese Maan died in 1697. The chronicle reports that Husain was consulted by the Porte for the succession of the Maan, and that he advised Istanbul to appoint Haydar Shihab for the leadership of Mount Lebanon. Haydar was still a minor in 1697, only twelve years of age.[19]

Haydar's uncle Bashir (the man whom the notables chose at Simqaniyya) was designated by the Porte as his tutor and is remembered as Bashir Shihab the First. In fact, the Porte agreed only temporarily to the rule of Bashir, who was the genealogically distant son of the sister of the last Maʿn. But the Porte accepted him merely as the tutor of the teen Haydar,[20] and the intrigue over the succession continued. Bashir died in 1707, reportedly poisoned by the by then twenty-one-year old Haydar.[21] Here also, the 1835 chronicle mentions a meeting of the notables to acclaim him, but unlike Simqaniyya, this was a typical, post-facto embrace of a decision taken at a higher level.[22]

There was no Ottoman readiness for the Emirate system giving way to a more collective decision, or disrupting the one-man rule over the villages and towns of Mount Lebanon whose chief task was to collect taxes and keep the peace. The various coastal cities returned to the normalcy of emir autocracy under close control by the Ottoman regional governors. Even the Simqaniyya

[18] '*thumma taqaddam bil-khidma al-mulukiyya wa sar qabbudji basha wa 'asha zamanan tawilan.* (He progressed in service to the monarch, became *qabuçi bashi*, and lived for a long time)'. Id. 5. *Qabuci* was an Ottoman court position akin to head chamberlain. Husain's career includes high positions in the central administration and an ambassadorship at the Mughal court in India. He even wrote a book on Sufism, *Kitab al-tamyiz*, Beirut: Dar al-shuruq 2001.

[19] Husain ibn Fakhreddin is reported to have died in 1697, which is the same year as the last local Maʿn. It may be that the last advice given to the Porte was the appointment of a Shihab, or that a nice story was fabricated that burnished Fakhreddin the Great's legacy with a son who has the last word a half century after seeing his whole family, including his father, mother, and brother, killed.

[20] Shihab, *Lubnan fi 'ahd al-Shihabiyyin* (Lebanon during the rule of the Shihab), above n.14, 3. In 1697, the Ottoman Sultan was Mustafa II (r.1695–1703).

[21] Id., 7: '*wa qil annahu fi dhalik al-hin dass lahu al-amir Haydar summan fi ba'd al-halwa. Li-anna al-amir Haydar kan fi dhalik al-awan qad adrak al-rushd wa-stahaqq rutbat al-wilaya*' (It is said that Emir Haydar put poison in some confectionery served to him. For Emir Haydar had by then become and adult and deserved of the power of governance).

[22] Id., 8. In 1707, the Sultan was Ahmed III (r.1703–1730).

gathering must be viewed as a fleeting occasion which marks in scholarship a mere symbolic founding date of modern Lebanon. Albert Hourani again:

> This was not exactly a free expression of autonomy. The Ottoman governor of Sidon wanted someone with whom to deal on matters of taxation and public order, and, rather than bringing in someone from outside, he needed someone who could command the loyalty of the local population, as an intermediary; this indeed was a common pattern of Ottoman rule.[23]

Nor is it apparent from the documentation who exactly those 'notables of Lebanon' were at Simqaniyya.[24] We do not have their names. All, or nearly all, belonged to the Druze community, the dominant and largest religious community then in Mount Lebanon.[25] Noteworthy was their coming together of their own accord and initiative to deliver a name to the ruler of Saida, who took it to the Sultan for approval. There seems to have been no effort at this point to include any of the other religious communities.

Limitations on the self-determination of these notables are evident. Istanbul did not confirm their choice immediately. A novelty, which appears first in the chronicle of 1835, is the change in terminology. The first chronicle c. 1700 uses the verb to choose ('*ikhtaru*, they chose'). The second (1835) and third (1860) chronicles, both post-French Revolution, use the verb *yantakhibu* and *yantikhibun* respectively, which means to elect. The slight shift

[23] Hourani, 'Political society in Lebanon, above n.6, 8.

[24] Shihab, *Lubnan fi 'ahd al-Shihabiyyin* (Lebanon during the rule of the Shihab), above n.14, 3, mentioning them generally: '*ijtama'at a'yan jabal lubnan lil-mashura*, the notables of Mount Lebanon met for consultation.'

[25] The complicated passage of Ma'n to Shihab is discussed by Abdul-Rahim Abu-Husain in 'The Shihab Succession (1697): A Reconsideration', in *Essays on Ottoman Civilization, Proceedings of the 12th Congress of the Comité International d'Études Pré-Ottomanes et Ottomanes, Prague 1996*, Prague: Oriental Institute 1998, 9–16, and in Yahya Koç, 'Yerel İktidar ve Denetim Bağlaminda i Şihāboğullari ve Cebel-i Şūf Emāreti (1697–1770) ('The Shehab dynasty in the Emirate of Mount Lebanon in the perspective of local power and control)' *Tarih Dergisi* (Istanbul), 69, 2019, 51–86 (with extensive abstract in English). Neither study yields further clues on the meeting at Simqaniyya, although Abu-Husain mentions 'Samaqaniyya' as 'the accepted account ... in Lebanese historiography' and confirms that the meeting was held with the Druze family leaders only (at 9), possibly with one Maronite sheikh (at 10). Both historians give more importance to the 1707 takeover of the Emirate by Haydar, and the 'Ain Dara battle in 1711 which secured the domination of the Shihab and their allies over their local competitors for the next century and a half.

in language signals the passage of the political-institutional vocabulary to the modern democratic era.

The events represent but a small blip in Ottoman history from the perspective of the Empire. The Ottoman archives suggest that the Simqaniyya episode was so insignificant to the Ottoman rulers that the meeting place does not even appear in the records kept in Istanbul, with the whole episode barely registering in their archives.[26]

The birth of Consultative Councils (Cairo 1829, Damascus 1832, Beirut 1834)

The symbolism of local notables choosing their Emir expresses a sense of 'public opinion' in a formal coming together of local leaders to 'choose' or 'elect' a *primus inter pares* who would succeed a deceased Emir with no obvious descendants. In the long life of Ottoman rule in Mount Lebanon, Simqaniyya remains a one-time event from an institutional perspective until the much later nineteenth century breaks. The Mount Lebanon Emir was an individual whose rule was subject to the will of the Sultan running a huge empire from Istanbul, and the Sultan sat way above caring for a provincial event such as the one taking place in tiny Mount Lebanon. In fact, the Lebanese Emirs did not usually report directly to Istanbul. They were under Ottoman absolute rule through various local relays, usually the governors from the coast (Sidon, Acre) or from the interior (Damascus), and they regularly sought their confirmation into power by higher-ups mostly moved by their ability to extract taxes and keep the peace in the territory (*muqata'a*) allotted to them, hence their names as *muqata'jis*, a rough equivalent of feudal landlords.[27]

[26] The late Abdul-Rahim Abu-Husain, *The View from Istanbul: Lebanon and the Druze Emirate in the Ottoman Chancery Documents, 1546–1711*, Oxford: Centre for Lebanese Studies 2004, produces and discusses at 23 and 64–6 a much later document, from January 1707, which mentions the order to appoint Haydar, despite the fact that 'the people (*ehali*) did not accept [him] because he is not forthright and will obstruct the collection of state money and cause losses to the treasury, and [also] because his treason is obvious.' Id., at 65. The appointment was contingent on Haydar's ability to pay the tax. Probably like all the local tax collectors cum rulers, the Porte distrusted him.

[27] For the confluence between the Emirate system and the feudal economy, we have several classic historical studies: William Polk, *The Opening of South Lebanon 1788–1840*, Cambridge: Harvard University Press 1963; Iliya Harik, *Politics and Change in a Traditional Society, Lebanon 1711–1845*, Princeton: Princeton University Press 196; Toufic Touma, *Paysans et Institutions Féodales chez les Druses et les Maronites du Liban du XVIIe siècle à 1914*, 2 Vols, Beirut: Librairie Orientale 1971.

Slow institutional progress came much later, when Ottoman rule was profoundly shaken by the Egyptian occupation of Muhammad 'Ali (1769–1848) whose son Ibrahim conquered the whole Levant in 1830–1.[28] Egyptian rule lasted almost a full decade (1831–1840).[29] Whilst formally under the nominal power of the Sultan, twice during the 1830s the Egyptians came close to defeating the Ottoman realm all the way to Istanbul. Muhammad 'Ali failed because of a combination of local insurrections and European military intervention. The stronger Western powers ultimately preferred a weaker Istanbul to a powerful Cairo. They eventually prevailed through gunboat diplomacy.

In the territories conquered during that decade, which he obviously intended to keep, Muhammad 'Ali sought to establish a whole new administration. This is where the nucleus of constitutionalism in Lebanon started, more precisely in the emergence of a governing council for the city of Beirut.

Egypt's occupation by Napoleon Bonaparte in 1798 is rightly associated with the emergence of the modern Middle East. The French expedition of 1798 was carried out, ostensibly, to embody and establish the 'civilising' ideals of the French Revolution. Its very first expression took the shape of a Council (*diwan*), consisting of nine notables taken from amongst the legal scholars (*'ulama*) and high functionaries. Napoleon ordered its establishment on

[28] Muhammad 'Ali, whose long and turbulent rule from 1805 until his death in 1848 made him 'the founder of modern Egypt', also conquered large parts of the Arab peninsula including the holy cities of Mecca and Medina, all the way to Yemen, as well as significant parts of Ottoman Europe, including Crete and parts of Greece (triggering the Independence revolt), the Sudan, and even parts of Somalia. These conquests have an institutional history of their own, not addressed here. For a map on the impressive extent of the territories Ibrahim conquered, https://upload.wikimedia.org/wikipedia/commons/6/67/Ottoman_Egypt.png. On Muhammad 'Ali generally, see the scholarship of Afaf Lufti al-Sayyed and of Khaled Fahmy.

[29] For Egyptian rule in the larger international scheme, see Caesar Farah, *The Politics of Interventionism in Ottoman Lebanon, 1830–61*, Oxford: Centre for Lebanese Studies 2000, 12–17 on domestic developments. More generally, for the impact on Lebanon, see Khalaf, *Civil and Uncivil Violence in Lebanon*, New York: Columbia University Press 2002, 62–79. Aboultaif, *Power Sharing in Lebanon: Consociationalism since 1820*, New York: Routledge 2019, 38–50; Fawaz Traboulsi, *A History of Modern Lebanon*, London: Pluto Press 2007, 12–13. Edmond Rabbath, *La Formation Historique du Liban Constitutionnel*, Beirut: Lebanese University Publications, 2nd ed. 1986 (original 1973), 196–200. Mas'ud Daher, *Al-Judhur al-Tarikhiyya lil-Mas'ala al-Ta'ifiyya fi Lubnan 1697–1861* (The historical roots of the communal question in Lebanon 1697–1861), Beirut: Farabi 2nd ed. 2009, 315–18, 422–8. For coverage of the 10-year period specifically, Khaled Ziadeh and Boutros Labaki eds, *Al-Manateq al-Lubnaniyya khilal al-Hukm al-Masri 1831–1840* (The Lebanese regions during Egyptian rule 1831–1840), Beirut: Dar Sa'er al-Mashreq 2022.

24 July 1798, the day following the conquest of Cairo, and requested that it meet daily to take care of sundry tasks. The decision reads:

> Bonaparte, member of the National Institute, General-in-Chief, orders:
>
> 1) Cairo shall be governed by a diwan composed of nine persons.
> 2) Shaykh al Sadat, al Sharqawi, al Sawi, al Bakri, al Fayyumi, al Arishi, Musa al Sirsi, the *naqib al ashraf* [head of the notables] Sayyid Umar (Makram), Muhammad al Amir, will go tonight, at five o'clock, to the house of Kiaya al Shawid. They will compose the diwan. They will appoint one of them as president, a secretary taken out of their midst, and two secretaries-interpreters who know French and Arabic. They will appoint a commission of three to oversee the markets and the supplies to the city. They will appoint a commission to bury all the dead who may be in Cairo and two leagues away.
> 3) The diwan will assemble every day at noon, and there will perpetually be three members who will be permanent.
> 4) There will be at the gate of the diwan a French guard and a Turkish guard.
> 5) General Berthier and the commander of the square will go tonight, at five o'clock, to the diwan to install it and make its members take an oath not to do anything against the interests of the army.[30]

The diwan, which did not function as intended because of the rapid popular resistance to the French occupation, provided nonetheless the seed for a different concept of governance. Although the members of this first diwan were chosen by Napoleon, the group was nevertheless collective and meant to represent important factions for consultative purposes. There would be further Napoleonic councils in Cairo and the provinces. In Cairo, two councils provided a daily link with the local population, under tight French control, and operated off and on through the troubled years of the French occupation of Egypt.[31] They disbanded when the Ottomans returned with the

[30] Citations and references in Henry Laurens, *L'Expédition d'Egypte, 1798–1810*, Paris: Armand Colin 1989, 92.

[31] For the 'general council (conseil général, *diwan 'amm*)', composed of 60 members and the smaller 14-member private council (conseil particulier, *diwan khass*), established by Napoleon in Egypt respectively on 7 and 8 October 1798, id., 143–8, 167.

help of the British in 1801, but lingered in collective memory to be revived by Muhammad ʿAli in 1829, when he appointed 156 notables to a *majlis al-shura* (consultative, or deliberative, council) under the leadership of his son Ibrahim:

> In the afternoon of 3 Rabiʿ al-Awwal 1245 [2 September 1829], the Consultative Council (*majlis al-shura*) met by order of our Efendi Muhammad ʿAli Basha. The Council was constituted by officials of the regions, scholars, and notable sheikhs of the country under the leadership of our Efendi Ibrahim to consider the administration of the country's matters.[32]

Al-Waqa'eʿ al-Misriyya, the first journal in Egypt printed in Arabic (1828, lasting to date as official gazette), started referring to the body as *Majlis al-mashura*.[33] The name *shura/mashura* stuck, and the Majlis was supposed to meet once a year. The first meeting in September 1829 lasted over several sessions, because the appointees came from faraway regions in a vast Egypt. There is no mention at this point of any need to include members of different religious groups. Distance forbade their continued presence in the capital. Staying in Cairo was unsustainable, and the Council appears to have faded quickly:

> This council, which could have been the nucleus of a parliamentary system, did not last long. There was not much trace of it during most of the rule of Muhammad ʿAli.[34]

[32] Text in Amin Sami (d.1941), *Taqwim al-Nil: Wa-Asma' man Tawallaw Amr Misr wa-Muddat Hukmihim ʿalayha* (The measuring of the Nile: and the names of those who ruled in Egypt and the duration of their rule), Cairo: al-Matbaʿa al-amiriyya, 3 vols, 1915–33, vol. 2 (1928), 349. (Hereinafter *Taqwim*). Officials of the regions, *ma'muri al-aqalim*. Country, *bilad*.

[33] It is on the texts of *Al-Waqa'eʿ al-Misriyya*, albeit without an explicit reference, that the *Taqwim*, a reference work for the nineteenth century in particular, bases its information. Other works confirm the source for the 1829 council as issue 49 of the *Waqa'eʿ*: see ʿAbd al-Rahman al-Rafiʿi, *ʿAsr Muhammad ʿAli* (The era of Muhammad ʿAli), Cairo: Maʿaref, 5th ed. (original ed. 1930), 517. See also Muhammad Hammad, *Qissat al-Dustur al-Masri* (The story of the Egyptian constitution), Cairo: Jazirat al-ward 2011, 23–4. Hammad mentions bylaws (*qanun tartibat*) for the High Council (*al-majlis al-ʿali*) of Muhammad ʿAli enacted on 23 Safar 1249/12 July 1823. The text, which consists of 12 points organising the internal working of the Council, is reproduced in id., 27–8.

[34] Rafiʿi, *ʿAsr Muhammad ʿAli* (The era of Muhammad ʿAli), above n.33, 522. The Council was preceded and followed by a plethora of councils established by Muhammad ʿAli as essentially advisory or as department and ministries of government. A little known proto-constitution, called *Siyasatnameh*, was also proclaimed. This *Qanun al-siyasatnameh* (literally the statute of policy lists) was proclaimed in Rabiʿ al-Thani 1253 (July 1837). Text in Hammad, *Qissat al-Dustur*

The Consultative Councils of the Levant under Egyptian occupation were different from the 1829 Cairo Council in their composition and in their mission. Egyptian historian Latifa Salem, who worked on the archives of Egyptian rule of the Levant in that period, mentions the emergence of several councils for cities of over 20,000 inhabitants. These 'institutions ... gave the Egyptian conqueror strong pillars for his rule ... and a comprehensive view of the effective cooperation from the larger forces in society. This is a matter which Syria did not know before, and this suggested form of administration followed European systems.'[35] While their members were also appointed by Muhammad 'Ali and operated under the leadership of his son Ibrahim, the Councils were specific to the main cities of the conquered territories.

The Beirut Council was not the first such institution in the territories conquered by the Egyptians. The first Consultative Council was established in Damascus two years earlier, in June 1832, with 22 members from amongst the city notables chosen by Ibrahim, notably including, along with 20 Muslims, one Christian and one Jew.

The founding charter of the Damascus Council, dated 15 Safar 1351/20 June 1832, reads:[36]

> Order was issued by military commander Ibrahim Basha on 15 Safar [1351/20 June 1832] to the persons mentioned hereinafter, who are the best-known families of Damascus-Syria and its grandees, notables and elders, to be members of the special council.[37]

al-Masri (The story of the Egyptian constitution), above n.33, 34–61, and digitally at University of Minnesota Human Rights Library, http://hrlibrary.umn.edu/arabic/Egyptian_Constitution/EG-CON.1837.pdf. It provides a long governmental charter for the realm, with a criminal code of sorts, and includes in section nine a *Majlis shura*, composed of the heads of various agencies and advisors to the ruler (*wali al-amr*). In Istanbul, the first basic text in the reformist era of the Tanzimat was announced in 1839 as the Gülhane edict. Note the correlation. The Egyptian 1837 text deserves a thorough study as a first proto-constitution in the Middle East.

35 Latifa Muhammad Salem, *Al-Hukm al-Masri fil-Sham* (Egyptian rule in Syria), Cairo: Madbuli 2nd ed. 1990 (1st ed. 1983), 79–80. One finds in the 1837 *Qanun al-siyasatnameh*, above n.33, an explicit reference in the establishment of the *majlis shura* to 'the way of European kingdoms.' (Article 9).

36 Text in Dawud Barakat, *Al-Batal al-Fateh Ibrahim wa Fathuh al-Sham 1832* (The conquering hero Ibrahim and his conquest of Syria 1832), Cairo: Wikalat al-sahafa al-'arabiyya 2021 (Original 1931), 49–50. Next excerpts all from these two pages.

37 Id. Military commander, sir, *'askar*. Who are the best-known families of Damascus-Syria and its grandees, notables and elders, *wa hum min ashhar 'a'ilat dimashq al-sham wa akabiriha wa a'yaniha wa shuyukhiha*. The special council, *al-majlis al-makhsus*.

The names of the Council members follow, all twenty of them Sunni. The last two designees are non-Muslim, but the religious denomination is not mentioned. They are referred to as *khawajas* (roughly equivalent at the time to 'sir'): '*khawaja* Rufayil al-Sarraf [Christian], and *khawaja* Mikha'il Kahil [Jewish], all in all 22 persons.'[38]

Then follows the rationale for the Council's establishment:

> Let it be known that in application of the *hadith* [the sayings of Prophet Muhammad] that 'each shepherd is responsible for his flock,' it was incumbent on us to look into the conditions of the flock, including all aspects of its rest and well-being, a matter which does not happen other than by the spread of justice and goodness, and by issuing judgments for them in a rightful way.[39]

Since local buy-in was needed to 'spread justice and goodness' in the newly conquered city, the order further explained that 'we have found best to form a special council from the sages and the informed amongst the notables and grandees and merchants to look into [contentious] matters, and discuss them, and for that we chose you from the public of Damascus-Syria, and allowed you to hear cases and to defer legal disputes to the noble law.'[40]

In the last sentence, the new Council appears as a jurisdiction standing in unnecessary competition with the long-existing judicial organisation of the qadi courts, so Ibrahim Basha made the distinction here between traditional and 'political-policy' disputes. The distinction was not said in so many words, of course, but the order addresses the tasks of the Council in non-judicial matters, dubbed matters of policy (*siyasa*), and the way its decisions and their implementations were to be carried out:

> As for the policy in other matters, decision is made upon your [collective] decision after the concertation and public exchange of opinions between the members of the council made openly.[41] Agreement in opinion [i.e., in

[38] Id. All in all 22 persons, *wa jami'uhum 22 dhatan*. Among the order's 22 names, twenty were Sunni figures with titles like *bey, agha, afandi, hajj, sheikh*. The last two members are distinguished by their non-Muslim 'title', *khawaja*. Note however that the religion is not expressly mentioned in the text, unlike in the later Beirut Council.

[39] Id., 'each shepherd is responsible for his flock, *kullu ra'in mas'ul 'an ra'iyyatihi.*'

[40] Id. Legal (*shar'i*), noble law (*shar' sharif*).

[41] Policy, *siyasa*. Openly, *jahran*.

> the resulting decision] commands implementation in accordance with that opinion. After an opinion [is agreed] a report is brought to our council [here meaning our office or court] for implementation.[42] This is done without bias or personal interest or arbitrary will or bias towards a grandee or a friend or a notable.[43] Anyone who hides his opinion for some reason or for refusing to criticise the words of someone who is more important than him amongst the Council's notables will have opposed our wish and drawn upon himself our blame.[44]

In other words, Ibrahim was encouraging the members of the Council to speak their minds 'without bias', in full equality among them within the Council, and requesting concurrence to the extent possible so that their decision could be implemented. This was a major departure from the tradition in the region, and he was aware of the novelty. Ibrahim's charter concludes with a terse threat: 'The present order is issued as a standard for you. Seek the acquiescence of the flock and the gratitude of honourable religious service. Beware, beware of contradicting it.'[45]

The Damascus Council, and those that followed, mark a departure in modern Middle Eastern constitutionalism. To increase their power in the territories they conquered, the Egyptian rulers selected influential notables in the main cities across the religious/communal spectrum. Tellingly, the Damascus Council's Christian and Jewish members were formally equal to their Muslim colleagues. This equality represents a significant break with the existing system. Muslims had been hitherto considered the unquestioned rulers, with other religious denominations remaining subordinate to them. A second break from traditional governance was to endow these councils with the task of addressing contentious matters of public interest, and of coming up, after proper deliberation, with a collective opinion which the ruler as holder of executive power would then execute.

The system initiated in Damascus was soon adopted and perfected in the other cities conquered by Muhammad 'Ali. We also have two years later,

42 Implementation, *tanfidh*.
43 Bias, *mayl*.
44 Id.
45 Id.

unnoticed in constitutional scholarship, the charter establishing the Council of Beirut in 1834. The text appears in an anonymous chronicle of the battles of Ibrahim Basha, in a book attributed to monk Antun al-Halabi (d.1864).[46]

Our proto-constitutional text is buried within this chronicle.[47] Here is how it starts:

> On the 1st of Ramadan [1249, 12 January 1834], an order from Ibrahim Basha was issued from Tripoli to the governor of Beirut requesting that the capitation average for each person, rich and poor, 90 piasters.[48]
>
> On the 11th of Ramadan, Ibrahim Basha arrived in Beirut with only ten people. Emir Amin [one of the sons of Shihab Emir Bashir II] came to his meeting in Beirut, where Ibrahim Basha ordered the collection of the capitation and a loan of 300 purses.[49]

First things first, securing the tax. Then follows the report which concerns us more directly:

> On 14 [Ramadan, 25 January 1834] Ibrahim Basha ordered the establishment of a Consultative Council (*diwan mashura*) in Beirut composed of 12 men from capable notables of Beirut, with no say to the governor henceforth except in accordance with the decision of the Consultative

[46] [Antun al-Halabi], *Hurub Ibrahim Basha al-Misri fi Suria wal-Anadul* (The wars of the Egyptian Ibrahim Basha in Syria and Anatolia), Asad Rustum ed., Heliopolis n.d. (1927?), 36–8. Asad Rustum compared the handwriting in the manuscript to letters found in the Patriarchal archives to the handwriting of monk Antun Halabi. (Id., 3) Halabi, according to Rustum who enquired about him with then Maronite Patriarch Howayek, was a close supporter of Emir Bashir II. See the short biography of Halabi and references at id., 4–6. The chronicle yields a wealth of information on the patterns of flights, battles, compromises and surrenders during a troubled decade of Egyptian rule, as well as on the social and institutional hierarchy of the time, by a chronicler supporting Emir Bashir. I owe the discovery of this text in 2000 to my cousin Hyam Mallat.

[47] Halabi, *Hurub Ibrahim Basha al-Misri fi Suria wal-Anadul*, above n.47, 36–8. The text appears is contemporaneous to Ibrahim Basha's rule over Lebanon. I suspect the Damascus and Beirut charters were also published in *al-Waqa'e' al-Misriyya*, but the early issues seem hard to find even in Egypt.

[48] Governor, *mutasallem*. Capitation, *farda*.

[49] Id., 36. Purse, *kis*, French 'bourse', is a unit of payment equivalent to 500 piasters (*qursh*) in the middle of the nineteenth century: 'En 1838, l'unité monétaire reste la piastre, apparue au milieu du XVIIè siècle, et qui n'a cessé de perdre de la valeur.' Salgur Kançal and Jacques Thobie. 'L'impossible homogénéisation du système monétaire ottoman', *Relations Internationales*, 99, 1999, 251–68, at 253. See also Albert Frey, *A Dictionary of Numismatic Names*, New York: The American Numismatic Society 1916, entry 'Beutel': '[M]eaning a purse, was a former Turkish money of account. The Keser, or Beutel of silver, was computed at 500 Ghrush [*qursh*] or Piastres.'

> Council [following] a letter from him to the members of the aforementioned Council.[50] [The Council is composed of] six Muslims (*sittat islam*) 'Abd al-Fattah Hamadeh Secretary of the Council, 'Umar Beyh[um], Ahmad al-'Aris, Hasan al-Barbir, Amin Ramadan, Ahmad Jallul, and six Christians (*sittat nasara*), Jibrayel Humsi, Bishara Nasrallah, Elias Menassa, Nasif Matar, Yusuf 'Ayrut, Musa Bustros.[51]

This moment in 1834 is remarkable, both because of the explicit mention in the Beirut Council of religious affiliation and because of the parity between Christians and Muslims, a parity which would endure in the general constitutional system of Lebanon. Importantly, there is no specific communal denomination within the Christian-Muslim segmentation. Muslim members are all most likely Sunnis, as Beirut did not have Shi'i residents at the time. The respective sect of the Christian appointees is not further defined, even though the names of the families, some of which are prominent today, are those of 'Greek-catholic' ('Ayrut) and 'Greek-orthodox' (Bustros). Ibrahim Basha sought a rough, general religious representation. This is a key moment. The population of Beirut at the time was roughly 50–50 Christian and Muslim, and Ibrahim Basha may have had a rough proportional representation in mind. Its logic developed in time into more specific communal denominations characterising the constitutional system in the country.

The Beirut Council's charter, probably drawing on the experience acquired in the Damascus Council, establishes in further detail the role of the Council and its decision-making mechanisms:

[50] Capable notables of Beirut, *akaber Beirut ashab fitna*. Decision, *hukm*.

[51] Halabi, *Hurub Ibrahim Basha al-Misri fi Suria wal-Anadul*, above n.47, 37. Secretary, *nazer*. Most of the family names on the Council remain associated with Beirut notability to date. Yusuf 'Ayrut, whose portrait is still in the family, was a close advisor to the Egyptian rulers. His appointment to the Beirut Council may not have lasted long, and the Yusuf Juju who is mentioned below is probably not the same person. In the 'Ayrut family lore, Yusuf came with Ibrahim Basha from Cairo, where the 'Ayruts thrived through the nineteenth and early twentieth centuries (Conversations with Marie-Antoinette and Charles Airut ('Ayrut), Spring 2022). A Cairo street still carries the name. 'Abd al-Fattah Hamadeh, effectively the head of the Council (*nazer*), also came from Egypt with Ibrahim. Information from the late Hasan Hallaq, in conversation in Beirut on 29 June 2022. The Annex of Jens-P. Hanssen, *The Effect of Ottoman Rule on Fin de Siècle Beirut, 1888–1914*, St. Antony's College, University of Oxford, Phd 2001, includes a useful 'who's who' of the main Beiruti families in the second half of the nineteenth century.

As for the business of the aforementioned Council:[52]

(1) A specific time is fixed every day for the meeting of the members of the Council, and upon their arrival, the registrar writes down their name in a list based on effective presence without attention to their station.[53]
(2) The registrar edits every day the business before him and submits it to the members of the Council when they arrive so that they complete it and so that business does not linger on from day to day.[54]
(3) If these business matters cannot be completed that day, the meeting the following day takes place sometime before the time agreed, enough to complete [unfinished work].
(4) Business which remains from the previous day is not listed in that day's order but on the day it is completed.
(5) When the registrar reads the claim/complaint, an answer is sought from the one among the Council members who is expert in that matter over the others, and the registrar thereafter takes the opinion of the others so that no one remains who has not spoken. If he finds a member of the Council has spoken with another member about a matter unrelated to the claim, he gives him a first then a second warning. If this is to no avail, the case is noted in the minutes of the meeting that so-and-so is busy with matters outside the [public] interest. The registrar must write whatever is decided by the Council and should not leave anything out; every time a decision is made it is written down to accord with the law.[55]

This order of business is far more sophisticated than the one established for the Damascus Council. In the first place, there is an insistence in the Charter that business needs to be carried out until completed. The text also shows the Council more clearly as an adjudicator of claims. The word for claim is the same as the one used in court. Within the Council, the registrar

[52] Business, *tartib.*

[53] Registrar, *kateb*. Presence, *hudur*. Station, *maqam*.

[54] Business, *ashghal.*

[55] Claim/complaint, *da'wa*. Every time a decision is made it is written down to accord with the law, *wa kull ma yataqarrar yakun maktuban wa la yataharrar illa alladhi muwafiq al-haqq*. Halabi, *Hurub Ibrahim Basha al-Misri fi Suria wal-Anadul* (The wars of the Egyptian Ibrahim Basha in Syria and Anatolia), above n.47, 36–7.

appears to hold the agenda and moderate the meeting. He notes the views of all members intervening in the matter at hand, starting with the ones with the greater expertise. The explicit attention to not recording rank and to including all who had not spoken seems to denote a significant effort to make the deliberation substantively productive. Recording the views of all participations was important to the Egyptian rulers:

(6) After the end of the meeting and business disposed of, and when a decision has been reached with the recommendation of all, the registrar writes it in draft.[56] He copies it properly the following day and files it in its appropriate place. It is then noted in the register of the Council, and the registrar takes these summaries every day to the Council after they are noted down, and he reads them at the top of his voice in the presence of all.[57] If they recommend a more appropriate opinion than the one presented, they change the summary, and the [new] dispositions are then presented to the Secretary of the Council, who seals them with the Council's seal.[58] After being registered, the recommendations are taken to the holder of the higher authority [Muhammad 'Ali, represented by Ibrahim, literally 'the master of the matter'] to brief and order those concerned [to implement] the decisions.[59] If His Excellency the ruler is present, then the honourable governor does the briefing.[60]

(7) The registrar holds two registers, the first including a copy of the Council's minutes of the report, the second including the summaries after they are sealed. The registrar must also keep the daily drafts in a bag.[61]

[56] Business, interests, *masaleh*. With the recommendation of all, *bistihsan al-jami'*.

[57] Register, *sijill*. Summaries, *khulasat*.

[58] If they recommend a more appropriate opinion than the one presented, *idha istahsanu ra'yan awfaq min alladhi taqaddam*.

[59] 'the master of the matter', *saheb al-amr*.

[60] The ruler, *hakemdar*. Governor, *mutasallem*. 'The recommendations are taken to the holder of the higher authority [Muhammad 'Ali] to brief and order those concerned [to implement] the decisions. If His Excellency the ruler is present, then the honourable governor does the briefing, *tasil ila saheb al-amr likay yashrah 'alayha ila ashabiha amiran bi-ijra' ma tadamman min al-hukm wa-idha kana sa'adat al-hakemdar mawjudan fa-yushrah min taraf mutasallem agha*.

[61] Id., 37–8.

In practice, the Consultative Councils dealt with various complaints and disputes that were brought to them on any given day. They discussed them and presented the concluding opinion of their deliberations agreed amongst them to the ruler or his deputy. At that point the outcome of their deliberations seems to have been taken as dispositive: 'Ibrahim Basha gave instructions of the need to follow the decisions of the Council in all matters'.[62] Specifically, he granted the Council 'judicial power in civil and commercial matters', and made clear that the decisions be executed when reached unanimously.[63]

Such judicial power contrasts with the long-standing rule of the normal shar'i courts, which are attested to the main cities of the Ottoman Empire with records available since the sixteenth century.[64] Ibrahim Basha's councils solving 'civil and commercial' disputes appear to be in competition with the normal courts, which had been working across the Ottoman Empire as an important locus for dispensing local peace through law.[65]

Other useful information in this Beirut Consultative Council charter is reflected in the names of the notable Beirutis of the time and the degrees of seniority within and beyond the *Diwan mashura* decision-making: *saheb al-amr, hakemdar, mutasallem*, the members of the Council, the secretary (*nazer*) and the registrar (*kateb*).

The flow of decision-making starts with a referral to the Council. This usually comes from the governor of Beirut, an Egyptian appointee, Mahmud Nameh.[66] The Council deliberates and tries to reach a unanimous decision after listening to the most knowledgeable member in the matter at hand, then to all members 'without attention to rank'. The decision is verified the following day (or later as matters tend to be protracted) and raised to the ruler

62 Salem, *Al-Hukm al-Masri fil-Sham*, above n.35, 81.

63 Id., 80.

64 See Chibli Mallat, *Introduction to Middle Eastern Law*, Oxford, Oxford University Press, 2007 (Hereinafter IMEL), 61–86 on Ottoman courts through the prism of the 1667 register of the Tripoli court.

65 There has been significant work from historians, anthropologists and gender studies experts on the Ottoman courts. See for the leading authors, id., 63 fn 228, 64 fn 229, 64 fn 232. For the Beirut shar'i court in the nineteenth century, see the overview of Hassan Hallaq, '*Al-Malameh al-'umraniyya wal-iqtisadiyya wal-ijtima'iyya wal-'askariyya fi Bayrut al-'uthmaniyya* (Urban, economic, social and military aspects in Ottoman Beirut),' *Tarikh al-'Arab wal-'Alam* (n.d.), 24–39, at 25.

66 On the governor (*mutasallem*) of Beirut Mahmud Nameh (or Nami), see Jens Hanssen, *Fin de Siècle Beirut; the Making of an Ottoman Provincial Capital*, Oxford: University Press 2005, 30–2.

for implementation. Although the positions are somewhat blurred in the record, the top decision-maker is Ibrahim Basha, *saheb al-amr* (as himself or as his father's representative), in his absence presumably the [general governor] *hakemdar* 'if he is present', then the governor of the city, the *mutasallem*. In the minutes of the Council, some fuzziness in competence and titles emerges. The *mutasallem* of Beirut is also referred to as *muhafez* in the minutes, to which we now turn.[67]

The Council's work in practice

Regardless of some confusion in the officials' denominations, surviving minutes of the Beirut Council show how the system worked in practice. In one long manuscript document from 1839, dated '11 j 1255',[68] two complaints are brought to the attention of the Council. Present at the meeting were

[67] A slightly different reading of the titles can be found in Farah, *The Politics of Interventionism in Ottoman Lebanon, 1830–61*, above n.29, 13–5. According to him, Emir Bashir, the chief ally of Ibrahim Basha, refused to assume the position of *hakemdar* in 1832, and Mustafa Sharif Pasha was appointed. In *Histoire de Beyrouth*, Paris Flammarion 2003, at 127–8, Samir Kassir writes that Emir Melhem [Haydar], who was close to Bashir II, was the first *mutasallem* of Beirut, and was replaced in 1835 by Mahmud Nameh. In the decision examined here, the *mutasallem* is certainly Mahmud Nameh, and *saheb al-amr* Muhammad 'Ali (via Ibrahim), with Mustafa Sharif Pasha perhaps the *hakemdar*. Of note in the chronicle of Halabi, *Hurub Ibrahim Basha al-Misri fi Suria wal-Anadul*, above n.47, at 24, an order (*marsum*) 'in early Jumada I 1248 [late September 1832]', with no clear authorship (but most likely by Ibrahim Basha), to Emir Bashir 'to appoint *mutasallems* in the cities.' The chronicler notes that Emir Bashir implemented the order by 'sending *mutasallems* to the cities, Emir Melhem [Haydar] to the city of Beirut, Emir Bashir the son of Emir Qasem to Saida, and Emir Hasan al-As'ad to Tyre. And he appointed with them people to help them for the gates and the citadels, one hundred and fifty in each city.' This suggests that Bashir accepted in fact the appointment of *hakemdar* in 1832, but that it did not last. Nor did Melhem, his chosen *mutasallem* in Beirut last long, since we know that he was replaced by Mahmud Nameh. Also of note is the greater importance of Damascus, where Yuhanna Bahri, a Syrian Christian, gained Ibrahim's trust and exercised considerable authority over the whole region under Egyptian occupation, as attested by several chronicles.

[68] 11 J [Jumada?] 1255, which would be 23 July 1839 if Jumada 1, a month later if Jumada 2. I was able to consult and copy the original text from Asad Rustum's papers. Rustum (d.1966), mentioned above for his work on the nineteenth century chronicles, was a remarkable historian. Amongst his many interests, he collected and edited a large set of documents from the then called Royal Archives – now National – archives in Cairo. His papers are available in the American University of Beirut Library, whose efficient staff I am grateful to for facilitating access to the documents and sharing their expertise in them. Those discussed in this section can be found in Asad Jibrail Rustum Collection 1701–2015, A.A.6.2.18, Box no. 11, Archives and Special Collections, American University of Beirut. The Ms of the minutes of 23 July 1839 consists of ten dense pages (hereinafter 'Ms Beirut Council', followed by the folio number), and is partially transcribed in Asad Rustum ed., *Al-Usul al-'arabiyya fi 'ahd Muhammad 'Ali Basha* (Arabic sources in the reign of Muhammad 'Ali Basha), hereinafter *Usul*, Beirut: American University of Beirut 1934,

'the Secretary'[69] and members Ahmad Jallul, Khalil Nasr, Yusuf al-Juju, Hasan al-Barbir, 'Abd al-Qader al-Jubayli, Ne'meh al-Tweini, Sa'id Darwish.' The hour of their arrival is also noted, all at 6 pm except Darwish at 6.15.[70]

The Council has two matters to discuss that day, for which the full record survived. One matter is a lengthy complaint involving the insolvency of one Ramia Khuri, on the insistence of the British consulate in Beirut acting in defence of the interests of a foreign creditor by the name of Held, probably an Englishman. The decision is convoluted and covers several pages.[71] The case arose when Held sought to force Ramia to return money which Ramia owed him in a commercial transaction. The consul wrote to the Beirut governor Mahmud Nameh, who referred the matter to the Council.[72] The Council made the required enquiries and wrote back to Mahmud. The last letter in the file is from Mahmud to the English consul Niven Moore.[73] He explained that enquiries had been made about Ramia Khuri's debt to Held, but that there were several other creditors, including Emir Bashir, as well as foreign ones. It was not possible, Mahmud continued, to force them to all appear and get to the bottom of the insolvency and the order of redistribution of the assets.[74] Yet all of the properties of Ramia Khuri had been attached, save perhaps the house of Ramia which had been deeded over to his wife.[75] At the end of his letter, the governor suggested that the consul should inform him if Held knew of any property of Ramia's that might have gone unnoticed.

Vols 3 and 4, 1934, 247–56, at 249. The names of the participants in the meeting appear on the top of page one of the Ms.

69 Secretary, *nazer*, but his name is not mentioned here. It appears later in the document as Sa'id Darwish.

70 The names of some members differ considerably from those listed above of the first CC in 1834, five years earlier. This suggests a quick system of replacement by the Egyptians, as well as a likely change in the number of members. 'Likely' because members might have been simply absent, but this does not appear in the record despite the charter's injunction to note absentees.

71 Ms Beirut Council, folios 4ff = Rustum, *Usul*, above n.68, 250–7.

72 Governor, *muhafez*.

73 Niven Moore was consul in Beirut between 1835 and 1841 (with an interlude in Aleppo) and between 1841 and 1848: see 'List of British Consular Officials in the Ottoman Empire and its former territories, from the sixteenth century to about 1860' July 2011, entry Niven Moore, at http://www.levantineheritage.com/pdf/List_of_British_Consular_Officials_Turkey(1581-1860)-D_Wilson.pdf

74 Assets, *tabeq*, the technical word for bankruptcy assets.

75 Rustum, *Usul*, above n.71, 252.

The matter may have not been fully solved in the exchange, but it shows where it ended with the Council, and sheds light on its decision-making process. The Council was first brought in on the case by the Beirut governor in reaction to the case raised before him by the English Consul. In turn, the governor asked the Council to investigate and find a solution. The information of the Council, which revealed its inability to decide further because it could not summon all the creditors, was then passed on to the governor, who in turn relayed the information to the English Consul. The property had been fully attached for the liquidation, but the liquidation process itself was stalled because of the absence of most creditors. The Beirut governor added his own advice to probably reassure the Consul of his personal attention to the matter. He suggested that Held enquire further about any other property of Ramia for it to be also attached.[76]

The Held case was a consular matter. It is one of many in the context of the capitulations providing redress for foreigners outside the local adjudication system. By that time, the European powers, especially the British and the French, were well established in the Mediterranean. Bonaparte's wars in Egypt and Palestine were still remembered, and the British had shown their firepower effectively to Muhammad 'Ali, checking his ambition to take over Anatolia in 1832, then in 1839–40. Egyptian armies had the upper hand against the Sultan's forces, but Muhammad 'Ali was bombed into submission. The long-standing capitulatory system had by then transformed from the original mutual diplomatic courtesy between European countries and the Ottoman powers into a one-sided protective system for European interests and residents in the Levant.

The Beirut CC also dealt with domestic issues. The first matter preserved in the archives for that meeting is eminently local and worth a closer look for its significance on the CC's procedure and power in decision-making. The Council examined a claim from the wife of Salama al-Dahhan to the governor, who again passed it on to the Council.[77] She mentions that her husband had been found guilty of theft in Acre ('Akka) some fourteen years earlier and

[76] Id., 256.

[77] Claim, *istid'a*. *Dahhan* is house painter, but we don't know from the report the name of his wife, even though she is the claimant. This and next excerpts from Ms Beirut Council, ff 1–3 = Rustum, *Usul*, above n.71, 249–50.

fined 'a sum of dirhams beyond his capacity'. In order to get her husband out of prison, she sold some of her own belongings in her father's house. The husband had to sell his farm[78] to a relative in Zuk Mikhayel (a coastal village 10 km north of Beirut) for 2500 piasters, but she rushed to the buyer, got it back at the same purchase price, and received a deed confirming that she had repurchased the property. The farm was hers now, not her husband's; he had recently relapsed in debt because the silk market had collapsed, leading 'to great loss'.

Meanwhile the farm had been taken over by the government, possibly because of an unpaid tax, but she explained that the property was hers and not her husband's. The deed, which was produced in the meeting, is the legal basis for her complaint to the governor, in which she claimed the return of the property to her, especially since her husband had physically beaten her and absconded, and she and her children were now totally destitute:'It has been a month. I have not heard from him, and I am still waiting. He left me with the children, your subjects, in total poverty. We have nothing to eat and no one opens the door for us. We have no shelter after God other than your care and pity.'[79]

The reason why the claimant could not dispose of the property was a government lien for a tax due and unpaid, the *miriyye* (relative to *miri*, 'the Emir's tax'). The abandoned wife of Salama al-Dahhan was asking for 'her' farm to be returned to her lien-free so that she could pay the remainder of the fiscal debt, as well as 'the price of the flour needed' to avoid starving. After all, she had a title to the farm, and she produced the repurchase deed as proof.

When the Council examined her petition at the request of the governor, various members made comments on the way to solve the problem. The register includes first a comment by member Ahmad Jalloul, then by member Yusuf al-Juju, and finally by the Council's Secretary, Sa'id Darwish. They discuss the deed, confirming its authenticity and the likely ownership of the

[78] *'awda*, which is a word from the period, linked to the silk industry which enriched (and then ruined) Mount Lebanon in the second half of the nineteenth century. The word has since faded from use. It is 'a type of farm which includes planted trees of silk mulberry, fruit and olives.' Hallaq, '*Al-Malameh al-'umraniyya wal-Iqtisadiyya wal-Ijtima'iyya wal-'askariyya fi Bayrut al-'uthmaniyya*,' above n.65, 31.

[79] Ms Beirut Council, ff 1–3 = Rustum, *Usul*, above n.71, 249. (your subjects, literally your slaves, *'abidukum.*)

petitioner. On the problem of the attached property, effectively confiscated because of the *miri* tax, the solution which the Majlis provides 'unanimously' was for the impending harvest of silk to be released to her – but mortgaged for the value of the tax owed to the treasury, set at 2600 piasters.[80] The report was destined to the governor (*hakemdar*) for action.

In modern terms, this is an administrative petition to the Council for state dispossession of a piece of property, complicated by a taxation dispute and assets' attachment. The members opined on the merits of the petition, and on the documents produced, namely the deed (*hujja*) of the petitioner about her alleged ownership of the farm.

This all sounds like a judicial proceeding. Although the case went to the Beirut CC, the normal court would have been a more appropriate forum. Members of the council are notables and not judges, and they sound in the text slightly out of their depth. It is also true that unlike a normal court, whose decision is binding, the 'judicial' power they have is not fully theirs, for they could only recommend a course of action to the general governor, the *hakemdar*, and not even directly to him since it was up to the Beirut governor who had passed on to them the initial petition to convey the Council's 'decision' to the higher authority.[81]

The conflict of jurisdictions is attested in Damascus, where the normal shar'i court was long established.[82] In the case of Beirut, we do not have reports from a local court extant before 1843, and our Council discussion dates from three years earlier.[83] A shar'i court in Beirut is attested only after the Egyptians

[80] Ms Beirut Council 2 in fine, Ms Beirut Council 3 top, eight signatures. Text not in *Usul*.

[81] Insofar as these two decisions appear to be administrative because the request is for the 'executive' authority to intervene – the local municipal power in the consular request, and the tax department for Salama al-Dahhan's wife – one could conclude that such matters came under the jurisdiction of the Beirut Consultative Council because of its state/administrative dimension. This explanation is unsatisfactory. In the Ottoman courts at the time, the separation between normal/shar'i and state/administrative jurisdictions did not exist, and normal courts included administrative claims in their judicial remit. The normal shar'i court was a 'court for all seasons' according to the registers: see IMEL, above n.64, 75–86 for administrative decisions before the Tripoli court two hundred years earlier.

[82] See Ferdinand Perrier, *La Syrie sous le Gouvernement de Méhémet-Ali jusqu'en 1840*, Paris: Arthus Bertrand 1842, 56–60.

[83] Hassan Hallaq was the first scholar to uncover the riches of the Beirut court *sijillat* (registers), for instance in *Al-Nahda al-Sina'iyya wal-Iqtisaddiyya wal-Tijariyya fi Beirut al-Mahrusa 1840–1914* (The industrial, economic and commercial revival in hallowed Beirut), Beirut: al-Nahda al-'Arabiyya 2019, esp. 195–210, where several original documents of the register are

left and the Council disbanded when Ottoman rule was restored.[84] In Tripoli, the reports are continuous since 1666, and conflicts between the local CC and the qadi court were inevitable. This was not alien to the classical age, where courts did not readily infringe on the powers of the ruler in police and criminal matters, but where the administration could be held responsible for private property violation.[85] A study of the registers of the Tripoli courts during Egyptian rule shows the efforts of Ibrahim Basha to curtail their previously wide adjudication to personal status/family disputes. It also shows a complicated division of labor between the Tripoli CC and the Tripoli shar'i court.[86]

Let us now look more closely at the charter of the Beirut Council.

Essentially, the presence of the members is requested to document, discuss, and decide on important daily affairs of the city, 'with the recommendation of all'.[87] Decisions are not taken immediately. There is no voting, but an extensive

published in facsimile. We have for instance a criminal decision about the request by the relatives of a man shot by the defendant to punish him for talion (*qisas*). The pistol shooting of the man had taken place in Tayyuneh (then 'near Beirut'), and the court agreed to administer the talion after various parties, including the police, were asked to testify. The testimony focuses particularly on the fact that the victim eventually died from the wounds deliberately occasioned by the defendant. Report in full facsimile at id., 195. The decision is from 1263/1846. Since there are no available decisions before 1843, it may well be that the Beirut court did not exist (or function) between 1834 and 1840, when the Council operated. This was not the case in Damascus and Tripoli, where courts had long been established. The overlap of jurisdictions disoriented the claimants, and significant confusion resulting from this overlap attested in the contemporaneous book by Ferdinand Perrier cited in the previous note.

[84] In addition to the Held and Dahhan cases, similar reports on disputes involving the British consulate are summarised in Su'ad Salim and Su'ad Merhej, '*Majalis al-mashura (al-shura) fi Lubnan Ayyam Muhammad 'Ali* (the Consultative council in Lebanon at the time of Muhammad 'Ali)', in Ziadeh and Labaki eds, *Al-Manateq al-Lubnaniyya khilal al-Hukm al-Masri 1831–1840*, above n.29, 487–99, at 495–6. One report adjudicated by the Beirut CC was about the ownership of a small boat moored in Beirut harbor that was in dispute between two locals, id. at 496.

[85] IMEL, above n.64, 79–82.

[86] Ghina Murad, '*Al-Hamla al-Misriyya wa Atharuha 'ala Wilayat Trablus* (The Egyptian campaign and its effects on the district of Tripoli), in Ziadeh and Labaki eds, *Al-Manateq al-Lubnaniyya Khilal al-Hukm al-Masri 1831–1840*, above n.29, 403–61, at 419 on the conflicts between the shar'i court and the newly established Consultative Council of Tripoli. I was not able to ascertain when the Tripoli Consultative Council was first formed. The earliest document attested in Rustum, *Usul*, above n.71, v.3–4, at 19–21, bears the date 15 Sha'ban 1251/6 December 1835. Since Tripoli was occupied by the Egyptians after Beirut, and witnessed an upheaval against the new rulers in 1834, the Council must have been formed that year or the following one. Like the Beirut Council, it also included Christian members.

[87] From the Beirut CC Charter, in Halabi, *Hurub Ibrahim Basha al-Misri fi Suria wal-Anadul* (The wars of the Egyptian Ibrahim Basha in Syria and Anatolia), cited above n.71, 39. I translate *istihsan* here as recommendation. The word *istihsan*, literally preference, is not as strong as decision, so 'recommendation' is a more appropriate translation here.

deliberation takes place, with expertise solicited first from the best-informed members, then from the whole Council. Once everyone has opined and the views converge into a recommendation, the comments and concluding results are written down. They are read again the following day to the Council, which might yet change the recommendation. Only then is it raised to the higher authorities for execution. The equality amongst members and attention to the expertises of each are remarkable.

The first five paragraphs of the Charter show Ibrahim Basha to mean business, while the role of the registrar in keeping order in the Council's work is rather amusing.[88] The fact that the minutes were preserved and ordered to be sent on a regular, sometimes daily basis to Cairo, shows the determination of Ibrahim Basha and his father to create an institution with real power and bureaucratic memory. Mostly, consultative councils with some decision-making authority help their rule align with some of their subjects' wishes; and if not all the subjects, at least the notables amongst them.

Beyond its historical value on daily life in Beirut in the 1830s, the CC Charter is important as the first official document establishing in law the communal equality of Muslims and Christians who are entrusted with public business: 'twelve members ... six Christian and six Muslim'. This dates Muslim-Christian parity in Lebanese constitutional decision-making back to 1834. Between the Beirut Council of 1834 and the Lebanese Parliament of 2022 there is little structural difference. Under Art. 24 of the Lebanese Constitution as amended in 1990, 'the positions are distributed ... in equal number between Christians and Muslims.'[89]

This could be a mere coincidence, but it is not. The communal template lives on to date, with few variations in the successive Councils' overall membership for almost two hundred years.

[88] Cited above, text cited at n.55, on recording a member's disruptive behaviour: 'If he finds a member of the Council has spoken ...'

[89] '*tuwazza' al-maqa'ed ... bil-tasawi bayn al-masihiyyin wal-muslimin.*'

3

The Entrenchment of Communalism and the Birth of the Electoral Principle (1840–1920)

> ... yet without Mount Lebanon there could be no broader politics ... Conflict in the Mountain did not begin today. Yet this is the region which, from 1864 to 1914, for fifty full years, lived an admirable peace.[1]

Ibrahim Basha's rule ended in 1840, and Egyptian troops retreated from the Levant never to return. The Egyptian withdrawal was the result of various revolts, in Palestine in 1834, and in Lebanon and Syria in 1838–9, combined with European military interventions and *ultimata* in support of the Ottomans under the leadership of England. This was a tumultuous, important period in the Middle East:

> After a year of tense deadlock over the 'Egyptian question', while the Pasha [Muhammad 'Ali] refused to return the fleet or withdraw his troops and, on the other hand, the sultan refused to grant him independence, Palmerston [the British Foreign Secretary] intervened and called a conference in London in July 1840. The 'Convention for the Pacification of the Levant' gave the Pasha an ultimatum to withdraw from Syria, Adana, Crete, and Arabia. When the Pasha still refused to comply, a British force landed at Beirut in September, defeated Ibrahim, and forced him to withdraw to Egypt.[2]

[1] '... mais sans le Mont-Liban aucune grande politique ne se ferait ... La turbulence de la Montagne n'est pas d'aujourd'hui; mais c'est aussi le pays qui, de 1864 à 1914, pendant cinquante ans entiers, a connu une paix admirable.' 'Doit-on le dire?', 7 March 1946, Pol Int 94–5. By 'grande politique', Chiha probably meant that all Lebanese politics must be anchored in the Mountain.

[2] Khaled Fahmy, 'Era of Muhammad Ali Pasha, in *The Cambridge History of Egypt*, vol. 2, *Modern Egypt, from 1517 to the End of the Twentieth Century*, M. W. Daly ed., Cambridge: Cambridge University Press 1998, 139–79, at 175.

In Mount Lebanon, most historians ascribe the first communal clashes to the enlistment and arming by Emir Bashir, at the request of Ibrahim Basha, of the Maronites against the Druze, the two main religious communities in the Lebanese mountain. The confrontation, which followed the withdrawal of the Egyptian conqueror, was to be repeated time and again in a tragic pattern of local and foreign alliances over the following two centuries:

> The greatest sacrifice which the Lebanese Christians offered their Egyptian friends was their fighting their Druze neighbours who stood against the Egyptian government (...) Ibrahim entrusted them with this mission [of bringing down the rebellion], and it was harder than the previous missions [which included the massive revolt in Palestine in 1834], because they were forced to fight their neighbours and former comrades. And they continued to resist until forced to yield.
>
> But this victory achieved by the Maronites for the benefit of their Egyptian allies cost them dearly. As soon as the Egyptians withdrew from Syria in 1840, the Druze started holding a grudge towards the Maronites, until they made a deal with the Ottoman rulers and carried out the horrendous massacres in 1845 and 1860, in which the Maronites lost a third of their population and a large part of their country.[3]

Persistent turmoil followed the Egyptian withdrawal, with peasant uprisings and communal – that is religious – strife recurring between 1840 and 1860.

The two kaïmacams' councils (1842–1860)

The violent dissensions between Maronites and Druze in the Lebanese mountain area continued under restored Ottoman rule.[4] To remedy a state

[3] Bulos Qara'li (d.1952), author of the first preface to Antun al-Halabi, *Hurub Ibrahim Basha al-Misri fi Suria wal-Anadul* (The wars of the Egyptian Ibrahim Basha in Syria and Anatolia), Asad Rustum ed., Heliopolis n.d. (ca 1927), presented in ch.2. The preface is signed and dated 25 May 1927 by 'Pastor Bulos Qara'li', at 8.

[4] For the period of the two *Qa'immaqamiyyas*, see generally Fawaz Traboulsi, *A History of Modern Lebanon*, London: Pluto press 2007, 24–40; Samir Khalaf, *Civil and Uncivil Violence in Lebanon*, New York: Columbia University Press 2002, 79–102; Aboultaif, *Power Sharing in Lebanon-Consociationalism since 1820*, New York: Routledge 2019, 50–2; Edmond Rabbath, *La Formation Historique du Liban Constitutionnel*, Beirut, Lebanese University Publications, 2nd ed. 1986 (original 1973), 205–20. Mas'ud Daher, *Al-Judhur al-Tarikhiyya lil-Mas'ala al-Ta'ifiyya fi Lubnan 1697–1861* (The historical roots of the communal question in Lebanon 1697–1861),

of affairs that threatened their restored rule, the Ottomans, prodded by the British, established a Consultative Council for the Mountain on 22 May 1841 in the spirit of those established the previous decade in Beirut and Damascus. By the summer of 1841 that new CC had collapsed under the weight of renewed armed clashes.[5] Eventually, another idea emerged: Istanbul agreed with the five European powers holding consulates in Beirut – Britain, France, Austria, Prussia and Russia – to divide Mount Lebanon into separate, northern and southern Kaïmacam Councils (KC).[6] The dividing line agreed on was the Beirut-Damascus Road, which had just been built.

The idea appears to have been Metternich's, as the foreign minister of a powerful Austria which, together with other European powers, had an increasing say in matters Levantine.[7] It is documented for the first time in a 1842 dispatch from Metternich proposing to divide the troubled mountain into two districts, with a Maronite and a Druze as their respective heads.[8] In the northern, dominantly Maronite region, the Porte appointed a local Christian kaimacam; in the southern, mixed region, it designated a local Druze leader. The arrangement generally held and jelled over three

Beirut: Farabi 2nd ed. 2009, 428–43; and the extensive archival work of Cesar Farah, *The Politics of Interventionism in Ottoman Lebanon, 1830–61*, Oxford: Centre for Lebanese Studies 2000, 52–553.

5 Caesar Farah, *The Politics of Interventionism in Ottoman Lebanon, 1830–61*, above n.4, 68–70.

6 Kaïmacam council, *majlis al-qa'immaqamiyya*. The kaïmacam means the official 'standing in the position of', here of the Sultan. I have generally adopted the spelling Kaïmacam (the post), Kaïmacamia (the institution) in the French diplomatic usage of the time.

7 Richard Edwards, *La Syrie 1840–62*, Paris: Amyot 1862, 87: 'M. de Metternich trouva un moyen terme qui consistait à établir deux administrations, l'une chrétienne et l'autre druze. Au mois de septembre 1842, cette nouvelle solution fut connue. (Mr de Metternich found a middle way which consisted in establishing two administrations, one Christian, the other Druze. In September 1842, this new solution became known.)' The 'Metternich solution' appears to have been adumbrated first in a meeting between him and Ali Efendi, the Ottoman ambassador to London, who stopped en route to see him in Vienna. Details in Farah, *The Politics of Interventionism in Ottoman Lebanon, 1830–61*, above n.4, 187.

8 'Résumé d'une conférence entre le ministre des affaires étrangères de la Sublime-Porte et les représentants des cinq puissances, tenue le 27 mai 1842 (16 rébiul-akhir 1258)'. These minutes form part of the 11-volume collection of diplomatic and other historical documents for the Ottoman Empire since the sixteenth century, compiled by Baron Ignaz de Testa, *Recueil des Traités de la Porte Ottomane*, Paris: Amyot then Bibliothèque Diplomatique, 1864–1911 (Hereinafter 'Baron de Testa, followed by the volume number). The minutes appear in vol. 3, 1878, 113–19. The report mentions the idea of Metternich in a dispatch (*dépêche*) which it dates on 17 May 1842, ten days before the meeting. Id., 116.

years under the so-called 'Règlement de Chekib Efendi', named for the then Ottoman foreign minister.[9]

The process leading to the adoption of the Règlement was staggered, in an almost trial and error exercise. At a meeting with the five European powers on 27 May 1842, 'the Turkish ministers, appearing to desire some progress, were asked whether the Porte would be opposed to a combination in which Druzes and Maronites would be placed under two separate leaders taken from their respective regions.'[10] The Turkish envoys demurred, expressing reservations about 'a measure which would be impossible to achieve, because Druze and Maronites live together in the same villages.'[11] But the participants agreed to give the matter further thought, and the Turkish side rallied slowly to the proposal.

While Istanbul and the European powers debated, communal discord and conflict dug in. Action was needed. In pursuit of the emerging understanding, the local commander of the Ottoman military contingent stationed in Sidon dismissed the ineffective Emir Bashir Shihab III. The Ottomans nominated on 1 January 1843 a Maronite emir as kaimacam for the Christian district and a Druze Emir for the Druze district. To no avail. The communal troubles which had broken out in 1841 flared up again in 1845 on a larger scale, highlighting the precariousness of the arrangement. But the framework for partition had the blessing of the international forces of the day, and it proved difficult to depart from the consensus. In 1845, the publication of the Règlement made the accumulated compromises official in a detailed document establishing the new regime of a Mount Lebanon divided geographically while the populations remained mixed, as the Turkish envoys had pointed out and warned against.

9 Full text of the Règlement as 'Instructions du commissaire de la Sublime-Porte (Chékib-éfendi) aux représentants aux conseils des deux kaïmacams, en date de fin octobre 1845 (fin-chéwal 1261),' Baron de Testa, vol. 3, 200–7. See also Rabbath, *La Formation Historique du Liban Constitutionnel*, above n.4, 212–14. Rabbath considers the Règlement as the first template of communal constitutionalism in Lebanon, but he did not know about the Beirut Council of 1834.

10 'Les ministres turcs ayant paru désirer quelques développements, on leur a demandé si la Sublime-Porte serait contraire à une combinaison par laquelle les Druses et les Maronites seraient placés sous deux chefs séparés pris dans chaque nation respective.' Baron de Testa, vol. 3, 118.

11 Id. Live together, literally fused together, *confondus*.

The Règlement took the form of 'instructions' (in Arabic *tartibat*, arrangements) from Chekib Efendi to members of each of the two KCs, giving their names, the roles of the officials in the two administrations, and a complicated dispute resolution mechanism with judges from the various sects also appointed to the Council. Unlike in the Beirut Council, where members were described generally as Muslims and Christians, the sectarian identity (rather than the religious one) was specified for each of the members and judges appointed.[12] This was a momentous innovation, which lasts until today: in the establishment of both KCs, a finer religious grain than the simple Muslim/Christian divide of the Beirut Consultative Council charter was adopted.

With the inherent instability of the arrangement, of which the Turkish participants to the May 1842 meeting had wisely warned, civil strife continued intermittently.[13] Repeated revolts led to the gradual introduction of ever-wider *electoral* consultation for membership in the governing councils, a feature absent from institutional structures until then but presaged, at village level, several years earlier, in 1820, when 'no less than 6000 insurgents from the villages of Kesrwan and Metn met in the village of Antelias [near Beirut] and accomplished the unheard of: they established a *wakil* (agent/representative) for each village represented in the assembly'.[14] In 1821 in the Jbeil (Byblos) region, insurgents claimed the right to choose their Emir themselves, with a 'convention' of the residents of the village of Bshe'leh entrusting the representation of their interests to a local *wakil*.[15] In Antelias in June 1840, referring to the precedent of the call to arms in the third year of the French revolution, and to the Greek rebellion against the Ottomans from 1821 to Greek Independence in 1830, the insurgents demanded elections to choose their representatives in a proclamation to 'the friends of the Nation (Amis de la Patrie)':[16]

[12] List of members of each kaïmacam, judges and substitutes, in Baron de Testa, vol. 3, 201–2.

[13] See text of the Turkish reluctance at n.10 above.

[14] Nadi Abi Rached, 'Les origines historiques du système électoral libanais', *Travaux et Jours*, 93, 2018, 21–45, at 23.

[15] Id., 24–5.

[16] 'Proclamation des insurgés du mont Liban à leurs compatriotes, en date du 8 juin 1840', Baron de Testa, vol. 3, 74–6: 'Amis de la Patrie' (at 74); comparison with the French who 'preferred to die rather than surrender ... and killed 150,000 men' (at 75, in an unexpectedly precise reference to

> To act with the dignity and strength which such grave circumstances require, a meeting of our most outstanding and enlightened men becomes necessary that we may include the wisdom and levelheadedness of free men in our decision-making.[17]

Freedom in decision-making translated in the next section into 'election' on a territorial rather than religious basis:

> This meeting shall be composed of five chiefs elected by a majority in each district, and they shall form among themselves all or in part a council established in a suitable place in order to arrive at a perfect system.[18]

In the final months of 1840, as Egyptian domination stood on its last legs, Emir Bashir II had succeeded in crushing the Antelias insurgency, making short shrift of the rebels' yearning for the democratic election of a governing council. As for the Règlement of Chékib Efendi formally establishing the Kaïmacamia in 1845, it was undone by its own complexity and proved ineffective in containing violence. Communitarian skirmishes persisted until a larger popular revolt in 1858, when Druze and Christians briefly joined forces against the feudal regime under the leadership of commoner Tanius Shahin (1815–1895).[19]

Like its predecessors in 1820 and 1840, the 1858 revolt is remembered as *'ammiyya'* – one of the 'commoners' movements'. They all reveal in their recurrence a 'national' propensity to break free from sectarianism, but the brief cross-sectarian appeal soon gives way to the return, with a vengeance, of the communal system. Revolts are rooted in a wide dismay resulting from

the *Soldats de l'an ii*); Greek rebellion (at 75–6). Text cited in part by Abi Rached, 'Les origines historiques du système électoral libanais', above n.14, 25.

17 'Pour agir avec la dignité et la force qu'une circonstance aussi solennelle exige, et pour mettre dans notre décision la sagesse et la pondération d'un peuple libre, il faut une réunion des hommes les plus marquants et les plus éclairés parmi nous.' Baron de Testa, vol. 3, 75.

18 'Cette réunion sera composée du cinq chefs élus à la majorité dans chaque district, et ils formeront entr'eux tous ou en partie un conseil érigé dans un lieu convenable pour obtenir une parfaite organisation.' Baron de Testa, Id.

19 For the 1858 revolt, see Antoine Charif Sfeir, *Genèse du Liban moderne 1711-1864*, Paris: Riveneuve 2013, 247–66; Traboulsi, *A History of Modern Lebanon*, above n.4, 29–33; Ussama Makdisi, 'Corrupting the Sublime Sultanate: The Revolt of Tanyus Shahin in Nineteenth-Century Ottoman Lebanon,' *Comparative Studies in Society and History*, 42, 2008, 180–208, and Yehoshua Porath, 'The Peasant Revolt of 1858–61 in Kisrawan,' *Asian and African Studies*, 2, 1966, 77–158. See also, the important work of Dominique Chevallier, *La Société du Mont Liban à l'Epoque de la Révolution Industrielle en Europe*, Paris: Geuthner 1971, 272–81.

heavy taxation or the forced enlistment of young men in the armed forces of Istanbul or Cairo, and these less- or non-sectarian revolts underlie the recurrent promise of a proto-national or national appeal, with its own continuity over time in collective memory. Large-scale popular revolts that include significant participation across the sectarian divide provide an alluring story from the bottom up. This persistent contradiction between 'the people' taking to the street and the communal bedrock of the political system through more than two hundred years of the modern history of the country has been noted:

> *The circumstances which impelled groups to resort to political violence were not necessarily those which sustained their mobilization and informed the direction and outcome of conflict.* All three uprisings [1820–1, 1840–1, 1858–60], as we have seen, were initially sparked off by a sense of collective consciousness and a concern for public welfare. Yet, all were deflected, at one point or another, into confessional hostility: Likewise, episodes of communal conflict, originally provoked by socioeconomic disparities and legitimate grievances, were transformed (or deformed) into factional or confessional rivalry.[20]

A strong factor in the larger 1858 uprising echoes movements provoked by taxes imposed on commoners and by threats to their personal security, including forced conscription, the world over.

> Again and again, in other words, struggles over 'divisible goods', i.e., contests of distributive justice as to who gets what and how much, are deflected into struggles over 'indivisible principles', those embedded in primordial loyalties and the inviolable attachments of faith, creed, community, and family. The enthusiasm for 'class' struggle and collective mobilization among Christian peasants in the North found little appeal among their counterparts in the Druze districts ... Expressed more concretely, confessional, local, and feudal allegiances continued to supersede other public and collective interests. A Druze remained a Druze first, a Jumblatti second, a Shufi third and then, a fellah or part of the *'ammah*.[21]

[20] Khalaf, *Civil and Uncivil Violence in Lebanon*, above n. 4, 68. Emphasis in original.

[21] Id. *'amma*, here the commoners, is also the word for 'public', 'generalised'. From it also derives the word *'ammiyya* as the revolt of the commoners, or the public, generalised revolt. The word has since fallen into disuse.

Social historians study the logic and rhythm of recurrent popular revolts which raised hope of institutional solutions to communitarian deadlocks in nineteenth-century Lebanon. These uprisings by commoners, most of whom peasants, appear more as a jacquerie limited in time than a revolution with an ideological inspiration. For our purposes, it is sufficient to note that cross-sectarian revolts were recurrent in the nineteenth century – in 1820, 1840, and 1858, mostly in the shape of peasants' uprisings against the feudal system. They are important in Lebanese history. But the revolts have not produced constitutional texts, despite attempts to formalise nascent leaderships into councils which, even whey they were formed, did not formally express popular representation.

Regardless of the limited and unstructured revolutionary appeal, a *longue durée* pattern emerges: the Lebanese peoples marched together time and again, from the 1820 *'ammiyye* of Antelias, through Independence in 1943, and up to the great upheavals of 2006 and 2019, the last also marked by social-fiscal grievances.[22] When the hope for radical break with communalism was dashed, the disagreement became more than simply socio-fiscal; conflicts assumed a far more alarming dimension:

> *[A] disconcerting but explicable inference stands out.* It is one with prophetic implications for the course and magnitude violence was to assume in the future. As long as the conflict remained a 'class' rivalry, exacerbated by fiscal pressures, socioeconomic disparities, political coercion and the like, it was comparatively bloodless. If and when, however, it was transformed or deflected into a confessional or communal hostility, the magnitude and intensity of violence became much more menacing.[23]

The Administrative Council (1861–1920)

The Kaïmacamia and its institutions were a casualty of the 1860 civil war. January to July 1860 saw bloody communitarian clashes that culminated in wide-scale massacres in the mountains all around Beirut before spreading to

[22] The upheaval of 2019 was triggered by the government's decision to increase the tax on the until then free use of WhatsApp. It is known as the Whatsapp revolt. It started on 19 October 2019, and remained active until the onset of the COVID pandemic in early 2020.

[23] Khalaf, *Civil and Uncivil Violence in Lebanon*, above n.4, 102. Emphasis in original.

southern and eastern Lebanon and then to Damascus.[24] The fighting ended only with military intervention carried out separately by the French and the Ottomans.

Once order was reestablished in late summer 1860, a new constitutional arrangement was deemed necessary to replace the two Kaïmacam Councils. An agreement was reached by Istanbul and the five powers the following year in a multi-nationally endorsed 'Protocol', accompanied by a proto-constitutional text which became known as 'Règlement Organique'.[25] An Amended Règlement Organique followed in 1864.[26]

The arrangements adopted in 1861 replaced the failed partitioning model of the last two decades and ushered in a long period of stability marred only by the brief insurrection in 1866 of a local notable called Yusef Karam.[27] The era came to be known as the Mutasarrifiyya (1861–1920).[28] Istanbul was

[24] Full study in Leila Fawaz, *An Occasion for War: Civil Conflict in Lebanon and Damascus in 1860*, Berkeley: University of California Press 1994. I examine the work of the tribunals set to punish the participants in the mass killings of Christians in Mount Lebanon and in Damascus in 1860–1 in *Philosophy of Nonviolence*, New York: Oxford 2015, 246–55.

[25] Règlement Organique is commonly used to distinguish the text from the 1843 Règlement de Chekib Efendi, the charter of governance agreed between the Ottomans and the five European powers in 1861. The 1861 Règlement Organique bears the signature of the European representatives, but it is the Sultan who decreed it. The word 'Protocol' is used for the side agreements that confirm the Règlement Organique, including later its modifications and/or additional implementation measures. All Règlements Organiques and accompanying and subsequent Protocols bear the signature of the European representatives and the Ottoman official in charge.

[26] For the original French text of the Règlement Organique and the first Protocol of 9 June 1861, see 'Règlement et protocole pour le mont Liban,' in Baron de Testa, vol. 6, 338–43. For the Arabic text, Asad Rustum, *Lubnan fi 'ahd al-Mutasarifiyya* (Lebanon in the era of the Mutasarrifiyya), Beirut: Nahar 1973, 35–41. The French text of the 1864 Règlement appears in full in another compilation of Ottoman laws and treaties, Artistarchi Bey (Grégoire) ed., *Législation Ottomane ou Recueil des Lois, Réglements, Ordonnances, Traités, Capitulations et Autres Documents Officiels*, Constantinople: Bureau du Journal Thraky: 1874, 204–10. Arabic text in Rustum, *Lubnan fi 'ahd al-Mutasarifiyya*, 55–60.

[27] Yusef [Yusuf] bey Karam (1823–1889) has remained an iconic figure in his native city of Ehden in North Lebanon. His brief political career was checkered and included armed participation in 1861 in the Druze-Maronite conflict, then an armed rebellion in 1866 when he stood up against the Ottomans. On both occasions, he took the route of exile when local and regional powers decided to end his bid for leadership. He died near Naples in Italy. Most books mentioned in the next footnote include a brief account of his revolt.

[28] There is significant literature on the Mutasarrifiyya. Books on this extensive period include Engin Akarli, *The Long Peace: Ottoman Lebanon 1861–1920*, Berkeley: California Press 1993; Rustum, *Lubnan fi 'ahd al-Mutasarifiyya* (Lebanon in the era of the Mutasarrifiyya), above n.26; Ahmad Tarabain, *Lubnan mundhu 'ahd al-Mutasarrifiyya ila Bidayat al-Intidab 1861–1920* (Lebanon from the Mutasarrifiyya era to the beginning of the Mandate 1861–1920), Beirut: Ma'had al-buhuth wal-dirasat al-'arabiyya 1968; John Spagnolo, *France and Ottoman Lebanon 1861–1914*,

again calling the shots, under the watchful eye of increasingly colonialist European powers which continued to sign onto regular and successive renewals of Protocols until the First World War.

In the new constitutional arrangements, Mount Lebanon, administratively landlocked and reduced to the area stretching from Tripoli in the North to Sidon in the South, and not including Beirut and the coastal cities, was governed by a non-Lebanese Christian Ottoman governor appointed by the Porte, assisted by a council of local notables known as the *Majlis al-idara* or Administrative Council (AC).

The governor or *mutasarref* reported directly to Istanbul.[29] He held executive power, originally for a period of three years, and could be dismissed at any time.[30] The first *mutasarref*, Dawud Basha, was appointed by the Porte and the European powers under the Protocol of 1861.[31] His appointment was renewed by a formal decision of the Porte with the agreement of the European powers on 6 June 1864, 'for a period of five years.'[32] The Protocol of 1868 appointed Franco Basha 'for a period of no less than ten years.'[33] No *mutasarref*

London: Ithaca Press 1977; Antoine Khair, *Le Moutaçarrifat du Mont-Liban*, Beirut: Publications of the Lebanese University 1973; Lahd Khater, *'Ahd al-Mutasarrifin fi Lubnan 1861–1918* (The Rule of the governors in Lebanon 1861–1981), Beirut: Publications of the Lebanese University 1967; Ussama Makdisi, *The Culture of Sectarianism. Community, History, and Violence in Nineteenth-Century Ottoman Lebanon*, Berkeley: University of California Press 2000; Wajih Kawtharani, *Al-Ittijahat al-Ijtima'iyya al-Siyasiyya fi Jabal Lubnan wal-Mashriq al-'arabi 1860–1920* (Social and political trends in Mount Lebanon and the Arab Levant 1860–1920), Beirut: Ma'had al-inma' al-'arabi 1976.

29 Article I of both Règlements ('gouverneur chrétien nommé par la Sublime-Porte et relevant d'elle directement.') *Mutasarref* was by then a common word for executive decision-making at the local level; see its use above during the Egyptian occupation. It is translated in the official documents as 'gouverneur'. The *mutasarref* is literally the one 'who makes dispositions', hence the name Mutasarrifiyya. The Ottomans appointed *mutasarrefs* in various regions in the Empire during the Tanzimat period.

30 Protocol of 1861, Baron de Testa, vol. 6, 344. Dismissal could not be ordered without a trial, however, and until the First World War, there was no appetite in Istanbul or elsewhere to upset the delicate balance in the Mountain.

31 Dawud Efendi, a Catholic Armenian-born diplomat, born Garabet Davoudian, was the first governor, *mutasarref*, id. 403. He ruled until his resignation in 1868, reportedly over the rejection by the Porte of his efforts to extend Mount Lebanon's boundaries. All eight subsequent Ottoman governors were Catholic. The Porte reestablished direct rule in 1916, as the Protocol arrangements were upended by the First World War, and appointed three successive Muslim governors.

32 Baron de Testa, vol. 6, 405.

33 Rustum, *Lubnan fi 'ahd al-Mutasarifiyya*, above n.26, 116. Franco died in the post in 1873. The ten-year period for Rustum Basha was formally confirmed in the Protocol of 1873. Id., 153.

stayed longer than ten years.[34] With the head of executive power changing regularly, an important pattern was established against the continuing rule of one single person. The ability and trustworthiness of the *mutasarrefs* varied considerably, but the limitation of the tenure ensured that bad governance did not turn into autocracy. The anonymous author of a diary in the first decade of the twentieth century noted 'the extraordinary interest among the government and the people' in both Syria and Lebanon 'for the changes in the *mutasarifiyya* and the appointment of its holders.'[35]

The rise of the electoral principle

The Administrative Council included a fine-grained communal representation reflecting the larger number of Christians in Mount Lebanon and the ever-rising influence of Europe. Meanwhile, Beirut and the coastal cities, as well as the Bekaa (Biqa') valley, returned to pre-Egyptian direct Ottoman rule under a governor (*wali*) appointed by Istanbul.

The AC was communal through and through. Art.II of the 1861 Règlement specifies the composition of the 'large Administrative Council' of twelve members with their communal denomination:

> Art. II. There will be for the whole Mountain a large administrative medjliss [*majlis*, council] composed of twelve members, two Maronite, two Druze, two Greek-Catholic, two Greek Orthodox, two Metwali [Shi'i], two Muslim [Sunni]. They are tasked with distributing taxes, controlling the management of revenues and expenses, and giving consultative advice on all the questions which the governor [the *mutasarref*] will ask them.[36]

[34] A useful list of *mutasarrefs* and relevant dates can be found in the Wikipedia entry 'Mount Lebanon Mutasarrifate', and in French with their communal/sectarian denominations in Rabbath, *La Formation Historique du Liban Constitutionnel*, above n.4, 236n.61 for the first eight (Christian) governors from 1861 to 1915, and 238n.62 by the last three (Muslim) governors, from 1915 to 1918. Appendix A in Akarli, *The Long Peace:Ottoman Lebanon 1861–1920*, above n.28, 193–9, provides a sharp summary of the life and tenure of the eight governors.

[35] Anonymous, *Yawmiyyat Lubnani fi Ayyam al-Mutasarrifiyya* (Diary of a Lebanese in the days of the Mutasarrifiyya), Selim Hishshi ed., Beirut: al-Mudiriyya al-'amma lil-athar 1973, 50.

[36] Art. II 'Règlement et protocole pour le mont Liban', Baron de Testa, vol. 6, 339. In French the word used for the AC is 'central'. In Arabic, the name for AC was to be 'large (*kabir*)'. Rustum, *Lubnan fi 'ahd al-Mutasarifiyya*, above n.28, 36.

In the language of political philosophy, the AC represents more of a 'threshold' representation than a proportional approach.[37] Because these were advisory, not decisional, 'threshold' bodies, the successive councils could take a deliberative approach, aiming at consensus, with the last word retained by the *mutasarref*. As the AC turned increasingly decisional, proportionality became more compelling. The number of Maronite members gradually increased over the six decades of the AC's life. By the First World War, the AC comprised 14 members, with a relative Maronite majority of four.

As an institution, the Administrative Council reproduced the model originally established in both the temporary kaïmacams and the Beirut Consultative Council. But unlike the loose arrangement in the Beirut Council representing Christians and Muslims generally, the AC defined the communal identity of each and every member, alongside the mantra that started with Muhammad 'Ali and the Ottoman reforms declaring that 'all [residents are pronounced] equal before the law.'[38] There does not seem to have been a Druze representative initially. This was probably because the Ottomans wanted to punish the Druze, who had 'won' the civil war in 1860, expelled a large number of Maronite residents, thereby triggering French military intervention. The punishment did not last. Absence of Druze representation was remedied with a Druze appointment on the Council in 1866.[39]

The Protocol was confirmed and amended in 1864 by the Porte with, as in 1845, Austria, Britain, France, Prussia, and Russia.[40] Successive Protocols

[37] For threshold representation, see Will Kymlicka, *Multicultural Citizenship*, Oxford: Oxford University Press 1995, 146–7.

[38] Baron de Testa, vol. 6, 340, Art.VII: 'Egalité de tous devant la loi, abolition de tous les privilèges féodaux.' De Testa reproduces the preparatory works through 1860–1, including successive projects and intensive epistolary exchanges between the six states concerned under the leadership of Ottoman foreign minister Fu'ad Basha, in an appendix at 346–404. Of note is that the whole of Syria was originally considered under successive projects, but with different governors for 'les provinces de Damas et de Saïda.' (Dépêche d'Aali-pacha à M. Musurus en date du 20 janvier 1861), id., 347. Starting in March 1861, the discussions focused on Lebanon. Id., 350 ('Protocole de la vingt-sixième séance de la commission de Syrie tenue à Beïrout, le 21 mars 1861').

[39] See below text of n.43.

[40] Arabic text of the Règlement as amended in the 1864 Protocol in at Rustum, *Lubnan fi 'ahd al-Mutasarifiyya*, above n.26, 56–61. French original text of the Protocol of 1864 in Baron de Testa, 405.

followed, agreed by the Porte and six powers (rather than the original five) after Italy was brought in following its unification in 1871.[41] The changes in the size of districts, judicial conflicts, and taxes, made only small dents in the sectarian system. The one lasting breakthrough achieved was the formal abolition of all feudal privileges.

For our purposes, the main change was the evolution of an ever wider *electoral* consultation for Administrative Council membership, a feature absent from institutional structures until then. Progress was gradual and intermittent. The 1861 Règlement Organique states in Art. XI that 'all the members of the courts and of the ACs, without exception, as well as the local magistrates, are chosen and designated by the leaders of their communities in agreement with the community's notables and are appointed by the government. Half of the members of the administrative councils will be renewed each year, and the outgoing members may be re-elected.'[42] The first members were appointed by the *mutasarref* after consulting the religious communities' leaders and the local notables.[43]

From then onwards, it was a case of two steps forward, one step back in terms of elections. In the 1864 remake of the Règlement Organique, Art. 10 introduced the two-tier mechanism for the *election* of the AC members:

[41] Akarli, *The Long Peace: Ottoman Lebanon 1861–1920*, above n.28, 71.

[42] Rustum, *Lubnan fi 'ahd al-Mutasarifiyya*, above n.26, 37. Baron de Testa, vol. 6, 341: 'Art. XI-Tous les membres du médjliss judiciaire et administratif, sans exception, ainsi que les juges de paix, seront choisis et désignés, après une entente avec les notables, par les chefs de leur communauté respective, et institués par le gouvernement. Le personnel des madjless administratifs sera renouvelé par moitié tous les ans, et les membres sortants pourront être réélus.'

[43] Names of the first AC appointed members at Rustum, *Lubnan fi 'ahd al-Mutasarifiyya*, above n.26, 80. Rustum notes that the Maronite Church was reluctant to cooperate, and the Patriarch refused to give names to Dawud arguing that 'his calling was spiritual and does not allow him to intervene in politics.' Id. 42. The text of an 1866 decree by the *mutasarref* appointing the Druze member of the AC for the Jezzine region was kept by the family, and is reproduced in Rustum, *Lubnan fi 'ahd al-Mutasarifiyya*, Id., 80: 'Mutasarrifiyya of Mount Lebanon Order number 22, *re* appointment of the members of the AC in Mount Lebanon: In Mart 1282 [Ottoman 'Rumi' calendar, corresponding to March 1866] the Mutasarrifiyya of Mount Lebanon appoints Daher Efendi 'Uthman, civil servant in [since] May [1]281 a resident of the village of 'Amatur in the caza of the Shuf in Mount Lebanon, from the Druze community (*tayifa*), aged 25, with a monthly salary of 1000 piasters, no more. [Signed] Dawud.'

> Judges are appointed by the *mutasarref*, in contradistinction to the members of the AC, who are elected (*yuntakhabun*) by the village sheikhs. The election (*intikhab*) of a sheikh is also done by the people of the village.[44]

This marks the birth, on institutional paper, of formal elections. The policy was enacted two years later, in 1868, at the beginning of the second *mutasarref*'s tenure. Village notables elected their representatives, the 'village sheikhs', to district level by 'signing petitions or "sealing" them, with the AC then looking into their validity and confirming the election'.[45] The process was staggered geographically. The very first election in the second-tier was carried out in the district of Batroun, where the Ottoman-appointed prefect (*qa'immaqam*) for the district

> brought together the village sheiks on December 1 [1868], and proceeded with the election [of the member of the AC] 'in all freedom in application of the order of HE [the *mutasarref*]' under the supervision of [with the knowledge of] the district's court. He [the *qa'immaqam*] then sent the election papers to the AC at the Mutasarrifiyya's headquarter. The votes were counted, and Sheikh As'ad Abu Sa'b won against his rival Jirijus Basim with 47 votes against 27, upon which the Council validated the election of Abi Sa'b.[46]

1868 was the first instance in the history of Lebanon when a true election was carried out. As in most countries at the time, the concept of universal suffrage was still distant, and the candidacy was heavily circumscribed. The representative of the village or town had to be 'over 30, to own property and to be capable of reading and writing'.[47]

[44] Arabic text at Rustum, *Lubnan fi 'ahd al-Mutasarifiyya*, above n.26, 59: 'Done with the knowledge of, *bi-ma'rifat* of the people in the village.' French text in 'Règlement du Liban en date du 6 Septembre 1864', 204–8, at 207: 'Les juges sont nommés par le gouverneur; les membres du Medjliss administratifs sont *élus* dans les arrondissements par les Cheikhs de village. Les Chéikhs de village sont *choisis* par la population de chaque village.' (Emphasis added). Note the fluidity in naming the 'election/choice' mechanism.

[45] Rustum, *Lubnan fi 'ahd al-Mutasarifiyya*, id., 80.

[46] This decision of the AC was then sent to the *mutasarref*, who confirmed the appointment. Rustum, *Lubnan fi 'ahd al-Mutasarifiyya*, Id., 124.

[47] Id. For a detailed description of the process, see Majed Khalil Majed, *Al-Intikhabat al-Niyabiyya 1861–1992* (Parliamentary elections 1861–1992), Beirut: al-Mu'assasa al-jami'yya lil-dirasat wal-nashr 1992, 12–13.

From the Batroun election of 1868 onwards, there were no more appointments. The Règlement Organique of 1861 had mentioned a renewable tenure of six years for AC members, with a rotation for a third of the AC every two years. Franco Basha (1868–1873) strengthened the election component of the AC by replacing four appointed members with four elected ones.[48] The elected delegates were then called in to the governor's residence to choose an AC member every time a post became vacant due to either death or resignation.

By the time the fourth *mutasarref*, Wasa Basha, was appointed in 1882, elections were proceeding apace every two years for four out of the twelve AC members as provided for in the Protocol.

The rising power of the AC as the legitimate representative of the Mount Lebanon constituencies prompted Wasa to undermine it by intervening directly in the election process.[49] Repeated interference by Wasa in the elections created a constant rift between him and the two pillars of his 'government party' – on one side, his administrative appointees and the AC members he helped to power; on the other, his opponents, often supported by the most powerful civil society institution in Mount Lebanon – the Maronite Church. Wasa's corruption was legendary.[50] His successor Na'um Pasha (1892–1902) tried to repair Wasa's sinister legacy and was seen as an honest and effective builder of infrastructure, but corruption dominated again under Muzaffar (1902–1907).[51] The third governor, Rustum (r. 1873–1883), had sought to

48 Rustum, *Lubnan fi 'ahd al-Mutasarifiyya*, above n.28, 125.

49 Akarli explains how the AC developed its only power, the veto over new taxation, with the support of the rich and powerful Maronite church, and how Wasa first tried to dismiss councilors who were not to his taste (a move which was categorically rebuffed by the Porte), then started manipulating all AC elections starting in 1885. Akarli, 'The Administrative Council', in Nadim Shehadi and Dana Haffar Mills eds, *Lebanon: A History of Conflict and Consensus*, London: I. B. Tauris 1988, 79–100 at 81–3 (for the veto power of the AC over taxation), 84–8 (manipulation of the elections).

50 One of the most famous distichs in Lebanese history is Tamer Mallat's (d.1914), poet and judge, on the death of Wasa in 1892: 'They say: Wasa has passed away/ I responded, for I knew;

Let coins ring of the marble of his grave/and I guarantee you he will come back to life.' Cited in Wajdi Mallat ed., *Chibli Mallat Poet of the Cedars, A School for National Identity*, Beirut: Raidi Press 1999, 80 (English section). For Tamer's stand, Hyam Mallat, '*30 huzairan 1892– Waqfat al-hazimiyya* (30 June 1892- Taking the stand in Hazmiyyeh)' in Tamer Mallat, *Diwan* (Collection of poetry), Beirut: Bada2e3 2016, 241–52. See for Wasa's son-in-law Kupelian's 'famous ... cupidity', Akarli, *The Long Peace: Ottoman Lebanon 1861–1920*, above n.28, 196.

51 On Muzaffar's governorate, see 'Abdallah al-Mallah, *Mutasarrifiyyat Jabal Lubnan fi 'ahd Muzaffar Basha* (Mount Lebanon's Mutasarrifiyat under Muzaffar Basha), Beirut: Khalifeh 1985.

introduce voting by secret ballot, but the reform did not take root.[52] Muzaffar took up the effort in 1902, and introduced a 'rudimentary form' of the secret ballot at both stages of the two-tier elections:

> Within a short time he [Muzaffar] introduced more 'democratic' procedures into the two stages of the Lebanese elections. For the first stage he implemented a rudimentary form of secret poll with ballot boxes for the election of village *shaikhs* by their largely illiterate villagers. Every voter was given as many tokens as there were candidates. All but of one these were black, the remaining token being white. Each candidate was assigned a box, and the villagers were asked to pass before every box to drop in a token. The white token being dropped into the box of their preferred choice. At the second stage, he brought about a substantial modification of procedures in time for the March 1903 elections of Administrative Councillors. He summoned the shaikhs to cast, in his presence, sealed ballots which were no longer required to sign.[53]

Progress towards genuine elections was slow until the Young Turks' revolt in 1908 ended the wider authoritarian rule of Ottoman Sultan Abdelhamid. 'How effectively the new election procedures were applied in different parts of the Mountain [in different periods] is difficult to tell, but some evidence suggests that the election became better organized, freer and more competitive'.[54] There was also institutional progress. In 1902 for instance, when the electoral system had taken root more firmly, first-tier representative sheikhs came from an electorate composed of male residents over 25 years of age who paid a franchise fee and had lived in the village or city neighborhood for the previous five years.[55] When a Protocol was added to the Règlement Organique in 1912, a notable new procedure was introduced: in addition to the village sheikhs, every hundred taxpayers in the town concerned voted for a representative to join the pool of AC members' electors.[56] With the slow but steady development

[52] Akarli, *The Long Peace: Ottoman Lebanon 1861–1920*, above n.28, 174.

[53] Spagnolo, *France and Ottoman Lebanon 1861–1914*, above n. 28, 224.

[54] Akarli, *The Long Peace: Ottoman Lebanon 1861–1920*, above n.28, 94.

[55] Details of the electoral laws in Majed Khalil Majed, *Al-Intikhabat al-Niyabiyya 1861–1992* (Parliamentary elections 1861–1992), Beirut: al-Mu'assasa al-jami'yya lil-dirasat wal-nashr 1992, 12–13.

[56] Akarli, 'The Administrative Council', above n.28, 94.

of its popular legitimacy, the AC had become an important locus of power which the *mutasarref* could no longer ignore.

Of considerable importance for the future of Lebanese constitutionalism, starting in 1865, the *mutasarref* appointed a Lebanese deputy chairman of the Council – despite the absence of such a position in the Règlement. The deputy chairman was always a Maronite, reflecting the community's demographic dominance in the Mountain. In time, as the Council's power and prestige increased, 'the deputy chairmanship of the Council became the most coveted position in the Mutasarrifiyya administration.'[57] This lies at the institutional origins of Maronite leadership as a feature of the Lebanese presidency in the twentieth and twenty-first centuries.

The distinct stability of an elected AC with an exclusively Lebanese membership, together with the rotation at the head of the executive, stand out in the Middle East where colonial incursion and Ottoman despotism mark the second half of the nineteenth century. The AC functioned throughout the relatively long period of peace in the region. While Ottoman governors were changed regularly, Mount Lebanon enjoyed institutional continuity because of its Administrative Council, a democratic feature which is to this day essential for ordered change at the top. In addition to the entrenchment of the concept of a 'governing council', the electoral principle for its membership marks a major development at the core of Lebanese constitutionalism. Slowly and surely, elections on the basis of communal representation became a tradition in Mount Lebanon and were strengthened by the rise of a parallel electoral process across the Ottoman Empire.

Elections in the Ottoman Empire

Institutional developments in the wider Ottoman Empire form the inescapable backdrop for electoral reforms in the local Ottoman provinces.[58] At the center of the Empire, the Sultan ruled in absolute until the Constitution

[57] Id., 83. The first deputy was 'Ammun 'Ammun, and had been appointed in 1865 by the first *mutasarref*, Dawud. Rustum, *Lubnan fi 'ahd al-Mutasarifiyya*, above n.28, 80.

[58] For still valuable summaries of the reforms at provincial and municipal level, Bernard Lewis, *The Emergence of Modern Turkey*, Oxford: Oxford University Press 2nd ed. 1968, 384–93 (Provinces), 393–400 (Municipalities); and Rustum, *Lubnan fi 'ahd al-Mutasarifiyya*, above n.28, 88–92 (Provinces).

of 1876. There followed two fleeting Empire-wide parliamentary elections in 1876 and 1877, but the spirit of reform was quickly killed. The Constitution was suspended in early 1878. It was revived in 1908, 30 years later.[59] Only after the Young Turks' revolution and the restoration of the Constitution did an elected Parliament bring together 'emissaries' from the whole Empire to legislate and control some of the state purse.[60]

At the provincial level, with several early attempts that did not yield tangible results,[61] the Empire had been organised in a pilot Velayat Law in 1864, with a considerably amended version in 1871 providing the most enduring text.[62] Its administrative sub-division of the Empire was confirmed in the

[59] The Constitution was slightly amended in 1909. For the Ottoman text of the 1876 Constitution see *Düstur*, 4, 2–20, hereinafter D., followed by the volume and page number. *Düstur* is the title of the eight-volume collection of Ottoman legislation, four main texts and four supplements, published in Istanbul from 1872 onward: *Düstur*, 1st series. 8 vols, Istanbul, 1289–1335 (1872–1917) and 1937–1943. An Arabic text before amendments can be found in Amin Khuri ed., *Al-Qanun al-Asasi* (The Basic Law), Beirut: Adab 1908; For an English text of the 1876 Constitution with the list of revised articles see https://iow.eui.eu/wp-content/uploads/sites/18/2014/05/Brown-01-Ottoman-Constitution.pdf. A better English translation of the Constitution was published by the Iraqi Ministry of Justice, together with other useful laws for this section, Iraqi Ministry of Justice, *Translations of the Ottoman Constitutional Laws, the Wilayet Administrative Law, the Municipal Law and Various Other Laws*, Baghdad: 1924 n.p., 1–9 (Cited here, together with other relevant electoral laws, as Iraqi Ministry of Justice, *Translations of the Ottoman Constitutional Laws*). For a more recent translation of the Constitution, together with a useful introduction, see Tillman Röder, 'The Separation of powers in Muslim countries', in Rainer Grote and Tillman Röder eds, *Constitutionalism in Islamic Countries*, Oxford: Oxford University Press 2011, 321–72, text of the Constitution and its amendments at 341–59.

[60] A section of the Constitution covers the Ottoman lower chamber, *hey'et-e mab'uthan* (Arabic *majlis al-mab'uthin*) in the original text, Arts. 65–80, translated in the English text as Chamber of Deputies, references in previous note. For an overview of the national elections, Hasan Kayalı, 'Elections and the Electoral Process in the Ottoman Empire, 1876–1919', *International Journal of Middle East Studies*, 27, 1995, 265–86.

[61] An earlier Sultanic *firman* (edict) for the administration of the provinces was decreed in 1852 to centralise the system with governors (valis) put in charge of the police and the administrations. Edouard Engelhardt, *La Turquie et le Tanzimat, ou Histoire des réformes dans l'Empire ottoman, depuis 1826 jusqu'à nos jours*, Paris: Cotillon 1882, 109. This was part of various attempts richly analysed in Jun Akiba, 'The Local councils as the origin of the parliamentary system in the Ottoman Empire', in Tsugitaka Sato ed., *Development of Parliamentarism in the Modern Islamic World*, Tokyo: The Toyo Bunko 2009, 176–204. In the pre-Tanzimat Empire, the word for province was *Eyalat*.

[62] Text of the 1864 Law of Velayats in D. 1, 608–24, of 1871 Law in Id., 625–51; English text of the Law as amended by 1914 in Iraqi Ministry of Justice, *Translations of the Ottoman Constitutional Laws*, above n.60, 35–48 (which I use here). French text of the 1864 and 1871 versions in Georges Young ed., *Corps de Droit Ottoman*, Oxford: Clarendon Press 1905, vol. 1, respectively at 36–45 and 47–69. Of note is that amendments continued until the First World War, with some variations on names and subdivisions of no particular relevance for our discussion.

Ottoman Constitution.[63] Under the authority of the Porte, the Empire was organised, from top to bottom, into provinces, districts, cantons, town clusters, and villages.[64]

The *Velayat* (province) was the main administrative region of the Empire. The key position was that of governor, the *vali*, who was 'the Chief Executive Official'.[65] He was appointed and dismissed at will by the Porte, and disposed of bureaucratic appointees to second him and implement his decisions.

Next were the districts, *livas*, also called *sancaks*,[66] governed by a *mutasarref.* Below them stood the *kaza* (canton, Arabic *qada'*), under an appointed *qa'emmaqam*. The next and lowest tier under the Law of Velayats consisted of the cluster of towns (*nahiyes*), headed by a *mudir* (director), and the smaller villages (Arabic *qaria*, pl. *qura*). Local notables in towns and villages chose one or more *mukhtars* (mayors), minor on-the-ground officials who reported to the Ottoman hierarchy.

The executive appointees at all these levels were beholden to their respective heads, with the *valis* at the top of the pyramid.[67] In turn the *valis* reported directly to Istanbul, with the Ministry of Interior formally in charge.

Three levels of governance are particularly relevant for our purposes. The lowest exercise of governance operated at the municipal level and developed separately from other administrative laws in a series of edicts which were amended and consolidated in an Empire-wide Law on municipalities in 1877. The second operated at the level of the provinces under the Velayat Law of 1864 and its amendments, esp. in 1871, with a complex hierarchical substructure and modes of appointments and elections. The third level was the

[63] The subdivisions appeared first in the 1864 Law of the Velayat, Art.1, and were incorporated (except for the two lowest tiers) in the 1876 Constitution in the section on '*Velayat*' (Provincial Administration, Arts. 108–112). The Constitution refers details of elections to special laws. The translation of the Turkish/Arabic terms varies: for instance in the first English translation, located on the internet and cited above n.60, Art. 109: 'A special law will settle on wider bases the election of the administrative councils of provinces (*vilayet*), districts (*sancak*), and cantons (*kaza*), as also of the Council General, which meets annually in the chief town of each province.' In the translation of the Iraqi Ministry of Justice, *Translations of the Ottoman Constitutional Laws*, above n.60, the text reads, respectively, Velayat, Liwa (not *sancak*), and Qadah.

[64] Art. 1 of the 1871 Law of Velayats, for the subdivisions and names of officials.

[65] Art. 20 of the 1871 Law of Velayats in the English version.

[66] The 1864 Law of Velayets uses *sancak*, D. 1, 608.

[67] Wilayet officials at Arts. 5 to 7 of the 1871 Law of Velayats, and their mode of selection and removal at Arts. 8–19.

Empire-wide national parliament under the provisions of the Constitution and electoral laws. Progress in the election and competences varied considerably between the respective levels, but they all formed part of the slow rise of the electoral principle. The reforms also reverberated differently between the center and the European and Arab dependencies of the Empire, with traces of that nineteenth century reorganisation remaining in some cases to the present day.

Within the vast Empire, the territory of modern Lebanon was roughly divided until the First World War between Mount Lebanon, with its relative autonomy and the continued oversight by the European powers over the Protocol and Règlement Organique during the Mutasarrifiyya, and the rest consisting of the eastern cantons (*qada'*) of the central Bekaa and of the south under the provinces of Damascus and Jerusalem. Most coastal cities, Beirut in particular, were part of the Province of Damascus then Beirut. Tripoli, which had remained an important city, was part of the Province of Aleppo. I consider the three relevant levels of institutional development briefly:

1. *Municipalities* (*baladiyyat*).[68] The first tier of representation developed on the Lebanese coast, which was city-based. Beirut grew significantly in size and economic importance to rival some of the other major Levantine cities.[69] In 1865, it returned to the hierarchical rule of the Empire as part of the Province of Damascus and became in 1888 the capital of its own province.[70]

With the precedent set by its Council of 1834, the concept of a municipal council lived on through its president. The municipal presidency was

[68] Text of the 1877 Law on Municipalities: Ottoman original in D. 4, 528–70. Arabic text in Muhammad al-Mashnuq, *Hukumat Beirut* (The Beirut government), Beirut: Masters 1995, 261–83; English translation in Iraqi Ministry of Justice, *Translations of the Ottoman Constitutional Laws*, 49–57 (with 1886, 1890, 1912 addenda at 57), which I use in this section (Law on Municipalities, followed by the article); French translation in Georges Young ed., *Corps de Droit Ottoman*, Oxford: Clarendon Press, vol. 1, 69–84, with 1886 and 1890 addenda at 84.

[69] Fine studies on Beirut in the second half of the nineteenth century include Jens Hanssen, *Fin de Siècle Beirut- The Making of an Ottoman Provincial Capital*, Oxford: Oxford University Press 2005; Samir Kassir, *Histoire de Beyrouth*, Paris: Fayard 2003; and the documentary works and analyses of Hassan Hallaq, including *Baladiyyat Bayrut al-Mahrusa (1840–1943)* ('Municipality of Beirut 1840–1943), vol. 1, Beirut: Dar al-nahda al-'arabiyya 2013; and *Al-Tarikh al-Ijtima'i wal-Iqtisadi wal-Siyasi fi Bayrut wal-Wilayat al-'uthmaniyya fil-Qarn al-Tase' 'ashar* (Social, economic and political history of Beirut and the Ottoman provinces in the nineteenth century), Beirut: Al-Dar al-jami'iyya 1987.

[70] They could not, however, be at the same time members of two councils. (Art. 7, 1877 Law on Municipalities.)

remarkably stable for the holders of the appointment, with several 'Egyptians' confirmed by the Porte to run Beirut after the departure of Ibrahim Basha and the governorship of Mahmud Nami.[71]

A parallel process was afoot, not surprisingly, for Istanbul. In the early 1860s, select neighbourhoods were considered in Istanbul as a pilot model for the rest of the city. The chic 'Sixth District' of Pera/Galata acquired recognition as a pilot model in 1868.[72] That very same year, Beirut received a similar status featuring significantly, the principle of elections. With some power over their budget, expropriation and taxes, experimentation with Istanbul's Sixth District and the Beirut municipality proved successful. Originally drafted in 1867, an Empire-wide law for municipalities was enacted in 1877.[73]

Municipal elections were irregularly held in two successive tiers, with candidacy limited by maleness, property and income-related franchise, and the close oversight of the Ottoman Ministry of Interior. In Beirut, the Ottoman governor dissolved the municipal council at least three times.[74] Still, after the law was consolidated in 1877, '[t]he municipal members were chosen in a long,

[71] Hanssen, *Fin de Siècle Beirut*, above n.70, 153–7 ('Continuity and change in the municipal presidency'); Hallaq, *Baladiyyat Bayrut al-Mahrusa*, above n.70, 75- 82. The first appointed president, Ahmad Pasha Abaza, was an officer of the Egyptian army. When elections were introduced in 1868, he was elected by the members, or rather confirmed by them, as the head of the Council. One successor was the son of Mahmud Nami, appointed by Ibrahim Basha from 1833 to 1840. See Hanssen, id. at 154 (with full composition of the Municipal Council from 1868 to 1908 at 145–6); and Hallaq, id. at 6 (with list of all Beirut 'governors' from 1831 to 2016 at 6–7).

[72] Since Gabriel Baer, 'The Beginnings of municipal government in Egypt', *Middle Eastern Studies*, 4, 1968, 118–40, scholarship on Ottoman municipalities has developed significantly, including Beirut in particular; see above references. The 'Sixth District' in Istanbul was reportedly named after the Sixth Arrondissement in Paris, which was considered the best-run and most affluent. See for instance Lewis, *The Emergence of Modern Turkey*, above n.58, 397.

[73] Text of the 1877 Law on Municipalities and translations above n.60. The most relevant sections on elections are Art. 4: Council membership between 6 and 12, elected for four years with half the Council changed every two years; Councilors must be Ottoman subjects and holders of property; The governor appoints the municipal president from amongst the councilors; and Arts. 18–38, section on the election of members: Art.18- the voter must be a resident, male, over 25 years of age, with no criminal record; Art. 19- a candidate must be over 30, pay 'at least 100 piasters *vergu* [the name of the tax] annually to the State on immovable property', and be able to speak Turkish; Art. 21- Formation of an Electoral Committee by 'imams, priests, rabbis and mayors/*mukhtars* of the mahalla [designated neighbourhoods]' who will call on the entitled voters of the mahalla to put forward entitled candidates (Art.23); Art. 30- On the day of the election, the voters will cast their votes by secret ballot for their preferred candidates to the extent of the number of positions that need to be filled; Art. 33- The candidates with the higher number of votes will be formally appointed by the Ottoman government.

[74] Hannsen, *Fin de Siècle Beirut*, above n.70, 151.

highly public, and, indeed, publicized process ...'[75] A complex filter mixing notability and electoral representation was formed by mayors/*mukhtar*s and religious leaders staffing the electoral committee.[76] This, one should remember, was the lowest tier in the Empire administration, so 'elections' should be appreciated as a stepping stone for more important national instances.

Nor was the communitarian framework ever absent in Beirut. In 1909, a brief division of the city between two municipalities obtained from intra-Sunni rivalries which were exploited by some Maronite circles to push for a separation between Christian east Beirut and Muslim west Beirut. The division did not work, and the city was reunited in 1911. Despite the rise in the number of Christians in Beirut, this was a traditionally Sunni city, and even when there was a chance for a Christian councilor to become municipal president in 1893, the position remained reserved for Sunnis.[77] Through the twentieth and twenty-first century, the municipality of Beirut kept this bi-communal trait, and succeeded, in its institutional expression of the city's residents, to keep the Shi'i community, despite its vastly increased number, at the capital's outskirts, literally the 'suburb', *al-dahiye*.

2. Provinces (*wilayat, velayat*).[78] Municipalities had trailed behind more important electoral developments in the Empire. In 1864, Grand Vizier Midhat Pasha (1822–1883), the most famous Ottoman reformist, introduced the Law of the Vilayets, which was amended several times thereafter, and put in effect in 1867. Midhat had studied the regional organisation of France, and the system was a calque of the French system, based on *prefectures*, with *vali* the equivalent of *préfet.*

In the immediate vicinity of Mount Lebanon's Mutasarrifiyya, the eastern regions including most of the Bekaa were *qada'/kaza*s which followed the Velayat of Damascus. The city of Beirut itself was initially part of the Damascus Province. As a *sanjak*, the region above the *kaza*, it was governed by a *mutasarref*. This made for a complex, evolving and intertwined system,

[75] For the first municipal elections in Beirut, with the councilors elected by an assembly of local notables, Id., 144.

[76] For elaborate details on the election process, Id., 150–3.

[77] Id., 155–6 (for the division of the city); for the appointment of a Muslim Sunni president despite a Christian councilor receiving a higher number of votes, id. at 151.

[78] I use here again the English text in Iraqi Ministry of Justice, *Translations of the Ottoman Constitutional Laws*, above n.60, 35–49 (Law of Velayets, followed by the article.)

further complicated by a rivalry with Tripoli and the separation between the Beirut and Damascus Provinces in 1888. That year, following two decades of lobbying by Beirutis in Istanbul, the Province of Beirut was created.[79] Before 1888, Beirutis elected councilors separately for the Beirut municipal council, sitting in Beirut, and for the Administrative Council of the Province of Damascus, sitting in Damascus. After 1888, they continued to elect councilors separately for the two councils.

Elections at the level of the province were confusing. In the latest iteration of the Law of Velayets in 1914, 'elections' of administrative councils had to be held at the levels of *velayet/wilaya, liwa, kaza/qada'* (Arts. 62, 63, 64 respectively). The same formula was used for membership of all three councils, with Ottoman bureaucrats and local dignitaries flanked by 'other elected members'. They were all under the control of the *vali*, who 'is responsible for the general administration of the *velayet*.' (Art.20) The way 'elected members' were 'elected' is not clear, but they were clearly outnumbered and outranked by numerous appointees.

Another chapter of the last version of the Law of Vilayets before the First World War covers the 'General Council', whose members are elected by the *kaza* on the basis of one member for every 12,500 of the male population. (Art. 103) The election of the General Council members was thoroughly communal: 'The number of Mohammedan and non-Mohammedan members of the Council shall be in proportion with the Mohammedan and non-Mohammedan populations of the Wilayet' (Art 103.2). Their two-tiered election takes place with the members 'elected by the secondary electors of the most recent Parliamentary elections and the Municipal Council of the *kaza* headquarters, who will elect jointly.' (Art. 104). The bulk of the General Council's tasks is budgetary (Arts. 121, 126 to 134), but both the decisions to hold the sessions and the substantive decisions of the General Council are under the control of the *vali*, who can veto any of the General Council's decisions (Art. 118 for the presidency of the sessions by the *wali*, Art. 135 for his veto power.)

Then there is a Wilayet Committee (*Anjuman*), which consists of four to eight members appointed by the General Council after the conclusion of

[79] For the constant lobbying and the decision of Sultan Abd al-Hamid to create the Beirut Province in February 1888, Hannsen, *Fin de Siècle Beirut*, above n.70, 45–50.

its annual session. They follow up on the decisions of the General Council for the budget and expenditures, again under the close control of the *wali*. (Art. 136 to 144).

The reader will be forgiven for glossing over these complicated rules governing elections at the level of the Ottoman provinces, and I should also mention a chapter on 'Special Wilayet', including Crete, or the regime of the Jerusalem Mutasarriffiya, which was distinct from Mount Lebanon's electoral system. In all cases, 'elected' councils were firmly subordinate to the Istanbul-appointed *wali*s. What matters for institutional memory is the principle of elections in the Law of Velayats, their always dual or multiple tiers, the narrow qualifications for voters and candidates, and a strong communitarian flavor.

3. *Majlis al-Mab'uthin* (Chamber of Deputies). The era of the Tanzimat had started with the Gülhane Edict in 1839, emulating Muhammad 'Ali's earlier reforms, and establishing the principle of equality between the subjects of the Sultan irrespective of religion. In time, an extensive set of edicts, laws, and codes was enacted after European fashion. With the spread of elections at municipal and provincial levels, the electoral principle culminated in the provisions on elections in the Ottoman Constitution of 1876. The reformist tide established an elected Empire-wide lower chamber of parliament which translates as the Chamber of Deputies.[80]

The 1876 Constitution, we saw earlier, did not live long. In early 1878, the restored absolute rule of Sultan 'Abd al-Hamid II dashed all democratic hopes. It was only in 1908, after he was removed by the Young Turks' revolt, that the Ottoman Empire returned to the constitutional arrangements suspended three decades earlier. Elections for the Chamber of Deputies were to be held within the provinces' delimitation every four years (Art. 69 and Art. 72 of the Ottoman Constitution), with 'one deputy for every 50.000 males belonging to the Ottoman nationality'. (Art. 65 of the Ottoman Constitution).

Similar to all the major Ottoman cities, Beirut and the coastal cities of Lebanon were represented in the Chamber of Deputies as part of the larger

[80] Again *hey'et-e mab'uthan* in Turkish, *majlis al-mab'uthin* in Arabic (literally council or assembly of the emissaries).

province to which they belonged. So were Tripoli, Jerusalem, Aleppo, Baghdad, and several similarly significant provincial towns all the way down to Jeddah, in addition to Benghazi in Libya, before the Italian invasion of 1912, and some provinces in a shrinking Ottoman Europe. In effect, electoral representation featured mainly residents of the large cities, who would rise later throughout the Arab liberal age as notables and politicians drawn from the former provinces of the Empire.

All in all, there were six elections to the Ottoman Parliament. They shared the well-established two-tier system and limited male franchise. They were based on, and benefited from, the structure, experience and subdivisions of the previous system established by the Law of the Velayats. After two hasty elections in 1876 and 1877 before the Constitution was suspended, the elections of 1908 were freer and far more representative. But later elections were marred by corruption and manipulation, the dominance of the Young Turks through the Committee of Union and Progress party, and the increasing travails of the Empire that culminated in the disaster of the First World War. All three subsequent elections suffered killer blows: the 1912 election was cancelled with the dissolution of parliament; the 1914 election was overtaken by the war; and the 1919 parliament became meaningless after the defeat of Turkey and the Allies' occupation of Istanbul in March 1920.

There was a further daunting dimension to elections in the Ottoman Empire. Unlike the Arab Levant, the Empire had, in addition to its religious-communitarian fracture, an ethnic and linguistic fracture fraught with complications. In 1908, communitarian quotas were integrated in the system, but the ethnic-linguistic representation in the Chamber marginalised Arab deputies. In 1912, an attempt to erase the communitarian quotas resulted in the collapse of Christian representation. In 1914, with the restoration of religious quotas and the exacerbation of Arab nationalism, Ottoman Christians fared better, but ethnic representation of the Arab Provinces declined again significantly. The 1912 and 1914 elections faced a further complication in the emergence of parties, with the battle between the two main political parties, the Unionists (Committee of Union and Progress, representing the military) and the liberal Ententists (Hurriyet ve Itilaf, Liberty and Entente) dictating campaigns and results. The introduction of political parties, hitherto absent from the Istanbul scene, reverberated across the Empire, adding its own novel weight to an already intricate electoral process.[81]

Mount Lebanon was never represented in the Majlis al-Mab'uthin. Despite attempts to see deputies sent to the Majlis, local opposition led by the Maronite Church and international opposition represented by France ensured the integrity of the Mutasarrifiyya's autonomous regime. Mount Lebanon guarded its *sui generis* institutions with its European guarantors.[82]

At a Lebanese national level, seen now in retrospect, the institutional story to be retained is one of continuity, occasional progress, and several setbacks of electoral representation to the present day. Yet the communitarian composition of any ruling council or head of the executive persisted and entrenched.

Ottoman elections were marred by interventions and interruptions tied to persistent turmoil within the Empire and at its fragile borders. No country that survived the partitioning of the Ottoman Empire was able to escape the heavy grip of European colonialism, or durably loosen the grip of the autocrat in power after independence. And like all other Ottoman elections in the second half of the nineteenth and first third of the twentieth centuries, and in much of the democratic world, universal suffrage was inconceivable until well into the twentieth century.

Yet the concept of governing councils developed in tangible fashion, and the electoral principle became the norm rather than the exception.

[81] This paragraph is a condensed account of various studies mentioned in this chapter, especially Kayalı, 'Elections and the Electoral Process in the Ottoman Empire, 1876–1919', above n.61, and his *Arabs and Young Turks: Ottomanism, Arabism, and Islamism in the Second Constitutional Period of the Ottoman Empire, 1908–1918*, Berkeley: University of California Press 1997; see also for Arab representation in the Ottoman Chamber of Deputies 'Ismat 'Abd al-Qader, *Dawr al-Nuwwab al-'arab fi Majlis al-Mab'uthan al-'uthmani 1908–1914* (The role of the Ottoman parliament 1908–1914), Beirut: Al-dar al-'arabiyya lil-mawsu'at 2006.

[82] To be more accurate, Jamal Basha, the Ottoman military ruler during the war, sought to efface the Mutasarrifiyya's separate status, and leaned on 'Ali Munif, the first non-Christian *mutasarref* appointed by the Porte without the European Powers' imprimatur, to send three deputies representing Mount Lebanon in the Istanbul Majlis in 1915. Kayalı, 'Elections and the Electoral Process in the Ottoman Empire, 1876–1919', above n.61, 280, writes that they were elected. Fu'ad Khuri, who mentions the name of the three deputies, says they were appointed. Fu'ad Khuri, *Al-Niyaba fil Lubnan min 1860 ila 1977* (Parliamentary membership in Lebanon from 1860 to 1977), Beirut: n.p. 1980. 62–3. Considering the war situation, their appointment is more likely, but it does not matter. By then, the Ottoman Parliament was a helpless institution, Lebanon was under direct military rule, and several members of the AC had been exiled, as we shall see in next section.

Franchise and the two-tier principle weakened popular representation. In Lebanon, both took a full century to be jettisoned in favor of universal suffrage. What was never jettisoned were the dominance of the executive branch and the strictly communitarian representation of the Lebanese religious groups.

Transitioning from Mount Lebanon to Great Lebanon

The constitutional system in Mount Lebanon, the heart of what would become the Grand Liban in 1920, persisted until the entry of Istanbul into the war against the Allies. The Administrative Council (AC) was dissolved by the Ottoman military ruler in 1915. Its local Lebanese component was led at the time by a Maronite notable, Habib Basha al-Sa'd, who had been appointed to the top Lebanese position of Mount Lebanon in 1902 by the Ottoman *mutasarref* as his deputy. After an interlude, Habib Basha was appointed again in 1913 as the deputy of the *mutasarref*. In March 1915, he was arrested when the AC was perceived as a threat to the dominance of the Ottoman military governor. Together with several other AC members, he was exiled to Anatolia for the duration of the war.

The clamor for constitutions as the mark of independence rose again at the end of the war, partly on the strength of the decisive contribution of the United States to the Allies' victory over the Central powers, and Wilsonian insistence on self-government for the territories which emerged after the dismemberment of the Austro-Hungarian and Ottoman empires.

Yearning for independence in the colonies was severely curtailed with the retreat of the United States after the US Senate rejected adhering to the League of Nations advocated by Woodrow Wilson. Taking advantage of the return of America to a policy of isolationism, and the collapse of Russia to communist rule, Britain and France implemented, with significant adjustments, the Sykes-Picot plans agreed during the war. In the Arab Levant, Britain took over present-day Israel/Palestine, Jordan and Iraq; France, Lebanon and Syria.[83]

[83] On the (in)famous Sykes-Picot agreements (1916) secretly dividing the spoils between France, Britain and Russia (which pulled out altogether from the scene after the Bolshevik revolution), to which Italy was added when it changed sides to rally the Allies, see in the large literature available e.g. David Fromkin, *A Peace to End all Peace: the Fall of the Ottoman Empire and the Creation of the Modern Middle East 1914–1922*, New York: Macmillan 1989. For a map of the Sykes-Picot

A particularly troubled period followed Ottoman collapse in 1918. The new military rulers started operating as a joint British-French command with British general Edmond Allenby at the head, and French colonel Philpin de Piépape as his second.[84] The troops commanded by Allenby took over Jerusalem in December 2017, then Beirut and Damascus in October 2018. The bulk of the French forces did not arrive immediately.[85] With the hiatus between the agreed Sykes-Picot map and military rule on the ground, the alliance between the British forces in the lead and the Arab forces in open revolt against the Ottomans, under the leadership of the Sharif of Mecca, translated into the establishment of an 'Arab government' in Damascus under Faisal. Faisal was the Sharif of Mecca's son, whom Allenby supported.[86] But the British did not allow Faisal to extend his rule to Beirut. A joint British-French command under Allenby included the dispatch of a French military vessel to Beirut to prevent the establishment of a Lebanese branch of the Arab government set up in Damascus.[87]

In Palestine and Transjordan, British occupation would continue until the independence of Jordan in 1946 and the formation of Israel in 1948. In Syria, the British tried to fulfil part of their promise of an Arab Kingdom to the Sharif of Mecca when the Sharif launched the Arab revolt against the Ottomans in 1916 with the iconic Lawrence. But the pre-agreed colonial division of the Levant eventually took precedence over the military map on the

divisions, https://www.britannica.com/event/Sykes-Picot-Agreement. In this section, I sought to underline the events which proved most significant institutionally.

[84] James Simon, 'The role of the Administrative Council of Mount Lebanon in the creation of Greater Lebanon,' *Journal of Third World Studies*, 1996, 13, 1996, 119–71, at 124–6; Antoine Hokayem, *Min Mutasarrifiyyat Jabal Lubnan ila Dawlat Lubnan al-Kabir 1914–1920* (From Mount Lebanon's mutasarrifiyya to the State of Great Lebanon 1924–1920), Beirut: al-Dar al-lubnaniyya lil-nashr al-jami'i 2018, 11–49.

[85] 'Forty-five thousand British officers and soldiers were stationed in Syria and Lebanon, compared with a French garrison of only 8,000, mostly colonial troops, the majority of whom were stationed in Cilicia'. Meir Zamir, *The Formation of Modern Lebanon*, Ithaca NY: Cornell University Press 1988, 56.

[86] For the quick advance of the Allenby troops, mainly Australian, and the conflictual reports on the conquest of Damascus, see Elie Kedourie, 'The Capture of Damascus, 1 October 1918', *Middle Eastern Studies*, 1964, 66–83; Hokayem, *Min Mutasarrifiyyat Jabal Lubnan ila Dawlat Lubnan al-Kabir 1914–1920*, above n.85, 117–30.

[87] Simon, 'The role of the Administrative Council of Mount Lebanon in the creation of Greater Lebanon,' above n.85, 122. Hokayem, *Min Mutasarrifiyyat Jabal Lubnan ila Dawlat Lubnan al-Kabir 1914–1920*, above n.85, 141.

ground, which the French adjusted in 1920 to their effective ground troop presence in the Levant. In the summer of 1920, they sent significant military contingents under the command of General Henri Gouraud to take over Lebanon and Syria.[88] Faisal was ejected from Damascus in July 1920 by the French, while his brother Abdallah was made Emir of Transjordan by Britain. Faisal would be later consoled by the British, when they appointed him King of Iraq in 1923.

In the grey period which followed the departure of the defeated Ottoman troops from Lebanon in late September 2018, Habib Basha, the *mutasarref*'s erstwhile deputy, had returned from exile and revived the dissolved Council, seizing Mount Lebanon's Government house (the Sérail) in Baabda on 7 October 2018. This was not pure bravado. In the void following the collapse of the Ottomans, various contenders emerged along two main fault lines: the first was between those who would be content only with full independence and those who were ready to accept the French mandate at least temporarily. A second fracture emerged between those who wanted Lebanon to be separate from Syria, and those who wished for the two territories to remain united.

As the void emerged after four centuries of Ottoman rule, the AC was in Lebanon the most representative institution, being elected and having a long institutional memory. Habib Basha was initially confirmed in position by the Anglo-French military command,[89] and the AC was even recognised in an official ceremony on 22 October 1918.[90]

This did not last. As France increasingly asserted its grip with British-led troops leaving the French area roughly delineated in the Sykes-Picot agreement, the nationalist positions of the AC hardened over 1919–20 in Lebanon and under the rule of Faisal's Arab Government in Syria. In Lebanon, Habib Basha and several other AC members took a nationalist line against foreign

[88] For Gouraud's role in Lebanon and Syria, Julie d'Andurain, *Le Général Gouraud- Un Destin hors du Commun, de l'Afrique au Levant*, Paris: Perrin 2022, 308–409. Gouraud arrived in Beirut on 21 November 1919 and took over command immediately. He proclaimed the Etat du Grand-Liban on 1 September 2020. For details see id., 341, 390–1, and discussion of the decrees organising the new state in next chapter.

[89] Khater, *'Ahd al-Mutasarrifin fi Lubnan 1861–1918*, above n.28, 198. See also Zamir, *The Formation of Modern Lebanon*, above n.86, 35–6; Rabbath, *La Formation Historique du Liban Constitutionnel*, above n.4, 270–1.

[90] James Simon, 'The role of the Administrative Council of Mount Lebanon in the creation of Greater Lebanon,' above n.85, 124–6.

'occupation', and the AC was active trying to affect the peace discussions in Paris through 1919 and 1920.

On 22 March 1920, the AC declared Lebanon's independence.[91] The declaration was ignored by the French. They were new to a complicated scene, and their assumption of full power was gradual. On 10 July 1920, an AC delegation to Damascus en route to France to present its demands was detained by Gouraud.[92] Tension rose and France went on the war path against all resistance to its rule in both Syria and Lebanon. On 12 July, General Gouraud dissolved the AC. Amid increasing tension with Faisal, and despite continued contacts between them, Gouraud was ordered by the French government to take the hard line in Syria as well.[93] On 8 March 1920, he marched his now considerable troops on Damascus to supplant the Syrian Arab Kingdom established by Faisal. On 24 July 1920, the Arab Kingdom's short life came to an abrupt end in the battle of Khan Maysalun on the outskirts of Damascus. Gouraud occupied Damascus the following day.

Under its new French rulers, 'Mont Liban' grew into 'Grand Liban' and then, in its current borders, simply into 'Liban'. French domination of Lebanon and Syria continued until the debacle of World War Two. From 1920 until then, both countries were under the firm control of France. Lebanon gained its independence in 1943, Syria in 1946.

Institutionally, two central features analysed in this part survived and matured. The first, initiated in the Beirut Council under Egyptian rule, was communal balance in governance, entrenched under the Kaïmacamia and the Mutasarifiyya. In the preparatory meetings between the Ottomans and the European powers to the Protocol and Règlement Organique, there was

[91] Id., 146.

[92] Khuri, *Al-Niyaba fil Lubnan min 1860 ila 1977* (Parliamentary membership in Lebanon from 1860 to 1977), above n.82, 103–4 (relating their arrest on 12 July and their exile to Corsica, where they spent three years). Akarli, *The Long Peace: Ottoman Lebanon 1861–1920*, above n.28, 17, and n. 55 for the names of the seven AC members arrested. On 29 November 1919, the AC requested the French to stop appointing administrators across the country and displacing the locals. On 10 July 1920, in preparation for their trip to lobby the Peace Conference in Paris, the AC issued a full nationalist 'proposal' for independence, somewhat backtracking on the declaration of independence in March. Texts in Khuri, *Al-Niyaba fil Lubnan min 1860 ila 1977* (Parliamentary membership in Lebanon from 1860 to 1977), above n.82, 101–4.

[93] D'Andurain, *Le Général Gouraud- Un Destin hors du Commun, de l'Afrique au Levant*, above n.88, 378–82.

a lively discussion on the person of the governor and the 'aggregation' or not of 'the races' – the religious communities.[94] The communitarian dimension was never called into question, and all participants took the Lebanese 'races' as a socio-political given.[95] The battle became one of numbers: which was the largest religious community or sect in any given territory under Ottoman rule?[96]

The second feature was the small but budding electoral representation initiated under the Mutasarrifiyya. Not surprisingly, it corresponded to the slow and cautious development of full and direct popular representation in government the world over, and across the shrinking and fragile Ottoman Empire.

[94] Baron de Testa, vol. 6, 'races' e.g. at 354, 365. In 1860 already, there was a dispute between the French, the English and the Ottomans on the qualifications of the governor. Although the possibility of an 'indigène' was floated, the Ottomans and the English representatives did not wish the Lebanese governor to be Maronite, a French request based on the argument that the majority of the population of the Mountain was Maronite. A compromise was reached after the English foreign minister, John Russell, suggested 'un seul pacha chrétien dans le Liban, qui ne serait pas originaire de la Montagne', Baron de Testa, vol. 6, at 379. The French floated on 28 May the name of 'Daoud-effendi, arménien catholique dont les relations avec l'ambassade de France sont excellentes', id. at 387. It was agreed by the Ottomans on 31 May, id., at 389.

[95] Baron de Testa, vol. 6, 345–404, see for instance first Project presented to the Commission at its meeting in Beirut on 28 March 1861, Arts. 1 and 2 ('désagrégation' proposed and 'séparation ethnographique des chrétiens et des druzes'), id. at 360.

[96] For a short description of the bias in counting numbers of religious communities' membership and the discrepancy in census amongst European consuls and the Ottoman government, see J.M. Wagstaff, 'a Note on some nineteenth-century population statistics for Lebanon', *Bulletin of the British Society for Middle Eastern Studies*, 13, 1986, 27–35. See in the classical work by Kemal Karpat, *Ottoman Population, 1830–1914*, Madison: University of Wisconsin Press 1985, at 4: 'The manipulation of population statistics for political purposes by various ethnic and religious groups was widespread and ingenious.'

PART TWO

THE LEBANESE CONSTITUTION OF 1926

4

The Constitution of 1926: Reconstructing the Timeline

> Given that the Lebanese are spirited and, by nature, restless, it is essential that their country's institutions provide stability ... This is something I have known for a while, in fact since the spring of 1926 when, as deputy of Beirut for minorities and in the aftermath of grave events in Syria, I worked late into the nights to design the Lebanese Constitution.[1]

The Commission Administrative and the Council of Representatives (1920–1925)

Freed from the dissolved Administrative Council (AC), General Gouraud proceeded with several decisions abolishing all previous institutions and establishing the foundations of the League of Nations' French Mandate in the new, post-war order.[2] His most famous decision took the shape of a

[1] 'Ainsi, dans la mesure même où le Libanais est mobile par la chair et l'esprit, il faut que les institutions de son pays soient stables ... Pour notre part, nous savons cela depuis bien longtemps, au moins depuis le printemps de 1926, lorsque, député de Beyrouth pour les minorités, nous fabriquions, au cours de studieuses veillées au lendemain de graves événements en Syrie, la Constitution libanaise.' Michel Chiha, 'A l'usage des 'réformateurs' libanais', 14 November 1952, Pol Int 252–3.

[2] On the emergence of the Lebanese Constitution, see in particular Edmond Rabbath, *La Formation Historique du Liban Constitutionnel*, Beirut: Lebanese University Publications, Beirut 2nd ed. 1986 (original 1973), esp. 379–402, with an important update in *La Constitution Libanaise: Origines, Textes et Commentaires*, Beirut: Publications de la Librairie Orientale 1982, 16–43; Antoine Hokayem, *La Genèse de la Constitution Libanaise de 1926*, Antélias: Les Editions Universitaires du Liban 1996, which is extensively based on documents in the French archives. See also the entry-based *Dictionnaire de la Constitution Libanaise*, by Béchara Menassa, Beirut: Nahar 2010. A repertory of the main French legal documents during the Mandate can be found in Youssef Takla, 'Corpus juridique du mandat français', in Nadine Meouchi and Peter Sluglett eds, *The British and French Mandates in Comparative Perspectives*, Leiden: Brill 2004, 63–100.

unilateral proclamation, Arrêté 318 dated 31 August 1920, which established the 'Grand-Liban' in its current borders. This was celebrated on 1 September with a grand ceremony in Beirut hosted by Gouraud.[3]

On 1 September also, Gouraud issued a much longer decree which drew a new administrative and political map of the country. It included his self-appointment as France's 'Haut-Commissaire', with a French 'gouverneur' under him at the head of the new French administration. The former AC gave way to a Commission Administrative (CA) of 15 members, raised shortly thereafter to 17. All were chosen on a communal basis. All were appointed by the High Commissioner.[4] The CA's power was purely consultative and its impact was, for the most part, short-lived and seldom noticed.[5]

A year and a half later, to strengthen France's power and rally support at home, Robert de Caix, the interim High Commissioner, dismissed the 'Commission Administrative' in Arrêté no 1304 of 8 March 1922.[6] Arrêté no 1304 bis, another lengthy order issued the same day, established the 'Conseil Représentatif' (CR, *al-majlis al-tamthili* in Arabic),[7] to be elected on the basis of communal representation. Arrêté 1307 of 10 March 1922 organised its election.[8] The Council's role was limited, for it did not command legislative power even on paper. Its importance lay in that its 30 members were to be

[3] Full text of the Proclamation in Rabbath, *La Constitution Libanaise: Origines, Textes et Commentaires*, above n. 2, 68–9. The ceremony took place at the Résidence des Pins, now the French ambassador's residence. For the ceremony, Julie d'Andurain, *Le Général Gouraud- Un Destin hors du Commun, de l'Afrique au Levant*, Paris: Perrin 2022, 390. There is an iconic picture of Gouraud flanked by religious dignitaries and other Lebanese notables on the steps of the Résidence. For a rich chronicle of the Mandate with a copious set of photographs, Pierre Fournié and Jean-Louis Riccioli, *La France et le Proche-Orient 1916–1946*, Paris: Casterman 1996.

[4] Arrêté 336 of 1 September 1920, extensive excerpts in Rabbath, *La Formation Historique du Liban Constitutionnel*, above n.2, 372–4.

[5] The Commission Administrative was headed by Daoud Ammoun (1867–1922): see Lynne Lohéac, *Daoud Ammoun et la Création de l'Etat Libanais*, Paris: Klincksieck 1978 (suggesting contra that the Administrative Council had more influence than usually admitted.)

[6] There are two Arrêtés 1304. The title of the first, short Arrêté 1304, stated unceremoniously the 'licenciement de la Commission Administrative du Grand-Liban (dismissal of the AC of Great-Lebanon).' Rabbath, *La Formation Historique du Liban Constitutionnel*, above n.2, 374.

[7] The title of the second Arrêté 1304, Arrêté 1304 bis, also taken on 8 March 1922, is 'portant création et organisant le fonctionnement du Conseil Représentatif de l'Etat du Grand-Liban (addresses the creation and organisation of the workings of the Representative Council of the State of Great Lebanon)'. Id., excerpts at 374–6.

[8] Full text of Arrêté 1307 (or Electoral Law of 1922) in Muhammad Murad, *Al-Intikhabat al-Niyabiyya fi Lubnan 1920–2009* (Parliamentary elections in Lebanon 1920–2009), Beirut: Publications of the Lebanese University 2013, Appendix 1, 466–79. It can also be found in the

elected, unlike the Administrative Commission which had been appointed, in its entirety, by the High Commissioner. In effect, the progress in AC practice in the later stage of the Mutasarrifiyya was revived, and elections took place in two phases – the first, on 7 May 1922 at the level of villages and city neighbourhoods where male citizens voted for their delegates, and the second on 21 May for the successful delegates to elect the 30 members of the new CR.[9]

Most Muslim Lebanese refused to participate in the elections of 1922 because they resented their separation from Syria, and because the French yoke was tight. France had effectively established direct rule by unilaterally issuing High Commission arrêtés in all walks of public life. The CR did not have legislative powers, let alone executive ones. It was designed to provide some representative legitimacy through elections, but its lasting contribution was the entrenchment of communalism by means of an electoral law. Arrêté 1307 establishing the first CR continued in its broad traits the AC system of the Mutasarrifiyya, rooting communalism in the representation of Lebanese voters through an electoral model that persists to date.

There was resistance to communalism. In addition to local nationalist figures who sought to rid the country of religion-based representation, the French Republic was by this time determinedly 'secular', *laïque*, with this *laïcité* strengthened in France by the laws of 1905 which sharply separated Church and State. Opposition to communalism in Lebanon was not restricted to the Lebanese. It was the subject of a fierce debate behind the scenes amongst the French administrators.

The attempt to de-communalise the system fell largely to Maurice Sarrail, former Commander of the French Third Army and High Commissioner to Syria and Lebanon from January to November 1925. Sarrail was viscerally anti-clerical and determined to do away with the prevailing system.[10] In order to undermine religious leaders whom he disliked, and to strengthen French

Official Journal (*al-Jarida al-Rasmiyya*), accessed here in facsimile through al-Mustashar, a private electronic data basis for lawyers.

[9] Id., Art. 6 of the Electoral Law of 1922 for the two turns. See next chapter section on Electoral templates.

[10] Hokayem, *La Genèse de la Constitution Libanaise de 1926*, above n.2, 173–83: 'Les maladresses de Sarrail au Liban.' On the complexity of decision-making in France leading to the dismissal of Sarrail, Pierre Fournié, 'Le Mandat à l'épreuve des passions françaises: l'affaire Sarrail (1925)' in Nadine Méouchy ed., *France, Syrie et Liban 1918–1946*, Damascus: IFPO 2002, 125–68.

power, he pushed for a gerrymandered, secular electoral system more in line with his *laïque* worldview and the interests of France. He was also brutal, stoking discontent in Syria and Lebanon which in October 1925 exploded into an uprising only defeated at the cost of more than 10,000 lives, the vast majority Syrian.[11] In Lebanon, he dismissed the Council of Representatives when it rejected his preferred candidate for governor of Lebanon.[12]

The archives of the Quai d'Orsay reveal the internal battle between Sarrail and the Secretary General of the High Commission, Verchère de Reffye, a battle which was ultimately decided against Sarrail by the French Minister of Foreign Affairs Aristide Briand, by then also the President of the Council of ministers. Briand personally enjoined Sarrail to retain both the communitarian law of 1922 and the electoral districts which had been drawn in its wake. The decision-makers in France were clear and peremptory. Sarrail was ordered to keep to the 'statu quo ante'.[13]

The election of the new CR was carried out in two phases, based on the template of the 1922 law. The first was held on 28 June 2005 and the second on 12 July, this time with a more significant Muslim participation.[14] By then, a much larger number of citizens of the new state had rallied to the idea of effective contribution to the workings of Great Lebanon, practically if not out of conviction. Like the short-lived AC, the CR comprised 30 members, all male, divided in regions on the basis of religious communities.[15]

11 On Sarrail and the 'great revolt' of 1925 in Syria, see Philip Khoury, *Syria and the French Mandate: The Politics of Arab Nationalism, 1920–1945*, Princeton: Princeton University Press 1987, 151–242.

12 Hokayem, *La Genèse de la Constitution Libanaise de 1926*, above n.2, 167–8.

13 All original texts in Id., 179–82, including: Letter of Reffye of 7 June 1925 about danger of tampering with the existing electoral law and circumscriptions; text of the attempt on 19 June by Sarrail to gerrymander on a more secular basis; Briand's firm telegram to Sarrail on 20 June with request of formal confirmation; final acceptance by Sarrail on June 25 of the 'statu quo ante' as ordered by Briand.

14 Rabbath, *La Formation Historique du Liban Constitutionnel*, above n.2, 385.

15 For the results of first and second turns, Majed Khalil Majed, *Al-Intikhabat al-Niyabiyya 1861–1992* (Parliamentary elections 1861–1992), above n.8, 30–7, with full names, regions and sects at 36–7: Out of the 30 members, 17 were Christian, 13 Muslim. More specifically: 10 members were Maronite, 6 Sunni, 5 Shi'i, 4 Orthodox, 2 Catholic, 2 Druze, one 'minorities' (meaning any other denomination than the communities accepted in law). This is the Beirut seat, which was won by Michel Chiha in 1925 and allowed him to sit on the CR and its various committees, including the one drafting the Constitution.

Sarrail was dismissed and recalled to France on 30 October 1925 amid growing international criticism of his suppression of the uprising against French occupation. His use of heavy weaponry culminated in a 48-hour air and land bombardment of Damascus and burning of its environs. Sarrail's successor, Henry de Jouvenel (1876–1935), a journalist and statesman aligned with the Left, arrived in Beirut on 2 December.[16] His mission was to end the bloody rebellion developing across Syria, and to complete the formal request of the League of Nations to grant Lebanon its 'Statut Organique', its Constitution, within three years – no later than 29 September 1926.[17]

On 4 December 1925, just two days after his arrival in Beirut, de Jouvenel signaled his intention to devolve significant power to the Lebanese. He enjoined that the recently elected CR be turned into a constituent assembly.[18] To their surprise, the CR members found that they were charged with the writing of the country's founding text. To this day, there have remained some doubts that France really intended to trust the Lebanese with the writing of the Constitution. A dispatch de Jouvenel sent to Paris on 6 January 1926

[16] On de Jouvenel, see the biography of Christine Manigand, *Henry de Jouvenel*, Limoges: Presses Universitaires de Limoges et du Limousin 2000, esp. at 201–28 for his tenure in Lebanon and Syria; and the preface and bibliography by Hugues Moreau, *Henry de Jouvenel- Répertoire Numérique*, Tulle: Département de la Corrèze, Archives départementales 2010. De Jouvenel was an 'honnête homme' in the French eighteenth century sense, multi-talented and encyclopedic. Both his written legacy, which consists of several books, and his unique diplomatic skills, especially his role in Rome in the mid-1930s, might have saved Europe from the formation of the Axis had it not been for his untimely and sudden death (perhaps less 'natural' than announced, conversation with Anne de Jouvenel, 30 September 2022) on a bench in the Champs-Elysées on 5 October 1935. On his strategy of bringing Italy to the side of France and against Germany in the early 1930s, see Manigand, *Henry de Jouvenel*, 229–73.

[17] 'Mandat de la SDN pour la Syrie et le Liban', signed in London on 24 July 1922, Art. 1: 'Le Mandataire élaborera dans un délai de trois ans à dater de l'entrée en application du présent mandat un statut organique pour la Syrie et le Liban.' Text available on https://mjp.univ-perp.fr/constit/sy1922.htm. The legal dimension of the French Mandate under the Société des Nations is considered in the present study only perfunctorily. More generally on the Mandates in the Levant, see Cyrus Schayegh and Andrew Arsan eds, *The Routledge Handbook of the History of the Middle East Mandates*, London: Routledge 2015.

[18] The declaration was followed on the same day by Léon Cayla's convocation of the CR to meet on December 10. Cayla was the first governor of Great Lebanon's. The call to start working on the constitution appeared so surprising to the Lebanese representatives that one member asked whether he understood correctly that the CR, and not the French government, would elaborate the Constitution. The response of Cayla was in the affirmative. See for both texts Rabbath, *La Formation Historique du Liban Constitutionnel*, above n.2, 391.

puts this controversy to rest once and for all. 'Since I tasked the CR of Great Lebanon *to write their own constitution ...*'[19]

With communal representation a hallmark of the CR, the template confirmed in the electoral law of 1922–1925 would carry through Lebanese constitutional life with no end in sight. The advocates of secularism continued to oppose the system, and to express serious reservations about the philosophy underlying it, then and now, without much success.

Enter Michel Chiha

The CR members lost no time in getting down to work once they realised that the new High Commissioner was serious about devolving powers. The new CR had been elected in the summer of 1925, and a 12-man Commission de Constitution, or Commission du Statut Organique (CSO), was elected from its members at its first plenary session on 10 December 1925. With lawyer Musa Nammur as president of the CR joining it ex officio, it became known informally as the Commission des Treize.[20]

One of the 13 CSO members was Michel Chiha, born in 1891 into a Catholic family in the village of Bmakkin near Aley in Mount Lebanon. Chiha was a young financier who had worked in Manchester for the banking and trade business of his family, and returned to Lebanon after the First World War from Egypt, where he studied law.

Despite their prominence in the constitutional history of Lebanon, the 'founding fathers' of the Lebanese Constitution have not been the object of serious biographical studies with the occasional exception.[21] A full account of the life of Chiha in particular is wanting, considering the richness of his

[19] 'Depuis que j'ai chargé le Conseil représentatif du Grand Liban *de faire lui-même la constitution ...*' Cited by Hokayem, *La Genèse de la Constitution Libanaise de 1926*, above n.2, 216. (Emphasis added.)

[20] Hokayem, *La Genèse de la Constitution Libanaise de 1926*, above n.2, 221–3; Rabbath, *La Formation Historique du Liban Constitutionnel*, above n.2, 391–3; Rabbath, *La Constitution Libanaise: Origines, Textes et Commentaires*, above n.2, 32–8. Names of the 12 members at 222 and 33 respectively.

[21] An extensive biography of CR member for Kisrawan Youssef al-Khazen can be found in Fadel Sa'id 'Aql and Riad Honein, *Al-Shaykh Yusuf al-Khazen, Fikr Sabaqa Zamanah* (Sheikh Yusif al-Khazen, a thought that preceded his time), Beirut[?]: n.p 1993. A comprehensive repertory of representatives and deputies since 1861was published by 'Adnan Daher, *Al-Mu'jam al-Niyabi al-Lubnani* (The Lebanese parliamentary dictionary), Beirut: Bilal 2007. The reader will find entries on every representative in the Council of 1925 mentioned here.

written legacy and the unanimous recognition during his lifetime of his stature as statesman.[22] A short, unpublished biography, written almost 70 years ago, summarises his political life.[23] It notes his law studies in Cairo, and his return to Lebanon in 1920 to take over the family business – the Pharaon and Chiha bank founded by his father Antoine in 1876.[24] In addition to refining his understanding of public finance in his role as banker, which explains the extensive budgetary clauses of the Lebanese Constitution, Chiha was elected to the Council of Representatives in 1925. But he grew quickly disenchanted with public office and refused to stand for office again in 1929. Yet his influence was critical at key junctures in the history of the country through his many lectures and editorials – first in *Le Réveil*, then as a columnist for the French daily *Le Jour*, which he bought in 1937, and then for the *Eastern Times*, Lebanon's first English-language daily which he founded in 1941. In addition to his authorship of the Lebanese Constitution, Chiha is remembered as a man of letters and a poet, but mostly as the author of incisive commentaries on domestic and regional affairs.[25] Politically he was a liberal, deeply committed to fairness in society, highly spiritual, and a man convinced of the special role of Lebanon at the junction of East and West, and as a unique link between the Arab world and Europe.[26]

[22] An interesting book focusing on Chiha is Mahdi 'Amel, *Madkhal ila Naqd al-Fikri al-Ta'ifi: Al-Qadiyya al-Filistiniyya fi Idiulujiyyat al-Burjwaziyya al-Lubnaniyya* (Introduction to the critique of sectarian thought: the Palestinian question in the ideology of the Lebanese bourgeoisie), Beirut: Dar al-Farabi 1980. The book is a Marxist critique of Chiha's thinking as the ideology of the merchant class running Lebanon at the time. 'Amel is the nickname of Hasan Hamdan, who was assassinated in 1987. In the same vein, though far more informative and subtle, see Fawaz Traboulsi, *Silat bila Wasl: Michel Chiha wal-Idiulujiyya al-Lubnaniyya* (Connections without link: Michel Chiha and the Lebanese ideology), London: Riyad al-Rayyes 1999. Neither however is a biography, and their 'class struggle' perspective misses the positive contributions of Chiha in constitutional and other reflections.

[23] Pierre Bart, 'Biographie [de Michel Chiha]', October 1955, Chiha Archive.

[24] Bought in 2016 by a larger bank, Banque Pharaon et Chiha remained the model of a small, discreet and trusted fiduciary for almost a century and half until it was taken over.

[25] An extensive record of Chiha's works, including his books and the full editorials grouped by year, can be found on the site of the Chiha Foundation, michelchiha.org, and in the bibliography at the beginning of this volume.

[26] This is encapsulated well in Francesco Mazzucotelli, "From Ottoman Lebanon to the French Mandate: The End of the "Long Peace"?", in Feroz Ahmad and M Hakan Yavuz eds, *War and Collapse: World War I and the Ottoman State*, Salt Lake City: University of Utah Press 2015, 1134–61, at 1144: "Michel Chiha, a Chaldean Catholic banker and intellectual, was the most prominent of the authors who advocated an image of Lebanon as a bridge between East and West, a place of conjunction for the Mediterranean civilizations of the past, French culture (assumed

Another prominent member in the CR was Chebl Dammous (Shibl Dammus), a central figure in the constitutional process and similarly neglected by biographers.[27] He and Chiha were part of a five-man subcommittee tasked on 14 December 1925 to draw up a timeline and program for the elaboration of the Constitution.[28] Two practical dispositions followed: the first came on 16 December, when Dammous was put in charge of preparing a detailed questionnaire to sound out leading members of society as popular input into the Constitution;[29] the second was the drafting of the constitutional text. This was the work entrusted to Michel Chiha.

The Dammous questionnaire was distributed to political notables, religious leaders, captains of industry, lawyers and other professionals to solicit

to be the historical heir of Greco-Latin civilization), and Arab civilization, which was considered only one of the facets of Lebanon's visage. Basing himself heavily on Toynbee's theories, Chiha theorised that the 'stimulus of pressure' made inevitable Lebanon's Mediterranean projection in a mercantile and business-friendly perspective that was the country's destiny." Although born a Chaldean, a small and ancient Christian community which lived in Iraq, Chiha ran for the minorities' seat as 'Latin', a Catholic group with few members. Chiha's thought is examined in Part III of this book.

27 Thanks to Amine Issa (Amin 'Isa), a remarkable archival legacy of Dammous has been salvaged, including documents on the questionnaire, as well as a large set of political and literary writings. (Hereinafter the Dammous Archive). A short document in this archive mentions his birth on 1 February 1871, a long sojourn in the United States, his return to Lebanon in 1908, and his work as lawyer, judge, journalist and politician. The document mentions that Dammous retired from politics after three tenures as parliamentary deputy and dedicated the end of his life to translating Shakespeare. He died on 18 January 1939. We also have a published translation from English to Arabic of Sa'id Hamadeh, *Al-Nizam al-Naqdi wal-Sarrafi fi Suria* (The monetary and cambist system in Syria), Beirut: American University of Beirut 1935. Hamadeh thanks Dammous for the translation in his preface.

28 Hokayem, *La Genèse de la Constitution Libanaise de 1926*, above n.2, 222. The other three members of the Committee for Beirut were 'Umar Da'uq, for the South Subhi Haydar, and for Mount Lebanon Rukoz Abu Nader.

29 The French version of the Dammous Report was published in 1927 and is available in full, both at Id., Annex 7, 342–53, and in Antoine Hokayem ed., *Documents Diplomatiques Français Relatifs à l'Histoire du Liban et de la Syrie à l'Epoque du Mandat 1914–1946*, Beirut: Les Editions Universitaires du Liban 2003–2016, 3 vols, 840–51. The third volume of the *Documents Diplomatiques* provides rich documents on the genesis of the Constitution and is entitled *Le Désengagement de la France de la Cilicie et l'Affermissement de son Mandat en Syrie et au Liban*. It is referred to hereinafter as 'DD3'. The Report mentions the date of 16 December 1925 for the decision of the 13 member-constitutional commission to 'consult the Lebanese people on the constitution which it was tasked to establish (consulter le peuple libanais sur la constitution qu'elle était chargée d'établir)', respectively at Hokayem, *La Genèse de la Constitution Libanaise de 1926*, above n.2, 342, and at DD3, 841. The original document in Arabic and several answers to the questionnaire are with Amin Issa, above n.27. To avoid multiple references, the Report is cited below as Rapport Dammous, with the numbering of the 12 questions and the page number in the Hokayem annex only.

their views on the forthcoming social contract.[30] It was printed and sent out by 28 December 1925, with answers requested before 15 January 1926. On 16 January, 78 responses had been received, of which were 18 rejections of the questionnaire itself, mostly from Sunni leaders who did not wish to legitimise a constitution recognising a Lebanon separate from Syria. The deadline was extended, and some names added. More answers came, including from both Sunni and Shiʿi personalities who had meanwhile decided that participation was preferable to a sterile boycott. Out of some 200 questionnaires, 132 responses were eventually returned.[31] A side but telling point which emerged from the consultation was the option for those who were polled to participate in the constitutional deliberations. One finds trace of this debate in a long article in *al-Maʿrad* in January 1926.[32] Unsigned, the article mentions 'that the HC expressed for the advisors [i.e. those consulted in the questionnaire] to have the right to vote, so what are the deputies waiting for to follow the desire of the Nation. Why the hesitation?'[33] In practice, it would have been difficult to upend the process to accommodate the idea.

A word on the content of the Dammous Report is in order. To help the CR delineate the basic principles of the Constitution, Chebl Dammous summarised the responses to his questionnaire, only some of which have survived.[34] The report includes the twelve questions posed, the number of people who responded, which answer to each question they selected and why, and a summary of the majority and minority opinions. The poll turned out

[30] The list of the type of *délégués* who were selected to receive the questionnaire appears in Rapport Dammous at 342–43, with a total of 189 addressees. In the 1974 Christmas-1975 New Year issue of the daily *al-Nahar*, an important file is consecrated to the genesis of the Lebanese Constitution. In addition to a long Arabic introduction by Edmond Rabbath, one can find pictures of some of 'the founding fathers', samples of Béchara al-Khoury's handwritten answers to the questionnaire, and various responses from Lebanese notables (with letters and petitions from various Sunni quarters rejecting the principle of a Lebanese Constitution against unity with Syria).

[31] Rapport Dammous, 343. For a thorough analysis of the responses, Rabbath, *La Constitution Libanaise: Origines, Textes et Commentaires*, above n.2, 16–32.

[32] '*Al-Majlis wal-dustur* (the chamber and the constitution)', *al-Maʿrad*, issue 14, September – December 1925, 8.

[33] Id.

[34] At the end of the Report, Dammous expressed his 'hope that the Council [of Representatives] will publish a Green Book in which all the responses received would be reproduced in their entirety.' Rapport Dammous, 352. No such compilation has emerged, and there is no trace yet of the full set of answers, but the Issa Archive includes a significant number of responses, including those of Béchara al-Khoury, who became the first president in Independent Lebanon in 1943.

to be massively favorable to a republic over a monarchy,[35] but divided over a parliamentary or presidential system.[36] A majority favored the establishment of a Senate, partly appointed and partly elected.[37] Many supported the idea of a president who would not be a mere figurehead, with 68 responders wishing to engage his responsibility directly before parliament, against 64 wanting to engage only the individual responsibility of the ministers.[38] All stood largely in favor of direct elections for the lower chamber, as opposed to the prevailing two-tier system.[39] They differed on the division of the electoral districts. Some wanted the 1922/1925 division to remain unchanged; other wanted districts tailored to their communities; still others favored larger districts, three or four for the whole country.[40] There was no direct reference to the French mandate, but 'self-government' was advocated to educate the Nation.[41]

While Dammous's questionnaire is significant from a sociological perspective, it revealed little that the drafters did not know already. But the mere fact of the exercise was important, giving stronger legitimacy for the CR to proceed with the constitutional text. The Constitution which ultimately emerged generally mirrors the main choices in the answers to the questionnaire.

The most telling aspect of the enquiry probably lies in the ambivalence shown towards communitarianism in the Constitution. To Question 6 – 'Should communitarianism be adopted as the basis for the allocation of seats in Parliament?' – only 11 opposed it outright on the ground that communitarianism was incompatible with 'a constitutional regime' and could not

35 Rapport Dammous, Question 1, 343–5.

36 Rapport Dammous, Questions 1, 2, 3, 344–7.

37 Rapport Dammous, Question 2, 345. Two questions were devoted to the Senate, Questions 9 and 10, at 351, with wide differences in the answers on number, type of election for the senators who were to be elected, and the length of the Senate term.

38 Rapport Dammous, Question 3, 346 (most supported a parliamentary system in theory, but a good half supported a president with real power). Questions 4 and 5, 346–7. (on the personal and collective responsibility of the ministers before Parliament).

39 Rapport Dammous, Question 7, 349–50. Question 7 was about the electoral system, with widely ranging answers, id., 350.

40 Rapport Dammous, Question 11, 351.

41 Rapport Dammous, Question 6, 344: "Ce régime enseigne à la Nation la pratique du 'self government'".

'constitute a form of government.'[42] This most distinctive socio-political feature of Lebanon was the subject of lengthy debate, neatly summarised by Dammous:

> The people consulted were unanimous in condemning, as a matter of principle, the so-called system of communitarian representation, which consists in distributing the seats in Parliament among the different religious communities in proportion to their size; they expressed their desire to see the bias which perpetuates this system disappear. Despite this, 121 responders advocated, not without great reluctance, they said, the communitarian system as the basis of representation.[43]

The democratic nature of the Lebanese consultation for their first Constitution cannot be underestimated. Respondents took it to heart, giving long and elaborate answers. The Dammous Archive has preserved a significant number of the full answers by some of the most prominent Lebanese of the first half of the twentieth century. It is doubtful that more comprehensive answers would be forthcoming if a similar consultation took place one hundred years later. Such is the weight of history, and the lasting imprint of the main ingredients of the constitution, that room for improvement or innovation would be as hard, if not harder, in a renewed exercise.

Michel Chiha as drafter of the Lebanese Constitution

As the responses were trickling down to Dammous and the CR, the focus shifted to writing the Constitution. Michel Chiha soon emerged as its key drafter.

The Chiha Papers on the Constitution (CCP) fill in a major gap in our knowledge of Lebanese constitutionalism. They provide a remarkable

[42] Rapport Dammous, Question 6, 349: 'Un pays qui se respecte et qui se croit digne d'adopter le régime constitutionnel ne peut s'attacher au système confessionnel.' Id.: 'L'esprit confessionnel ne peut pas constituer une forme de gouvernement.'

[43] Rapport Dammous, Question 6, 348: 'Les personnes consultées ont été unanimes à condamner, en principe, le système dit de la représentation confessionnelle, qui consiste à répartir les sièges au Parlement sur les différentes communautés religieuses proportionnellement à leur nombre, ils ont exprimé le désir de voir disparaître les préjugés qui nous attachent encore à ce système. Toutefois 121 délégués ont préconisé, non sans une grande répugnance, ont-ils dit, le système confessionnel comme base de la représentation.'

documentation on the elaboration and progress of the text, not least because they solve a century-long riddle about who the drafters were, and whether the Constitution was initially composed in Arabic or in French. As Edmond Rabbath noted, 'The question of who wrote the original Constitution of 1926 and where [i.e. in France or in Lebanon], and in what language, never fails to fuel controversies that have become chronic.'[44]

Thanks to the CCP, we finally have an answer to these persistent, lingering mysteries surrounding the 'dean of the constitutions of the Middle East.'[45] The first draft of the text was written by Michel Chiha in Beirut, in French, in early 1926. The manuscript version comprises 85 articles.[46] It is in Chiha's hand, as are the copious annotations of three consecutive typed drafts. This discovery ends speculation that has persisted for a century. It confirms Michel Chiha as the author of the original version of the Lebanese Constitution, in French, in Beirut.

The Constitution as it was finally enacted in May 1926 was the result of a more collective process. Precise conclusions are sometimes difficult to reach because of the absence of dates in the manuscript, the typed drafts and the corrections. There was no central CR secretariat that kept documents and exchanges, at least as far as we can tell. We do not know exactly when Chiha's first manuscript was written and eventually completed.

Previous to this first manuscript draft, several projects had circulated for the organisation of Lebanon within the larger Mandate encompassing Syria, An 'avant-projet de statut organique préparé par le Département', the legal section of the French foreign ministry, dated 22 December 1924, covers all the states of the Mandate across Lebanon and Syria,[47] with only eight articles

[44] 'Mais la question de savoir qui a rédigé la Constitution originale de 1926 et où, et en quelle langue, elle a été rédigée, ne laisse toujours pas d'alimenter des controverses devenues chroniques.' Rabbath, *La Constitution Libanaise: Origines, Textes et Commentaires*, above n.2, 13. Evidence that the question remained without answer can be found in the title of the thoughtful article of Fabienne Quilleré-Majzoub and Tarek Majzoub, 'Recherche les véritables auteurs de la Constitution libanaise de 1926 désespérément ...', *Revue française de droit constitutionnel*, 131, 2022, 641–60.

[45] The Lebanese Constitution is described as the 'doyenne des constitutions du Moyen-Orient' by Rabbath, *La Constitution Libanaise: Origines, Textes et Commentaires*, above n.2, 3.

[46] DOC 1, in Chiha's handwriting, stops at Art 86, which is torn after the first truncated word / aucu/.

[47] Other than the State of Great-Lebanon (capital Beirut), the other 'States' are the states of Syria (capital Damascus), of the Alaouites (capital Lattaquieh), and of the Djebel (mountain) Druze

on 'l'Etat du Grand Liban'.[48] The text has little resemblance to what emerges eventually as the Chiha drafts and, ultimately, the 1926 Constitution. This is also the case for several other documents in the French archives, including the 'Projet de Statut organique limité au règlement mandataire élaboré par le Département, 4 janvier 1926',[49] in which Lebanon figures largely as part of the larger Syrian union governed *in toto* by France.

Rather than the text of the Projet itself, it is the date which is meaningful. By January 1926, de Jouvenel had tasked the CR to go ahead with a constitution for Lebanon only. The various Avant-Projets which dealt with the whole territory controlled by France, necessarily making the sections relevant to Lebanon short and general, became moot.[50] The Syrian provinces under the Mandate would have to wait while the Lebanese Constitution took shape. One should therefore discard the 4 January 1926 texts, and all their predecessors that came from Paris. Those who wrote the Projet of 4 January were lagging way behind parallel and more important developments in Beirut.

Constructing the puzzle of the constitutional timeline: chronology and dates

In the remainder of this chapter, I propose a timeline for the construction of the Constitution between 4 December 1925, when de Jouvenel and Cayla

(capital Soueida). 'Second avant-projet du Département, juillet 25', Annex 5 of Hokayem, *La Genèse de la Constitution Libanaise de 1926*, above n.2, 331–40 (40 Arts).

48 Annex 3 of Hokayem, *La Genèse de la Constitution Libanaise de 1926*, above n.2, 316–24 (54 Arts), Arts 40 to 47 bis on Lebanon at 322–3. Another common reference is to the Paul-Boncour committee, whose work was also marginal to the constitutional text and is discussed in next chapter.

49 Id., Annex 8, 353–7. See also Annexes 4 to 7, 324–53.

50 The limited influence of these texts on the Statut Organique across the Lebanese-Syrian Mandate is confirmed by various actors, for instance Robert de Caix in an extensive report entitled 'L'organisation donnée à la Syrie et au Liban de 1920 à 1923 et la crise actuelle', dated October 1926, and published in full by Gérard Khoury, *Une Tutelle Coloniale, Le Mandat Français en Syrie et au Liban- Ecrits Politiques de Robert de Caix*, Paris: Belin 2006, 394–456. Written for a new High Commissioner, the report is remarkable for its colonial spirit, and for the colourful perception by de Caix of some actors in the field. Chiha is considered highly talented, de Jouvenel conceited and contradictory, and it is clear that the author's antipathy towards de Jouvenel passed under silence his achievement of the Lebanese Constitution. See at 425 on the confidence-inspiring quality of Chiha and his 'incontestable patriotisme'; at 442 on 'la nomenclature pompeuse de M. de Jouvenel'; at 444 on 'la politique sautillante de M. de Jouvenel'; and at 441 for the only mention of the Lebanese Constitution, a mention which is critical of the clause in Art. 2 which prevents the country from being dismembered.

formally entrust it to the CR, and 23 May 1926, when the CR completed its votes on the Constitution in the early hours of the morning.

The puzzle is daunting to assemble, and a brief reminder of the sources consulted might help. In addition to the contributions of the main historians and jurists who worked on the French archives, I rely on the Chiha Constitutional Papers,[51] de Jouvenel's archives in Corrèze and his papers in Paris,[52] two Lebanese daily newspapers, *L'Orient* in French and *al-Ma'rad* in Arabic, and the Arab-language weekly *al-Ahrar al-Musawwara*.[53] I tried to reconstruct as precisely as possible the timeline of 'how things actually were' – *wie es eigentlich gewesen*' – in the well-known words in the nineteenth century scholar Leopold von Ranke, a founder of modern source-based history.

As *terminus ad quo*, 4 January 1926 suggests that there is no Lebanese constitutional draft yet, and if there was, Paris was unaware of it. We also have amongst Chiha's CP one document which, unlike all other main documents, is dated. This is a letter dated 28 December 1925 from a young Paris law graduate named Gabriel Menassa, who appended a draft model for a

[51] The 29 documents in the CCP are cited DOC followed by the number.

[52] Fonds de Jouvenel in Corrèze ('Corrèze'). Papers of de Jouvenel in Paris with Anne de Jouvenel ('AJ').

[53] The dailies are the *Ma'rad*, founded in 1921, and *L'Orient*, founded in 1924. The period covered in December 1925 to May 1926.

Al-Ma'rad was owned and published by Michel Zaccour (d.1937) between 1921 and 1936, sometimes daily, sometimes two or three times a week. I am grateful to Makram Zaccour, Michel's son, and his namesake grandson Michel, who kindly put at my disposal the full pdf set of the Ma'rad. I refer here to the set as '*al-Ma'rad (original)*', in contradistinction with facsimile collection of *Al-Ma'rad*, published in two volumes, 1921 to 1929, and 1929 to 1936. (Basim al-Jisr and Mas'ud Dahir eds, Beirut: Nahar n.d.).The facsimile published edition, which consists of a choice of issues, is cited here simply as *al-Ma'rad*. On Michel Zaccour, see Alexandre Najjar, *L'Enfant Terrible, Michel Zaccour (1896–1937)*, Beirut: L'Orient-Le Jour 2010.

L'Orient was owned by Gabriel Khabbaz (d. 1944), with George Naccache (d. 1972) as chief editor, and continues to run as *L'Orient-Le Jour L'Orient* and *Le Jour*, which was bought by Chiha in 1937, fused in 1971. I am grateful to Nayla de Freige, the Président-Directeur Général of *L'Orient-Le Jour*, who put at my disposal the full archives of the paper, and to the newspaper's archivist, Sylva Chaer, who quickly spotted the most important text in that period. The other contemporaneous newspaper source examined is *Al-Ahrar al-Musawwara* (courtesy of Ziad Chebib), a semi-satirical weekly. The *Ahrar* was published by Gebran Andraos Tueini (d.1948) in 1926 and 1927. The facsimile collection of 50 issues was reprinted by his son Ghassan (d. 2012) at Dar al-Nahar in 1995. All these papers were strongly nationalistic, with courageous owners and editors defending Lebanon's full independence and the liberty of the press.

constitution (DOC 22). The draft, he wrote to Chiha, was culled from a 'diplome' on Lebanon and the French mandate he had completed the previous year.[54]

In addition to the letter by Menassa, the other dates of which we are certain pinpoint the emergence of two sub-committees for the Constitution. On 10 December, Chiha was appointed to the 13-member Commission du Statut Organique (CSO);[55] and on 14 December to the smaller 'committee of five' which was tasked by the CR with the timeline and planning.[56]

We then have the record of a brief report of the conclusions of a plenary CR meeting dated 6 January 1926 with lapidary but important directives given to the drafters, including 'a republican form of government', 'a bicameral parliament', the 'irresponsibility [i.e. the immunity] of the head of state' and some details on individual ministers' responsibility; and, for communal purposes, the 'repartition of seats by rite [i.e. religious community].'[57] In a matter of

[54] See in next chapter the section on Menassa and the Annex to his letter.

[55] The word 'Commission du Statut Organique' appears in the Mandate of the League of Nations (French SDN), which, as mentioned, comes formally into effect on 29 September 1923 and gives three years to France to complete a 'Statut organique' (Art. 1, text and sources in next chapter). Statut Organique was the official name until the Lebanese text emerged in May 1926 as the Constitution, together with a shift from Grand-Liban to République libanaise (Art.101 of the Constitution of 1926, unchanged to date). One can detect in the daily papers in the first months of 1926 a slow but steady shift away from 'statut organique (*qanun asasi*)' to 'constitution (*dustur*)'. Grand Liban becomes Liban in the 1943 amendments.

[56] Hokayem, *La Genèse de la Constitution Libanaise de 1926*, above n.2, 220–2. The minutes of the 10 December 1925 meeting which appointed the 'Commission des 13' and their names are published in Anwar al-Khatib, *Al-Dawla wal-Nuzum al-Siyasiyya- Dustur Lubnan 1* (The State and political norms 1) Beirut: n.p 1970, 3–6. Also present at that meeting was Léon Solomiac (d.1960), the head of the civil cabinet of the High Commissioner and his representative, who assured the CR members again that they were in charge of writing the Constitution, with the exception of 'the rights of the mandatory State defined by the express statement of the High Commissioner.' Id., 3–4. At the 14 December 1925 meeting, the five-member subcommittee was appointed by the 'Commission des 13' to prepare for a larger consultation of the notables of the country. Hokayem, *La Genèse de la Constitution Libanaise de* 1926, 222; Meir Zamir, *The Formation of Modern Lebanon*, Ithaca NY: Cornell University Press 1988, 207.

[57] 'Gouvernement à forme républicaine.

Chef d'Etat irresponsable.

Ministres individuellement responsables pour les décisions prises par leurs départements respectifs; collectivement responsables pour les décisions arrêtées en Conseil des ministres; le vote défavorable au ministre devra regrouper les deux tiers des membres plus un.

Parlement composé de deux chambres.

Répartition des sièges par rite.' Full text, with reference to 'the day of 6 January 1926', in Hokayem, *La Genèse de la Constitution Libanaise de 1926*, above n.2, 232.

dates certain, we then have a reference ten days later to a French record of a CSO meeting held on 15 February to discuss the Senate.[58]

For the sake of clarity, let me recap the main dates in the chronology, from the statement of de Jouvenel on 4 December 1925 to mid-February 1926:

Preparations
4 December 1925 to 15 February 1926

4 December 1925- De Jouvenel informs the CR of his decision that the Lebanese should write their constitution.
10 December- First plenary meeting of the CR, election of 13-member CSO.
14 December- CR Plenary meets to decide on the drafting plan, designation of a subcommittee of five members, including Chiha and Dammous, to prepare work timeline and program.
16 December- Dammous tasked with preparing national questionnaire.
28 December- Dammous questionnaire sent out.
28 December- Letter of Menassa to Chiha.
6 January 1926- Plenary CR meeting for the general structure of Constitution.
16 January- Meeting of the CSO to discuss the responses to Dammous questionnaire which had been received. Responses continue to trickle down for another two months.
5 February- mention of the appointment of two (or three)-member drafting subcommittee, including Chiha.
15 February- CSO meeting to discuss the Senate.

A grey area: mid-February to mid-March

From 15 February to mid-March, the sources available give little indication as to progress. This is due to a number of reasons.

During this period, the whole country is concerned with the Syrian revolt, which erupted in August 1925 against French mandated rule in Syria and

[58] Hokayem, *La Genèse de la Constitution Libanaise de 1926*, above n.2, 233. In its issue 6 dated 15 February 1926, at 4, *Al-Ahrar al-Musawwara* mentions that the 'Committee for the Statut Organique (*lajnat al-qanun al-asasi*)' was continuing its work on the basis of the answers to the Dammous questionnaire.'

Lebanon. The press reports extensively on the progress of France's merciless counter-attack, then on the rebellion's slow collapse.[59] Day after day, developments in Syria dominate the news agenda, taking up roughly two-thirds of newspaper coverage.

At the same time, all newspapers, including *al-Maʿrad* and *L'Orient,* suffer the censor's heavy hand in a feverish atmosphere further inflamed by the extension of the revolt to Hasbaya and other parts of Lebanon, and by sympathy and admiration for the anti-colonial rebel Sultan al-Atrash, the leader of the uprising in Syria. *L'Orient* is the most heavily hit by censorship which puts it out of business from 23 February to 22 March.[60] Articles censored in *al-Maʿrad* are highlighted with a picture of a pair of scissors.[61] Other papers keep going with sometimes large gaps between lines, also the work of the censor.

Censorship continues until the Constitution is adopted. It ceases after the election of the first President of the Republic, Charles Debbas, on 26 May, and the formation of the first government on 29 May.[62]

A second reason for the wave of censorship was attacks against High Commissioner Henry de Jouvenel for his 'Damascus speech', a talk he gave in Damascus on 6 February referring to 'les Etats-Unis de la Syrie et du Liban.'[63] A tempest of protests followed in Beirut, especially in Lebanese Christian

[59] The collapse is marked by the occupation of Suwayda (Soueida) in the Druze Mountain of Syria on April 25. On April 27, *L'Orient*'s full front page is about 'La Prise de Soueida'.

[60] On 23 March 1926, the owner of *L'Orient*, Gabriel Khabbaz, writes in a front-page note to the readers that the paper had been suspended on 23 February 'for political considerations', but that de Jouvenel's 'liberal temperament' did not accept censorship lightly. The upshot was a compromise where the censor, a Mr. Beusher, could simply cut the passages he disliked rather than ban the paper altogether.

[61] On 4 March, the front page of *al-Maʿrad* is adorned with a caricature of the censor, *al-Maʿrad (original),* 4 March 1926. The censorship is related mostly to the events in Syria, where battles are raging. And in the issue of *al-Maʿrad (original)* on 8 April, at 2, the editor complains about the excessive use of the censor, who cut out a report stating that 'the deputies came out from the [constitutional] advisors' meeting murmuring that they would have been spared a headache if they had not been debating them in that meeting ... since the draft of the Constitution had been written, the matter was over and the HC read it'.

[62] *Al-Maʿrad (original),* 6 June 1926, 2, writes that 'the censorship over newspapers is at last over', thanking the new president for this, and 'strongly regretting that the rulers (*al-sulta*), and in particular the HC Monsieur de Jouvenel, the distinguished journalist, left his colleagues in journalism with their hands tied while the CR was busy writing the Constitution'.

[63] Full text in French in the frontpage of *L'Orient,* 9 February 1926, and again, in the fuller version provided by the HC office, on 10 February, 2. The controversial formula appears in that second version: 'La France ... sera la conseillère technique qui guidera *les Etats-Unis de la Syrie et du Liban* dans la voie du progrès moderne.' (Emphasis added)

circles, including the nationalist papers opposed to French colonial rule. *Al-Ma'rad* and *L'Orient* devote several indignant articles to the speech. Officials at the High Commission in Beirut including de Jouvenel himself tried to calm the protest by suggesting that the speech was misunderstood, and that he never meant to consider Lebanon other than fully separate from Syria.

Several reports show Michel Chiha's personal concern. On 12 February, *L'Orient* mentions a meeting of the CR two days earlier, with a text it said was signed by Chiha and seven other deputies, all Christians, querying the formula.[64] On 20 February, the front page of *L'Orient* asks again: 'What is the response of the High Commission to the question posed on 10 February by Mr. Michel Chiha and seven deputies?'[65] This is followed by legal arguments by Chiha about the relations between Syria and Lebanon being mere treaties, therefore not binding until the concerned parties have formally agreed them. De Jouvenel being away on an important trip to Ankara to finalise the borders between Turkey and Syria, it is Solomiac who answers:

> Mr. Michel Chiha has been kind enough to ask me what meaning should be given to the words 'United States of Syria and Lebanon' used by the High Commissioner on the occasion of his speech in Damascus: he [Chiha] thinks that they should be interpreted in the sense that Mr. Briand, President of the Council [of Ministers], gave to them when he spoke on his return from Locarno of the United States of Europe.
>
> I agree with Mr. Chiha.[66]

The public row continues through February, so jolted by the Damascus speech were Lebanese nationalists and the Maronite Church.[67] The speech

[64] *L'Orient*, 12 February 1926, 2.

[65] *L'Orient*, 20 February 1926. The original letter to Léon Solomiac is signed by Miichel Chiha and seven deputies (Corrèze 5J-148035) and the response of Solomiac is available at Corrèze 5J-148036. It appears in the minutes of the CR meeting dated 18 February 1926 (Corrèze 5J-148034).

[66] Id.: 'M. Michel Chiha a bien voulu me demander la signification qu'il fallait attribuer aux termes « Etats Unis de la Syrie et du Liban » employés par le Haut-Commissaire à l'occasion de son discours de Damas: il pense qu'il convient de les interpréter dans le sens que M. Briand, Président du Conseil, leur donnait en parlant, à son retour de Locarno, « des Etats Unis d'Europe. »
Je suis d'accord avec M. Chiha'. Léon Solomiac was the chief of cabinet of the HC.

[67] I mention here the public row. The private spat between de Jouvenel and Chiha, and its consequences, are discussed extensively by Antoine Hokayem, see next chapter n.2 and corresponding text.

was clearly a major distraction for the constituents. For what is the value of the commitment to the CR made by the High Commission on 4 December, and what is the point of its intensive work on a Lebanese constitution, if Syria and Lebanon are to be 'united'?

Solomiac's reassurance was not sufficient to calm the atmosphere. On 24 February, de Jouvenel himself denies news of a fusion between Lebanon and Syria, since 'the Lebanese entity is working today on drafting a constitution and not a single change is possible unless the Lebanese Nation expresses its wish to have it changed through a decision by its parliament'.[68]

Despite this controversy, work on the Constitution continued in committee. In the scattered documentation on the preparatory works, we know that the CSO had regular meetings, both internal and with civil society representatives. On Monday 8 March, *al-Ahrar* reported on 'the Constitution and the Chamber of Deputies':

> Since we mention the CD, we report that the Constitutional Committee [the CSO] continues its work, and that the active opposition [of Sunni Muslim circles] at the beginning has now lost its animosity, and that groups [of civil society] have coalesced around it and expressed their views, except for the Association of Journalists, the Bar and the Order of Physicians. The Committee has almost finished reading the answers it received [the answers to the Dammous questionnaire] ... It appears ... that the Committee tries its best to write a constitution which fulfils all conditions found in [world] constitutions to avoid leaving any ground for criticism.[69]

The march of the constitutional draft

Where do the CCP sit in this geopolitical jigsaw? A definitive answer is not possible, as we do not have dates for the drafts or information about their internal circulation. We can rely nonetheless on the CCP's internal coherence and on the language, marginal comments, and amendments in the draft versions, and sequence them with some accuracy.

[68] *Al-Ma'rad (original)*, 24 February 1926, 2. (The Lebanese entity, *al-kiyan al-lubnani*)

[69] *Al-Ahrar al-Musawwara*, issue 9, 8 March 1926, 3.

From mid-February to mid-April 1926, the initial Chiha manuscript and eight other major versions are typed, retyped, and annotated, providing the most important source to understanding the making of the Lebanese Constitution. The novelty of the Chiha CP is the safekeeping for history of at least ten original drafts which we have in full, or almost in full, and which include corrections and comments by Chiha, but also comments in other readers' hand, in the margins of DOCs 1 to 8. We also have in the CCP the longish typed document of unsigned 'Observations' (which I entitle 'Souchier observations' DOC 9)[70] and other typed and unsigned drafts (which I entitle the 'Trad/Chiha drafts' DOCs 23 and 24),[71] as well as shorter documents which add some marginal information to the language and concern of the drafters.[72]

In parallel, various testimonies record the progress of the Dammous questionnaire since its distribution in mid-January. Dammous's report does not bear a date, but there is a suggestion that it was available at least as a workable version in the first half of February 1926.[73] We also know that on 5 February 1926, a smaller committee of two (or three?), including Michel Chiha, was tasked to write 'the Avant-Projet of the Constitution.'[74]

[70] See in next chapter the sẹction on 'Souchier and French expertise'.

[71] The Chiha/ Trad drafts, if my hypothesis is confirmed, are best inserted before or after DOC 5. To avoid an additional complication to the already disorienting jigsaw, and because my conclusions are tentative, I prefer to list them in the chronological reconstruction *after* the 'Souchier observations.' (DOC 9)

[72] The CCP include a typed version of the Avant-Projet (DOC 11), which differs in one article only from the Avant-Projet sent to Paris by de Jouvenel on 18 April. DOC 11 includes 106 articles, whereas the Paris Avant-Projet includes 105 Articles. The text sent to Paris deletes two articles on the composition of the Senate with the number of elected and appointed senators left blank (DOC 11, Art.24) and limited measures on the electoral mechanisms (Id., Art. 25). It replaces them with one laconic phrase: 'Art. 24: Une loi ultérieure fixera le vote d'élection au Sénat (A later law will determine the vote of the Senate)'.

[73] The DD editors added an approximate date. DD3, 840: '[1ère quinzaine de février 1925]', with the text in brackets added by the editors. 1925 should read 1926.

[74] Hokayem, *La Genèse de la Constitution Libanaise de 1926*, above n.2, 231. Hokayem refers to this smaller committee as one with either two or three members. At fn.3, he suggests that the second member was Chebl Dammous, and that Souchier may have been the third member. In the case of Dammous, Rabbath correctly notes that Dammous was 'de culture américaine, ne connaissant pas le français'. Rabbath, *La Formation Historique du Liban Constitutionnel*, above n.2, 392, so whether he was formally on the Committee or not, he could not have interacted with Chiha's French drafts timely and/or comfortably. An amusing conversation about Dammous learning French at the time is reported in *Al-Ahrar al-Musawwara*, issue 6, 15 February 1926, 10: '[Dammous]: I have been learning French for a month ... I want to be in direct contact with the decision-makers (*uli al-amr*) and since they don't know my language, I am learning theirs ... He

Who sat on this crucial subcommittee? Was it a sub-committee of two or three members, and who other than Chiha was on it? We do not have records of the deliberations of that smaller three- or two-member sub-committee, if it were ever functional.[75] The first extant draft of the Constitution is obviously the work of a single person, and, as we shall see in next chapter, Chiha's first handwritten text and the final text of the Constitution correspond both in structure and in the phrasing of several articles that survive to this day.[76]

In that subcommittee of two or three, membership remains shrouded by the documentary foliage extant. Several names are mentioned by various sources. Chiha was the only Council representative whose name is universally acknowledged as a member of the drafting committee(s). Musa Nammur, the president of the CR and head of the CSO, must have had an easy access to the texts, but he would have been too busy for daily contributions, for the work of the CR continued as normal with a busy agenda.

added, laughing: I build for the future. Lebanon is getting Frenchified (*Lubnan sa'er ilal-tafarnus*) and I do not want to be a stranger.'

75 The Corrèze and Anne de Jouvenel documents did not yield decisive texts, but the Corrèze Fonds has an extensive collection of minutes of the CR plenary meetings, dated and appended by Solomiac (Cote 05J-138). Some of the minutes mention work on the Constitution tangentially, such as the replacement of CR member Fu'ad Arslan by member Jamil Talhuq on the CSO, but the CR deals with other matters within its jurisdiction such as infrastructure and road works. It is hard to imagine that the CSO minutes simply did not exist, for Dammous in particular mentions several times during the final debates in the CR that an issue was considered 'in committee'. The Chiha CP do not include them (or make reference to them), but there is in the Corrèze archives a minute of a meeting of the CSO with religious delegates, albeit not one of the CSO itself. I suspect that any surviving set of the Arabic minutes remains in family archives, either Musa Nammour's or Chebl Dammous's, but I did not find them in the Dammous archives held by Amin Issa. If the CSO minutes were taken, and held, in French and/or in Arabic, they have not yet been found.

76 As for the participation of Paul Souchier or any other French personality in the drafting sub-committee, it is doubtful in the light of de Jouvenel's insistence that the Lebanese 'own' their Constitution, for Souchier to have been sitting on a formal committee. Souchier, as we shall see, actively participated in the preparatory works, but not as drafter of the Lebanese part of the Constitution. The French civil servants were clear from day one about reserving to the French 'the rights of the mandatory State defined by the express statement of the High Commissioner'. This makes Souchier, in all likelihood, the main author of that part, which is completely deleted from the Constitution after Independence in 1943. The Lebanese part is therefore Chiha's, with the active participation of the other Lebanese 'founding fathers' (mainly Nammour, Trad and Dammous), and with side yet important observations by the HC and Souchier, which we examine next chapter.

The other drafts

The name of Greek-Orthodox deputy for Beirut Petro Trad (1886–1947) appears in several accounts as drafter.[77] Trad was a French-educated lawyer and major figure throughout the French Mandate, including briefly as president of the Republic in 1943. We can almost say for certain that he was formally part of the 'two-person committee'. But there is no mention of his name in the CCP.

We have an intriguing clue as to Trad's role from an external source – an article published in *al-Maʿrad* on 16 April:[78]

> What we know is that the CSO, which is composed of 12 persons, entrusted four members to draft the constitution, and that the four members asked two of them Mssrs. Petro Trad and Michel Chiha, to do the work. *Each one wrote a draft separately.*[79]

This last sentence is crucial. We have seen that membership of the 'two- or three-person sub-committee' has remained unclear, and that several testimonies point to Petro Trad as being 'the other man' on the committee. If the report of *al-Maʿrad* is accurate, then each of the two men wrote a draft separately.

Where then is Petro Trad's separate draft? It does not surface in any of the studies and documents available, with one possible proviso: it might be included in Chiha's constitutional papers, without his name appearing on

[77] In *Al-Niyaba fil Lubnan min 1860 ila 1977* (Parliamentary membership in Lebanon from 1860 to 1977)), Beirut: n.p. 1980, 111, Fu'ad Khuri writes that the 'two rapporteurs (*al-muqarrirayn*)' were Michel Chiha and lawyer Petro Trad'. This is also mentioned by Zamir, *The Formation of Modern Lebanon*, above n.56, 207, and by Béchara El-Khoury (the former Lebanese president and brother-in-law of Chiha) in his memoirs, *Haqa'eq Lubnaniyya* (Lebanese truths), Beirut: Awraq Lubnaniyya 1960, vol. 1, 133. It is confirmed in the final deliberations of the plenary CR, which include a passage where Trad self-refers 'to the two rapporteurs and to the Commmitee' as he explains what they argued and decided on the matter of the mandate of the president. Ahmad al-Zein ed., *Mahader Munaqashat al-Dustur al-Lubnani wa Taʿdilatuh 1926–90* (Minutes of the discussions about the Lebanese Constitution and its amendments), Beirut: Publications of the Chamber of Deputies 1993, 48. Another passage shows Dammous referring to Trad as rapporteur (id., 59)

[78] '*Al-dustur aydan* (The Constitution again)', *Al-Maʿrad (original)*, 16 April 1926, 1–2. The article yields significant information on the progress of the preparatory works, see below at n.106 and accompanying text.

[79] Id. Emphasis added.

it, in the shape of two longish documents, DOC 23 and 24 (110 Articles each), which are full drafts of a constitution and are difficult to place anywhere on the timeline of the Chiha-centered drafting exercise in the rest of the CCP.[80]

Are DOCs 23 and 24, entitled 'Constitution de l'Etat du Grand Liban', the Petro Trad drafts? It is impossible to say for certain, and it is hard to conclude that they are exclusively Trad's. A close examination of these two texts and the eight first Chiha documents suggests that DOCs 23 and 24 are the fruit of a possible collaboration between Chiha and Trad meeting more than once, reading and discussing the articles, with, as a result, what I suggest to call the Chiha/Trad drafts.[81] An alternative hypothesis is that DOC 25, which consists of 54 articles, was contributed by Trad as a fully separate draft proposal, before or during the time when Chiha was elaborating his first versions (DOCs 1 to 4) This would leave the time and sequencing of DOC 25 unknown. In the absence of further sources, the suggestions presented here remain speculative.

Like the Chiha/Trad drafts, and unlike the Menassa letter, DOCs 19, 20 and 21 are three incomplete 'preparatory documents' which are difficult to place.

DOC 19 starts with the line 'Ch.IV Du Pouvoir Executif'.[82] It is handwritten by Chiha and is heavily corrected. If the missing articles surface, DOC 19

[80] DOC 23 is clearly the earlier version. DOC 24 differs slightly from DOC 23 in the first 90 or so articles, with 'Council of Representatives' replaced by 'Chamber of Deputies', but the differences in the last sections are more significant.

[81] Part of the conclusion reached here rests on the fact that Chiha's drafts are never longer than 96 articles (without the Mandate and transitional part), whereas the Chiha/Trad drafts consist of 103 articles for the corresponding domestic part (with an additional 7 articles on Mandate and transition, a section left to the French to draft). Speculation that Chiha edited the Trad draft is also based on the fact that DOCs 23 and 24 are separate texts which cannot be integrated in the rest of the successive Chiha versions. They are autonomous in some parts, yet partly similar, or exactly similar, in others, when compared to the language of the articles we find in the Chiha DOCs which follow the first manuscript (DOC 1). Like other documents such as the Menassa letter (DOC 22 see below) and a draft whose author is also unknown (DOC 25), I suspect that Trad passed them on to Chiha, who integrated what he thought useful (or what he and Trad agreed to be useful). This can be also supported in the X-crossed passages on the Chiha/Trad texts, as when someone checks that the particular section or article has been taken into account.

[82] DOC 19 consists of five pages, Arts. 50 to Art.73. There are no articles 1 to 50, and a page seems missing after page 1 (the last article is Art. 50 bis, and the next page starts with Art. 59).

would probably be DOC 0. Its most telling part consists of a few lines at the end of page 4, which lists topics that Chiha jots down for later development, namely:

Revision of the Constitution
Special provisions for Parliament sitting in Congress
Judicial power
High Court of Justice
Finances
Transitional Provisions (DOC 19)[83]

These six topics are taken up in the later documents and developed in the very sequence in which they appear in the final text of the Constitution.

DOC 20 is entitled 'Projet de Constitution Libanaise, Titre Premier, Pouvoir Exécutif', and includes 19 articles over three pages. DOC 21 is a copy, but it is typed on a different machine and includes 29 articles. Other than 'x's in the margin, as in DOCs 23 and 24, which suggest that Chiha checked that his drafts had taken these articles on board, there is little of interest in these documents.

Together with the Menassa letter (DOC 22), the two Chiha/Trad drafts (DOC 23 and 24), and the shorter anonymous draft (DOC 25), the various drafts constitutions (or sections of draft constitutions) that are kept in the CCP can be listed together under the heading 'Preparatory Documents'. This conclusion is reflected in my arrangement of the CCP.

Picking up the documentation sequence again in the light of these texts: For a better approximation, I now turn to the printed texts of the draft Constitution in the CCP. There are four such printed documents (DOCs 12, 13, 14, 15).

The first two, DOCs 12 and 13, are 'Avant-Projets' and consist of 108 articles. They are identical, in French, with the second version including corrections by hand.[84] They constitute a replica of DOC 11, with slight

[83] 'Révision de la Constitution; Dispositions spéciales au Parlement siégeant en Congrès; Du pouvoir judiciaire; Haute cour de justice; Des finances; Dispositions transitoires'. DOC 19.

[84] The title page of DOC 12 ('CONSTITUTION LIBANAISE- AVANT-PROJET') is missing in DOC 11.

modifications and additional articles.[85] The most important addition is a new article in the section on 'Finances',[86] and the language is also edited in various places.

The two other printed versions, DOCs 14 and 15, are in Arabic. DOC 14 comprises 107 Articles with an addendum (*dhayl*) consisting of one article, Art. 43.[87] DOC 15 is a consolidated, final Arabic version of the Constitution, printed in full under dark green cover, and entitled *al-dustur al-lubnani* (the Lebanese Constitution).[88] It is clean and carries no written comments. It comprises 102 articles, with a list of errata at the end.[89] It was probably printed immediately after the deliberations of the CR on 19 May, and before the version published in the Official Journal on 25 June. The version of the Official Journal incorporates the errata signaled in DOC 15.

85 An article is added to the section in the 'Dispositions communes aux deux chambres,' and another article is inserted (Art.44, DOCs 12 and 13) about the right of a member of parliament to address a question to a member of the cabinet, relegating details to the internal regulations of each, but it is crossed out in DOC 13. It becomes Art. 37 in the final text, with amendments removing the need to refer details to the Chambers' internal regulations.

86 In DOCs 12 and 13, Art. 94 is new, and allows the president to request additional expenditures under particular conditions to the annual budget. Art. 93 introduces several conditions regarding any increase in expenditures.

87 Article 43 is the translation of Art. 44 in DOC 12, and the other 107 articles are translations of the corresponding articles of that document. This means that DOC 14 as the translation of the printed French DOC 12 must have been circulated soon after DOC 12 was completed, while the French version was circulated in copies of which we have one with comments, which is DOC 13. Another indication of the sequence can be concluded from the corrections in DOC 14, in handwriting, to the text of DOCs 12, 13. They include a handwritten note in the margin of Art. 59 requesting 'correction of the translation (*tashih al-tarjama*)'. The comments are in two different handwritings at least. This suggests that several DOCs circulated at the same time and that they overlapped.

88 The front page also mentions the printing press, 'Matba'at al-adab, y. j. [*ya'jim*] Beirut'.

89 DOC 15 is the final Arabic version of the Constitution, except for the errata, which were fixed in the Arabic version of the Official Journal text on 25 June, a month after the adoption of the text. It is also the basis for the French version of the Constitution published several months later, in the French section of the Official Journal on 12 October 1926, and in the annual 1926 report of the League of Nations, both referenced by Hokayem, *La Genèse de la Constitution Libanaise de 1926*, above n.2, footnote at 380 (Hokayem also published the final French text, id. at 380–91). Henry de Jouvenel appeared before the League of Nations to defend his achievements on 17 June (*L'Orient*, 19 June 1926), and must have had the final French version with him to entrust to the League. The delay in the publication of the final French text remains mysterious. Rabbath, *La Formation Historique du Liban Constitutionnel*, above n.2, 397, n.2, suggests that the League did not consider the Constitution to be binding until 1930, but this does not mean that a final text had not been produced before it by de Jouvenel. Nor does it explain why publication of the French text was delayed until October.

Intensification of the process and the publication of the draft

As the CCP begin to circulate within limited circles, press interest in the preparation of the Constitution is back to its pre-censorship level. On 22 March, newspapers report that the CSO met to hear its members on the responses to the Dammous questionnaire. 'The delegates requested that when the draft of the Constitution is ready, they be reconvened to discuss it once more'.[90]

On the same day, *Al-Ahrar al-Musawwara* reports extensively on the Constitution, with a precision suggesting that the main guidelines, and even some fine details, were circulating in town. The longish article sheds light on authorship, circulation, discussions with the French advisor(s), and content.[91]

A surprising dimension of the article is the accuracy of its information:

> About the Constitution we [the author of the article] say that the Committee devoted to the presidency of the State 'an elastic' (*marina*) article, which is not bad, making it a condition for the president to be among those who are elected and who elect, limiting in this way the right to the presidency to the Lebanese. It then discussed the ministries and limited them to seven. It also made the minister alone responsible before Parliament.[92]

These three dispositions are present in the very early Chiha drafts. In particular, the issue of the nationality of the president weighed on the process as the top power structure of the Mandate included, under the HC, a governor who was French – at that time Léon Cayla. With the Constitution prominently featuring a president, the position of governor became redundant. The president being Lebanese was an early feature of the Chiha drafts and was considered

[90] Zamir, *The Formation of Modern Lebanon*, above n.56, 213. At note 127, Zamir references an archived document entitled 'Séance tenue le lundi, 22 mars 1926 à 10 heures par la Commission du Statut Organique.' This is the text # 5J-148136 in Corrèze, which mentions that the CSO met that day with 'delegates from various [religious] communities in Lebanon'. One of the Maronite delegates requests the enactment of family laws (statut personnel) for each community. Another delegate requests that the Lebanese emigrants be consulted on the future constitution and that they be represented in the CD. Consulting emigrants is a recurrent demand during the period, but CR President Nammour answered that it was not easy to hold such consultation, and that there was no example in any constitution allowing an emigrant to sit in the national legislature.

[91] *Al-Ahrar al-Musawwara*, issue 11, 22 March 1926, 3, under the title '*madha fil-dustur* (What is in the Constitution?)'.

[92] Id., column 2.

through the debates a major achievement of the Lebanese in their fight for self-determination.[93]

By 24 March, *L'Orient* is back. It mentions several Lebanese meetings for the Constitution to hear the religious communities' representatives, one of whom required that the full project be submitted again to them when complete.[94] On 25 March, an article refers to a meeting of the CSO the previous day to hear the other deputies, with 'many absent'.[95]

On 25 March also, *Al-Ma'rad* publishes a frontpage article 'for the sake of the Constitution':[96]

> *We have read a version of the draft constitution* which representative Michel Chiha has written in the name of the CSO, and we understand that it has been submitted to the HC.[97]

This is followed by a three- or four-line gap, no doubt the work of the censor. Then come a short encomium to Chiha, and, on the next page, a long passage translated from a French book on the role of the presidency in the Third Republic. The *Ma'rad* article's author, its editor in chief Zaccour most likely, published the translation 'because the draft has strong echoes of the spirit of the French Constitution, especially with regard to the president of the Lebanese Republic'.[98]

This short comparative note, we shall see in the next chapters, is not correct: the Lebanese presidency, powerful as it was from the beginning, has little to do with the effete presidency in the Third Republic. But the

[93] In DOC1, the qualifications of the president are said to be the same as those of deputies (Art.52), who must be Lebanese (Art.27). This makes the extensive debate in the press on the nationality of the president, which continued into and after March, somewhat redundant. It is likely that the journalists as well as some representatives missed the effect of the combined articles.

[94] *L'Orient*, 24 March 1926, 2.

[95] *L'Orient*, 25 March 1926, 2.

[96] *'fi sabil al-dustur'*, *Al-Ma'rad (original)*, 25 March 1926.

[97] Id. Emphasis added.

[98] Id., 2. The long passage, where the author criticises the weakness of the French presidency in the Third Republic, comes from a book by Stéphane Lauzanne (1874–1958), *Les Hommes que j'ai Vus*, Paris: A. Fayard et Cie 1920. Lauzanne was a prominent journalist, and the co-editor in chief in 1906, with de Jouvenel, of the center-left daily *Le Matin*. See Hugues Moreau, *Henry de Jouvenel- Répertoire Numérique*, above n.16, 7. Lauzanne became increasingly radical on the right in the 1930s and was imprisoned after the Second World War for collaboration with the Nazis.

25 March date of the article is telling, as is the assertion that a copy of the Constitution was shared by Chiha with *al-Ma'rad*. There is no reason to doubt the veracity of the newspaper report. It confirms that a draft of the constitution had begun to be shared by Chiha outside the High Commission and the CR, and that he showed it at least to Zaccour. Other newspapers, like *al-Ahrar*, had not seen it.[99] We cannot ascertain which of Chiha's drafts was shared with Michel Zaccour, but the *Ma'rad* report on 25 March means that an advanced draft text was in circulation in Beirut in the last week of March 1926.

On 26 March, *L'Orient* writes that high civil servants and judges met with the CSO.[100] On 29 March, *al-Ahrar*'s front page is entitled 'the Constitution on stage'.[101] It features an artist's drawing of three members of the CD on a dais, with four 'advisors' in front of them turning their back to the 'audience' and a prompter telling them what to say.[102] On April 5, the paper mentions that the 'parliamentary committee' has finished hearing from the 'advisors ... the high officials in the State', but that it focused in particular on 'the summary ... by general rapporteur Chebl Dammous.'[103]

On 9 April, a front-page article in *L'Orient* rues the vacuity of a debate raging amongst reporters and editorial writers over 'la représentation confessionnelle' of the 'authors of the Statut [Organique]'. The author of the text concludes, sagely, that to rid the country of communalism, 'it is hearts that need correcting – not texts.'[104]

[99] See issue 12 of *Al-Ahrar al-Musawwara*, dated 29 March 1926, where Chiha is also mentioned as the author of the draft: 'Talks about the constitutional project which was written by the Committee [probably the 13-member Committee] are hovering (*hamat*), but no-one can say a true word about it because the project which Deputy Michel Chiha wrote is still under study, and the Committee has not taken a final decision about it.' At the end of the report, Gebran Tueini (probably) writes: 'We shall not say a word before seeing it'.

[100] *L'Orient*, 26 March 1926, 2. From 30 March to 2 April, *L'Orient* published in four instalments of a 'projet de Constitution' authored by 'Dr Eyoub Tabet', also sent to the HC. This is the same text which was sent to Chiha, see Ch.5 n.107.

[101] '*Al-dustur 'alal-masrah* (The Constitution on stage)', *Al-Ahrar al-Musawwara*, issue 12, 29 March 1926.

[102] *Al-Ahrar al-Musawwara*, issue 13, 5 April 1926, 4.

[103] Id. There is confusion here between the Dammous questionnaire and the draft constitution, but the article shows the continued centrality of Dammous in the process. The passage laments, in the continued policy request for transparency in the paper, the fact that the full draft had not been made public.

[104] *L'Orient*, 9 April 1926.

Four days later, starting on 13 April, *L'Orient* publishes, in five consecutive instalments, the full 'Projet de la Commission du Statut.'[105] This was a first in a French-language newspaper, but there appears to have been a simultaneous – if not slightly earlier – scoop by the Arabic-language *al-Ahwal*. On 18 April 1926, under the title 'The Constitution Again', *Al-Ma'rad* writes: 'Our sister newspaper *al-Ahwal* opened the battle by publishing the draft constitution, but the presidency of the CR responded that the published version was not the official [Arabic] version'.[106]

By 19 April, the whole draft has been published in French in *L'Orient*. It corresponds to DOC 11, the consolidated, 'clean' version of DOCs 6 through 8.[107] An Arabic translation, not an official one, was surely available at the time: *al-Ma'rad* had written three days earlier that the CSO was meeting regularly, including with Souchier, 'to study the draft, which was typed and distributed to the members in French, and was sent for translation'.[108] A workable first translation in Arabic of such an important (and rather short) document could not have taken more than a day or two.

On the strength of the texts visited so far, we can formulate the following hypothesis: Chiha finished the first draft (DOC1) by early February and started receiving comments from the CSO and a limited group of French officials. (DOCs 2 to 5). DOCs 2 to 5 were therefore available on or around February 15, and Docs 6 to 8 circulated in restricted French and Lebanese circles between the second week of February and the first half of March. The clean copy of DOC 11 was made available in wider circles in the second half of March or the first week of April, reaching *L'Orient* on 12 April. An Arabic version was published also around the same time in *al-Ahwal*.

105 *L'Orient*, issues of Tuesday 13, Wednesday 14, Friday 16, Saturday 17, Sunday-Monday 18–19 (there is no paper on Thursday 15 April).

106 '*Al-dustur aydan* (The Constitution again)', *Al-Ma'rad* (*original*), 16 April 1926. *Al-Ahwal* was founded by Khalil al-Badawi in 1891 and is said to have been the first Arabic newspaper which appeared twice daily, in the morning and in the evening. Badawi then fell on hard times; the paper was sold in 1909, then re-appeared intermittently. Philippe de Tarazi, *Tarikh al-Sahafa al-'arabiyya* (History of the Arabic press), Windsor: Hindawi 2023, rpt of 1913 edition, 272–4. I was not able to find issues of *al-Ahwal* at the time.

107 There is however a final section missing since the newspaper's serialised publication stops at Art. 91. In DOCs 6 to 8, page 14 stops at Art. 91, and the remaining articles (Arts. 92 to 96) are on page 15. So either the editors of the paper missed the last page, or it was not given to them. The final sections on the Mandate and transitional dispositions are also missing.

108 *Al-Ma'rad (original)*, 16 April 1926.

A reconstruction of the drafting progress so far can be summed up as follows:

Phase 2- Progress of the constitutional draft February to 18 April 1926

January to mid-February- 'Preparatory works' and documents, including foreign constitutions, the Menassa project, a partial draft by Chiha (DOC 19), the two other anonymous typed short drafts (DOCs 20 and 21), and the 'Chiha/Trad' drafts (DOCs 23 and 24).

Ca first half of February- Chiha completes the first draft (DOC 1).

Second half of February- DOC 1 is typed and three additional typed versions (DOCs 2 to 5) circulate amongst the members of the CSO – probably also amongst French figures in the High Commission.

Through March, improved typed drafts (DOCs 6 to 8) circulate in Beirut. CSO members meet regularly. Comments from French HC officials (including de Jouvenel DOC 6), and from CSO members are added in the margin of these typed versions.

Paul Souchier (probably) comments extensively on the drafts in a set of 'observations' (DOC 9), a few only are taken on board by Chiha (DOC 11).

Last week of March- first week of April- DOC 11, a clean version of DOCs 6 to 8, adds in a final, separate section, the French Mandate provisions and the 'dispositions transitoires' to the work of the Lebanese drafters.

End March-first week of April: DOC 11 circulates in Beirut with ad hoc Arabic translations, probably without the last section on the Mandate.

13–19 April- Publication of constitutional draft in *L'Orient*, in five instalments. Unofficial Arabic translation is published in *al-Ahwal*.

18 April- finalised Avant-Projet sent by de Jouvenel to Paris.

On 18 April 1926, when High Commissioner Henry de Jouvenel sends 'the Avant-Projet of the Constitution' to Paris, it is a finished text.[109] This Avant-Projet included at the end two sections about the role of France that were of

[109] Discussion in Hokayem, *La Genèse de la Constitution Libanaise de 1926*, above n.2, 230–2.

signal importance for the French mandatory power. They did not survive colonial rule. The sections appear after the domestic section of DOC 11, in slight but clearly different colour of paper. They were almost certainly written by the French experts, probably Paul Souchier. They do not appear in the document published by *L'Orient* on the same day, and it is probable that the High Commission did not wish them to be distributed or discussed in Lebanon at the time lest a nationalist reaction develop prematurely.[110]

What happens then to the deliberations, since the constitutional cat is out of the bag?

After publishing the last instalment of the Projet in the weekend of 18–19 April issue, the editors of *L'Orient* note on 20 April that there will be much to comment on — and that they are starting by asking why the drafters, 'after examining European constitutions', put the minimal age for senators at 35 when the age was 40 in France.[111]

On 22 April, *al-Ma'rad* confirms the intensification of the CSO meeting, with 'sessions going into the night to study the constitutional draft'.[112] On 23 April, *L'Orient* reports a meeting of the CSO the previous day, 'attended by Mr. Souchier', where deputy Subhi Haydar (from Baalbeck) makes a fuss by requiring that his region, together with the city of Beirut, be removed from Great Lebanon. The editor is quick to criticise the request and cites the first article of the published Projet on the established boundaries of the country.[113] The same issue mentions a report in the Arabic press on the need to elect the senators, with *L'Orient* correctly predicting that the first Senate would, on the contrary, be appointed by the HC.[114] The following day, the editors once more lament the fact that 'sectarianism [is] made obligatory'.[115]

On 8 May, *L'Orient* publishes a full front-page article headed 'Histoire d'un Article 103'.[116] This is a draft article on transitory measures in the final section of the Constitution, stating that the Council of Representatives turns

[110] When a draft constitution for Syria was completed the next year after the Revolt had subsided, it was rejected by the nationalists because of a text similar to the Lebanese final sections.

[111] *L'Orient*, 20 April 1926.

[112] *Al-Ma'rad (original)*, 22 April 1926.

[113] *L'Orient*, 23 April 1926.

[114] Id., 2.

[115] *L'Orient*, 24 April 1926, 'le Sectarisme rendu obligatoire.'

[116] *L'Orient*, 25–26 April 1926.

into the Chamber of Deputies when the Constitution is adopted, and that it continues its four-year mandate until 1929. The paper deplores this self-prorogation.[117] It announces at the same time that the 'CSO has just finished its work', and that 'interesting debates' on the Constitution 'will start next week'.[118] On 10 May, *Al-Ahrar* harps on the question of the nationality of the president, incorrectly informed that he might not be Lebanese. On 19 May, *L'Orient* announces, also incorrectly, that the final debates of the CR will take place 'tomorrow'.[119] They started in fact at 10 am that same day.

The last phase: the debates in the CR and the adoption of the Constitution

On approximately 18 April therefore, the official Avant-Projet reached Paris. Final comments from France on the text, all touching on the future role of France in Lebanon, were sent back from Paris by Prime Minister Briand on 12 May.[120] After a brief exchange of telegrams between Briand and de Jouvenel between 12 and 17 May, the text's Lebanese provisions were left undisturbed. De Jouvenel explains in his correspondence with Briand that France's concerns

[117] *L'Orient*, 25–26 April 1926. For the purpose of dating and the circulation of documents, Art. 103 appears as Art. 101 in the Avant-Projet sent to Paris on 18 April, Hokayem, *La Genèse de la Constitution Libanaise de 1926*, above n.2, Annex 9, 358–69. In DOC 13, the 'Avant-Projet complet' features the text in Art. 102. This confusion in numbers suggests that the addition of the Mandate and Transitional sections was made public in the week following 18 April, and that several versions circulated at the same time, each with a different number of articles. In both the final draft presented to the CR on 19 May, and the text adopted on 23 May, Article 103 became Article 97.

[118] *L'Orient*, 8 May 1926, 2.

[119] *L'Orient*, 19 May 1926.

[120] The French government knew the importance of the Constitution, and correspondence at the highest level on this issue took place between Briand, the French Foreign Affairs ministry in Paris and de Jouvenel, the High Commissioner in Lebanon. See details of the last phase in Hokayem, *La Genèse de la Constitution Libanaise de 1926*, above n.2, 235–48. The French naturally cared most of all about the role of France in the Constitution. In the manuscripts and typed versions of the Chiha papers, France is mentioned only in the first article as deputised to govern Lebanon by the League of Nations, 'mandataire de la Société des Nations'. France's role as the League of Nations' mandatory power was a question of importance at the time but is now of mostly historical interest. The result was a clear-cut division between an international law-colonial dimension, which did not last, and the domestic-constitutional arrangements, which did. The French role figures as Title V in the April Avant-Projet, and as Titles V and VI in the final May text. On 22 May 1926, Paul Souchier restated France's right, as mandatory power, to near-total control, including the right to suspend the Constitution, which it exercised regularly from 1926 to 1943.

had all been taken into account in the Avant-Projet, and Briand appears to have been swayed. The final approval from Paris arrived on 17 May.[121]

We do not have an extant text in Arabic before 19 May, even though Arabic drafts must have circulated early on, since several members of the CR did not know or were not comfortable with French. As will be discussed in the next chapter, all printed texts available and those in the CCP appear to miss Art.95, which is the defining article for the communitarian trait of the Lebanese Constitution (DOCs 1 to 14). The final agreed-upon draft distributed to the CR members, in Arabic and/or in French, shortly before they met to discuss it in plenary on 19 May, remarkably, includes it.[122]

The Arabic text was discussed article by article and put to the vote in eight plenary meetings of the CR over four days, from 19 to 22 May. We know that a simultaneous or quasi-simultaneous translation was provided since we have occasional interventions by Paul Souchier on the record. Souchier's interventions in the final debates are few and far-between, except for his concluding speech where he reserved all security and foreign powers to the High Commissioner.[123] These exorbitant powers of France have been made irrelevant since the country became independent. The other articles of the Constitution have not.

The final CR debate, which entailed an article-by-article discussion followed by a vote, sheds light on the interests and views of various CR members.[124] Yet, despite several comments, queries, and suggestions, there were ultimately few changes to the text in the plenary discussions. Shortly after midnight on 23 May, the deliberations of the CR concluded. Later that day, de Jouvenel

[121] Hokayem, *La Genèse de la Constitution Libanaise de 1926*, above n.2, 268.

[122] French text as Annex 10 in id., 379.

[123] The stern declaration of Souchier at the close of the deliberations can be found in Hokayem, *La Genèse de la Constitution Libanaise de 1926*, above n.2, Annex 11, 392, and as 'Déclaration de Paul Souchier, Représentant du Haut-Commissaire, à la 8ème séance du Conseil Représentatif (Discussion des articles de la Constitution', 22 May 1926, DD3, 890–2. Arabic text in Ahmad al-Zein ed., *Mahader Munaqashat al-Dustur al-Lubnani wa Ta'dilatuh 1926–90* (Minutes of the discussions about the Lebanese Constitution and its amendments), above n.77, 84–5.

[124] They are discussed next chapter. For the full text of the deliberations, which were carried out in Arabic, see Zein ed., *Mahader Munaqashat al-Dustur al-Lubnani wa Ta'dilatuh 1926–90* (Minutes of the discussions about the Lebanese Constitution and its amendments), above n.77, 16–84.

announced that the constitution was complete. In a telegram sent to Paris the same day, he writes that he had just 'promulgated' the Constitution.[125]

The final text was published in the Official Journal(s), in Arabic and in French, respectively on 25 June and 12 October 1926.[126]

Table 4.1 below summarises the full timeline reconstructed in this chapter:

Table 4.1 A timeline of the Lebanese Constitution

4 December 1925 to 25 May 1926

Phase 1- Planning and committees set-up
4 December 1925 to 15 February 1926

4 December 1925- Henry de Jouvenel informs the CR of his decision that the Lebanese should write their constitution.
10 December- First plenary meeting of the CR, election of 13-member CSO.
14 December- CR Plenary meets to decide on the drafting plan, designation of a subcommittee of five members, including Chiha and Dammous, to prepare work timeline and program.
16 December- Dammous tasked with preparing national questionnaire.
28 December- Dammous questionnaire sent out.
28 December- Letter of Menassa to Chiha.
6 January 1926- Plenary CR meeting for the general structure of Constitution.
16 January- Meeting of the CSO to discuss the responses to Dammous questionnaire which had been received. Responses continue to trickle down for another month.
5 February- mention of the appointment of two (or three)-member drafting subcommittee, including Chiha.
15 February- CSO meeting to discuss the Senate.

[125] 'Le Conseil représentatif du Grand-Liban a voté solennellement, hier soir, le dernier article de sa constitution que je viens de promulguer …' telegram of de Jouvenel to the 'Département' [at the Foreign affairs ministry] dated 23 May 1926, text in Hokayem, *La Genèse de la Constitution Libanaise de 1926*, above n.2, 276.

[126] The Arabic text can be found in Zein ed., *Mahader Munaqashat al-Dustur al-Lubnani wa Ta'dilatuh 1926–90* (Minutes of the discussions about the Lebanese Constitution and its amendments), above n.77, 84 with footnote 3 mentioning the publication of the Constitution on 25 May 'at pp. 1–6 of Addendum (*mulhaq*) 1984 to the Official Journal'. This is a mistake. I was able to confirm the date in the Mustashar (electronic data base for lawyers), which reproduces the published version in a special, separate Addendum: the date is 25 June, not 25 May. The date of the French text, with the strange lag in its publication in the French version of the OJ, can be found in Hokayem, *La Genèse de la Constitution Libanaise de 1926*, above n.2, 380. See also the section on 'Ratification' in the next chapter.

Table 4.1 Continued

Phase 2- Progress of the constitutional draft
February to 18 April 1926

Mid-January to mid-February- 'Preparatory works' and documents, including foreign constitutions (DOC 16), the Menassa project (DOC 22), a partial draft by Chiha (DOC 19), the 'Chiha/Trad' drafts (DOCs 23 and 24), and another anonymous draft (DOC 25).
First half of February- Chiha completes the first draft by hand (DOC 1).
Second half of February- the manuscript is typed and three additional typed versions (DOCs 2 to 5) circulate amongst the members of the CSO – probably also amongst French figures in the High Commission.
Through March- improved typed drafts (DOCs 6 to 8 consolidated in DOC 11) circulate in Beirut. CSO members meet regularly.
Ca mid-March- Comments from French HC officials and from CSO members (DOCs 6 to 8), including de Jouvenel (DOC 6). Paul Souchier comments extensively in a set of 'observations' in DOC 9.
25 March- copy of the draft shared with *al-Ma'rad.*
Last week of March, first week of April- Paul Souchier adds the second part of DOC 11 on the French Mandate to the Lebanese section.
End March-first week of April- A printed version (DOCs 12, 13) of DOC 11 circulates in Beirut with ad hoc Arabic translations.
13–19 April- Publication of the Lebanese part of DOC 11 in *L'Orient*, in five instalments. Arabic unofficial translation is published in *al-Ahwal.*

Phase 3- From constitutional draft to Constitution
18 April to 23 May 1926

18 April- finalized Avant-Projet sent by de Jouvenel to Paris.
19 April to 11 May 1926- Avant-Projet studied in Paris by French Prime minister Aristide Briand and his team.
Around the same time- Continued press and committee discussions in Beirut.
Second half of April, early May, printed documents are prepared for the CR for its final debate. Changes in printed documents (DOCs 12, 13, 14) show that they are completed after the Avant-Projet is sent to Paris.
12–17 May- French correspondence between Paris and Beirut.
17 May- Approval by Aristide Briand of the Avant-Projet.
Shortly before 19 May- A version missing in our Documents, which does not correspond to the Avant-Projet, includes a major article, Art.95, which constitutionalizes communitarianism in the Lebanese Republic.
19 May- Arabic and French versions, which include Art.95, are discussed in plenary.
19–22 May- CR plenary article-by-article discussion, occasional amendment, and vote.
23 May- 1.30 am- The CR approves the final, consolidated text.
23 May- de Jouvenel mentions that he 'promulgated' the Constitution in a telegram to Paris.

5

The Constitution of 1926: Structure and Inspiration

It is because there is no country like it that we can be assured that Lebanon will remain similar to itself.[1]

Table 5.1 compares the overall structure of the Constitution adopted in May 1926 with that of the first Chiha Ms.

The resemblance between the two is striking. In the final debate, the Lebanese representatives adopted the structure and the titles used by Chiha in his very first draft.

LEJ(F)ARC: the Lebanese version of the 'Atlantic constitution'

We now need to provide a more granular examination. I have argued in a previous book that constitutional law as a discipline has not improved much on the template adopted in the first two constitutions of the modern State: The Constitution of the United States of America (1787) and the first Constitution of France (1791), both part of the Atlantic Revolution.[2] The late eighteenth-century template includes the sections covered, in no particular order, by the acronym LEJ(F)ARC:

[1] 'C'est parce qu'il n'existe aucun pays qui lui ressemble qu'on peut être assuré que le Liban demeurera semblable à lui-même.' Michel Chiha, 'L'Originalité du Liban', Pol. Int. 310.

[2] Mallat, *Philosophy of Nonviolence*, New York: Oxford University Press, chapter 10 'Constitution-writing: LEJFARC's universal template', 153–74. For the emergence of the concept of 'the Atlantic Revolution', Jacques Godechot and Robert Palmer, 'Le problème de l'Atlantique du XVIIIe au XXe siècle', *Relazioni del X Congresso Internazionale di Scienze Storiche, Roma, 1955, vol. 5. Storia Contemporanea*, Firenze: Sansoni, 1955, 175–239; and Jacques Godechot, *Les Révolutions 1770–1799*, Paris: Presses Universitaires de France 1963, esp. 1–4.

Table 5.1 Chiha's first draft and the Lebanese Constitution compared

Constitution du 23 mai 1926	Constitution du Grand Liban (Chiha Constitutional Papers, DOC 1)
Titre premier – Dispositions fondamentales	Titre 1er – Dispositions fondamentales
Chapitre premier – De l'Etat et du territoire	Ch. 1er De l'Etat et du Territoire
Chapitre 2 – Des Libanais, de leurs droits et de leurs devoirs	Ch. 2. Des Libanais, de leurs droits et de leurs devoirs
Titre II – Des pouvoirs	Titre 2: Des pouvoirs
Chapitre premier – Dispositions générales	Ch. 1er Dispositions générales
Chapitre 2 – Du pouvoir législatif	Ch. 2. Du Pouvoir Législatif
Chapitre 3 – Dispositions relatives aux Chambres	Ch. 3. Dispositions communes aux deux Chambres
Chapitre 4 – Du pouvoir exécutif	Ch. 4. Du Pouvoir Exécutif
Titre III	Titre 3: Dispositions relatives au Congrès
A. Election du président de la République	a) Election du Président de la République
B. Révision de la Constitution	b) Révision de la Constitution
C. Fonctionnement de l'Assemblée	c) Fonctionnement du Congrès
Titre IV – Dispositions diverses	Titre 4: Dispositions diverses
A. Haute Cour	a) Haute-Cour
B. Finances	b) Finances
Titre V – Dispositions relatives à la puissance mandataire et à la Société des Nations	
Titre VI – Dispositions finales et transitoires	

L for legislative power

E for executive power

J for the judiciary as separate and independent part of government

(F) in parenthesis, for federalism in countries like the US or Germany where this mode of regional distribution of power was adopted, with the parenthesis indicating that federalism is rejected or ignored in other constitutions, including those adopted in France and in Lebanon.

A for amendments. A constitution establishes a contract between the people over an undefined period of time. Amendments are eventually needed, and the text itself usually permits them under a special procedure.

R for ratification. Ratification is important when a constitution is first completed but soon fades into oblivion. Both A and R tend to be short and are of secondary importance to the other sections needed in any constitution.

C for citizen rights. This list of fundamental rights, also known as basic rights, forms the core of citizens' entitlement with respect to the state and its agencies. It also marks the parameters of the rights of citizens with regard to each other. In the original Constitution of the United States, this section is known as the Bill of Rights and was added in 1790 as an annex to the main text. But citizen rights are more commonly written at the beginning of the constitution.

I proceed now with a more precise examination of the 1926 text on the basis of the LEJ(F)ARC template, starting with C, which appears in the first section of the Lebanese text.

C The Citizen's basic rights

Within the LEJ(F)ARC model, C, on the rights of the citizen, is laid out early in the Lebanese Constitution.[3] The first chapter defines the country's territory,[4] the inalienability of any part of that territory,[5] the prohibition of a change in administrative districts other than by legislation,[6] the republican nature of the regime,[7] and Beirut as the country's capital.[8] The second chapter establishes the contours of Lebanese citizenship,[9] equality before the law,[10]

[3] Title I, Dispositions Fondamentales:

Ch.1 De l'Etat et du Territoire, Arts. 1 to 5 of the Lebanese Constitution of 1926 = DOC 1 Arts. 1 to 4 in the Chiha Constitutional Papers.

Ch.2, Des Libanais, de leurs Droits et de leurs Pouvoirs, Arts. 6 to 15 of the Lebanese Constitution of 1926= DOC 1, Arts. 5 to 14 in the Chiha Constitutional Papers.

In this chapter, the articles of the finalised Constitution of 1926 are cited by default, with articles of the Chiha drafts precede by = and cited as (DOC) number and the number of the article.

[4] Art. 1 = DOC 1, Art. 1.

[5] Art. 2 = DOC 1, Art. 2 sentence 1.

[6] Art. 3 = DOC 1, Art. 2 sentence 2.

[7] Art. 4 = DOC 1, Art.3. Chiha adds its parliamentary form, see Ch.7 section on 'the nature of the constitutional regime'.

[8] Art. 4 sentence 2 = DOC 1, Art. 4.

[9] Art. 6 = DOC 1, Art. 5. Art. 5 of the Constitution of 1926 describes the national flag, which did not appear in the first Ms. Chiha inserts if for the first time in DOC 5.

[10] Art. 7 = DOC 1, Art. 6.

freedom as a basic principle,[11] religious freedoms,[12] a free (as in private) educational system,[13] Arabic and French as official language(s),[14] merit as the sole basis for public employment,[15] freedoms of expression, press, assembly and association,[16] the inviolability of one's home,[17] the protection of property and timely compensation for its expropriation.[18]

L Legislative power, J Judiciary

Title II, Des Pouvoirs, is the same in both documents.[19] It comprises in both a first chapter entitled 'Dispositions Générales',[20] which includes a brief definition and basic attributions of all three powers – legislative, executive and judiciary. The first article explains that L, legislative power, is exercised by the two Assemblies, the Senate and the Chamber of Deputies.[21] E, executive power, belongs to the President of the Republic and his ministers.[22] Laws can be introduced by the President, the CD, or the Senate.[23] The next article concerns the judiciary, J, considered a 'power' as well, with 'indispensable guarantees' for the judges.[24] Chapter 1 closes on designating the right of the citizen to participate in elections at age 21.[25]

11 Art. 8 = DOC 1, Art. 7.
12 Art. 9 = DOC 1, Art. 8.
13 Art. 10 = DOC 1, Art. 9.
14 Art. 11 = DOC 1, Art. 10.
15 Art. 12 = DOC 1, Art. 11.
16 Art. 13 = DOC 1, Art. 12.
17 Art. 14 = DOC 1, Art. 13.
18 Art. 15 = DOC 1, Art. 14.
19 Title II, Des Pouvoirs, Arts. 16 to 72 = DOC 1 Arts. 15 to 72.
20 Title III, Des Pouvoirs, Ch.1 Dispositions Générales, Arts. 16 to 21 = DOC 1, Arts. 15 to 20.
21 Art. 16 = DOC 1, Art. 15. I use L to refer here to the Legislature comprising both chambers.
22 Art. 17 = DOC 1, Art. 16.
23 Art. 18, DOC 1, Art. 17.
24 Art. 19 = DOC 1, Art. 19. The Article numbering is the same here in both texts, because Art. 18 of the Constitution (= DOC 1, Art. 17) was added to the previous article. In the initial Chiha Ms. as well as in the Constitution of 1926, there is only one article about J, judicial power. Other dispositions about the judiciary only come with the High Court in charge of the trial of the president and the ministers, but with no constitutional court/council, an American invention which did not become current in Europe until much later, and was introduced in Lebanon as Art. 20 in the Ta'ef constitutional amendments of 1990.
25 Art. 21 (age for the voter at 21) = DOC 1 Art. 20 (age for election at 20). Note the slightly more trusting age in Chiha's text. Ensconcing the elector's age in the Constitution made it difficult to effect a change later by simple legislative enactment, in contrast with the rest of the electoral system.

Also under Title II, a longer chapter on L follows in both texts. Title II, Chapter 2, 'Legislative Power', remains in its overall structure and articles similar in both the Chiha Ms. and the text adopted in 1926. With the abolition of the Senate the following year, major amendments were made to simplify the legislative process with only one Chamber remaining.[26] A comparison between the text adopted in 1926 and the initial Chiha Ms. shows how similar in sequence the respective versions on L are. This is also true of E on the role of the president and the ministers, where the articles correspond generally, but where some changes were enacted during the drafting process.

Because it reveals a genuine discussion among the representatives who participated in the final debate, the examination of the substantial changes across the texts is more telling than those articles which remained generally untouched. It shows the tension between different options along the drafting process. Unlike the previous articles, the arrangements regulating the two Chambers were altered in significant ways when the Senate was abolished the following year.

Under L, composed initially of two legislative assemblies, no major change appears in the general composition of the Senate. Some senators were to be elected, and some appointed by the President.[27] The prerequisites to be a senator appear next,[28] followed by the suspension of Senate meetings upon the dissolution of the CD.[29]

One sharp bifurcation between the two texts appears in the next section, entitled 'b) Chambre des Députés' in the Chiha draft. It is replaced in the Constitution by a Chapter 3 entitled 'Dispositions relatives aux Chambres'. This is probably because the original text had mentioned the parameters for electing both the Chamber and the Senate. A later intervention by de Jouvenel requested their removal: the CD was to be elected according to the 1922–25 electoral law.[30] There are no further provisions on the election of the members of the CD, which the Constitution left to be decided and amended by law.

[26] Title II, Chapter 2, Du Pouvoir Législatif, Arts. 21 to 48 = DOC 1 Arts. 22 to 48.

[27] Art. 21 = DOC 1 Art.22.

[28] Art. 23 = DOC 1 Art.22. The candidate must be Lebanese and over 30 years of age. He does not need to be resident in Lebanon.

[29] Art. 25 = DOC 1 Art.25. A section of Art. 30 on the need to elect a new CD within three months was moved here from its earlier location in Art. 25 of DOC 1.

[30] See Ch.6 on de Jouvenel's annotations.

This deferral is common to world constitutions even today. The choice of the elected senators, and their number, was moved to the end of the constitutional text.[31] Instead of Chiha's more balanced section on the Senate, which was then followed by a text common to both chambers, the constitutional text adopted in May 1926 merged them in Chapter 3.[32]

Both chambers, the Chamber of Deputies and the Senate, were required to meet in Beirut;[33] individual members of parliament were considered to be representative of the whole country;[34] incompatibility in membership among different national positions was addressed[35] as were several provisions on the validation of the election;[36] the organisation of meetings;[37] and majority quorum and votes in the two L assemblies and their joint sessions.[38] A parliamentary bill which is rejected once may not be presented again in the same session.[39] Deliberations in the chambers are public.[40]

The next set of articles is also similar in many ways in the two versions. They hold that a deputy can only question a minister about conduct in office under certain conditions,[41] and that a deputy or senator may not be investigated or prosecuted for his opinions or his vote in the course of his duties.[42] The procedure about parliamentary confidence in the government is glossed over,[43] though a majority in both chambers is needed to bring down the government.[44] Each chamber sets its own internal regulations.[45] Each chamber elects its president, vice-president and secretaries.[46]

31 For details, see Ch. 6 in the section on the Senate.
32 Arts. 31 to 36 = DOC 1 Arts. 35 to 42.
33 Art.26 = DOC 1 Art. 31.
34 Art.27 = DOC 1 Art. 32.
35 Art.28 = DOC 1 Art. 33. There is a telling difference here with the final text, which allows a senator to be a minister. Chiha disallows membership in both.
36 The long article by Chiha establishing a tribunal of verification in case of dispute about the results of the elections was simplified in the text adopted, which has each Chamber organising its own verification. Art.30 = DOC 1 Art. 34.
37 Arts. 31, 32, 33 = DOC 1 Arts. 35, 36, 37.
38 Art.34 = DOC 1 Art. 38.
39 Art.38 = DOC 1 Art. 42.
40 Art.35 = DOC 1 Art. 39.
41 Art.37 = DOC 1 Art. 42.
42 Art.39 = DOC 1 Art. 43.
43 The 'question de confiance' is mentioned in passing in both texts, Art. 36 = DOC 1 Art.41.
44 General voting principle at Art.34 = DOC 1 Art.38.
45 Art.43 = DOC 1 Art.47.
46 Art.44 = DOC 1 Art.47 second sentence.

E Executive Power

A full chapter is devoted to E, executive power.[47] While the exact same number of articles appears in both texts, some articles are shuffled around. Most confirm, either verbatim or in spirit, Chiha's skills in constitution-drafting.

The similarities between the two texts include the election of the president of the republic, by a majority by the CD and Senate meeting in Congress, and the length of his term.[48] The president must swear 'an oath of fidelity to the Lebanese Nation and to the Constitution' before taking the reins of power.[49] He promulgates laws voted by the two chambers and is in charge of their application.[50] He may issue individual pardons, but amnesties require a law.[51] He negotiates treaties and ratifies them. Treaties on finance and commerce must first be approved by the two chambers, as must any treaty that impacts national life for more than 12 months.[52]

The most critical power of the president is to name and dismiss ministers at will and to oversee the council of ministers and the administration. He also designates, by default, holders of positions in the administration not provided for by law, and he presides over official occasions.[53] The president must co-sign all his 'acts' with the relevant minister.[54]

The president promulgates all laws within a month of the L chambers transferring legislation to the council of ministers, with the period reduced

[47] Title II, Du Pouvoir Exécutif, Arts. 49 to 72 = DOC 1 Arts. 50 to 72. In the CCP, DOC 19, entitled 'Du Pouvoir Exécutif' and written in Chiha's hand, consists of slightly less articles (Arts. 50 to 70) and is clearly a draft preceding DOC 1 (see argument in Ch.4).

[48] Art. 49 = DOC 1 Art.50. In the original Chiha text, the president is elected by an absolute majority, and the length of the mandate is set at five years. He can be reelected, so there is no term limitation. In the text of the 1926 Constitution, the president must be elected by 2/3 of the votes of the two chambers in the first turn, and if not by majority in a second voting turn. His term is for three years, and can be renewed one time only.

[49] Art. 50 = DOC 1 Art.53. The oath is not specified by Chiha in DOC 1 and appears in his handwriting only in Art. 57 of DOC 8. The president's oath is taken up in the Constitution in the exact terms written by Chiha.

[50] Art. 51 sentence 2 = DOC 1 Art. 54 sentence 2.

[51] Art. 51 sentence 2 = DOC 1 Art. 54 sentence 2.

[52] Art. 52. There is no mention of treaties in DOC 1. They appear in DOC 5, added in Chiha's handwriting as Art. 59.

[53] Art. 53 = DOC 1 Art.55.

[54] Art. 54 = DOC 1 Art.56.

to five days when the chambers label the law 'urgent'.[55] He can request the chambers to reconsider a law he rejects, but must promulgate it if it is returned to him by a majority vote in each chamber.[56] If both confirm the law in plenary assembly, which the president may call upon in case they disagree, he must yield and promulgate it.[57] He can adjourn the meeting of the chambers for one month, but he cannot adjourn the meeting twice in the same session.[58] Another critical presidential power is the right to dissolve the CD under some conditions.[59]

The rest of the articles in the chapter on E establish the criminal responsibility of a president for high treason or violation of the constitution, and his indictment by the CD with at least three quarters of its members, upon which a constitutionally formed 'Haute Cour de Justice' tries him.[60] If indicted, he may no longer exercise power.[61] If the presidency falls vacant for any reason, the Council of ministers takes charge and assumes all the powers of the presidency.[62]

[55] Art. 56 = DOC 1 Art.58.

[56] Art. 57 = DOC 1 Art.53.

[57] Art. 58 = DOC 1 Art.58. Chiha's text is slightly different in the sequencing. A third sentence in Art. 58 only says that the president can ask for a new deliberation. The sentence was moved to the end of Art. 57 in the adopted constitution. Art. 58 appears as Art. 65 in an insertion made by Chiha in DOC 5.

[58] Art. 59 = DOC 1 Art.59.

[59] Art. 55 = DOC 1 Art.57. In the Constitution of 1926, the substantive conditions are three, alternatively: 1) if the CD refuses to meet despite repeated requests by the president; 2) if the CD rejects the budget with the intention to paralyse the government; 3) if the CD takes decisions which might work against the Mandate or the Constitution. Chiha's original text is not encumbered by these conditions, but he includes as formal condition the agreement of the Senate, which also figures in the Constitution of 1926. A sentence reading 'par décret pris en Conseil des ministres' is struck out in DOC 1 but is reintegrated in the final text, which adds the three substantive conditions for the dissolution. In both cases, a similar language is used for the election in the two chambers within three months upon a chamber's dissolution. This appears in by DOC 1 as Art. 30. In the text of the Constitution, Art. 55 refers back to Art. 30, which is couched in similar terms, but there is a mistake in numbering because the relevant article in the final text is Art. 25. This mistake again confirms Chiha's text as the Ur-model.

[60] Art. 60 = DOC 1 Art. 60. In the first Chiha text, there was no mention of criminal responsibility. It appears for the first time, in his handwriting, in DOC 5. The Haute-Cour has a special section devoted to it under Title IV b.

[61] Art. 61 = DOC 1 Art. 61.

[62] Art. 62 = DOC 1 Art. 62. In the original text, Chiha proposes that the 'Secretary of State' take over, and in a variant in parenthesis, 'les ministres agissant collectivement'.

In the next set of articles, the Constitution moves on to the 'civil list' of the president,[63] the role and responsibility of ministers,[64] and their right to attend parliamentary sessions.[65] It gives relatively extensive coverage to their questioning by the L members and their trial for high treason or abuse of power. Since the president cannot be removed by L other than in exceptional circumstances, the question of the political responsibility of the minister arose for the drafters, including Chiha, as one which is specific to a minister as opposed to the Council as a whole. As we saw in the question of confidence above,[66] the constitutional drafter skirted the issue, and the focus on the individual responsibility of the minister was privileged in the text.[67]

Of the articles just described, two initially drafted by Chiha do not appear anywhere in the Constitution.

In Art. 64 of DOC 1, Chiha proposes that government membership never exceed seven ministers. In Art. 66, he limits the members of the legislative chambers allowed to become ministers to two only. Neither provision was preserved. The omission of these constitutional safeguards is unfortunate, especially the innovative in Chiha's proposal in Art. 64 to limit the size of the cabinet to seven members. Attention to a more cohesive cabinet with a maximum of seven ministers is a healthy note of caution to prevent bureaucratic proliferation in Leviathan.

In the second case about preventing membership in the cabinet and in the CD in Chiha's proposed Art. 66, the embryo of separation between E and L, with a maximum of two L members being permitted in E, fell by the wayside, never to be revived. The right of a deputy to be also minister has undermined

[63] The president's salary and expenses are limited by Art. 63 of the final text, which prevents both being changed in any way during the president's term. This provision is absent from DOC 1. Chiha introduces it by hand as Art. 70 later, in DOC 5. His original wording is the rather English 'liste civile', which is replaced in the final text adopted by the more French 'dotation.'

[64] Arts. 64 and 66 = DOC 1 Arts. 63 and 66.

[65] Art. 67 = DOC 1 Art. 67. They may also delegate attendance to a civil servant in their ministry.

[66] At n.43 and accompanying text.

[67] These dispositions on the individual minister's responsibility can be found in the Constitution in Arts. 68, 69, 70, 71 and 72, with Art. 68 also referring back to Art. 37, on the right for any deputy to formally accuse any minister. They are adopted almost verbatim from Chiha's Arts. 68, 69, 70, 71, 72, with a minor exception in Art. 71, where Chiha adds to the indictment by the CD of the minister before the Haute Cour de Justice by the CD: '[L]a Chambre charge un de ses membres de soutenir l'accusation devant ladite Cour'. Chiha's text is also more elegant in that he does not refer the reader to a previous article.

the principle of the separation of powers and damaged the stability of the cabinet ever since.

A, R, 'final and transitory dispositions'

In Chiha's outline, Title III is entitled 'Dispositions Diverses'. He had clearly in mind matters which do not belong under the first two titles, but this idea did not quite work out as planned. In the first place, the subsections under Title III are not called chapters, as in the previous titles, creating some dissonance in the outline. Title III itself was entitled 'Dispositions relatives au Congrès', and the subsections, inserted in smaller print after the articles, were marked 'a) Election du Président de la République'; b) Révision de la constitution; and c) fonctionnement du Congrès'.[68]

The text of the Constitution adopted Chiha's subdivisions. Through the drafting process, no one seems to have paid attention to the lack of symmetry between successive Titles. With other small editorial mistakes,[69] it is probable that there was never a dedicated secretarial bureau to streamline the successive versions and ensure that the final constitutional text was free of embarrassing errors.[70]

Amendments, presidential elections, and reunion of the two chambers in Congress

Amendments of the Constitution are included in Title III b, which is preceded by an important 'section a' organising the election of the president in Title III. It includes three articles which underline the importance Chiha gave to the top

[68] Looking more closely at the first manuscript, one can notice that /Ch/ was crossed, so Chiha tried perhaps first to use /chapter/ instead of a b c. Maybe he thought that the sections were too short to be called chapters. The imbalance remains to date, with Title III bizarrely left unnamed.

[69] Like the reference to the wrong number of Article 30, above n.59.

[70] The absence of a Lebanese (or French) secretarial bureau for the duration of the drafting process also explains why the CCP in the Chiha archive is not yet held in national archives. The absence of a central site preserving the most important documents in the institutional history of the country makes dating particularly difficult. During the final deliberations, a good (but not comprehensive) minuting takes place under Simon Shukri, 'the head of the Secretariat of the Council of Deputies, *ra'is sikritariyat al-majlis al-niyabi*', Ahmad al-Zein ed., *Mahader Munaqashat al-Dustur al-Lubnani wa Ta'dilatuh 1926–90* (Minutes of the discussions about the Lebanese Constitution and its amendments), Beirut: Publications of the Chamber of Deputies 1993, 15, 22. I found no trace of Simon Shukri with reference to the Constitution elsewhere.

constitutional position in the country. These articles were reproduced almost verbatim in the text adopted in May.

Art. 73 requires the two chambers to meet at least once a month before the end of the presidential term and no less than ten days before the end of the term. Art. 74 concerns a vacancy in the presidency following death, resignation, or judicial condemnation of a president before the end of his term. In that case the Chambers are to meet immediately to elect a successor.

Chiha anticipated an additional scenario, where the CD had been dissolved when the presidency falls vacant. In that case, Art. 74 requires 'the electoral colleges' to proceed 'without delay' with the election of the deputies.[71] Once this is completed, the two chambers meet immediately to elect a new president.

Art. 75 reinforces the mechanism to prevent any vacancy in the presidency. It requires the two chambers meeting in Congress 'to do nothing else' but elect a president.

The similarity in numbers and content between the articles in the first Chiha manuscript and the text adopted in May 1926 is uncanny. The three articles were adopted almost verbatim in the Constitution in May 1926 and have remained unchanged to date, with the exact same numbering as in the first Chiha manuscript.[72] These articles sit uneasily in this Title III and would have naturally complemented Art. 49 on the election of the president at the beginning of E. Still, their length and separate presence in the text give an aura of gravity to the election of the president. This arrangement is the more remarkable considering the massive hurdles over a full century to holding free and regular presidential elections.

[71] Art. 74 of the present text continues to mention 'electoral colleges' which no longer exist.

[72] There were two small changes in these texts. One change to Art. 74 was introduced by Chiha in DOC 5 where he removed /jugement/ and wrote the more comprehensive /pour toute autre cause./ The second was introduced in the early evening of 21 May 1926 by Yusuf al-Khazen and Chebl Dammous, who realised that the timing of the meeting was not precise enough. Dammous suggested adding /and two months at most/ to the first clause of Art. 73. The suggestion was adopted by the majority of the CR. Zein ed., *Mahader Munaqashat al-Dustur al-Lubnani wa Ta'dilatuh 1926–90*, above n.70, 63.

A Amendments

Articles 76 and 77, which form Title III b, organise amendments to the Constitution.[73] In the Constitution adopted in 1926, the first article allows both the president and the two chambers to request an amendment. The articles to be amended must be identified and the language of the amendments precise. Adopting the amendment is conditioned first on a two-thirds majority vote in both chambers. Art. 77 requires then that the two chambers meet in Congress to deliberate and pass the amendment with a 31-vote majority out of a total of 46 members.

Chiha's original text differs in two ways from the text adopted in May. In Art. 76, Chiha allowed the chambers to move forward on the amendment by a majority of the vote, conditioned however on the presence of three quarters of deputies for the quorum. He did not include the second Article mentioning a majority of 31 votes in Congress,[74] which renders any amendment extremely difficult to carry out and awkwardly inserts a number which was bound to change over time with the increase of the population.

This section b of Title III, entitled 'Révision de la Constitution', was subjected to various changes after the first Chiha Ms. In the text submitted to the CR final deliberations, Art. 76 demanded 'an absolute majority' of votes in the Chambers rather than two-thirds. The change to the majority of two-thirds was introduced during the plenary session of the CR. Chebl Dammous supported Jamil Talhuq's reservation on allowing a constitutional amendment to be decided by a simple majority of deputies and senators:

> The Constitution cannot be like a feather in the wind. The Constitution is foundational. It is not right for it to be subject to an overhaul from time to time. In other countries, amendments have required a two-thirds decision to be solid. I support Talhuq.[75]

[73] Corresponding to DOC 1 Arts. 76 and 77.

[74] 'Pour être valables, les délibérations doivent avoir été prises à la majorité de 31 voix'. This addition was proposed by Dammous and adopted unanimously. Zein ed., *Mahader Munaqashat al-Dustur al-Lubnani wa Ta'dilatuh 1926–90*, above n.70, 64. The amendment became irrelevant when the Senate was abolished in 1927.

[75] Zein ed., *Mahader Munaqashat al-Dustur al-Lubnani wa Ta'dilatuh 1926–90*, above n.70, 64.

The amendment proposed by Talhuq and Dammous was adopted unanimously.[76]

The last two articles of Title III (Title III section c) concern the work of the chambers when they meet in Congress. Art. 78 puts the leader of the Senate in charge. Art. 79 requires an absolute majority of the members of each Chamber as quorum for the Congress, and for the decisions to be taken by an absolute majority of votes.[77] This section disappeared in the first series of amendments in 1927 which abolished the Senate and jettisoned the idea of a Congress altogether.

Titles IV and V- Miscellania

Title IV is entitled 'Disposition diverses' in the initial manuscript and in the text adopted in May 1926. The first section of Title IV consists of one article only, establishing the High Court in charge of putting presidents and ministers on trial.[78] The second section is about 'finances'. As we saw, Chiha's first Ms. stopped at Art. 85, in the middle of the section on finances, and part of Art. 86 is torn out. The full text of the missing articles emerges only in DOC 5, in addition to three new articles on the budget.[79] From then on, all versions include 96 articles, which form the domestic side of the Constitution. The French rulers just needed to insert a Title V on the Mandate without disturbing the Lebanese draft.[80]

[76] Id. Jamil Talhuq was a physician and the representative for the Druze seat in Mount Lebanon.

[77] The text of Chiha put the quorum for Congress at 'three quarters minimum (les trois quarts au moins)', but he then struck the clause out and replaced it by 'majorité absolue'. (Art 77 DOC 1)

[78] Art. 80 = DOC 1 Art. 80. Constitutional violations by the president or a minister are mentioned at Arts. 60, 61 and Art. 71, respectively, in both the Constitution and DOC 1.

[79] As will be developed in the discussion on the Budget, the comments in DOC 3 written by Chiha at the beginning of the section on Finances mention 'Concessions, Emprunt (V Constit. Egypt)' [i.e. 'Voir la Constitution de l'Egypte'], and another comment at the end reads 'Concessions, impôts, traités'. The three articles in Chiha's hand in DOC 5 address, respectively, the 'impôt', 'emprunt' and 'concession'.

[80] In the next chapter I discuss briefly these five articles of Title V, which are found in none of the eight CCP versions (DOCs 1 to 8).

'Title VI- Final and transitory dispositions': R, Article 95, the Mandate

Title V defined the role of the Mandatory power, and was drafted by the French High Commission. Another important title was also added – Title VI, a hodgepodge of 'final and transitory measures' which condensed in the last part of the Constitution important sections that had previously been scattered throughout the draft versions.

The most delicate issue, namely the principle of communitarianism as the backbone of the system, can be found here. Art. 95 became notorious for its encapsulation of the communitarian system, although in subtle and ambiguous terms. This measure was dubbed 'transitory ... with the aim of bringing justice and harmony',[81] but it was reinforced by the express communitarian composition of the Senate.[82] The first Senate's 16 members were to be directly appointed by the High Commissioner for its first term, which would run until the end of 1928.[83]

Other 'transitional' arrangements change the name of Council of Representatives to Chamber of Deputies by the end of its current mandate,[84] and the name of the country from 'Great Lebanon' to 'Lebanese Republic'.[85] The first president of the Republic was to be elected by the two chambers within a month of the appointment of the Senators.[86]

What about R, for ratification, another key piece for any constitution in our LEJ(F)ARC template? Ratification was simply missed, creating a

[81] Title VI, Art. 95: 'A titre transitoire et conformément aux dispositions de l'article 1er de la Charte du Mandat et dans une intention de justice et de concorde, les communautés seront équitablement représentées dans les emplois publics et dans la composition du ministère sans que cela puisse cependant nuire au bien de l'Etat'. Extensive discussion on substance is carried out of this key article in next chapter.

[82] Art. 94. Art. 99 organises the election by the Senate of its president and bureau.

[83] Art. 98. It should be recalled that out of the 16 members of the Senate, nine members were to be elected in two terms, and seven were to be appointed by the High Commissioner (Art. 22) The first term of the Senators was never completed, since the Senate was abolished in a constitutional amendment a year later.

[84] Art. 97.

[85] Art. 101.

[86] Art. 100.

conundrum that scholars only noted much later.[87] Normally a constitution comes into effect when published in the official gazette, which would be done immediately considering the importance of the text. Yet the Arabic text appeared in the *Official Journal* only on 25 June 1926, and the French text on 12 October.[88]

So there were no explicit dispositions on a ratification process, or on the date for the Constitution to take effect. The one clue which appears in the very last sentence of the final article, Art. 102, states that 'all legislative dispositions contrary to the present Constitution are abrogated'.[89] Without a precise date, and with the use of the present tense of the verb 'to be', the formulation would logically mean that the Constitution abrogates all contrary legislation 'henceforth'. But the precise date would still be missing. 'Henceforth' could mean that the new Constitution kicks in with the final vote of the CR, when the meeting officially ended at 1.30 am on Sunday 23 May. Or it could mean its proclamation that same day by Henry de Jouvenel. Since the French Mandate was under the aegis of the League of Nations, one could also conceive of the Constitution being enacted upon formal confirmation by the League, or upon the end of the Mandate.

None of this was spelled out in the adopted text, but it did not matter. The Constitution was immediately applied by the High Commissioner, who appointed the 16 communally distributed senators (Art. 96) on 24 May, one day after it was approved by the CR.[90] The Congress, composed by the CD and the Senate, elected the first president, Charles Debbas, on 26 May.[91]

[87] Rabbath correctly notes the oddity and discusses it at some length in *La Formation Historique du Liban Constitutionnel*, above n.2, 396–7.

[88] See discussion and references in previous Chapter, n.126 and accompanying text.

[89] Art, 102, second sentence: 'Toutes les dispositions législatives contraires à la présente Constitution sont abrogées.'

[90] Following the transitory disposition of Art. 98 of the Constitution, Rabbath, *La Formation Historique du Liban Constitutionnel*, above n.2, 400, mentions the appointment of the senators by de Jouvenel on 24 May. Hokayem gives 25 May as the date of their appointment, *La Genèse de la Constitution Libanaise de 1926*, above n., 276. According to Muhammad Murad, *Al-Intikhabat al-Niyabiyya fi Lubnan 1920–2009* (Parliamentary elections in Lebanon 1920–2009), above n.8, de Jouvenel issued Arrêté 305 bis on 24 May appointing the Senators. Their names and communities are presented in Id., 96–8.

[91] Charles Debbas (1885–1935), a lawyer by profession, and a Greek Orthodox Christian (the second largest Christin community in Lebanon), was elected on 26 May 1926, with 45 votes of the Congress (out of 46). He was reelected in 1929 by 44 deputies (the Senate and the Congress had been merged into the CD). The first government was formed on 29 May, with seven

De Jouvenel left Lebanon on 27 May, never to return. Debbas formed his first government on 29 May.

Outside influence: Lebanese (Menassa, Trad ...), French (de Jouvenel, Souchier, Duguit ...)

There remain two intriguing sets of questions about the composition of the constitutional text. Anyone with some experience in constitutional drafting knows the importance of a few common characteristics in the design of a constitution.

The first is the model of inspiration which informs the various sections covered by the two-century-old LEJ(F)ARC template. It is inconceivable that a text emerges without resting on some previously written charter or textual model, oftentimes with some texts composed *a contrario* – as, for example, when comparing the US Constitution of 1787 with the much looser union under the Articles of Confederation of 1777. Until decolonization in the 1960s, the template was sometimes provided by the constitution of the colonising state, such as France with its African colonies, or, in case of foreign occupation, by the US-inspired German Constitution after the Second World War. The cases of Germany and Japan underline the variety of applications despite the model of the occupying state, for instance the strong federalist structure of Germany as opposed to the continued centralization of Japan. Inspiration is therefore often composite, and this is also the case of the Lebanese Constitution.[92]

Another factor is timing. A constitutional scholar can write up the most alluring charter, but his work will always be subject to long- and short-term constraints. Long-term, the Constitution of Lebanon could not jettison the deep communitarian imprint characteristic of the country and the region. Short-term, it was conceived in a period of the nascent country's history that had to accommodate various idiosyncrasies mostly related to Lebanese

ministers under the presidency of Auguste Basha Adib. Rabbath, *La Formation Historique du Liban Constitutionnel*, above n.2, 400.

92 There is understandably a vast literature on the topic, see for instance Michel Rosenfeld and Andras Sajo eds, *Oxford Handbook of Comparative Constitutional Law*, Oxford: Oxford University Press, 2012; Tom Ginsburg and Rosalind Dixon eds, *Comparative Constitutional Law*, Cheltenham: Edward Elgar 2011.

factionalism and French domination. I discuss in the next chapter the communitarian straitjacket of time immemorial in the Orient, as well as some of the Constitution's Lebanese quirks and French interventions in the form of suggestions, advice, or diktat. Communalism was the proverbial elephant in the constitutional room, hovering over the delegates and only occasionally mentioned, usually with a sigh. In the rest of this chapter, the shorter-term context is discussed, including the comparative constitutional set-up at the time, an intriguing letter in the Chiha archive, other Lebanese jurists' input, French expertise generally, and the fleeting shadow of a major constitutional scholar of the Third Republic, Léon Duguit.

Menassa, Trad, and other Lebanese figures

Where did Chiha draw the framework for his text from?

The Lebanese Constitution is often said to relate to the Third Republic as the 'natural' model for drafters steeped in French law and subject to direct French control.[93] This perception needs to be adjusted.

In Chiha's CP, we find various constitutions, including the Egyptian Constitution of 1923, as well as the Lithuanian, Latvian (French Lettonie), Finnish and Romanian Constitutions, all enacted in the early 1920s. (DOC 16) The structure of the Lebanese Constitution does not follow any one of them specifically. Nor could it follow the French Republic's constitutional structure, since the French Constitution at the time was an assemblage of three successive basic laws which were brief and disjointed.[94] The case of the Belgian Constitution of 1831 is more compelling. An edition of the text was available in 1923 in a book edited by Jean Servais and E. Mechelynk.[95] The outline of the

[93] See in particular Rabbath, *La Constitution Libanaise: Origines, Textes et Commentaires*, above n.2, 49–58, 'Les modèles d'inspiration', discussing the 'debt' of the Lebanese Constitution to the models of the French Third Republic, the Belgian Constitution of 1831 and the Egyptian Constitution of 1923.

[94] Despite the disjointed construction of the 'Constitution of 1875' in these three laws, the Third Republic endured 75 years. Treatises on an already long constitutional life of the Third Republic were many. In addition to Duguit, whose learned treatise was extensive, probably the most famous French expert on constitutional law at the time was Adhémar Esmein (d.1913), whose second volume of *Eléments de Droit Constitutionnel Français et Comparé*, Paris: Sirey 7th ed. 1921 was a major reference on the Third Republic in Chiha's time. See Esmein's introductory chapter in vol. 2, 3–33, on the three laws making the Constitution of 1875.

[95] Jean Servais and E. [Edouard] Mechelynk eds, *Code Civil Précédé de la Constitution Belge*, Bruxelles: Bruylant 1923.

Belgian Constitution bears an uncanny resemblance to Chiha's drafts. This is also true of some common language, for instance Article 11 of the Belgian Constitution on the sanctity of private property and its equivalent in Chiha's first draft (DOC 1) and in the 1926 Constitution.[96]

In the sources used by Chiha, one unexpected discovery in his papers is a letter by a young man, Gabriel Menassa, to which is appended a constitutional model. Like the Belgian Constitution, Menassa's constitutional model inspired the structure of the Lebanese Constitution as reflected in the divisions discussed above as LEJ(F)ARC.

In the previous chapter, I mentioned Menassa's letter dated 28 December 1925, in passing, to better approximate the chronology of the constitutional timeline.[97] Gabriel Menassa was a recent graduate from the then Ecole Libre de Sciences Politiques (now known as L'Institut d'études politiques de Paris, SciencesPo), who went on to become a lawyer and a macro-economist.[98] From his early career, he left us an entire book on *Les Mandats A et leur Application en Orient: Il Faut Convoquer les Assemblées Constituantes*.[99] As its title indicates, the book is mostly concerned with the French mandate over Lebanon and Syria. The main argument of the book calls for the establishment of a Constituent Assembly to draft it. It has little bearing on the substance of the constitution that emerged.

Menassa's appendix, however, was based on another part of his research for a 'Diplôme' at Sciences Po. In his cover letter to Chiha, he explains that this 'Avant Projet de la Constitution Libanaise', which he attaches to the letter,

[96] On expropriation, Article 11 of the Belgian Constitution states: 'Nul ne peut être privé de sa propriété que pour cause d'utilité publique, dans les cas et de la manière établie par la loi, et moyennant une juste et préalable indemnité'. Chiha's first draft is exacly the same, minus the redundant 'et de la manière': Article 14:'Nul ne peut être privé de sa propriété que pour cause d'utilité publique, dans les cas établis par la loi, et moyennant une juste et préalable indemnité'. The Constitution of 1926 keeps Chiha's formulation, which has remained untouched since: 'Article 15. Nul ne peut être privé de sa propriété que pour cause d'utilité publique dans les cas établis par la loi et moyennant une juste et préalable indemnité.

[97] Menassa's ketter and appendix form DOC 22 in the CCP.

[98] See Gabriel Menassa and Joseph Naggear, *Plan de Reconstruction de l'Economie Libanaise et de Réforme de l'Etat*, Beirut: Editions de la Société libanaise d'économie politique 1948, a large book. On Menassa, including his later closeness to Chiha, see Nadim Shehadi, 'The Idea of Lebanon: Economy and state in the Cénacle Libanais 1946–54,' Papers on Lebanon 5, Oxford: Centre for Lebanese Studies 1987, 20–2.

[99] Paris: Jouve 1924.

'represents the first part of [his] thesis for the Diploma of the Ecole Libre des Sciences Politiques, a thesis which [he] defended on 16 June, and which [I] have unfortunately not published yet'. (DOC 22) The thesis in question was probably the Mémoire 'defended on 16 June' 1925 which survived, at least in part, in a six-page manuscript found at Sciences Po.[100]

The letter would have been received by Chiha in Beirut a few days later, just as the first discussions about the Constitution were starting with the CR.[101] Menassa writes to 'Monsieur le Député' that 'he hopes that [Chiha] will take into account some of the views that [Menassa] exposes in this humble work'.[102] The 'Annex' to the letter is entitled 'Avant Projet de la Constitution Libanaise', and consists of 110 Articles signed 'Gabriel Menassa, Licencié en Droit de l'Université de Paris. Diplômé de l'Ecole des Sciences Politiques'.[103]

A comparison of the structure and the articles in the Menassa Annex shows that Chiha adopted Menassa's outline,[104] which was also the general structure of the Belgian Constitution, no doubt an easily accessible model which Menassa also resorted to. Chiha picked and chose amongst the

[100] The thorough research to assist me in the archives of Sciences Po by Anne Brigot-Laperrousaz added a rich 'Menassa archive' to the genesis of the Lebanese Constitution. It shows that the 'thesis' he mentions in his cover letter to Chiha was not a doctoral thesis, but more likely a simple 'Mémoire' (which earned him the title of 'Diplômé'). This thesis consists of six handwritten pages used for the Annex he sent to Chiha.

[101] The Messageries Maritimes was the travel company in charge of the post, and secured a regular line from Marseille to Beirut, via Alexandria. It took five days for Henry de Jouvenel to reach Beirut when he was appointed: 'Le 27 Novembre, il quitte Marseille à bord du Sphinx, fait escale à Alexandrie, puis accoste à Beyrouth le 2 décembre'. Hugues Moreau, *Henry de Jouvenel-Répertoire Numérique*, Département de la Corrèze, Archives départementales, Tulle 2010, 7.

[102] 'J'espère que vous voudrez bien prendre en considération certaines des vues que j'expose dans cet humble travail.' (DOC 22).

[103] Menassa might have known Chiha personally. He certainly knew of Chiha as a key person in the drafting process, considering that the entrusting of the constitution to the CR was official since 10 December. They met and worked together thereafter, and their relationship developed over the years, attested in a document of 1943 establishing the 'Conseil de la Société Libanaise d'Economie Politique', which includes the names of both Michel Chiha, described as 'Licencié en droit; Directeur de Banque; Administrateur de Société; Ancien député,' and Gabriel Menassa, described as 'Avocat à la Cour; Ancien Sous-Secrétaire d'Etat aux Affaires Economiques; Diplômé de l'Ecole Libre des Sciences Politiques; Titulaire des Diplômes Supérieurs d'Economie Politique et de Droit Privé'. Document in the Chiha Archive dated 6 April 1943. See also below n.108, Menassa's letter to Chiha of 26 April 1926.

[104] The Table at the head of the chapter shows how the final outline of the Constitution of 1926 is an almost exact calque of to the first version of Chiha (DOC 1). In turn, the two texts adopted the almost exact outline of the Belgian Constitution.

formulation of various articles and improved on them as he saw appropriate. In Menassa's annexed constitutional draft, there is one comment in Chiha's hand, and, more tellingly, black, red and blue marks against each article. This suggests that Chiha read the text at least twice, crossing out long sections which he considered inapplicable, or unnecessary, and integrated others in his draft.[105] With this unexpected trove, we have an additional layer of information to add to the Travaux Préparatoires of the Lebanese Constitution.

The way in which Chiha followed up on Menassa's letter is typical of his treatment of other communications he received regarding the constitution: he reads the text sent to him, marks passages to be incorporated in some way in his evolving draft, and puts small 'x's or writes a few words, including 'non' in the margins of the articles. This is true of the partial drafts (DOCs 20 and 21), and of the two documents I call tentatively 'the Chiha-Trad drafts' (DOCs 23, 24).[106] In addition, Chiha received in late March a full printed text of a draft Constitution from Ayyub Tabet, which had been completed the previous summer at the request of former High Commissioner Maurice Sarrail.[107] In the case of Tabet, unlike the Menassa letter in late December, the study arrived too late to have any impact on a draft Constitution which was well advanced in April. This is also the case of another letter by Menassa in the

[105] Some of the articles marked are included, sometimes verbatim, in his formulation of the corresponding articles in his manuscript. This is mostly the case in Chapter 1, 'De l'Etat et du Territoire', and Chapter 3, 'Des Libanais et de leurs droits', next to which Chiha inserts 'et devoirs'. The two titles appear also verbatim in the initial manuscript and remain to date in the Constitution, together with the overall outline followed by Menassa. Later chapters in Chiha's first draft and the corresponding articles in the Constitution are not as close to Menassa's Annex, but the structure and content are similar generally. I am grateful for the private communication of Ms Brigot-Laperrousaz, above n.100, for the details and various documents she found in the Sciences Po archives, and her rich comments on the material. Comparing the articles in Menassa's Annex reveals many similarities with the initial Chiha Ms.

[106] See previous chapter for timeline and details.

[107] DOC 26, which is a printed booklet by Dr. Ayyub Tabet, '*Mashru' al-Nazam al-Asasi li-Dawlat Lubnan* (Draft of a basic law for the State of Lebanon)', Beirut: al-Sabah 1926, consists of 74 articles. A French version was published in *L'Orient* in four instalments from 30 March to 2 April 1926 (see previous Ch.4 n.100). The Arabic booklet includes on its front page the mention that the text is 'a response to the request of HE the former HC General Sarrail in a letter dated 29 August 1925', and a handwritten dedication to Michel Chiha dated 25 March 1926. There is little if any influence from this text on the Chiha drafts, which he received too late. On Tabet, a forgotten figure from the Mandate period and briefly president in 1943, see Shereen Khairallah, *Dr Ayyub Tabet (1875–1947)*, Beirut: Dergham 2014.

Chiha Archive, dated 26 April 1926.[108] By then a complete Avant-Projet was being discussed in the French Cabinet.[109]

Souchier and French expertise

French context and influence can hardly be gainsaid in the emergence of the Lebanese Constitution. It was a part of colonial baggage which has its roots in the nineteenth century during the slow dismemberment of the Ottoman Empire. 'Representative' councils can be traced to those which Napoleon established in Egypt, themselves vague predecessors of Muhammad Ali's 1829 Egyptian Council and the councils created in the Levant during the decade of Egyptian occupation.[110]

A new colonial format in the shape of a 'Mandate' was established by the League of Nations. At least in theory, the Mandate would differ from a colony by 'educating' local populations yearning for full independence. The League required France and England to write 'Statuts Organiques' for countries that would later be admitted to the League as full members. We have several proto-constitutional texts in 1924–5, resulting in particular from the Commission Paul-Boncour which was tasked by Aristide Briand, then Minister of Foreign Affairs, to elaborate the 'Statut Organique' formally required from the 'Mandate A' colonisers.[111] None of these texts directly

[108] Two-page typed letter from Gabriel Menassa to Michel Chiha, 26 April 1926 (Chiha Archive). The letter is focused on several budgetary amendments, which Menassa proposes with the support of US constitutional references. They did not affect the Constitutional draft.

[109] The 25 December 1925 Avant-Projet of Menassa (DOC 22) and the April 1926 text of Tabet (DOC 26) are not mentioned in the plenary debates of the Council of Representatives in May.

[110] Discussed in Chapter 2.

[111] On the Joseph Paul-Boncour Commission, Fabienne Quilleré-Majzoub and Tarek Majzoub, 'Recherche les véritables auteurs de la Constitution libanaise de 1926 désespérément …', *Revue française de droit constitutionnel*, 131, 2022, 645–7, 651–2; Rabbath, *La Constitution Libanaise: Origines, Textes et Commentaires*, above n.2, 13–15, and, extensively, Hokayem, *La Genèse de la Constitution Libanaise de 1926*, above n.2, 123–63. Joseph Paul-Boncour, who died age 99 in 1972, was at the time a deputy in the French parliament. The main contribution of his Commission, which met only three times according to Rabbath, is the determined request of its president to carry out the proper consultation of the local population before the Statut Organique is drafted. Hokayem, *La Genèse de la Constitution Libanaise de 1926*, at 129, 150. The idea had been made current in the Levant by the so-called King-Crane Commission, which was sent by the US government to the region in 1919 to advance Woodrow Wilson's support for self-determination in the colonies. The King-Crane Commission's report is dated 28 August 1919 and is based on the consultation of the local populations in Palestine, Lebanon and Syria. Report available for instance on https://history.state.gov/historicaldocuments/frus1919Parisv12/d380;

affected the Constitution, although they encouraged some enlightened French administrators to facilitate the Mandate countries' path to independence.

In 1925, Henry de Jouvenel added his unique touch to Lebanese history. He separated Lebanon's constitutional process from those of the other 'states' which had also come under French control in the larger Syria. And he entrusted it to the Lebanese 'to own' their constitution, in modern parlance. With the withdrawal of French penmanship, the Constitution was distinctly Lebanese in Chiha's hand and in its CR's escort to completion in the five months of constitutional iteration from January to May 1926.

Thanks to the CCP, France's role during the constitutional process is now much clearer. French influence took three forms.

One was the HC clearly reserving for France the writing of the clauses relative to the Mandate, which form the bulk of Title V of the Constitution.[112] Title V, together with any reference to France or the Mandate, was abolished upon independence in 1943.[113] This Title consists of five articles which mention the tutelage of France as 'puissance mandataire' under the aegis of the League of Nations in accordance with Art. 22 of the 'Pacte de la Société des Nations et de l'Acte du Mandat'.[114] It gives France the last word on Lebanon's

original text and collection of extant petitions in http://dcollections.oberlin.edu/digital/collection/kingcrane/. The report was officially released only on 2 December 1922.

112 'Titre V, Dispositions relatives à la puissance mandataire et à la Société des Nations', Arts. 90–94.

113 This facilitated their 'bulk' deletion in the constitutional law of 9 November 1943, excepting Art. 93 on the clause required for agreement between Lebanon and neighbouring countries giving France the power to arbitrate any conflict. The article was abolished only in 1947 after all remaining French troops left the country. Because the French Mandate section was appended to the Chiha draft, there was no need for renumbering the first 89 articles (out of a total 102 Articles) that precede Title V.

114 Art. 90. Art. 22 of the Covenant of the League of Nations, part of the Treaty of Versailles signed on 28 June 1919, reads in relevant part: 'Certain communities formerly belonging to the Turkish Empire have reached a stage of development where their existence as independent nations can be provisionally recognized subject to the rendering of administrative advice and assistance by a Mandatory until such time as they are able to stand alone. The wishes of these communities must be a principal consideration in the selection of the Mandatory. (...) In every case of mandate, the Mandatory shall render to the Council an annual report in reference to the territory committed to its charge'. Original text available on https://libraryresources.unog.ch/ld.php?content_id=32971179. The 'Acte du Mandat' refers to the charter of the 'Mandat de la SDN pour la Syrie et le Liban', which was approved by the League of Nations' Council on 24 July 1922 and made effective on 29 September 1923. The section most relevant to the future Lebanese Constitution is Article 1: 'Le Mandataire élaborera dans un délai de trois ans à dater de l'entrée en application du présent mandat un statut organique pour la Syrie et le Liban'. This meant that the latest date for

eventual membership of the League as a fully independent state.[115] This is followed by an article which allows France to intervene in the event of any tension between Lebanon and its neighbours.[116] In an unusual last article, it projects some Lebanese diplomatic representation in Paris and other cities abroad with a large Lebanese diaspora.[117] The arrangement signals both the attention of the French authorities to the significant Lebanese diaspora and the domestic Lebanese pressure to bring the diaspora into the national fold.

A second expression of French influence lies in the in-margin comments made to some of the texts, of which De Jouvenel's, although few, are the most interesting.[118] There is, too, the correspondence between the French authorities in Beirut and Paris. The most telling is the acceptance by Aristide Briand of Henry de Jouvenel's argument that the Lebanese part of the Constitution was adequate and should not be altered, and that the Mandate clauses added to the successive Chiha versions corresponded to Briand's vision of the role of France during the Mandate.[119] Souchier's declaration on 23 May 1926 confirms in stark terms this paramount role of France in matters dear to French decision-making.[120]

Of special value, because it is the most extensive and technical, is a typed document of six pages entitled 'Observations sur le projet de Constitution' (DOC 9). Together with the handwritten comments on the developing CCP versions (DOC 1 to 8), I discuss what I call the 'Souchier Observations' in the next chapter as part of the substantive analysis of the building blocks of the Constitution through the iterations of Chiha's first draft.

a Statut Organique/Constitution, which de Jouvenel succeeded in honouring, was 29 September 1926.

115 Art. 91 of the Lebanese Constitution.

116 Art. 93.

117 Art. 94. It is unfortunate that 'the diaspora' mentioned in this article was jettisoned together with the full Title V, therefore depriving it of constitutional recognition. Throughout the private and public discussions during the constitutional process, the local Lebanese were set on giving an active role to the diaspora in the Constitution (see Ch. 4), but their efforts were thwarted, inadvertently, when Art.94 was abrogated. It was only in 2006, following an initiative within the Cedar Revolution, that the electoral law included the vote of Lebanese abroad in parliamentary elections. But the diaspora remains unrecognised constitutionally.

118 They are discussed extensively in next chapter.

119 See for copious excerpts of the correspondence between Briand and de Jouvenel, Hokayem, *La Genèse de la Constitution Libanaise de 1926*, above n.2, 262–8.

120 On Souchier's address, see previous chapter, n.123.

Is it Souchier who authored these 'Observations'? And what version of the *Projet* do they concern?

It is useful first to briefly present the man whose name appears recurrently in the constitutional march, and who is the probable author of that unsigned document.

Paul Souchier (1887–1938) was a magistrate given leave of absence from the French Conseil d'Etat after de Jouvenel requested he join him in Beirut to give expert advice and guidance to the CSO in Beirut. He arrived in Lebanon on 19 January 1926 and was the main French legal advisor on the Constitution throughout the period of its drafting.[121] All sources confirm his active participation throughout.[122] Chiha and Nammour are reported to have met regularly with Souchier, whose name appears regularly in the Arabic and French press.

Several examples have been cited before.[123] A further example appears in *al-Ahrar* of 22 March on 'what is in the Constitution':

> We learnt that the rapporteur of the Committee [probably the CSO], Mr Michel Chiha, has met several times, together with the president [of the CR, Musa Nammour], with Mr Souchier, who is in charge for the [High] Commission in organising [*tanzim*] the Constitution. It is said that the discussion turned on the introductory formulation for the relationships between the Mandate and the local government. This formulation will take the form of a letter which the High Commissioner will address to the Council after it completes the Constitution. The Council would then accept it and put it in the Preface.[124]

[121] *L'Orient*, 'Paul Souchier', 20 January 1926, 2. In a telegram from de Jouvenel to the Department of Foreign Affairs in Paris, dated 12 April 1926, DD3, 855, the HC requests the prorogation of Souchier's mission until 1 June.

[122] Before the discovery of the CCP, much importance was given to Souchier, in large part on the basis of the memoirs of a lawyer called Jean-Louis Aujol (d.2002). See Souchier's role in Rabbath, *La Constitution Libanaise: Origines, Textes et Commentaires*, above n.2, 42–3, and Hokayem, *La Genèse de la Constitution Libanaise de 1926*, above n.2, 243–8. Aujol was the personal secretary of de Jouvenel. In *Un Avocat dans le Siècle, de Poincaré à Mitterrand*, Paris: Gazette du Palais 1988 (Kindle), 37–8, he ascribes the leading role in drafting the Constitution to Paul Souchier, but the two pages recollecting events a half century later are filled with mistakes. For instance, work on the Constitution starting only in March, the dubbing of the text as the 'De Jouvenel-Souchier' Constitution, or secondary figures like Emile Khoury amongst the main Lebanese protagonists. This position regarding Souchier is no longer tenable, as will become clear in the discussions below.

[123] Above, Ch. 4.

[124] *Al-Ahrar al-Musawwara*, issue 11, 22 March 1926, '*madha fil-dustur* (What is in the Constitution?)', 3 column 2.

This extract confirms Chiha's leading role as the key drafter. It also confirms the collegiality of the work since Nammour is involved throughout, as president of both the CR and the CSO. It confirms, again, that the French left the domestic sections to the Lebanese while keeping control of 'the Preface', which turned into Title V and VI 'final dispositions' of the constitutional text.

Why do we say Souchier is the likely author of the 'Observations' (DOC 9)? Only he could have written the document, for several reasons. First is the detached, deferential tone of the comments, as opposed for instance to de Jouvenel's peremptory tone in DOC 6. Then there is the technical, juristic nature of comments on several articles, with some explanation as to why he is suggesting deletions, amendments, or additions. Unlike other officials in the High Commission, Souchier was a specialist of public law, and returned to his work as judge (maître des requêtes au Conseil d'Etat) at the end of his Lebanese assignment.[125] Third is the absence of any other serious candidate. The author of the document knows about earlier discussions and was in the know of the constitutional march. It is hard to imagine that anyone in France could have made such elaborate, precise comments on the draft. The only possible alternative is that Léon Solomiac (1884–1960), de Jouvenel's main assistant and his 'chef de Cabinet' in Beirut, wrote the comments. But Solomiac had a lot to do as 'delegate to the High Commission', and documents show that he operated on a higher policy level. Unlike Souchier's profession as a jurist, Solomiac's whole career was in the French administration, mainly in the colonies.

The 'Souchier Observations' (DOC 9) consist of six pages of remarks on the second batch of the CCP.[126] No doubt Souchier followed the discussions closely, but the drafting committee ended up mostly as a Michel Chiha one-man show, with Chiha sending the drafts to some members of the CR and selecting French officials for comments, all of which only marginally altered the text. Chiha ignored some observations, and incorporated others.[127] Contrary to received wisdom in the scholarship about Souchier's co-authorship,

[125] Souchier was judge at the Conseil d'Etat from 1923 to 1934, and reappointed at the Conseil in February 1938, just before his death. He also exercised various administrative jobs, finishing as Préfet of the Bouches-du-Rhône in 1936.

[126] DOCs 5 to 8, then consolidated in DOC 11.

[127] See the discussion of the substance of the Souchier Observations in next chapter.

or even his strong imprint, the claim of the important Lebanese part of the Constitution ascribed to him is not supported by the documents.

One should also mention the chemistry among the Lebanese constituents, which can be followed in their plenary discussions on 19–22 May, but also the chemistry between Chiha and the main French actors. Chiha was close to Robert de Caix (1869–1970), who played a leading role in Lebanon between 1919 and 1923, including with two terms as interim High Commissioner, and remained in touch with Chiha after he left the country to represent France at the League of Nations.[128] In November 1925, two years after de Caix had left the country, Chiha publicly acknowledged his appreciation of the man: 'I had the honour of knowing and meeting Mr. de Caix long enough (as did many of our compatriots) to be able to attest to his feelings about and his perfect loyalty towards Great Lebanon. M. de Caix, whose formidable intellect is well known, has rendered and continues to render services to Great Lebanon which it would be unfair to ignore'.[129] In a long note written in 1926, de Caix expresses, in turn, his admiration for Chiha: 'Such would undoubtedly be the policy of men like Michel Chiha and his friends, if we knew how to inspire confidence in their undeniable patriotism ...'[130]

A similar chemistry was missing between de Jouvenel and Chiha. We mentioned the 'public row' over de Jouvenel's speech in Damascus on 6 February about 'the Etats Unis du Liban et de la Syrie', a phrase which was widely interpreted in Lebanon as France's abandonment of a Lebanese entity remaining separate from Syria. There was also a corresponding 'private spat', reconstructed by Hokayem on the basis of the French archives, according to

[128] For a rich biography of de Caix and a large selection of his writings, see Gérard Khoury, *Une Tutelle Coloniale, Le Mandat Français en Syrie et au Liban- Ecrits Politiques de Robert de Caix*, Paris: Belin 2006.

[129] Michel Chiha, 'Correspondance', *Le Réveil*, 10 November 1925: 'J'ai eu l'honneur de connaître et de fréquenter suffisamment M. de Caix (et beaucoup de nos compatriotes sont dans le même cas) pour être en mesure de témoigner de ses sentiments à l'égard du Grand-Liban et de sa parfaite loyauté. M. de Caix dont chacun connaît les hautes qualités intellectuelles a rendu et continue de rendre au Grand-Liban des services qu'il serait injuste de méconnaître'.

[130] Robert de Caix, 'L'organisation donnée à la Syrie et au Liban de 1920 à 1923 et la crise actuelle' (October 1926), in Khoury, *Une Tutelle Coloniale, Le Mandat Français en Syrie et au Liban- Ecrits Politiques de Robert de Caix*, above n.128, 435: 'Tel serait sans doute la politique d'hommes comme Michel Chiha et de ses amis, si on savait inspirer confiance à leur incontestable patriotisme ...' 'Such (*Tel*)' is in reference to 'the moral consolidation' that a High Commissioner should give to Lebanon as an independent State.

which the HC was embarrassed and annoyed by Chiha 'going public' over the issue.[131]

The controversy did not ultimately affect the Constitution, but it might explain why Chiha was absent from the final plenary meeting of the CR in May 1926, 'with an excuse' on grounds of health that was recorded in the minutes of the meeting.[132] His absence was noted by Rabbath.[133] It might have resulted from the bad blood between Chiha and the HC. But it could also be that Chiha, having completed his main task in the midst of intensive discussions and comments on his draft, wanted his Lebanese colleagues to have their say, unimpeded, at the close of the process. It is not impossible that he was unwell, as he claimed. Personal chemistry matters in history, but it is often hard to fathom. Between Souchier and Chiha, the meetings and discussions were no doubt numerous; between de Jouvenel and Chiha, they were rarer, given the position of the HC and his preoccupations during the large insurrection in the French-mandated territories of Syria and parts of Lebanon. Another document shows the high regard in which officials held Chiha: he was the only Lebanese whom de Jouvenel appointed on 23 December 1925 to a Commission tasked with 'examining ways of correcting the increase in the price of fuel'.[134] That, of course, was before the February falling out.

Chiha and Duguit

Last but not least is the influence of a leading French constitutional scholar whose name appears in the Chiha documents. This was Léon Duguit (1859–1928), a formidable constitutionalist who is little known at present, partly because the Constitution of 1958 adopted a presidential form which was

[131] Hokayem, *La Genèse de la Constitution Libanaise de 1926*, above n.2, 251–6 (on de Jouvenel's speech in Damascus on 6 February mentioning 'Les Etats Unis de Syrie et du Liban', the commotion which followed in Lebanon on the fear of remaining joined with Syria, and the letter of protests by Chiha to Solomiac, dated 10 February, which were relayed to de Jouvenel while he was travelling in Syria and Turkey). From Turkey, where he was informed of Chiha's letter, de Jouvenel sent a telegram expressing his pique at Chiha not coming to him first, and for sending his letter while he was away. Text of the telegram dated 18 February 1926, at id., 254–5.

[132] Zein ed., *Mahader Munaqashat al-Dustur al-Lubnani wa Ta'dilatuh 1926–90*, above n.70, 16.

[133] 'Mais le fait saillant est, qu'à tous les débats, qui s'ouvrirent dans la matinée du mercredi 19 mai, pour s'achever dans la nuit du dimanche 23, Michel Chiha eût été absent.' Rabbath, *La Constitution Libanaise: Origines, Textes et Commentaires*, above n.2, 41.

[134] Letter from the HC to Chiha, dated 23 December 1925. Chiha Archive, Document 16–22.

not at the heart of his writings during a characteristically parliamentary Third Republic.[135] In DOC 10, which consists of two pages of notes, Chiha appears to be responding to comments by Duguit or by someone sharing Duguit's comments. We know that de Jouvenel and Duguit knew each other, given the sustained correspondence between the two families.[136] What transpires from the available texts suggests that de Jouvenel may have passed on to Duguit a copy of the draft he had commented on (DOC 6), and that Duguit's reaction was transmitted orally to Chiha in the course of discussions with de Jouvenel and/or Souchier. DOC 10 might therefore be a set of notes summarising this communication.

The verso page in DOC 10 includes a set of brief points. One is an outline of the main two powers, and their relations with each another and 'against the executive'.[137]Another point suggests that the Senate should have the same powers as the Chamber, but 'facultatifs', optional.[138] Yet another sentence suggests that the cabinet 'should not be necessary under a collective responsibility', since the government is 'a coalition government by definition', and that it does not require therefore a president.[139]

The more interesting part of the Duguiy document is the front page. For convenience, here is its typed version of Chiha's handwritten notes:

> The President of the Republic 'secures and oversees the execution of the laws'. Criticism of M. Duguit – formulation obscure, it can be put into practice only with possessing the power of regulation.

[135] Duguit's writings were extensive, including a five-volume treatise on constitutional law, *Traité de Droit Constitutionnel*, Paris: Boccard then Cujas, 3rd ed. (first edition 1911), 5 vols, 1927- n.d. On Duguit in English, see Matthew Mirow, 'Léon Duguit: (1859–1928)', in O. Descamps and R. Domingo eds, *Great Christian Jurists in French History*, Cambridge: Cambridge University Press 2019, 358–71.

[136] Hokayem, *La Genèse de la Constitution Libanaise de 1926*, above n.2, 246 n.1.

[137] DOC 10: 'Conflits a- Chambres contre exécutif b- Chambres entre elles'.

[138] DOC 10: 'Sénat avec pouvoirs étendus pareils à ceux de la Chambre mais facultatifs'. *Facultatifs* is more accurately translated here as secondary or supplementary. The note adds: 'Une sorte de droit d'évocation aux conséquences limitées, some type of right of evocation with limited consequences.'

[139] DOC 10: 'Exécutif ... Sans responsabilité collective inutile parce que a- Gouvernement de coalition par définition ... Donc pas de président de conseil en titre, parce que ses collaborateurs ne pourraient pas lui survivre.' (The Executive [should remain] without collective responsibility, [which is] useless because a- [it is] a coalition government by definition ... So no official president of the council, because his collaborators could not survive him.) On the usefulness of a president of the council in the presence of a president of the republic, see Ch. 7, section on the emergence of a bicephalous executive.

> Duguit: functions of the State — legislative, administrative, jurisdictional
>
> Functional – Representative Gt [Government] – a general formula implying [that the representative government is] parliamentary.
>
> Separation of powers? Contested
> Collaboration of State organs
>
> Mr Duguit – supporter of two assemblies
> by two-degree vote for certain countries in our outline [text unclear]
>
> Mr. Duguit: 'The President of the Republic personifies the Government.'[140]

Let us try to make more sense of this enigmatic text. In the first draft of the Constitution (DOC 1), Art. 54 mentions that the president of the republic 'secures and oversees the execution of the laws'.[141] Duguit's reported criticism is that this 'formulation is obscure, and can be put into practice only with [the president] possessing the power of regulation'.[142] As a consequence, DOC 5 integrates the criticism by entrusting the president with 'regulatory powers' in line with Duguit's recommendation. The text adopted in May 1926

[140] DOC 10:

Le Président de la République 'assure et surveille l'exécution des lois'. Critique de M. Duguit-formule obscure qui ne s'applique que par la possession du pouvoir de réglementation de l'Etat.

Théorie: législative
(Duguit: fonctions de l'Etat; — législative, administrative, juridictionnelle

Fonctionnel – Gt [Gouvernement] représentatif- formule générale implique parlementaire.

Duguit – Séparation des pouvoirs? Contestée
Collaboration des organes de l'Etat

M. Duguit – partisan de deux assemblées
au suffrage à deux degrés pour certains pays dans le plan [text unclear] du nôtre

M. Duguit- 'Le Président de la République personnifie le Gouvernement.'

[141] Art. 54 DOC 1: 'Il en [les lois] surveille et assure l'exécution'. The typed versions (DOCs 5 to 8) mistakenly repeat the verb 'assure'.

[142] DOC 10: 'Critique de M. Duguit – formule obscure qui ne s'applique que par la possession du pouvoir de réglementation.'

reproduces the formulation. It is adopted from DOC 5 onwards with the president expressly endowed with the 'pouvoir règlementaire'.[143] This suggests, chronologically, that DOC 10 arrived to Chiha just after DOC 4.[144]

The most alluring part of the Duguit document is the section entitled 'Theory'. Against the dominant Montesquieu trope, the three powers for Duguit are 'legislative, *administrative*, and jurisdictional'. These powers are 'the functions of the state'. By '*fonctionnel*' Duguit meant that 'the general formula implies [that the representative government is] parliamentary'. This is not explained further, but the formula finds its explanation in Duguit's constitutional treatise:

> In the scholarship nowadays dominant in France and abroad, one distinguishes three great functions of the State: the legislative function, the administrative function, and the jurisdictional function. One should not say judicial function, because this word must be used exclusively, in a formal sense, to designate a certain category of civil servants.[145]

Duguit pursues this distinction by presenting 'a general notion', from a purely 'material' perspective, 'for each of these functions'.[146]

First, 'the State exercises a legislative function ... every time it formulates a normative or constructive statement'. This is what Duguit calls *acte-règle*, which is objective, general and normative. Secondly, the State exercises an administrative function in all instances where it accomplishes an *acte-condition*, or conditional act, whereby its agents work to ensure a proper public service provision in the case of substantial and material acts. Thirdly and last, 'the State resolves questions of law [*droit*] raised before it'.[147]

This is a sophisticated and novel theory of the separation of powers, more accurately called 'the separation of functions' to justify, in Duguit's eyes, the legitimacy of government as parliamentary. In another passage in his lengthy

[143] From DOC 5 onward, Art 51 reads: 'Le Président de la République ... en [les lois] assure l'exécution: il dispose à cet effet du *pouvoir réglementaire* sans pouvoir modifier les lois elles-mêmes ni dispenser de leur exécution.' (Italics added)

[144] Here again, I preferred to keep DOC 10 with the 'preparatory files', since it would otherwise disturb the flow of the full drafts constituted by DOCs 1 to 8.

[145] Duguit, *Traité de Droit Constitutionnel*, above n.137, vol. II, 156.

[146] Id.

[147] Id.

Treatise, he clarifies this point: 'In short, one has confused two totally different points: the point concerning the separation of powers and the point concerning the separation of functions'.[148] This is reflected in the Chiha document with, appropriately, a further point under 'théorie' separating the three functions. There, the separation of powers is followed by a question mark and the word 'contestée.'

How is this theory reflected in Chiha's Constitution? One significant change was that Chiha ascribed *regulatory* powers to the president as opposed to the formulation of *executive* power used previously.

The adjustment was not sufficient to build a novel constitutional theory in the Lebanese Constitution. For Chiha to espouse Duguit's more sophisticated theory rejecting separation of powers and replacing it with separation of functions, he should have substituted all mentions of 'powers' in his draft with 'functions', and set the various 'powers' of each of the organs of government under an altogether different structure. This would have been truly revolutionary, since 'separation of functions' never made it into modern constitutional design, including in subsequent French constitutional texts and elsewhere in the comparative constitutional world. Considering the limited room that constitutionalism allows outside Montesquieu's hallowed formula, it was impossible for Chiha to replace the formula with Duguit's sophisticated new theory of the 'collaboration of the organs of the State' on a 'functional' basis making the line of separation one of functions between a legislature issuing an *acte-règle* and an administration issuing 'an *acte-condition* (...) to ensure a proper public service provision in the case of substantial and material acts'.[149]

[148] Id., 661.
[149] Id.

6

Building Constitutional Blocks: The Communitarian Straitjacket

Impossible to put in the Constitution if one does not wish to see it violated, which would be very serious.[1]

Blocks, as in a building or a Lego construction, are a metaphor. The bricks, adobes or blocks in the construction of a constitution come in words which affect the future of the country in a unique way. No surprise when, like sacred texts, they become in need of meaning, *deutungsbedürftig*.[2] They are ever interpretable. The central difference in the interpretation of the two genres is that sacred texts may not be amended.

The previous chapter addressed the overall structure of the Lebanese Constitution, as well as some attendant documents to its birth. This chapter and the next one look more closely at the themes of the Constitution in its distinct development through the main controversies which surface as Chiha constructs his text. They also address some of the exogenous factors that accompanied its construction.

A lasting straitjacket

With the drafting process better delineated chronologically, and the Lebanese version of the LEJ(F)ARC template described, our concern is now with substance. First is the way in which communal constitutionalism prevailed despite

1 'Impossible à mettre dans la Constitution si on ne veut pas la faire violer, ce qui serait très grave.' Henry de Jouvenel (DOC 6).

2 The concept of *Deutungsbedürftigkeit* (need for exegesis) is used extensively by John Wansbrough in *Qur'anic Studies* (1977) as 'characteristic of sacred language'. Cited here in Andrew Rippin's edition, New York: Prometheus 2004, cite at 118. See the section on *Deutungsbedürftigkeit* at 148.

the known reluctance of several members of the CR and many French overseers by virtue of their attachment to the Third Republic's version of *laïcité*.

On the face of it, all citizens are equal, and all public positions allotted according to merit. The very first version of the Chiha manuscripts reads:

> Article 6. All Lebanese are equal before the law. They equally enjoy civil and political rights and are equally subject to obligations and public duties.[3]

An additional article establishing the Lebanese flag was introduced in DOC 5. This became Art. 5, and the subsequent versions were renumbered consequently. The handwritten text inserted as Art.5 reads: 'The Lebanese flag is blue, white, red, with a cedar on the white part',[4] obviously drawn in the colours of the French flag. It was slightly changed in the first available Arabic version, by hand, to say 'with equal vertical bands',[5] and remained unchanged until Independence, when the French *tricolore* was jettisoned. The blue band was replaced by another red one and the three bands were drawn horizontally.[6] With the added Art.5 on the flag, original Art. 6 was renumbered starting DOC 5 and became Art.7:

> All Lebanese are equal before the law. They equally enjoy civil and political rights and are equally subject (*asujétis*) to obligations and public duties without any distinction of race or religion (*sans aucune distinction de race, ni de religion*).[7]

[3] 'Tous les Libanais sont égaux devant la loi. Ils jouissent également des droits civils et politiques et sont également assujettis aux charges et devoirs publics.' This appears as Art.6 of the first Chiha Paper (DOC 1). Of anecdotal and chronological interest is Chiha's striking out the word /soumis/ and replacing it with /assujettis/ (DOC 1). In the first and second typed versions, the typist wrongly wrote /assujettis/ as /asujétis/ (DOCs 2 and 3). Then a slight change occurs: /sont égaux/ becomes /libres et égaux/, and /assujétis/ is struck out and replaced by /soumis/, with an important clause added in Chiha's hand at the end of Art.7: /, sans aucune distinction de race et de religion/ (DOC 5). In the next set, Chiha notices the spelling mistake and inserts an additional /t/ in /assujétis./ (DOC 7). In the Avant-Projet of 18 April 1926, as well as in the text presented to the CR on 18 May for discussion, this corrected version is adopted, and we have /assujettis/ with double /t/ and without the accent on the /e/.

[4] 'Le drapeau libanais est bleu, blanc, rouge, en bandes verticales égales avec un cèdre sur la partie blanche.' Inserted in Chiha's hand, DOC 5.

[5] with equal vertical bands, *aqsamanan 'amudiyya mutasawiya* (DOC 14).

[6] The flag of 1926 and the flag of 1943 (which remains unchanged) can be found in the entry 'Flag of Lebanon' in Wikipedia. An iconic drawing of the flag, dated 11 November 1943 with the signatures of the main figures of independence, is reproduced in the article with the title 'Flag as drawn and approved by the members of the parliament during the Declaration of Independence in 1943'.

[7] The added clause /sans aucune distinction de race, ni de religion/ appears in DOC 5, and remains in the text until the final CR plenary discussion in May. It became eventually /sans distinction aucune/.

This remained the text of Art.7 until the CR plenary discussions in May. Both the misspelling of 'assujétis' and the added clause 'sans aucune distinction de race, ni de religion' provide a useful example of the iteration in Art. 7 until a change occurs in the plenary meeting. On the morning of 20 May 1926, a debate took place over three suggested changes to the article by various CR members.[8] Representative Ibrahim Mundher suggested first 'that there is no need for the expression "race and religion".' Then Chebl Dammous intervened: 'I would amend the article as follows: "without distinction as to region"'. Finally, CR member Youssef al-Khazen suggested: 'And I add to it "male and female", after the mention "all Lebanese".'[9]

After a brief discussion, the reference to region suggested by Dammous was dropped, but the two other suggestions were put to the vote. With only three members in support, mention of 'male and female' was defeated.[10] But the amendment suggested by Mundher to delete reference to race or religion was carried out unanimously. It remains unchanged to date:

> Art.7- All Lebanese are equal before the law. They equally enjoy civil and political rights and are equally subject to obligations and public duties without any distinction.[11]

In the wider context, Art.7 responds to the secularist penchant of several French and Lebanese protagonists for equality of all citizens before the law in all civil and political rights 'with no distinction whatsoever'.[12] Despite its lasting appeal for the equality of all before the law, a basic tenet in Chiha's world-view, the clause remained largely inconsequential institutionally, as had many previous such attempts under Egyptian and Ottoman rule. In 1839, the first

[8] Ahmad al-Zein ed., *Mahader Munaqashat al-Dustur al-Lubnani wa Taʿdilatuh 1926–90* (Minutes of the discussions about the Lebanese Constitution and its amendments), Beirut: Publications of the Chamber of Deputies 1993, 24–5 for the discussion of Art.7.

[9] Id., 24. Race is *jins*, religions is *din*, region is *mantaqa*, and male and female is *dhukur wa inath*.

[10] Id., 24–5. It is unfortunate that the suggestion of Khazen was rejected, with its potential consequences on both female voting and candidacy. In 1957, during the presidency of Camille Chamoun, a change of the electoral law finally allowed all women to vote in Lebanon. The first woman MP is Myrna Bustani, who succeeded her father Emile, killed in a plane accident in 1963.

[11] 'Tous les Libanais sont égaux devant la loi. Ils jouissent également des droits civils et politiques et sont également assujettis aux charges et devoirs publics, sans distinction aucune'.

[12] In the final French version, the place of 'aucune' moves somewhat inexplicably from 'sans aucune distinction' to 'sans distinction aucune'. This more elegant formulation might have been the correction of a French official or the typist's creative initiative.

Ottoman rescript had declared all subjects of the Sultan equal. In practice, the rule of the Sultan was organised into a Muslim Sunni dominion. In Lebanon, the equality of Art. 7 never prevented communalism from prevailing.

In fact, the difference in law based on communal belonging is asserted in the very same section of the Constitution. The separate family and inheritance laws between the sects (including significant differences between Sunni, Shiʿi and Druze communities) was acknowledged and constitutionalised in Art. 9: '[The State] shall also guarantee that the personal status and religious interests of the population, to whatever religious sect they belong, shall be respected'. The emergence of this controversial text, which consecrates in law the different treatment of Lebanese citizens in key aspects of their lives, does not appear in any version up until and including the Avant-Projet sent by Henry de Jouvenel to Paris on 18 April 1926.[13] It surfaces out of nowhere in the text submitted to the CR for discussions on 19 May.[14]

In the plenary discussions, the clause is queried by CR member Youssef al-Khazen, who asks what 'the State shall guarantee' in Art.9 means. Dammous responds with two arguments: 'The intent in the expression confirms Art. 6 of the Mandate charter. The objective is that the communities (*tawa'ef*) have been used for 600 years to exercise their own regime of personal status, and the Mandate of the League of Nations guarantees this, so does the present Constitution'.[15]

It is probable that the pressure of religious leaders was the source of the sudden addition, which took place therefore sometimes later in April or early May. While it is true that Art.6 of the League of Nations' Charter for the Mandate over Syria and Lebanon (1922) stipulates that '[r]espect for the personal status of the various peoples and for their religious interests shall be fully guaranteed',[16] Dammous's argument about the Mandate sounds like a forced

[13] Reproduced in Annex 9 in Antoine Hokayem, *La Genèse de la Constitution Libanaise de 1926*, Antélias: Les Editions Universitaires du Liban 1996, 358–69, at 359; it is also not mentioned in the latest versions in the CCP, namely DOCs 11 to 13, but appears in DOC 14.

[14] Annex 10 in Antoine Hokayem, *La Genèse de la Constitution Libanaise de 1926*, above n.13, 369–80, at 370.

[15] Zein ed., *Mahader Munaqashat al-Dustur al-Lubnani wa Taʿdilatuh 1926–90* (Minutes of the discussions about the Lebanese Constitution and its amendments), above n.8, 26.

[16] In English: 'French Mandate for Syria and the Lebanon', *The American Journal of International Law*, 17, Supplement: Official Documents (July 1923), 177–82 (Art.6). In French: 'Le respect du

rationalization of an eminently sectarian constitutional clause which every discussant must have seen as an impairment to the equality of citizens before the law. Communalism in family and inheritance laws is a Middle Eastern problem which finds strong echoes in India and other mixed-religion countries.[17] It adds considerable legal weight to an already heavy communitarian straitjacket.

Communalism in the legislative branch

The way communalism became entrenched can be read in the developments of the text from the first Chiha draft through the final shape of the Lebanese Constitution. Despite remaining unsaid, communalism suffuses the composition and resulting power of a Congress consisting of a Senate and a Chamber of Deputies on its basis.

From the very first manuscript, no doubt in conformity with de Jouvenel's wishes, Chiha includes both a Chamber of Deputies and a Senate in a parliamentary system. The first Document provides a replica of the French Third Republic's bicameral constitutionalism with a Chamber of Deputies and a Senate.[18] This also corresponds to the Ottoman tradition since the 1876 Constitution had both a Majlis al-Mab'uthin, the elected lower chamber of the 'emissaries' of the Empire to Istanbul, and an upper chamber of notables, Majlis al-A'yan, appointed by the Sultan.[19]

The emergence of the Lebanese Senate was also partly the expression of de Jouvenel's own attachment to the French Senate, in which he sat until his death in 1935. Yet Chiha was fully aware that a Senate made little sense in a small country like Lebanon, where a dual chamber unduly complicates decision-making in an already entangled communal system. Almost immediately, the upper chamber appeared redundant and cumbersome. The many

statut personnel des diverses populations et de leurs intérêts religieux sera entièrement garanti'. Hokayem, *La Genèse de la Constitution Libanaise de 1926*, above n.8, Annex 2, 310–16.

17 There is a large literature on personal status laws in Lebanon (and other countries), see for instance Marie-Claude Najm, *Principes Directeurs de Droit International Privé et Conflit de Civilisations*, Paris: Dalloz 2005. For the transformation of these issues into 'acid tests' in the form of the 'scarf/veil' controversies, see my *Philosophy of Nonviolence*, New York: Oxford University Press 2015, 181–90.

18 Title II a, 'Le Sénat' (DOC 1, Arts. 21 to 25).

19 Ottoman Constitution of 1876, Art. 42. 'The General Assembly is composed of two chambers: the Chamber of Notables or Senate, and the Chamber of Deputies.' English text of the constitution available at https://iow.eui.eu/wp-content/uploads/sites/18/2014/05/Brown-01-Ottoman-Constitution.pdf. Discussed in Ch. 3.

articles devoted to the Senate in the 1926 Constitution disappear in the very first constitutional amendments, adopted a year and four months later. The fusion of the two assemblies into one Chamber of Deputies ended the short life of the Senate.[20]

As far as institutionalised communalism went, the membership of both the Senate and the Chamber of Deputies is thoroughly communal in the Constitution adopted in 1926.

Under Art. 22, the Senate is composed of 16 members, seven of whom are designated by the president ('head of state'), and the rest elected. Art. 96 specifies the religious community of each of the 16 Senators, in proportion to the census of 1922, which was also the basis for the CR distribution. The final version of Art. 96 distributes the Senators into '5 maronites, 3 sunnites, 3 chiites, 2 grecs-orthodoxes, 1 grec-catholique, 1 druze, 1 minoritaire', so 9 Christians and 7 Muslims'.[21] When de Jouvenel appointed the senators, he chose Muhammad al-Jisr (1881–1934) to head it, a religious Sunni notable from Tripoli and a former qadi.

Article 22 established the designation by the president of almost half the senators, undermining the principle of popular representation. This is not the case for the lower chamber. Under Art. 24 of the Constitution, all the members of the lower chamber are elected in conformity with the CR's electoral law of 1922/1925.[22] The Chamber of Deputies, which is the new name of the

[20] The Amendment is dated 27 October 1927 and signed by President Charles Debbas and President of the Council of Ministers Bechara al-Khoury. Arabic text in Zein ed., *Mahader Munaqashat al-Dustur al-Lubnani wa Ta'dilatuh 1926–90* (Minutes of the discussions about the Lebanese Constitution and its amendments), above n.13. 181–97. Of interest in Lebanese constitutional history is the potential use of an upper chamber to dilute communalism. The allure of bicameralism, which resurfaced in the 1989 Ta'ef agreement, seeks a balance in legislative power between a lower chamber elected on a non-sectarian basis alongside an upper Senate with a communal composition, in some new form of 'religious federalism' (Amended Art.95). Bicameralism is a persistent institutional calque, and the evanescent Lebanese Senate reappeared at the end of the twentieth century as the major constitutional rearrangement of legislative power in Ta'ef, which is discussed further in Ch. 11.

[21] De Jouvenel designated all 16 Senate members in accordance with Art. 98, but this arrangement was designed to operate only once. Art. 98 planned for the nine elected senators to be voted in by the people before end of 1928. This arrangement became moot when the Senate was scrapped in the 1927 Amendment. The 16 senators were just added to the CD as deputies.

[22] See for the full text of Art. 24 below at n.24. When the Senate was abolished, the only elected institution with universal (male) suffrage, was and remains to date the Chamber of Deputies, aka the Lebanese parliament or national assembly.

Council of Representatives under the express provisions of Art. 98 of the 1926 Constitution, was fully elected, but it was also communitarian.

Could the profoundly communal character of the legislature have been avoided, or at least tempered? Let us look more closely at the progress of the texts, first for the Senate and then for the Chamber of Deputies.

Senate

Chiha's proposed Senate is partly elected and partly designated by the president. Art. 21 of DOC 1 reads: 'The Senate is composed of 23 members, including seven members who are appointed by the Head of State and 16 members elected'.[23] The initial formulation of Art. 24 is subtle:

> In order to ensure *a proportional representation satisfying the traditions of the Lebanese people*, the distribution of senatorial seats will be as follows:
>
> Elected Senators: [left blank]
> Appointed Senators: [left blank]
>
> The surplus of what relates to the election of the Senate will be regulated by the electoral law.[24]

The number of senators is left blank, with 'representation satisfying the traditions of the Lebanese people' a back entry to communitarianism. The sentence appears in Art. 24 of the manuscript and of the three subsequent typed versions (DOCs 1 to 4), but it is altered by hand in the next version (DOC 5) and the article renumbered 25: 'In order to ensure representation *in accordance with custom*, the distribution of senatorial seats ...'[25] 'Custom' replaced 'traditions', with little practical difference between the two.

[23] 'Le Sénat est composé de 23 membres dont 7 nommés par le Chef de l'Etat et 16 élus.' Art.21 of DOC 1. There is a *variante* which appears in the first typed version, as /(Variante: 7 élus et 10 nommés ou le contraire)/.

[24] Emphasis added. Art. 24 in DOC 1 and DOC 2. 'Afin d'assurer une *représentation proportionnelle satisfaisant les traditions du peuple libanais*, la répartition des sièges sénatoriaux se fera de la façon suivante:

> Sénateurs élus: [left blank]
> Sénateurs nommés: [left blank]

Le surplus de ce qui a trait à l'élection du Sénat sera réglé par la loi électorale'.

[25] 'Afin d'assurer une représentation *conforme à la coutume*, la répartition des sièges sénatoriaux ...' (underlined in original)

The next typed version (DOC 6) was annotated by de Jouvenel himself, no less. The comments are in black ink, alongside further comments in red by Chiha.[26] In red therefore, Chiha fills in the void after 'elected senators and designated senators' with a detailed communitarian affiliation of the seven senators in each category with the first letter or two for each.

The void is filled for each community as follows:

Mar ... Sun. Ch. g.o D. g.c. Min

standing for Maronite, Sunni, Shi'i, Greek Orthodox, Druze, Greek Catholic, Minorities (DOC 5). The annotations in red must have preceded those of de Jouvenel, who crossed out the two articles. The next version available (DOC 7) reduces the denomination of the senators to three: M. (for Maronite), S. (for Sunni) and C. (for Shi'i), followed by 'etc'. DOC 8, with the annotations of Chiha, introduces a major change: Art. 25 is deleted and replaced with Art.23, which says that 'the surplus related to the Senate will be fixed in the electoral law'.[27] The senators are therefore not to be chosen or elected on an explicitly communal basis. The issue was left to the 'electoral law'. As a consequence, de Jouvenel's suggestion to delete communal representation was taken on board, but the principle of communal distribution was simply pushed to the 'transitory' title at the end of the Constitution.

The disappearance of the Senate within a year of the adoption of the Constitution makes these subtle adjustments academic. They remain interesting insofar as they show the clear-headed mind of Chiha, who knew that a Senate would unduly complicate the already byzantine affairs of government, and that it would likely be subject to the same communal constraints that the country's 'custom and traditions' imposed on the CD. If both the CD and the Senate are to be sect-based, what is the point of the Senate?

[26] Because I was familiar only with Chiha's handwriting, the authorship for all other handwriting notes in the Chiha Papers could not be ascertained. The exception in DOC 6 was possible thanks to the privileged friendship with Anne de Jouvenel, Henry's granddaughter and longtime keeper of his written legacy. I contacted her when I suspected the comments in an unusual handwriting might have been Henry de Jouvenel's because of their peremptory and flowery turn-of-phrase. She immediately assured me that it was her grandfather's. Phone and WhatsApp exchange with Anne de Jouvenel, 22 July 2022.

[27] 'Le surplus de ce qui a trait aux élections du Sénat sera réglé par la loi électorale' (DOC 8), Art.23.

We have several documents which show Chiha's sense of the unnecessary complications of an additional upper Chamber. In an article published in 1950, he reminisced about the cumbersome Senate: 'The Senate of 1926, wanted by Henry de Jouvenel, lasted exactly one year ... After twelve months, political life was so poisoned by the new assembly that the Senate had to be abolished'.[28] And on 12 January 1954, in an article also published in *Le Jour*, he wrote: 'When they talk to you about a senate added to what we have, we may wonder whether we are not sinking in either a sweet or a violent folly'.[29] In Chiha's CP, we also find an undated typed document in Arabic, from which the first page is missing, stating that any amendment to reintroduce the Senate is unnecessary, because it proved cumbersome for legislation, 'especially for the passing of the budget law'.[30]

The proposed abolition of the Senate was agreed upon in the first set of amendments passed on 17 October 1927. This is only a year and a half after the adoption of the Constitution and the departure of de Jouvenel, who was replaced by Henri Ponsot, a High Commissioner who was far less attached to an upper chamber for legislative power.

Regardless, the Senate could have been envisaged early on as a secular/non-communal institution in contrast with a communal CD (or vice-versa), especially since some of the senators were to be appointed. Yet the Lebanese 'traditions' or 'custom' in the very first versions defeated whatever secular window might have been briefly opened at the time. But the idea of two chambers, one elected in a communal manner, the other secular without consideration to communities, hovered over Lebanese constitutionalism for a long time. It was formally adopted in 1990.[31]

[28] Michel Chiha, 'Pour faire réfléchir', *Le Jour*, 16 June 1950: 'Le Sénat de 1926, voulu par Henry de Jouvenel, dura exactement un an ... Au bout de douze mois, la vie politique était tellement empoisonnée par la nouvelle assemblée qu'il fallut supprimer le Sénat'.

[29] 'Quand on vous parle d'un sénat ajouté à ce que nous avons, on se demande si on ne sombre pas dans une folie douce ou furieuse'. *Le Jour*, 12 January 1954.

[30] DOC 29, p. 2: '*wa khususan qanun al-muwazana*'.

[31] This is one of the major changes introduced in the Constitution in 1990, in accordance with the Ta'ef Agreement the previous year. The two chambers appear in Arts. 22 and 24 of the Constitution as amended but have not been put into effect more than 30 years after the amendment, for the Senate has yet to be established.

Chamber of deputies

The Constitution adopted on 23 May includes only two texts under the section 'Chambre des Députés,' Arts. 24 and 25. Art. 25 is marginal. It requires new elections to be held within three months in the event that the CD is dissolved. In contrast, Art. 24 entrenches the communitarian basis of the CD by reference to the 1922/1925 electoral law:

> The members of the Chamber of Deputies are elected in accordance with the provisions of Arrêté No. 1307 of March 10, 1922, which will remain in force until the drafting of a new electoral law by the legislative powers.[32]

We have encountered this important piece of the constitutional puzzle as the communitarian electoral arrangements regulated by Arrêté 1307 of 1922.[33] The 30 members of the CR were distributed 'in proportion to the number of each sect in the country'.[34] In 1925, the law was re-enacted, unchanged, following the tug-of-war between High Commissioner Maurice Sarrail and the higher powers in Paris informed by opponents of the change in Beirut to keep strictly to 'the statu quo ante' for the election of the CR that summer. The determined wish expressed in Paris to see the 1922 law unchanged in 1925 persisted through the final constitutional deliberation. Art. 24 was confirmed on 20 May 1926 by a large voting majority during the plenary debate of the CR.[35]

[32] 'Les membres de la Chambre des députés sont élus conformément aux dispositions de l'arrêté No 1307 du 10 Mars 1922 qui restera en vigueur jusqu'à l'élaboration d'une nouvelle loi électorale par les pouvoirs législatifs.' (Art. 24 of the Constitution). As a reminder, the electoral law of 1925 is the same as its 1922 predecessor.

[33] Arrêté 1307 (or Electoral Law of 1922) in e.g. Muhammad Murad, *Al-Intikhabat al-Niyabiyya fi Lubnan 1920–2009* (Parliamentary elections in Lebanon 1920–2009), Beirut: Publications of the Lebanese University 2013, Appendix 1, 466–79.

[34] Id. Art. 1 of the Law of 1922, which specifies that the governor (*al-hakem*) would decide on the distribution.

[35] Zein ed., *Mahader Munaqashat al-Dustur al-Lubnani wa Ta'dilatuh 1926–90* (Minutes of the discussions about the Lebanese Constitution and its amendments), above n.8, 39. Only CR members Subhi Haydar and Nagib Sa'd oppose it (with no explanation recorded in the minutes). There is a slight and insignificant change in the French text from 'autorités législatives' in the text submitted on 19 May to the CR, and the text adopted in the Constitution, 'pouvoirs législatifs'. In Arabic, '*sulta ishtira'iyya*' covers both, but the change in the French text suggests some last-minute editing without the formal approval of the CR.

As a consequence, the most distinctive component of the Constitution remained effectively unwritten. Communitarianism happened, so to speak, outside the Constitution, with changes every now and then depending on the legislators' majorities and executive impulses, yet never impugning its hold. This arrangement is not a complete oddity in modern constitutions, where the basic text usually says little about parliamentary elections and leaves them open to changes always dictated by demographic shifts. The Lebanese particularity is that electoral legislation never reached the point of putting into question the sectarian distribution of seats.

This also means that the constitutional text bore no mention of religious communities, a tribute to the subtlety of the drafters and their determination to keep the option of secularism live. The subtlety was lost in Ta'ef, which subjected the Constitution to an important symbolic change. The amended text of 1990 explicitly mentions religious community affiliation as an 'equal number between Christians and Muslims' in Parliament.[36] This calque, which we traced back to 'the six Muslim and six Christians' in the Charter of the Beirut Consultative Council of 1834, had been muted in the 1926 Constitution, where it was incorporated only by reference to the electoral law (Arrêté 1307 of 1922).

In DOC 1, Chiha does not mention the Arrêté. The section on the Chamber of the Deputies includes five articles, Arts. 26 to 30.

Article 26 reads:

> The members of the Chamber of Deputies are elected by universal suffrage and by majority list vote with one deputy for every 20,000 inhabitants of the same district. The fraction of district equal to or greater than ... inhabitants, shall be entitled to one deputy. Districts ~~with fewer~~ ... persons will be counted together and will be entitled to one deputy.[37]

[36] '*bil-tasawi bayn al-masihiyyin wal-muslimin*'. (Art. 24 of the Lebanese Constitution as amended in 1990).

[37] 'Art. 26 Les membres de la Chambre des Députés sont élus au suffrage universel et au scrutin de liste majoritaire à raison d'un député pour 20.000 habitants d'une même communauté. La fraction de communauté égale ou supérieure à ... hab., aura droit à un député. Les communautés comptant moins de [/moins de/ crossed] ... personnes seront comptées ensemble et auront droit à un député.' (DOC 1) Note that *communauté* in Chiha's text should not be read as religious community but as electoral district or circumscription.

Article 27 specifies that the length of a deputy's mandate must be four years. It sets out the conditions for candidacy – Lebanese nationality, at least 25 years of age, no criminal record.[38] Article 28 then provides:

> In order to ensure proportional representation that satisfies the traditions of the Lebanese people, the distribution of seats in the Chamber of Deputies taking into account the latest census will be as follows ------------------------------
> -- A law will modify if necessary the numbers set out in this article when a new census is made.[39]

Rather than by reference to the Arrêté 1307, Art. 29 determines that 'electoral districts are those which exist at the moment'.[40] Chiha notes the need to keep to the 'proportional representation satisfying the traditions of the Lebanese people', in other words communalism, and the geographical districts drawn by the electoral law even when a new census is eventually conducted. Art.30 regulates the dissolution of the CD and gives three months to elect a new chamber.[41]

In DOC 2, which includes handwritten marginal comments whose author is unknown, a comment brings Chiha's attention to the redundancy ('double emploi') between Art. 26 and Art. 27. Chiha takes the suggestion on board,

[38] 'Art 27 La durée du mandat de député est de quatre ans. Pour être député, il faut être libanais, âgé de 25 ans et ne pas être déchu de ses droits civiques tels que définis par la loi électorale.' (DOC 1).

[39] 'Art. 28 Afin d'assurer une représentation proportionnelle satisfaisant les traditions du peuple libanais, la répartition des sièges à la Chambre des députés en tenant compte du dernier recensement se fera de la façon suivante--
Une loi modifiera s'il y a lieu les nombres fixés à cet article quant un nouveau recensement sera fait.' (DOC 1).

[40] 'Art 29 Les circonscriptions électorales sont celles qui existent actuellement. Les sièges tels que répartis à l'article précédent seront attribués aux circonscriptions comme suit -------------------------
---Une loi modifiera s'il y a lieu l'attribution des sièges effectuée à cet article quand un nouveau recensement sera fait.' ('Art 29 Electoral districts are those that currently exist. The seats as distributed in the previous article shall be allocated to the constituencies as follows--
A law shall, if necessary, amend the allocation of seats made in this article when a new census is made.') (DOC 1).

[41] 'Art 30 En cas de dissolution de la Chambre des députés, l'acte de dissolution doit contenir convocation des électeurs pour des élections nouvelles devant avoir lieu dans un délai ne dépassant pas trois [/quatre/ crossed out] mois.' ('Art 30 In the event of dissolution of the Chamber of Deputies, the act of dissolution must contain the convocation of voters for new elections to be held within a period not exceeding three [/four/ crossed out] months') (DOC 1).

inscribing in the margin of DOC 4: 'Arts. 27 and 28 and 29 modified and reduced to 27 and 28'.[42]

These five (then four) articles remained until the printed version in Arabic reduced the section to the two articles adopted in the final text.[43] The four articles also appear in the text of the Avant-Projet sent to Paris on 18 April.[44] The change reducing the five (then four) longish articles to the two articles ultimately adopted in the Constitution takes place therefore between 18 April and 19 May 1926, when the version presented to the full CR for adoption retains reference to the Arrêté, whilst leaving open the possibility of a later law changing it. This is one of the few changes to the text between 18 April and 19 May.

The comments of de Jouvenel on the inappropriate mention of a communal Senate within a constitution were not repeated in the section about the deputies in the version which he annotates (DOC 6). The two articles finally adopted confirm the view that the French teams in Paris and Beirut had remained aware of the dispute between Sarrail and the French supporters of the 'statu quo ante' with an explicit reference to the Arrêté instead of the more elegant formula proposed by Chiha which refers to 'the existing law'.

To sum up on communalism in legislative power: despite the equality established between all citizens under Art. 7, members of both chambers of parliament yielded to the communal 'traditions' of the country. A religious sect-based electoral template was imposed on Chiha and de Jouvenel, whatever their misgivings about communal constitutionalism as a principle. The weight of Lebanese history was too difficult to jettison. But the formulation was more subtle in the initial texts, since Chiha's 'existing law', meaning the Arrêté 1307 of 1922, was open to a change which never happened, whereas Arrêté 1307 was too specific to allow a secular window out for the election of deputies.

[42] 'Arts 27 et 28 & 29 modifiés [underlined twice] et réduits à 27 et 28' (DOC 1).

[43] The four articles (Arts. 24 to 28) appear in all documents previous to the final text submitted on 19 May to the CR, including the printed French and Arabic texts of the Avant-Projet (DOCs 12 and 13, in French, DOC 14 in Arabic).

[44] Annex 9 of Hokayem, *La Genèse de la Constitution Libanaise de 1926*, above n.7, at 371 (Arts. 24 and 25).

Communalism in the judiciary, the cabinet and the administration

In the judicial branch, there is no mention at all of communalism. The available texts dedicate only a few lines to judicial power. This is Art.19 in DOC 1, where the 'judges are independent', and 'judicial power functions within the frameworks of a status established by law which gives essential guarantees to litigants …'[45] Like other articles, the numbering of the article is pushed back by the addition of Art.5 on the flag, and it becomes Art. 20 starting in DOC 5. Art. 20 is the same a hundred years later. But irrelevance of religious communities for the talents of a judge is systematically defeated by the communalism that grips the entire institutional system.

This raises the question of communalism in the executive branch, and across the administration. It appears in the version finally adopted in one brief yet key text on 'final and transitory provisions' within Title VI. This is the famous Art. 95 in Lebanese constitutional lore. It provides the backbone of communalism as the constitutional principle on which the whole system is based:

> Article 95 – On a provisional basis and in accordance with Art. 1 of the Charter of the Mandate, and with the intention of justice and concord, communities will be represented equitably in public employment and in the composition of the government, without prejudice to the interest of the state.[46]

Art. 95 was adopted by the Council on 22 May, in its last session.[47] The article did not appear in the earlier CCP versions. The documents stop in the manuscripts and typed versions at the Title on Financial Arrangements, which discusses taxes and the budget (DOCs 1 to 8). Art.95 surfaced late, sometime

[45] 'Les juges sont indépendants dans l'exercice de leur magistrature. Le pouvoir judiciaire fonctionnant dans les cadres d'un statut établi par la loi et assurant aux justiciables les garanties indispensables …'

[46] 'A titre transitoire et conformément aux dispositions de l'article 1er de la Charte du Mandat et dans une intention de justice et de concorde, les communautés seront équitablement représentées dans les emplois publics et dans la composition du ministère sans que cela puisse cependant nuire au bien de l'Etat.'

[47] Zein ed., *Mahader Munaqashat al-Dustur al-Lubnani wa Ta'dilatuh 1926–90* (Minutes of the discussions about the Lebanese Constitution and its amendments), above n.7, discussion and adoption of Art. 95 by a majority of 16 present against 6, at 74–7.

between 18 April 1926, when the Avant-Projet was sent to Paris by de Jouvenel without it, and 19 May 1926, when the final constitutional draft was submitted for discussion to the full Council of Representatives.

Could one conclude that Chiha tried to reduce the impact of communalism by seeking to limit it to legislative power, namely the Senate and Chamber of Deputies, while sparing the administration and the executive branch from the communal straitjacket?

For the answer to this question, we must examine the issue in the constitutional articles on the cabinet first, then on the administration at large.

Council of ministers

Already in the very first manuscript by Chiha, traces of Art. 95's 'language' appear regarding the Cabinet's composition. The issue surfaces in Art. 64, which we encountered in the previous chapter as a forward-looking text about preventing bureaucratic proliferation, a healthy measure which was eventually defeated. Art. 64 reads in the very first manuscript:

> There cannot be more than seven ministers, including the secretary of State, who is a minister in the same way as the others.[48] (Variant: apportion the seats). *In the composition of the Ministry, the communities are represented* insofar as the public interest does not oppose it. In the event that the President of the Republic is indisposed, the Secretary of State chairs the meeting of the Council of ministers.[49] (DOC 1, my emphasis)

[48] This '*secrétaire d'Etat*' becomes '*Ministre d'Etat*' starting DOC 17 (the word in Arabic is '*amin al-dawla*'). In the Avant-Projet of 18 April 1926 published as Annex 9 of Hokayem, *La Genèse de la Constitution Libanaise de 1926*, above n.7, Art. 59 at 364, it is back to 'Ministre d'Etat'. In the printed constitutional draft (DOC 28), he is for the first time called 'president, *ra'is*) in Art. 53. In the version presented to the CR (Hokayem, *La Genèse de la Constitution Libanaise de 1926*, Id., Annex 10, at 374), Art.53 adopts 'président du Conseil des Ministres', a title which is confirmed in the 1926 text and remains to date an important feature of bicephalism at the top of the executive branch.

[49] 'Il ne peut y avoir plus de sept ministres y compris le secrétariat d'Etat qui est un ministre au même titre que les autres. Dans la composition du Ministère, les communautés sont représentées dans la mesure où l'intérêt public ne s'y oppose pas. (Variante: Répartir les sièges) En cas d'empêchement du Président de la R.[épublique] le Secrétaire d'Etat est le président de séance au Conseil des Ministres.' There is a slight correction in DOC 3, handwritten in red: 'insofar as the public interest allows it, *dans la mesure où l'intérêt public le permet*'.

The intercalation 'Variant: apportion [or distribute] the seats' signals the option to mention the sects in each Ministry. The next versions take up the idea and develop it starting with DOC 4. Handwritten under/(Variante: répartir les sièges)/, appears the following precision: 'The four dominant communities are necessarily represented'.[50]

In light of DOC 5, these were probably meant to be the Maronite, Sunni, Shi'i and Greek Orthodox. In DOC 5, the expression/Variante: Répartir les sièges/is crossed out by hand, with the following text introduced opposite now-renumbered Art. 72:

> In the composition of the Ministry, the communities are represented insofar as the public interest allows it. The distribution is normally as follows: a Maronite, a Sunni, a Shiite, a Greek-Orthodox, a Druze, a Greek-Catholic, and a Representative of Minorities.[51]

In the next version which de Jouvenel comments on, and where the passage is inserted at now Art. 72 (DOC 6), the High Commissioner singles out the passage with a single, peremptory sentence:

> Impossible to put in the Constitution if one does not wish to see it violated, which would be very serious.[52]

Probably as a result of this harsh comment, the next version is reshuffled. Moved away from treatment in 'Fundamental principles' and 'Executive power', communalism in the Cabinet is relegated to the 'transitory' principles which include Art. 95. This transfer comes much later, in a version which circulated in April-May 1926 and which has not surfaced yet. It is only in the constitutional draft put to plenary deliberations of the CR on 19 May when we encounter it the first time.

[50] 'Les quatre communautés dominantes sont nécessairement représentées' (handwritten comment next to Art. 64 in DOC 4).

[51] 'Dans la composition du Ministère, les communautés sont représentées dans la mesure où l'intérêt public le permet. La répartition est normalement la suivante: un Maronite, un Sunnite, un Chiite, un Grec-Orthodoxe, un Druze, un Grec-Catholique, et un Représentant des Minorités' (DOC 5). Seven ministers are inscribed as the upper limit for the cabinet, with Chiha and unknown commentators trying to make the number of ministries correspond to the main sects in the country in Art.64 (renumbered as Art.72 in DOC 5).

[52] 'Impossible à mettre dans la Constitution si on ne veut pas la faire violer, ce qui serait très grave.' (DOC 6). Cited above n.1.

Since the article was anything but transitory, a subtle formulation by Chiha was inadvertently lost in the shuffling process. The Cabinet composition had been envisaged by Chiha to be communal, it is true, yet without assigning any ministerial portfolio to a specific community. This had resulted in two 'secular' provisions.

I mentioned the first provision, which is budgetary and prevents ever larger cabinets weighing on the State coffers. The concern was real, and financial scarcity affected the work of both the French and Lebanese elite throughout the Mandate. Even the resignation of HC Henri Gouraud, the founder of Great-Lebanon, was mainly caused by the slashing of his budget.[53]

The second provision is more subtle. It carries secular potential because the important portfolios *rotate* among the seven sectarian denominations. All ministers are equal, so all communities are represented in the cabinet without one community member necessarily holding an important or strategic portfolio forever. Had the limited number chosen by Chiha prevailed, the cabinet would have ended with a maximum of seven ministers and a natural rotation of the seven ministries among the communities. The limitation of the cabinet to seven members in the original draft, together with the representation of the seven main communities (including the 'minorities' category), would have allowed a Druze, or a 'minority' member like Chiha himself, to hold the defence or foreign ministry, or conceivably the presidency of the Council of ministers, on an equal standing with other ministers chosen from larger communities.

These two forward-looking provisions were paradoxically lost as a result of de Jouvenel's opposition to expressly inscribing communalism in the Constitution and the consequent reshuffle which lost them in the final text. The move away from communalism at the heart of executive power was scuttled when the number of ministers increased, sometimes to as many as 30, in addition to 'ministers without portfolios' added only to redress any perception of communitarian imbalance in the cabinet. When the formation of the Council of ministers put no limit on portfolios,

[53] Julie d'Andurain, *Le Général Gouraud- Un Destin hors du Commun, de l'Afrique au* Levant, Paris: Perrin 2022, 405–8.

the larger sects took control of the most important ones on the basis that they are more important numerically. This is not to say that a cabinet of seven, including a prime minister, would free the constitutional system from the communal straitjacket. But it would give some room for talent over identity.

What about communalism in the administration in the Chiha drafts?

Administration

As it does not appear as a full article in any of the versions of the Chiha archive and does not figure in the Avant-Projet sent to Paris by de Jouvenel on 18 April, Art. 95 emerging on 19 May 1926 to entrench communalism in the Constitution appears sudden and surprising, as if it were parachuted in by some higher decision-maker before being submitted to the CR for final discussion. A closer look at the Chiha Constitutional Papers suggests a more nuanced explanation of its emergence.

In the first four versions, one finds the following language in Art. 11:

> Civil servants are chosen for their efficiency and personal merit, whilst taking established practices into account, wherever possible, as long as this does not damage the interest of the State. Legislation will secure the legal status of civil servants (DOCs 1 to 4).[54]

In one of the early comments on this first typed draft (DOC 2), the unknown annotator, who is probably French (Souchier, or Solomiac?), put a question mark in the margin of Art. 11. He was rightly surprised by the vague expression 'taking established practices into account, wherever possible'. This requirement to take communalism on board stood in contradiction with the next clause about not harming the *bien* (good, interest) of the State. This contradiction persists to date. It was always resolved by 'practices' being considered communitarian rather than national. Hardly a position in the government, even in the lower rungs of the administration, is filled without regard to the communitarian identity of the civil servant appointed.

[54] 'Les fonctionnaires sont choisis pour leur compétence et leur mérite personnel en tenant compte dans la mesure du possible des usages, sans cependant que cela puisse nuire au bien de l'Etat. Une loi assurera aux fonctionnaires un statut légal'. DOC 4 has a slightly different arrangement in the last sentence.

The communitarian bent increased in subsequent drafts. In the second typed draft (DOC 5), the following heavily corrected and recorrected mention in Chiha's handwriting is inserted at Art.12:

> All Lebanese citizens have equal access to all public employment, according to their merit and ability and the conditions established by law.
>
> *However, given the custom in Lebanon and in the intention of justice* [crossed out: *equity*] *and concord, communities will be equitably represented in public employment, without prejudice to the interest of the state.*[55] (insertion in Italics)

Here again appears the exact language later adopted in Art. 95, this time for the administration. There is nonetheless clear resistance to the communitarian principle. A handwritten comment, not in the hand of Chiha, appears in the margin next to the corresponding passage in the next draft (DOC 6):

> This does not fit in with a Constitution. It renders the Constitution invalid the very moment it takes effect. This [constitution] is to include Lebanon within civilization. What about competency? What about merit? It [competency] is allocated by community. Blatant contradiction.[56]

This was undoubtedly de Jouvenel's handwriting, showing the High Commissioner weighing in again directly on the constitutional draft before him. It provides the most tangible indication of his active interest in the Lebanese Constitution. De Jouvenel's keenness to rid the Constitution of religious identities is confirmed in another instance. When it came to the communitarian composition of the Senate in Art.25, de Jouvenel crossed the entire article out and added an exclamation mark.

[55] 'Tous les citoyens libanais sont également admissibles à tous les emplois publics, sans autre motif de préférence que leur mérite et leur compétence et suivant les conditions fixées par la loi'.
Toutefois étant donné la coutume au Liban et dans une intention de justice [crossed out: équité] et de concorde, les communautés seront équitablement représentées dans les emplois publics, sans cependant que cela puisse nuire au bien de l'Etat' (DOC 5. Inserted text in Italics).

[56] 'Cela ne se met pas dans une Constitution. C'est la rendre caduque au moment même où on l'établit. C'est mettre le Liban dans la civilisation. Et la compétence, et le mérite? On la répartit par communauté. Contradiction criante' (DOC 6). Note the antiquated language of 'civilised and uncivilised countries', and the emotional mistake in de Jouvenel 'putting Lebanon within civilization' when he meant that the clause needs to be struck out because it would prevent Lebanon 'from being put within civilization'.

De Jouvenel was not alone in expressing his surprise at the language of communalism. In the document entitled 'Observations sur le projet de Constitution' (DOC 9), which I suggested above was written by Paul Souchier, the very first comment is about Art.12:

> Article 12- I would suggest deleting the second paragraph. [which starts '*However, and given the custom in* Lebanon', cited above at n.55.] Proportional representation of communities should be limited to the two chambers.[57]

The observation expresses the technical language of an expert jurist.[58] It suggests that communal representation ought to remain in the two chambers, but should not be forced on appointments in the civil service lest merit and competency be lost. The observation also fulfils de Jouvenel's desire to lighten the communitarian imprint in his comments on Chiha's draft.

We must now examine Art. 12 more closely to understand the battle over communalism in public service since its appearance in Chiha's handwriting (DOC 5) cited above, with him crossing out the typed text of the previous, milder reference in the corresponding articles in DOCs 1 to 4. This key clause in DOC 5, '*communities will be equitably represented in public employment,*' is limited to public employment, but it provides the base for the extension of communalism at all rungs of the executive.

To appreciate the the contest over the communalism of the Lebanese Constitution, we must follow the tracks of Art. 12 in the subsequent versions. The formula of Art. 12 is typed in DOCs 5 to 8. Souchier suggests its removal in his first observation (DOC 9). From DOC 11 onwards, the Article includes both the merit principle, and, in parenthesis, the communal clause: '(However, and given the custom in Lebanon and in the intention of justice [crossed: equity] and concord, the communities will be equitably represented in public employment, without prejudice however to the interest of the state)'.[59] In the margin of DOC 13, which is a copy of DOC 12, Chiha

[57] 'Article 12- Je serais d'avis de supprimer le deuxième alinéa. La représentation proportionnelle des communautés devrait être limitée aux deux chambres' (DOC 9).

[58] Chiha wrote in the margin a number of 'Non' on several of these 'observations.' He clearly remained in charge of the domestic side of the Constitution.

[59] French text above at n.55.

crosses out Art.12's communal passage. The communitarian straitjacket seems by then to have been spared the civil service.

The version of the Avant-Projet of 18 April 1926 sent to Paris does not include the text in Art.12.[60] Thereafter, the passage does not resurface until the final draft passed on to the Council is discussed in plenary starting 19 May. Someone, somewhere, revived the principle and added it in the shape of Art.95 to the document distributed for final deliberations. It includes the civil service, along with the composition of the government, under the principle of communal representation: '[C]ommunities will be represented equitably *in public employment* and in the composition of the government'.

The three added words made communalism also prevail for administrative appointments. Administrative and judicial appointments have remained communitarian to this day. The provisional, transitory caveat ('On a provisional basis, *à titre transitoire*') opening the article endured. 'Il n'y a que le provisoire qui dure', as goes the French saying.

Conclusion

The patchwork that resulted from an odd dance between the texts by Chiha and the various interventions, especially the comments of de Jouvenel, reveals the heavy imprint of religious communalism on the Lebanese Constitution of 1926. It can be summarised as follows:

For legislative powers, representation in both the CD and the Senate was subjected to sectarian Lebanese 'traditions' or 'customs'. Despite the clear inclination of both Chiha and de Jouvenel to temper communal entrenchment, the seats in both chambers were assigned to specific religious communities, indirectly for the deputies (by reference to the communitarian electoral laws of 1922/1925, Art. 24) and directly for the Senate (Art. 96).

For executive power, communalism was retained both for the Cabinet and the administration under Art. 95, encompassing them in an elliptic and allegedly 'transitory' formula. Appointments in the judiciary followed suit. The article became the expression of the Lebanese constitutional system and its main distinctive feature among the world constitutions. It was also the continuation of a process of institutionalised communitarianism which our

[60] Hokayem, *La Genèse de la Constitution Libanaise de 1926*, above n.7, Annex 9, at 359.

documentary trail traced back to 1834. The chance of a rotation government limited to seven ministers fell by the wayside as the constitutional march proceeded and the articles reshuffled. With that fall, the constitutional window onto a less sectarian and leaner government was firmly shut. It might have been shut anyway, but we shall never know.

Far more certainly, the Lebanese Constitution, then and now, proves the vainness of the originalism v. interpretivism debate, with the former looking into 'the four corners of the constitutional text' for its application, compared to interpretivists allowing far more leeway in their understanding of the constitutional text. Article 95 belongs to both. Interpretivists will find it easy to single out the word 'provisional' to move outside the four corners of the text and redraw the electoral map against communalism. The originalists, or literalists, will insist that meaning is to be found strictly in the text, and that only a formal constitutional revision removes the loaded 'transitional' wording.[61]

Regardless of its interpretations, the scope of the constitutional system conceived under Art. 95 is also Middle Eastern. It poses severe theoretical and practical challenges to world constitutionalism, challenges which we discuss in the last part of the book.

[61] This paragraph was added upon a query by John Borneman, who noted that the Lebanese Constitution provides a clear example of a text 'stuck in an originalist mode'. The debate bespeaks the difficulty of a deep Middle Eastern culture expressed in religious texts which are by definition sacred and immutable. Consistent with previous work, I find the opposition between an originalist (literal) v interpretivist (looking outside the four corners of the text) reading of the constitution alluring but not decisive. One can read a constitutional text in an originalist or interpretivist way without necessarily being pigeonholed as conservative (literal, originalist) or progressive (liberal, interpretivist). Even the clarity of the Qur'anic verse allowing polygamy has been interpreted in modern societies, in law and in fact, as supportive of monogamy in an evident *contra legem* yet persuasive reading. It was persuasive enough in Tunisia to ban polygamy because it is conditioned on treating all wives equally, with the condition deemed in the same verse to be impossible. *Mutatis mutandis*, one can dismiss the communalist trait of the Lebanese Constitution by arguing that both 'the transitional nature' introducing Art. 95 and the principle of the equality of citizens in Art. 7 must be read literally. At the same time, one is hard put negating communalism considering the remainder of Art. 95. In both cases, literalism/originalism and interpretivism can be used to advance one's preferred reading.

7

Building Constitutional Blocks: Modern Constitutionalism

> The President of the Republic 'ensures and oversees the execution of the laws.'
>
> M. Duguit's criticism: a vague formula which can only be implemented if the State holds regulatory powers.[1]

This chapter continues the discussion of the building blocks in Michel Chiha's Constitution, this time with reference to modern constitutional issues as opposed to the communalism dictated by the deep structures of the past. I discuss the nature of the constitutional regime and the form of government it establishes, the dual nature of the executive, as well as Chiha's interest in getting the budget constitutionalised. A final building block discussed in this chapter considers the electoral template dictated periphrastically by the Constitution.

In the course of deciding the appellation of the heads of the executive branch, Chiha was confronted with two challenges. The first concerns the nature of the regime: presidential or parliamentarian; the second, the distinction between the presidency of the Republic/State and the presidency of the Council of ministers, also known as the Prime Minister.

The nature of the constitutional regime

The mantra to date in works on the Lebanese constitution is that the country is a 'parliamentary republic'. This denomination has a long pedigree, but

[1] 'Le Président de la République 'assure et surveille l'exécution des lois'.
Critique du M. Duguit: formule obscure qui ne s'applique que par la possession du pouvoir de règlementation de l'Etat.' DOC 10.

the qualification comes with surprises. No doubt Lebanon is a republic, as opposed to a monarchy. But is it truly parliamentarian?

In Art. 3 of Chiha's first manuscript, the parliamentary dimension is mentioned expressly: 'Great Lebanon is a Republic and its government has a parliamentary form'.[2] Yet Chiha realised quickly that it was problematic to call a constitution 'parliamentarian' when the president wielded so much power in it. Already in the second typed version (DOC 3), 'parliamentarian' is struck out by hand. It also gets struck out in the typed versions DOCs 4 and 5 and disappears from the second round of drafts (DOC 6 to DOC 8, DOC 11). Thereafter, there is no mention of the form of government or of the nature of the regime beyond its being 'republican'. In the Constitution adopted in May 1926, Art. 3 reads: 'Le Grand Liban est une République'.

This is the occasion to discuss more closely what sort of political-constitutional regime Lebanon adopted in 1926. When constitutional amendments were enacted following the Ta'ef agreement more than sixty years later, the newly inserted preface to the Constitution included a clause harking back to the beginning. In the new Preface, the constitutional system is expressly considered 'parliamentarian'.[3] Whether the Ta'ef amendments accord with a parliamentary government need not detain us here.[4] In 1926, the regime was not defined constitutionally as parliamentarian.

In parliamentary regimes, the people go to the polls to elect a parliament with the understanding that parliament then chooses a head of the executive. Usually known as the Prime Minister,[5] she and the cabinet under her hold full executive powers. In the archetypal parliamentary regime of the UK, there is no president and the PM derives her considerable power from the majority in Parliament whose MPs are elected by the people. Because the UK parliament

[2] 'Art. 3: Le Grand-Liban est une République et son gouvernement a la forme parlementaire' (DOC 1).

[3] Ta'ef amendments in 1990, Preface §c: '*Lubnan jumhuriyya dimuqratiyya barlamaniyya* (Le Liban est une république démocratique parlementaire)'.

[4] On Ta'ef remaining heavily presidential, see my argument in *Al-Ri'asa al-Lubnaniyya Baynal-ams wal-Ghad* (The Lebanese presidency between yesterday and tomorrow), Beirut: Nahar 1998, 21–6.

[5] In Arabic, the translation of 'prime minister' is not literal, except in Morocco, where the Prime Minister is *al-wazir* (minister) *al-awwal* (first, or prime). Elsewhere he (or she, eventually) is 'the president (or head) of the council of ministers, *ra'is majlis al-wuzara*.

is dominated by two parties, voters also express their preference for the Prime Minister when they vote for their MP.

When there is a president in a parliamentary regime, as in Germany, the president has no legitimacy beyond that of the members of the chamber(s) who choose him. His powers are mostly limited to honorary representations of the State. This was also the case of France under the Third Republic where, despite the initially considerable power of the presidency, the Prime Minister ended up conducting executive policy.[6]

Presidential regimes are those in which the president derives his legitimacy from a direct mandate of the people in a vote dedicated to his election. The typical example is the United States, which Chiha knew well. The separation of powers tends to be strict. The cabinet which the president appoints cannot be removed by Congress. The president is fully and exclusively in charge of executive policy, domestic and foreign. Originally the US president was voted in by the electorate in two rounds, hence the aberration of the US 'electoral colleges' that persists to date. But his election was always separate from the elections for the Senate and the Chamber of Representatives. This is all summarised by Chiha in an article 'on the presidential regime'.[7] As a consequence of acquiring his legitimacy directly from the people, the legitimacy of a US president is bolstered considerably, as are his powers. But he can never dissolve parliament.

These basic features were well known to Chiha. His sharp understanding prevented the Constitution from being wrongly categorised as parliamentarian. The president is powerful throughout the text. From the first manuscript version through the final version adopted in May, the president's executive prerogatives are wide. He is referred to as 'Head of State,'[8] and as the formal

[6] During the Third Republic, the Presidency of the Council of Ministers (qua Prime Minister), bizarrely, did not exist formally in the three constitutional laws of 1875. An attempt to correct the constitutional record was led by Gaston Doumergue in 1934 failed, see below Ch. 8, section on 'The dominance of executive power'. Instead, the position, which was not formally endowed with personnel and a budget, was covered finally by the Law of 24 December 1934. See generally Guillaume Tusseau, *Droit Constitutionnel et Institutions Politiques*, 4th ed., Paris: Seuil 2022, 185. The controversy reached Lebanon and elicited Chiha's reaction; it is discussed in next chapter.

[7] 'Sur le régime présidentiel', 24 July 1952, Pol Int 238–42.

[8] 'Chef de l'Etat', Arts. 21, 75, 76 = DOC 1, Arts. 22, 55, 76. The mention of 'Chef de l'Etat' appears haphazardly in the Chiha Ms. and subsequent texts. It is probably unintentional and betrays Chiha's resistance to considering the French HC as the formal head of the state. Souchier does not

head of the executive;[9] he presides over the Council of ministers, names and dismisses all ministers, including the Prime Minister (also known as 'President of the Council of Ministers', see bicephalism below); as head of the Executive, he appoints all civil servants.[10]

On the legislative side, he holds the right to introduce bills, as do the members of the two assemblies, but he is the only official who can promulgate a law;[11] he may call the chambers to meet in extraordinary sessions during which he imposes his agenda;[12] he can request the reexamination of a law voted by the chambers, and he may adjourn their meetings for a month.[13] He can dissolve the CD after consulting the Senate;[14] and he appoints a sizeable number of senators.[15]

The Lebanese Constitution of 1926 is therefore clearly more of a presidential constitution than a parliamentary one. Only the election of the president is in the hands of parliament, making the form of government at best mixed. Once elected, the president wields vast powers, only marginally curtailed by the CD. Parliamentary oversight over the budget remains weak, as will be shown in the section on the budget below. In practice, legislation was mostly initiated and controlled by the government.

Presidential dominance was not lost to the Council of Representatives. They discussed it extensively. In the final debate, CR members accepted it both in line with the *mutasarrifiyya* tradition, and more mundanely because a powerful president would better stand up to the whims of the High Commissioner. Evidence of this attention to the enhancement of the status of the Lebanese president vis-à-vis the French HC can be found in an exchange between CR member Youssef al-Khazen and Paul Souchier. This is when Khazen proposed

notice the inconsistency and refers to 'Chef de l'Etat' in a comment on Arts. 76 and 77 (DOC 9). In 1990, the beginning of Art. 49 was amended to state that 'the President of the Republic is the Head of State and the symbol of the Nation's unity'.

9 Art. 17 = DOC 1 Art. 16.

10 Arts. 51, 55 = DOC 1 Arts. 51, 24.

11 Art. 18 = DOC 1 Art. 17. The text of the Constitution does not give the Senate the right to introduce a bill. The deletion occurred between the Avant-Projet of 18 April, where this prerogative of the Senate figures, and the text submitted to the CR plenary on 19 May, where it no longer appears.

12 Art. 33 = DOC 1 Art. 37.

13 Art 59 = DOC 1 Art. 59.

14 Art. 55 = DOC 1 Art. 57.

15 Art. 22 = DOC 1 Art. 21.

an addendum to Art. 53 of the Constitution on the powers of the president to include 'representation by the president of the country at home and abroad'.[16]

Souchet had no immediate reaction to the proposed amendment, probably because he was waiting for the translation. CR members Ibrahim Mundher, Mas'ud Yunis and Georges Zouein continued meanwhile the conversation about the wide power the Article gave the president to appoint ministers and civil servants. Souchier, who by then has received the translation, asks 'what the objective of Sheikh Khazen's proposed amendment was'.

Khazen: I mean that the president, if he travels to Paris, represents the country [Lebanon] there.

Souchier: Your amendment contradicts Art. 3 of the Charter of the Mandate.

Khazen: But with regard to the country exercising the Mandate [France], if he travels to Paris, does he not represent the country [Lebanon]?

Souchier: He represents the country [Lebanon] in Beirut and within the country. As for his representation abroad, it is up to the country exercising the Mandate [France], and the president represents the country [Lebanon] through that country [France exercising the Mandate].

Souchier's convoluted answer was not too convincing. The minutes then report that the discussion continued between the two men, with Khazen asking for the debate to be postponed until the 'declaration on the Mandate'. The majority opposed him, and the text as it stood was agreed by all over his dissent.

When the 'declaration' came, on the last day, Souchier issued a simple diktat.[17] The HC's powers overrode practically every prerogative of every

[16] Ahmad al-Zein ed., *Mahader Munaqashat al-Dustur al-Lubnani wa Ta'dilatuh 1926–90* (Minutes of the discussions about the Lebanese Constitution and its amendments), Beirut: Publications of the Chamber of Deputies 1993, 57. Id. for all quotes of the CR plenary debate in the next paragraphs.

[17] Declaration of Souchier in French in Antoine Hokayem, *La Genèse de la Constitution Libanaise de 1926*, Antélias: Les Editions Universitaires du Liban 1996, Annex 12, 392; for text in Arabic, Ahmad al-Zein ed., *Mahader Munaqashat al-Dustur al-Lubnani wa Ta'dilatuh 1926–90* (Minutes of the discussions about the Lebanese Constitution and its amendments), Beirut: Publications of the Chamber of Deputies 1993, 83–4, together with Souchier's reminder that

Lebanese official, in addition to allowing him to appoint, at will, advisors to assist in exercising his vast powers domestically and abroad.

In the CR plenary, there was pushback in favor of a larger role for Parliament, with rich discussion of Art. 55 and the president's power to dissolve the CD. In the form submitted to the CR, the text is close to Chiha's original, more compact formula. It ended up being much longer because of two additional paragraphs concerning 'reasons' for dissolution. Chiha's original text was approved, with additions italicised below:

> The President of the Republic may, by reasoned decree taken in the Council of Ministers, and with the assent of the Senate expressed by a three-quarters majority of the members composing this Assembly, dissolve the Chamber of Deputies before the legal expiry of his mandate. *The grounds on which the President of the Republic can dissolve the Chamber are:*
>
> 1. *Refusal of the Chamber to meet in ordinary or extraordinary session notwithstanding two successive convocations called by the Head of State.*
> 2. *Rejection of the budget with the intention of paralyzing government action.*
> 3. *Making decisions that may rally the country against the mandate or the constitution.*
>
> In this case, the electoral colleges meet as provided for in Article 30 and the new Chamber is convened within ten days of the proclamation of the election result. *A second dissolution cannot take place for the same reason as the first.*[18]

the CR members were to be merely informed, since 'there was no room for [dis]approval' of the declaration. Id., 83.

[18] 'Le Président de la République peut, par décret motivé pris en Conseil des ministres, et sur l'avis conforme du Sénat exprimé à la majorité des trois quarts des membres composant cette Assemblée, dissoudre la Chambre des députés avant l'expiration légale de son mandat. Les motifs pour lesquels le Président de la République peut dissoudre la Chambre sont:

1. Le refus de la Chambre de se réunir en session ordinaire ou extraordinaire nonobstant deux convocations faites successivement par le Chef de l'Etat.
2. Le rejet du budget dans l'intention de paralyser l'action du gouvernement.
3. Le fait de prendre des décisions susceptibles de soulever le pays contre le mandat ou la constitution.

The three conditions added to curtail the president's power of dissolution can be called 'the Dammous amendment'.[19] The amendment was triggered in the CR's afternoon session of 22 May by Georges Zouein calling for renewed discussion of the matter of dissolution. This was taken up by Jamil Talhuq, who reminded his colleagues that dissolution had not been discussed in earlier sessions. CR President Musa Nammour then read the relevant section of Art. 55, and Zouein, supported by his colleague Youssef al-Khazen, launched into a lengthy diatribe on the difficulties which the Third Republic had encountered on the one occasion it had attempted to dissolve parliament, in 1875.[20] Zouein's disquisition was cut down unceremoniously by the minute-taker, who reports one sentence only, on Zouein's unease with the right of the president to dissolve parliament: 'In my view', Zouein said, 'when a disagreement takes place between the executive power and the legislative power, both powers need to put themselves up [for re-election] to the Nation'.[21]

Several CR members expressed their agreement with Zouein, generally on similar grounds. At this point Dammous intervened, relating the lively discussion about the Article 'in committee'.[22] This was, he explained, 'like the knot which Alexander cut'. The knot was cut, Dammous said, by dissolving parliament while retaining the government of the day lest both fall 'and chaos ensues'.[23] What then? Well, he went on, it is difficult to compare the situation of Lebanon with that of European countries, because Lebanon has not reached the stage of having political parties. Without pressure from political

En ce cas, les collèges électoraux sont réunis comme il est prévu à l'article 30 et la nouvelle Chambre est convoquée dans les dix jours qui suivent la proclamation des résultats des élections. Une deuxième dissolution ne peut pas avoir lieu pour le même motif que la première'.

19 Lengthy discussions on Art. 55 in the CR at Zein ed., *Mahader Munaqashat al-Dustur al-Lubnani wa Ta'dilatuh 1926–90* (Minutes of the discussions about the Lebanese Constitution and its amendments), above n.17, 78–81.

20 Zouein at Id. at 79, Khazen at 80.

21 Id. 79.

22 *'al-lajna'*. Dammous, id. 79. This is an important incidental indication on the committee discussions, without further details unfortunately. These committee discussions are not available in the documentation of the drafting process, but the passing mention of Dammous shows the seriousness of the pre-plenary debates 'in committee'. There are several other instances in the CR debates on 19–22 May to previous deliberations 'in committee', including by Souchier, showing that he attended some. There are no details on the occasion, date or nature of these committees in the available archives.

23 Id. 80.

parties, there is no way to force a lazy Parliament to do its work other than by the executive threatening to dissolve it.

Khazen then intervened again, deflecting the debate somewhat with two awkward comparisons: why remove a parliamentarian when the president may not dismiss a judge by executive power? Why, then, would a parliamentarian be required to go home, he who has a general mandate from the Nation?[24]

It was getting late. The CR agreed to take a break for dinner, and the meeting resumed at 10 pm. It picked up Dammous's mention of the alternative formulation, as well as other options raised by Khazen, Subhi Haydar and 'Umar Bayhum. They were read, but we do not have their text in the minutes. The president brought the debate to a close, and three options went to the vote: a full deletion of the Article, and the two unreported proposals by Haydar and Bayhum. All were defeated and the president then put Dammous' formulation to a vote. It was approved by all except Haydar and Bayhum. This became Art. 55 as adopted in the 1926 Constitution, cited above, with the right given to the president to dissolve Parliament under the three conditions added to the original text of Chiha.[25]

The prospect of rendering it easier for the president to dissolve the CD would resurface soon after the Senate was abolished in 1927. The three conditions were then deleted in an amendment effected in 1929. The by then unfettered right given to the president to dissolve parliament consecrated the dominant presidential nature of the regime. The president was now able to designate and dismiss all ministers, *and* to dissolve parliament upon approval by a Council of Ministers over which he presided. In 1988–9, the use of this amendment triggered one of the worst constitutional crises in the Lebanese wars. In a constitutional coup, the commander-in-chief of the army, who had been appointed prime minister at the end of the former president's term, unilaterally dismissed the cabinet and dissolved Parliament. Two opposed governments arose, with the crisis solved only after a massive military attack two years later to dislodge the main coup protagonists. As a result, both the presidential

[24] Id. 80.

[25] The three conditions are cited in text accompanying n.18 above.

prerogative to appoint and dismiss ministers at will, and the right to dissolve Parliament, were removed at Ta'ef.[26]

The adoption of the Dammous amendment by the CR, on the last day of the plenary, shows how the main representatives had understood that parliament's role and legitimacy were no less important than the president's, and that the latter should not be given the freedom to dissolve parliament. Sixty years later, the loss of this informed, premonitory constaint, would cost the country dearly.

Eventually, the Lebanese system turned out to be neither fully parliamentarian nor fully presidential in received legal categories, but leaned heavily towards the latter in practice. Meanwhile, another particularity of the Lebanese Constitution slowly emerged in the journey of Chiha's draft, namely bicephalism in executive power.

The emergence of a bicephalous executive

Dual leadership at the helm has long been a characteristic of constitutions. Constitutional monarchies are based on designated dynasties with King, Emperor, Sultan sitting as the head of state for life, and his powerful and revocable subordinate running the country's daily affairs. The gamut of bicephalism is wide. Even in absolutist countries, a division of labor develops naturally when the administration expands and policy becomes complex, such that the absolute ruler requires a capable aide – the grand viziers of the Ottoman Empire and the chancellors of the French kings. In a republic, dual headship can take the form of an honorary president supported by the leader of the executive branch, as in the president and the president of the council of ministers in the French Third Republic, or a president and a chancellor as in the German Constitution of 1949.

The Lebanese tradition was familiar with bicephalism well before the 1926 Constitution, since the local Emir, however powerful in his farm-taxing realm, was subordinate not only to the Sultan in Istanbul, to whom he had little or no access, but to Ottoman-appointed governors (*wali, wulat*) in coastal cities like Sidon or Acre, sometimes even in the regional metropole of Damascus.

[26] The crisis split the country in two and resulted in the return to full Syrian military control of Lebanon.

During the Mutasarrifiyya, there was no president in Mount Lebanon's Administrative Council, as the *mutasarref* remained the official and effective ruler of the region. Slowly, as we saw when discussing the Mutasarrifiyya, a Lebanese vice-head of the AC emerged. Similarly, in the early years of the Mandate, the Haut Commissaire was flanked by a Gouverneur of Lebanon.

This was the legacy that fell to Chiha and his colleagues. The Lebanese public was living bicephalism at the top every day, and the duality continued throughout the Mandate. Well after the Constitution was enacted, the High Commissioner ruled in the name of France and took all key decisions, while a president of the Republic elected by the Chamber of Deputies was in charge of marginal issues.

Was it useful to distinguish in the Constitution between a president and a prime minister and thereby complicate executive decision-making? Was it necessary for a president of the republic, the holder of executive power, to be flanked by another 'president of the council of ministers', also known as the prime minister?

Constitutional practice eventually adopted bicephalism, but successive constitutional drafts show much hesitation amongst the drafters. The process establishing bicephalous power at the top of the executive was halting during the drafting period; once adopted, however, the bicephalous nature of the regime proved inexorable, in large part because of communalism.

We can start our demonstration of this argument with Art. 53 of the 1926 Constitution, which reads in relevant part that '[t]he President of the Republic appoints and dismisses the ministers amongst whom he appoints a president of the Council of ministers'.[27]

The formulation remains awkward in the original French (and in my English literal translation). Redundancy betrays the dilemma that the constitutional drafters faced. Not only is '*a* president' slightly derogatory, but the last five words in the phrase are unnecessary. Of note in Chiha's manuscript, the p in /president/ of the Council of Ministers is in lower case. This suggests that the position was not as highly considered as that of the President of the Republic. The lowercase president was subordinated to the uppercase

[27] 'Le Président de la République nomme et révoque les ministres parmi lesquels il désigne un président du Conseil des ministres'.

President in practically all decision-making since the P can dismiss p the same way he can dismiss, at will, the other ministers.

Turning to Arabic now. Arabic does not know capital letters. The article reads in literal translation:

> *ra'is al-jumhuriyya yu'ayyen al-wuzara' wa yusammi minhum ra'isan wa yuqiluhum.*
>
> The President of the Republic appoints the ministers and he appoints a President among them and he dismisses them (Art. 53).

Again, the formulation is awkward. Why was it difficult to fix the language in Arabic and in French?

The answer is not merely linguistic. Let us follow the development of the text since Chiha's first draft.

In the very first manuscript under 'Title II- Des Pouvoirs, Ch1[er] Dispositions Générales', Chiha writes: 'Executive power belongs to the President of the Republic assisted by a Secretary of State and ministers under the conditions established by the present Constitution'[28] (DOC 1). In the text, he crosses out two expressions. The first is 'et à ses ministres' after 'Président de la République'. Had it remained, the text would have read: 'Executive power belongs to the President of the Republic assisted by his ministers ...', and the Lebanese form of government would have been closer to the American model, with a cabinet headed by the president who dismisses its members at will. The second crossed-out expression was more important. Under 'Secrétaire d'Etat', Chiha wrote, in parenthesis, then crossed out, 'président du conseil', with both the p of 'président' and c in 'conseil' in lower case.

Art. 55, Title II.4 of the Constitution, provides a sharper text: 'The president of the Republic appoints and dismisses the Secretary of State and the other ministers; (...) he presides over the council of ministers'.[29]

Here also, an alternative formulation is crossed out in Chiha's text: 'Le président de la République nomme et révoque le Secrétaire d'Etat président

[28] Le pouvoir exécutif appartient au Président de la République assisté par un Secrétaire d'Etat et des ministres dans les conditions établies par la présente constitution' (DOC 1 Art.16).

[29] 'Le président de la République nomme et révoque le Secrétaire d'Etat et les autres ministres; (...) il préside le conseil des ministres' (Art. 55 of the Constitution).

~~du Conseil~~ et les autres ministres ~~sur la proposition du Secrétaire d'Etat~~; (...) il préside le conseil des ministres' (DOC 1). The two deleted clauses show that the 'Secretary' was originally the president of the council of ministers in Chiha's mind, and that his role was mostly perfunctory since he only proposes a list of ministers from which the president chooses those he wishes to appoint.

The name then changes as documents proceed. We have an incoherent replacement of Ministre d'Etat by Secrétaire d'Etat (and vice-versa) through the various versions.[30]

The uncertainty remains until the intervention of Souchier (DOC 9).[31] Taking up Art. 17 in the version 'Minister of State' which appears in the four successive DOCs 5, 6, 7, 8, his comment in the margin of Art.17 reads: 'Replace everywhere "Minister of State" with "president of the Council of ministers".'[32]

This complicated deconstruction shows, I think, the reason why we end up with the awkward formulation of Art. 53 in the Constitution with which we started the discussion.

Again, the matter is not merely one of style. The successive changes led to the disappearance in the text of the Constitution of both 'Secretary' and 'Ministre d'Etat', and their replacement by 'the president of the Council of ministers'. Both the President of the Republic and the President of the Council

[30] In more detail, here are the changes, though they are hard to understand without having the manuscripts in hand:

In DOCs 3 and 4, Chiha crosses out 'Secrétaire' and replaces it with 'Ministre' (Art. 16). This is also changed in the same way in Art. 55. DOC 5, where the same typed text is renumbered because of the addendum of the article on the flag, the corresponding Arts. 17 and 60 have the same crossed out 'Secrétaire' d'Etat and its replacement by 'Ministre' d'Etat.

In DOC 6, the one annotated by de Jouvenel, the text is completely retyped. It integrates the change to 'Ministre d'Etat' in both Arts.17 and 60. The clause 'il préside le conseil des Ministres' is crossed out by hand in red ink, so probably by Chiha. This is again crossed out in DOC 7, and the new typed version in DOC 8 finalises the article in a clean manner, without hand-written deletions. 'Secrétaire d'Etat' is used again, as a mere assistant to the president of the Republic, in the manuscript of DOC 19, and the incomplete typed documents on the 'Pouvoir Exécutif' (DOCs 19, 20, 21), which we I have suggested that they probably preceded the first manuscript version as general preparatory drafts.

[31] Souchier's position comes after a point in the Duguit Document where a president of the council is considered redundant. See Chapter 5, section on Chiha and Duguit.

[32] 'Art. 17.- Remplacer partout 'le ministre d'Etat' par 'le président du conseil des ministres'. (Souchier, DOC 9).

of ministers are *ra'is* in Arabic. Chiha's ambivalence triggered Souchier's comment about the need to streamline the text. The consequences were significant on the dualist nature of the executive. Souchier's correction led to the bicephalous character of the Lebanese Constitution in executive power, with endless disputes and deadlocks to date with two 'presidents'. For after a brief period where the country knew two Christian 'presidents', one of the Republic, the other of the Council of ministers,[33] the dominant logic of Christian-Muslim communalism eventually froze the first presidency into a Maronite position, and the second presidency into a Sunni one. The non-written arrangement is known as the 1943 National Pact (*mithaq watani*). We pick up the story later, when bicephalism turns into a series of enduring deadlocks under the communitarian straitjacket.

Chiha's budgetary concerns

The Lebanese Constitution is budget top-heavy. It includes a full section on 'Finance' with nine articles (Arts. 81 to 89). Considering how short the constitution,[34] it reflects the personal attention of Chiha to budgetary matters.

Chiha was a financier as well as a jurist, professionally a man of banking and numbers. The public finance section in the Constitution, from the first draft (DOC 1) on, is much longer than the one found in the constitution of the Third Republic, which includes financial and budgetary provisions perfunctorily. In the three laws forming the 1875 Constitution of the French republic, only two articles mention finance. The first article does so amongst a myriad other prerogatives of the President.[35] The second article, on the powers of the Senate, specifies that '... finance laws must first be introduced in

[33] As mentioned previously, Charles Debbas, a Greek Orthodox, was elected by the CR in 1926 as the first President of the Republic. Béchara El-Khoury, a Maronite, was chosen by Debbas as the first President of the Council of ministers. Throughout the Mandate, changes occurred in the religious denomination of the holders of both positions, but the presidency was always Christian.

[34] 102 short articles upon its adoption, far less when the Senate was suppressed in 1927, and 90 articles when the Mandate articles were removed upon Independence.

[35] Art. 8 §2, Art. 8 §2, Constitution de 1875, IIIe République- Loi constitutionnelle du 16 juillet 1875 sur les rapports des pouvoirs publics: 'Les traités de paix, de commerce, les traités *qui engagent les finances de l'Etat*, ceux qui sont relatifs à l'état des personnes et au droit de propriété des Français à l'étranger, ne sont définitifs qu'après avoir été votés par les deux chambres ...' (Emphasis added.)

the Chamber of Deputies and voted on by it'.[36] There are no other financial clauses in the text.[37]

Chiha saw otherwise. If not from the Third Republic, where did this lengthy section on the budget come from?

We know that Chiha was familiar with the Egyptian Constitution of 1923, an Arabic copy of which we find in his papers, along with four other contemporaneous constitutions, all adopted after 1920: Lithuania, Latvia (French Lettonie), Finland and Romania (List at DOC 16).

On budgetary arrangements, the Egyptian Constitution includes a full section on finance, and it is clear that Chiha relied mostly on this text.[38] A section on finances is common in constitutions enacted at the time. Except for the Latvian Constitution of 1922, where the budget is addressed briefly in Art. 66, and only in passing in two other articles (Arts. 73, 81), extensive budgetary clauses appear in the Lithuanian Constitution of 1922 (Arts. 91 to 96), in the Finland constitution of 1919 'on the form of government' (Arts. 61 to 74), and in the Constitution of Romania of 1923 (Arts. 109 to 118), all collected in a special folder of Chiha's papers (DOC 16).

These budgetary texts are generally similar in all these constitutions, and the section on finance in the Lebanese Constitution would be familiar to a constitutionalist in any of these countries. The close similarity is evident from the very first Chiha manuscript. DOC 1 includes six articles.[39] The first five articles state that a tax can be established, modified or annulled only by law (Art. 81); that the budget is annual and written into law for the following year (Art. 82);[40] that

[36] '... les lois de finances doivent être, en premier lieu, déposées à la Chambre des députés et votées par elle Art. 8 §2, Constitution de 1875, IIIe République- Loi du 24 février 1875 relative à l'organisation du Sénat.

[37] It also turns out in the minutes of the CR discussions that Paul Souchier thought that budgetary articles should not be included in the Constitution. Souchier: 'I said [in committee] that articles dealing with finance do not have a place in the constitution.' Zein ed., *Mahader Munaqashat al-Dustur al-Lubnani wa Ta'dilatuh 1926–90* (Minutes of the discussions about the Lebanese Constitution and its amendments), above n.17, 68. The CR members devoted a long discussion to the section in Finance. Id., 66–72.

[38] Egyptian Constitution of 1923, *maliyya*, Arts. 134 to 145.

[39] We saw that Art. 86, the sixth article of the Finances section and the last one in DOC1 had only one word (/Aucu/), with the rest of the paper torn out. See DOC 1 and Ch. 4, n.46.

[40] Equivalents in Art. 66§1 Lettonie (Latvia Constitution of 1922); Lithuania Constitution of 1922, Arts. 91 and 94; Finland Constitution of 1919, Arts 65, 67; Romania Constitution of 1923, Art. 109. Egypt Constitution of 1923, Arts. 134, 138.

it is drawn up for the legislators' examination and vote, article by article, in the October session (Art. 82). If parliament fails to approve it in March, the government may fall back on the previous budget (Art. 84).[41] Any additional expense incurred by the government when the two chambers of parliament are not meeting must be submitted for approval at the next legislative session (Art. 83).[42]

In DOC 5, an article is added at the beginning of the Finances section about the need to levy taxes only for the public interest, in a uniform manner across all Lebanese territory (DOC 5 Art. 89). Two additional articles develop marginal remarks on 'concessions' and 'borrowings' (with a comment by Chiha: 'see Constit. Egypt'), and 'treaties' in the margin of DOC 3. The full texts are included by hand in DOC 5 and renumbered (Arts. 95, 96). In the clean, retyped copies that follow (DOCs 6, 7, 8), these three articles complete the section. One appreciates the concision and clarity of Chiha's style, and his synthetical abilities. With one exception, the texts remained virtually untouched until their adoption in May 1926.

This one exception, which will weigh on the adoption of the budget in subsequent troubled times, appears in a substantive change in the course of drafting. It first surfaces in a marginal comment next to Art. 93 in DOC 7. The comment says '1/12 *provisoire*' but is struck out. It does not appear to be in Chiha's handwriting, but Chiha includes it in the next typed version (Art. 93, DOC 8). In the final text of the Constitution adopted in May, by then renumbered, Art. 86 reads:

> If the Chambers have not voted the budget of the next financial year before its start, taxes, contributions, fees, dues and other revenues continue to be collected as before and the expenses are incurred monthly *on the basis of the provisional twelfth of the previous financial year*, increased by additional and permanent supplementary appropriations and diminished by permanent reductions until the promulgation of the new budget.[43] (Emphasis added.)

[41] Similar articles only in Egypt's Constitution of 1923, Art. 142, and in Romania's Constitution of 1923, Art. 114.

[42] Equivalents in Art. 66§2 Lettonie (Latvia Constitution of 1922); Lithuania Constitution of 1922, Arts. 91; Finland Constitution of 1919, Art. 66; Romania Constitution of 1923, Art. 114. No equivalent in Egypt's Constitution of 1923.

[43] 'Art. 86- Si les Chambres n'ont pas voté le budget d'un exercice avant l'ouverture de cet exercice, les impôts, contributions, taxes, droits et autres recettes continuent d'être perçus comme précédemment et les dépenses sont engagées mensuellement sur la base du douzième provisoire de

The 'provisional twelfth' was an addendum which had by then become customary in the Third Republic. It must have been suggested to Chiha by a French jurist familiar with budgetary practice in France, most likely Souchier.[44] Rather than risking shutting down institutions and suspending payments for the coming year if the budget failed to be voted in time, 'the twelfth' was devised to allow salaries and other pressing expenses to be continued by a unilateral government decision. This could be repeated as needed to prevent the shutdown of institutions with civil servants left unpaid. Confirmation by parliament would come later when the budget was eventually approved.

Post hoc confirmation of 'the twelfths' is in fact the only option available, since it is inconceivable to retrospectively defund items already paid for by the government.[45] In Lebanon, 'the provisional twelfth' was a mechanism destined to become a mainstay of the budget. Instead of extending the previous year's budget, adding expenses monthly proved a necessary tool after the country became independent. This became a lasting feature for deadlocked institutions, until a decision of the Constitutional Council in 2017 invalidated the practice as unconstitutional.[46]

Electoral templates

Michel Chiha inherited an uncompromisingly communitarian electoral law. This was the law of 1925 under which he and the 29 members of the CR were elected. The law of 1925 was itself the calque of the law of 1922 that saw the emergence of the first CR as a body elected on a communitarian basis. Both CRs followed the results of the census carried out in 1921, and assigned seats in proportion to the size of each sect in the population. The distribution of seats in the CR of 1922, replicated in 1925, is summarised in Table 7.1 for

l'exercice précédent, majorées des crédits additionnels et supplémentaires permanents et diminuées des réductions permanentes, jusqu'à la promulgation du nouveau budget'.

44 Handwritten comment in DOC 9 at Art. 93.

45 As a measure of doubtable democratic legitimacy since it impinged on the central role of parliament in controlling budgetary laws, it was discontinued in the French Fifth Republic.

46 It took almost a century for the recognition of the legal necessity to complete the budget in time, which is now acknowledged as a constitutional rule by the Lebanese Constitutional Council, Decision of 22 September 2017, available online on the site of the Lebanese University, ul.edu.lb. The last section reads: 'The Constitutional Council agrees unanimously ... that refraining from the adoption of an annual budget and from the completion of appropriations for every year constitutes a flagrant violation of the Constitution'.

*Table 7.1 Population and number of seats; 1925 Council of Representatives/1926 Chamber of Deputies**

	Maronite	Sunni	Shi'i	Orthodox	Druze	Catholic	Protestant	Others	Total
Beirut	Pop.17763	32882	3274	12672	1522	4256	544	4907	77820
Deputies	1	2		1			1 minorities		5
Tripoli	2076	26094	3	6824	10	186	185	764	36153
Deputies		1							1
North Lebanon	52719	23594	451	28932	11	962	298	844	107791
Deputies	2	1		1					4
Mount Lebanon	97368	9333	7523	15519	33478	8801	1207	569	73798
Deputies	5			1	2				8
South Lebanon	17255	13397	62796	5673	3519	11242	1334	629	115945
Deputies	1	1	3			1			6
Bekaa	11980	19506	30900	11789	5102	17015	547	723	97562
Deputies	1	1	2	1		1			6
Total	Pop.199181	124786	104947	81409	43633	42462	4215	8436	609069
	10	6	5	4	2	2		1 minorities	30

* Muhammad Murad, *Al-Intikhabat al-Niyabiyya fi Lubnan 1920–2009* (Parliamentary elections in Lebanon 1920–2009), Beirut: Publications of the Lebanese University 2013, 87.

*Table 7.2 Communitarian composition of legislative chambers 1922–2025**

	1922	1925	1929	1934	1937	1943	1947	1951	1953	1957	1960	1964	1968	1972	1991	1992–
Sunni	6	9	9	5	13	11	11	16	9	14	20	20	20	20	22	27
Shi'i	5	8	8	4	11	10	10	14	8	12	19	19	19	19	22	27
Druze	2	3	3	2	4	4	4	5	3	4	6	6	6	6	8	8
Alawite	0	0	0	0	0	0	0	0	0	0	0	0	0	0	2	2
Maronite	10	15	15	7	20	18	18	23	13	20	30	30	30	30	30	34
Orthodox	4	6	6	3	7	6	6	8	5	7	11	11	11	11	11	14
Catholic	2	3	3	2	4	3	3	5	3	4	6	6	6	6	6	8
Armenian Orthodox	0	0	0	1	2	2	2	3	2	3	4	4	4	4	4	5
Armenian Catholic	0	0	0	0	0	0	0	1	0	1	1	1	1	1	1	1
Minorities	1	2	1	1	2	1	1	1	1	1	1	1	1	1	1	1
Protestant	0	0	0	0	0	0	0	1	0	0	1	1	1	1	1	1
Total	30	46	45	25	63	55	55	77	44	66	99	99	99	99	99	128–

* Id., 456, adjusted to 2025.

the first Chamber of Representatives, renamed Chamber of Deputies by the Constitution:

The template has lived through the French Mandate and since Independence in its main general traits. Table 7.2 tracks the template through successive Chambers:

The 1922/1925 law marks a turning point in Lebanese institutional history. For the first time, the system was based on universal (male) suffrage for Lebanese nationals aged at least 21, listed on the electoral register in their voting district, paying taxes, and able to read and write.[47] The election was a two-stage process,[48] following the precedents set in Mount Lebanon and in the Ottoman elections.[49] This changed only in 1934, when the electoral system gave way to the direct election of all candidates by habilitated (male) voters.[50] But control by the HC remained in sundry ways until Independence: dissolution of Parliament, suspension of the Constitution, unilateral amendment, appointment of deputies.

The number of deputies varied significantly over the years, more often upwards than downwards.[51] The 16-member Senate established by the Constitution lasted only one year, and its members were integrated into the CD, so 46 in total.[52] The CD was then diminished by one seat to 45 between 1929 and 1932. The number was drastically reduced in the third Chamber, also partly elected, with 25 MPs from 1932 to 1937. In 1937–39, by then a one-stage system for the election, the CD's size increased to 62. After the war interlude, Independence in 1943 allowed elections to be fully free from

[47] Law of 1922/1925, Arts. 6, 26. Text of Arrêté 1307 (or Electoral Law of 1922) in for instance Muhammad Murad, *Al-Intikhabat al-Niyabiyya fi Lubnan 1920–2009* (Parliamentary elections in Lebanon 1920–2009), Beirut: Publications of the Lebanese University 2013, Appendix 1, 466–79.

[48] Id., Art.6.

[49] Discussed in Chapter 3.

[50] L.R./ Arrêté 1, OJ 2916, 12.1.1934, in full in Majed Khalil Majed, *Al-Intikhabat al-Niyabiyya 1861–1992* (Parliamentary elections 1861–1992), Beirut: al-Mu'assasa al-jami'yya lil-dirasat wal-nashr 1992 55–57, 'one-tier' election at 56.

[51] All numbers and dates can be found on the parliament's website, tab '*lamha tarikhiyya lil-majlis al-niyabi* (historical outline of the CD)', at https://www.lp.gov.lb/CustomPage?Id=9.

[52] When the first amendment fused the two chambers into one, Art. 51 of the Constitutional Amendment Law, Qanun ta'dil al-dustur al-lubnani (17 October 1927), was added as a temporary article, see text in Zein ed., *Mahader Munaqashat al-Dustur al-Lubnani wa Ta'dilatuh 1926–90*, above n.17, 185.

French interference, with deputies no longer appointed. The electoral law adjusted the number of parliamentarians to 55 in 1943, with an arithmetic formula of *khamsi/sitti mukarrar*, or five/six repeated, as the basis of increase (or decrease) to preserve the Muslim Christian balance *rebus sic stantibus*. The ratio of six Christians to five Muslims was retained in all subsequent elections until 1972, which was the last parliamentary election held before 1992 because of the protracted troubles between 1975 and 1990.[53] While the assignment of the top three positions between the three largest communities remained unchanged, the number of deputies in Parliament would be augmented from Independence to 1992, as rule of thumb, by the same formula of a multiple of five deputies for Muslims (Sunnis, Shiʿis and Druze), and a corresponding multiple of six for the rest of the communities, principally Christian. Maronites came first as the largest Christian community, then by order of size, Greek Orthodox, Greek Catholic, Armenians divided in smaller Orthodox and Catholic churches, in addition to 'minorities', which comprises everything else, including Syriac Catholics, Protestants, and Jews.

All the communally designated seats had been fixed according to the official census carried out in 1932. Before the Mandate, there had been various censuses, accurate enough but not official.[54] The Law of 1922 was based on an official census completed on 31 January 1922, which allowed the communitarian distribution of seats calculated on the basis of a roster of the Lebanese nationals entitled to vote in the new territory carved out by France.[55]

Similar to all countries where groups with unalterable traits form distinct minorities, numbers in these groups are important for all kinds of discriminatory practices, including constitutional ones. A census is always a major exercise. The fact that the last official Lebanese census was carried out in 1932, and

[53] With the increase in the population, the five/six ratio applied to the seventh parliament (77 members from 1951 to 1953), to the ninth parliament (66 from 1957 to 1960) and to all parliaments between 1960 and 1976 (99 members).

[54] For census of the Lebanese population of Mount Lebanon and its sectarian distribution in the nineteenth century, Dominique Chevallier, *La Société du Mont Liban à l'Epoque de la Révolution Industrielle en Europe*, Paris: Geuthner 1971, 50–1 (1840), 62 (1860).

[55] Census mentioned in Art. 4 of the Law of 1922: 'The number of voters amongst the population is that of the sons of Great Lebanon whose names have been registered in Registers A and B of the census registry, in addition to all those whose names appear in Registry E on condition that they have been paying to the State one of the decreed taxes'.

never revisited since, is easily understood. A state-ordered census commands a corresponding redistribution of seats for the various communities. With the sense of decline of Christians relative to Muslims, and the perceived rise of the Shiʿi community in particular, neither the Christian nor the Sunni traditional leaderships found usefulness in a new census.[56] Few politicians or religious leaders outside the Shi'i community would allow a census that gives an official stamp acknowledging the demographic ascendancy of the Shi'is.

As elsewhere, demographic changes developed slowly over the twentieth century. All 30 CR members had been elected on the basis of the 1922/1925 template, and the faint attempt to do away with communal quotas by HC Maurice Sarrail and the anti-clerical and hardcore secularists in France and in Lebanon was defeated. There was therefore a vested interest in keeping the same electoral format, which persists to date in its core communitarian principle.

* * *

Electoral laws never come in a void, and their progress, in the absence of a revolution, is glacially slow. On the democratic side of the balance, universal suffrage enshrined under HC Ponsot in 1934 removed the two degrees hampering the direct connection between the citizen's vote and his parliamentary representative. This was followed by the post-Independence political leadership eliminating appointed deputies, and the extension of voting to women. On the negative side of the balance, in addition to skewing the electoral law in favor of the sitting president's faction (in 1948, in 1957, and in 2017), parliamentary elections have been marred by irregularities of various gravity ranging from stuffed ballots to militias controlling the outcome no matter the circumstances.

[56] The census of 1932 confirms the trend in the previous 1922 Census of the slow decline of Christians relative to Muslims. Numbers in Muhammad Murad, *Al-Intikhabat al-Niyabiyya fi Lubnan 1920–2009* (Parliamentary elections in Lebanon 1920–2009), Beirut: Publications of the Lebanese University 2013, at p. 32 for the Census of 1922 and at p. 35 for the Census of 1932. In 1932, Maronites were at 29 pc, down from 32 pc in 1922; Sunnis at 22 pc, up from 20 pc in 1922, and Shiʿis at 20 pc in 1932, up from 17 pc in 1922. The numbers are complicated by the category of Lebanese emigrants counted in or excluded from the census. See Thibaut Jaulin, 'Démographie et politique au Liban sous le Mandat', *Histoire et Mesure*, 24, 2009, 189–210.

Irrespective of these common distortions of electoral processes, a specific structural flaw in the dysfunction of Lebanese democracy came with the reinforcement of the communitarian principle by two social-historical realities which the Constitution does not mention.

The first is the absence of political parties. Already in 1926, the CR members were well aware of the fateful absence of that key component of constitutional life. The country was young, and political leaders rose to the occasion soon thereafter, as haphazard factionalism characteristic of the early years gradually made room for the institutionalisation of differences in political parties. Throughout the period of the Mandate, efforts were directed at forming parties without obvious ties to communities. Sharply opposed factions emerged during the Mandate around two key figures and their parties, Béchara El-Khoury, Lebanon's first post-Independence president (1943–1952),[57] and Emile Eddé, who was president in the last years of the Mandate (1936–41).[58] Other smaller parties emerged during the Mandate, but political life was dominated by the two Maronite politicians, and the institutional opposition naturally focused on the most important constitutional position in the country, the presidency. During the Mandate, the battle between Khoury's constitutionalists (*dusturi*s),) and their rivals (Eddé's '*kitlawis*') revolved around the presidency under the watchful eye of the French HC.

Of importance here is that even when political parties formed and developed, both their constituencies and their actions were molded by the communitarian straitjacket. The two parties just mentioned were massively 'Maronite', and others which followed also bore a communitarian overtone which they were unable to shed. A few parties, like the Communist party and the Syrian National Party, *al-hizb al-qawmi al-suri*, sought to dissipate such heavy communitarian weight in their membership and appeal, but it is a fact that no one significant party succeeded in freeing itself from the communitarian stigma.

Why were political parties in Lebanon unable to transcend commu-

[57] Biography in Walid 'Awad, *Bishara al-Khuri Faris al-Mawarina al-'arab* (Béchara El-Khoury knight of the Arab Maronites), Beirut: Dar al-Afkar 2009.

[58] Biography in Michel Van Leeuw, *Émile Eddé (1884–1949): Aux Sources de la République libanaise*, Paris: Geuthner 2018, 2 vols.

nitarianism over a hundred years of political life? I suggest that the reason is based, structurally, in the electoral law.

In theory, the Constitution was neutral, as we saw, and in the 102 articles adopted in 1926 there is not a single mention of Christianity, Islam or Judaism, let alone the smaller constituent groups. Only in 1990, when the major amendments approved in Ta'ef were included in the text, did Article 24 make express mention of parity in Parliament between Christians and Muslims. Elsewhere the text remained neutral throughout.

This is why the electoral law is so important. Without it, the Constitution remains meaningless in its most characteristic trait. This often-overlooked fact is easily illustrated: when elections take place, a candidate will not be seeking a seat just in a district, whether large (*muhafaza*) or small (*qada'*). He or she will be the Maronite or Shi'i candidate for Baabda, or the Sunni seat of Tripoli. Unlike the national presidencies, which operate in a communitarian manner without specific mention in the Constitution or in legislation, the parliamentary pillars of Lebanon are openly communitarian. This is why the electoral template is key. Since the councils of Beirut in 1834 and of the two kaïmacams in the next decade, the assignment of representation in the councils, those appointed first and those elected afterwards, has been openly communitarian. We have seen how the electoral principle began to be applied, haltingly, during the Mutasarrifiyya.[59] The electoral laws initiated in 1922 sealed this tradition within a tight system retaining blunt communitarian assignments through the Mandate and Independence eras.

Other than changes to the electoral laws which affect districting, list- and proportionality-related electoral computation, the communitarian straitjacket remained.[60] This explains why the hopes of some major political actors and the

[59] See Ch 3.

[60] Other than the several laws suspending Parliament or extending its tenure, the main changes in electoral laws since their timid adoption in the Mutasarrifiyya and the first election in 1868 can be summarised as follows:

1902, secret ballot;
1922, vote carried out 'nationally', i.e. for a full council rather than for the piecemeal election of one candidate;
1934, adoption of the one-tier system, where voters choose a candidate and not a member of an electoral college;
1943, suppression of elected deputies (reintroduced briefly in 1992);
1957, suffrage extended to women;

population at large in moments of national upheavals in fulfilling the equality promised by Article 7 of the Constitution were easily dashed. Political competition is stacked by the electoral law communitarian principle. All reforms are vitiated by the immovable sectarian command of the electoral law.

This also explains the difficulty of establishing political parties which are not community-based. When a large popular wave appears for a while intent on transcending sectarianism, the communitarian electoral principle sweeps it aways. The national trans-communal mood in the country is undermined by the next election, which continues to be sectarian. When the voter comes to the electoral booth, he confronts again a box on his ballot vote which forces the seeker of a parliamentary seat to don his or her sectarian hat whether she wants to or not. Whether the voter or the candidate want it or not, the seat or seats in the circumscription are assigned on a sectarian basis.

There is a second structural flaw in the communitarian straitjacket. It operates beyond parliamentarian representation and affects the top positions of government. A communitarian parliament could in theory disregard the 'need' for the president of the Republic to be Maronite, the Speaker (more accurately the President of the Chamber of Deputies) to be Shi'i, and the Prime Minister (more accurately the President of the Council of Ministers) to be Sunni. After all, unlike the electoral law for parliamentary seats, these positions are not expressly assigned to the respective communities in any text, legislative or constitutional. In Lebanese history, none of the top positions were limited to a particular community before Independence.

The explanation as to why only a Maronite can be president resides, again, in the electoral template, albeit under a different logic. The presidency of the Republic is by far the most powerful position in the constitutional system devised by Chiha. The position was never expressly assigned for Maronites, as we saw with Debbas and some of his successors during the Mandate. Why is it therefore that after Debbas, almost all elected presidents in the country have

1960, electoral districting based on the smaller *qada'*;
1991, adaptation of the parity between Christian and Muslim MPs;
1992, return to a *muhafaza*-based system (more accurately a mixed *qada'-muhafaza* system);
2017, introduction of a system based on *hasel* (minimal number of votes) and *sawt tafdili* (preferential vote) that undermines majority voting. A useful summary can be found in Saba Zuraiq, '*Al-dimuqratiyya 'al madhbah qawanin al-intikhab* (Democracy at the altar of electoral laws)', *al-Nahar*, 13 October 2022.

been Maronite? The response is, generally, that a 'constitutional custom' has formed over time. This explanation has some merit, but it is insufficient.

The more mundane reason for only Maronite candidates becoming president is arithmetical. A Muslim candidate had no chance to muster the votes needed in a parliament with a majority of Christian members. This arithmetic gap between Christians and Muslims became larger as more members were added to parliament. Throughout the Mandate, the fight on the sectarian allocation of seats continued. It was cemented during the run-up to Independence in 1943 with the six/five formula, which we described earlier, and which may be attributed to Major-General Edward Spears, the commander of the British forces which defeated the French Vichyists in power in Lebanon in June 1941.[61] The formula endured until 1990. Among the 30 members of the first CR/CD in 1926, 17 were Christian and 13 Muslim. In a Parliament composed of 99 deputies, as it was between 1960 and 1992, 54 Christian deputies outnumbered their 45 Muslim counterparts more significantly than when the CR elected its first president in 1926. And within the Christian majority, Maronites outnumber significantly the Greek Orthodox, the next largest community.

Without a political earthquake to reshuffle the political deck, it is hard to imagine how the arithmetical dominance of Maronites in parliament could have been challenged to impact the presidency. The constraint is quasi-mathematical, for once the top seat was assigned de facto to the Maronite community, the other seats could only follow.

For the secularist, there remains a silver lining. Why the country did *not* collapse into sectarian regions is also explained by the nature of the electoral laws. Despite occasional attempts to create a more stringent electoral communitarianism in the shape of Sunnis voting exclusively for Sunnis, or Greek Orthodox voters exclusively for Greek Orthodox, the sociological reality and a national consciousness have prevented a turn to the worse. While it is possible to conceive of such a system, since electoral registers are detailed enough to mention each voter's community, most districts are mixed, and a strict

[61] 'After much discussion I got them [the Muslim local and regional protagonists] to agree to a new decree, which gave 30 seats to the Christians and 25 to themselves and the Druzes', Edward Spears, *Fulfilment of a Mission, Syria and Lebanon 1941–1944*, London: Leo Cooper 1977, 213. More on the 1941 war in Ch. 8.

communitarian correspondence between the voter and the elected deputy would prove even more absurd than the present arrangements. In this case, not only would deputies be Maronite, Greek Orthodox, or Sunni, but each voter would be Maronite, Greek Orthodox and Sunni. The country has so far been spared this even more radical application of communalism. In theory therefore, the possibility remains of making Lebanon even more sectarian by having members of a given community elect only members of their own community.

One should note another silver lining which renders the existing structure less communitarian. This is the fact that the three top constitutional positions are competitive within the respective communities. The presidential contest nearly always sees fierce competition among Maronite contenders. The natural (and healthy) competition makes it unlikely for all Maronites to vote for the same candidate. It is therefore the other, non-Maronite deputies, who eventually decide who the president will be.

This silver lining supporting national rather than communitarian comportment in the top three positions is also true at the voting level. The deputy in a circumscription, often a mixed one, fights for his seat against another deputy from the same religious community. But there are subtle differences depending on the size of some districts and their mixed nature. Maronite candidates in the Maronite heartland do not rely on the very few non-Maronite votes in their districts, whereas a Maronite contender in a mixed district with a massive Shi'i constituency opposed to him is unlikely to prevail even if all the Maronites in the district vote for him.

Overall, both silver linings, at the top and at the bottom, are incapable of trumping the communitarian dominance of the constitutional system. Varying combinations have been put forward, such as considering a Christian-Muslim presidential ticket, but they remain insufficient to undermine the basic arithmetic in the process of electing MPs or the three presidential positions in the Republic.

A final trait of the Lebanese electoral template needs to be mentioned. Seen from the perspective of a citizen called on to cast her ballot on election day, how does the choice in the voting booth appear to the voter?[62]

[62] The secrecy of the vote, as mentioned in Ch. 3, was introduced the first time during the Mutasarrifiyya in 1873 under Rustum Basha (Asad Rustum, *Lubnan fi 'ahd al-Mutasarifiyya*

The system has varied over the years, but one element has remained constant: in addition to being communal, the voting was 'plural'. The plural vote is the one usually cast by the Lebanese voter for a list of candidates defined by their religious denomination, where he selects for instance a Mount Lebanon list of three Maronites, two Druzes, a Sunni, and a Greek-Orthodox. This was described ironically by Chiha once. A candidate to the Chamber of Deputies at the time, it is not clear who from Chiha's text, had been adamant in his advocacy of a 'plural vote' as the dominant mantra of his campaign. Chiha expressed surprise at his enthusiasm of suddenly discovering a 'plural vote' which had been a feature of communal list-based elections prevailing at least since the 1922 electoral law:

> It is possible not to find in the plural vote prodigious advantages such as our zealous fellow-citizen discovers in it; it is even permissible to think that this obsolete thing, if it were possible, would lead to nothing despite the extreme difficulties resulting from the demographic composition of Lebanon; *but what is striking is that, the Government has used the plural vote for its own account for twenty-five or thirty years in such a way that in the end* it has replaced all the doctors, all the mandarins, all the graduates, all the intellectuals, all the owners and all the fathers of families in the country.
>
> This is what must first be considered; in terms of plural voting, voting several thousands of times, it's brilliant. One has never achieved better anywhere.[63]

In Lebanon, the communitarian system has meant that there has never been a one-seat electoral district. There is invariably a roster of candidates

(Lebanon in the era of the Mutasarrifiyya), Beirut: Nahar 1973, 174). But it was not systematic, and it was only 30 years later, under Muzaffar, that its adoption firmed up.

63 'On peut certes ne pas trouver dans le vote plural les avantages prodigieux que notre zélé concitoyen y découvre; il est permis même de penser de cette chose désuète que, si elle était possible, malgré les difficultés extrêmes résultant de la composition démographique du Liban, elle ne conduirait à rien; *mais ce qui frappe, c'est que ce vote plural, le Gouvernement en a disposé pour son compte depuis vingt-cinq ou trente ans de telle manière* qu'en définitive il s'est substitué à tous les docteurs, à tous les mandarins, à tous les diplômés, à tous les intellectuels, à tous les propriétaires et à tous les pères de famille du territoire.

C'est cela qu'il faut d'abord considérer; en fait de vote plural, voter plusieurs milliers de fois, c'est brillant. On n'a jamais mieux fait nulle part.' 'Variations sur la loi électorale', 16 August 1947, Pol Int 83.

on a list. 'Plurality' is structurally embedded in the communitarian electoral system. The only exception arises if a deputy dies early in his term of office, requiring a vote to fill the vacant seat.[64] While lists are a basic feature of any proportional representation election, the system is thoroughly communitarian in Lebanon.

Within the electoral communitarian constraint, the size of electoral circumscriptions, their boundaries and constant re-districting add their own complications. The electoral laws since Independence have varied between dividing the country between smaller *qada'*s and the larger *muhafazat*s, with limited gerrymandering within each as the boundaries of both have tended to remain stable since the Mutasarrifiyya. (Beirut was a special case, because it was not part of the Mutasarrifiyya, therefore never a *qada'*). The difference between *muhafaza* and *qada'* is important because of the much smaller size of the *qada'*, with two paradoxical effects. In the absence of nation-wide, all-community parties, the battle fought in a *qada'*-based districting is local rather than national, with uneven coalitions tailored to the size of the electoral district. The smaller the circumscription, the more local the vote because of the more direct relationship between a candidate and his local audience of voters. In this sense, the vote is more democratic in a *qada'* since it expresses the stronger ties between candidate and constituency. When the circumscription is large, as in the *muhafaza*, the expression of a vote gets diluted in the larger number of voters and seats. Of note is that in both cases, populations are mixed community-wise, with some extremely mixed and others extremely homogenous. This renders the candidates' tactics for winning very different. In general terms, this means that a candidate in a large circumscription is forced to belong to a coalition list decided at a distance from the voters. In a smaller circumscription, he has more control over the chances of winning if his local roots are strong enough to secure the more limited number of voters. But the size of districts is not the most important factor since voting started in the nineteenth century. For it is the communitarian element that dominates, manifested in a voting process based on competing lists of candidates with seats allocated according to communities and with the names of the candidates and their religious denomination spelled out.

[64] This is constitutionally prescribed in Art. 41 = Chiha Art. 43.

Conclusion

The constitutional deck was stacked from the beginning. Election particulars lay outside the remit of Chiha's Constitution, and there was little he could do to remove the communitarian straitjacket. Nor was there much leeway to even loosen it.

Is the move towards less communalism possible at all? Contrary to the received view, we have established that the electoral law is key to understanding the perpetuation of communitarianism in government. Changing the electoral law to a non-communitarian one is viewed with fear – the fear of Christian communities, already outnumbered by Sunnis and Shiʿis, that the present parity in parliamentary seats, seen as a loss of earlier power, would be whittled away by demographic changes further disfavoring Christians. This is probably the most difficult hurdle on the path of an 'ethnolysed nation', where differences in ethnicity and other 'natural' traits are melted in the proverbial common pot of individuals as naked, pure, self-standing citizens in law.[65] Despite the written advocacy at Ta'ef for a lower chamber elected on a non-communal basis, it is hard to see how an electoral law can allay the fear of Lebanese Christians, and Christian Maronites in particular, of being made politically redundant through their numbers.

Time, Chiha thought, would turn the country of Lebanon into a nation. There were moments in Lebanese history when a nationalist spirit prevailed over sectarianism. In living memory, the two street revolutions in 2005–6 and 2019–21 offered hope as individuals-in-their-community shed sectarianism for a palpably national identity which briefly fused them as full citizens in the common public space. The occasions were lost for reasons that need to be examined more attentively elsewhere. Similar occasions might occur again, in a moment of enlightened reform or in another revolution, but the default deck is always stacked.

[65] The chemistry inspired concept of 'ethnolyse" was coined by Robert Fossaert: 'Surely, at the cost of decades (or centuries) of alternating eruptions and lulls, the survivors of statal implosions – in Africa and elsewhere – will learn to live together. Present Europe is itself born of similarly savage *ethnolyses*, which are finally formative of Europe's nations. But the fact does not authorise any indifference, for medieval age resurgence is insufferable with the media coverage that it elicits before the world'. Robert Fossaert, *L'Avenir du Socialisme*, Paris: Stock 1996, 239.

PART THREE

CHIHA AFTER THE CONSTITUTION

8

The Constitution Undermined

A viable constitution beyond the Mandate.[1]

Once a constitution is up and running, it takes on a life of its own. In Lebanon, a century of constitutional life can be analysed under various types of periodization. Like other countries in the world, the ride was bumpy.

The most formal approach is to follow the sequence of amendments to the Constitution and its occasional suspensions by decisions of the HC or the President.[2]

Another periodization covers all successive parliaments starting with the CR becoming the first CD (1926) and the second CD fusing Parliament and Senate (1927). In a total of 22 CDs, the full century witnesses, not always continuously, four CDs from 1926 until 1943, and 18 CDs since Independence.[3]

[1] 'Une constitution viable en dehors du Mandat' (DOC 10).

[2] The sequence includes:

1927 (Senate suppression),
1929 (strengthening of the presidency),
1932 (full suspension, CD dissolution),
1934 (partial reinstitution of executive power, parliamentary elections),
1937 (CD dissolution and parliamentary elections),
1939 (full suspension and CD dissolution),
1943 (abolition of Mandate, end of nomination of deputies, free CD election),
1947 (CD early dissolution and election),
1975 (adjustment of presidential term with the onset of the civil war, beginning of repeated extensions to existing CD),
1990 (end of the civil war and Ta'ef amendments),
1992 (CD appointed deputies),
1996 and 2004 (forced extension of presidential terms),
2014–2016 (first presidential void),
2022–2025 (second presidential void).

[3] This includes a period of two years without Parliament upon its dissolution by HC Ponsot in 1932, Majed Khalil Majed, *Al-Intikhabat al-Niyabiyya 1861–1992* (Parliamentary

A more technical way considers the successive electoral laws in the life of the republic.[4] Sometimes, the electoral law does not change from one parliamentary cycle to another, but when it does, consequences are inevitable for the number of deputies, districting, or the mode of electoral representation.[5] The two most positive changes in the electoral system were the ending of two-tier elections in 1934 and the extension of the vote to women in 1957.[6]

One can also envisage the division of constitutional life according to the presidents elected, and/or the successive prime ministers and cabinets.[7] Schoolchildren in Lebanon are taught the names of the successive *mutasarrefs* in an awkward acronym made up from the first letter (in Arabic) of their first names.[8] A similar mnemonic acronym for the presidents, based on their last names, would be overbearing, for there have been too many since 1926.

elections 1861–1992), Beirut: al-Mu'assasa al-jami'yya lil-dirasat wal-nashr 1992, 53; and a repeatedly extended life for the thirteenth CD between 1972 and 1992 during the Lebanese wars.

4 Successive electoral laws varied the number of deputies considerably. To sketch the sequence drawn in the previous chapter: The electoral laws of 1922 and 1925 had 30 members for the CR turned CD in 1926, 46 deputies in 1927 when the Senate was disbanded and its 16 members added to the existing CD, 45 in 1929, only 25 between 1932 and 1937, 62 between 1937 and 1939 when Parliament was suspended, then 55 for the first and second CDs of Independence in 1943, 77 in 1951, down to 44 in 1956, and 66 from 1957 to 1960. The electoral law of 1960 fixed the number at 99, which remained until Ta'ef in 1989, where the number was adjusted to 108 deputies under the new parity between Christian and Muslim MPs, but this figure was ignored when the 1991 electoral law raised the number to 128 for the 1992 elections. Data from various sources, including the Lebanese Parliament site, '*lamha tarikhiyya lil-majlis al-niyabi*' tab, https://www.lp.gov.lb/CustomPage?Id=9. A useful summary can be found on the aljazeera.net site, Jana al-Duhaibi, '*Ta'arraf 'ala tasalsul al-hayat al-barlamaniyya al-lubnaniyya mundhu 1832 hatta intikhabat 2022* (Learn the sequence of the life of Lebanese Parliament from 1832 until the 1992 elections)', 12 May 2022.

5 Districting and redistricting oscillated mostly between the smaller *qada'* and the larger *muhafaza*. The mode of election, always communitarian, varied between lists with the voter's right to choose one or more names on the list (known as *tashtib*, deleting), fixed lists, and lists with preferential names.

6 Decision 2 of 1934 by HC de Martel, text in Majed, *Al-Intikhabat al-Niyabiyya 1861–1992* (Parliamentary elections 1861–1992), above n.3, 257 (Art. 5 at 258: one-tier election and secret ballot across the country); Law of 24 April 1957 under President Camille Chamoun, Id., 278–85 (Art. 21 at 280 for voting rights extended to women).

7 http://www.pcm.gov.lb/arabic/charts.aspx?pageid=266, on the site of the Lebanese Parliament for Presidents of the Council and the ministers since Independence. The site lists all the governments which received a vote of confidence along with their *bayan wizari*, the inaugural ministerial statements announcing their programs.

8 Lebanon saw 18 *mutasarrifs* in from 1861 to 1918, 10 presidencies (with eight presidents) during the Mandate period, and 15 presidencies from 1943 to 2025.

The succession of heads of states is nonetheless educational, a healthy reminder of the democratic importance of change at the top.

A more general periodization selects important breaks in the life of the Republic. In one perspective, 1926 marks the birth of a first Lebanese republic. Independence in 1943 starts the life of a second republic. In 1989, at Ta'ef, a third republic brings the country out of its long wars with major amendments including prospective changes for a less communitarian fourth republic. Another perspective recognises only two republics: a first starting in 1920 upon the declaration of Great Lebanon by the French occupiers or in the 1926 Constitution; a second starting either with Independence in 1943 or after Ta'ef in 1989.

Last and not least, the tragic history of the country conjures up a periodization based on foreign occupation, in full or in part, of the national territory: France during the Mandate (1920–1943), with a hiatus in the Second World War between the Vichy government (1940–1941) and the Free French (1941–1943). In the era of Independence, an American maritime force landed in 1958, Palestinian guerillas launched military actions across the Southern border against Israel between 1968 and 1978, and a long military domination by Syria lasted from 1976 to 2005, with an interlude in the summer of 1982 during which the Israeli army occupied Beirut. Alongside Syrian military control in the rest of the country ran an Israeli occupation of parts of South Lebanon from 1976 to June 2000.

None of these periodizations is particularly satisfying, but they give a sense of the many bumps in the century-old ride. For our purposes, this chapter follows changes in the Constitution during Chiha's life, together with his reactions to some of the building blocks identified in the previous chapters.

Suspension(s) and restoration(s) of the Constitution during the Mandate

The Constitution was never formally suspended after independence in Lebanon, even during the country's long wars, in a telling contrast with its repeated suspensions during the much shorter French mandate. During the Mandate, the Constitution was suspended in part or in full by High Commissioners for a good ten out of the 17 years between its adoption in 1926 and Independence in 1943. Chiha as key drafter of the Constitution naturally resented its transformation into an empty vessel.

The first suspension lasted from 1932 to 1934. The main reason why High Commissioner Henri Ponsot (HC 1926–33, d.1963) resorted to this drastic measure was a disagreement over the presidency when Charles Debbas's second term came to an end. In the original text of the Constitution, the term of the president was limited to a maximum of two consecutive terms of three years, six years in total. Elected in 1926, and reelected in 1929, Debbas could not seek a third term, and a heated campaign pitting Maronite contenders Béchara El-Khoury and Emile Eddé eventually resulted in Eddé supporting a third candidate, Tripoli deputy Muhammad al-Jisr. Jisr was the Sunni Muslim leader whom de Jouvenel had appointed President of the Senate in 1926, and he became Speaker (formally 'President' of the CD) after the two Chambers were merged in 1927 upon the Senate's abolition. We saw how various Christian circles, especially the Maronite Patriarch, opposed the presidency going to a Muslim in 1932. This is when Henri Ponsot intervened to suspend the Constitution.[9]

Three justifications were given in Ponsot's decision to suspend the Constitution: the need to limit budgetary expenses, the drastic 'economic imbalance' created by the international economic crisis, and a troublesome presidential election around the corner.[10] In an internal note found in Chiha's papers, Ponsot explained his 'hurried' decision to suspend the Constitution more bluntly: 'It was a matter of preventing Lebanon giving itself a Muslim President'.[11]

[9] Further on this episode, see Fawaz Traboulsi, *A History of Modern Lebanon*, London: Pluto Press 2007, 91; Edmond Rabbath, *La Formation Historique du Liban Constitutionnel*, Beirut: Lebanese University Publications, Beirut 2nd ed. 1986 (original 1973), 416–7. On Ponsot, see Général Catroux (who played an important role during the second world war), 'Un grand ambassadeur: Henri Ponsot', *Revue des Deux Mondes*, 1963, 538–47, 539–44 (Ponsot's role in Lebanon and Syria). The article by Catroux is telling for his complete disregard of Henry de Jouvenel and the Lebanese Constitution.

[10] Arrêté 55/LR on 9 May 1932. Text of the Arrêté in French in *Bulletin Mensuel*, 1.2.1934, 72–3.

[11] 'In other circumstances, however urgent it was in some respects, we could have waited a few months. This would have allowed me to explain myself beforehand in Paris. But the house was on fire, and it was to avoid that Lebanon gave itself a Muslim President'. ('En d'autres circonstances, pour urgent que cela fût à certains égards, on aurait pu attendre quelques mois, et cela m'eût permis de m'en expliquer au préalable à Paris. Mais le feu était à la maison, et il s'agissait d'éviter que le Liban se donnât un Président musulman'.) Letter from Ponsot to the Minister of foreign affairs, 27 May 1932, 2. (Chiha Archive, reference MC1932–09.jpg and -10.jpg)

Despite, or because of, the subtle 'transitory' nature of Art. 95, the Constitution never apportioned the very top positions, including the presidency, in the rigid communitarian form increasingly adopted after 1932 and consecrated in 1943 by the so-called National Pact. Allowing the democratic process to continue might have been an opportunity to avoid communal entrenchment in Lebanon's highest position. Debbas was not a Maronite and he would have been succeeded by a Sunni president, suggesting a trend at odds with the rigid distribution that took hold eventually at the top. The HC's intervention prevented a turn towards a more secular constitution at a key point in the young republic's life.

Ponsot suspended the Constitution on 9 May 1932 without jettisoning the political leaders. Executive and Legislative powers were suspended 'temporarily'.[12] The president went out of the door but came back through the window. Charles Debbas was appointed president of the Council of ministers by the HC, and Ponsot kept issuing unilateral Arrêtés in all walks of political life.

The CD's work was stopped, leaving Debbas and his government apparently in charge, but Ponsot stood above him with 'a Board of Directors' whom he named and dismissed at will.[13] Art.2 of Arrêté 55/LR 'temporarily and partially suspending the Statut Organique de la République Libanaise' stipulates that 'a Head of Government' is designated by the HC. This 'Chef du Gouvernement' exercises executive power with the support of the Mandatory Power and is assisted by the 'Conseil des Directeurs des Services Généraux' in the various departments of government (Art. 3). All the ministers were dismissed, and the 'Directors' became a fixture of the system until Independence, establishing top-down control for the benefit of the HC.[14] The

[12] Arrêté 55/LR on 9 May 1932, Art. 1: 'Est suspendue, à titre temporaire, l'application de la Constitution Libanaise pour ce qui touche à l'organisation et le fonctionnement du Pouvoir exécutif et du Pouvoir Législatif'. Text of the Arrêté in French in *Bulletin Mensuel*, 1.2.1934. This was followed by Arrêté 56/LR, id. 73–4; Arabic text in Majed, *Al-Intikhabat al-Niyabiyya 1861–1992* (Parliamentary elections 1861–1992), above n.3, 53–4. Art. 1 of Arrêté 56/LR retained for Debbas his 'present title' of president: 'M. Charles Debbas est chargé, avc son titre actuel, des fonctions de Chef du Gouvernement.'

[13] The Arabic translation of the 'Conseil des Directeurs des Services Généraux' was *Majlis mudiri al-dawa'er al-'amma*. Majed, *Al-Intikhabat al-Niyabiyya 1861–1992* (Parliamentary elections 1861–1992), above n.3, 54.

[14] Arrêté 56/LR of 9 May 1932, above n.12, Art. 4.

Board of Directors provided a local sounding board and additional power for the HC, who also relied on a set of top French advisors in the administration to relay his decisions. The Directors are the least known officials of the Mandate, despite an importance which is acknowledged in some memoirs by successive High Commissioners.[15] Left to fight secondary battles over the crumbs, the Lebanese kept mobilising for the restoration of the Constitution, including with a new party led by Béchara El-Khoury, which called itself the Constitution Party (*'hizb al-ittihad al-dusturi*, the constitutional unity party').

The pattern of suspending the Constitution continued throughout the Mandate. From Ponsot onwards, the HCs picked and chose what bits of the Constitution were useful to them at any given time. This brought even more havoc to the fragile constitutional rule.

When Debbas resigned on 2 January 1934,[16] the successor to Ponsot, Damien de Martel (HC 1933–1939, d.1940) disregarded the constitutional requirement for the president to be Lebanese and appointed a Frenchman as acting president in his place.[17] He then proceeded with a full overhaul of the constitutional system. The Constitution was eviscerated. De Martel replaced its main sections (Titles 2, 3, and 4) with a complete text of his own. The 49 articles of Arrêté 1/LR on 2 January 1934 were so wide-ranging that the charter was even described by one author as a new 'constitution'.[18] It reinforced the powers of the previous Head of Government – renamed President – and flanked him with a 'Secrétaire d'Etat' whose title was revived from the early Chiha drafts.

[15] On the directeurs' key role in support of the HC, see e.g. instance Gabriel Puaux, *Deux Années au Levant- Souvenirs de Syrie et du Liban, 1939–1940*, Paris: Hachette 1952, 57 (Kindle).

[16] See Debbas's letter of resignation dated 2 January 1934 suggesting that the objectives sought in 1932 had been achieved, and the acceptance by HC de Martel on the same day, in *Bulletin Mensuel*, 1.2.1934, 39–40. Debbas died in Paris in November 1935.

[17] This was Antoine Privat-Aubouard, who was acting president for less than a month, from 2 January to 30 January. Then the HCs returned to the established rule that the president be Lebanese. Privat-Aubouard was a member of the colonial administration. When he died in Beirut on 9 October 1934, the French daily *La Croix* ran on a short notice under the title of 'Mort d'un gouverneur des colonies', where he is described as 'délégué auprès du gouvernement du Liban', *La Croix*, 10 Octobre 1934 (from the gallica.bnf.fr site).

[18] Majed correctly describes the decree of de Martel as a '*dustur*, constitution' of replacement, *Al-Intikhabat al-Niyabiyya 1861–1992* (Parliamentary elections 1861–1992), above n.3, 55.

De Martel's institutional overhaul was supported by a series of three Arrêtés decreed on the same day.[19] In Arrêté 2, he restored the CD by enacting a full electoral law which has one remarkable feature compared to the two-tier election prevailing since the Mutasarrifiyya: 'Voting is universal and direct'.[20] One-tier elections to a third CD with diminished powers were held in January 1934.[21]

Under Arrêté 3, the HC appointed Habib Basha al-Sa'd as president.[22] De Martel also appointed seven members in a CD which he reduced to 25 deputies. A French head of government was designated to oversee the new elections.[23] The Directors were kept in place. This strange organisation replaced the Constitution of 1926 with a puzzle of texts forming an even more pliable tool in the hands of the HC.[24] The Directors are again mentioned in Art. 6 of de Martel's 'constitution' of 1934, jointly with the Secrétaire d'Etat as 'Conseil de Gouvernement'.[25]

[19] The text of the Arrêtés can be found in *Bulletin Mensuel*, 1.2.1934, 40–51. On de Martel, see Chiha's derogatory column on the nickname earned by de Martel's 'fantasies' as 'le Chinois': 'Les méthodes de M. de Martel s'inspiraient de plus des secrètes violences de la Russie. M. de Martel avait institué ce régime "d'oukases et de Caucase" qu'on n'a pas oublié. (The methods of Mr de Martel were inspired additionally by the secret violent acts of Russia. Mr. de Martel had established this regime of 'ukazes and Caucase' that we have not forgotten)'. Chiha, 'Les Souvenirs de M. Gabriel Puaux', *Le Jour*, 26 July 1952.

[20] Art. 6 of Arrêté 2/LR of 2 January 1934: 'Le suffrage est universel et direct'. The next sentence makes the vote secret.

[21] Arabic text of the electoral law of 1934 for the third CD and results of the elections in Majed, *Al-Intikhabat al-Niyabiyya 1861–1992* (Parliamentary elections 1861–1992), above n.3, 55–63. Replacement of the two-tier election with one at 56.

[22] We encountered Habib Basha al-Saad (1867–1942) as the highest Lebanese official in the Mutasarrifiyya's Administrative Council. He was exiled to Turkey during the First World War for his nationalist positions. During the Mandate he occupied key positions in the Republic, including all three top presidencies.

[23] See Youssef Takla, 'Corpus juridique du mandat français', in Nadine Meouchi and Peter Sluglett eds, *The British and French Mandates in Comparative Perspectives*, Leiden: Brill 2004, 89; Rabbath, *La Formation Historique du Liban Constitutionnel*, above n.9, 421–4, esp. 422 n.58 summarising the Arrêtés.

[24] A 'Note remise par de Martel' to Chiha is dated October 1934 (Chiha Archive, reference MC1934–07.jpg and 03-jpg). The title is in the handwriting of Chiha, which suggests that the HC shared the telegram he sent to the Ministry of foreign affairs with Chiha, perhaps to explain why the presidential contest was frustrated by the HC. In this note to the Quai d'Orsay, de Martel appears satisfied with the application of a 'constitution promulguée à titre provisoire' and explains that his appointment of Habib Basha al-Saad as president is because of his loyalty, but also because of the animosity between the Lebanese leaders which he witnessed in the presidential contest.

[25] *Bulletin Mensuel*, 1.2.1934, 40.

The political tension between the French Mandatory power and the people it ruled over shifted in the following three years to treaty-seeking discussions with a view to independence of the Mandate territories. Between 1934 and 1936, all institutional discussion was focused, in Lebanon and Syria, on concluding a Treaty with France which would allow the Mandates to be formally ended, with Syria and Lebanon gaining independence and joining the League of Nations. To avoid a complete divorce with France, the Treaties were to include military arrangements allowing France, as a world power, to retain influence on the ground. This model, pioneered by Great Britain in Iraq in 1930 and in Egypt in August 1936, further undermined the meaningfulness of Lebanon's young Constitution.

The French Treaty with Syria was signed in Paris on 9 September 1936 and the Treaty with Lebanon a few weeks later.[26] For reasons of French domestic politics, neither was ever put to the French National Assembly for approval, and the agreements were not ratified. That complication came later. In 1936, rising popular discontent over continued French occupation subsided in both countries with the treaty prospects, and the more relaxed atmosphere led de Martel to restore the Lebanese Constitution on 24 January 1937. A new CD of 63 members was elected in October 1937.[27]

The parliamentary election was preceded by a heated presidential election pitting the two new poles of Maronite leadership, Béchara el-Khoury and Emile Eddé.[28] Eddé won, pushing Khoury and his Dustur party

[26] Extensive discussion of the treaties in Rabbath, *La Formation Historique du Liban Constitutionnel*, above n.9, 425–40; texts of the Franco-Syrian Treaty of Friendship and Alliance and of the Franco-Lebanese Treaty of Friendship and Alliance of 13 November 1936, in Ministère des Affaires Étrangères (France), *Rapport à la Société des Nations sur la Situation de la Syrie et du Liban* (*Année 1936*), 201 and 229 respectively. The Franco-Syrian Treaty is also available in Arabic on the Syrian modern history site, at https://wp.me/pdHyhC-Ya. The Franco-Lebanese Treaty was also published in *Correspondance d'Orient*, December 1936, 'Traité d'Amitié et d'Alliance entre la France et le Liban', 544–6.

[27] Rabbath, *La Formation Historique du Liban Constitutionnel*, above n.9, 440–1. Majed, *Al-Intikhabat al-Niyabiyya 1861–1992* (Parliamentary elections 1861–1992), above n.3, 63–5, for the texts related to the new electoral law passed in 1937.

[28] The curious sequence in holding the election of the president before the election of the CD illustrates the selective choice by de Martel of parts of the Constitution that he chose fit. De Martel had appointed Habib Basha al-Sa'd as president when he suspended the Constitution in 1934. The 30 January 1936 presidential elections pitting Khoury against Eddé came in the wake of the HC's restoration of the elected presidency by Arrêté 1/LR on 3 January 1936. This is why presidential elections preceded the parliamentary elections of October 1937.

into opposition until 1943.[29] Political life in Lebanon had been revived, but the feverish situation in Europe took its toll and the renewed life of the Constitution was halted by the outbreak of the Second World War.

A few months after a new HC, Gabriel Puaux (1939–1941), arrived in Beirut in the first week of January 1939, war broke out between France and Germany.[30] The high-handed Puaux suspended the Constitution on 21 September 1939 and took over. The CD was dissolved again, but the President of the Republic and the Directors were kept in place. From 1939 until independence four years later, France's representatives in Lebanon ruled 'à coup d'arrêtés'.[31]

Ponsot, Damien de Martel and Puaux exercised full colonial power in their administration of Lebanon. They opposed de Jouvenel's style in all aspects and cared little for the Lebanese Constitution, which they suspended and manipulated at will. They also kept up the practice of unelected directors running as their sounding board for the Lebanese republic, and as pliable instruments in both Lebanese and Syrian affairs.

See for dates and comment, Rabbath, *La Formation Historique du Liban Constitutionnel*, above n.9, 440–1.

29 Text summarising the 1937 CD electoral provisions, and results of the elections, in Majed, *Al-Intikhabat al-Niyabiyya 1861–1992* (Parliamentary elections 1861–1992), above n.3, 65–72. One third of the deputies were appointed by the HC. Eddé narrowly won the presidential election of 20 January 1936.

30 Gabriel Puaux (d.1970), an eccentric and awkward diplomat, worked on a plan to appoint a son of ibn Saud, the head of the newly established Kingdom of Saudi Arabia, king of Syria. Puaux looked down on the locals as lacking in 'civilization'. He left a colourful memoir of his stay in Lebanon and Syria, *Deux Années au Levant- Souvenirs de Syrie et du Liban, 1939–1940*, above n.15. See for instance at 35 on the monarchy episode: 'Was it appropriate to maintain the republican form and the parliamentary system in Syria? We had dealt with a political party opposed to the French mandate. What guarantee of stability did we find there for the future? Was it not necessary to expect, in the Syrian parliament, a perpetual one-upmanship on the road to absolute independence? It is to the detriment of our rights and our interests that this evolution continues. How to put a stop to it, if not by a coup whose heinous nature, in the eyes of the whole world, would fall on us? Why not make Syria a kingdom? A treaty concluded with a monarch would have a much greater chance of lasting: it would bind not a man or a party, but a dynasty. A friendship would be forged between France and the Syrian crown, much more stable and more effective, because it is more human than a theoretical legal commitment'.

31 Rabbath, *La Formation Historique du Liban Constitutionnel*, above n.9, 447.

Second World War and Independence

After war broke out in Europe in 1939, developments on the battlefield dominated the course of events in the Middle East, as elsewhere. Conditions throughout the Orient deteriorated rapidly in the wake of the German occupation of Paris in June 1940 and the pro-German coup in Iraq on 1 April 1941. The British military command, headquartered in Cairo for the duration of the war, reacted swiftly in Iraq and restored the rule of the monarchy within one month, but the fragile truce in the Levant was shattered.

In Lebanon, where a French mini-civil war was taking place between the Pétain regime and the Free French led from Algiers by General Charles de Gaulle, Britain launched an invasion to oust Vichy rule under Pétain-designated High Commissioner Henri Dentz.[32] Despite unexpectedly tough resistance by the Vichyists, Lebanon and Syria were overrun in June 1941.[33]

With the historic defeat of France, French colonial rule was bound to end in the Levant. Quasi-simultaneous declarations by the British commander stationed in Cairo and the French Delegate-General (so-named to avoid using 'High Commissioner') designated by the Free French government stated that Lebanon and Syria were now 'sovereign and independent'.[34] A wave of independentist hope engulfed the country, supported by British officials who

[32] After Puaux was recalled, Philippe Pétain, head of the Vichy regime now in charge of France, appointed Jean Chiappe as HC on 25 November 1940. Chiappe was killed on his way to Lebanon when his plane was shot down over the Mediterranean on 27 November 1940, probably mistakenly by Italian planes engaged in an air battle with the British Air Force. General Henri Dentz was then appointed HC, and he supported Vichy against de Gaulle and the British forces, which he fought determinedly in 1941. Dentz surrendered in July 1941 and returned to France. He was tried after the war and condemned to death. De Gaulle commuted his sentence, and he died in the prison of Fresnes in 1945.

[33] On this little-known war, which was costly in both human (about 10,000 military dead) and economic terms, see Henry de Wailly, *Syrie 1941, La Guerre Occultée*, Paris: Perrin 2006. Like several works on the Mandate, the book covers the foreign dimension, with little about the impact of the war on Lebanese caught between a fight to the death of two opposing French leaderships they had little to do with.

[34] Proclamation of Lebanon's independence by Delegate-General George Catroux on 8 June 1941 text at Albert Hourani, *Syria and Lebanon- A Political Essay*, New York: Oxford University Press 1946, 240–1, in French at 371–2; this was repeated by Catroux of 26 Nov 1941, text in Hourani, id., 250–2. The French made independence contingent on a new treaty. Britain's recognition was straightforward. On the 'variously assigned' dates for the end of the Mandate, see Stephen Longrigg, *Syria and Lebanon under French Mandate*, London: Oxford University Press 1958, 317.

did not mind depriving the French of their two Levantine colonies. Whoever remained of French power wielders dillydallied, including de Gaulle. Little happened in 1941–2, with few changes in the Lebanese ministries and a rapid succession of short-lived Lebanese presidents – and a French president who remained in place for five days![35] They were all appointed by the French Delegate-General under the watchful eye of the new British military occupiers.[36]

Under domestic and international pressure, mainly British but supported by Arab countries which had won independence, the Free French restored constitutional government to Lebanon in January 1943. Parliamentary elections were held in late August and early September. For the first time since 1926, there were no 'députés nommés'. All the deputies were elected.[37]

This fifth CD, which would be the first one post-Independence, was composed of 55 MPs, 30 Christian and 25 Muslim, confirming the communitarian six to five ratio.[38] In turn, the CD unanimously elected Béchara El-Khoury to the presidency on 21 September 1943, and Khoury appointed the pan-Arabist Sunni Riad al-Sulh as Prime Minister. The pair moved forward towards full independence despite threats from the French Delegate-General Jean Helleu,

[35] In succession, after Emile Eddé's term (1936–1941): Paul-Hippolyte Arlabosse (President from 4 to 9 April 1941); Alfred Naccache (9 April 1941 to 18 March 1943); Ayyub Tabet (18 March 1943 to 22 July 1943; Petro Trad (22 July 1943 to 21 September 1943); Béchara El-Khoury (21 September 1943 to 11 November 1943), and Emile Eddé again, for ten days, until Independence, from 11 November 1943 to 22 November 1943.

[36] General Georges Catroux (d. 1969) succeeded Dentz as Delegate General (July 1941 to June 1943). He restored the Constitution, suspended by Puaux in September 1939, on 18 March 1943. Rabbath, *La Formation Historique du Liban Constitutionnel*, above n.9, 474–5. Catroux was followed by diplomat Jean Helleu (June 1943 to Dec. 1943, d.1955), the last French representative of the Mandate period able to issue legally binding decisions in Lebanese and Syrian affairs. After Delegate General of diplomat Yves Chataigneau's brief term (1943 to Jan 1944, d. 1969), the last Delegate-General, General Paul Beynet (Jan. 1944 to Sep. 1946, d.1969), proved particularly brutal. Additional British pressure and nonviolent resistance by Lebanese and Syrians precipitated the final withdrawal of French troops in April 1946.

[37] Texts and results in Majed, *Al-Intikhabat al-Niyabiyya 1861–1992* (Parliamentary elections 1861–1992), above n.3, 74–82. On 'députés nommés, see below n.42 and accompanying text. The elections were held in two phases (not two tiers) on the basis of the larger *Muhafaza* district, with five such districts in the country, and candidates gathered in lists (with the usual communitarian distribution). In the first phase, the candidate who received a majority of the votes against his communitarian opponent succeeded. In the second turn, a relative majority sufficed. Id., at 74–5.

[38] See Longrigg, *Syria and Lebanon under French Mandate*, above n.34, 329, on then President Ayyub Tabet's attempt to double the number of Christian MPs. Tabet (d.1947), a Protestant, was appointed president by Delegate-General Catroux for a short period, March to July 1943.

who had replaced Free French representative General Georges Catroux and was instructed by de Gaulle to hang on tight to French colonies.

Lebanese resistance to France reneging on its 1941 promises grew, and the CD could not be deterred from proceeding with a constitutional amendment that removed all articles referring to France, the Mandate, and the League of Nations.[39] The deputies approved the amendments unanimously on 9 November 1943. Helleu was not pleased. The President of the Republic and the President of the Council of ministers were arrested at dawn on 11 November 1943 and jailed in the Eastern town of Rashayya. Riots followed and massive public opinion in favor of independence carried the day, bolstered by a three-day ultimatum issued on 19 November by British officials in Cairo.[40] Political prisoners were released, and the Presidents' leadership restored on the morning of 22 November. Lebanon has since celebrated its Independence on that date.[41]

An overbearing Mandate

Despite the paralysis of constitutional life during the Mandate, and with the HC issuing countless decisions without Parliamentary consultation or approval, Parliament was not formally disbanded every time the Constitution was suspended. It kept its own rhythm of ups and downs dictated by a host of political factors. Its representativity was impaired as early as 1927 when a significant number of MPs were appointed by the French HC, a practice which Chiha had denounced sarcastically as a bizarre invention.[42] In 1943, the CD

[39] Changes of Art. 1, declaring Lebanon a sovereign state; Art.11, removing French as an official language; Art. 52, full Treaty powers to the Lebanese State; deletion of the whole of Part V on the Mandate and the League of Nations (Arts. 90–4); removal of reference to the Mandate in the last Part entitled 'Concluding and Temporary Provisions) in Arts. 95 and 102.

[40] The ultimatum was delivered by Major-General Edward Spears, 'First British Minister to the Levant', to the Free French on 19 November: see for instance Fawaz Traboulsi, *A History of Modern Lebanon*, above n.9, 108. Spears left a posthumous account on the period, *Fulfilment of a Mission, Syria and Lebanon 1941–1944*, London: Leo Cooper 1977. He notes at 274 the difference between the one dead Frenchman, 'being a soldier shot by an officer for refusing to obey an order to fire at an unarmed crowd' and 'the Lebanese casualties in Beirut, Sidon and Tripoli (a striking illustration of the difference between French provocation and Lebanese restraint): 16 to 22 killed and 66 to 95 wounded.'

[41] On the last stretch to Independence, see also Longrigg, *Syria and Lebanon under French Mandate*, above n.34, 332–3. Rabbath, *La Formation Historique du Liban Constitutionnel*, above n.9, 474–93; Ghassan Tueni, Fares Sassine, Nawaf Salam, *Kitab al-Istiqlal* (The Independence book), Beirut: Nahar 1998.

[42] 'Députés nommés.' Chiha, 'Pour faire réfléchir', *Le Jour*, 16 mai 1950.

was freely elected, for the first time, without the shadow of French colonialism hovering over it. It was able to usher in formal independence, followed by the withdrawal of the last French troops three years later. Unlike the terms of the aborted Franco-Lebanese Treaty of 1936, France's final withdrawal left Lebanese sovereignty without any restriction.

All this while, Michel Chiha had been under no illusions about the limitations imposed by the Mandate. In 1934, in the face of yet another proposed reform of executive power, he spoke his mind plainly:

> In fact, there is only one authority in Lebanon: that of the High Commissioner. The High Commissioner has absolute, limitless powers. He can suspend chambers, dismiss ministers, legislate as it pleases him, and, without a coup d'état, he suspends constitutions. Next to his own, the powers of the late padishah look pale and insignificant.[43]

The veto power of the French High Commissioner, 'ten times stronger' in Lebanon than in Egypt,[44] played havoc with Lebanese decision-making:

> All past, present, and future constitutional freedoms of Lebanon – and of Syria – have been granted to us by the Mandate, and granted on a provisional basis. The existing imbalance between the different powers has certainly not been, nor is likely to be, for the benefit of Parliament. The Mandate retains a permanent right of veto: no one dreams of contesting this right. On the contrary, it will be an element of guarantee and stability: moreover, the donor has the possibility in law, and the means in fact, to take back his donation whenever he pleases and however he likes.[45]

[43] 'En fait, il n'y a au Liban qu'une autorité: celle du Haut-Commissaire. Le Haut Commissaire a des pouvoirs absolus, sans limites. Il peut suspendre les chambres, renvoyer les ministres, légiférer comme il lui plait et, sans coup d'état, il a suspendu des constitutions. A côté des siens, les pouvoirs de feu le padichah semblent pâles et insignifiants'. 'La réforme de l'Etat au Liban', *Le Jour*, 3 November 1934. Padichah refers to a Persian and Ottoman sultan/shah/emperors with no limits whatsoever to their power.

[44] Id.: 'In law, Egypt is an independent country. The British High Commissioner does not hold a tenth of the powers of his colleague in Syria and Lebanon. (En droit, l'Egypte est un pays indépendant. Le Haut-Commissaire britannique n'y dispose pas de la dixième partie des pouvoirs dont dispose son collègue en Syrie et au Liban)'.

[45] Id.: 'Toutes les libertés constitutionnelles du Liban – et de la Syrie – passées, présentes et futures nous sont concédées par le Mandat, et concédées à titre provisoire. Et le déséquilibre existant entre les différents pouvoirs, ce n'est certes pas au profit du Parlement, qu'il s'est produit, ou risque de se produire. Le Mandat conserve un droit de véto permanent: ce droit, personne ne songe à le lui

Mandatory power was absolute; whatever it granted it could take back. No one in Lebanon or Syria was fooled by grandiloquent statements of colonial magnanimity. 'Protectorate' in Morocco and Algérie française, like 'mandate' in Syria and Lebanon, were weasel words masking the strict subordination of indigenous, national, and local will to the colonial master.

Chiha went on record several times criticising the suspension of the Constitution. In 1935, he expressed popular disappointment with the Mandate:

> *Because we believed it to be a Mandate intent on our liberation*, we trustingly accepted fifteen years of changes in government and all manner of constitutional amendments. A fact which the mandatory authority must acknowledge is that any advance in our country's emancipation can only come about through genuine power-sharing. How much longer can the Mandate deny us this?[46]

And again in an open letter to HC de Martel a few weeks later:

> We ask that the Lebanese be allowed to undertake, in Lebanon, the urgent task of rebuilding their own nation. We have been waiting for this to be granted for twenty years and yet, as easy as it is to grant, for twenty years a response has failed to come.[47]

It does not come as a surprise that Chiha disliked the repeated suspensions of the Constitution. In his archives, we find a series of letters and telegrams from HCs Ponsot and de Martel explaining or justifying the suspension. In the first, addressed to the prime minister and minister of foreign affairs on

contester. Au contraire, il constituera un élément de garantie et de stabilité: de plus, le donateur a la possibilité en droit, et les moyens en fait, de révoquer sa donation quand il lui plaira et à son gré'.

46 '*Parce que le Mandat que nous avons accueilli était un Mandat libérateur*, nous avons accepté, avec confiance, pendant quinze ans, les changements de gouvernements et de constitutions les plus divers. ... Nous savons, et le Mandat ne peut ne pas le reconnaître, que la marche vers l'émancipation ne commencera pour nous qu'avec la participation réelle au pouvoir. Le Mandat pourrait-il nous la refuser plus longtemps?' 'Démocratie et dictature au Liban', *Le Jour*, 30 January1935. Emphasis in original, as in all subsequent citations of Chiha.

47 'Nous venons demander qu'on permettre à des libanais d'opérer au Liban la reconstruction nationale qui s'impose ... Il y a environ vingt ans que nous attendons une réponse, pourtant facile à donner, et il y a autant d'années que cette réponse ne vient pas.' 'A Son Excellence le Comte de Martel', *Le Jour*, 25 February 1935.

13 May 1932, Ponsot explains that his decision to suspend the Constitution four days earlier had been well received by the population, and that a stream of communications in support of the decision had come 'from all over Lebanon'.[48] In fact the unilateral suspension did not sit well in France either, where his high-handedness was not considered warranted. A communication to Paris by Ponsot, dated 27 May 1932, acknowledges the 'legitimate impatience of the Department [in the Ministry]' with the suspension of the Constitution and explains that the suspension was necessary for the reforms needed.[49] On 4 January 1937, his successor, de Martel, announced to the ministry of foreign affairs that he had revived the Constitution and hoped that the new president, Emile Eddé, would carry out the reforms needed to limit the growth of the 'appareil gouvernemental', remedy 'l'instabilité ministérielle', and 'stem the 'surenchère financière'.[50]

Chiha did not react to all the vicissitudes affecting the Constitution which he had 'worked late nights' to complete.[51] When at last the Mandate was in the throes of Lebanese riots which culminated in Independence, he had this to say about empty words:

> Formulas which, in our eyes, had become mere words, gave way to a vision, to a less artificial notion of things. All these words: mandate, principal, agent, have become tired, exhausted. They no longer resembled themselves, or resembled what the Law thinks of them, or what schools teach. In our eyes, they were nothing more than a pack of fictions, a collection of masks, an absence of faces.[52]

48 ... 'de tous les points du Liban'. Telegram from Ponsot to The President of the Council and Foreign Affairs Minister; 13 May 1932 (Chiha Archive).

49 Letter from Martel to the Minister of foreign affairs, 27 May 1932: 'la légitime impatience du Département' (Chiha Archive).

50 Martel to Direction politique et commercial of the Ministry of foreign affairs, 4 January 1936 (Chiha Archive).

51 Cited in Ch. 4, text accompanying n.1.

52 'Des formules qui, à nos yeux, n'étaient plus que des mots, qui ne pouvaient plus être que des mots, ont fait place à une vision, à une notion moins artificielle des choses. Tous ces vocables: mandat, mandant, mandataire, fatigués, épuisés, ne ressemblaient plus à eux-mêmes, à ce que le Droit en pense, à ce que l'école enseigne. Ils n'étaient plus à nos yeux qu'une somme de fictions, qu'une collection de masques, qu'une absence de visages'. Chiha, 'D'une révision', *Le Jour*, 9 November 1943, Pol Int 40–1.

This was Chiha's unambiguous comment during the tense period in November 1943 which ended that month in Independence. The Mandate was full of Orwellian wording. This did not mean that it was all bad. The French presence in Lebanon did not trigger the same animosity it did in Algeria or Vietnam. Chiha and most of the political actors in Lebanon kept a sense of nuance, together with a conviction that self-government was inevitable, that the French were disingenuous, and that they would eventually leave.

Chiha's appreciation of the Mandate came with the constant concern that Lebanon would be sacrificed to regional or international interests decided by France, in particular because of France's domination over both Lebanon and Syria. At various points in the Mandate, including in de Jouvenel's awkward reference to the emerging Lebanese Constitution as part of a larger 'United States of Syria', those Lebanese who believed in a fully sovereign state, separate from Syria, remained apprehensive until Independence in 1943. Considering the military interventions of Syria in Lebanon starting in the mid-1970s and their domination over the country until 2005, the apprehension is not misplaced.

The dominance of executive power

Clear and compact as the Constitution was, amendments to its text were not well-crafted. With the problems of 'designated deputies' high on his mind, Chiha is also on record commenting on several other changes that affected 'his' constitution through the Mandate and into Independence.

The Constitutional Law of 1927 brought several changes to the original text. It was followed by yet another set of amendments in 1929, which significantly affected the term of the presidency. The major effect of the successive changes was to increase the power of the president.

In the 1927 amendments, the president was allowed to designate a third of the deputies (Art. 24), force the Chamber to reconsider a law (Art. 57), impose the adoption of the budget if the CD missed the end of year deadline (Art. 86), and open new credits unilaterally, up to a certain limit (Art. 85). An oddity in modern constitutionalism, the president could also declare a bill 'urgent' and promulgate it as law if the CD did not reject it within forty days (Art. 58).[53]

[53] Unlike the final plenary sessions in May 1926, Michel Chiha was in attendance during the discussions of the Amendments in 1927. In his only intervention in comment to Art. 58 on 'urgent bills', Chiha did not oppose the proposed amendment, telling those who opposed it that

On the other hand, the fog that characterised the individual and collective responsibility of ministers was removed by the express adoption of the Council of ministers' collective responsibility (Art. 66).[54]

The Constitutional Law of 1929 further strengthened presidential powers. A significant amendment extended the terms of the presidency from three to six years (Art. 49). Another significant amendment gave him the right, with the assent of the Council of ministers, to dissolve the CD by decree (Art. 55). The previous cumbersome conditions for the dissolution of parliament by the president were abolished.[55]

There is no trace of Chiha intervening in the 1929 debate. He was no longer a deputy and was under no illusions about the cosmetic nature of these constitutional amendments. In 1934, a proposal had percolated all the way from France with the aim of further strengthening the Lebanese executive in the name of efficiency. This was known as the Doumergue reform. Gaston Doumergue (d.1937) was President of the Council of ministers in France, a position which did not exist formally in the Constitution of the Third Republic,[56] and he sought to strengthen the executive against legislative power. His appeal to revise the French Constitution by correcting the formal absence of the Prime Minister/President of the Council of Ministers in the constitutional texts, and by augmenting the powers of the Prime Minister, notably in the right to dissolve parliament unilaterally, was eventually defeated.[57] Chiha did not find it

Parliament could still defeat any such urgent bill within 40 days. Ahmad al-Zein ed., *Mahader Munaqashat al-Dustur al-Lubnani wa Ta'dilatuh 1926–90* (Minutes of the discussions about the Lebanese Constitution and its amendments), Beirut: Publications of the Chamber of Deputies 1993, 150.

[54] Rabbath, *La Formation Historique du Liban Constitutionnel*, above n.9, 405–6, esp. n.40 on the invention of 'urgent' laws in the Constitutional Law of 17 October 1927. Zein ed., *Mahader Munaqashat al-Dustur al-Lubnani wa Ta'dilatuh 1926–90* (Minutes of the discussions about the Lebanese Constitution and its amendments), above n.53, 97–9 (minutes of the debate in the Senate), 101–78 (minutes of the extensive debate in Congress). The debate on the superfluous dimension of Senate was robust. It took place over five sessions on 13–14 October 1927, in the presence of Solomiac.

[55] Rabbath, *La Formation Historique du Liban Constitutionnel*, above n.9, 407–9. Zein ed., *Mahader Munaqashat al-Dustur al-Lubnani wa Ta'dilatuh 1926–90* (Minutes of the discussions about the Lebanese Constitution and its amendments), above n.53, 191–4 (Debates on 23 and 27 April 1929).

[56] Guillaume Tusseau, *Droit Constitutionnel et Institutions Politiques*, 4th ed., Paris: Seuil 2022, 185.

[57] Marc Simard, 'Doumergue et la réforme de l'Etat en 1934: La dernière chance de la République', *French Historical Studies*, 16, 1990, 576–96 (Constitutional revision was made impossible by the dominant fear of an authoritarian presidency).

excessive in the case of France, but he was concerned about a contagious impact on Lebanon, which he opposed in an op-ed:

> M. Doumergue's reform does not consist in suppressing national representation, or paralyzing its action, or establishing a dictatorship; it tends to give more authority and stability to Executive power in order to restore the balance broken by the Chambers and to their advantage. But here! The least informed mind will immediately detect the impossibility of applying the same reasoning in a country under a Mandate.[58]

Why did Chiha believe that it was different for a 'country under Mandate'? He thought, correctly, that there would be little point in any such change, considering how much the executive, the President in particular, is tightly controlled by the HC. The Lebanese situation was considerably different from the French case:

> Let us add that the Lebanese executive, whatever it is, tends to be confused with [legislative] power. When it [the executive] is only an emanation [of legislative power, since Parliament elects the president], as is currently the case, the question does not arise. Even when it is not an emanation, the direct dependence in which it finds itself with regard to the Mandate, the daily contact [with the French authorities] and a thousand other reasons, make this confusion impossible to avoid.[59]

Within the Lebanese separation of powers, Chiha argued, the balance works to the constant advantage of the executive. His initial intuition to refuse describing the system as parliamentarian proved right again. A significant part

[58] 'La réforme de M. Doumergue ne consiste pas en effet à supprimer la représentation nationale, à paralyser son action, ou à établir une dictature; elle tend à donner plus d'autorité et de stabilité au pouvoir Exécutif pour rétablir l'équilibre rompu par les Chambres et à leur profit. Mais ici ! L'esprit le moins averti décèlera du premier coup l'impossibilité d'appliquer le même raisonnement dans un pays sous Mandat.' Chiha, 'La réforme de l'Etat au Liban- Parlementarisme sous mandat, l'exemple égyptien,' 3 November 1934 (MichelChiha.org, Tab Editorials, November 1934).

[59] 'Ajoutons que l'exécutif libanais, quel qu'il soit, tend à confondre avec ce pouvoir. Quand il n'en est que l'émanation, comme c'est actuellement le cas, la question ne se pose pas. Même quand il n'en est pas l'émanation, la dépendance directe dans laquelle il se trouve à l'égard du Mandat, le contact quotidien et mille autres raisons, rendent cette confusion impossible à éviter.' Chiha, 'La réforme de l'Etat au Liban- Parlementarisme sous mandat, l'exemple égyptien,' Id.

of his interventions after the Constitution was adopted dwelt on the need for parliamentarians to step up and fully assume their functions:

> *In short, the Chamber in Lebanon must make a greater effort to learn its duties and carry them out.* It must learn the business and to practice it in less questionable conditions. As it currently behaves, it opens itself up in every possible way, and it's no wonder it is the subject of irony and pamphleteering.[60]

Chiha lamented on several occasions the dominance of the executive branch over the CD:

> If an institution is necessary in Lebanon, it is the Chamber of Deputies. And it is not for the love of democracy; it is because Lebanon is a country of associated communities (none of which constitutes a majority on its own).[61]

For Chiha, the CD was important not only as a counterbalancing power. It had, or at least it was supposed to have, a particular role as the privileged locus of discussion in the country: 'The Chamber of Deputies is an essential part of political life. Associated religious minorities (as is the case here) need *collective representation* in order to remain associated'.[62] It is in the CD that all elements of what we now call civil society meet.

Another aspect of the CD's importance for Chiha was its multifaceted role. In addition to providing an agora for national representation and inclusive debate, 'always necessary if there is to be peace',[63] it was also needed for its counter-balancing effect within the separation of powers:

60 '*En bref, la Chambre au Liban doit travailler plus pour arriver à connaître ses devoirs et à les remplir*. Elle doit faire effort pour apprendre le métier et pour l'exercer dans des conditions moins critiquables. Comme elle se présente, elle prête le flanc, de toutes les façons, et il n'est pas étonnant qu'elle appelle l'ironie et le pamphlet.' 'Le Gouvernement et la Chambre', 7 August 1947, Pol Int 138.

61 'Si une institution est nécessaire au Liban, c'est bien la Chambre des députés. Et ce n'est pas pour l'amour de la démocratie; mais bien parce que le Liban est un pays de communautés associées (dont aucune d'ailleurs ne représente à elle seule la majorité).' 'Une institution nécessaire', 24 October 1946, Pol Int 114–15.

62 "La Chambre des députés est un élément essentiel de la vie politique. Des minorités confessionnelles associées (c'est bien le cas chez nous) ont besoin pour demeurer associées d'une *représentation collective.*' 'A propos de la Chambre', 30 August 1944, Pol Int 54–5.

63 '[I] faudra toujours que nous ayons une Chambre pour avoir la paix.' 'Une institution nécessaire' (24 October 1946), Pol Int 116.

> The Executive is so strong in Lebanon (contrary to a childish and tenacious prejudice) that it will always be in its power to attenuate passions instead of flattering them.[64]

Within the communal system, the CD was essential to avoid becoming hostage to the country's clerical institutions. Outside the CD, the interests of the people are expressed by their religious leaders, a recipe for failure to transcend the communal straitjacket.

> *In Lebanon, the Chamber of Deputies, a necessary meeting place and a symbol of the desire for coexistence, is the epitome of balance and harmony.* Its absence has always led to a brutal return to communalism. Its disappearance has regularly had the effect of moving political debate to the church, the mosque and the synagogue.[65]

Time and again, Chiha would encourage the deputies to take their role seriously and convey their constituents' interests with lively debate amongst all parliamentarians. Only these deliberations could ensure a common space and a national debate. It was not up to the cabinet to fulfill this role, because the cabinet was often the product of the victory of one faction over another.

The abolition of the Senate

It took less than a year before the redundancy of the Senate was acknowledged. In the very first amendment introduced on 17 October 1927, every article mentioning the Senate was deleted, starting with Article 16. Art. 16 established that legislative power was to be exercised 'by two bodies: the Senate and the Chamber of Deputies'. There is 'only one body', the amended text said simply, 'the CD'. The significant number of articles amended in 1927 underlines the desire to do away with the complications caused by the existence of two chambers.[66]

[64] 'Et l'Exécutif est si fort au Liban (contrairement à un préjugé puéril et tenace) qu'il sera toujours en son pouvoir d'atténuer de ce côté les passions au lieu de les flatter'. Id.

[65] '*Au Liban, la Chambre des députés, lieu de rencontre nécessaire, symbole du vouloir vivre en commun, est la condition même de l'équilibre et de la concorde.* Son absence a toujours signifié automatiquement le retour brutal à l'organisation confessionnelle. Sa disparition a régulièrement eu pour effet de transporter le débat politique dans l'église, dans la mosquée et dans la synagogue'. Id.

[66] The other amended articles concerning the Senate are Arts. 18, 22, 23, 26, 27, 28, 29, 30, 31, 32, 33, 34, 35, 37, 38, 39, 40, 41, 42, 43, 44, 45, 46, 47, 48, 49, 51, 52, 53, 54, 55, 56, 57, 58, 59, 60, 66, 67,

Chiha was opposed to the Senate from the beginning. In 1950, he laid out the grounds for his opposition. A discreet and understated character, he never vaunted his central role in drafting the Constitution. But despite his reluctance to put himself forward, he did not hesitate in the late 1940s to express his annoyance with renewed attempts to create a Senate he believed was meant to empower new officials for petty political advantage: 'If the Government is thinking of manufacturing a Senate in order to appoint new officials, we might as well acknowledge this right now'.[67]

The controversy over the Senate provides a rare occasion on which Chiha claimed authorship of the Constitution outright, with a side jibe against de Jouvenel:

> We talk about these things because we have lived them. I was deputy for Beirut at the time, and I drafted this Constitution myself, a constitution which experimented with a Senate because of pressure from Henry de Jouvenel, himself a senator in France. There was no reason to be so obstinate. As always happens, reality triumphed over theory at lightning speed. Despite this, every precaution was taken in the Constitution to ensure that the Senate was as little cumbersome as possible.[68]

De Jouvenel enjoyed good relations with his peers in the French Senate and believed the upper chamber had a calming role. While his personal preference no doubt played a part, the existence of a Senate with seven of 16 members appointed by the HC also strengthened the hand of France in Lebanon.

Yet Chiha might have been too harsh towards the High Commissioner's alleged obsession with a Senate. The concept of an upper chamber was common in the region. The Egyptian Constitution of 1923 created a Senate, and memories of the 'Chamber of notables' (*Hay'at al-a'yan*) within the Ottoman

68, 73, 74, 75, 76, 77, 78, 79, 80, 84, 85, 86, 87, 96, 98, 99, 100. One gets a sense of the size of the constitutional overhaul in 1927.

[67] '[s]ic'est pour faire des nominations que le Gouvernement songe à fabriquer un Sénat, autant voir les choses dès maintenant sous ce jour.' Chiha, 'Pour faire réfléchir', 16 June 1950, Pol. Int 202.

[68] 'Nous parlons de ces choses parce que nous les avons vécues. Nous étions député de Beyrouth alors, et nous avions rédigé nous-même cette Constitution où il fut inévitable de faire l'expérience du Sénat, sur le désir pressant d'Henry de Jouvenel, lui-même sénateur en France. Il n'y avait pas de raison de s'obstiner. Mais, comme il arrive toujours, la réalité triompha de la théorie avec une rapidité foudroyante. Et dans la Constitution pourtant, toutes les précautions avaient été prises pour que le Sénat fût aussi peu encombrant que possible'. Id., 201–2.

Congress were still strong in the Sunni elite of the coastal cities of Lebanon. Tripoli and Beirut had participated in Ottoman elections several times and dispatched their deputies to the Majlis al-mab'uthin, the lower chamber of the Empire. The Ottoman upper chamber also included 'Lebanese' members appointed by the Porte.[69]

In the course of 1926, the complications the Senate inflicted on the machinery of government soon deadlocked the political process. With no parties yet and no party discipline, the fractiousness of both chambers led to painful legislative shuttles with all the delays and impasses inherent in a dual chamber system. These complications, especially on urgent budgetary deadlines, were noted by Chiha:

> The Senate of 1926, which Henry de Jouvenel wanted, lasted exactly one year. It was appointed in its entirety by the High Commissioner and composed of sixteen elders selected from the city's most virtuous men. After twelve months, political life was so encumbered, so poisoned by the new assembly, that the Senate had to be scrapped.[70]

Whilst the country's political life, already byzantine and cumbersome because of communalism, was further complicated by the Senate, two results obtained from its rapid suppression. One was short-term. The other emerged much later.

The short-term consequence was the undermining of the CD's legitimacy. Because France sought to keep the HC's role in appointing some members in the legislature, however few, a major democratic rule was broken.

[69] In the first Ottoman legislature after the revolution which deposed Sultan 'Abdal-Hamid in 1908, the upper house/senate (*hay'at al-a'yan*, literally the chamber or committee of notables) included several names associated with 'Lebanon', like the later Mount Lebanon *mutasarref* Ohannes Basha, a high Armenian civil servant (appointed *mutasarref* in 1912, resigned in 1914); Fethi Franco Basha, the son of the third *mutasarref* Franco (1868–1873), and Sulaiman al-Bustani, mentioned in Chapter 1 as the author of a book on the 1876 Ottoman Constitution. For details on the rich Ottoman parliamentary experiment between 1908 and 1914, see Aykut Kansu, *The Revolution of 1908 in Turkey*, Brill, Leiden 1997; *Politics in Post-revolutionary Turkey, 1908–1913*, Brill, Boston 2000.

[70] 'Le Sénat de 1926, voulu par Henry de Jouvenel, dura exactement un an. Il était entièrement nommé par le Haut-Commissaire et composé de seize pères conscrits parmi les hommes les plus vertueux de la cité. Au bout de douze mois, la vie politique était tellement encombrée, elle était tellement empoisonnée par la nouvelle assemblée qu'il fallut supprimer le Sénat.' Chiha, 'Pour faire réfléchir', above n.67, Pol. Int 201.

With the 16 senators appointed by France now added to the CD's 30 members, in a unified Chamber, all 46 deputies saw their legitimacy weakened. The Lebanese Congress, which elected the president and was a joint legislator, was suddenly undermined to the tune of one-third. Chiha noted the emergence of appointed legislative members as a severe blow to democracy: 'The result was the unplanned addition of senators and deputies that ended in a wonder the world has never seen: appointed deputies'.[71] Chiha's quip was more than just sarcasm. He, and most of his Lebanese colleagues, saw how the HC's designation of members to a chamber that was supposed to reflect the will of the people stripped popular representation of its core meaning.[72]

The abolition of the Senate and the consequent appointment of non-elected members to the CD did not go without protest from several members of the joint meeting of the chambers to discuss and pass the amendments. As recorded in the minutes of the session, deputy after deputy expressed his dismay at the recycling of Senators as appointed deputies by constitutional amendment.[73]

This was the short, one-year life, of the Lebanese Senate. Its longer-term fate and its problematic impact on constitutional rule show obduracy in collective institutional memory. The idea of a Senate persists. From time to time in the twentieth century, resuscitating the Senate is mooted as a possible panacea to some of the problems of Lebanese political life. A Senate was eventually integrated in the Ta'ef accords of 1989 and formally introduced in a set of amendments to the Constitution in 1990. Art. 22, which had been abrogated by the Constitutional law of 1927, was reintroduced with an updated role for a Senate:

[71] 'Le résultat fut une addition imprévue de sénateurs et de députés qui aboutit à une merveille inconnue dans le monde: les députés nommés'. Id.

[72] See for instance intervention of Fu'ad Arslan during the debate over the first amendment of the Constitution on the morning of 13 October 1927: '... we find ourselves before a project establishing appointment [of the deputies], in which the sacred right of the people is lost. This is the only right left to the people. If we deprive them from this right, we would have betrayed their trust in us'. Zein ed., *Mahader Munaqashat al-Dustur al-Lubnani wa Taʿdilatuh 1926–90* (Minutes of the discussions about the Lebanese Constitution and its amendments), above n.53, 107; see also speech by Chebl Dammous in the afternoon of 13 October, id., 124.

[73] Id., 101, rejection by Fu'ad Arslan, Chebl Dammous, Emile Eddé, Georges Zouein, Muhammad al-Jisr.

> With the election of the first Chamber of Deputies on a national, not sectarian, basis, a Senate shall be established in which all religious communities are represented. Its powers shall be limited to national matters of major importance.[74]

The Senate's revival in the Ta'ef texts, followed by a freeze on its establishment, attests to the widespread ambivalence which persisted between its emergence in 1926 and its abolition a year later. Compounding the undemocratic parachuting of senators into the not yet one year-old CD, the disregard for minimal constitutional stability played havoc with the rule of law. Regular suspensions of the Constitution during the Mandate vitiated the democratic essence of the regime and impaired the importance of continuity in the social contract which a constitution expresses in writing. One easy way out was to abolish the upper Chamber. Some 60 years later, the easy way out for the Ta'ef participants was to reestablish the Senate as the solution to sectarianism, without much thought given to the reasons which led to its abolition in 1927. Nor did they understand that the complication of an added legislative chamber would not resolve the far more deleterious communitarian apportionments at the head of the executive.

Budgetary developments

We saw in the previous chapter the importance Chiha gave the budget while drafting the Constitution. A man of the Enlightenment, Chiha had many strings to his professional and scholarly bows. As a banker, he knew how to read economic data, evidently scarce at the time in Lebanese public finance. His interest in budgetary matters appears strongly in the relatively large set of articles in the Constitution devoted to the matter.[75] Few of his peers knew much about such technical matters.

[74] French text: 'Avec l'élection de la première Chambre des députés sur une base nationale et non confessionnelle, un Sénat sera créé où seront représentées toutes les familles spirituelles. Ses attributions seront limitées aux questions nationales d'intérêt majeur' (*al-'a'ilat al-ruhiyya*, literally 'spiritual families' in the Arabic original). On the 1989 Ta'ef agreement and the Senate, see Ch. 11.

[75] See Chiha noting the constitutional details on the budget in a long 1949 editorial: 'Au titre IV de la Constitution, il y a un article 85, un article 87, un article 88 que ceux qui nous gouvernent feraient bien de relire. Il y en a d'autres ... (In Title IV of the Constitution, there are an article 85, an article 87, an article 88, which those who govern us better read. There are others ...)'. 'Finances dominicales', 23 January 1949, PEL 114–19, at 118–19.

During his term as deputy between 1925 and 1929, and before resigning his position in Parliament, Chiha was tasked with drawing up the first two budgets of the Republic, in 1927 and in 1928. The summaries of the annual budgetary law which he presented to his colleagues express his annoyance with the absence of reliable data and the lack of professionalism in public finance:

> Although slightly weightier than the previous year, the 1929 budget does not stand out. Like its predecessors, it is peppered with vague headings and brief summaries that give the overall impression of a fragmentary effort. The introduction is thin. With a complete absence of financial detail, it does nothing to suggest what should come next. The Chamber simply must address the absence of any significant economic figures and even fewer relevant financial figures. It seems we are not in the habit of dealing with financial statistics, which is not surprising as they are laborious and require perseverance and conscientiousness. Surely this is not beyond our capabilities?[76]

And again the following year:

> No statistical evidence or informal figures are available for submission, not to the General Public but to the Chamber and the Government itself. This explains the absence of coherence, the absence of a global perspective, and the absence even of a general idea on where things stand. In short, we can produce a budget but not a balance sheet, or we can produce a very poor balance sheet based on an unreliable inventory.[77]

Chiha's frustration with the data available was inevitable considering how thin budgetary laws were in these early years. The first Budget Law passed on 26 April 1927 consists of 31 short articles, most of them adjusting taxes to other currencies – the Turkish-Ottoman mejidiye, the French franc, the Lebanese-Syrian lira.[78] Two articles summing up the annual exercise starting

[76] 'Summary of the 1929 Budget Report to the Chamber of Deputies Presented by Mr. Michel Chiha', in http://michelchiha.org/about-michel-chiha/finance-economy/government-budgets/, citing excerpts from articles in *Le Réveil*, 14 and 17 December 1928.

[77] '1929 BUDGET – Salient Points', http://michelchiha.org/about-michel-chiha/finance-economy/government-budgets/, n.d.

[78] The law is available in five small pages, *Al-Majalla al-Qada'iyya/Revue Judiciaire* 7, 1927, 161–5 without annexes.

1 January 1927 mention 1.219.270 Liras in revenues and expenses (Arts. 3 and 4). This was equivalent to ca 60,000 French francs, to which the Syrian-Lebanese pound was pegged since 1920, with this value reconfirmed in 1924.[79]

In 1927, the totality of the published budget was therefore equivalent to 41,000 Euros a century later, a small sum even by the standards of the tiny Lebanese economy.[80] But the real figures do not appear on the budget presented to Parliament. The French had secured control, without accountability, of taxes levied on customs, the most important sources of revenue in the young Lebanese state. Throughout the Mandate period, custom revenues amounted to approximately 90% of state revenues and were wholly controlled by the mandatory power.[81]

Money always matters. We mentioned how Henri Gouraud quit his responsibilities in Lebanon as HC in 1922 when the French government slashed the budget for Lebanon and Syria.[82] Ten years later, the official reason for Ponsot's suspension of the Constitution in 1932 was budgetary. In addition to the fractious politics over the presidency, Lebanon was severely affected by the international economic crisis that followed the collapse of Wall Street in 1929. Ponsot explained the problem, in economic terms, to the Mandate Commission sitting in Geneva: 'Overall, the recovery effort is reflected in the following figures: the actual savings made during 1932 are of the order of 8 to 10 million francs. The budget for Lebanon for 1933 will probably be limited to 84 million compared with a forecast of 102 million for the previous year'.[83]

[79] See for a brief history of the currency, https://www.bdl.gov.lb/about-banque-du-liban.html.

[80] For conversion operations, 'Convertisseur Franc-Euros', at https://www.insee.fr/fr/information/2417794 (consulted April 2023).

[81] '[The budget common to Lebanon and the Syria 'states', which was managed by the High Commissioner] revenues were largely raised from customs revenues collected directly by the *Office des douanes* under the direct control of the High Commissioner (between 80 and 90 percent)'. Joelle Abi-Rached and Ishac Diwan, 'The economic legacy of the French Mandate in Lebanon', *Economic Research Forum*, Cairo, Working Paper 1614, November 2022, 6. (In French 'Ce que l'économie du Mandat a légué au Liban', *Revue du Droit Public*, 139, 2023, 60–81.)

[82] Julie d'Andurain, *Le Général Gouraud- Un Destin hors du Commun, de l'Afrique au Levant*, Paris: Perrin 2022 (cited above Ch.3), at 404 for figures (French budget for Lebanon and Syria: 180 millions francs in 1920, 120 million in 1921, 50 millions 1922).

[83] 'Dans l'ensemble, l'effort de redressement se traduit par les chiffres suivants: l'économie effectivement réalisée au cours de l'année 1932 est de l'ordre de 8 à 10 millions de francs. Le budget pour le Liban pour 1933 se bornera probablement à 84 millions contre une prévision de 102 millions pour l'exercice précédent'. Rapport SDN 1931, cited by Rabbath, *La Formation Historique du Liban Constitutionnel*, above n.9, 417.

After 1929, Chiha realised that parliament had little or no control over state finances. There is no significant comment available from him on the topic until after Lebanese independence in 1943. In 1944, he published an article on how to pass a fair budget and engage in healthy public finances.[84] In 1949, a common concern in two successive articles is the lack of transparency so long as the government indulges in secretive and unauthorised expenses.[85]

A leitmotif in Chiha's articles is the CD's dereliction of its parliamentary duties. Only Parliament can ensure that the budget is fair and transparent, Chiha explained. Part of its sacred duty is to inform its citisens, 'the good people':[86]

> *We, Lebanese citizens, (and it is the right of everyone) wish to know all the resources of the State and the use to which they are put. We request that an account be given to the Chamber. We are making this individual petition a public act.*[87]

Parliament was particularly important for Chiha, not only to counterbalance the power of an increasingly dominant executive power, but also to lighten communal entrenchment which, in the absence of a common agora, pushes citizens to fall back on their religious leaderships. His attachment to basic democratic principles, which we develop next, was always remarkable. Part of this attachment, naturally for a consummate liberal, was to freedom.

[84] 'Prévisions budgétaires et autres', 12 January 1944, PEL 13–15 (on Beirut and the fiscal targeting of merchants). Chiha was worried about overtaxing, in particular what he considered a specific punishment of Beirut and its merchants.

[85] On lack of transparency and the role of Parliament, 'Les finances de la République', 15 January 1949, PEL 109–14 at 111; 'Finances dominicales', 23 January 1949, PEL 114–19 at 115, 116, 117.

[86] 'Le bon peuple', in 'Les finances de la République', above n.85, 110.

[87] '*Nous, citoyens libanais (et c'est le droit de chacun) nous demandons à connaître toutes les ressources de l'Etat et l'emploi qu'on en fait. Nous formulons le vœu qu'à la tribune de la Chambre on en fasse la lecture. Nous faisons de cette pétition individuelle un acte public.*' Id., 118.

9

Chiha's Worldview

> We believe this morning, after the calm meditation of the night, that it is permissible to doubt everything, but not the delicate sensibility of a Lebanese people who have for so long renounced everything that Political Economy calls property and wealth, privileging the freedom to choose their own friends and gods.[1]

The French connection

Recently elected as a deputy of Beirut, Michel Chiha was thirty-six when he was thrown into a public career which started on the high note of constitutional drafting. We have no trace of any major writing of his before then.[2] His law studies in Cairo during the war enabled him to work as a lawyer, but the bar association of Beirut was founded only in 1920, two years after

[1] 'Nous pensons ce matin, après la calme méditation de la nuit, qu'il est permis de douter de tout, mais non de la sensibilité frémissante de ce peuple libanais qui a si longtemps renoncé à tout ce que l'Economie Politique appelle biens et richesses pour préférer à tout cela la liberté de choisir ses amis et ses dieux'. Michel Chiha, 'D'une révision' 9 November 1943, Pol Int 40.

[2] The Chiha archives include five articles published in *Le Réveil* before 1926. He published with Henry Debbané a magazine/journal during their law studies in Cairo, *Les Ebauches*. The collection has survived in the general Chiha Archive. It consists of a magazine, fully in French, published twice a month. *Les Ebauches* was published in Alexandria and distributed in Cairo and in Paris. The cover page of the first issue of *Les Ebauches* is dated 1 June 1916: see Claude Doumet-Serhal and Michèle Hélou-Nahas eds, *Michel Chiha 1891–1954*, Beirut: Fondation Michel Chiha 2001, 43. The last issue, numbered 21–22, is dated September 1917. The issues are available in two bound volumes, the first in 480 pages, the second in 324 pages. Chiha wrote under various pseudonyms (Tite, Em. Say., M.C., Thaumaste ...) a third to a half of each issue of *Les Ebauches*. The magazine is a literary publication with poems, epistolary exchanges, book reviews, and short stories, all genres which the young Chiha practised on it pages. There is, oddly, barely a reference to the raging World War at the time. An exception is the publication of a lecture by 'R. S.' on 'Les lois de la guerre', *Les Ebauches*, 1st year, issue 19–20, June 1917, 199–216. An editorial note explains that the lecture by 'our collaborator and friend R.S.' had been, 'très applaudie, à l'Université Populaire du Caire'. Id., 199 n.1.

his return, and he did not practise law at the bar despite the survival of his official membership in a document in the Chiha Archive. Since his return to Lebanon, he seems to have been focused primarily on the financial affairs of the family bank.

Chiha was fully conversant in Arabic, his native language, but did not publish any work in Arabic. This was not unusual during the French Mandate, nor is it unusual a century later. The Lebanese francophone and francophile intelligentsia interact intensively, then and now, with official representatives of France, as well as with a large network of schools and colleges which operate mainly in French.[3] The law school of Saint Joseph's University (USJ in its French acronym) remains a major reservoir of officials and politicians amongst the Lebanese lawyers whom it trains in French and Lebanese law through the four years of undergraduate studies required for the degree.

In addition to the exclusive dispensation in Lebanon of French law studies in the first half of the twentieth century at Saint Joseph's University, it was uniquely difficult, during the Mandate, to accede to top positions in the Lebanese administration and in government without being able to deal comfortably with the French administration.[4] This was reflected in Art. 11

Chiha cooperated also with *La Revue Phénicienne*, founded by Charles Corm (1894–1963), who had, as the title of the *Revue* suggests, a view of Lebanon as a unique, non-Ottoman, non-Arab, heir to Phenicia (*La Revue Phénicienne*'s four issues were published in 1919, and were reprinted in facsimile, Beirut: Dar An-Nahar 1996). The *Revue* appeared also briefly to be pro-Greater Syria: see Henri Lammens's front article in issue 4, Christmas 1919, 'Histoire de la nationalité syrienne', 193–207, vaunting the coherence and unity of Syria through the ages. The paradox is explained by the fact that the French were initially inclined to englobe Syria as one entity under the Mandate as drawn by Sykes-Picot. Chiha contributed, in the style of *Les Ebauches*, three articles of literary and mystical flavour, 'Entretiens de Patrice', in the second, third and fourth issues, respectively at 91–2, 135, 258.

[3] For the birth of a lasting Lebanese 'Francophonie', see Daniel Lançon, 'Exil, Terre natale, terre rêvée: Naissance de la Francophonie littéraire libanaise dans et par la Grande Guerre', in Carole Dagher and Myra Prince eds, *De la Grande Guerre au Grand-Liban*, Paris: Geuthner 2015, 151–84.

[4] Saint Joseph's University (USJ in its French acronym) produced most of the governing elite in the better part of twentieth century Lebanon. A sprawling Jesuit higher education institution, USJ teaches a large set of disciplines, including medicine, engineering, business and humanities, mostly in French. USJ's direct American competitor, the American University of Beirut, never trained Lebanese lawyers despite its wide range teaching in other fields. Law was exclusively taught in Lebanon at Saint Joseph's until the founding of the country's national university in the 1950s. Furthermore, a US law degree is exclusively a post-graduate degree ('graduate' in American parlance) since Harvard Law School, under the deanship of Christopher Langdell, added in the late nineteenth century two then three years for a Juris Doctor degree for a graduate student to become

of the Constitution, which considered both Arabic and French to be official languages.[5] Arabic was often disparaged in French schools during the Mandate, with the notorious *bâton* given as a punishment to the student who spoke Arabic during the break. This negative recollection may be an exaggeration, but it conveys the atmosphere of French cultural dominance through most of Michel Chiha's life. While Arabic is the native language of most Lebanese, French remains widely used when it comes to research and publishing. Other writers in French include internationally-acclaimed literary figures like Georges Schéhadé, Chucri Ghanem, Charles Corm, later Nadia Tueni, Amin Maalouf, Charif Majdalani and Wajdi Mouawwad, and French-educated leaders starting with the first Lebanese president, Charles Debbas, several times president Emile Eddé, later his son Raymond, the socialist leader Kamal Joumblat, and USJ rector Sélim Abou.[6] Several Lebanese presidents were trained at Saint Joseph's and/or studied law in France. The tradition of cultural excellence in French persisted in the country, with children of the Lebanese elite adding English as a third language since its accelerated rise as world lingua franca in the late twentieth century.

After the Constitution was enacted, Chiha wrote prolifically, in French. His books include regular columns, in addition to lectures and essays on domestic and international topics, ethics, history, and the economy, even a

a lawyer. The unusual pattern extended quickly to all accredited law schools in the US, but it remains mostly an American exception in the world. This is why USJ remained without a competitor in Lebanon for the dispensation of a law degree, whereas medicine, business and several other disciplines were also taught in the older American University of Beirut. On the recruitment of French and, later, of Lebanese French-speaking professors at USJ, see Catherine Fillon, 'Le Jésuite, l'universitaire et le politique: stratégies de recrutement du corps enseignant de l'école Française de droit de Beyrouth (1913–1939)' in Jean-Christophe Aven et Frédéric Audren eds, *Les Facultés de Droit de Province aux XIXe et XXe Siècles*, 3 vols, Toulouse: Presses de l'Université Toulouse 1, Vol. 3, 2012, 115–38. On the history of the school of law at Saint Joseph's see Jean Ducruet, *Livre d'Or de la Faculté de Droit, Sciences Politiques et Economiques, 1913–1993*, Beyrouth: Publications de l'Université Saint-Joseph de Beyrouth 1995.

[5] In Chiha's first draft, Art. 10 (DOC 1). Constitution of 1926, Art.11.

[6] Kamal Joumblat, who was assassinated in 1977, left a posthumous book in French, *Pour le Liban*, Paris: Stock 1978. Sélim Abou (d. 2018) was at the forefront of Lebanese nonviolent resistance to Syria's domination, leaving a set of commemorative annual lectures given on the anniversary of Saint Joseph's and collected in *Les Libertés*, Beyrouth: USJ Press 2003 (see my English translation and preface in *Freedoms*, Beirut: USJ, 2005). The other writers mentioned represent a mere sample of a rich Francophone legacy in literature, with dozens of works published.

collection of poetry.[7] He gathered a museum-grade collection of antique seals from the Near East.[8] In addition to this wide array of intellectual and professional interests, it is no surprise that he kept a critical eye on 'his' Constitution until his death in 1954. The genesis of the Constitution and his comments on public life after its enactment are informed by his erudition in history and in literature, together with a sophisticated knowledge in law, which he practised occasionally as arbitrator; and in economics, which he exercised daily at the bank, and in his advice on budgetary matters and public finance in the country.

Contrary to the generally received notion of Chiha standing against Arabic and Arab culture, he expressed in this wide-ranging historical vision a strong attachment to the language:

> Arabic is a magnificent language. It is the language of millions of people; we would not be ourselves if we, Lebanese of this twentieth century, refuse to master it as we have for a hundred years.[9]

An article published in 1952 by the *Bayrut* newspaper disparages Chiha's understanding and use of Arabic.[10] The slightly circular argument was that Chiha did not publish in Arabic, hence did not know the language well; and

[7] Works in ten vols collected at Editions Trident: see references at the beginning of the book, and the bibliography. For the scholarship on Chiha's thought, in addition to the books of Mahdi 'Amel and Fawaz Traboulsi cited in the previous chapter, see Michelle Hartman and Alessandro Olsaretti, '"The First Boat and the First Oar": Inventions of Lebanon in the Writings of Michel Chiha', *Radical History Review*, 86, 2003, 37–65, esp. at 55 on the social-moral aspects of his thought; Jean Salem, *Introduction à la Pensée Politique de Michel Chiha*, Beirut: Samir 1970; Kais Firro, 'Lebanese nationalism versus Arabism: From Bulus Nujaym to Michel Chiha', *Middle Eastern Studies*, 40, 2004, 1–27; Nabil Khalifa, *Michel Chiha, Awwal Anbiya' Lubnan wa Akher Anbiya' Falastin* (Michel Chiha, the first Lebanese prophet, and the last prophet of Palestine), Byblos: Markaz biblos lil-dirasat 2013.

[8] Claude Doumet-Serhal, *Sceaux et Cylindres Orientaux: la Collection Chiha*, Freiburg, Switzerland: Editions Universitaires 1992.

[9] 'L'arabe est une langue magnifique et c'est la langue de millions d'hommes; nous ne serions pas nous-mêmes si nous renoncions, nous Libanais de ce vingtième siècle, à en devenir les maîtres comme nous le fûmes depuis cent ans'. *Liban d'Aujourd'hui* ('LA'), Beirut: Editions du Trident, original 1942, rpt 2008, 49.

[10] Unknown author, '*Al-ustadh Chiha wal-lugha al-'arabiyya* (Mr Chiha and the Arabic language)', Beirut, 24 November 1952: 'If Mr Chiha knew Arabic well, it would have been more appropriate for him, especially since he criticises the styles of Arabic, to do so in Arabic, and give the good example to direct the children of Arabic towards the better contemporary style. Since he did not, then it is our right to reject his criticism, and consider Mr Chiha no expert in the matter.' Available on the Chiha site.

that if he did know Arabic, then it is most odd that he never wrote or lectured in Arabic: 'We cannot forgive him for lecturing to his people in a foreign language. André Maurois, for instance, who writes and lectures in America and England in English, would never allow himself to give lectures to the French, and to write for the French, in the language of Shakespeare'.[11]

The criticism is misplaced. No doubt Chiha was more comfortable in French than in Arabic, but his Arabic was excellent, and not only to carry constitutional discussions in various committees and in parliament. We have a remarkable eulogy in Arabic written in his hand upon the death in 1950 of a friend, the Tripoli leader 'Abd al-Hamid Karameh.[12] His command of the language allowed him to read Arabic poetry. A paean to a Lebanese poet who wrote in the vernacular, Michel Trad (d.1998), can be found in a Chiha column where he cites him as well as another major figure of modern Arabic poetry, Sa'id Aql (d.2014), and translates some of their verses while applauding their creative break with the traditional poetical canons.[13]

This all is besides the point which really matters. In his writings, Chiha was rightly critical of the way Arabic was suffocated by empty rhetoric. Expressing again his attachment to the language, he raised a legitimate concern about the mother tongue becoming stultified in its daily use and the way it is taught:

> [B]ut if the proponents of the Arabic language, and we are among them, want it to live because it is not only an instrument of poetry but also a means of power, they must understand that it cannot live with windows closed, and that vast supplies of oxygen around it must be renewed (as, under analogous conditions, is the case for all languages).[14]

[11] Id.

[12] Undated Arabic eulogy in his hand, in two pages, on file with author from the Chiha Archive. Karameh died on 23 November 1950. The text is eloquent, the final paragraph reads: '*Inna al-'atifa al-hayya takhruq hijab al-mawt. wa halil-mawt illa hayatun ab'ad ghawran min al-hayat?* (Living emotion pierces the veil of death. Is death other than life deeper than life?)'

[13] 'There are a few of them now, with us, who liberate the noble Arabic language from the austere laws and allow it to run free in the meadows. (Ils sont quelques-uns maintenant, chez nous, à libérer la noble langue arabe de lois austères pour lui permettre de courir les champs.)' Chiha, 'Un poète de chez nous', 6 January 1952, available on the Chiha site.

[14] '[M]ais si les tenants de la langue arabe, et nous en sommes, veulent qu'elle vive parce qu'elle n'est pas seulement un instrument de poésie mais aussi un moyen de puissance, il faut qu'ils comprennent qu'elle ne peut pas vivre les fenêtres fermées, et qu'il faut que de vastes provisions d'oxygène autour d'elle se renouvellent (comme, dans des conditions analogues, c'est le cas pour toutes les langues).' 'Les langues sont une richesse', 7 November 1944, Pol Int 63.

What are these closed windows?

> The present and future glory of the Arabic language requires that thousands of the most educated and learned Lebanese not be condemned to silence today; it requires, for a time and until the necessary effort is made for Arabic to become *the preferred language of all*, so that the Lebanese express themselves as they can and as it pleases them.[15]

Chiha was expressing his concern that Arabic, as it was taught, would not be simple enough for children and adolescents to understand. Its dominantly stilted style at the time made natives feel estranged from their mother tongue because of the gap between classical and spoken Arabic (*fusḥā* and *dārej*), and because of the sacrifice of the spoken language to classical Arabic's elaborate and sometimes trying forms. The problem remains pressing across the Arab world because of the persistent hiatus between spoken vernaculars and written, classical Arabic. Here also, Chiha comes out as a visionary reformist.

Nor was Chiha impervious to the weakness of the newly established League of Arab States. Elsewhere, he remarked that the Arab world, of which Lebanon was part, is still insignificant in terms of power: '*The countries of the Arab League, to which we belong, what are they alone, in the world today?* In terms of strength, next to nothing, it must be said with honesty and courage.'[16]

Chiha maintains that this weakness can and must be remedied. We are at the end of the Second World War, when the few independent countries in the Arab world have just come together in the Arab League, except for the French colonies in North Africa. At the time, there were only 40 million citizens in the Organisation:

> Now, therefore, *the 40 million men of the countries of the Arab League find themselves living in the very birthplaces of History, which are, together with Ancient History, the starting point for the teaching of the historical past across*

[15] 'La gloire présente et future de la langue arabe exige que des milliers de Libanais parmi les plus instruits, les plus savants ne soient pas aujourd'hui condamnés au mutisme; elle exige, pendant un temps, jusqu'à ce que l'effort légitime que l'on tente pour que l'arabe devienne à haut degré *la langue éminente de tous*, que les Libanais puissent s'exprimer comme ils le peuvent et comme il leur plaît'. Id., 63–4.

[16] '*Les pays de la Ligue arabe, et nous en sommes, que sont-ils à eux seuls, dans le monde d'aujourd'hui*? Sur le plan de la force, à peu près rien, il faut le dire avec honnêteté et courage'. (1950) VPL 103. Emphasis in original, as in all subsequent citations of Chiha in this chapter.

> *the West*. This is the tight link, the natural link that we do not see enough (any more in the West than in the Middle East) and which is the key to an inescapable solidarity.[17]

This does not prevent the immense potential for the Arab world of which Lebanon is a member:

> *Both geographically and historically, they [the Arab countries] are a priceless reality*. If they cannot do much by themselves, their strength lies in necessarily intelligent and comprehensive policies. *On their own, they comprise a network of roads and crossroads they are unable to defend*; and oil, often referred to as 'industrial fuel and politically explosive', lies beneath them in deep deposits.[18]

In sum, it is incumbent on Lebanese to master Arabic alongside Western languages, to shed its rhetorical bent and the awkwardness it conveys to the youth. Mastering Arabic is not only a literary and economic must. It is a political 'necessity'.[19]

Literary distinction in the Arab world is a matter of pride for Lebanon, whose poets, journalists and writers have carried the torch of excellence:

> *It must be our legitimate ambition to know it and to teach it at an advanced level, in order to be able to continue to give the Arab world its greatest writers, greatest journalists and greatest poets, as well as standing and prestige.*[20]

[17] 'Or donc, *les 40 millions d'hommes des pays de la Ligue arabe, se trouvent habiter les lieux de naissance mêmes de l'Histoire, lesquels sont, avec l'Histoire ancienne, au point de départ de l'enseignement du passé historique dans tout l'Occident*. Voilà le lien profond, le lien naturel qu'on ne voit pas assez (pas plus d'ailleurs en Occident qu'en Proche-Orient) et qui est la clé d'une solidarité inéluctable'. Id.

[18] '*[S]ur le plan de la géographie comme sur le plan de l'histoire ils sont une réalité sans prix*. S'ils ne peuvent pas beaucoup par eux-mêmes, leur force est dans une politique intelligente et compréhensive qui est celle de leur destin. *Ils représentent ensemble un nœud de routes et de carrefours dont ils sont incapables de défendre le passage*; et le pétrole, 'combustible industriel et matière explosive politique' comme on l'a appelé souvent, est dans leur sous-sol en nappes lourdes'. Id.

[19] LA 46 (1942).

[20] 'Ce doit être pour nous une ambition légitime de la connaître et de l'enseigner de façon tout à fait supérieure, de manière à conserver avec notre prestige et notre rang la chance de toujours donner au monde arabe ses plus grands écrivains, ses plus grands journalistes et ses plus grands poètes'. LA 48. Chiha lived during the Nahda, the Arabic literary Renaissance which flourished in the first half of the twentieth century, with Cairo and Beirut at its heart.

The second necessity is economic. Noting already the riches of Lebanese industries as chiefly intangible (commerce, communications, banking), he warns that Arabs must not fall behind in the 'neighbourhood' – meaning Palestine/Israel:

> More and more teachers and students are arriving from different places. The teaching of theology, for example, has led to the establishment of seminaries; the teaching of medicine, clinics and hospitals, with their clientele coming from near and far. We should be careful about the increasingly threatening competition in our neighbourhood and must improve our techniques and our disciplines rapidly if we do not want to be left behind.[21]

The third necessity is political, a 'means of power'.[22] Polyglotism and racial mixing result from trade routes which have existed for centuries. 'Merchants have disseminated languages and information. They are and always have been polyglots. *They will increasingly be so*'. [23]

It would be unnatural as well as detrimental if polyglotism were lost: 'Don't we see right away that a country like ours, if it is not bilingual (and even trilingual if possible) is quite simply decapitated?'[24]

Longue durée

The multiplicity of languages dovetails, in Lebanon's position at the heart of the Arab world, with the longue durée experience of the country with overbearing neighbours. Chiha cites historian Gaston Maspéro: 'Syria [meant here to include Lebanon] is so placed that it can only be independent on the condition that it does not have powerful neighbours'.[25] With trade comes conquest,

[21] 'Professeurs et élèves venant de directions en général différentes se sont multipliés. L'enseignement de la théologie, par exemple, a créé le séminaire; et l'enseignement de la médecine, la clinique et l'hôpital, avec leur clientèle venue de près et de loin. Notons que sur ce dernier terrain s'affirme de plus en plus dans notre voisinage une concurrence menaçante et que nous devons améliorer rapidement nos techniques et nos disciplines si nous ne voulons pas être dépassés'. LA 48.

[22] 'moyen de puissance', cited above n.14.

[23] 'Les marchands ont répandu les langues et les nouvelles. Polyglottes depuis l'origine ils n'ont pas cessé de l'être. *Ils le seront de plus en plus*'. (1951) VPL 113.

[24] 'Mais ne voit-on pas tout de suite qu'un pays comme le nôtre, s'il n'est bilingue (et même trilingue s'il se peut) est tout simplement décapité?' LA 50.

[25] 'La Syrie est ainsi placée qu'elle ne peut être indépendante qu'à la condition de ne pas avoir des voisins puissants.' LA 31. Gaston Maspéro (d.1916) was a leading historian of ancient Near Eastern civilizations, which he taught at the Collège de France. Chiha probably quotes from the

and with conquest, disruption, misery and dependence. This was obvious to Chiha and his contemporaries, who were just emerging from a fierce First World War in which Turkish, English and French armies settled their bloody scores on Lebanese soil. '*Our long history*', Chiha wrote in 1944, '*is fertile in events of all kinds. Through the teaching of ancient history, it is known to the entire world. It is part of the heritage of civilised people.*'[26]

The core of Chiha's political-historical views can be found in a long essay, *Liban d'Aujourd'hui*, written in 1942 and published in 1949.[27] The essay is a rich survey of what history means for the country. The book's historical perspective stretches back to antiquity.

Lebanon is both blessed and plagued, Chiha explains, by a vocation that has been determined by geography since the beginning of time:

> Phoenicia presents itself as a narrow passage between Africa and Asia, with the great and virtually impenetrable desert of Syria spreading out beyond Lebanon (...) It was, for those who controlled it, an open door either on Africa or on Asia, a '*marche*' which was a rampart for itself and the launch pad for a future invasion ...[28]
>
> To apply it to the present, what should we change about this definition? Nothing, it seems, except that the desert has been crossed in every direction, roads have multiplied, become wider and more vital, and constantly await the vehicles most suited to imperial service.[29]

11th edition of his *Histoire Ancienne des Peuples de l'Orient*, Paris: Hachette 1912 (original 1895), at 341.

26 '*Elle [our long history]*', '*Elle [our long history] est fertile en événements de toute nature. A travers l'enseignement de l'histoire ancienne, elle est familière à tout l'univers. Elle fait partie du patrimoine de l'humanité civilisée*'. 'La leçon du passé', 1 September 1944, Pol Int 60.

27 In LA, at page 8, Chiha mentions that the text was originally a lecture at the Cercle de la Jeunesse Catholique de Beyrouth in the spring of 1942, and 'a servi de conclusion à une suite de sept conférences sur *le Liban au cours de l'histoire*'. These seven lectures do not seem to have survived and were probably given by other lecturers.

28 'La Phénicie se présente comme un passage étroit entre l'Afrique et l'Asie, puisqu'au-delà du Liban s'étend le grand désert de Syrie pratiquement infranchissable (...) C'était, pour celui qui la possédait, une porte ouverte soir sur l'Afrique, soit sur l'Asie, une '*marche*' qui constituait un rempart pour soi-même et un point de départ à une invasion future ...' LA 16–7. '*Marche*' literally step' in medieval France a demarcating, frontier province.

29 'Pour l'appliquer au présent, que devrions nous changer à cette définition? Rien, il semble, sinon que le désert a été franchi de toutes les manières, que la route s'est multipliée, qu'elle est devenue plus nécessaire et plus large, et qu'elle attend sans cesse les véhicules les plus perfectionnés pour un service impérial'. LA 17.

In the first paragraph of the quotation, Chiha cites a then-famous French historian of Phenicia.[30] In the second part he extrapolates from this concept of '*marche*' an argument for the 'key position' of Phenicia-Lebanon as the obligatory crossroad in an immense territory stretching from Lebanon in Western Asia all the way to China:[31] 'Ending in China, in Peking, the "yellow crusade" of which we keep a remembrance, had Beirut as Asian point of departure; it is in fact the shortest route'.[32] This is the East-West axis Asian terrestrial route, which ends in Lebanon. The other geographical axis is the route running North-South from Europe down to Egypt and the Arabian Peninsula, 'the one of the Orient-Express, which comes from the North.'[33]

These time-honoured trade routes north-south and east-west do not constitute the only geographical determinants of Lebanese history. Lebanon's position at the intersection of the then-known world also determined the character of its inhabitants: not only their propensity to trade, but also their polyglotism and the ensuing mix of cultures vehiculated by the cumulation of languages. Take the case of the Crusades:

> Beirut, for example, occupied around the middle of May 1100 by King Baudouin, will belong to the Franks until July 1291, i.e. more than 180 years, and the Frankish period as a whole will last all that time. But since 1918, barely twenty-five years have passed. This tells us what the 180 years of the Frankish kingdom represents in time.[34]

[30] Georges Conthenau, *La Civilisation Phénicienne*, Paris: Payot 1928, at 37–8. Conthenau (d. 1964) was a prolific author, in charge for a long time of the department of Near East antiquities at the Louvre. Chiha also cites him in an editorial, 'L'Histoire et la vie', 4 April 1950, PEL 148.

[31] Key position, 'position clé', LA 17.

[32] 'Pour aboutir en Chine, à Pékin, la "Croisière Jaune", dont nous avons gardé le souvenir, eut Beyrouth pour point de départ asiatique; c'est en effet le plus court chemin'. LA 17–18. 'La Croisière Jaune refers to a then celebrated land vehicle expedition organized by André Citroen, the owner of the car brand bearing his name, from Beirut to Beijing. It started in Beirut on 4 April 1931 and ended in the Chinese capital on 12 February 1932: see entry 'Croisière Jaune' in the French version of Wikipedia for futher references.

[33] 'celle de l'Orient-Express qui vient du Nord'. Id. 19.

[34] 'Beyrouth par exemple occupé vers le milieu de mai 1100 par le roi Baudouin, appartiendra aux Francs jusqu'en juillet 1291 soit plus de 180 ans, et la période franque dans son ensemble durera tout ce temps-là. Or depuis 1918, vingt-cinq ans à peine se sont écoulés. Rendons-nous compte par là de ce que les 180 années du royaume Franc représentent dans le temps'. LA 38.

These two centuries of Crusader occupation by people from all over the medieval Occident, including Scandinavia, led to 'mixed marriages' and new 'familiar' languages,[35] with polyglotism as an enduring constituent trait. This, Chiha repeats, is an important legacy for the country to hone and develop.

But Lebanon's geographical position has its negatives. The most traumatic event was the double blockade during the war – by land from the Turks, preventing grain reaching Mount Lebanon and the coast, and by sea from the Allies. A third of the civilian population perished in the worst recorded famine in the country's history.[36] Famine ravaging the country was the latest example of this geopolitical weakness.

Chiha himself saw Lebanon's position as a bane as much as a boon as far back as the 10th century BCE when there was evidence of Phoenicia-Lebanon being sandwiched between 'world powers':

> At the beginning of the 9th century BC[E], the wars of conquest and the great invasions resumed. From the demographic point of view, their result is to parade between the Euphrates and the Red Sea the triumphant armies of new empires, which have themselves become 'world' powers. It is an uninterrupted movement, with brutal jolts, which invariably finds Phoenicia-Lebanon and Syria at the center of each adventure. The ebb and flow leave

[35] Id. 'Mariages mixtes' is taken from Belgian Jesuit historian Henri Lammens (d. in Beirut in 1937), who wrote a well-known history of Syria, *Syrie: Précis Historique*, Beirut: Imprimerie Catholique 1921. The Chiha description of mixed marriages refers to Lammens's *Précis*, vol. 1, 241: 'Dans les principautés d'Antioche et d'Edesse, ces mariages de '[l]a noblesse franc-syrienne' furent nombreux'. And at 242, Lammens quotes Fouchet (or Foulcher) de Chartres (d. in Jerusalem in 1127), a priest who took part in the first crusade and wrote a chronicle entitled *Historiae Hierosoliemitana*, translated as *Histoire des croisades*, Paris: n.p. 1825. Available at http://catalogue.bnf.fr/ark:/12148/cb372999811. The original quote appears at Ch. LXII: '[I]ls parlent diverses langues, et sont déjà tous parvenus à s'entendre. Les idiomes les plus différents sont maintenant communs à l'une et à l'autre nation, et la confiance rapproche les races les plus éloignées.' Referenced by Lammens, Foulcher's quote is close but not identical to Lammens', then Chiha's: 'Les langues sont devenues familières', 'communes aux citoyens des deux nations'.

[36] The famine during the First World War is one of the major traumas in modern Lebanese history. For details and further references, Youssef Mouawad, 'Jamal Pacha, en une version libanaise', in *Maronites dans l'Histoire*, Beirut: L'Orient des Livres 2017, 143–76 (Original 2006); Id., 'La famine occultée et la Grande-Guerre de 1914–1918 au Liban', in Carole Dagher and Myra Prince eds, *De la Grande Guerre au Grand-Liban*, Paris: Geuthner 2015, 37–60.

> their human alluvium everywhere and the entanglement of races becomes ever more complicated and accentuated.[37]

Chiha then brushes in a few captivating pages the history of the country under Assyrian occupation, through the conquest of Alexander, the Roman, Byzantine and Persian rivalries and domination.[38] With the advent of Islam, he writes, a new trait of particular importance emerges: religious communalism.

> By force of circumstance, with a nascent Islam, the main label of an individual who, under the domination of Byzantium, was national (one was or was not a citizen of the Empire), and became denominational. Political Islam obviously stems from religious Islam. The Caliph is the Commander not of Syrians or Arabs or Egyptians or Andalusians, but of believers. What we sometimes impute to a kind of fatality, without thinking much about it, finds its starting point in a historical fact. From now on, the ethnographic factor is coupled with a communal factor which becomes more critical. And political Islam automatically includes the various denominations that are under its authority by attributing to them a tiered system of family law dispositions with their varying duties and rewards.[39]

Is Chiha right that communalism starts only with Islam structuring religious sects into so many groups under one dominant Muslim government? Was Christian Byzantium national rather than religious? Probably not, from my perspective if not Chiha's, for the religion-government nexus is so strongly

[37] 'Au début du IXe siècle avant notre ère, les guerres de conquête, les grandes invasions reprennent. Leur résultat du point de vue démographique est de faire défiler entre l'Euphrate et la Mer Rouge les armées triomphantes de nouveaux empires, devenus à leur tour des puissances "mondiales". C'est un mouvement ininterrompu, aux secousses brutales, qui trouve invariablement Phénicie-Liban et Syrie au centre de chaque aventure. Le flux et le reflux laissent partout leurs alluvions humaines et l'enchevêtrement des races se compliquent et s'accentue'. LA 32–33.

[38] LA 31–6.

[39] 'Par la force des choses, avec l'Islam naissant, l'étiquette principale des individus qui, sous la domination des Byzance, était nationale (on était ou on n'était pas citoyen de l'Empire) devient confessionnelle. En effet, l'Islam politique procède évidemment de l'Islam religieux. Le Calife est le Commandeur non des Syriens ou des Arabes ou des Egyptiens ou des Andalous, mais des croyants. Ce que nous imputons quelquefois, sans y réfléchir beaucoup, à une sorte de fatalité, trouve son point de départ dans un fait historique. Désormais, la question ethnographique se double d'une question confessionnelle qui prend le dessus. Et l'Islam politique dénombre automatiquement les confessions diverses qui sont sous son autorité en leur attribuant une hiérarchie de statuts personnels à servitudes et privilèges variables'. LA 36.

associated with the Near East since recorded antiquity that Islam appears merely as the latest major religion to add its own weight, both domestically and internationally, to an already entrenched religion-based system.[40]

This can be read in the Qur'an, in particular the Qur'anic verse which underlines both the autonomy of religious communities and the principle that religious laws should not transcend their respective boundaries.[41] Whether the region previous was religion-based or not, Chiha is right in tracing communalism at least to the advent of Islam. Contrary to the received notion that the Ottomans first established communalism in the so-called '*millet* system', a great historian of Cairene archives in the ten to thirteenth century has demonstrated how the Jewish community in Cairo retained a large dose of self-government whilst paying an exacting tax (the *jizya*) to the Muslim government to which it was subordinated in the public sphere.[42]

There was a further distinctiveness to Lebanese geography. Here also, in Chiha's wide historical brush, the determinant is the mountainous nature of the country that weighed heavily on its social structure. For that determination, he cites Toynbee:

> The contemporary English historian Arnold Toynbee makes an incisive observation in his great work, *A Study of History*.[43] Among the fundamental motives of the evolution of human history he counts what he calls 'the spur of necessity', or 'the pressure stimulus', in other words the stimulus of constraint, 'a continuous external pressure'. In short, this is what Lebanon has always had to endure. *This is what has always made us live 'dangerously'*, making our lives difficult, most recently in the vicinity of Turkish provinces under the sway of Constantinople; with this additional result, visible to the naked eye, that our mixed villages, Christian and Druze for example, which,

[40] For the argument that religion was a key political factor since the Ancient Near East, see my *Introduction to Middle Eastern law* (Oxford: Oxford University Press 2007), section on 'Middle Eastern legal calques', 16–32, and Part IV of the present book.

[41] Q v: 44, a long verse which enjoins in the received interpretation each of the different religious communities to stick to their law, see also references in *Introduction to Middle Eastern law*, above n.40, 33 n78.

[42] Samuel Goitein, Samuel Goitein, *A Mediterranean Society: the Jewish Communities of the Arab World as Portrayed in the Documents of the Cairo Geniza*, 5 vols, Berkeley: University of California Press 1967–88. See also Ch.11 for the discussion of the still 'political-theological' Middle East.

[43] Chiha refers to *The Geneses of Civilization*, Oxford: Oxford University Press 1934, vol. 2, in Toynbee's celebrated 12 volume work, published between 1934 and 1961.

thank God, have long fraternised, are often of a stronger mettle than those villages where there are only Druze or Christians. Hard life leaves a decisive mark on those it touches. It teaches good ethics and sharpens the will. It strengthens character and makes a man sharper and better. But all Lebanese literally have *sea and mountains as their joint homeland*. They are a breed of mountaineer-navigators, very different to those who surround them. Even if we wished this was not the case, it would not be different.[44]

In another passage, he cites and translates the great English historian at length:

> "*In modern times, the highlanders of Lebanon have emulated the historic exploits of the Phoenician islanders of Tyre and Aradus by seeking their fortune abroad and making livelihood as traders and shop keepers far and wide* (Toynbee: A Study of History, T. II p. 56)." ...
>
> *THE ENTIRE LEBANESE ECONOMY IS ADUMBRATED IN THESE LINES.*
>
> "*In the light of the local precedents it looks as though the Lebanese were stimulated to emulate the Phoenicians by the barrenness of their native mountain, while the agreeableness of the Jabal Ansariah has inveigled the Nusayris into vegetating in a Philistine sloth*" (Toynbee, id.). This brings us, as you see, back to the stimulus of pressure.[45]

[44] 'L'historien anglais contemporain Arnold Toynbee fait dans son grand ouvrage: « A Study of History » (Une Etude de l'Histoire) une observation incisive: il retient parmi les mobiles fondamentaux de l'évolution historique des peuples ce qu'il appelle « l'aiguillon de la nécessité »: « the stimulus of pressure », autrement dit le stimulant de la contrainte, « a continuous external pressure » (une pression de l'extérieur continue). C'est en somme ce que le Liban a toujours eu à subir. *C'est ce qui nous a toujours fait vivre « dangereusement »*, en nous faisant la vie dure, en dernier lieu dans le voisinage de provinces turques aux ordres de Constantinople; avec ce résultat complémentaire, visible à l'œil nu, que nos villages mixtes, chrétiens et druzes par exemple, qui, grâce à Dieu, depuis longtemps fraternisent, sont souvent d'une race plus forte que ceux où il n'y a que des druzes ou des chrétiens. La vie dure marque un peuple d'une façon décisive. Elle enseigne les mœurs et elle aguerrit; elle trempe les caractères et fait plus vite et mieux d'un homme, un homme. Mais tous les Libanais ont littéralement pour *patrie conjointe la mer et la montagne*. C'est une race de montagnards navigateurs, très différente de ce qui l'entoure. Nous voudrions qu'il en fût autrement, nous ne le pourrions pas'. (1953) VPL 146–7.

[45] Emphases and caps in original. Chiha provides both the original English text and his own translation into French, at id.: "Dans les temps modernes, les montagnards du Liban ont rivalisé avec les exploits historiques des insulaires de Tyr et d'Aradus, en cherchant fortune à l'étranger et en trouvant leurs moyens d'existence dans le commerce comme marchands et boutiquiers, au loin et partout. (Toynbee: A Study of History, T. II p. 56)." ...

Chiha's mountain is highly consequential for Lebanon, whose elevated summits and deep canyons provide relatively secure regions for persecuted minorities and individuals of all kinds, not only Christian:

> In parallel, a little before or after, dissidents of orthodox Islam, followers of new sects entered Lebanon and Syria from the north and south and occupied, one community after another, a natural bastion considered as a refuge. This is typical. Ismailis, Nusairis, Druze, Shi'is: they were always threatened, persecuted minorities who perched on their part of the mountain, as the Christians had done and continued to do. Where the communities settled then, with a few variations, they are still today. *We must take note how, at home and around us, as an easily explainable phenomenon, the mountains are the stronghold of minorities.*[46]

Not surprisingly, a sustained criticism of Chiha is his conception of the country as an assemblage of minorities.[47] Chiha's political-constitutional hallmark is the stubbornness of the communal system in Lebanon, to which he gives in this passage a historical depth. With the stability of the Ottoman Empire, Christian minorities took shelter from the prosecution all around them: 'It is the persecution in other lands that attracts clerics and laity to Lebanon,

TOUTE L'ECONOMIE LIBANAISE EST EN PUISSANCE DANS CES LIGNES DU GRAND HISTORIEN ANGLAIS.' [Aradus (Arwad in Arabic) is a small island off present Syria's coast.]

« A la lumière des précédents locaux, il semble que les Libanais aient été poussés à rivaliser avec les Phéniciens par la stérilité de leur montagne natale, tandis que la douceur du Jabal Ansariah (la chaîne alaouite, au nord) a habitué les Nossairis à végéter dans l'indolence des Philistins (c'est-à-dire des Palestiniens au sud). Cela nous ramène, vous le voyez, au stimulant de la contrainte (the stimulus of pressure)'. VPL 154.

[46] 'Parallèlement, un peu avant ou après, des dissidents de l'Islam orthodoxe, des fidèles de sectes nouvelles s'introduisent par le nord et par le sud au Liban et en Syrie et occupent, une communauté après l'autre, un bastion naturel considéré comme un refuge. Cela est caractéristique. Ismaïlis, Nosaïris, Druzes, Chiites: il s'agissait toujours de minorités menacées, persécutées qui se perchaient chacune sur sa montagne, comme avaient fait et continuaient de faire les Chrétiens, Où elles étaient alors, à quelques déplacements près, elles sont encore aujourd'hui. *Constatons que, chez nous comme autour de nous, par un phénomène facilement explicable, les montagnes sont le fief des minorités.*' LA 38–9.

[47] Most iconic in Lebanese memory the criticism of Georges Naccache, 'Deux négations ne font pas une nation', *L'Orient*, 10 March 1949. Also published in a collection of his columns, *Un Rêve Libanais (1943–1972)*, Beirut: Fiches du Monde arabe 1983, 52–8. Famously, Nacchache and Chiha traded criticism across the editorial pages of their respective newspapers, *L'Orient* and *Le Jour*.

ultimately all the leaders of the Eastern Christian rites. We only have to look around us to see them'.[48]

In this wide historical brush, Chiha joins historian Albert Hourani in his description of modern Lebanon as solidification of the properly 'Lebanese' dynasties from the Maʿns to the Chehabs:

> Then came the Ottomans, before whose eyes was soon born a Lebanese dynasty really worthy of the name, these amazing Maans, followed by the Chehab, who understood the profound originality of this country and its singularities, and had an instinctive knowledge of its destiny and of a Lebanese tradition steeped in blood.[49]

There are strong sociological-theological elements in the formation of minorities in Lebanon, both typical of the religious Orient. From a sociological perspective, Chiha explains, men of religion came to Lebanon as pilgrims, as missionaries, and as scholars:

> But the interest in us shown by the West and the rest of the world has other explanations too. *From the viewpoint of faith*, nothing was more natural than seeing missionaries coming to us. Nor could the high spiritual authorities whom we obey ignore our proximity to the Holy Places where, in various forms, the one God is worshipped. Let us immerse ourselves here in ancient history, in the history of religions, in sacred history. *The cleric came to us in the threefold form of the pilgrim, the missionary and the scholar*. From here a discipline grew, which, little by little, became its own raison d'être.[50]

[48] 'Ce sont les persécutions chez les autres qui attirent au Liban clercs et laïcs et finalement tous les chefs des rites orientaux chrétiens. Nous n'avons que regarder autour de nous pour les constater.' LA 41.

[49] 'Puis viennent les Ottomans, cependant qu'en face d'eux naissait un peu plus tard une dynastie libanaise vraiment digne de ce nom, ces Maans étonnants prolongés par les Chéhab, qui eurent conscience de l'originalité profonde de ce pays à travers ses singularités avec une connaissance pour ainsi dire instinctive de son destin et la tradition libanaise dans le sang.' LA 40. On Hourani and the early formation of modern Lebanon, see Ch. 2.

[50] 'Mais l'intérêt qui nous est porté par l'Occident et par le reste du monde obéit aussi à d'autres mobiles. *Sur le plan de la foi*, rien n'était plus naturel que de voir des missionnaires venir vers nous. Les hautes autorités spirituelles auxquelles nous obéissons ne pouvaient pas ignorer non plus notre proximité des Lieux Saints où, sous des formes diverses, le Dieu unique est adoré. Nous baignons ici dans l'Histoire ancienne, dans l'Histoire des religions, dans l'Histoire sainte. *Le clerc est venu à nous sous la forme triple du pèlerin, du missionnaire et du savant*. De là est né un enseignement qui, petit à petit, en se développant, est devenu une raison d'être en soi.' LA 47.

From a more theological perspective, the Orient is steeped in belief, liturgy, religious exegesis, and faith. This also underscores the richness and foibles of the religious mosaic which is unique to the country:

> We are, let us not forget, in this Orient always in ferment and literally sick with intelligence and exegesis, a promised land of restless minorities, a high place from which all prayers rise freely to the brightest, starriest sky. Such that we have become a religious mosaic without equivalent on earth, and *such that, in the nation as in the city, we describe ourselves only through our belief or our liturgy*. This last singularity has as its main raison d'être today, together with the formidable strength that that comes from habit, the instinctive mistrust of the weak and the fear by some of being dominated by others. No one would speak of minorities if he did not himself fear a majority. But sometimes *in some areas* the fear becomes excessive and illusory. *Diversity in ancestry and faith has to a great degree created diversity in ethics and in laws as the personal status regimes* [the different family laws of the communities] *illustrate. As we are, we would, I think, be regarded as an impossibility by reason alone if we did not exist with that quiet assurance which we oppose to philosophers.*[51]

Never too far from the fierce urgency of now, Chiha seizes the moment to warn again of the impending consequences of 'the neighbourhood' threatening the advances made by the Lebanese in educational and scientific terms as a modern prolongation of the theological curriculum. The mountain and its

[51] 'Nous sommes, ne l'oublions pas, dans cet Orient toujours en fermentation et littéralement malade d'intelligence et d'exégèse, une terre promise des minorités inquiètes, un haut lieu d'où montent librement vers le ciel le plus transparent, le plus étoilé, toutes les prières. De sorte que nous voilà devenus une mosaïque religieuse sans équivalent sur la terre, *et qu'à l'intérieur de la nation et de la cité, nous ne savons plus nous nommer que par notre croyance ou notre liturgie.* Cette dernière singularité a de nos jours pour principale raison d'être, avec la force redoutable qui naît de l'habitude, la méfiance instinctive des faibles et la crainte des uns d'être dominés par les autres. Nul ne parlerait de minorités s'il ne redoutait lui-même une majorité. Mais il arrive que, *dans certains domaines,* la crainte devienne excessive et illusoire. *Et la diversité dans l'ascendance et dans la foi a fait en bonne partie la diversité dans les mœurs et dans les lois comme les statuts personnels en témoignent. Nous serions je pense, tels que nous sommes, considérés par la raison pure comme une impossibilité si nous n'existions pas avec cette tranquille assurance que nous opposons aux philosophes.*' LA 45–6. The last sentence is cryptic, but Chiha probably means that his considered view of constitutional life as communitarian jars with the equality of individuals defended by the philosophers of the Enlightenment. This does not prevent him from finding comfort in the weight of history against the philosophers' 'pure reason'.

minorities are only one of the two factors that make Lebanon unique. The other is the sea. Resting his argument on Toynbee again:

> "*While the Philistines were browsing on the Shephelah* (Shephelah is the littoral, we would say in Lebanon the 'Sahel, *al-Sahel*' of Palestine)[52] *like sheep in clover and were moving inland, at their peril, in search of pastures new, the Phoenicians whose maritime horizon had hitherto been restricted to the short range of the coastwise traffic, between Byblos and the Delta of the Nile, now launched out into the open sea and won a second home for the syriac civilization in the western basin of the Mediterranean and on the coasts of the Ocean beyond*" (Toynbee, id. p. 52).
>
> *THE WHOLE LEBANESE DESTINY IS IN THIS PARALLEL MADE BY TOYNBEE*; our politics, our trade, our industry, our monetary and financial policy.[53]

Together, the sea and the mountain combine to make Lebanon what it is and what it has been since the dawn of recorded time: partly 'a seafaring nation'[54] with its far travels, international commerce, and cosmopolitanism. Its large population of emigrants attests to this unchanging trait. And then stands the mountain, making the country the refuge of 'associated minorities'.

In the natural geography of Lebanon, the human element is the most important.

'Economics'

From the long section on public finances in the Constitution, and his interventions in parliament during his deputyship, we know that Chiha favored an informed and balanced budget. As a banker, he cared for accurate data

[52] Parentheses by Chiha.

[53] Again, Chiha cites the English original, translates it to French, and provides explanations in the parenthesis: 'Tandis que les Philistins broutaient dans le Shephelah comme des moutons dans le trèfle et avançaient vers l'intérieur, à leurs périls, à la recherche de nouveaux pâturages, les phéniciens, dont l'horizon maritime avait été jusque-là restreint aux limites étroites du trafic côtier entre Byblos et le Delta du Nil, se lancèrent sur la haute mer et fondèrent une seconde patrie pour la civilisation syriaque (syriaque se dit en principe, vous le savez, de la langue araméenne) dans le bassin occidental de la Méditerranée et au-delà, sur les côtes de l'Océan. *TOUT LE DESTIN LIBANAIS EST DANS CE PARALLELE DE TOYNBEE*; notre politique, notre commerce, notre industrie, notre politique monétaire et financière'. VPL 155.

[54] Toynbee's English cite by Chiha, VPL 152.

and appreciated healthy accounts.[55] Chiha displays the caution of a good accountant when it comes to the State's indebtedness and profligacy:

> *We, fortunately, do not entrust valuable money, land and companies to a flawed State.* We lend little to the State because we fear its prodigality and failings. It is better for the State to make itself a debtor as little as possible, [otherwise it becomes] an entity which undermines society when it has spent too much. It is when the State can no longer pay that it devalues, that it empties its budget of its substance, stupidly destroying, without discrimination and without pity, savings, legacies and social frameworks.[56]

Beyond this robust approach to accounts, Chiha was not impressed by economics, and his view of the discipline is more that of a humanist than an arithmetician. His thoughts on economics appear in various writings. His *Propos d'Economie Libanaise* is not a treatise.[57] Like his two collections of *Essais*, it provides a sample of his daily columns on the Lebanese economy and on economic principles. It should be read alongside other writings bearing on the discipline.

The espousal of a caritative understanding of economics adorns the title of a contribution by Chiha to a French journal on classics in 1950, 'Economy and humanism'.[58] After criticising the violence of an economic system based on slavery in the classical world, and on the machine in the modern world, he expresses his attachment to the protection of the spirit of free human enterprise, as opposed to 'the brutal businessman'.[59] The lecture concludes on a call

[55] See sections on budget in chs. 6 and 7.

[56] '*Chez nous, heureusement on n'expose pas la valeur de la monnaie, celle de la terre et celle des entreprises aux défaillances de l'Etat.* On prête difficilement à l'Etat parce qu'on redoute les prodigalités et les déconfitures de l'Etat. Et il vaut mieux que l'Etat se rende débiteur le moins possible. Celui qui ébranle la société, quand il a trop dépensé. C'est quand l'Etat ne peut plus payer qu'il dévalue, qu'il vide son budget de sa substance, détruisant stupidement, sans discrimination et sans pitié, l'épargne, les patrimoines et les cadres sociaux.' VPL 116.

[57] *Propos sur l'Economie* ('PEL') is a collection of editorials by Chiha on economic topics. It appeared in 1965 in a first edition at Trident, with an introduction ('propos liminaire') by him at 9–11, suggesting he had made the choice of the articles published in the book before his death in 1954.

[58] Michel Chiha, 'Économie et Humanisme', *Bulletin de l'Association Guillaume Budé*, 12, 1950, 55–74.

[59] Id., 74: 'l'homme d'affaires brutal'.

for a new economy which is informed by 'humanism' and which moves the needle from an 'économie politique' to an 'économie poétique.'[60]

Chiha's skepticism towards economics as a 'science' appears clearly in *Visage et Présence du Liban*:

> *Political economy remains a relative and confused science.* It must be interpreted as one interprets the oracles of Sibyl. Political economy, as all Lebanese know, is for us like the languages of Aesop. It contains the best and the worst. *We can live and we can die by it.* Everything depends on the use we make of its hypotheses, its experiments, its calculations of probability. If it acknowledges us as a creative people, a people truly outside the norm, we can respect its suggestions and its counsel; but if it wants to subject us to brutal demolition, as in a street façade, then we shall oppose it. An eternal principle sheds light on the whole debate: "*The letter kills, but the Spirit gives life*".'[61]

The limited value of the discipline also comes from the uniqueness of the Lebanese situation. In the 'Introduction' to *Propos d'Economie Libanaise*, Chiha explained that 'the scientific arsenal of international economists may appear deceptive and pointless for a country like ours; I am enough of an economist and financier to bear strong witness to this truth'.[62] This is because '*all Lebanese legislation, all Lebanese economic policy, must take into account one essential factor: Lebanese activity abroad and with foreign countries.* This has been the secret of our prosperity for tens of centuries'.[63]

[60] Id.

[61] '*L'économie politique est encore une science relative et confuse.* Il faut l'interpréter comme on interprète les oracles de la Sibylle. L'économie politique, que tous les Libanais le sachent, est pour nous comme les langues d'Esope. Elle contient le meilleur et le pire. *Nous pouvons vivre et nous pouvons mourir par elle.* Tout dépend de l'usage que nous ferons de ses hypothèses, de ses expériences, de ses calculs de probabilité. Si elle reconnaît en nous un peuple original, un peuple vraiment hors série, nous pouvons rechercher avec respect ses suggestions et ses conseils; mais si elle prétend nous aligner au prix des démolitions brutales, comme on fait des façades d'une rue, alors nous nous élevons contre elle. Un principe éternel éclaire tout le débat: "*la lettre tue et l'esprit vivifie*".' VPL 158. The last citation is Saint Paul's, 2 Corinthians 3:6.

[62] 'L'arsenal scientifique des économistes de l'univers peut paraître illusoire et vain pour un pays comme le nôtre; nous sommes suffisamment économiste et financier nous-même pour pouvoir en témoigner avec force'. PEL 10.

[63] '*Toute la législation libanaise, toute la politique économique libanaise doivent tenir compte d'un facteur congénital: l'activité libanaise à l'étranger et avec l'étranger.* C'est le secret de notre prospérité à travers des dizaines de siècles'. VPL 158–9.

Lebanon's history is conjured up here once again. Lebanon is 'unique in the world'[64] because of its small size and its peculiarity as maritime republic with a mountainous backdrop. Agriculture cannot be relied on, nor can industry. Lebanon has little in common with countries that have vast land and raw industrial riches. This leaves services, trade, banking, culture and tourism as the core of Lebanon's added economic value regionally, and the Lebanese diaspora as a constituent part of the country's prosperity internationally.

Chiha's economic thought has usually been approached from two contrasting perspectives. The first, started by Marxist writer Mahdi 'Amel and construed more closely against Chiha's texts and the Mandate period by Fawwaz Trabulsi, is a critique from the left – a radical one by the former, an Althusserian communist assassinated in 1987, and a more nuanced one by the latter.[65] Both are right in that Chiha had little inclination for state interventionism in the mode of a socialist take-over of the instruments of production and distribution, and that he generally supported the service sector over the industrial sector. When Chiha dealt with the Soviet Union or French socialist experimentation under Léon Blum, it was clear that he did not like the combative view of socialism as class struggle or Blum's original view of labor as exploitation.[66] It is also true that his focus was more on the geo-political weight of Russia than on its domestic economic policy, which stood at total odds with his.[67]

The second perspective, which takes the works of Chiha at closer face value, appears in an article by two Lebanese economists.[68] The article is a useful

[64] 'un pays unique au monde', PEL 10.

[65] Mahdi 'Amel (nickname of Hasan Hamdan), *Madkhal ila Nqd al-Fikr al-Ta'ifi: Al-Qadiyya al-Filistiniyya fi Idiulujiyyat al-Burjwaziyya al-Lubnaniyya* (Introduction to the critique of sectarian thought: the Palestinian question in the ideology of the Lebanese bourgeoisie), Beirut: Dar al-Farabi 1980, esp, 45–151 (On Chiha as 'representative of Lebanese bourgeois ideology'); Fawaz Traboulsi, *Silat bila Wasl: Michel Chiha wal-Idiulujiyya al-Lubnaniyya* (Connections without link: Michel Chiha and the Lebanese ideology), London: Riyad al-Rayyes 1999.

[66] On Léon Blum, see e.g. 'L'Appel au travail de Léon Blum', 4 January 1947, Essais II, 21–3, at 23: 'M. Léon Blum, sur le déclin de l'âge, peut faire plus de bien à la France qu'il ne lui fit de mal avec ses chimères d'antan (Mr. Léon Blum, as he is getting older, can do more good to France than he did with his chimeras in the past.') Blum was the president of the Council of ministers in France in 1936–7 at the head of the Front Populaire, then briefly back in power in 1946–7.

[67] For instance 'Le retour de Moscou', 24 April 1947, Essais II, 89–91 (On US–Soviet rivalry).

[68] Rayan Haykal and Nizar Hariri, 'La pensée économique de Michel Chiha: Variations sur le thème de la liberté', *Travaux et Jours*, 86, 43–72.

round-up of Chiha's main themes and their liberal bent. They include his non-technical view of the field of economics, more in the mode of Montesquieu than Adam Smith, and his focus on the distinct Lebanese features at the heart of his economic views. This approach is the more convincing one. There is no need to second guess Chiha. His views are quite transparent.

We have seen Chiha's geo-political determinants in sea and mountain, and their comparative advantages in the economy in his reading of regional history to date. Within Lebanon, two other traits are particularly alluring: human capital with its educational and cosmopolitan nexus, and the limited role of the State.

Human capital and *Etat-moins*

Human capital is key to Chiha's economic vision: 'We know that in all wealth, the key is man.'[69] Lebanon is '*a small country, certainly: a very small country; a small nation perhaps, but not a small people*.'[70] This explains the repeated need in Chiha's writings on more citizens, and on more educated citizens:

> At this point we must confess our sin. If we are in dire need of prosperous trade, thriving industry, and flourishing agricultural life (it is in the agricultural sector that the dangers are smallest), if we need merchants and industrialists, top men in commerce and finance, *we need more citizens*. What is happening in Palestine should serve as a lesson to everyone.
>
> *If Lebanon does not begin to mass-produce citizens, it may in the long run be threatened*. Four thousand years of political and social life make this clear.[71]

In Chiha's mind, the citizen is first and foremost the educated citizen:

> *For Lebanon, the time for quality has come, quality in everything: in the produce of the soil, in the work of the hands, in manufactured products, in*

[69] '... et nous savons que de toutes les richesses, la première c'est l'homme'. '150 Libanais au kilomètre carré', 21 August 1944, PEL 24.

[70] '*Petit pays, assurément: très petit pays; petite nation peut-être, mais non point petit peuple.*' (1951) VPL 140.

[71] 'Nous devons sur ce terrain avouer notre péché. S'il nous faut de toute nécessité un commerce prospère, une industrie vivante, une vie agricole épanouie (c'est dans le secteur agricole que les dangers sont les moins grands), s'il nous faut des marchands et des industriels, des hommes de commerce et de finance de grande classe, *il nous faut davantage des citoyens*. Ce qui se passe en Palestine doit servir à chacun de leçon.

Si le Liban ne se met pas à fabriquer des citoyens en série, il peut à la longue être menacé Toute l'histoire l'établit à travers quatre mille ans de vie politique et sociale.' VPL 73.

> *services, in intellectual and scientific achievements. Along with the best worker and the best foreman (priceless in all endeavors) we need the best teacher, the best doctor, the best lawyer and, at the same time, the best teaching, the best hospital, the best justice and the rest.* Because everything connects and is linked.[72]

From this need ensues another principle:

> The rule that must be defined here is the following: *The welcome we give to the foreigner must be at least as liberal and fraternal as that which he gives us or that we expect of him: Your 'neighbor as yourself'.* Xenophobia in Lebanon leads to slow death; *it is a form of suicide.*[73]

This is true first domestically. The opening of Lebanon to the world economy is another leitmotiv in this vein.

> We do not acknowledge sufficiently that the material well-being of the Lebanese, insofar as it exists, is due mainly to resources coming from abroad. This is of the greatest social interest.
>
> The Lebanese earns little from his fellow Lebanese: but the profits he makes abroad allow him to maintain a lifestyle which astonishes foreigners.[74]

The Lebanese diaspora, not surprisingly, forms part of this cosmopolitan vision of Lebanon, and the line is thin between the Lebanese inside and those who find their economic calling abroad: '*All Lebanese legislation, all Lebanese*

[72] '*Pour le Liban, le temps de la qualité est venu, la qualité en tout: dans les produits du sol, dans le travail des mains, dans les produits fabriqués, dans les services, dans les manifestations intellectuelles et scientifiques. En même temps que le meilleur ouvrier et que le meilleur contremaître (précieux en tout), il nous faut le meilleur professeur, le meilleur médecin, le meilleur juriste et, parallèlement, le meilleur enseignement, le meilleur hôpital, la meilleure justice et le reste.* Car tout se touche et s'enchaîne'. 'Règles et consignes', 20 April 1950, PEL 339 This article concludes PEL with an optimistic call for Lebanon's creative future.

[73] 'La règle qui se dégage ici est la suivante: L'accueil que nous faisons à l'étranger doit être au moins aussi libéral et fraternel que celui qu'il nous fait ou que nous attendons de lui: "Ton prochain comme toi-même". La xénophobie au Liban entraîne la mort lente; c'est une forme de suicide'. VPL 159.

[74] 'On n'observe pas assez que le bien-être matériel des Libanais, dans la mesure où il existe, a surtout pour origine des ressources venues de l'extérieur. Cela est du plus haut intérêt sur le plan social. Le Libanais gagne peu du Libanais son concitoyen: mais les profits qu'il fait à l'étranger lui permettent de maintenir ce train de vie dont l'étranger s'étonne.' 'Un aspect de l'économie libanaise', 26 August 1952, PEL 228.

economic policy, must take account of one essential factor: Lebanese activity abroad, and Lebanese activity with abroad'.[75]

Chiha describes Lebanon's cosmopolitan *émigrés*, a perennial feature of the workforce ever since the second half of the nineteenth century, with a poetical simile, likening them to 'these large seabirds which bring food to their young ones from the world over.'[76]

> *If the Lebanese, in large numbers, did not enrich themselves year after year in the four corners of the world, the Lebanese who do not leave the country would no doubt have a far harsher life. If one wants a Lebanese equilibrium, the Lebanese, and most importantly the sociologist and the tax collector, must never forget this.*[77]

In addition to his conservative suspicion of the State and its propensity to overspend, Chiha was generally a supporter of what a present-day economist calls 'L'Etat moins'.[78] The smaller the State, the less interventionist, the better:

> When one works for the State, when the profits accrue to the State and when it is the State that pays and plugs the holes, one can take it as probable that there will be few profits and that the dimensions of the holes will increase.[79]

[75] '*Toute la législation libanaise, toute la politique économique libanaise doivent tenir compte d'un facteur congénital: l'activité libanaise à l'étranger et avec l'étranger*'. VPL 159.

[76] '... ces grands oiseaux de mer qui, du grand large, rapportent à leurs petits leur pâture'. Chiha, 'Un aspect de l'économie libanaise', 26 August 1952, PEL 230.

[77] '*Mais si des Libanais, en grand nombre, ne s'enrichissaient pas chaque année aux quatre coins du monde, les Libanais qui ne quittent pas le pays auraient la vie beaucoup plus dure sans doute. Si l'on veut un équilibre libanais, il faut que les Libanais, le sociologue et l'homme du fisc en premier lieu, n'oublient jamais cela*'. Id.

[78] *L'Etat-Moins* is a concept developed by Robert Fossaert (d.2015) in *Les Etats*, vol. 5 of *La Société* (8 vols, Paris: Seuil et al 1978–1996), 142–55, see at 144: 'If the term STATES-PLUS [ETATS-PLUS] is to be summed up as the series of States from 1 to 14 [Fossaert elaborates the history of states in their classification in history from 1 to 14, of which the Soviet Union was the latest form at the time], born of social 'statification' (*étatisation*) — a series of which new forms will no doubt increase — we can call STATES-MINUS [ETATS-MOINS] the series of future forms of State-in-the-process-of-decline (Etat-en-voie-de-dépérissement).' And at 155: 'The idea that democracy is ultimately the power of the people exercised for the people by the people themselves, may indeed begin to take shape in the State-minus.' See also his *L'Avenir du Socialisme*, vol. 8 and final of *La Société*, Paris: Stock 1996, 295–7, at 144: 'In line with such momentum, the withering away of the State is the only perspective opposable to the drift towards the all-State, because the dispersion of decision-making centers and the resulting democratic tensions replace the concentration of State power in a useful manner'.

[79] 'Quand on travaille pour l'Etat, quand c'est à l'Etat que reviennent les profits et quand c'est l'Etat qui paie et qui bouche les trous, on peut tenir pour probable qu'il y aura peu de bénéfices et que les dimensions des trous iront grandissant'. 'Nationalisations', 1 March 1947, PEL 52.

Within this decreased role of the State, Chiha sides clearly with a policy of laissez-faire:

> *Freedom forms the very basis of the policies that suit us and the economy that we need. Legitimate freedoms are those that are backed by order.* This is where we are in innate opposition to totalitarianism of all kinds. We are truly the land of free enterprise and the friends of its supporters, wherever they are. In this way will Lebanon fulfill its mission (it does have one), whether it is a question of the country itself, of the countries of the Arab League, of Mediterranean countries, and finally of what international commitments permit in this world, with or without the United Nations.[80]

This view of the laissez-faire State also reflects the importance of the diaspora in the economic well-being of the country. The diaspora will not help if the State is not liberal enough to accommodate its international activities and 'its various endeavours, whatever they may be':

> This is elementary logic. *The State will have to accept this. It will have to renounce a traditional economic and financial policy and have the courage to embrace the furthest limits of liberalism;* (...) *The ideal is to let the Lebanese travel as they please, yet by providing them with a country adapted to their nature, a country that invites them not to leave, and, surely, to return.*[81]

Wider horizons: Poetry, Palestine, etc.

One would be remiss in restricting Chiha's intellectual interests to the French Mandate and its development in the country, to the reading of Lebanese history, or to economic policy. Rather, his persona looks anachronistic. He multi-tasked before it became fashionable. Chiha was a polymath who

[80] '*La politique qui nous convient, l'économie qu'il nous faut, c'est la liberté qui est leur base même, ce sont les libertés légitimes, dans l'ordre.* C'est par là que nous sommes en conflit congénital avec les totalitarismes quels qu'ils soient. Nous sommes le pays même de la libre entreprise et les amis de ses partisans où qu'ils soient. A ce prix le Liban remplira sa mission (car il en a une), qu'il s'agisse de lui-même, des pays de la Ligue arabe, des Méditerranéens, et de ce qu'enfin, avec et sans les Nations-Unies, le devoir international permet dans l'univers'. (1951) VPL 140.

[81] 'Dans leurs métamorphoses insaisissables, toutes les formes du travail. Cela est de logique élémentaire. *L'Etat devra se faire une raison. Il faudra qu'il renonce à une politique économique et financière conformiste et aille bravement aux dernières limites du libéralisme*; (...) *L'Idéal c'est de laisser le Libanais voyager à sa guise, mais en lui faisant un pays adopté à sa nature, un pays qui l'invite à ne point partir, et, sûrement, à revenir*'. VPL 138.

took journalism to heart with regular chronicles, developed the family bank with signal success, used his lawyerly skills to arbitrate commercial disputes,[82] and wrote poetry.[83]

Last and not least, there is Chiha the regional seer. His concern with the emergence of Israel over the ruins of Palestine led to editorials in the 1940s and 1950s numerous enough to fill a book.[84] The texts of some of his collected articles in *Palestine* are simply prophetic, in a subtle but robust prose, with nary a speck of dust three-quarters of a century later:

> The most probable hypothesis for Palestine, in the event that the [world] powers insist on their decision, is a Hundred-year war (with frequent and possibly far-ranging repercussions in the West). A worst hypothesis would be a world war which would find its starting point in this fiery core (a more dangerous one than the Balkans).[85]

The diagnosis was right. In another famous passage, Chiha writes:

> *The decision to divide Palestine by creating the Jewish State is one of the worst errors of contemporary policy. A matter which appears inconsequential will have the most startling consequences. It is not unreasonable to write that this small matter will shake the earth to its foundations.*[86]

[82] There is in his archive several references and a rich correspondence on an arbitration case involving the Asfar family, an arbitration where he clearly played a leading role.

[83] Chiha's poetry is collected in *La Maison des Champs*, Beyrouth: Fondation Chiha 2nd rpt 1994 (first print 1965). It includes several poems, mostly in traditional rhyming verse, in a mix of bucolic, love and spiritual themes and a dominantly elegiac tone. The original version was published in 1934 in the presses of the *Revue Phénicienne*.

[84] *Palestine*, Beirut: Fondation Chiha rpt 1994 (original 1957). See Samir Khalaf, 'Michel Chiha and the Struggle for Palestine', talk at conference on 'The Lebanese system: A critical assessment', American University of Beirut, 18–19 May 2001 (on file with author).

[85] 'L'hypothèse la plus probable pour la Palestine, au cas où les puissances s'obstineraient dans leur décision, c'est une guerre de Cent ans (avec des répercussions fréquentes et peut-être très étendues en Occident). Une hypothèse pire serait une guerre mondiale qui trouverait dans ce foyer d'incendie (plus dangereux actuellement que les Balkans) son point de départ'. 'Horizon sans soleil', 18 December 1947, Pal 79.

[86] '*La décision de partage de la Palestine par la création de l'Etat juif est une des erreurs les plus considérables de la politique contemporaine. D'une chose apparemment petite, les conséquences les plus surprenantes vont sortir. Et ce n'est pas offenser la raison que d'écrire que cette petite histoire contribuera à ébranler la terre dans ses fondements*'. 'Une politique aberrante', 5 December 1946, Pal 74.

Chiha's solution is also right, at least for those who increasingly believe that it should extend to the whole of historic Palestine, without dividing it into two or more states, under a constitutional system not too dissimilar to the Lebanese conviviality of 'associated minorities':

> *For a reasonable man who sees things from the summit of Mount Hermon, Christians, Muslims and Jews should be able, in Palestine, to live together as citizens of the same State, enjoying absolutely equal rights, with the benefit of personal status* [different family laws] *extended to all.* This is the sensible solution, this is the humane solution which would lead Palestine to a miraculous level of organisation and prosperity. Yet, as often happens, it is precisely the most reasonable and the most logical that gets rejected.[87]

The Lebanese reference is explicit: 'All told, with careful adjustments suited to Palestine, it is the Lebanese solution. In a country of associated minorities, it is the coming together within a joint assembly that accomplishes the will-to-live together'.[88]

The freedom canopy

Under the variety of his world vision and interests stands Chiha's unwavering attachment to liberty. One finds his belief in liberty repeated time and again: 'We can't say it enough: this country needs to have its doors open to the world ... It loses its balance if freedom is persecuted.'[89] 'It is only when individual freedom is guaranteed that a people can be said to be free. All the

[87] 'Pour un homme raisonnable et qui verrait les choses du sommet de l'Hermon, *chrétiens, musulmans et juifs devraient pouvoir, en Palestine, vivre ensemble comme des citoyens d'un même Etat, jouissant de droits absolument égaux, avec le bénéfice de statuts personnels étendus.*

C'est la solution normale, c'est la solution humaine; et qui conduirait la Palestine à un point d'organisation et de prospérité miraculeux. Mais, comme il arrive souvent, c'est justement ce qui est le plus raisonnable qu'on repousse et c'est le plus logique qu'on rejette.' 'Perspectives palestiniennes', 8 February 1947, Pal 35.

[88] 'Tout compte fait, avec les méfiances propres à la Palestine, c'est la solutions libanaise. Dans un pays de minorités associées, c'est une assemblée commune qui fait le vouloir-vivre en commun'. 'Les chances de la raison en Palestine', 7 October 1946, Pal 30. On a later occasion, when the Israeli Declaration of Independence (14 May 1948) was imminent, he proposed a federal solution in one State. 'Pour en sortir', 13 March 1948, Pal 90.

[89] 'On ne le dira jamais trop: ce pays a besoin d'avoir ses portes ouvertes sur le monde ... Il perd son équilibre si on y persécute la liberté'. 'Principes d'Economie politique', 17 August 1948, PEL 97.

rest is literature.'[90] A 1944 Chiha column on 'De la Liberté' is an unwavering paean to freedom:

> From the top of this dais, we are invited to take an interest in freedom. Such a call cannot fail to move: it is the human condition that hangs in the balance.
>
> Of all that concerns us, nothing comes before freedom. Our horizons open or close depending on whether we are denied freedom. And what would man be if he were not free? ... less than the sparrow in the wind, less than the oak in the forest. Yet there is this freedom, this privilege in creation, this honour, this right, this personal exercise of proud sovereignty. There is this remarkable faculty of being able to say: I want or I oppose, I reflect, I bow, I accept, or, on the contrary, I discuss and I do not want. A creature thus made, how to conceive it otherwise than in the image of God and as the living fruit of the breath of divinity?[91]

Freedom is considered a defining principle, rooted in history, without which Lebanon does not make sense.[92] Freedoms must be exercised responsibly, and the democratic system allows people to flourish without harm to others:

> We love democracy as much as anyone else; but we cherish temperance with it. Freedom has no friend more passionate than us; but we do not know freedom without temperance and without constraints. We say the world needs to breathe, but letting it empty its lungs won't make it breathe better.[93]

[90] 'C'est seulement quand la liberté individuelle est garantie qu'on peut dire qu'un peuple est libre; tout le reste est littérature.' "La Prise de la Bastille et le 'bon tyran'", 14 July 1944, Essais I, 70.

[91] 'Du haut de la chaire, on nous invite à nous intéresser à la liberté. Un tel appel ne peut pas ne pas émouvoir: c'est la condition humaine qui est dans la balance. De tout ce qui nous préoccupe rien ne se place avant la liberté. Nos horizons s'ouvrent ou se ferment suivant qu'on nous la refuse. Et que serait l'homme s'il n'était pas libre? moins que le moineau dans le vent, moins que le chêne de la forêt. Mais il y a la liberté, ce privilège dans la création, cet honneur, ce droit, cet exercice personnel d'une souveraineté altière. Il y a cette faculté insigne de pouvoir dire: je veux ou je m'oppose, je réfléchis, je m'incline, j'accepte, ou, au contraire, je discute et je ne veux pas. Une créature ainsi faite, comment la concevoir autrement qu'à l'image de Dieu et comme le fruit vivant du souffle de la divinité?' 27 February 1944, 'De la Liberté', Essais I, 27–8.

[92] See the previous chapter on the historical roots of freedom in Lebanese history in Chiha's worldview. Further on a similar perception by early European travellers, Hyam Mallat, *Le Liban, Emergence de la Liberté et de la Démocratie au Proche-Orient*, Paris: Geuthner 2014, 132–9.

[93] 'Nous aimons, quant à nous, la démocratie autant qu'aucun autre; mais nous chérissons la mesure avec elle. La liberté n'a pas d'ami plus passionné que nous; mais nous ne connaissons pas de liberté sans équilibre et sans contraintes. Nous disons qu'il faut que le monde respire, mais ce n'est pas en

One can multiply these statements of faith. They were not only domestic. Chiha was consistently critical of Hitler and Mussolini. A year only after Hitler's takeover, he wrote on 9 August 1934: 'The press is dying in Germany. It is in vain for Goebbels to personally invite journalists to criticise the regime. The editors think of concentration camps and suicides. And they find it safer to keep quiet'.[94] A month later, in September, he underlined 'the rupture of Germany with all the moral forces in the world' and denounced its persecution of the Jews and Russia's persecution of the Orthodox.[95] In the *Eastern Times*, the English Daily which Chiha founded in 1941, the tone against the Axis is sharp from the very beginning. In an editorial introducing the paper in the second issue, Emar, a likely pseudonym of Chiha, writes:

> Never in the history of mankind was there such a period of uncertainty. Never before did the angel of doom cast such a sinister shadow upon civilization. Whatever may be the changes in the geographical state of the world, let us always remember that there is something more important at stake- FREEDOM.[96]

le laissant vider ses poumons qu'il respirera mieux'. 'L'Idéal et le possible', 22 February 1946, Pol Int 91.

94 'La presse se meurt en Allemagne. Goebbels lui-même aura beau convier les journalistes à critiquer le régime. Les rédacteurs pensent aux camps de concentration et aux suicides. Et ils trouvent plus sûr de se taire'. 'La 'trêve des partis, M. Doumergue et la presse allemande,' 9 August 1934 (Text on Chiha.org). Note the early reference to the concentration camps.

95 '... la rupture de l'Allemagne avec toutes les forces morales du monde ... Il n'y a pas un opprimé dans un coin de la terre qui ne puisse espérer d'Elle [Papacy], à un moment donné, aide et protection; les juifs persécutés en Allemagne, comme les Orthodoxes persécutés en Russie'. 'Les forces morales et l'Allemagne', 5 September 1934 (Text on Chiha.org).

96 Emar, 'The Eastern Times- A changing world', *The Eastern Times*, 29 September 1941. Contrary to the received notion of his Francophone attachment, Chiha was in many ways more of an Anglophile since he spent part of his youth learning the silk trade in Manchester (conversations with Isabelle Doumet Skaf, February 2024). The first issue of *The Eastern Times* is dated 28 September 1941, and the last issue 9 March 1946. In total, 1678 issues were published. They constitute another treasure in the Chiha Archive, promising to research a local Middle Eastern perspective that covers the Second World War and the beginning of the Cold War from Lebanon. The English is excellent throughout.

10

Chiha's Nation

Lebanon is a country of associated religious minorities.[1]

'Associated religious minorities' v. 'nationalism'

The weight of Lebanese history is a constant referral for Michel Chiha's present. Communalism, as we saw in his summary of Lebanese history, is partly the product of centuries of attachment to freedom, with the rugged Lebanese mountains allowing persecuted groups relative shelter. Tolerance is the hallmark of Lebanon's long history. 'Associated minorities' need tolerance to coexist. This is where communalism finds the country's persistent yearning for freedom and balance:

> *Despite several mistakes and abuses, it is communalism that has taught Lebanon tolerance. It is the close proximity of religions and liturgies, the long habit of living together, the esteem, mutual friendship and deep understanding of each other that have led us to the equilibrium we enjoy today.*[2]

Chiha describes Lebanon in several writings as a country of minorities. This is the hallmark of his political theory. In a text entitled 'Philosophie du confessionalisme au Liban', he starts with a definition of communalism:

[1] Le Liban est un pays de minorités confessionnelles associées'. 'Continuité et mouvement', 30 November 1943, Pol Int 44 (full passage cited below n.3)

[2] '*Malgré beaucoup d'erreurs et d'abus, c'est le confessionnalisme qui a enseigné au Liban la tolérance. C'est le voisinage immédiat des cultes et des liturgies, c'est la longue habitude de vivre en commun, c'est la fréquentation, l'estime, l'amitié réciproques et la connaissance approfondie des uns par les autres qui nous ont conduits à l'équilibre où nous sommes*'. 'Philosophie du confessionnalisme au Liban', 1 September 1954, Pol Int 305. Emphasis in original, as in all subsequent citations of Chiha.

> *Confessionalisme* is 'the narrow attachment to a religious *confession*'. This is the dictionary definition, and it fits us. But communalism in Lebanon has another meaning. It is the guarantee of equitable political and social representation for associated religious minorities.[3]

This trait, for Chiha, is as real as it can be beneficial. It makes Lebanon special on the world stage:

> *THE CASE OF LEBANON IS UNIQUE IN THE WORLD: a country of refuge in essence, being Mediterranean and on the threshold of Asia, maritime and mountainous at the same time; a country whose very diverse population is at root composed of a long line of men and families persecuted for their beliefs, for their ideas; a collection of communities in faith, each with its own personal status [family law].*[4]

In a 1952 editorial a month later, he repeats that

> Lebanon is a country of associated confessional minorities. In it, all minorities must find their place and obtain their rights. This is the raison d'être of this country and its originality.
>
> This is why nothing is more fatuous than saying, for example, that our Armenian compatriots are in some danger. All we ask of each other is to behave like good Lebanese.[5]

I was not able to trace the Armenian community-related occasion for this article, and the second paragraph of the quote is an expressive application to Lebanon's Armenians in Chiha's understanding of the country's modus

[3] 'Le confessionnalisme est 'l'attachement étroit à une confession religieuse'. C'est la définition du dictionnaire et il est clair que c'est chez nous le cas. Mais le confessionnalisme au Liban signifie autre chose. Il est la garantie d'une représentation politique et sociale équitable pour des minorités confessionnelles associées'. Id. 303.

[4] 'LE CAS DU LIBAN EST UNIQUE AU MONDE: un pays refuge par essence, parce que méditerranéen et au seuil de l'Asie, maritime et de montagne à la fois; un pays dont la population très diverse à ses sources est faite d'une longue suite d'hommes et de familles persécutés pour leurs convictions, pour leurs idées; une collection de communautés confessionnelles ayant chacune son statut personnel.' 'Vérités Libanaises', 14 October 1952, Pol Int 246–7.

[5] 'Le Liban est un pays de minorités confessionnelles associées. Toutes les minorités doivent y trouver leur place et y obtenir leurs droits. C'est la raison d'être de ce pays et c'est son originalité.

C'est pourquoi rien n'est plus ridicule que de raconter par exemple que nos compatriotes arméniens y sont menacés de quelque péril. Tout ce qu'on demande aux uns et aux autres, c'est de se comporter en bons Libanais.' 'Continuité et mouvement', 30 November 1943, Pol Int 44.

vivendi. In tune with previous immigrations of minorities, the community reflects a phase in early twentieth century history when Armenians fleeing Turkish brutality were anxious about their new surroundings, in part because they were the only group in Lebanon who kept their mother tongue alive and active. They came to the country in two main refugee waves: one following the Turkish genocide in the First World War, the other after Turkey occupied the *sanjak* of Alexandretta after the French surrendered it to them in 1939 in the face of strong nationalist opposition from Syrians and Lebanese.[6] Chiha was asking Armenians 'to behave like good Lebanese', in other words to operate, like other Lebanese, as a community like others.

A country of minorities, therefore, but also a country of Lebanese citizenship under the modern and universal format of nationalism. Over the hundred years since Chiha's Constitution, this simple equation dominates Lebanese society and continues to define its political and constitutional life. The individual citizen is a member of a religious-sectarian community, which operates as a collective agent between the citizen and the state. But the citizen also operates as an individual in relation to the State. It is the combination of these two traits which defines Lebanese constitutionalism for Chiha. While a frustrating fact, it is a hard fact nonetheless. Why turn one's back on this stubborn reality?

> Why want to modify, brutally, the product of centuries? By what strange mental process is secular bias given a more important role than general human intelligence?[7]

Chiha provides no easy solution to Lebanese sectarian inequality, in large part because he is conscious, as a student of Lebanese history, that only time is capable of assuaging differences and creating a nation. 'Wisdom is gleaned from

[6] In 1939, the Armenians left the historical city of Antioch and the *sanjak* when the French ceded the region to the Turks mostly in order to keep them from joining the Axis. High Commissioner Gabriel Puaux relates the episode in *Deux Années au Levant- Souvenirs de Syrie et du Liban 1939–1940*, Paris: Hachette 1952 (Kindle), 43–9 (On the political interests of France to keep on good terms with a neutral Turkey, to which the Antioch region was simply ceded, causing the panicked departure of Armenians from the sanjak).

[7] Pourquoi vouloir modifier brutalement ce que les siècles ont fait? Quelle bizarrerie de l'esprit prétendra mettre le préjugé laïque au-dessus d'une position plus générale et plus humaine de l'intelligence?' 'Philosophie du confessionnalisme au Liban' (1954), Pol Int 184.

the reassuring lesson of time'.[8] But time cannot be gaged, so Chiha expressed his belief in its healing role without being confident that it would necessarily go in the right direction: '*Over time, these differences may fade and slowly disappear.*'[9] This is immediately followed by a doubt:

> *Currently, the raison d'être of Lebanon lies precisely in the communal balance which characterises it and which is seen most of all at the level of legislative Power. If we are to reform, let us begin by moving away from religious ties towards an administration that performs according to merit. It feels so much more natural.*[10]

Commenting in 1943 on the ministerial declaration of the first post-Independence government, he sounded hopeful: 'It seems to us, whatever people say, that time has done its work, beneficent, calming work.'[11] A month later, he was back to being cautious: 'Time needs to pass. Prejudices must be overcome, wounds must heal, affection must be rebuilt'.[12]

Ultimately, caution was balanced by hope. This base line never changed:

> CONFESSIONALISM IN LEBANON IS A STRUCTURAL PHENOMENON; *no amount of violence will change that; it is time alone which will modify it, or not.*[13]

For Chiha, a move away from confessionalism is contingent on several factors. One is the need to relieve Lebanon of the weight of its two powerful neighbours: throughout the Mandate, it was Syria which represented the greatest risk to

[8] '[L]a sagesse qu'inspire la leçon apaisante du temps.' 'La leçon du passé', 1 September 1944, Pol Int 61.

[9] '*Avec le temps, ces différences peuvent s'atténuer et lentement disparaître*'. 'Philosophie du confessionnalisme au Liban', above n.7, 185.

[10] '*Actuellement, la raison d'être du Liban est justement dans l'équilibre confessionnel qui le caractérise et qui se manifeste d'abord sur le plan du Pouvoir législatif. Pour nous réformer, commençons par renoncer à la confession en faveur du mérite à l'intérieur de l'administration. Cela paraît tellement plus naturel'.* Id.

[11] 'Il nous semble, quoi qu'on dise, que le temps a fait son oeuvre, une oeuvre bienfaisante, une oeuvre de pacification des esprits.' 'Bref commentaire sur la déclaration ministérielle' 8 October 1943, Pol Int 36.

[12] 'Mais il faut que du temps s'écoule. Il faut que les préjugés tombent, que les blessures se ferment, que les sentiments se retrouvent.' 'D'une révision', 9 November 1943, Pol Int 41.

[13] 'LA POSITION CONFESSIONNELLE AU LIBAN EST UN PHÉNOMÈNE DE STRUCTURE; *aucune violence n'y changera rien; c'est le temps seul qui la modifiera, ou qui ne la modifiera pas.*' 'Politique intérieure et doctrine politique', 3 May 1953, Pol Int 270.

the Lebanese entity; after Independence, with the rise of Israel, Chiha issued warning after repeated warning against the worrying developments south of the border.[14]

His conclusion is that for time to heal, there must be peace with Lebanon's neighbours and efforts to stem violence among its own communities:

> Let it be well understood; for us, peace is not only the opposite of war; it is not a state of apparent disarmament, it is not order that does without the consent of the people; *it is the genuine peace that results from fair policies which prohibit all violence against any minority whatsoever in this country of minorities.*
>
> *All Lebanese communities must be united in the community that is Lebanon in order to resolve* the serious problems that confront the world today, problems which are evidenced and echoed in Lebanon; and in order to administer this country with the proactive, tolerant and patient wisdom of the leaders of old, among them the great Fakhreddine.[15]

The regional factor is not, however, the major impediment to the Nation prevailing over communities. It is the domestic one that is key.

Chiha's nationalism

Chiha's constitutional philosophy was constantly drawn by his hope and determination to see nationalism prevail over communalism. The vision is expressed in a text of 1936:

> We cannot remedy denominational and social anarchy in Lebanon by deliberately ignoring the political. All that sectarian belief gains is a loss to the Nation.

[14] See section on Palestine in Ch. 9.

[15] 'Qu'on nous comprenne bien; la paix pour nous ce n'est pas seulement l'opposé de la guerre; ce n'est pas un état de désarmement apparent, ce n'est pas l'ordre qui se passe à la rigueur du consentement des citoyens, *c'est la tranquillité profonde résultant d'une politique équitable qui s'interdit toute violence contre la minorité quelle qu'elle soit, dans ce pays de minorités.*

Il s'agit de regrouper dans la communauté libanaise toutes les communautés libanaises, et pour résoudre les grands problèmes dont l'univers retentit et dont nous avons ici les manifestations ou les échos, d'administrer ce pays avec la sagesse active, tolérante et patiente de ses chefs d'autrefois, du grand Fakhreddine par exemple'. 'Equilibre et mesure', 16 May 1946, Pol Int 97. Fakhreddin II Ma'n (d.1635), see Ch. 2, is the most iconic Emir in the history of Lebanon.

> On the other hand, all that the Nation gains can only contribute to attenuating, at the confessional level, the disorder to which we are the unhappy witnesses.[16]

Other than time and the extrication of Lebanon from regional overbears, a tall order already, how could nationalism save the country from the inequity and fractiousness of sectarianism?

We find in a late conference at the Cénacle, a year before Chiha's death, one of his more subtle elaborations on the subject.[17]

Looking at the communal conundrum in a positive light, he considers the association of religious groups forming Lebanon 'a collective form of self-love'.[18] The definition appears mystical, and expresses the spirituality of Chiha's worldview. Contrary to the leftist criticism of Chiha as a hardcore capitalist, with a predilection for commerce over industry, his attachment to Christianity is rooted in a caritative approach to society that keeps a healthy distance from Mammon:

> We are then faced with a duality, a kind of separation of the legacies: on one hand, things that can be fixed by money, and, on the other, at a completely different level, those that are fixed by greatness. From this comparison, from this choice, we deduce, immediately and without any hesitation, that *the primacy of the spiritual* carries the day.[19]

[16] 'On ne peut pas remédier au Liban à l'anarchie confessionnelle et sociale, en ignorant délibérément ce qui est d'ordre *politique.* Tout ce que l'idée confessionnelle gagne, *c'est la Nation qui le perd.*
Mais à l'opposé, tout *ce que la Nation gagne* ne peut que contribuer à atténuer, sur le plan confessionnel, le désordre dont nous sommes les témoins attristés'. 'Introduction à une politique libanaise', 2 July 1936, Pol Int 20.

[17] 'Présence du Liban', 29 October 1953, VPL 149–52. On the Cénacle, where Chiha gave several lectures, see Nadim Shehadi, *The Idea of Lebanon: Economy and state in the Cénacle Libanais* 1946–54, Papers on Lebanon 5, Oxford: Centre for Lebanese Studies 1987. For the leading role of Chiha in the forum, see 8–10, 18: 'It's all in Chiha'. A selection of Arabic and French lectures at the Cénacle appears in a rich collection put together by Dar al-Nahar as *'Ahd al-Nadwa al-Lubnaniyya- Les Années Cénacle*, Beirut: Nahar 1997. Chiha contributed to the circle of the Cénacle four talks, 'Valeurs' in 1948, 'Le Liban dans le monde: Perspectives d'avenir' in 1951; a reading of poetry ('Récital de poésie') in 1953; and 'Présence du Liban' in 1954.

[18] 'Nous avons nommé le nationalisme qui est une forme collective de l'amour de soi.' Id. 149.

[19] 'Nous nous trouvons alors devant une dualité, une sorte de séparation des patrimoines: *ce qui, d'une part, peut se résoudre par de l'argent*, et d'autre part, sur un plan tout différent, *ce qui se résout par de la grandeur.* De cette comparaison, de ce contraste qui s'impose à notre raison, résulte tout de suite et sans hésitation, *la primauté du spirituel.*' 'Valeurs', VPL 59.

Chiha's spirituality is also religious. It can be found in various writings, and in his poems in particular.[20] Mysticism and love, a classical Christian theme, merge in 'A la Mémoire d'Anna de Noailles', and in 'Prière'.[21] In his analysis of nationalism, however, 'self-love' is not merely a projection of the core theology of the Catholic church. The concept of 'self-love' engenders a circumspect view of nationalism. A 'generous and explosive interpretation of nationhood is', he says, a dangerous idea in the world today, a world in which nationalism can be devastating. Criticising Maurice Barrès's 'perfectly authentic and moving nationalism whenever the question of Lorraine, the place of his birth, is concerned', such 'acute nationalism' is no longer appropriate, for it 'can appear too passionate and has little validity'.[22] In blunt terms, 'we must differentiate between pervasive, insensitive nationalism, and what is a most legitimate and noble national sentiment in one's love of his country.'[23]

This is followed by another Jean Monnet-like vision of European v. French or German nationalism:

> The last twenty-five years, have witnessed an overwhelming, extreme nationalism that is no longer acceptable. To this day, however, a Frenchman and a German cannot love Europe more than they love France and Germany. Similarly, before Washington and the United States came into being, there was a kind of jealous nationalism among states, even though they were still so young.[24]

[20] Chiha's poetry was collected in *La Maison des Champs*, Beirut: Revue Phénicienne 1934 (1st ed.); second augmented edition in 1964, rpt Fondation Chiha 1994.

[21] Id., respectively at 87; 91–2; earlier, in *Vers Anciens*, untitled, at 15: 'Aimer, souffrir. Voici que vous naissez ensemble (To love, to suffer. You are born together)'. Later, in 'Voir', poem dated 25 December 1950, at 133: 'Tomber aux pieds de Dieu, brisé, pantelant, dans un long cri d'amour (To fall at God's feet, broken, halting, in a long cry of love'. Anna de Noailles (1876–1933) was a celebrated poet and novelist of the early twentieth century.

[22] 'nationalisme aigu'; 'Le nationalisme d'un Maurice Barrès, par exemple, parfaitement authentique et émouvant quand il s'agit de la Lorraine, sa terre natale, peut de nos jours paraitre trop passionné et moins rigoureusement valable', VPL 152. Maurice Barrès (1862–1923) was a leading politician or extreme nationalism in France, and a literary figure.

[23] 'Il nous faut établir la différence entre un nationalisme systématique et buté et ce qu'il y a de plus légitime et de plus noble dans le sentiment national et dans l'amour de son pays'. 'Présence du Liban' (1953), VPL 147.

[24] 'Jusqu'à ce dernier quart de siècle, il y eut partout un nationalisme aigu qu'on a maintenant dépassé; mais un Français, un Allemand ne peuvent pas aimer encore la patrie européenne comme ils aiment respectivement la France et l'Allemagne. De même, avant Washington et les Etats-Unis,

Mutatis mutandis, 'ideological' or' excessive nationalism is out of place. Its inappropriateness is true against the call for Arab unity, a fixture of a period spanning the formation of the League of Arab States in 1945 until two decades after Chiha's death.[25] In Chiha's view, there is no harm in coordinating one's own legitimate interests with a neighbour's, as with Lebanon and Syria, for instance.[26] But too rushed a union of Arab countries is a sure recipe for division, and would be no different from the division which 'made the Umayyads victims of the Abbasids'. Equally undesirable is nationalism on a larger scale arising from the division of the world into two or three blocks: 'What if Asia were to become a single country from here to Kamchatka? How could one be ready to die for such a huge area?'[27]

Between the Charybdis of communalism and the Scylla of nationalism, Chiha did not venture a final judgment, even if he ultimately opted for Lebanon as a nation. Lebanon is lucky, he writes, because 'thanks to the grace of the Gods, the country is the size of a province.'[28] It allows both an attachment to a recognizable space, a person's 'home, his meadow, and his loves', as well as 'the desire to become "citizen of the world"' because of the siren call of the sea.[29] Citing the Renaissance poet Joachim du Bellay, a French diplomat in Rome longing for the calm beauty of his native Loire, Chiha explains the lure of the local, the 'provincial', and the peace it inspires.[30]

d'un Etat américain à l'autre, quoique les Etats d'alors fussent bien jeunes, un nationalisme jaloux existait'. Id. 150.

25 Probably described best in Fouad Ajami, *The Arab Predicament: Arab Political Thought and Practice since 1967*, Cambridge: Cambridge University Press, 1981.

26 For instance: '*Our task and that of Syria together, our future task, is to develop on these slopes forests and human settlement, which gives us as a border something other than desert and wind.' (Notre tâche et celle de la Syrie ensemble, notre tâche future, est de développer sur ces versants un peuplement forestier, puis humain, qui nous donne pour frontière autre chose que le désert et le vent)*'. 'Présence du Liban', VPL 148–9.

27 'Nationalisme idéologique', 'exaspéré'; 'Une rupture se produirait, pareille à celle qui fit des Ommeyades les victimes des Abbassides'; 'même si [le monde] n'est plus fait que de deux ou trois 'forces' collectives'; 'Quand l'Asie, d'ici jusqu'au Kamtchatka, ne serait-plus qu'un seul pays, comment voudrions-nous donner notre vie pour elle?' Id. 152.

28 'Par la faveur des dieux, le Liban a les dimensions d'une province', Id. 151.

29 'sa maison, son champ et ses amours', 'avec l'ambition de devenir « citoyen du monde »'. Id.

30 Id. 150–1. Joachim du Bellay's (d. 1560) famed poem in *Les Regrets* ('Heureux qui comme Ulysse') on the yearning to go home is likened to the 'song of the exile', of the emigrant', of the Lebanese in the far-off Americas' ("le chant même de l'exilé, de l'émigré, celui des Libanais des 'Amériques' lointaines.")

The fusion of mountain and sea in Lebanon adds to the attraction of the country. True, Lebanon is Arab, as well as a bridge at the crossroads of Europe and Asia, and the Middle East. Yet it is a 'Mediterranean republic before all else'.[31]

The fact that Lebanon is tiny allows the Lebanese citizen to 'know every hamlet, every peak, every canyon' in his country. Size matters.[32] Smallness is not always a blessing for a country, as Chiha knew all too well. His reading of history had shown that Lebanon was cursed as a passage for conquerors across the ages, and the country suffered through most of Chiha's life from the instability and ambitions caused by its neighbours.

Chiha also realised that globalisation was complicating an already charged picture. Localism, provincialism, even nationalism in its traditional association with a recognised nation-state, are all balanced by 'a shrinking world' and a planet which is getting steadily smaller because of the 'effects of extreme speed' accelerating emigration.[33] Torn between the call of the mountain and the call of the sea, between 'local' nationalism and a regionally- or internationally-driven nationalism, between Lebanon's residents and its diaspora, Chiha's preferred scale is local. His attachment to home and his bend to the mystical are channeled into 'the fraternal intimacy' of his collection of poetry – *The House of the Meadows*.[34]

Looking for constitutional temperaments to communalism

As a member of one of Lebanon's smallest religious sects which, together with a number of other small sects, had been known since the electoral law of 1922 as 'minorities' (*aqalliyyāt*), Chiha had no access to the three highest positions of state. These became reserved for the 'troika': a Maronite president of the Republic, a Sunni President of the Council of ministers, or Prime Minister, and a Shiʿi President of the Chamber of deputies, or Speaker.[35] Chiha was also an unlikely candidate for the more insignificant ministry, as well as key

[31] 'république maritime méditerranéenne avant tout'. Id. 147.

[32] '... hameau par hameau, crête par crête, vallon par vallon.' Id. 150–1.

[33] 'un globe qui rétrécit'; 'effets de l'extrême vitesse.' Id. 150, 151.

[34] *La Maison des Champs*, see previous chapter on Chiha as poet.

[35] The freezing of the top positions came in the later stage of Chiha's life, after Independence. But even early on, as denominationally 'Latin' (a community considered as one of the 'minorities'), he had no chance to access any significant position in the constitutional system.

embassies abroad and important positions in the administration and the military. He could therefore not celebrate a communal system which excluded him and others like him despite their obvious talent.[36] We saw how lively the debate over communalism was during the drafting of the Constitution, and how its bipolar reality weighed on the country. The 'disorder' and 'anarchy' to which Chiha was 'the unhappy witness' is an integral part of the communitarian system. This also explains why time was Chiha's hope for a move away from the strict communalism. Not only because of the weight of history, but also because he believed rushed alternatives risked causing more harm than good, Chiha was eminently conservative, honing and protecting tradition insofar as it appears beneficial. But he was not averse to change, and worked hard for a Lebanese nation that gains what communalism loses.

Yet his vision is not merely abstract, historical, and theoretical. As the careful crafter of the Constitution, Chiha's philosophy was more than a vague hope of seeing the nation come of age.

One aspect of his resistance to communalism appears in his repeated concen for merit in administrative recruitment. Administrative jobs, from top to bottom, were increasingly allocated on a communal basis, according to Art. 95 of the Constitution. As this became the norm after Independence, Chiha repeatedly expressed his principled opposition to communal entrenchment in the civil service.

> Here, finally, what matters is foresight and moderation. We understand that elective and political representation has to be communal for as long as is necessary. At the same time, however, we consider it legitimate and necessary that we should have more understanding and more flexibility at the administrative level and that there should not always be an unfair mix of civil servants. PROPORTIONAL PRESENCE IN THE ASSEMBLIES THAT MAKE THE LAWS REMAINS A STRUCTURAL NECESSITY. AS REGARDS THE ADMINISTRATION, IT IS IN EVERYONE'S INTEREST THAT IT RECRUITS THE BEST PEOPLE.[37]

[36] Edmond Rabbath (1902–1991), the distinguished constitutionalist on whom we have relied so often in this book, is another example. He was a member of the Syrian-Catholic 'minority' and was never appointed to a meaningful governmental position in the country.

[37] 'En cette matière enfin, tout est clairvoyance et pondération. Que la représentation élective ou proprement politique soit confessionnelle le temps qu'il faudra, nous le comprenons parfaitement.

There was another mechanism for the ethnolysis of communities, in the shape of a meaningful separation of powers in which Parliament should rise above its fractious behavioral pattern. We noted how Chiha harbored no illusions about the dominance of the executive in government, a deficiency compounded by the fact that Parliament had largely abdicated the balancing role given it by the Constitution:

> *In Lebanon, the Government* [the Council of Ministers], *whatever its make-up, has great responsibility for Parliament*. To the extent that the government is disinterested in it, to the extent that it ignores it, to the extent that it avoids it, *Government destroys Parliament*; even more so when it buys individual votes with favors. We have seen more than once how ministerial instability in this country is rarely because of Parliament. Rarely has Parliament withdrawn its confidence in a cabinet. *When a cabinet goes, it is usually because it has worn itself out.*[38]

Chiha often laments the weak backbone of deputies:

> The history of contemporary Lebanon has shown very clearly that every time Parliament has collapsed, the principle of representation has died a violent death, and communal leaders have taken over. *Automatically*, one or more Sanhedrins came into being. It is in the nature of things. *Whenever the community has no political representatives, it is the religious leaders who, naturally, take over*. And then, instead of calming down and folding into the life of the nation, as befits this country and this century, communal issues revive and rub against each other.[39]

Mais, parallèlement, nous tenons pour légitime et nécessaire qu'il y ait chez nous plus de compréhension et d'élasticité sur le plan administratif et qu'on n'exige pas, à tous les instants, un dosage de fonctionnaires inhumain. UNE PRESENCE PROPORTIONNELLE DANS LES ASSEMBLEES QUI FONT LA LOI RESTE UNE NECESSITE DE STRUCTURE. POUR L'ADMINISTRATION, C'EST L'INTERET DE TOUS QU'ELLE RECRUTE LES MEILLEURS'. 'Sur le confessionnalisme', 9 December 1952.

38 '*Au Liban, le Gouvernement, quel qu'il soit, porte largement la responsabilité de la Chambre*. Dans la mesure où il se désintéresse d'elle, dans la mesure où il l'ignore, dans la mesure où il la fuit, *il la détruit*; davantage encore en obtenant ses votes au prix de faveurs individuelles. Nous avons constaté plus d'une fois que l'instabilité ministérielle dans ce pays est rarement imputable à la Chambre. Rarement la Chambre a retiré sa confiance à un Gouvernement. *Quand le Gouvernement s'en va, c'est généralement qu'il s'est épuisé par le dedans*'. 'Le gouvernement et la chambre', 7 August 1947, Pol Int 137–8.

39 'L'histoire du Liban contemporain a montré jusqu'à la plus extrême évidence que toutes les fois que l'Assemblée a disparu, toutes les fois que le principe de la représentation est mort de mort

Another secularising role of Parliament provides a counterweight to the communities themselves, through the parliamentarians' ability to represent the entire nation:

> We are, as is well known, among those who have a strong belief that since Lebanon is made up of communal minorities, there must be a permanent balance among them if Lebanon is to thrive. This balance is found in national representation. It is in the CD that we must look for it.[40]

There is a dimension of repetition in Chiha's views over time, as he was constantly attempting to moderate the more damaging facets of communalism by various means, such as orienting the political process towards strengthening Lebanon as a united nation by taking a healthy distance from its neighbours, or relying on the diaspora as a unifying, common external factor. Other mechanisms he sought were domestic: a merit-based administration, and an active role of deputies using Parliament as a national agora against fractious communal representation. This constant attention to balancing fractious politics with national principles is at the heart of his democratic beliefs, which he also expressed in a set of 'principled stands'.

Chiha's 'positions de principe'

Chiha is remembered for a number of principled stands taken at various pivotal moments in his life, as 'positions de principe'.[41] Some of these stands derive from his private life. One little-known event concerned his betrothal to his cousin Marguerite Pharaon in 1926. The marriage was strongly opposed by Marguerite's mother, who did not consider him worthy of her and remained

violente, l'autorité proprement confessionnelle s'est substituée à l'Assemblée, et *automatiquement* un ou plusieurs sanhédrins ont pris naissance. C'est la nature des choses qui le veut. *La confession, quand elle n'a pas de représentants politiques, ce sont les chefs religieux qui, naturellement, la représentent.* Et alors, les questions confessionnelles, au lieu de se tempérer et de se fondre dans la vie nationale, comme il convient en ce pays et en ce siècle, rebondissent et s'exaspèrent'. 'A propos de la chambre', 30 August 1944, Pol Int 56.

[40] 'Nous sommes, on le sait, de ceux-là qui soutiennent avec une extrême vigueur que le Liban étant fait de minorités confessionnelles, il faut entre elles, pour que le Liban vive, un permanent équilibre. Cet équilibre c'est dans la représentation nationale, c'est dans la Chambre qu'il le faut chercher.' nationale, c'est dans la Chambre qu'il le faut chercher.' 'Liban «confessionnel»', 26 January 1945, Pol Int 81.

[41] 'Propos dominicaux: les positions de principe', *Le Jour*, 5 November 1950.

estranged from the couple and their three daughters for several years. Michel and Marguerite eloped for their wedding. It took a long time before he was accepted by his in-laws, well after he had proven himself a leading public intellectual, banker and writer, widely respected by the Lebanese and French elites alike.

Chiha took principled stands on other memorable occasions, such as his public opposition to the French High Commission over the speech of Henry de Jouvenel in Damascus on 'the United States of Syria and Lebanon.'[42]

Chiha's constitution was resolutely republican, as was his view of Lebanon as 'a maritime republic' since Antiquity. This did not stop him ruing the disappearance of Europe's kings after the Second World War. He noted the collapse of monarchies in southern Europe, often replaced by anarchy and instability, and their persistence in Belgium, Holland, and the Nordic countries, where democracy was more firmly rooted.

He sought to elucidate the paradox. Northern countries are comfortable with their monarchs, he explained, because these monarchs play a distant, withdrawn role of national cohesion and security when, and only if, needed. 'We do not say that monarchy is good for all countries. This would be idiotic (...) But we can suggest the following rule: *a monarchy will survive better, as a positive thing, in countries where every citizen feels that he is king*. This being the case, there is no room for envy'.[43] In similar vein, he drew a clear line between constitutional kings and tyrants: 'There are peoples who need a republic and others who need a king (on the English model). As for the tyrant, be he royal or plebeian, it is certain that he is no longer wanted anywhere'.[44] A special encomium is devoted to the future Queen Elizabeth II on her eighteenth birthday, and his regret that France never allowed a woman to be queen.[45]

[42] Discussed in Ch. 4.

[43] 'Nous ne disons pas de la monarchie qu'elle est bonne pour tous les pays. Ce serait une sotte erreur (...) Mais on peut proposer la loi que voici: *la monarchie subsistera le mieux, et comme un bienfait, dans le pays où chaque citoyen se sent roi*. Il n'y a plus place dans ce cas pour l'envie'. 'Le sort des rois', 14 May 1946, Essais II, 11. See See also his column denying the possibility of a 'good tyrant', 'La Prise de la Bastille et le 'bon tyran'', Essais I, 69.

[44] 'Car il y a des peuples à qui il faut la république et d'autres à qui il faut un roi (du modèle anglais). Quant au tyran, couronné ou plébéien, il est bien sûr que nulle part on n'en veut plus'. 'Monarchie et démocratie', 3 April 1946, Essais II, 72.

[45] 'Reines ...', 26 April 1944, Essais I, 49–51.

Chiha was a strong supporter of an active role for women in public life. Several of his editorials stress this commitment: '*If women, in Lebanon, wish to have a say in matters of State, insofar as their nature allows, we support them …*'[46] Women, he said, 'were not born to stay silent'.[47] His argument was twofold. One was a point of gender equality:

> After all, a woman is man's companion, she is not his inferior; her initiatives are often better than his. She is often a very stabilizing presence. She is more sensitive to order and disorder. Like him, she works, far more than used to be the case, to earn a living.[48]

Chiha's second point is the excellence of women as carers, both in public life and charitable work:

> In terms of social work, she has a head start on us. In social assistance, she is far more involved than us; in devotion to charitable organisations, she is at the front; she is the one who responds to suffering; in giving spiritual help, she again leads the way.[49]

Two conclusions derive from this 'principled stand'. One is that 'it is time for women to have their place in political life. A place compatible with their dignity'.[50] The other is that the greatest countries find a place for women. In this regard, Asia lags behind Europe and the Far East behind Western Asia, including Lebanon.[51]

The Khoury episode. The public stand Chiha is most remembered for occurred between 1948 and 1952. His brother-in-law Béchara El-Khoury,

[46] '*Si la femme, au Liban, veut se mêler des choses de l'Etat en limitant son rôle aux possibilités de sa nature, nous sommes pour elle.*' 'Le rôle de la femme', 31 December 1950, Pol Int 215.

[47] 'Les femmes ne sont pas nées pour être muettes.' Id.

[48] 'Car, enfin, la femme est la compagne de l'homme, elle n'est pas sa sujette; ses initiatives sont souvent plus heureuses que les siennes. Elle est souvent un facteur d'équilibre plus grand. Elle est plus sensible à l'ordre et au désordre. Elle travaille elle aussi et il lui arrive plus que naguère de gagner sa vie.' Id., 214.

[49] 'Sur le plan des œuvres, elle est en mouvement avant nous. L'assistance sociale, c'est elle plus que l'homme; le dévouement aux organisations charitables, c'est elle d'abord; la sensibilité à la souffrance, c'est elle; le service du spirituel, c'est elle encore.' Id.

[50] 'Il est temps que, chez nous, la femme ait sa place dans la vie politique. Une place compatible avec sa dignité.' Id.

[51] 'Les plus grands pays ont mis la femme à son rang. En cela l'Asie est en retard sur l'Europe et l'Extrême-Orient sur l'Asie occidentale.' Id.

married to Chiha's sister, Laure, and the politician who best personifies Lebanese independence, had been elected to the presidency in 1943. By then, the Constitution had been amended to limit the mandate of the president to six years, so Khoury could not seek a second term for at least another six years.[52] Because of his closeness to the president, both as friend and as kin, Chiha found himself in a bind.[53] He chose democracy. In a long article entitled 'Sur la révision de la Constitution' and published on 13 April 1948, Chiha opposed the amendment Khoury wanted in order to extend his term and to remove, 'for the one and only time', the clause in Art. 49 of the Constitution that excluded a second consecutive presidential tenure.

As he took a public stand on the matter, Chiha acknowledged his unique closeness to the president, but criticised what he calls Khoury's 'distressing way of treating constitutional matters and public affairs':[54]

> We acknowledge the ties of kinship, affection, long intimacy, a shared life and joint activities, and the common struggles that bind us to the Head of State, over such a long period that we have trouble remembering it all, a period that covers a lifetime. If it were only a question of giving free rein to brotherly, human feelings, we would be quite happy for the Republic and for ourselves.[55]

[52] The original Art. 49 of 1926 reads: '... La durée de la magistrature du Président est de trois ans; il n'est rééligible une troisième fois qu'après un intervalle de trois années.' In his first version, Chiha gave five years to the president, and he could be reelected forever. (Art. 50 DOC 1) In DOC 5, Chiha inserted by hand the major limitation which remains to date: 'Il n'est rééligible qu'après un intervalle de cinq années' (Art. 55 in DOC 5). The five-year mandate remained until the CR met to discuss the final draft. Art. 49 was discussed at length on 21 May 1926. In the wake of the debate, the majority voted for the amendment proposed by 'Umar Da'uq, whereby the presidential term, renewable once, was decreased from five years to three. Ahmad al-Zein ed., *Mahader Munaqashat al-Dustur al-Lubnani wa Ta'dilatuh 1926–90* (Minutes of the discussions about the Lebanese Constitution and its amendments), Beirut: Publications of the Chamber of Deputies 1993, 46–50. The length of presidential tenure was finally extended to a non-renewable six years in a 1929 constitutional amendment.

[53] A long eulogy by Béchara El-Khoury shows his deep attachment to and profound respect for Chiha. Noting Chiha's general disdain for politics, Khoury relates that Chiha disliked so much the campaign for the deputyship of Beirut in 1925 that he wanted to abandon it, and that he remained in the race only to be faithful to his commitments to the two other members of his electoral list, 'Umar Da'uq and 'Umar Bayhum. Khoury, typed eulogy dated 30 December 1954, Chiha Archive. See below on the Beirut electoral list.

[54] 'Cette façon de traiter la matière constitutionnelle et les affaires publiques a quelque chose d'affligeant.' 'Sur la révision de la constitution', 13 April 1948, Pol Int 149.

[55] 'On sait les relations de parenté, d'affection, de longue intimité, l'existence commune, l'activité, les luttes communes qui nous lient au Chef de l'Etat, depuis un temps pour nous quasi immémorial,

And yet, he continued,

> This is a question of principle, an exceptional event; it is a point upon which the future of the State quite literally depends. This is why, putting aside the man we are (who would listen to his heart and his inclinations), it is the citizen who has the duty to speak. Someone who writes for the public every day, and who assumes certain moral responsibilities, does not have the right in these circumstances to keep silent about what he thinks.[56]

This was a difficult moment for Chiha, and Khoury ignored his message. In an article entitled 'Preuves de maturité', written after the nonviolent 'White Revolution of 1952' forced Khoury out before the end of his second term, Chiha congratulated the country on electing a new president.[57] When Khoury finally resigned, Chiha expressed his relief that Parliament would meet to elect a new president. Insisting once again on the need for moderation and wisdom, '*for Lebanon is not a country to be ruled by whims and coups d'état*',[58] he stressed the importance of abiding by democratic principles and the constitutional rule of law:

> Developments at home are evolving in the best possible way. The Constitution is respected. The Chamber will meet on Tuesday to elect the new Head of State. *Lebanon is giving proof of maturity in domestic politics*

depuis un temps qui représente une vie. S'il ne s'agissait pour nous que de laisser se manifester le sentiment humain et fraternel, nous nous montrerions tout à fait heureux pour la République et pour nous'. Id.

[56] 'Mais c'est une question de principe qui se pose; c'est d'une procédure d'exception qu'il s'agit; c'est un point auquel peut être subordonné littéralement l'avenir de l'Etat. C'est pourquoi, bien avant l'homme que nous sommes (et qui mettrait en mouvement son penchant et son cœur), le citoyen a le devoir de parler. Quand on écrit pour le public tous les matins, quand on assume les responsabilités morales d'un certain degré, on n'a pas le droit en une telle circonstance de taire ce que l'on pense'. Id.

[57] 'Preuves de maturité', 20 September 1952 (and not 1951, as in the wrong date in the text) Pol Int 147. Chiha did not mention the large popular movement that led to Béchara El-Khoury's resignation, in a short, nonviolent revolution which is known in the country as '*al-thawra al-bayda*' (the White Revolution). The forced extension of the presidential mandate of Khoury had come with an atmosphere of corruption associated mostly with his brother Selim, nicknamed 'Sultan Selim'. On the corruption in the Khoury household, see Eyal Zisser, 'The Downfall of the Khoury administration: A dubious revolution', *Middle Eastern Studies*, 30, 1994, 486–511, at 497. For a more subtle analysis, Farès Sassine, 'Chute d'un président ou la révolution de septembre 1952', *Ecrits I*, Beirut: L'Orient des livres 2022, 167–79.

[58] '*Car le Liban n'est pas un pays à coups de tête et à coups d'Etat.*' 'Preuves de maturité', Pol Int 147.

> *which is a reassurance for the present and a guarantee for the future. This, more than anything else, is what matters.*[59]

Chiha's lesson, alas, would not be often heeded. More presidential elections in the ensuing century have been subjected to anti-constitutional manipulations. Several Lebanese presidents have sought to extend their mandate by undermining the Constitution with a 'once and exceptional amendment', or to prevent its application if the result went against them. Well into the twenty-first century, deadlocks leading to forced delays and forced extensions proved to be inordinately devastating for the country.

Elections. We saw how unforgiving Michel Chiha was of a system which invented the concept of 'appointed deputies'. Although crude violations such as stuffing ballots or preventing rivals from running were generally shunned, elections in Lebanon have tended to be marred by corruption, the heavy hand of sitting presidents, opportunistic redistricting, and foreign interventions. Occasionally, as in 1925 and 1943, then from 1960 to 1972, parliamentary elections were generally free and fair, but financing remained a key factor, even when clauses in the electoral law required caps on expenditures and transparency in the disbursement of electoral funds.

Chiha tended to hold his peace in the generally corrupt, and colonially crippled electoral exercises of the Mandate years, and he realised early on that those electoral laws reinforced sectarianism and worked against the building of the nation. When he was elected deputy of Beirut in 1925, it was his first and last foray into public office. Even that occasion proved hard to his principles. It is worth recalling that before Chiha won a 'minority' seat in Beirut, he was so reluctant to pursue the campaign that he thought it better to withdraw his candidacy. He explained the reason – his personal unease with communitarianism – in a draft letter to the Governor of Lebanon, which remains in the Chiha Archive:

> Having entered the electoral struggle with the sole purpose of serving, at the express desire of many people from all the communities of Greater Lebanon

[59] L'évolution de la situation intérieure se fait dans les conditions les plus raisonnables. La Constitution est respectée. La Chambre se réunira mardi pour élire le nouveau Chef de l'Etat. *Le Liban donne en politique intérieure des preuves de maturité qui sont un apaisement pour le présent et une garantie pour le futur. C'est cela, par-dessus tout, qui comptait*'. 'Preuves de maturité', Pol Int 147.

who honoured me with their trust and friendship, it seems to me today, in full conscience, that it is no longer possible to continue with my initial decision.[60]

The letter seems to have never been sent. Not wanting to let down the other two candidates on his list, ʻUmar Bayhum and ʻUmar Daʻuq, Chiha stayed in the race.[61]

We saw that the dilemma Chiha faced is rooted in the electoral system, which stamps the candidate with his sectarian identity and forces him to run within a sectarian list. Serving 'all the communities of Greater Lebanon' looks like the utter oxymoron. The list system – either 'open' lists from which voters could choose whomever they wanted, or 'closed' lists obliging voters to vote for the full roster – is crushing for the 'nation' when its electoral system runs on communal bases rather than on party lines. This feature, which the strait-jacket of electoral communalism makes so difficult to shed, remains dominant in Lebanon more than a hundred years after the laws of 1922/1925, *pace* the Mutasarrifiyya, established it as the political nerve of Lebanon.

In 1947, as a new electoral law was being debated, Chiha expressed the gap between the official reason for its introduction (more transparency) and the problem of trust in the country:

> If one takes precautionary measures on all sides, it is because one is wary of his fellow man and of the state. An Indian scout's mistrust. It's a funny thing where you have to defend yourself against the amorality of the democratic government and of the people who decide. Acknowledging this requires a lot of hard work. For what is universal suffrage if magic tricks and an absence of principle run riot? Yet one must accept that all countries experience change; in democratic institutions as well as in people.
>
> *When citizens go to the polls in Switzerland, in England, in Norway, why are they afraid neither of each other nor of the State?*[62]

[60] 'Entré dans la lutte électorale avec le seul dessein de servir, sur le désir formel d'un très grand nombre de personnes appartenant à toutes les communautés du Grand-Liban et qui veulent bien m'honorer de leur confiance et de leur amitié, il m'apparaît aujourd'hui qu'en conscience, il ne m'est plus possible de persévérer dans ma décision première'. Manuscript letter from Chiha to Lebanon's Governor, Léon Cayla, July 5, 1925. Chiha Archive, Document 16–25.

[61] See above Béchara al-Khoury's comment on the episode in his eulogy of Chiha, n.55.

[62] 'Si l'on prend des précautions de tous les côtés, c'est parce qu'on se méfie de ses concitoyens et de l'Etat. Une méfiance de peau-rouge. Drôle de situation où il faut se défendre à la fois contre

If Lebanon is so different from countries where elections are honoured and trusted, it is because of the combination of an immature electorate and manipulations of elections by the executive:

> The bad example we have been dealt came from above, a long time ago. It has come to be seen, quite wrongly, as legitimate and capable. A political regime which is smart and authoritarian has no hesitation in supporting universal suffrage when, on the contrary, it means to rip it up and rig the vote: 'Why should the drink matter as long as one gets drunk'.[63]

This is a serious problem for Chiha: the West depicts elections as a silver bullet for countries like Lebanon where a politically uneducated public is still not alert to electoral manipulation. Yet the West itself is far from being saved by electoral grace. Chiha considered 'the 40-degree latitude' a dividing line between mature democracies in northern Europe and their pale imitations in southern European countries:

> Thus the institutions of England (and of Iceland before it) have spread around the world without anyone knowing if they would fit in below 40° degrees latitude, down to the tropics and the equator.[64]

The consequence of the theory is sweeping. Like Italy, Greece, even France, Lebanon and 'the East' stand below the 40-degree line:

> Let us say it again, very clearly: *In most of the East, citizens, electors and legislators are still in need of (political) education.*[65]

l'amoralité du gouvernement démocratique et du peuple souverain. Mais la constatation du fait appelle un effort d'éducation pressant. Qu'est-ce, en effet, que le suffrage universel si l'absence de principe et si l'art du prestidigitateur en font leur affaire? Mais il faut reconnaître que, d'un pays à l'autre, tout change; l'institution démocratique et les hommes.

Pourquoi les citoyens, quand ils vont aux urnes en Suisse, en Angleterre, en Norvège, n'ont-ils pas peur les uns des autres et de l'Etat? 'Variations sur la loi électorale', 16 August 1947, Pol Int 83.

63 'Chez nous le mauvais exemple est venu de haut et de loin. Il a pris depuis longtemps un air équivoque de légitimité et de savoir-faire. Un régime politique astucieux et autoritaire va sans hésitation au suffrage universel quand il nourrit l'intention perverse d'en faire litière et de truquer le suffrage: « Qu'importe le flacon pourvu qu'on ait l'ivresse ».' Id.

64 'Ainsi les institutions de l'Angleterre (et de l'Islande avant elle) ont fait le tour du monde sans que l'on sût jamais si vraiment elles s'acclimateraient tout à fait à partir du 40° degré de latitude, en descendant jusqu'au niveau des tropiques et de l'équateur'. Id.

65 'Répétons-le clairement: *un peu partout en Orient, l'éducation du citoyen, de l'électeur et du législateur reste à faire*'. Id.

The Swiss example

Overall, Chiha's understanding did not move much constitutionally after 1926. His belief in small government coupled with the largest possible degree of political freedom remained at the heart of his liberal vision. As time went by, he came to see Switzerland as the best model for Lebanon. In a 1947 article entitled 'L'Exemple Suisse', he drew parallels between the communities of Lebanon and the cantons of Switzerland:

> Lebanon's Chamber of Deputies is, in essence, an original example of federalism. *Like Switzerland, which has cantons, our cantons are religious communities. The former are based on territory, the latter are based on legislation which regulates their individual status.* In both cases, they are social and political entities that wish to remain separate. The whole political apparatus in Switzerland would be much simpler if cantons agreed to disappear. But they do not want to, and they have compelling reasons for not wanting to. The situation is provisionally the same for our communities (because the truth is not always in centralization and unity).[66]

The article again urged a stronger role for the CD in order to balance communal powers:

> It is because the Chamber of Deputies is a fundamental institution in Lebanon that parliament should not be ridiculed. If it puts up a poor defence to ridicule, or if it lends itself to it, this is most regrettable. (One is respected to the extent that one deserves it, and the people are quick to distrust whatever they find grotesque.)
>
> *We have often explained that our Chamber of Deputies, more than the expression of a democracy, is the meeting place of associated religious communities.*

[66] 'L'exemple suisse', 30 July 1947, Pol Int 135–6: La Chambre des députés, au Liban, représente au fond un aspect original du fédéralisme. *Comme en Suisse, il y a des cantons, il y a ici des communautés confessionnelles. Les premiers ont pour base un territoire, les seconds seulement une législation*, l'adhésion à un statut personnel. Ce sont, dans les deux cas, des aspects de la vie sociale et politique qui ne veulent pas se confondre.

En Suisse, si les cantons acceptaient de disparaître, tout l'appareil politique serait simplifié. Mais ils ne le veulent pas et ils ont des raisons décisives pour ne pas le vouloir. Le cas est provisoirement le même pour nos communautés (car la vérité n'est pas nécessairement dans la centralisation et dans l'unité)'.

> It is the country's demonstration of the 'desire to live in common', of the will of the State for common management. If we renounce this model, we immediately fall back on religious assemblies, into a Sanhedrin.[67]

In his mature writings, Chiha often drew a comparison with Switzerland, to the extent that the model for the Lebanese constitution ended up being closer to the Swiss system than to the various constitutions he studied in 1926.[68]

But is Lebanon a replica of Switzerland? The concept of 'communitarian federalism' has gained traction over time, but it remains a stretch to liken Lebanon's religion-based communities to Switzerland's language-based cantons.[69] Lebanon is not a federation. A federation requires two chambers and all federations, the world over, are territorially defined. Since 1848, Switzerland has adopted a territorial-cum-linguistic bicameralism, where the Assemblée Fédérale in charge of legislation has two chambers: the Conseil National, which represents the citizens proportionately to their numbers, and the Conseil des Etats, which represents the Cantons.[70] Chiha was doubtful about bicameralism and the Senate, which was cancelled, with his full support, in the very first revision of 1927.

Yet he was right in likening Lebanon to Switzerland in other major aspects. Had his original draft survived with its two legislative Assemblies (like Switzerland) and their joint election of a president (like Switzerland) who heads a Council of Ministers limited to seven members (like the Swiss Conseil Fédéral),[71] it would have been remarkably similar to the constitutional structure of Switzerland. There would have been major differences still, not least that

[67] Id., 134–5: 'C'est parce que la Chambre des députés est au Liban une institution fondamentale qu'il ne faut pas la ridiculiser. Si elle-même se défend mal contre le ridicule, si elle s'y prête, il faut le déplorer. (On se fait respecter dans la mesure où on le mérite et l'ironie du peuple s'exerce volontiers sur ce qui lui paraît grotesque).

Nous expliquons depuis longtemps que la Chambre des députés, chez nous, avant d'être l'expression d'une démocratie, est le lieu de rencontre de communautés confessionnelles associées. Elle est la manifestation officielle du « vouloir vivre en commun », de la volonté de gestion commune de l'Etat. Si nous en sortons, nous tombons instantanément dans les assemblées religieuses, dans un sanhédrin'.

[68] See Chapter 7.

[69] For a comparison, Mark Farha, *Lebanon- The Rise and Fall of Secular State under Siege*, Cambridge: Cambridge University Press 2019, 89–94.

[70] Successive Swiss constitutions were enacted in 1848, 1872 and 1999. For a summary of the system, Guillaume Tusseau, *Droit Constitutionnel et Institutions Politiques*, 4th ed., Paris: Seuil 2022, Ch.11.

[71] The Conseil Fédéral is Switzerland's executive arm of government and has seven members.

the Lebanese Senate of 1926 was representative of communities and not of territories, and that the president was a far more powerful figure than his Swiss counterpart, who rotates every year and operates only as *primus inter pares*.

The comparative exercise in constitutional design is always approximative, and there is no reference in Chiha's 1926 archives to the Swiss Constitution of 1872 then in place. Nor is there a copy of the Swiss constitution alongside the other constitutions found in his files. He probably did not pay much attention in 1926. Yet rather than the French, Belgian, Latvian or Egyptian models, Chiha made in his later years repeated mention of 'the Swiss example':

> In Lebanon (and this is true of almost all countries), the Chamber of Deputies is an essential element of political life. Associated confessional minorities (as is the case with us) need to remain associated through *collective representation*.
>
> None of them, in fact, could dominate the others without jeopardizing the very existence of the State. The oft-cited Swiss example is conclusive here. Switzerland, the most democratic country in the world, maintains an impressive number of governments and assemblies in the name of peace and collective well-being.[72]

On 22 May 1954, a few weeks before his death, Chiha published a short reflection on constitutionalism in Lebanon. On Switzerland, he had this to say:

> The Constitution of Switzerland, which is very similar to that of the United States and was inspired by it, provided for two Chambers – the equivalent of the House of Representatives and the Senate in the United States. They are the Council of States, made up of two representatives per canton, regardless of the numerical or territorial size of the canton, and the National Council. Switzerland, a democratic country par excellence, is not a country *with a presidential regime because power there is not individual but 'collegial'*.

[72] 'Au Liban (et cela est vrai de presque tous les pays), la Chambre des députés est un élément essentiel de la vie politique. Des minorités confessionnelles associées (c'est bien le cas chez nous) ont besoin pour demeurer associées d'une *représentation collective.*

Aucune d'elles, en effet, ne pourrait dominer les autres sans mettre en péril l'existence même de l'Etat. L'exemple suisse souvent cité est à ce point de vue décisif. La Suisse, qui est le pays le plus démocratique du monde, maintient au nom de la paix et du bien-être collectifs un nombre impressionnant de gouvernements et d'assemblées'. 'A propos de la Chambre', 30 August 1944, Pol Int. 30.

> The Swiss Federal Council exercises power collectively ... The President of the Swiss Confederation, elected each year, holds a position mainly of courtesy; he is, in fact, merely the first among equals.
>
> Remembering these facts is useful in a country like Lebanon where everyone talks about the Constitution without having read it, and about the 'presidential regime' without knowing what it is.[73]

With the re-emergence of a Senate in the Ta'ef agreements of 1989, the Swiss federal system has risen again as the closest model for constitutional reform in Lebanon. The problem, as we shall see in next chapter, is that little else resembles the Swiss system.

[73] 'La Constitution de la Suisse, qui ressemble beaucoup à celle des Etats-Unis et qui s'en est inspirée, a prévu justement deux Chambres qui sont l'équivalent aux Etats-Unis de la Chambre des Représentants et du Sénat. Ce sont le Conseil des Etats, composé de deux représentants par canton, quelle que soit l'importance numérique ou territoriale du canton, et le Conseil national. La Suisse, pays démocratique par excellence, n'est pas un pays de régime présidentiel parce que *le pouvoir y est non point individuel mais 'collégial'*.

Le Conseil fédéral suisse exerce le pouvoir collectivement (...). Le Président de la Confédération suisse, élu chaque année, a plutôt une situation de courtoisie; il n'est, en fait, que le premier entre ses pairs.

Le rappel de ces choses a son utilité dans un pays comme le Liban où tout le monde parle de la Constitution sans l'avoir lue, et du 'régime présidentiel' sans savoir ce qu'il est.' 'Ce qu'est le 'Régime présidentiel américain', 22 May 1954, Pol Int 180–1.

PART FOUR

CONSTITUTIONALISM AND GROUP REPRESENTATION

11

Lebanese Constitutionalism and the Political-Theological Middle East

> We are in this East, let us not forget, always in ferment and literally sick with intelligence and exegesis, a promised land of anxious minorities, a high place from where all prayers rise freely into the clearest, starriest sky.[1]

Michel Chiha wrote the Lebanese Constitution in 1926. This makes it the sole surviving constitution in a sea of persistent regional trouble. In 1979, whatever remained of the Persian *Mashruteh* of 1905–1906, the grand old man of Middle Eastern constitutions still standing, was swept away by the revolution in Iran. Why the survival and continuity of the Lebanese Constitution after the passing of Chiha in 1954, how it is rooted far in the past of the Middle East, and how it stands in comparison with the region's other constitutions, are the subject of this chapter.

The depth of Middle Eastern constitutionalism

Borrowing the title of the chapter from Spinoza's famous *Theological-Political Treatise* (1670), my analysis underlines the unique place of religion in the Middle East, and therefore of theology as the quintessential canopy of its politics. In a region where written records extend back to the end of the third millennium BCE, religion has always been bedrock for the political imagination of society. Writing on the earliest Mesopotamia, a Sumer/Akkad scholar explains why:

1 'Nous sommes, ne l'oublions pas, dans cet Orient toujours en fermentation et littéralement malade d'intelligence et d'exégèse, une terre promise des minorités inquiètes, un haut lieu d'où montent librement vers le ciel le plus transparent, le plus étoilé, toutes les prières'. LA 46.

> [I]n the spheres reflected in our documents *Mesopotamian religion is politics*. From the earliest times historical statements are couched in religious metaphors, and this alone is enough to show that their ideological statements were important on a purely secular level.[2]

The political-theological nexus has always been a tightly knit compact, and social segmentation along religious lines a fixture of public life ever since.[3] Citizens are not merely individual subjects; they are also defined by their religious 'communities'. Modern Middle Eastern constitutionalism faces a reality, deeply rooted in its past, which continues to weigh on its peoples.

Not only does this trait strike root as a Middle Eastern calque since antiquity, but its continuity is attested at various moments of a long history. One scholar of the earliest Christian period confirms the irrelevance of secularism in the tragic triangle composed of Pontius Pilate as Roman prefect in Judea, Caiaphas as Judean Grand Priest, and Jesus, a Galilean native from Nazareth. In the most famous trial in history, Pilate wants to punish Jesus for 'sedition', Caiaphas wants to punish Jesus for 'blasphemy', and Jesus responds that his realm, and his law, belong to neither Roman nor to Judean/Jewish law. Yet all three laws, including Roman law, are religious:

> On a purely lexical register, characterization of sedition as a 'secular Roman crime' is confused. Pre-Christian Roman law had no place for the term 'secular'; there are no 'secular' rights, or crimes, in pre-Christian Rome. The legal use of the term 'secular' (*saecularis*) emanates from Christian chanceries in late antiquity, and the word 'secularity' (*saecularitas*) was put into circulation by the late Medieval, Latin-rite Christians.
>
> In a technical sense, Jesus could not have been condemned for a secular offence, since no offense in first-century Roman law is called 'secular'. But for that matter, no offence in first-century Judean law is called 'religious'.[4]

[2] Nicholas Postgate, *Early Mesopotamia*, London: Routledge 1992, 479. Emphasis added.

[3] In a Western context, the masterpiece of Lucien Febvre on *Le Problème de l'Incroyance au 16ème Siècle- La Religion de Rabelais*, Paris: Albin Michel 1937, demonstrates society's inevitably religious daily life in early Renaissance Europe.

[4] David Loyd Dusenbury, *I Judge No One: a Political Life of Jesus*, New York: Oxford University Press 2023, 203 (fns omitted).

Fusion and confusion between religious and secular law continued through the ages. The 5th-century Syro-Roman Code shows how, well before Islamic law came of age in the 8th–9th century, law was inextricably linked with religion.[5] This segmentation persisted naturally with the advent of Islam.

In his 1942 survey of Lebanese history, Michel Chiha ascribed to Islamic rule the transformation of a more secular governmental mode, epitomised by the Byzantine Roman empire in the West and the Sassanid Persian Empire in the East, into a stricter religious-communal system. Regardless of whether the two large Empires defeated by the Islamic conquests of the 7th century were 'secular' in a modern understanding, there is little doubt that the religion-defined group, and within it, the religious/sectarian community, predates the arrival of Islam.

Political-theological segmentation can be seen in great detail in the case of Egypt in the 10th to 13th centuries through the prism of the Jewish communities of Cairo, and the wider Muslim world in which they operated. In his masterly study of the Jewish communities of the Arab word, Samuel Goitein describes this political-theological coupling is as a 'medieval religious democracy'.[6] In the last century of the Ottoman Empire's long life, when the democratic revolutions of the late eighteenth century rocked Europe and the Middle East, this was conceptualised into the millet system,[7] which is a calque of previous Middle Eastern systems: the Sultan rules and deputises bureaucrats and judges, while recognised or tolerated religious communities govern their members in ways that do not threaten or impinge on his authority. Various councils of state, generally known as *diwan* (plural *dawawin*, antechambers), advise the Sultan and carry out his orders. Any 'privy council' acts on the command of the ruler. Members of the diwan are appointed and dismissed by him at will.[8] And whereas the Middle East in the classical age

[5] On the religious dimension of the Syro-Roman law book, see my *Introduction to Middle Eastern Law*, Oxford: Oxford University Press 2007, 22–32.

[6] Samuel Goitein, *A Mediterranean Society: the Jewish Communities of the Arab World as Portrayed in the Documents of the Cairo Geniza*, 5 vols, Berkeley: University of California Press 1967–88, vol. 2, *The Community*, 1971, 5.

[7] Ottoman *Millet*, an originally Arabic word (*milla*), is attested for hundreds of years as meaning (religious) community: see the discussion on related terms in the section 'a terminological detour, Sect, community, confession, rite', in Chapter 1.

[8] On *Diwan al-mazalim* as a special semi-judicial iteration of the ruler's diwan, see my 'A Middle Eastern tradition', in Peter Cane et al. eds, *Oxford handbook of comparative administrative law*, Oxford: Oxford University Press 2021, 97–116.

allowed members of minorities to express themselves through a complicated system of group representation, the unquestioned dominance of one caliph or ruler undermines the democratic credentials of classical Middle Eastern societies.

Consultation was a constant, and enduring, feature within minorities, and a common one from the leaders of these minorities up to the Caliph, Shah or Sultan at the top. It survives most clearly in the associated minorities of Chiha's constitutional theory. The Lebanese Constitution stands as a stubborn template of historically deep social structures across the Middle East which consider the citizen always as individual-in-a fixed-religious group. Democracy as equality between individuals is bound to fail in a communal system.

Goitein was excessive in his enthusiasm about the Middle East as a 'medieval democracy' in the 10th–13th centuries. For there were no elections. And there is no democracy without elections.

Disruptive elections

The obvious way to promote representation, all the way to full representation of the people, is through fair, regularly held elections to ensure democratic change of the rulers. Although there may be several persons contesting a coveted official position in classical Middle Eastern/Muslim history, the concept of a competitive election with participants casting a vote with a relative or absolute majority in favor of one candidate winning is so far unattested. In an investigation which I carried out into government manuals of the classical Islamic age, an unexpected process came to light concerning the way in which communities chose their leaders, a system which to some degree foreshadows modern-day elections. This is the forgotten *istihama* (from *sahm*, share) or vote by shares, with the voters casting physical objects such as pebbles in a recipient, with each pebble representing one unit/share in a defined ensemble which is the receptacle. The candidate receiving the most pebbles/shares wins. The concept did not take root in practice.[9] The theoretical conception of a

[9] On the concept of *istihama*, see 'Introduction: Three circles and a few promises (with Elham Fakhro)', in *Promises of constitutionalism in the Gulf States*, *al-Abhath*, Special issue 70, 2022, 5–27, at 25–7.

competition arbitrated by shares is an exception which confirms the rule: the absence of any significant electoral practice in the pre-modern Middle East.

This should not come as a surprise, and the absence of voting was also true in the West until the Enlightenment. It took hundreds of years for 'social choice' to morph into 'election'. For our purposes, an election can be defined as an arithmetical operation carried out in a relatively short time to compute votes cast with the objective of choosing one or more winners among competing candidates in a pre-agreed ballot under a majoritarian system, with the acceptance of the winner(s) by all candidates as a matter of course. Like the elephant in the room, this complicated definition claiming accuracy and comprehensiveness will not add much to the simple voter's practical understanding of what an election is: namely, your candidate is elected if he, or she, wins a majority of the votes that are added to yours. There is no gainsaying the immense advance constituted by elections in the slow progress of humankind for the people's representation in the State. Elections are one, late form of social choice, intimately associated with the concept of democracy as a system in which critical pool of equal voters inexorably grows to become 'universal suffrage'.

Steps toward enfranchisement, on the road to democratic representation under universal suffrage as accepted in the twenty-first century, were slow, hesitant, often marred with reversals. The enduring ways of disenfranchisement also mean that elections are ever more perfectible on the road to fairness.

'Un monstre ingouvernable'

In light of the glacial move of humankind towards democracy, how has the Lebanese experiment fared since 1926?

A century after Chiha and his colleagues drafted the social contract, Lebanese constitutionalism remains the prisoner of a profound paradox. At one end of the paradox, all factions and all political leaders swear by the Constitution and the need to apply it. Even the radical groups sitting on the extremes have rallied to the mantra of upholding the Constitution. This acknowledgment has not yet reached maturation, and there is no constitutional core of principles that does not transcend petty factionalism depending on an extreme group or leader's narrow interests. But even 'extremes' in Lebanon are counterintuitive, for they are not merely right and left extremes.

Extremism among groups operates dominantly *within* a communal setting spanning the 18 or so legally recognised sects in the country and dominated by the three larger communities: Maronite, Shiʿi, Sunni. The political leader of one community is extreme when he sets his or her community up against another community to advance his personal interests, violently if necessary. Even without resorting to violence, his leadership is defined electorally by the seats he commands within his community, which is set by default separate and opposite the other communities. The result is extreme Maronites, extreme Sunnis, extreme Shiʿis dominating the political scene in times of tension. Even when tension is not stoked by the more extreme candidate in order to increase his chances at the ballot box, any candidate remains boxed in his community by default.

After Independence, when the president became a Maronite by constitutional custom, and the prime minister a Sunni, in times of crisis the association of minorities used to freeze the country into a Muslim-Christian binary. The binary figure receded steadily after the 1990 Ta'ef constitutional amendments into a triangle formed by Maronites, Sunnis and Shiʿis as the three largest religious communities in the country. This triangle has been described in popular and slightly derogatory wisdom as 'troika'. For the ordinary Lebanese citizen, the troika is represented constitutionally by the president of the Republic, the president of the Council of Ministers, and the president of the Chamber of Deputies, all three defined by religion. The troika is the embodiment of structural deadlock. The central problem of communalism in government is that it does not require its leaders to be extreme for the dual or multiple system of representation to freeze into ungovernability.

In short, one aspect of the Lebanese constitutional quandary rests on a power-sharing consociational Constitution which all Lebanese factions have increasingly rallied around in the pretense to, need for, or intimate belief in, upholding.

The other aspect of the quandary is that it does not work. The communal State of representative government, undergirded by a Lebanese Constitution forged in 1926, freed from colonial shackles in 1943, and revisited in 1989–90 with significant amendments, has become '*un monstre ingouvernable*'.[10]

[10] Editorial, 'Liban: l'Etat, monstre ingouvernable', *Le Monde*, 30 November 2020.

The ungovernability of a system based on an association of minorities is deeply rooted. Whether it is encapsulated in two communities, Christian and Muslim, or three, Maronite, Sunni and Shi'i, or in even more granular arrangements down to the fractiously detailed representation in the cabinet, parliament, the judiciary and the administration of all or nearly all communities, the system is blocked at each and every turn.

A bullet-like reading of contemporary history

Lebanese history since 1926 is a chain of snags in the system. What makes the country even more ungovernable is the fact that intra-communitarian disputes are often the reason why the system becomes blocked. During the Mandate, the young Constitution was undermined by the difficulty of the Chamber of Deputies voting on a successor to the first president from amongst Christian leaders. Greek Orthodox president Charles Debbas was reelected in 1929 for a second three-year term, as allowed by the Constitution at the time, to avoid a brutal contest between Christians. In 1932, the rift between the two leading Maronite contenders, Béchara El-Khoury and Emile Eddé, led to the 'risk' of Tripolitan Muslim leader Muhammad al-Jisr taking over the Republic's helm. Prodded by the Maronite Patriarch, 'Christian' France reacted by suspending the Constitution, and we saw how HC Henri Ponsot extended Debbas's mandate, adding insult to injury with the fig leaf of Debbas's appointment as President of the Council of ministers whilst retaining his title as President. After the death of Debbas in 1935, the rivalry between Béchara El-Khoury and Emile Eddé dominated the Chamber of Deputies' microcosm for the next 15 years. Eddé prevailed between 1936 and 1941, then El-Khoury between 1943 and 1952.

As in *Hamlet*, the foreigner is called in when the locals are at daggers drawn. Military-backed French 'arbitration' under the Mandate would recur time and again, prompted by intra-Maronite rivalry over the presidency. This was repeated in 1958 by the brief American 'arbitration' when the US Marines landed in Lebanon and secured the presidency of the head of the army, General Fouad Chehab, against the ambition of his predecessor retaining power in the face of an armed insurrection resisting him.[11] The constitutional system was

[11] On the presidency of Fouad Chehab, see in the bibliography the books of Bassem al-Jisr and Nicolas Nassif in Arabic, and of Stephane Malsagne in French, and the site FouadChehab.org. On the Marines in Lebanon in 1958, Irene Gendzier, *Notes from the Minefield: United States*

undermined again by the rise of the Palestinian armed movement in Lebanon after 1967, and the split in the country between 'Muslim left' and 'Christian right', but the battle remained most acute over the holder of the presidency. Syrian military 'arbitration' intervened to appoint its preferred Maronite presidents between 1976 and 1992, with a significant interlude of a 'counter-arbitration' by Israel invading Lebanon and occupying Beirut in 1982, thereby forcing on the country two successive presidents, the first one assassinated before taking over. Amidst a succession of internal wars and foreign armed interventions, the next episode of ungovernability saw the presidency turn into the battleground between Maronite contenders backed by Iraq and Syria (1988–90), with the temporary victory of Syria benefiting from its alignment with the West when the Iraqi ruler occupied Kuwait in 1990. Syrian military domination lasted until 2005, when the Lebanese Cedar Revolution weakened Syria's control and forced its troops out of the country. Subsequent presidents have remained an expression of outside domination, Iranian rather than Syrian.[12] Power balance changes, and the person of the head of state changes with it.

One recalls that the denomination of a Maronite president was never inscribed formally into the text. The received constitutional custom, unwritten, is the so-called National Pact (*al-mithaq al-watani*) struck by Béchara al-Khoury and the President of the Council, Prime Minister Riad al-Solh, in 1943, whereby the president would be forever Maronite and the PM forever Sunni. When the historically marginal status of Shi'is inherited from the Ottoman Empire was terminated by official recognition of the community by the French in 1926, as the Constitution was being drafted, the seeds of the modern troika were sown.[13]

Intervention in Lebanon and the Middle East, 1945–1958, New York: Columbia University Press, 1997.

12 I did not see useful to list the immense bibliography which covers that period, the later part having been lived by my generation in a fifty-year long war that persists in fits and starts since 1975. In addition to the works of Harris, Khalaf and Traboulsi (see bibliography), which extend (almost) to the present, two books by seasoned British journalists capture some of the ongoing violence, Robert Fisk, *Pity the Nation: Lebanon at War*, Oxford: Oxford University Press 1990 (for the 1975–90 period of the war); David Hirst, *Beware of Small States: Lebanon, Battleground of the Middle East*, London: Faber and Faber 2010 (up to 2009); and specifically on the Cedar Revolution of 2005, my *March 2221. Lebanon's Cedar Revolution- An Essay on Justice and Non-violence*, Beirut: [Lir] 2007, and Michael Young, *The Ghosts of Martyrs Square*, New York: Simon and Schuster 2010.

13 On Shi'i positioning during the French Mandate for and against the Grand Liban, see Tamara Chalabi, *The Shi'is of Jabal 'Amil and the New Lebanon*, New York: Palgrave-McMillan 2006,

Chiha saw the downside of a communal constitution, as did most of his contemporaries. One of his persistent responses was "time". He, and many others, hoped that the passage of time would privilege Nation over Sect. But time can also have the opposite effect, and Chiha knew it. One early, tragic example is the near-total disappearance of Jewish citizens in Lebanon, mostly in the aftermath of the Arab defeat by Israel in 1967, and accelerating with the outbreak of civil war in 1975. A community which dwindles to a few souls cannot claim representation in government. The principle also holds true for larger communities when demographics shift. The last official census was carried out in 1932, six years after the Constitution was put in place. Following on the previous census of 1922, upon which the first electoral law of the Council of Representatives was based, it was clear that Christians were losing numerical ground to Muslims.

When it comes to the game of numbers, change is always troubling in a democracy. A republic, also known as a democracy, representative system, or majority rule, finds itself undermined by changes in numbers and their perceptions by the usually dominant groups who see themselves assailed by rising 'minorities' or weakened by extensive emigration. This is a solid, universal rule. Its manifestation in Lebanon, at its most basic, is the illegitimacy of Christian dominance when Maronites are no longer a relative majority and Christians no longer an absolute majority. But the reality is more complex because of the triangle of three large communities, as opposed to the binary system that prevailed before 1975. It does not compensate the Christians or the Maronites for their loss of power, but it makes it sometimes secondary to the rivalry between Sunnis and Shiʿis.

One issue revolves around territory and borders. Like other modern-day countries, Lebanon was carved out of the Ottoman Empire. United Syria, pan-Arab unity, pan-Islamic unity, all meant to include Lebanon by their proponents, drove part of an important debate on where the country lay exactly: alone, within Syria, within the larger Levant, within the Arab world, within the Mediterranean, within Asia, within the Islamic world? There were

esp. Chapter 5, 'Out of the margins: Political and religious integration', 115–38, and the official recognition of Shiʿis, granted by the French High Commissioner as one of the religious communities in the country for the first time in its history, in a decree issued on 27 January 1926, Id. 130. This was Henry de Jouvenel.

also active Christian groups who advocated a return to a smaller Lebanon where Christians would remain a numerical majority. This option was dubbed derogatorily Marounistan. It remains alive and takes other forms, including calls for federalism understood as a loose confederation with a hapless central government and hardened border crossing between the federated regions.[14]

The relationship with Lebanon's immediate neighbours, Syria in particular, has remained fraught since the Mandate. Michel Chiha penned several columns on this relationship. Whilst he was supportive throughout of clearly defined territorial and political independence for Lebanon, including any form of economic union with Syria, he left room for close economic, even monetary, relations with Syria.[15]

In relation to his fierce 'Lebanism', a puzzling qualification in the very first article of Chiha's earliest manuscript is telling: 'Great Lebanon is a unitary independent republic'.[16] The word 'unitaire', which remains in the text today, reflects the troubled context of the country in 1925–6, in between the calls for a fusion with Syria and the separation of parts of the country, especially Tripoli, from the Lebanese map fixed in 1920.

Most countries have known threats to the integrity of their territory at some point in their history.[17] The trouble that comes with Lebanon's neighbours never seems to be over.[18] As rued by the first president of the Lebanese Constitutional Council, 'it is an unfortunate fact, but a fact nonetheless, that Lebanon's neighbours are not Sweden and Norway'.[19] Occupation under-

[14] The spirit of the 'Marounistan' allure in the late 1970s is best conveyed by Jonathan Randal, *Going All the Way: Christian Warlords, Israeli Adventurers, and the War in Lebanon*, New York: Viking 1983. On the often misunderstood concept of federalism in the Middle East, see my 'Federalist Dreams for the Middle East', *Lawfare*, 16 August 2018 (online).

[15] Economic ties with Syria are discussed in several op-eds by Chiha, generally with caution about Lebanon being drowned into a larger territory it does not control, but with support for developed economic exchanges.

[16] 'Le Grand-Liban est un Etat unitaire indépendant'. (DOC 1, Art. 1) = 'Le Liban est un Etat indépendant, unitaire et souverain'. Constitution of 1926, Art. 1.

[17] In comparative lore, when countries are threatened in the integrity of their territory, insistence on the integrity and unity of a country is expected. The most famous antecedent appears in the successive French constitutions. The Constitution of 1791, which was enacted when France was a monarchy, mentions that 'the Royaume est un et indivisible'. (text adopted by the Assemblée Constituante on 4 September 1791).

[18] See my short article, 'Trouble with the neighbours', *Index on Censorship*, 5, 2000, 158–60; and the telling title of Ghassan Tueni's book, *Liban, Une Guerre pour les Autres*, Paris: Lattes 1985.

[19] Wajdi Mallat (d.2010), in private conversations.

mines constitutions. The dominance of Damascus after Ta'ef sapped Lebanese democracy for a quarter of a century, and the consequences did not end when Syrian troops were forced out by the 2005 Cedar Revolution. In the South meanwhile, Lebanese territory under Israeli occupation persisted, also for a quarter of a century, until armed resistance forced Israel out in June 2000. North of the receding line of Israel's military occupation, Syria ruled with an iron fist. The three main positions at the top of the country, and several others across Lebanon's government and the administration, were filled at the behest of Syria's rulers.

While the rise of Lebanon the nation-state continues to be troubled by its close and less close neighbours, its continuity within its 1926 borders is no longer in doubt. Or, in more cautious terms considering the persistent turmoil of the Middle East, they are no longer the subject of serious debate. The crux of the ongoing existential controversy is how to govern the territory within these borders. There can be no discussion of reform while the dark shadow of foreign countries obscures the local scenery, nor can it take place seriously so long as the State does not recover its monopoly of violence.

With all these caveats, Lebanese constitutionalism calls for some speculative anticipation.

There has been no dearth of reform programs, especially constitutional ones, over the last century. Before and during the recorded constitutional debates, and in Chiha's papers, the central discussion was about the equality of citizens in the public space, both as electors and elected. The discussion could not escape the apportionment of positions at the top and in the administration through the prism of communities.

The debate has not moved an inch since 1926. In support of full equality and regard to merit over identity stands a deep secular appeal. One can find it adumbrated in 1925 in the anti-clerical, Third Republic-style beliefs of Maurice Sarrail – beliefs which, as High Commissioner of the Levant, he sought to implement in a communities-free electoral law. The penchant for secularism is also an expression of nationalism in its basic traits. As Chiha put it: what the communities lose, the Nation gains. The belief forms part of a liberal philosophy which marks the European Enlightenment's detachment from religion. It has deepened over two centuries astride the dominant cleavage between left and right, albeit tempered by more refined divisions.

Being on the right did not necessarily entail a defence of a religion-less government, and therefore a religious communities-less one. In France, most self-styled Republicans since the advent of the Republic in 1871 have been, by and large, on the right wing of the political spectrum, yet sometimes more markedly secularist than some adherents of the 'socialist' aspects of caritative Christianity. In Lebanon, the left dominated the public debate over constitutional reforms from Independence to the onset of the war in 1975. It advocated full-fledged secularism in the three branches of government and across the administration. Despite enjoying substantial popular support, peaking in the first weeks of 1976, the call for secularism led nowhere. Since then, egalitarian advocacy of secularism faded as an impossible utopia against the rise of political Islam, Christian retrenchment, and extreme Judaism. Secularism was rekindled in Lebanon in the large street protests of October 2019, and in Israel four years later on the occasion of a fight over the Israeli Supreme Court. Herein lies a *longue durée* secular pendulum to heed.

The pluses of communal constitutionalism

Whilst stating the deformity of an ungovernable monster, important caveats need to be taken into account when judging how democratic a country is, including relatively fair elections and the reality of free speech in Lebanon in contrast to the vast majority of Middle Eastern countries. Free speech in Lebanon is contingent on the communal system, and the system is averse to the rule of one person, despite the strong powers originally associated with the presidency. This is because checks and balances operate on a communal basis. When a person criticises a ruler, she is at the same time criticising a community leader. In practice, this allows the member of another community to be shielded by its own – also communal, leader. As a fiercer political debate sets in, all political leaders, and their supporters, become the subject of criticism from other political leaders, and their supporters. While sectarianism deepens, the cacophony of criticism blurs the debate by making it free. Freedom in Lebanon is powerfully served by the communal system.

There are other positives to constitutional sectarianism, not least that the Lebanese deputies, who are elected by a constituency larger than their own community, formally represent the whole country. This is true throughout the electoral districts for deputies, and for the three top positions in the Constitution. As noted in one subtle analysis of the Lebanese political regime, 'the criterion of accountability of the executive before the Chamber of Deputies must be analysed in the light of an essential fact, which is institutionalized communitarianism or even the institutionalization of communitarianism. The effects of the latter have no doubt been reduced by the list system (the electoral college being unique within each constituency), *and by the fact that each deputy is elected by voters foreign to his own community*.'[20]

Because several deputies are elected in large, mixed constituencies, they need to cater to an electorate not exclusively of the same denomination as theirs. This is equally true by-and-large for the troika, which is elected by Parliament. When there is an election by parliament of the president, Maronite candidates are pitted against other Maronite candidates, since only a Maronite Lebanese can be president. This enhances the chances of the Maronite candidate who can draw the largest number of votes from non-Maronite deputies. This is true *mutatis mutandis* for the two other top positions, with contenders competing with candidates from the same community. Such a reality is intrinsic to the system and represents electorally the less communitarian facet of a communitarian system.

This necessary collaboration, from the point of view of democratic representation, ensures a measure of national cohesion to the country. At the top, representation by contenders belonging to the same community is reinforced by constitutional checks and balances. This factor allows the country minimal social cohesion, while reproducing the structural weakness and fissiparousness inherent to sectarianism. Whence the usefulness of the word consociationalism, which, by conjuring up consensual agreement, allows constitutional vetoes by a section of society against the 'tyranny of the majority' over decision-making in the state. If not agreed by major communities, any legislative or

[20] '... [l]e critère de responsabilité de l'exécutif devant la Chambre des députés doit être analysé à la lumière d'une donnée essentielle, le communautarisme institutionnalisé ou encore l'institutionna lisation du communitarisme. Sans doute les effets de ce dernier auraient pu être amoindris par le scrutin de liste (le collège électoral étant unique à l'intérieur de chaque circonscription) *et par le fait que chaque député est élu par des électeurs étrangers à sa propre communauté*'. Maurice Flory et al. eds, *Les Régimes Politiques Arabes*, Paris 1990, chapter on Lebanon by Bahgat Korany, 314–15 (emphasis added).

administrative decisions of the state are blocked and their effectiveness stifled.[21] The formal as well as practical manifestation of this constitutional reality can be observed at work daily in Lebanon under the dual signature of the president (qua Christian Maronite) and the Prime Minister (qua Muslim Sunni) for all decrees, following the imprimatur of Parliament and its Speaker (qua Muslim Shiʿi) when laws are also concerned.

Ta'ef

It is time to look at the constitutional amendments enacted in 1990. Constitutional amendments are the truest revelators of the success of the reformists. Ever since the end of French tutelage in 1943, they have all failed to change the system. The one exception came in the 'Ta'ef Accord', agreed among warring Lebanese factions meeting under Saudi aegis in 1989 to mark the (relative) end of the civil and foreign wars in and over Lebanon. The domestic part of the agreement was incorporated in formal constitutional amendments the following year.[22] Ta'ef's main changes limited presidential power in the bicephalous system and established a constitutional council, both of which have been enacted since. For our purposes, it mostly provided a hypostatised 'secular' reform which remains 'pie in the sky' more than thirty years later.

Lebanese constitutionalists, and political leaders by-and-large, converge on a common understanding of Ta'ef.[23] They tend to agree that the president

[21] There is no exact equivalent in Arabic to the concept of consociationalism. The nearest expression is *al-dimuqratiyya al-tawafuqiyya*, concordance (as in the Swiss 'démocratie de concordance') or consensual democracy.

[22] Technically, these are two different types of agreement. Ta'ef was signed by most of the warring lords of the day, together with other less embattled leaders, under the sponsorship of the Kingdom of Saudi Arabia. The initial text of Ta'ef is known as *Wathiqat al-wifaq al-watani*, the Document of national accord. The amendments were introduced in the Constitution the following year by a vote of the deputies under Art. 77. The Ta'ef agreement included a foreign dimension, which was essentially the withdrawal of Syrian troops to the Biqaʿ Valley by December 1992, a commitment which was not honoured. It also included a number of domestic arrangements. These were by and large incorporated verbatim in the Constitution in 1990.

[23] The text of the Ta'ef agreement is sometimes appended to the Constitution. It is also available separately on the Lebanese presidency website. The minutes of the Ta'ef meetings were never released by then Speaker Hussain al-Hussaini, who passed away in 2023, so we do not know the details of how the resurgence of a Senate came about. Scholars have been generally hampered by the absence of the minutes, but see John Donohue, 'Changing the Lebanese Constitution: A Postmodern History', *Cardozo Law Review*, 50, 2008–2009, 2509–34; Joseph Maila, *The*

of the Republic's powers were diminished, and that Christians in Lebanon were deprived of their previously superior dominance. They also agree that the constitutional system was enriched by the introduction of a constitutional council on the French model, tasked with rejecting laws in violation of the Constitution. They also support the general mantra that the unfulfilled reforms required by Ta'ef should be implemented.

The crux of the constitutional debate, we saw in our analysis of the 1926 texts, vests in Art. 95 of the Constitution. The crux of the Ta'ef road out of the constitutional deadlock vests in its replacement.

The reader will recall the original text of the article:

> Article 95- On a provisional basis and in accordance with Art. 1 of the Charter of the Mandate, and with an intention of justice and concord, communities will be represented equitably in public employment and in the composition of the government, without prejudice to the interest of the state.[24]

Ta'ef replaced it with the following verbose amendment:

> Article 95- Once elected on a half-half basis between Muslims and Christians, Parliament must take the necessary measures to abolish political sectarianism according to a staggered plan [*marhali*, i.e. in stages], and establish a national committee led by the President of the Republic, which includes in addition to the presidents of Parliament and of the Council of ministers, political, intellectual and social personalities.
>
> The task of the committee is to study and propose ways apt to suppress sectarianism, to present them to the CD and the Council of Ministers, and to follow through the implementation of the staged plan.

Document of National Understanding: A Commentary, Centre for Lebanese Studies, Oxford: Center for Lebanese Studies 1992; Nawaf Salam, *Ab'a min al-Ta'ef* (Further than Ta'ef), Beirut: Jadid 1998; Fu'ad Yunis, *Nazariyyat al-Tawafuqiyya Bayn al-Ta'sil wal-Tatwir- Dirasat Halat Lubnan* (The theory of consociationalism between tradition and development: A study of the Lebanese case), Beirut: Halabi 2024, with bibliography of Arabic works at 577–90.

24 'A titre transitoire et conformément aux dispositions de l'article 1er de la Charte du Mandat et dans une intention de justice et de concorde, les communautés seront équitablement représentées dans les emplois publics et dans la composition du ministère sans que cela puisse cependant nuire au bien de l'Etat'. Post-Independence amendments removed the clause referring to the French mandate.

In the transitional period:

a- The communities (*tawa'ef*) shall be represented in an equitable manner for the composition of the Cabinet.

b- The rule of communal representation is abolished, and merit and expertise will be adopted for public office, the judiciary, military and security institutions, and public and mixed institutions, in accordance with the requirements of national accord, with the exception of the first-class positions and their equivalent. These positions will be considered on a parity basis between Christians and Muslims without dedicating any position to any particular community and will respect both the merit and expertise principles.

In addition to Art. 95, two important articles in Ta'ef are Art. 22 and Art. 24. The first creates a Senate dependent on the mechanism established by the process detailed in Art. 95:

> Article 22- With the election of the first Chamber of Deputies on a national non-sectarian basis, a new Senate shall be established in which all religious communities are represented. Their power shall be limited to high national causes.

Art. 24 of 1990, in turn, confirms parity in Parliament between the two largest religions, with additional segmentation based on sects and geography.[25] From

[25] Art. 24 is also long and slightly redundant with new Art. 95: 'The Chamber of Deputies consists of elected representatives whose number and the manner of the election are determined by the electoral laws in effect.

Until the Chamber of Deputies issues an electoral law shorn of the communal constraint [*al-qayd al-ta'ifi*, with *qayd* meaning both communal constraint and voters' registration], representative seats are distributed according to the following rules:

a. Equally between Christians and Muslims.
b. Proportionally between the communities of both sides [i.e. the various Christian denominations, the largest being the Greek-Orthodox and the Melkite Catholics, and, on the Muslim side, Sunnis, Shi'is, Druzes, and 'Alawis.
c. Proportionally among districts.

Exceptionally, and for once only, representative seats vacant at the date of publishing this Law, and all seats created by the electoral law are filled by appointment by a two-thirds majority of the National Unity Government, in implementation of the equality between Christians and Muslims, according to the National Accord Document [Ta'ef]. The electoral law shall provide details for the application of this Article'.

an electoral perspective, the iconic 6–5 ratio for Christian to Muslim deputies in the parliament could no longer hold, considering the turmoil of the past fifteen years, the demographic decline of Christians, and the political blunders of the Maronite leadership. It was replaced in Ta'ef by an equal number for both, in an eerie replica, 150 years on, of the Beirut Council of 1834.

These articles remind us how relevant is electoral law in the game of numbers. We have seen how electoral laws since 1922 have gone through a succession of traumatic and often arbitrary changes. This began with the Council of Representatives at 30, then zigzagged between 25 and 99. The change in 1992 was slightly less arbitrary. In order for Ta'ef to create parity between Christians and Muslims in the Chamber of Deputies, the number of deputies, which had remained stable at 99 (54 Christians to 45 Muslims in the 6–5 ratio), was increased to 108; this increased the number of Muslim deputies to reach parity with their Christian colleagues.[26]

Several changes adumbrated by Ta'ef increase the complexity of an already crowded decision-making structure.

The first difficulty concerns the proposed re-establishment of a Senate, and the relationship when it comes to legislation between a secular CD and a communal Senate. In several bicameral countries, the matter is resolved by a shuttling process. In the case of the 1926 Constitution, the CD and Senate were supposed to meet on various occasions in Congress. This lasted one year and proved unworkable: the Senate only added a layer of complication to an already byzantine and often deadlocked system. We saw how Chiha was opposed to the idea of a Senate. It is not clear that the Ta'ef constituents gave much consideration to the likely deadlock.

A second difficulty passed over the head of all the Ta'ef constituents: namely secularism in the Executive. When equality and merit are supposed to define the Republic, as stated in Art. 7 of the Constitution and unchanged since Chiha wrote it in 1926, decision-making in the executive should be secular. Ta'ef prevaricated. Except for the new Art. 95's mention of merit and expertise for 'first-class positions and their equivalent' in top administrative

[26] Ta'ef determined the number of deputies at 108 (double the 54 Christians since 1960), but the 1992 electoral law increased it to 128. The increase was likely due to the Syrian government's wish to strengthen the small sect of Muslim 'Alawis in the North by increasing the number of CD deputies overall in order to justify the creation of two 'Alawi seats when none existed before.

posts, an amendment which remains largely ignored with the entrenchment of communalism in Lebanese society and government, the three presidencies are not mentioned specifically. Were they to be considered for change, such a proposal would immediately hit a dead wall. Parity, which is supposed to be the rule if and when Arts. 24 and 95 apply, confronts the basic triad of the presidencies with a binary principle.

The third difficulty also passed over in silence by Ta'ef, concerns the shape and mechanisms of an electoral law intended to result in a secular CD. When Paris recalled Sarrail from Syria in 1925, the French had decided to prevent him hastily undermining the communal system with a secularised and gerrymandered electoral law. The 1926 Constitution confirmed the status quo. The schizophrenic attitude of the 1926 constituents remains true one hundred years later. Like them, (almost) everybody in Lebanon expresses opposition to communalism while at the same time frowning on any limitation of their community's power. This fear is not irrational, as we shall see when comparing Lebanon with the rest of the region. Despite its monstrous ungovernability, Lebanon's communal template has worked better than *all* other countries of the political-theological Middle East.

Good luck to the constitutionalist who seeks to devise a secular electoral law accepted both by the population at large and by entrenched religious leaders. There have been various attempts to come up with a better electoral law, but all have failed.[27] Probably the greatest challenge is in devising a national electoral law which allays the fear of groups cohering in a religious community, especially amongst Lebanese Christians. Considering the demographic trends, it may be impossible to devise.

Lebanese and Middle Eastern constitutionalism

In a broader frame, the global route to the Lebanese Constitution started in the US Constitution of 1787 as the first written consecration of the social

[27] All effective or attempted changes to the electoral law since 1926 were conceived under the communal canopy. Even the 'Boutros national commission for electoral reform' (named after its head, statesman Fouad Boutros, d. 2016), which was tasked with providing options to improve the electoral system, took communalism as a given. For a general description of the recommendations of the Commission, see Arda Ekmekji, 'Confessionalism and Electoral Reform in Lebanon', Aspen Institute Papers, 2012, 9–12.

contract in a republic. Written constitutions became the norm for the great majority of Western states and were slowly adjusted and adopted in the rest of the world.

To recall an earlier discussion, in the Middle East, constitutional documents are extant in Egypt since 1829 and 1832 in the Levant, but received scholarship puts the earliest proto-constitutional text in Tunisia's basic law of 1861 following a bill of rights of 1857, itself a calque of the Ottoman Khatti-Hemayun of 1856. Both Ottoman 'rescripts', the earlier one called Gülhane in 1839, the later one Khatti-Hemayun, were shaped as bills of rights, but a full constitution was adopted formally only in 1876. It was suspended almost immediately by the Sultan and came back to life in 1909 when the Young Turks took over, with the election of a parliament across the Empire that lasted until the First World War. Meanwhile, a constitutional process in the other important empire, Persia, was under way from 1905 until 1911. In that year, the Shah suspended a parliament elected on the basis of the constitutional text of 1906, and essentially froze the process until the 1979 Revolution swept the Persian Constitution away together with the Pahlavi dynasty. Parallel developments took place in Egypt, from 1829 through the Constitution of 1923, which was followed by a spate of constitutions until the one established in the wake of the 2011 Revolution.

Whether in Tunis, Cairo, Beirut or Istanbul, all these texts were initially inspired by the European Enlightenment, including the checkered legacy of the French Revolution which came to Egypt in the form of a skewed republican France. The new texts were introduced by a brutal Napoleonic occupation which marks the birth of the modern Middle East in 1798.

Within two long centuries of Middle Eastern constitutionalism, the Lebanese text of 1926 provides by its longevity a unique template in comparative constitutional law. As we have seen, it was described by Michel Chiha as an 'association of minorities'.

On a theoretical level, the expression is doubly imprecise. Lebanon may be an association of minorities sociologically or historically, but it was never exactly so constitutionally. 'Association of minorities' is imprecise because if all the 'minorities' were associated, then the term minority is wrong, for what is the majority in this case? It is not enough to say that the largest numerical group is the majority, or even a relative majority, because there is no majority in a country defined as an association of minorities. When he wrote the Constitution, Chiha, in his wisdom, knew that Christians could not impose their will even though they were the numerical majority at the time. He also knew that 'association of minorities' was an approximative concept.

There is another reason why the concept is imprecise. 'Associated' is an elastic term. Chiha's constitution, like any constitution, is forced to superpose the Montesquieu separation of powers under the LEJ(F)ARC template. When Chiha superposed it on 'minorities', he effectively introduced a layer of Montesquieuan order onto a fluid description of numerically uneven groups defined by religious denomination. Chiha might have used the word minorities to avoid bluntly saying 'sect'. The minority he meant is a social unit defined by its members' cohesion in their specific sub-unit, which is the sect, or the confession, or the community, or the *milla*, or the *ta'ifa*, all words having the same connotation here which is always religious. Whatever the terminology, the system as conceived in the Lebanese Constitution does not give, constitutionally, a superiority or dominance to one group over the other, even if the group is as small as Chiha's own 'Latin' community. While the size of community naturally matters, the constitutional system in Lebanon is an 'uneven association of equal groups', a 'living togetherness' of groups being defined by their members' sectarian birth, without any one group deemed superior to any other.[28] This is fundamentally different from the Ottoman millet system, the heyday of the Caliphate, or the pre-Islamic Near and Middle

[28] 'Vivre-ensemble', for the Arabic *ta'ayush*, has been a prominent trope of the twenty-first century, put forward in particular by secular activist leader Samir Frangieh (d.2017), see for instance his *Voyage au bout de la Violence*, Beirut: L'Orient des Livres 2011, 137–50. The term 'vouloir vivre en commun', similar to 'vivre ensemble' is an old topos which harks back at least to Renan's definition of the nation in a seminal talk in 1882: 'A nation is a soul, a spiritual principle. Two things, which are in truth one and the same, constitute this soul, this spiritual principle. One is in the past, the other in the present. One is the shared possession of a rich legacy of memories; The other is the current consent, *the wish to live together*, the will to continue to assert the legacy that one has received undivided. (Une nation est une âme, un principe spirituel. Deux choses qui, à vrai dire, n'en font qu'une, constituent cette âme, ce principe spirituel. L'une est dans le passé, l'autre dans le présent. L'une est la possession en commun d'un riche legs de souvenirs; l'autre est le consentement actuel, le *désir de vivre ensemble*, la volonté de continuer à faire valoir l'héritage qu'on a reçu indivis.)' Ernest Renan, 'Qu'est-ce qu'une Nation?', Paris: Calmann Lévy 1882, 27 (online version on Wikisource, emphasis added). The fact is that any social pact is meant to allow people to live together, so 'to wish living together' is redundant with the concept of a constitution. No constitution is conceivable, as a matter of principle, without the constituents wishing to live together.

East, where Islam, specifically the Sunni school dominant in Istanbul, was officially superior in recognition and power to all other denominations.

Empirically, the fact that the Lebanese text survived better than all other constitutions in the region does not negate the difficulty in governance that the country exhibits. Considering the country's persistent turmoil, coups d'état and wars, this may be a coincidence and the argument may not fully hold. Yet Lebanon did not jettison its Constitution. Does this mean that the Lebanese constitutional regime, ungovernable as it may be, remains superior to other constitutional systems in the region?

The answer is affirmative in both practice and theory. In practice, the Middle East is characterised by the dominance of autocrats, whom the traditional separation of powers has been incapable of constraining despite the extraordinary hopes sown by the so-called Arab Spring.

In comparison with the dominance of autocracies, rendered even more brutal and cynical by the failure of the 2011 revolutions, the Lebanese constitutional system offers significant advantages in legal-civilisational terms. In contradistinction to a sectarian separation of powers, the blanket secularism of constitutions based on the equality of all citizens allows little or no institutional check on the ruler in power. Despotism trumps secularism. In the same logic, communalism trumps despotism. The paradox should now be easily understood. By preventing the emergence of a single leader in the country without any countervailing opponent under the guise of 'secularism', the Lebanese system bars the advent or entrenchment of autocracy, which by definition is the rule of one. In Lebanon, there can be no one ruler in the presence of competing religious communities which respond to different leaders. The constitutional sect-inscribed rejection of a sole leader represents a key safety valve preventing the emergence of dictatorship in the country as has occurred elsewhere in the region. The acknowledged constitutional dimension of sectarianism in the foundational Lebanese text prevents the dominance of authoritarianism that is so prevalent in other parts of the Middle East.

One could argue that it is easy to compare Lebanon favorably in a region where all other Arab countries, in addition to Iran, Afghanistan, and Turkey, have been for the past century mired in despotism. The superiority of the Lebanese constitutional system over these Middle Eastern states is empirically easy to defend. But can one push the envelope further, and defend the proposition that Lebanon's association of minorities is superior constitutionally to Israel's vaunted Westminster-style democracy?

Considering the convergence between the level of democratic indicators in both Lebanese and Israeli societies as expressed in a significant degree of freedom of expression and the recurrence of meaningful elections resulting in periodic change at the top, which constitutional model is preferable for societies divided on religious/communitarian lines? Is the operation of Lebanon's 'sectarian democracy' not preferable to a 'majoritarian democracy' which, like Israel's, systematically discriminates, at all levels and with different degrees of violence, against the non-Jewish sections of the populations whose lives it controls?

The question can be put differently. Given that the Israeli system has been largely immune to, or oblivious of, the demands of its non-Jewish population over the almost 80 years of its existence as an independent country, is the century-old Lebanese model of sectarian constitutionalism not a more inclusive model?

Michel Chiha certainly thought so. In 1946 already, it was crystal-clear to him that Lebanon's constitutional configuration was superior to Israel's. We cite again, and expand on, his most emphatic paragraph:

> The formula [for Israel-Palestine] that we have been strongly advocating for so long is the very one proposed in London. It is reason itself: *a single government, a single assembly, separate personal status* [family laws] *widely understood.*
>
> Ultimately, acknowledging the specific concerns over Palestine, it is the Lebanese solution [which is superior]. In a country of associated minorities, it is a shared assembly that fosters the desire to live together.[29]

An extensive exercise in comparative constitutionalism between the Israeli and Lebanese models needs to be taken up elsewhere. Too short a review does not do justice to an existential problem on both sides of the Galilee, with a

[29] 'La formule que nous préconisons depuis si longtemps avec force est celle-là même qui est proposée à Londres. Elle est la raison même: *un seul gouvernement, une seule assemblée, des statuts personnels très largement compris.*

Tout compte fait, avec les méfiances propres à la Palestine, c'est la solution libanaise. Dans un pays de minorités associées, c'est une assemblée commune qui fait le vouloir-vivre en commun'. 'Les chances de la raison en Palestine', 7 Octobre 1946, Pal. 30. Emphasis in original.

'Jewish and democratic state' to the south and 'an association of communities' to the north.

Constitutional windows out of communalism

On the larger regional scene, an earlier book on nonviolence in the Middle East revolts of 2010–2012 presents ways out of the communitarian deadlocks with the following summary:

> Rethought federalism and separation of powers, a different calling for the judge, rotation of official positions, multiplication of mediations, the civil society lens, women's 'natural' representation in power: all these categories thought anew deserve to be investigated as the next constitutional frontiers of the philosophy of nonviolence in the Middle East and beyond.[30]

Each item just listed designates one alluring constitutional frontier which any Middle Eastern country can and should explore. In the light of Chiha's concern for the nation over the community, these ways forward can be expanded considerably. But I will limit this closing section to a few words on each of these forward windows in relation to Lebanese and comparative constitutional law.

Rethought federalism and separation of powers. Federalism being by nature territorial, communitarian federalism finds it hard to reconcile its place with a rich legacy that covers the whole field of comparative constitutional law, especially the constitutional layer added by federalism to the classic separation of powers. Personal law, which is religious-communal, appears characteristically fluid in contrast with territorial law, which is geography-based and more stable. Populations of different sects and religions are far too imbricated territorially to make communitarian federalism work. In addition, people move around. The only serious federal experience in the Middle East started taking shape in Iraq in the 2005 Constitution, and its constitution is territorial. It is far from clear that the new social contract has been successful, let alone that Iraq is a real federation under federalism's established canons. Like the projected Lebanese Senate in the constitutional amendments of 1990, the Iraqi Federal Council promised constitutionally in Iraq has not been established almost a quarter of

[30] Chibli Mallat, *Philosophy of Nonviolence*, New York: Oxford University Press 2015, 209. (Hereinafter PNV)

a century later.[31] A transversal separation of powers in federal terms begs the question of the dispensability of a communitarian separation of power in a country which includes two major fractures: one national-linguistic between Arabs and Kurds, the other communal between Shiʿis and Sunnis. A Federal Council also adds to the immense complications of judicial, legislative and executive decision-making when there are two legislative chambers. Yet federalism is in the Middle East air, and likely to endure through the twenty-first century and beyond.[32]

A different calling for the judge puts judicial power center stage, including to arbitrate federalism and government branches, somewhat at the margins of Chiha's constitutional world which gave little attention to a judicial branch considered at the time to be largely toothless and irrelevant to parliamentary supremacy. The US Supreme Court has meanwhile changed the world comparative scene, and Lebanon experiments with more failure than success with a Constitutional Council introduced by Ta'ef. The wisdom of powerful judges might ease entrenched communal problems, but it could also exacerbate them. Generally, the Middle Eastern tradition weighs against the judiciary's ability to move the constitutional ship forward. This includes Lebanon and Israel, where the judicial branches remain unable to eradicate a sometimes brutal discrimination against subordinated communities despite the relative independence of the leaders of the top courts and, occasionally, their genuine efforts to end it. One promising avenue forward to a less communal and more national government, is a sage, knowledgeable, strong judiciary. The reform needed is a big, slow-moving, long-term project.[33]

Multiplication of mediations goes hand in hand with both the massive structural mediation system that is federalism and sundry more modest mediations, including the various rungs of government ('state' in federalism, district, municipality ...). Parliaments are the natural anchor of mediation at the intersection of state and civil society. At one point also, supreme courts

[31] On the Federation Council, see my *Iraq: Guide to Law and Policy*, Austin: Aspen/Kluwer Law International, 2009, 237–42.

[32] PNV, 159–60, 203–6.

[33] PNV, 198–203.

are asked to streamline the cacophonic mess of 'acid tests',[34] matters of intense emotional polarisation. Such multiplication of mediations softens the hard edge of communal disputes, ranging from the headscarf, the *get* (the Jewish law repudiation), *talaq* (the Islamic law repudiation) and other obviously gendered fault lines, to violent confrontations among religious communities seeking domination. For non-elected judges, dealing with this range of conflicts may be too much to ask, but it is vital to include their mediation in social and political crises. Their skill will be apparent, for better or for worse, when an 'acid test' hits their docket.

The multiplication of mediations comes with the multiplication of identities. In Lebanon and the wider Middle East, a dominant identity is the citizen's religious sect. In the United States, it is race. In Switzerland or Belgium, it is language. In the world at large, it is gender. In all countries, it can also be region-based: Quebecois in Canada, Kurds in Iraq, Arabs in separate cities in Israel-Palestine. And there are transnational identities, which the acceleration of globalisation comforts. Humans are by nature defined by multiple identities, yet these identities are seldom taken into account constitutionally. This may be understandable under the definition of democracy as a republic of equals, but it deserves to be revisited in the light of our conclusions. The law lags far behind the promise of plurality. A multiple rather than a single constitutional acknowledgment tempers the dominance of the one, singular identity. It is increasingly probed under 'the plural society' label. Multiple identities are not easy to put in place constitutionally, but some soft legal form, as in constitutional review by the judiciary, offers roads forward.

Rotation of official positions. We come here to an ancient Roman Empire-style triumvirate model and variations thereon. This is about rotation at the top of the executive branch, and Robespierre was right to worry about the danger that multiple heads pose for the unity, and governability, of a country. The rotation of presidential posts might work in the European Council of

[34] PNV, 178–88, on acid tests. They are defined in PNV as those moments of intense emotional polarisation (for instance a woman's scarf/veil in France, Iran ...) when the subject-matter is *a priori* of minor importance. These tests are navigated by society in various ways, and the advocacy is for keeping the courts out of it as much as possible, for other mediations to take place. At one point, however, the judiciary, and at the top a country's supreme court, might have to say its word. Here is where the enlightened and wise judge is needed for a successful mediation of an emotionally charged and seemingly irrational social controversy.

the EU's constitutional system alongside other more traditional institutional mechanisms, but the European model is in crisis, and triumvirates did not survive republican Rome.

I find the concept of rotation at the top useful nonetheless, on the basis of the brief yet signal success of the Iraqi Governing Council in 2003–4, with a 12-member Council rotating its president monthly.[35] In the council of ministers of Chiha's first drafts, the rotation was possible in a cabinet limited by the Constitution to six or seven members with no particular denominational sect, inevitably triggering their rotation over time. The idea did not even reach the May 1926 vote by the full Chamber of Deputies. Revived, it could attenuate the communal straitjacket of the Lebanese troika. Rotation within Lebanon's established troika is a feeble exercise, but a rotation within a six or 12-member cabinet would be a different matter. In Switzerland, as Chiha noted on several occasions, the annual election of the President of the Confederation from within the seven members of the Federation Council has succeeded in helping keep the country stable and united.

As for the civil society lens, this is more within the precinct of the public intellectual legacy of Chiha than for matters technically constitutional. As a principle, a State is defined by its constitution while civil society is defined in opposition to the State. This explains why the term 'civil society' is only exceptionally, and only recently, mentioned in any world constitution.[36]

Government–elections–parties: a constitutionally elusive triangle

So much for constitutional windows in heavily segmented nations hampered by religious-communal constitutionalism, a vast program if any. The other leitmotiv of our investigation concerns the central role of electoral processes in any constitutional system, even if little is said about elections in a constitution.

[35] On the concept of rotation, PNV, 148; On the Iraqi Governing Council, see *Iraq: Guide to Law and Policy*, above n.31, 28–9. The Presidency of the EU's European Council rotates among member states every six months.

[36] PNV 165–71, including Robert Fossaert's definition of civil society at 166–8, with the references, and countries whose constitution explicitly mention 'civil society', PNV, 172–4. I leave 'women's "natural" representation in power' in the quote at n.34 above for more ample discussion in Chapter 13.

Together with the immense variety of electoral laws, sharply contrastive realities of the electoral principle suggest that a heuristic approach to electoral reform is a wiser route than high theoretical principles destined for quick collapse. The combination of elections and communalism is probably the most immoveable object in the constitutional field. Combining Chiha's 'plural vote' with a 'secular list vote' is a testing challenge when all electoral lists are communal.

Universal suffrage is not enough. For equality as the basis of Tocqueville's democracy, universal candidacy is also required. To reverse Chiha's formulation, 'what communalism gains, the nation loses'. A communal electoral law straitjackets the Nation with its quotas and limitations on national representation.

I wish to push the argument further with a third side of a hard-to-fathom triangle: in addition to communalism and electoral processes, there are constitutional difficulties arising from parties. What a communal electoral system prevents is the very possibility of a national political party. Electoral communalism makes it uniquely hard to reform the national system without losing its soul. This was demonstrated in the course of our journey in this book.

Should one conclude that the deadlocks wrought by the triangle government-elections-parties are impossible to overcome in a communal system because of its shifting constituent parts?

Yes is my provisional answer. There is a near or next-to-near impossibility for a party to transcend its communal overtone within the straitjacket of communal elections. Only in rare revolutionary instances is it conceivable for the national spirit to blow briefly over the communal fracture, and even then, as Samir Khalaf has shown in several works, the citizen's political agency soon relapses into the deadlock of the community.[37] Nor can education, even over time, remove communal blinders. Education has its limits when it comes to identity. Leaders coming from communal electoral systems regularly deal with public issues in a national rather than sectarian manner, and when the individual-in-a-religious-community casts his vote, he also votes for candidates

[37] See in particular Samir Khalaf, Khalaf, *Civil and Uncivil Violence in Lebanon*, New York: Columbia University Press 2002, discussed in Ch. 3.

belonging to other communities. This does not prevent the communal straitjacket, as argued in this book, from prevailing constitutionally.

National parties are doomed to fail in a communal system, barring a revolution enlightened enough to channel the brief national spirit into a cohesive structure. In the normal course of Middle Eastern societies, parties are forced to be communal when the electoral system is communal. Government in its three branches is then inevitably communal. French republicans, otherwise hard-core secularists, had reached this conclusion in 1924–5 when express directives from Paris sided with Chiha's vision of Lebanon against the attempt by High Commissioner Maurice Sarrail to force secularism on the country.

The triangle beyond the Middle East

Do the difficulties inherent in the triangle Government-elections-parties apply to 'normal', non-communal constitutions? The answer is a qualified no. In the Middle East, electoral laws and the party system undermine each other because they are both communal. The problem in Western countries is less fundamental, but it is real.

Competitive elections, rather than the principle of elections, did not apply to the presidency in the United States until 1796. Even in 1820, James Monroe ran unopposed, as had George Washington before him in 1789 and 1792. In an extreme contrast, the French revolutionaries considered competitive elections as the holy grail after the birth of the first National Assembly in 1789. In the first years of the Republic, even judges in revolutionary France were elected, as were deputies in the National Assembly and mayors in local precincts. Together with the immense variety of electoral laws, these sharply contrastive realities of the electoral principle suggest that a trial-and-error approach to reforming elections is a wiser route than high theoretical principles that fall apart on the hard rock of reality.

As regards parties, one should remember that the founding fathers in the early experiments in the Atlantic Revolution, both French and American, were wary of 'factions'. Yet there is no clear line between a party and a faction constitutionally, even if parties tend to be better structured and longer-lasting in political-historical terms. Faction and factionalism were simply derogatory signifiers for party, hence the negative connotation which remains associated to date with 'partisanship'.

Parties are a problem for democracy, not only in consociational countries like Lebanon. A modern democracy is inconceivable without parties. Yet parties distort electoral representation by their very presence. For independent candidates, electoral success is nearly impossible. Nor are individual party members their own agents in their share of the people's representation in government. They are not simple individuals elected by their respective districts, but individuals-in-a-party voting to have their party represented in government.

Parties, too, are poorly representative of society at large. In most countries today, a small fraction of voters are card-carrying members of any political party. Even within this group, few individuals are active militants. The rest may express their preferences at the ballot box for a party they are not signed up to, but they are limited by the impossibility of casting their vote for other than for the parties on offer.[38] Votes are often cast against a party that is abhorred, or even just tolerated, rather than for a party individuals belong to or support at arm's length. Votes cast just to prevent the victory of another candidate are purely utilitarian.[39]

There is also often significant abstentionism when voting is not compulsory. This opens a uniquely alluring political theory window, for only rarely have authors accepted that a human being is *not* political. *Zoon politikon* – man as a political animal – has impoverished public philosophy considerably since Aristotle expressed it in his *Politics*. A rare, contrarian view, holds that human beings are not necessarily political animals by nature, and considers the absence of voting a healthy sign in society. After all, many people do not vote because a victory of one party does not change their life significantly enough to bother going to the polls.

[38] Citizens at the ballot box can of course decide to spoil their vote in favor of their national version of the Official Monster Raving Loony Party, but this just proves the point. It is sufficient to say that those who vote do not need to be members of the party for which they vote. The argument that elections are needed because not all citizens can take part in government is further weakened, on the practical level, by Laurence Tribe's distrust of 'vote' smothering 'voice'. See Laurence Tribe, *Constitutional Choices*, Cambridge MA: Harvard University Press 1985, 193.

[39] Local and national referenda might attenuate the dominance of parties, but they do not work well because of their natural limitations. Machinery to set up a referendum is heavy, and the result is limited in time and topic. Switzerland succeeds somewhat in combining referenda and the normal vote for representation in power, but referenda remain fraught with question marks about their very wisdom. Democracy is a daily flow which can never be fulfilled either by elections or referenda.

In fairness to Aristotle, the celebrated paragraph in *Politics* focuses far more on speaking man than on political man: 'Now the reason why man is more of a political animal than bees or any other gregarious animals is evident. Nature, as we often say, makes nothing in vain, and *man is the only animal whom she has endowed with the gift of speech*.'[40] In this reading of Aristotle, man is political because he speaks. *Zoon politikon* is less alluring socially than *homo loquens*, which one finds in the literature. Constitutional scholarship which insists on the *deliberative* dimension of constitutionalism belongs to this Aristotelian school. It pays closer attention to *homo loquens* than to *zoon politikon*.

My final point suggests probing this avenue further. Building differently on Aristotle, when a human being speaks, some of the speech is about politics, the rest about something else. Fair enough. What if humans can dispense with politics altogether? What if politics is so secondary and insignificant to a citizen that he or she deliberately chooses to speak, interact, build, create, work, relax, deal with children and grandchildren, rather than *care* for politics?

The better scholarship on nonviolence now grants that men and women should no longer *suffer* for their politics. What if the citizen has a *right* not to care for politics?

[40] Aristotle, *Politics* 1253a, Jowett's translation in *The Politics of Aristotle*, Oxford: Clarendon Press 1885, vol. 1, 4. Emphasis added.

12

Constitutional Frontiers: The Lebanese Constitution and the World

The unitary doctrine, which is excellent in France, would be meaningless and wrong in other countries, and the more so in the Levant.[1]

With the help of the Chiha papers, this study examined the constitutional tradition in Lebanon from the early nineteenth century to the present, in its two central expressions. The first, the entrenchment of communalism in the constitutional texts; the second, the rise of an electoral system reinforcing group representation. They are both key in the comparative and historical fields the world over for the understanding of constitutionalism and democracy.[2]

[1] '[L]a doctrine unitaire, excellente en France, serait un contresens et une faute dans la doctrine unitaire, excellente en France, serait un contresens et une faute dans d'autres pays et plus qu'ailleurs dans le Levant.' Chiha, 'Géographie et politique', *Le Réveil*, 2 November 1921.

[2] Institutional history covered in the present book has not included the judiciary which presents, depending on the archives extant, a unique view of social problems and soft balancing of executive power by the courts. A pioneering work on the registers (*sijills*) courts of Tripoli in the seventeenth century is Khaled Ziadeh's *Al-Sura al-Taqlidiyya lil-Mujtama' al-Madini* (the traditional image of urban society), Tripoli: Manshurat ma'had al-'ulum al-ijtimia'iyya 1983. Works on Beirut courts by Hassan Hallaq in the second half of the nineteenth century have also advanced bottom-up perspectives that litigants provide in their everyday conflicts: see Chapter 3, n.85 above. The discovery of the decisions of my great uncle, poet and judge Tamer Mallat (d.1914), with over 100 full cases in one register, suggests that the intersection between legal institutions and social history will yield considerable scholarship in the years to come. Tamer Mallat, *Ahkam* (Judgments), Beirut, Bada'e', 1999. A rich court documentation, with good samples in various law reporters, is of easier access from the early twentieth century to date, although jurists tend to remain divorced in their approach to case-law from the more comprehensive view provided by social scientists. The set of court decisions available, and those expected to surface as the discovery of new judicial archives from pre-modern societies, will considerably change our view of the rule of law in the region and in other non-Western countries where it will be carried. But it will not bear much on the theory of governance.

We have used various perspectives to understand the Lebanese Constitution. One focused on its genesis in light of the new documents found in the Chiha Constitutional Papers. Another was the general LEJ(F)ARC template common to written constitutions worldwide ever since the Atlantic Revolution. A third perspective came in a more granular comparison of the articles from the first Chiha manuscript to the text approved in May 1926. A fourth perspective was more general, taking its cue partly from the 1697 Simqaniyya meeting to the present. A fifth line of investigation delved into the spirit of the Constitution by way of Chiha's prolific, albeit not systematic, works. The previous chapter added an examination of the Constitution culminating in the Ta'ef agreement and subsequent constitutional amendments, together with a comparison of Lebanese constitutionalism within its Middle Eastern neighbourhood.

This chapter puts Lebanon's constitutional model to a wider jury. The approach focuses on communities, or 'groups', under a more abstract theory. The next chapter builds on the research advanced here to provide a revised view of democracy.

Before doing so, it may be useful to offer a further perspective on key constitutional concepts common to all democracies and integrated in Chiha's Constitution.

On democracy

Understood in universal terms, basic democratic concepts can be divided into three:

1. *Liberty*. Liberty is a fundamental concept in all constitutions. Its written consecration with the French Revolution in the Declaration of the Rights of Man and the Citizen coincided almost to the day with its US promulgation in the Bill of Rights. Under cover of Reason's superior status in the formulation of speech and speech-acts, every word uttered is protected by freedom of expression as the default principle in a democracy. The various accepted exceptions are limited and decided by an independent judiciary. Two exceptions are common: slander, which remedies the speech-defamed plaintiff with monetary compensation in a civil suit; and immediate violence-inducing speech, couched in civil-law countries in a

more elastic 'violation of public order' and complicated by the category of 'hate speech', both punished criminally. Both are exceptions to the unfettered right of a person to say in public what he or she has in mind.

2. *Separation of powers*. Whilst the absence of a principle of majoritarian vote in choosing a leader might have remained absent for centuries, a common nemesis to peaceful exercise and transfer of power did exist from time immemorial: the tyrant, the despot, the dictator, the absolute king, shah or sultan. In short, the autocrat. Institutionally, one-man rule is a dominant figure of history, and the story is far from over. Autocracy extends to the group or political party which operates under one-man leadership, with totalitarianism the extreme expression of autocracy. This explains why Montesquieu's concept of the separation of powers represents a fundamental break in the history of constitutionalism. Once you have three branches of government, none can dominate the other, since the principle prevents one person from heading two or all three branches of government at the same time. There is no place for the autocrat in a constitution that respects the separation of powers.[3]
3. *Equal vote*. Nor is there place for an autocrat if competitive elections operate normally. Like Montesquieu's unique discovery of a new constitutional horizon, voting as a principle of representation came late in public life. Unlike the separation of powers in *L'Esprit des Lois*, voting as a constitutional device of unique portent does not have a mother founding figure. The principle of competitive elections in which the loser accepts the majority's vote even if it disfavors him has developed heuristically.

The electoral principle defines the republic *qua* democracy in the modern age. It was foreshadowed by Condorcet designing expressive modes of elections on a theoretical level.[4] That, however, was more Condorcet the mathematician

[3] Montesquieu, *De l'Esprit des Lois* (1748), xi, 6: 'All would be lost if the same man, or the same group of principals, of noblemen, or of the people, were to exercise these three powers: the power to make laws, the power to execute public dispositions, and the power to judge crimes and disputes between individuals. (Tout serait perdu, si le même homme, ou le même corps des principaux, ou des nobles, ou du peuple, exerçaient ces trois pouvoirs: celui de faire des lois, celui d'exécuter les résolutions publiques, et celui de juger les crimes ou les différends des particuliers).'

[4] Condorcet, *Essai sur l'Application de l'Analyse à la Probabilité des Décisions Rendues à la Pluralité des Voix*, Paris: Imprimerie royale, 1785.

than Condorcet the political philosopher who graced the French Revolution.[5] Democracy in late eighteenth century US-parlance, and in the *République* of 1792 France, were introduced by the American and French revolutionaries, who saw elections as the holy grail of the new order defined by the people's right to be represented in government. In systems that also espouse basic freedoms, it took two centuries for democracy to settle into universal suffrage. The great Republican *philosophe* himself, Jean-Jacques Rousseau, did not see it coming. 'Law as the expression of the general will' does not readily translate in law as the majority vote of the people represented in an assembly.[6] Democracy in the *Federalist Papers* tradition, the equivalent of republic in the Condorcet tradition, was way short of universal suffrage.

How does Chiha's constitution, and the constitutional legacy in Lebanon, integrate these three iconic poles of democracy: liberty, separation of powers, and equality?

1. *On liberty*, like all democratic constitutions, the Lebanese Constitution admits freedom's absoluteness as default principle. From the very first manuscript, Chiha included three articles on liberty. Art. 8 establishes the protection of individual freedom, and ties to it the principle *nullum crimen sine lege*.[7] The second is the absoluteness of the freedom of conscience.[8] The third mentions freedom of expression, freedom and the press, and freedom of reunion and association.[9] This shared value the world over

[5] Condorcet, *Esquisse d'un Tableau Historique des Progrès de l'Esprit Humain*, Paris: Librairie philosophique J. Vrin, 1970. Original 1793–1794.

[6] Rousseau, *Du Contrat Social (1762)*, II, 6 ('De la loi'): 'How can a blind multitude, who often do not know what they want, because they seldom know what is good for them, carry out themselves so great and difficult an enterprise as a system of legislation? (Comment une multitude aveugle, qui souvent ne sait ce qu'elle veut, parce qu'elle sait rarement ce qui lui est bon, exécuterait-elle d'elle-même une entreprise aussi grande, aussi difficile qu'un système de législation ?)'

[7] Constitution, Art.8: 'Personal freedom is guaranteed and protected by the law ... No one can be arrested, jailed or suspended except according to the rules of the law. (La liberté individuelle est garantie et protégée ... Aucune infraction et aucune peine ne peuvent être établies que par la loi.)' These two sentences were not modified since the very first Ms., DOC 1, except that the original numbering was Art. 7.

[8] Constitution, Art.9: 'La liberté de conscience est absolue'. Same text in DOC 1, Art. 8.

[9] Constitution, Art.13: 'The freedom of opinion, expression through speech and writing, the freedom of the press, the freedom of assembly, and the freedom of association, are all guaranteed within the limits fixed by law. (La liberté d'exprimer sa pensée par la parole ou par la plume, la liberté de la presse, la liberté de réunion et la liberté d'association, sont garanties dans les limites fixées

should not come as a surprise. Chiha's whole philosophy is built on liberty: 'Lebanon lives on liberty and would die without it'.[10]

2. *Separation of powers* in Lebanon is the same on paper as that in the universal LEJ(F)ARC template. In the course of our reflection on the separation of powers, we detected two key variations on the principle: one minor, the other major.

The first, minor variation, is a gloss obtaining from the passing mention of Léon Duguit and the reconstruction of his contribution to constitutional discussion in Lebanon, namely the specificity of administrative regulatory power in contradistinction to executive governmental power.[11] The civil service is usually subordinate to the executive. More significantly, unlike the cabinet in the executive branch, membership of the civil service does not draw its legitimacy from the people, nor is it supposed to. Duguit's suggested recognition of administrative power as a somewhat distinct category in the Lebanese Constitution was brushed away by Chiha and his colleagues as too unconventional. Its enduring importance in separating the administration from the executive branch has yet to be acknowledged, anywhere in the world, as a new theory of the separation of powers. This theory is needed more than ever but is not easy to develop constitutionally.

The second variation is major. The traditional, functional separation of powers as conceived in the LEJ section of the LEJ(F)ARC building blocks of constitutionalism, is fundamentally distorted in Lebanese communalism. In Lebanon, the separation of powers' traditional prophylactic role against despotism is secondary to the protection from autocracy provided by communalism. Chiha was sophisticated enough to weigh all the poles of reference for the sectarian straitjacket as opposed to merit-based citizenship. To repeat: 'We are among those who maintain, forcefully, that since Lebanon is composed of confessional minorities, there must be a permanent balance between them

par la loi.)' Original Art. 12 in DOC 1: '[L]a liberté de la presse, la liberté de réunion et la liberté d'association, sont garanties dans les limites fixées par la loi.'

[10] 'Le Liban vit de la liberté et mourrait sans elle'. PEL, opening citation.

[11] See Ch. 5, section on Chiha and Duguit.

for Lebanon to thrive'.[12] At the same time, '[t]his balance is found in national representation; it is in Parliament that we must seek it. For the rest, should we not start weeding out prejudice and allow the machinery (of Parliament) more flexibility?'[13] Chiha was always disappointed in the Lebanese Parliament, which, falling short of its role in the country, weakened the principle of separation of powers.

3. *Equal vote* in the Lebanese Constitution was restricted to the communitarian *mora* which prevailed in 1926. The discrepancy between citizen and citizen-in-his-community remains the greatest challenge for Lebanon. Chiha's mantra is summarised in the now familiar warning, also a lament: 'All that the confessional idea gains *is what the Nation loses*'.[14]

As a prelude to the more ambitious chapter that follows, redefining democracy, I propose to clear some of the bramblebush in the much larger debate on secularism and on group subordination. The first ground clearing exercise probes the limits of secularism; the second introduces the better US constitutional debate on 'historically subordinate groups'.

On secularism

The word secularism rarely appears in Chiha's work, and his deep Christian faith may go some way to explaining why a secularist worldview disturbed him. At the same time, the word *laïcité* came to Lebanon amid heated controversy in a France where the Dreyfus affair had dominated a good part of the first part of the twentieth century. Anti-clericalism rooted in the radical aspects of the French revolution, which the Third Republic developed excessively, was hardly acceptable for Chiha, even if one senses his occasional impatience with

[12] 'Nous sommes de ceux-là qui soutiennent avec une extrême vigueur que le Liban étant fait de minorités confessionnelles, il faut entre elles, pour que le Liban vive, un permanent équilibre'. Michel Chiha, 26 January 1945, Pol Int 81.

[13] 'Cet équilibre c'est dans la représentation nationale, c'est dans la Chambre qu'il le faut chercher. Pour le reste, ne faut-il pas laisser tomber lentement le préjugé et donner plus de souplesse aux rouages de la machine ?' Id.

[14] 'Tout ce que l'idée confessionnelle gagne, *c'est la Nation qui le perd*'. Chiha, 2 July 1936, Pol Int 20, cited in Ch. 10, n.16.

'the Sanhedrin'.[15] Secularism French-style did not, and still does not, sit well in Lebanon or elsewhere.

Understandably, the move towards Nation away from religious community is a move to secularism, in abstract to merit over identity. The philosophical question is blunt: is it a necessity for the State to be secular for it to be democratic?

Kantian philosophy and its contemporary legal expressions answer in the affirmative. Secularism is a necessity of the public space vis-à-vis the state. Since the individual is the core agent of the polis, his or her duties and rights are defined by the Kantian 'moral law within me' on the basis of reason.[16] For Kant, the moral law within us derives from our reason, not our faith. This determines the position of the citizen vis-à-vis state, society and constitution, only under the criterion of reason. This position cannot be determined by religion.

The Middle East fails these two foundational tests, since the moral law within us and its public constitutional expression require a distance from religion that communalism rejects. Neither Middle Eastern societies nor their states are secular. This is not so much because of codifying some version of the shari'a or halakha as 'a' or 'the' active source of all laws, an Egyptian creation of the 1980s which found its way to several other constitutions, or the exclusive assignment of the presidency to a Muslim, which can be found even in the constitution of Tunisia's post-2010 Revolution, let alone the Jewish nature of the Israeli State.[17] These discriminatory traits can and should be dispensed with, the more easily dispensable since they often make little difference to the country's rule of law in practice.[18] Yet the constitutional translation of

[15] See citation in Chapter 10, n.39 and n.67.

[16] Kant's famous formula on 'the moral law within me' appears in the conclusion to his *Critique of Practical Reason* (1788). Also, in Abott's translation (Gutenberg Project), at bk2 ch2 s5, 'The existence of God as a postulate of pure practical reason': '[The summum bonum] may be called faith, that is to say a pure rational faith, since pure reason (both in its theoretical and practical use) is the sole source from which it springs'.

[17] Egypt, Constitutions of 1980 and of 2012, Art. 2; Tunisia, Constitution of 2014, Art. 74; Constitution of 2022, Art. 88; Israel, Declaration of Independence 1948, and Basic Law: Israel as the Nation-State of the Jewish People, 2018.

[18] In the case of Egypt and Tunisia, there would be little practical consequences if the articles mentioned in the previous note were omitted. This is less true of Israel, where the problem is not so much the halakha, which like the shari'a in neighbouring countries, is more of a cultural than a legal corpus in all matters except family law. The 2018 Basic Law: Israel as the Nation-State of the

the country's communitarian set-up and spirit matters. It stands at the direct opposite pole of the Kantian test of citizenship.

The Middle East fails the secular test on an analytical basis which is Chihan, and which undermines the Kantian universal citizen as autonomous subject. The Kantian bedrock of citizenship is objectively frustrated because another source of agency operates between the individual and the state, which is her community. This constitutional reality is hardly comparable to Western countries, which all provide their more or less extreme version of secularism.

Paradoxically, a citizen does not have to be spiritual to belong to a religious community. A spiritual form of secularism can also be found in the Middle Eastern citizen regardless of her particular faith. And yet, spiritual as any citizen can be, there is no place for an agnostic or an atheist in Lebanon, whether they are 'secular' or 'spiritual'. One is born and remains Maronite, or Sunni, or Druze even if one is a professed sceptic, nay even if one is profoundly anti-church and other clerical temples. In Israel, there are myriads of 'secular Jews'. This does not change the sectarian build of the country. It is irrelevant to constitutional life in the living-together communal contract imposed on all.

The reader will by now be familiar with this paean in Chiha's vision and its constitutional expression in Lebanon. There is in addition a nuance of importance when the group is defined by religion as opposed to race or wealth. Unlike other markers of difference between citizens elsewhere, the specific theology and rituals of a given religious sect engulf the believer in the tenets of that sect within a cultural/ideological frame of reference which is not shared with the believer in the tenets of another denomination. The theology of Sunnis is profoundly different from the theology of Shi'is, let alone from the theology of Christians or Jews. All of these theologies are at the same time bridged by a so-called Abrahamic commonality. This is a foundational paradox specific to religion with its elastic and all-embracing concepts, but its treatment is better rooted in the field of comparative philosophy than in comparative constitutionalism. Still, it is worth a detour which I have taken elsewhere.[19]

Jewish People elicits grave consequences of an apartheid nature in the express subordination of non-Jews to Jews by Jewish Israelis.

19 Mallat, *Philosophy of Nonviolence*, New York: Oxford University Press 2015, 190–7.

Minority, community, group: the better US scholarship

To proceed meanwhile with a slightly less abstract constitutional comparison, the theoretical envelope, based on the Middle Eastern communities' constitutional agency, needs a push along two conjunctive terms: minority and group. The Middle Eastern/Lebanese community is, in Chiha's terms, a 'minority'. I first argue that 'group' is a better fit.

A bibliography on 'minorities', as on 'community' or 'group', would fill shelves of a library of international and constitutional law, sociology, anthropology or international relations. As we pick up the difficult exercise adumbrated at the outset of the book, some terminological choices need to be made here, to be explored more closely in the next chapter.

Minority is a standalone concept, a concept which Chiha's vision of the 'State as an association of (religious) minorities' intuits but fails to see more fully in universalist terms. In an association of minorities forming Lebanon the nation-state, there is no majority. Chiha's minority does not exist against a majority, for there is simply no majority in Lebanon. Nor does the word minority appear in the Lebanese Constitution, even if the presence of *de facto* communities characterises the apportionment of power amongst them by the constitutional text. In fact, the term minority seldom appears in any constitution. For comparative purposes then, and in order to better approximate its reality, one must first move from the term 'minority' to the word 'community'.

English community, French *confession*, Arabic *ta'ifa*, are words referring in the Middle East to religious sects. This is because they are effectively sectarian-religious at a basic societal and legal level rather than at the level of the wider theological canopy under which the three monotheist religious set themselves. Already in our opening chapter, we noted the polysemy of the term *ta'ifa*, and some of its equivalents, such as sects in English, *rites* and *confessions* in French, *races* even in some nineteenth century documents, *milla* in Turkish and Arabic, *jama'a* in early Islam. Such assembly of individuals is defined by religious affiliation, which translates poorly in comparative constitutionalism. The 'Law and religion' discipline does not provide an adequate basis for the comparative exercise. It misses, for our constitutional purposes, the legal boundaries specific to the religious/sectarian sub-'community' constitutive of Middle Eastern states. This is the first mismatch. We have been talking throughout the book, instead, of 'Law and religious sect'. 'Law and religion' also misses the necessarily thicker legal exercise of how religions (or sects) project their language and ideology onto their believers. Protestantism and Catholicism or Orthodoxy, Sunnism and Shi'ism, Reform and conservative Judaism have very different theologies, acid tests and 'buzzwords' that are meaningful to their adherents.

How can one overcome all these differences in a thick comparative approach?[20] First, and in the same way we just moved from the term 'minority' to the word 'community,' a more effective concept for this social configuration is 'group'. A 'group' is more of a fact than a 'community', in the sense that it does not necessarily entail the self-consciousness in belonging that a community does. Group may be more inchoate than community; it is no less real when defined by religion, sect, race, colour, gender, language, history, or even by the territory in which its members are legally circumscribed. The word connotes a neutrality which community and minority lack. It is also more encompassing. A constitution is not supposed to discriminate between and against 'members of a group on the basis of race, gender etc.' rather than between and against 'members of a community, or minority, etc'. True, there is loss of specificity occasionally, but a theory of groups is more universal than a theory of communities or minorities.

So group it is.

Secondly, finetuning the terminology helps but it may not be worth the effort to parse the exercise ad infinitum. One needs to move to a more substantive debate on equal groups and of the individuals-in-that-group.

In this universal debate, the discussion I find most alluring theoretically in constitutional terms is American. An elaborate thinking on the constitutional place of groups, in contradistinction with naked individuals, has taken place under two landmark *plateaux* of constitutional scholarship in the US. The first concerns subordinated groups and equality, a theoretical approach whose demonstrative force anchors my discussion.[21] The second is distrust in

[20] Paul Kahn, 'Comparative constitutionalism in a new key', *Michigan Law Review* 101, 2003, 2677–705. The concept of thickness has been developed in comparative legal theory to mean comparative questioning of legal texts within a large institutional and cultural context.

[21] The most representative article, in a sea of scholarship, remains Owen Fiss, 'Groups and the Equal Protection Clause', *Philosophy and Public Affairs*, 5, 1976, 107–77.

a democracy that discriminates in favor of the group remaining in power, and further discriminates against groups defined by their insularity and persisting victimisation.[22] Both are firmly rooted in the unique historical subordination of the United States' Black or Afro-American group.

Owen Fiss's 'Groups and the equal protection clause' was published in 1976, against the disturbing history of US racism and the then promising consolidation of the civil rights movement.[23] The article makes the argument that 'the equal protection clause' – a clause which appears as part the major constitutional amendments enacted after the War of Secession –[24] supersedes the simplistic association of equality among individuals. When individuals are part of a group, and the group elicits public treatment which is detrimental to the individual by virtue of his being a member of the group, the law which considers the individual without reference to the group fails to see the larger, more adequate picture. For purposes of constitutional equality, the individual-in-the-group displaces the individual per se.

As one central consequence of Fiss's approach, the equality expressed and sought for the individual citizen in all constitutions and in all human rights declarations cannot ignore the group's *subordination* by other groups in the majoritarian system. Constitutional mechanisms protect the equality of the group member; they do not abstract or extract the individual from that group. This is true for the Black community in the United States, but is also true for other subordinated communities, also called 'disadvantaged' in the article. Extrapolation is easy in American history. This is the case with respect to Chinese immigrants at the turn of the nineteenth century (colour), Catholic and Jewish Americans until the 1960s (religion), and until now Latinos (race/language), Indian/Native Americans (race, colour, pre-American history),

22 My preferred work, again in a sea of sophisticated contributions, is John Hart Ely, *Democracy and Distrust*, Cambridge, MA: Harvard University Press 1980.

23 Full of progressive appeal, the practical incidence of the article was undermined by the rise of a conservative tide which has dominated the world since, and was reflected in the US Supreme Court's retreat from the civil rights' breakthrough over two decades as the 'Earl Warren court'. Warren, who died in 1974, was Chief Justice between 1953 to 1969.

24 In a series of constitutional amendments that followed the defeat of the secessionist Southern States, slavery was formally abolished (Thirteenth Amendment 1865), equality was constitutionally protected (Fourteenth Amendment 1868) and discrimination on the basis of race or colour outlawed (Fifteenth Amendment 1870). It took almost a century for the break to be put into effect by the constitutional scrutiny of the Supreme Court.

Women (gender and history), each a group which is or has been historically subordinated to, and disadvantaged by, the ruling White/Caucasian Male Group (colour, race).

Constitutional powers, with the judiciary in the lead for the American constitutionalist, are all meant to effectively protect the group against the simplistic understanding of its individual membership as the defining unit of democracy. With the impossibility for the subordinated group to seek redress at the voting booth, it was mainly the courts' role to fight subordination by managing equitably the tension between the principle of equal citizenship and the unequal citizen in the subordinate group:

> The redistributive aims served by the group-disadvantaging principle – the elevation of at least one group that has spent two centuries in this country in a position of subordination – may simply override [...] supposed institutional advantages.[25]

This passage at the end of the article shows the particular concern for the United States' Black community, victim of a two centuries-long subordinating disadvantage starting with the structured kidnapping of Blacks during the slave trade through constitutional slavery and continued colour-based subordination. The passage focusing on the specific role of the judiciary privileges the anti-discrimination principle over normal 'institutional' mechanisms of individual equality, with a 'redistributive aim' as a central tool of redress against the 'group-disadvantaging' structure of democracy.[26] Redress includes ways to prevent or correct structural subordination based on a proactive understanding of the equal protection clause, for instance in preferring members of the disadvantaged group in employment recruitment, electoral redistricting to

[25] Owen Fiss, 'Groups and the Equal Protection Clause', above n.21, 175.

[26] Id. Fiss's article is rich and sometimes elusive, which combines jurisprudence, US case law, and philosophy. In his later writings, the language has been more fixated on 'the anti-subordination principle.' I had the benefit of Owen Fiss's comment on an early draft of parts of this book, where he suggests a general convergence of our enquiry, but where he notes more importantly that his theory departs from the US Constitution, whereas mine does not. This readily acknowledged approach, which is directly inspired by this jurisprudential philosophy, stands outside a strict judicial framework which represents Fiss's self-limited US ambit despite its universal appeal. This is further elaborated in Chapter 13.

strengthen the group's vote, and by conferring special treatment such as state funding to the group.

After Fiss, and under the same progressive philosophy, the second landmark *plateau* for constitutional comparison derives from John Hart Ely's *Democracy and Distrust*, especially in the chapter entitled 'Facilitating the representation of minorities'.[27] His analysis provides another powerful standard in comparative law for the individual-in-the historically-subordinate-group.

Ely roots the rationale for the courts' judicial review in the celebrated *Carolene Products* 'footnote 4'.[28] The case's iconic value for constitutional scholarship comes in this obiter footnote, written by Justice Harlan Stone (d.1946). Stone starts by cautioning that one should not read too much into the footnote:

> It is unnecessary to consider now whether legislation that restricts those political processes which can ordinarily be expected to bring about repeal of undesirable legislation, is to be subjected to more exacting judicial scrutiny under the general prohibitions of the Fourteenth Amendment than are most other types of legislation.[29]

In this alluring yet elusive turn-of-phrase, Stone opens up the courts to investigating (sometime in the future) a 'more exacting scrutiny' that will 'repeal undesirable legislation' under the Equal Protection Clause of the Fourteenth Amendment.[30] The same negative turn-of-phrase serves the demure and non-committal judge to express what became a constitutional prophecy:

[27] Ely, *Democracy and Distrust*, above n.22, Chapter 6, 135–81. I had an early interest in the book which brought me to interview John Hart Ely in 1985 in Stanford. See my '*Fin-nazariyya ad-dusturiyya al-amirkiyya al-mu'asira: Robert Bork wa John Hart Ely*' (On contemporary American constitutional law: Robert Bork and John Hart Ely), *Proche-Orient Etudes Juridiques* (Beirut), 1987, 9–26. Ely died in 2003.

[28] *United States v. Carolene Products Company*, 304 U.S. 144 (1938), fn 4. The *Carolene Products* factual case is relatively insignificant. It concerns a company trading with milk in a way which violated legislation passed under the New Deal to restrict its 'normal' distribution across state lines. As part of the atmosphere of state intervention in the era of the New Deal, the Court decided not to invalidate the milk-related statute, because it considered, against its previous attitude in matters of economic legislation and interstate commerce, that the legislator had the right to apply such constraints if their purposes are reasonable.

[29] Id.

[30] The Fourteenth Amendment comprises five sections. The first includes the so-called Privileges and Immunities Clause, which prohibits their 'abridgement' for all US citizens; the Due Process Clause which requires a judicially overseen process before 'a State' deprives 'any person of life, liberty

> Nor need we enquire whether similar considerations enter into the review of statutes directed at particular religious, ..., or national, ..., or racial minorities ...; whether prejudice against discrete and insular minorities may be a special condition, which tends seriously to curtail the operation of those political processes ordinarily to be relied upon to protect minorities, and which may call for a correspondingly more searching judicial inquiry.[31]

What are the issues which Harlan Stone thinks the court might one day consider? The anticipation is for the court to consider a more 'searching inquiry' of laws that violate the Equal Protection Clause of the 14th Amendment when they harm 'particular religious, or national, or racial minorities.' This is the basis of a plethora of decisions starting twenty years later, under the leadership of Earl Warren. The first and most famous case is *Brown v. Board of Education*,[32] which struck down racial segregation in schools in Kansas. *Brown* was followed by a large number of decisions heeding the philosophy of the footnote by exercising a 'strict scrutiny' review of any legal or governmental disposition, at local or national level, which discriminates, directly or indirectly, against Black Americans. The case and its progeny energised the rise of the civil liberties movement under the leadership of Martin Luther King, and progress in the court jurisprudence and King's nonviolent movement reinforced each other.

In short, the court will strike down any law or administrative measure that discriminates against, or appears to discriminate against, such 'discrete and insular minorities'. The reason is the intrinsic shortcoming of 'the operation of those political processes ordinarily to be relied upon to protect minorities'.

and property'; and the Equal Protection Clause which prevents the 'State' from 'deny[ing] to any person ... the equal protection of the laws'.

31 *United States v. Carolene Products Company*, above n.28. Even for the American constitutional student, the language is hermetic. In US constitutional theory, the footnote has developed to mean that the Supreme Court must annul legislation which is suspect of racial discrimination. This is the so-called 'strict scrutiny' principle. In Ely's argumentation, the footnote bloomed into a full, two-pronged constitutional theory. The first is the protection of minorities. The second is the need for the Supreme Court to 'cleanse the political process' by preventing 'those who are in' from using their legislative and regulatory powers to keep 'those who are out out.' Ely, *Democracy and Distrust*, above n.22, Chapter 5, 'Clearing the channels of the political process', 105–34. This is marginal to Lebanese communalism, albeit important to comparative constitutionalism at large to help make certain that 'the one-man one-vote' principle becomes 'one-person one-voice' constitutional rule. This means the need to protect the ordinary voter's voice from being smothered by mega voices drowning his by their disproportionate reliance on money.

32 *Brown v. Board of Education of Topeka*, 347 U.S. 483 (1954).

In plain words, the majoritarian rule is a structural obstacle to minorities protecting themselves by way of the ballot box.

A few examples will clarify this shortcut: a law prevents Blacks from marrying Whites. Unconstitutional.[33] An electoral law waters down the votes of a Black neighbourhood by way of re-districting. Unconstitutional.[34] A clause in the purchase of a house prevents it being re-sold to a 'non-Caucasian'. Illegal.[35]

The theory rooted in the footnote goes beyond the skin's arbitrary hues. It calls for protecting not only racial but also 'religious' or 'national' groups, by considering 'prejudice against discrete and insular minorities [to] be a special condition'. A special condition for what? For the court's intervention to invalidate official measures taken by the State, viz. any public authority in the federal or state system when it prejudices a minority group which is discrete, that is, identifiable by generally unchangeable traits, and insular, that is, surrounded by high boundaries and marginalised by the majority. Such measures are considered unconstitutional *a priori* under the Equal Protection Clause. They are subject, in the court's language, to a 'strict scrutiny test' that invalidates them without further ado. In the same spirit, the Court will *not* invalidate a 'reverse discrimination' legal or administrative disposition which favors a member of a historically subordinate group or law.[36]

The court's strict scrutiny test concerned dominantly the American Black community. This is important insofar as the Black group in the US, considering the almost total annihilation of Native Americans, has remained in terms of numbers the most important 'discrete and insular minority' in the country. Discrete because it is obviously identifiable as colour of skin-anchored and self-conscious as a group, and insular because it is structurally marginalised by its inherent arithmetical incapacity in mustering the votes needed to redress

33 *Loving v. Virginia*, 388 U.S. 1 (1967) (invalidating, as late as 1967, a 1924 anti-miscegenation laws punishing criminally interracial marriage in the State of Virgina).

34 *Gomillion v. Lightfoot*, 64 U.S. 339 (1960) (striking down state redistricting laws that deny equal protection to African-Americans).

35 These are known as 'restrictive covenants'. In restrictive covenants, new owners could not resell the house to a Black purchaser, so the clause was effectively made inoperative by the courts. In *Shelley v. Kraemer*, 334 U.S. 1 (1948), these clauses were not considered unconstitutional, but they were not enforceable judicially. It was only in 1968 that federal housing legislation made all such racial restrictions formally illegal.

36 Reverse discrimination (referred to by Fiss as 'redistributive') has its own checkered history in US law, with sharp reversals of the doctrine in the twenty-first century which keep the controversy live.

legal discrimination by the non-Black majority. Despite the readiness of Justice Stone to open judicial review to other discrete and insular groups that are described as 'national' and 'religious', Native Americans as self-described 'Nation(s)' do not quite fit the bill. Their treatment was always peculiar in law.[37] Even the 'religious' category, rife as it was with the anti-Jewish and anti-Catholic (of late anti-Muslim) biases, is complicated by a more nuanced balancing test than the one the Supreme Court has reserved for Black Americans since Earl Warren.[38]

In sum, the above treatment under the theory of 'equal groups' and of 'discrete and insular minorities' appears extremely parochial, very US American, in large part because the theory is rooted in two special features of America's institutional makeup: slavery, and the US Supreme Court. This combination can be matched nowhere else.

And yet: while the debate at the heart of American society might appear as an immense distraction in our Lebanese and Middle Eastern discussion, the treatment of historically subordinate groups is at the center of a fundamental tension, probably the most fundamental modern tension, in all societies and inside all states. The battle over group equality is joined: 'To sum up, *Brown* both reflected and propelled the development of human rights protection internationally ... It propelled an evolution yet unfinished toward respect, in law and in practice, for the human dignity of all the world's people'.[39]

[37] This unique area of US law has its own scholarship, including a *Restatement of the Law, Law of American Indians* (2022), rooted in the creeping annihilation, forced displacement, and structural corralling in 'reservations' of a large number of the original inhabitants of the US.

[38] In cases on the separation under the US constitution of state and religion ('First Amendment: Congress shall make no law respecting an establishment of religion, or prohibiting the free exercise thereof', section known as 'the Establishment Clause'), the courts have developed the so-called *Lemon* test, named after U.S. Supreme Court decision *Lemon v. Kurtzman*, 403 U.S. 602 (1971). Under this tripartite test, a law favoring or disfavoring religion is valid on condition that it has 'a legitimate secular purpose; second ... its primary effect must be one that neither advances nor inhibits religion'; and third, 'the statute must not foster "an excessive government entanglement with religion"' (at 612–3, citation omitted). This was a Rhode Island law which supported church schools' increase in teacher salaries. The court found that the first branch of the test was not violated, but invalidated it because of the 'excessive entanglement' of the State.

[39] '*Brown v. Board of Education* in International Context', Speech by US Supreme Court Associate Justice Ruth Bader Ginsburg (d.2020) at the University of Pretoria, 7 February 2006, https://www.supremecourt.gov/publicinfo/speeches/sp_02-07a-06.html

Back to Lebanon

Comparing the US example with the Chiha-Lebanese template, the Lebanese constitutional system does not rely on the judiciary to protect the individual-in-the-group, *a priori*, in *absolute*, as well as *proactively*:

- *A priori*, because the Lebanese judiciary does not play a role since Lebanese groups are structured and recognised in a clearly delineated format, bolstered by so-called personal status laws which define the individual-in-the-group and grant him or her specific legal and political attributes and duties vis-à-vis the State.
- *In absolute*, since constitutional protection is provided to the individual-within-his-community irrespective of the majority (even if there were an identifiable one), and irrespective of other groups since they all stand as equal in 'the association of minorities'.
- *Proactively*, because the protection is shaped by an end result, which is the forced representation of the group in power through some of its members. A communal separation of powers becomes the overarching reference for the individual's protection. Not surprisingly, judicial protection rising to the level of legislative interloper upsets both the traditional Montesquieuan system of separation of powers and Rousseau's belief in the common will of the people being expressed in the laws that they pass. It also risks creating an ungovernable monster by undermining the principle that the majority decides, which results in no one being able to decide. But it leaves no community outside the fabric of government, and therefore no individual-in-the-community unrepresented in power, in particular in executive power.

This all suggests that the Lebanese and American systems do not compare well. Like all comparisons, the granularity matters, and the granularity here is somewhat dense. Still, I wish to defend the choice on an abstract level which goes to the heart of democracy, in a prelude to the more universal set of proposals redefining republicanism, also known as democracy. This lays the groundwork for the radical theoretical and practical proposal to redefine democracy in the next chapter.

The longish detour in the constitutional subordination of the individual-in-a-historically-disenfranchised-group is warranted by the same problem in

Lebanon and in the United States, in Malaysia as well as Chile, Switzerland or Poland. Brecht once said that the smallest unit in society is not one person, but two, putting his finger on the universal problem which democracy faces. Namely, if the smallest unit in society is not just one but a number of citizens, then representation in government, that is, in decision-making, or in forcing some citizens to obey orders or follow regulations that the other set of citizens decide by majority vote, such representation will always be to the advantage of the majority. A constitution might failsafe the individual trapped in his minority group with an array of rights which no majority, however large, can violate, but the ordinary work of government is premised on the majority decision. A panoply of rights does not prevent the majority group from prevailing in decision-making, and the corresponding minority group from failing in the game of numbers.

Let us now slightly adjust the comparative lens. In any nation state where the 'national' does not correspond to the linguistic, or religious, or gendered, or disabled, society produces units, groups, which are in the minority from a governmental decision-making perspective. We have seen the evidence in Lebanon and the Middle East, based on religion. In Malaysia, the problem is in the Chinese and Indian minority groups v the Malay Bumiputra. In Switzerland, the segmentation is chiefly linguistic. In Chile, in Poland, or in Japan, the absence of an apparent minority suggests either that the problem is less acute and that the country has succeeded enough in its ethnolysis for an ethnic or otherwise differentiated minority group not to be laden with a heavy minoritarian problem; or that the dominance of the superordinate group is so great that the problems of the minority are hidden to the public eye. The segmentation and contrasting ethnolysis are either time- and context-sensitive, often the result of massacres in a long history, or temporary, since population movements inevitably disrupt ethnolysis. More fundamentally, 'minority' status is always constructed socially. The next chapter examines what makes a group a 'minority', and we shall see that it is not necessarily a question of numbers.

Meanwhile, I invite the reader to consider a rapprochement between Lebanon and the United States, focusing on Blacks in the US and the various religious denominations in Lebanon. A member of the Sunni – or Shi'i, or Druze, or Maronite, or Armenian-Catholic – community in Lebanon fares under Chiha's constitutional hundred-year-old system better than a US Black citizen has fared in more than two hundred years of American constitutionalism. The comparison is still favorable today, despite the civil rights movement, the Supreme Court's array of judgments in favor of Blacks in the 1950s to the 1970s, and Congress's actions through a long list of federal laws actively supported by various successive administrations. No doubt the formerly disenfranchised Black community has made qualitative progress on the route to equality, but the subordination of the-individual-in-the-community remains palpable in American society when it comes to the group identified as 'Black'.

Would the Black citizen have fared better in the United if she or he as individual-in-the-Black-group was protected by a Chiha-like system? In most of US history, it would be hard to say no. We can push the argument further. Would the Black citizen in America *presently* not fare better if America were constitutionally an association of groups where an individual's membership in that discrete and insular minority is protected by Lebanese-style constitutionalism, in the same way that a Shi'i, a Sunni, a Christian Maronite, or a Druze, is protected in Lebanon under Chiha's Constitution?

If we distill the term 'group' out of the terms 'minority' and 'community', the Lebanese constitutional system provides an inbuilt protection which is more efficient for the member of an identified disadvantaged discrete group than the American constitutional system. Whatever the other group or groups does, there is a nucleus of political rights for a historically victimised group which cannot be touched, most importantly the representation of its members in parliament, and their effective representation in the executive branch. These forms of representation always remain, even if the other group or groups hold a numerical majority in the country. A group cannot fully subordinate another group, regardless of numbers.

Is 'American democracy' more democratic than 'Lebanese democracy'? Does Chiha's system protect groups against marginalisation more than the system established by the American founding fathers?

* * *

Lebanon has proved, years and decades on end, to be ungovernable. The fight between its communities is as constant as their long-institutionalised life. The rays of hope which occasionally unite the nation have been soon put out by an entrenchment of the communities and their leaders' mutual distrust and violence. Fernand Braudel introduced to historical research the concept of *longue durée*, which he alternatively ascribed to geography and to economic cycles. A no less tangible dimension of longue durée is institutional, reflecting the slow adjustment of a country's institutions, barring rare moments which result from a national shock like a revolution. Revolutionary breaks, when they succeed, occasionally bring about a full overhaul of the system. Even then, it usually takes a long time for the change to jell. In constitutional terms, the break with more than a thousand years of near absolute monarchy in France in 1789 took a good century to bring in a lasting republic. The glacial pace of constitutional progress applies the world over.

In Lebanon's *longue durée*, individual egalitarianism never prevailed over communitarianism. In the two centuries of institutional communalism of emergent Lebanon, institutional change followed major traumas. The Egyptian occupation in 1830 saw the first adjunct governing councils established in Beirut and Tripoli; the recurrent civil strife between 1840 and 1860 led to the entrenchment of communalism in the dual *Qa'emmaqamiyya* council; the massacres of 1860 produced the *Mutasarrifiyya* and a sectarian Administrative Council, while the Ottoman Empire slowed its long decline with a halting system of elections in Mount Lebanon and across a shrinking realm; famine and wide-scale destruction in the First World War led to the displacement of Ottoman rule by the French army and the adoption of a republican model; the large revolt in Syria spilling over to Lebanese territory led to the adoption of the Constitution in 1926; the Second World War allowed Lebanese Independence and a string of constitutional amendments for self-determination; and the long civil war of 1975–90 came to a momentary end with the Ta'ef Agreement which adopted parity between Muslims and Christians in parliament in the 1990 constitutional amendments.

On many of these occasions forms of mass mobilization in revolutionary modes and moods arose, spilling onto the street in various ways to create a national oneness. The recurrent peasant-based communes/*'ammiya*s in the nineteenth century culminated in a call in the 1858 revolt for a republic, a *jumhuriyya*. Historians have studied popular awakenings, but they have not pinpointed the connection with the resulting constitutional change beyond some general statements regarding the end of feudalism in the course of the nineteenth century, or the search for self-determination and the pushback against foreign domination in the twentieth and twenty-first centuries.

In the twentieth and twenty-first centuries in Lebanon, major popular revolts against the ruling system also carried strong calls for equality and expressed rejection of communalism. The 'Nation' transcended the communities on several occasions and the revolts were no longer dominated by the peasantry. The Lebanese elite rose as one in 1920 to assert independence against the French, and in 1943 to gain independence. In 1952, a large nonviolent revolt restored democratic rule by forcing the president into resignation. Six years later, in 1958, another coalition rose against his successor for similar reasons. Until 1958, the revolts were mostly bloodless. That year, the rebellion took up arms, but the fight quickly subsided when the president was eventually dislodged following the military intervention of the United States. In 1975, another revolt, which had national-secular yearnings in its early months, soon collapsed into a long era of communal violence and regional wars that have yet to come to an end.

Revolt struck again in the twenty-first century. Twice in the first two decades of the second millennium of the common era – the third if there were a Phoenician/Canaanite calendar – a large cross-section of the Lebanese population rose in a nonviolent rebellion against the established order. In the first case, in 2005–6, the 'Cedar Revolution' succeeded in forcing the Syrian army out of the country without hurting a single Syrian soldier. This rebellion failed to translate its massive street presence into a national movement that transcended communalism. In the second case, in 2019, the revolt which accompanied the collapse of the financial system expressed a more determined rejection of communalism. Its core rebel groups came out expressly in support of secularism and radical change. The revolt produced a scattered group of MPs elected on the basis of their popular appeal for a more secular form of politics, but it failed to qualitatively change the communal system.

It could be reasonably concluded from two hundred years of communal governing councils, from the Beirut Consultative Council of 1834 to the Lebanese National Parliament post Ta'ef, that Nation-averse communalism will be triumphant until the end of time. This is also true of the wider Middle East, where society is defined since its recorded beginnings by religious segmentation.

When Chiha spoke of time as the assuager of communalism, he spoke with both hope and considerable skepticism. The Middle East appears stuck in its religious communities.

Another major institutional element, tied to our study of the Chiha constitution, stands in the way of change: the electoral system. As soon as elections take place, the large revolutionary coalitions which bring hope to the Nation come up short. In the Spring of 2005 and in the Spring of 2022, national parliamentary elections were carried out, a process that forced each citizen to retreat into his community. All parliamentary candidates had to adopt a candidacy wrapped in an openly sectarian fold. A rebel, secular, candidate for the district of Baabda could run only with the label of candidate for the Shiʿi, or the Maronite, Baabda seat. And when parliament elects a president, its speaker, or the prime minister, its members must choose a Maronite President, a Shiʿi Speaker, and a Sunni Prime Minister. The straitjacket of communal electoralism is not a benign side effect of the system. It is essential to its reproduction.

The various electoral laws studied in the course of our journey have been strictly communal. So far, we have seen no example of an electoral law where this scheme can be defeated by a mechanism that salvages the separation of powers resulting from communalism yet ensures the full equality of individual citizens coterminous with the meaning of republic/democracy, understood the world over as the rule of a majority of equal voters.

Nor can electoral laws be imagined outside a society whose politics are mediated by political parties. Here also, constitutions have little to say, and Lebanon is no exception. Usually, there is a brief clause in a constitution which considers the freedom of association to be unimpeachable. Freedom of association covers political parties as well as trade unions, schools and universities, and sundry non-governmental associations. The rest is left to the details found in laws and regulations.

The Lebanese public is not indifferent to the need for full equality, but all secularist reforms have so far been nipped in the bud. Although breaching the communal straitjacket seems impossible, one hopes that this avenue is not totally shut. The problem is that the reproduction of community-based parties dovetails with the reproduction of community-based elections.

There is a deeper problem which political parties add to the already complex situation of majoritarianism, and which the previous chapter presented as the elusive Government-elections-parties triangle. The problem is universal. With the end of the capitalist-socialist rivalry between the US and USSR, political parties are not faring well, and those in the Western world are veering towards unhealthy extremism. Lebanon is not immune to this trend, with the added complication that the communal constitution and the electoral system make it difficult for a political party to emerge at a national level. If the structural reality makes it hard, if not impossible, for national parties to form in Lebanon, then the way out of communalism through such parties is further compromised.

Should one conclude that there is no way out?

A tangible effort was made in 1989 at Ta'ef. It resulted in the most substantive institutional amendments since 1927. In the legislative branch, Christians and Muslims were considered formally at par. In the executive branch, the President's powers were curtailed, and the Speaker's term extended, with a new balance dubbed a 'troika' by both ruling and ruled people. In the judicial branch, a Constitutional Council was created.

It is not enough. The texts of Ta'ef, the National Accord Agreement and the amended 1990 Constitution, themselves admit that the new arrangements are not sufficient, and call for the continuation of the constitutional deliberation to reduce communalism in the country. Ta'ef resuscitated the Senate and promised to create a bicameral Parliament. The Senate is to be elected on a communal basis like the CR, while the CR would be elected on a non-communal basis. The President was tasked with forming a constituent committee to examine further measures to end (although more likely tame) the communal system.

A quarter of a century after Ta'ef, Lebanon does still not have a Senate. Lebanon still does not have a secularly elected CR, and four successive presidents have chosen not to form the constituent committee.

13

Democracy Redefined

> Our country, by its structure, is different from all others. Those who transplant western and eastern theory here rather foolishly overlook this – or pretend to.[1]

Our reflection has not ventured forward enough.

I have noted the communal grip in the Middle East and rued its projection worldwide as a threat to the human equality of individuals at the very basis of democratic theory, whilst underlying some advantages of communalism. At best, the 'communal pluses' appear as a recourse against dictatorship when the autocrat relies on his community to exclude all others from power.[2]

This was not all. The analysis in this book found solid terrain in constitutional theory on 'groups and equal protection', in particular the constitutional protection of 'discrete and insular minorities'.[3] But the theoretical grounding investigated so far was rooted negatively. Protection of minorities is approached in the better developed legal literature from the limited perspective of the constitutional judiciary, in which courts are tasked with providing counter-majoritarian measures to legislatures, grounded in enumerated constitutional rights. Another rich strand of scholarship comes from

[1] 'Notre pays, par sa structure, est différent de tous les autres. Cela, on l'ignore (ou on feint de l'ignorer) quand on transplante ici un peu follement, les théories de l'Occident et de l'Orient'. 'Pour un retour au réel', 30 June 1946, Pol Int 103.

[2] See Chapters 11 and 12. As a reminder, the examples of Sunni Ba'thism in Iraq under Saddam Hussein or 'Alawi Ba'thism in Syria under the Asad family are telling of the empty 'secular' pretense and its grotesque consequences. In the two previous chapters, I argued that most other countries in the Middle East, including Israel, fail the call of democracy, and that Western democracies, including the United States, undermine subordinate groups in a way the present theory seeks to remedy in a more radical approach.

[3] On this conceptual coining by Owen Fiss and John Hart Ely respectively, see Ch. 12.

political scientists on consociationalism, who often use Lebanon as a typical illustration.[4] The two traditions meet occasionally, but the lack of a common language, which also prevents a more rigorous combination of the best of both traditions, has prevented a fuller theory from developing.

The approach I choose in this final chapter amalgamates constitutional-legal and political-scientist language, with the emphasis in the book on the former, and the emphasis in this chapter on the latter.[5] It is based on the genealogical obduracy of two hundred years of Levantine history and four thousand years of Middle Eastern law. It uses Michel Chiha's communal constitutionalism as the anchor of comparison. Chiha's philosophical conception of government, which is vindicated by a uniquely enduring constitutional practice, entrenches the principle that government *must* represent every

[4] The consociational propositions tend to be heavily empirical, with 'characteristics' of democracy strewn over several variables, including electoral systems, federalism and even central banking. For an example by the main herald in the field, Arend Lijphart, *Patterns of Democracy: Government Forms and Performance in Thirty-Six Countries*, New Haven: Yale University Press 2nd ed. 2012. I have not found enough of a focus on subordinated groups in the writings of the leading Western theoreticians of democracy responding to Seyla Benhabib in her edited *Democracy and Difference*, Princeton: Princeton University Press 1996, despite the fact that she raised the question in her 'Introduction- The Democratic Moment and the Problem of Difference, 3–19, at 10: 'However, if what are to be represented are groups rather than ideas, views, and belief systems, this model of representation raises another set of quandaries: can groups be treated as homogeneous entities? If principles of representation are distributed along group lines, which aspects of group identity should be given the most preference in public modes of representation?' The reader will find the propositions in the present book to be more radical than those discussed by the contributors to Benhabib's book, including Iris Marion Young, who questions individual equality as universal at best ('Communication and the Other: Beyond Deliberative Democracy', id. at 120–37).

[5] Amongst numerous political scientists, my discussion acknowledges the pioneering work of Hanna Pitkin historically, *The Concept of Representation*. Berkeley: University of California Press 1967 (discussing several forms of representation beyond the political-electoral one), and Jane Mansbridge at present. See Mansbridge, *Beyond Adversary Democracy* (Chicago: University of Chicago Press 1980, on other types of participation in the public arena), and her taxonomy of multiple forms of participation in 'Rethinking representation', *American Political Science Review*, 97, 2003, 515–28, and 'Clarifying the Concept of Representation', *American Political Science Review*, 105, 2011, 621–30. This strand of political science scholarship has extensively studied the concept of representation beyond the more formal one which is discussed here (including for women). It carries a sustained focus on the relationships between those elected and those voters who entrust them with power as theorised in 'the deliberative democracy' school, also developed by Seyla Benhabib. I suggest that my reading is both more skeptical (deliberative processes in democracy are so evident that they turn out to be less important than their advocates suggest) and more radical (the ultimate proof in the democratic pudding is whether government represents society in its individual-in-the-subordinated-group quality). Representation is also explored in a rich corpus of French scholarship, where the concept of 'miroir' is prevalent.

individual-in-a-group, with group defined as religion, more accurately as sect qua religious sub-community.

Building on these scholarly traditions, I would like to sketch the contours of a theory which I will call Democracy, with a capital D to distinguish it from a prevailing theory of democracy with a lower-case d. Capital d Democracy is one where *needed* constitutional representation at large gives way to the *necessary* constitutional catering in government for the individual-in-the-subordinate-_____-group. Filling in the blank is Democracy's central theoretical challenge.

Representation *in* government is a major frontier of constitutionalism. I am not referring here to the great divide between direct and representative democracy, which eighteenth century political philosophers, Rousseau in particular, had to confront for a constitutionalisation of the people's general will into sovereignty by way of a social contract. After the yearning of the Renaissance for Athenian democracy as the paragon representative model of public life – Greek democracy did not know a sharp line between representing and being represented since all Athenian free male citizens participated in the agora as decision-makers – representative democracy won the historical day. This is not an insignificant achievement in the progress of human societies, and it is now an incontrovertible *acquis* of constitutional science.[6] There is no going back on the concept of 'separation of powers' which Montesquieu introduced single-handedly in 1748 on the basis of his observations of political life in England, or the rule of the majority as a simple definition of democracy which developed with the Atlantic Revolution.

Universal suffrage is also a major *acquis* of human progress. It is both the *summum* and the *sine qua non* rule for the people's representation in constitutionalism. Under a social contract defined by the boundaries of a nation-state, all citizens of age, male and female, vote for their representatives and thereby confer legitimacy to their presence and participation in government. A representative in government, an elected official, is voted in, by dint of a majority of votes cast in his favor, against the representative of another citizen, who loses to the winner's votes after they are counted. This is simple enough. It is

[6] I borrow the term *acquis* here from EU constitutionalism, in the sense that legal achievements which have been acquired can never be reversed.

the essence of the social contract 'of the people, by the people, for the people', the genial genius summary of democracy as coined by Abraham Lincoln and Frenchified by Charles de Gaulle a century later.[7]

Yet there are several disconnects, of which the individual-in-the-historically-subordinate-group is the defining one in my proposed theory of Democracy. I will mention some such disconnects briefly.

An early set of disconnects stems from the paradox of the voter and his representative's faithfulness. In Robespierre and his contemporaries' language, the voters are his *commettants*. They commit to him, and he commits to acting for them. In representative democracy, constitutions and constitutionalists have long underlined this disconnect by rejecting the legal liability of the elected representative when accused of betraying his *commettants*. Yet the problem of unfaithfulness remains.

Representation's disconnects are also acknowledged in the dilution of the individual electoral vote under a panoply of measures: gerrymandering, high barriers to party representation in the electoral law, the gamut of electoral laws from first-past-the-post to proportional representation, skewed results adumbrated in the Condorcet paradox, federalism, the role of money in the elections, etc. All these matter to proper representation in government. They distort the integrity of the individual vote and are the subject of an immense and fruitful body of scholarship. Some of these issues were addressed in the previous chapter. They are not of concern to me here. I am focused on a more fundamental disconnect, which I formulate provisionally as follows: when the group to which an individual belongs is subordinated to the ruling group in government, Democracy fails if the individual-in-the-group is not

[7] Abraham Lincoln (Gettysburg address, 9 November 1863): see the original formulation by Daniel Webster (d. 1852) in a Senate speech in 1830 cited by Garry Wills, *Lincoln at Gettysburg: The Words that Remade America,* New York: Simon & Schuster 1992, at 119 (Kindle Edition): 'It is ... the people's Constitution, the people's government, made for the people, made by the people, and answerable to the people ... I hold it to be a popular government, erected by the people; those who administer it responsible to the people; and itself capable of being amended and modified, just as the people may choose it should be'; Charles de Gaulle (Press conference in London, 27 May 1942): 'La démocratie se confond exactement, pour moi, avec la souveraineté nationale. La démocratie c'est le gouvernement du peuple par le peuple, et la souveraineté nationale, c'est le peuple exerçant sa souveraineté sans entrave.' Cited e.g. in Véronique Alibert-Fabre, 'La pensée constitutionnelle du Général de Gaulle à 'l'épreuve des circonstances', *Revue Française de Science Politique*, 40, 1990, 699–713, at 702.

effective in ending their subordination even when represented in proportion to the subordinated group's size.

Proponents of classic universalism defined by the equality of individuals shrug their shoulders. For them, the individual-in-the-group is the individual-in-the-nation. There is in equality no intermediary group between individual and government. People are equal as individuals, as citizens. They are not equal through the mediation of any group. Democracy starts and ends with the individual. Any other configuration undermines equality, representation, and citizenship. In the world system of nation-states, this is why the Middle East appears for the universalist to be civilisationally retarded. The erasure of the mediation of religious groups (bad) lies at the basis of democracy (good). Against the segmentations of tribes or sects (bad), the Rawlsian veil of ignorance that makes all equal under law is the answer (good). Religious segmentation (bad) is trumped by secularism (good).

I note here that even for religious subordination, from the historical divide between Protestants and Catholics in Ireland to the great fracture on all the frontiers of Muslim societies, and within Muslim-majoritarian (or Buddhist-, or Hindu-, or Jewish- majoritarian) countries, or the Orthodox/Catholic frontiers in Eastern Europe, the Chiha vision remains appropriate across large swathes of the planet.

Yet I would like to push the argument beyond religious segmentation. For a theory of Democracy, one should not be blinded by the religious prism. It is easy to recall that the nineteenth century, and a good part of the twentieth, were dominated by the bloody fractures, domestically and internationally, created by 'nationalities'.[8] Religious segmentation is only one hurdle among many on the way to equality, and no different in nature from segmentation between free men and slaves, which lingers on heavily in the colour of

[8] Bertolt Brecht's story of Mr K is an eloquent criticism of exacerbated nationalism: 'Mr K did not think it necessary to live in any particular country. "I can go hungry anywhere", he said. But one day, he went through a town occupied by the enemy of the country in which he was living. One of the enemy's officers came towards him and forced him to step off the pavement. Mr K stepped off and became aware that he was furious with this man, and not only with this man, but even more with the country from which the man came. So that he wished it could be wiped off the face of the earth. "Why", asked Mr K, "did I become a nationalist for that moment? Through encountering a nationalist. That's why stupidity must be stamped out, for it makes stupid the one who encounters it".' Original German in *Kalendergeschichten*, Berlin: Bertelsman n.d. (ca 1948), at 125 ('Vaterlandslieb, der Hass gegen Vaterländen').

a member-in-the-skin-group across the planet. In addition to the continuing subordination of the descendants of slaves and of the few remaining members of decimated non-Christian groups known as natives in the Americas and elsewhere, in a phenomenon universally abhorred as racism, the subordination of members-in-a-different-group is varied and stubbornly enduring. Simply proclaiming equality of all under the law, as a silver bullet solution, is naive, inadequate, and therefore wrong.

No illustration is more evident than the representation of women in government and their equal influence in power vis-à-vis men: How could there be a Democracy when the community of women who form about half of society and the citizenry, is not represented in government by their membership in, give or take, half the cabinet, half the legislature, half the judiciary, and half the administration, national and regional? Suffice it to see the increasingly negative reaction to photo opportunities in government summits across the globe which include an occasional colourful and lonely dress in an ocean of dullish grey suits with colour-shy ties.

Without gender parity *in* government, there is no Democracy. But even this presence may not be sufficient. Democracy acknowledges that women are equal not simply when they are entitled to vote like men, but when they are active in government in numbers and influence equal to men. The integrity of Democracy rests on women in power representing women and men through the sinews of power in society, rather than on women in society simply having exercised their right to vote or even sitting in government on a par in numbers with men.

Upon this simple illustration, I propose now to construct two language shifts for my proposed theory of Democracy.

The first shift is linguistic: taking up the constitutional discussion adumbrated in the previous chapter, the community of women is a *group*. In the world, and in the nation-state where universal suffrage rules, they form a distinct group within the larger community of citizens. To adjust the 1938 *Carolene Products* formula of the US Supreme Court, women are a discrete and insular group.

A second corollary shift results away from the terse fact of numbers. Women are a political minority, not a numerical one. One can keep the idea of women as 'minority' only if by minority we mean that they are a minority in power, or in society at large; and women are a minority in power because they have been, over millennia of recorded history, subordinate to men. This is also why the concept of subordinate group is preferable to the concept of subordinate minority.

I take the gender example to be for now largely accepted in terms of descriptive representation as formal representation in government, as opposed to the effective and efficient use of power, which is more difficult to pin down. A Black man in the United States better represents Black men against white domination only as a general rule, and this is true well into the twenty-first century for women the world over, Kurds in Turkey, or gay men in Central Africa. In all these situations, when one group is numerically dominant and in a position of historically subordinating other groups straitjacketed in immutable traits, Jane Mansbridge's conclusion strikes the right rule for the corresponding subordinate group: 'When such a trait is not represented descriptively for unjustifiable reasons (the group is unjustly subordinate), then, for as long as that subordination continues, that group should be descriptively represented in proportion to its presence in the population'.[9] Democracy builds on this conclusion as a *sine qua non*, a necessary but not sufficient one.

I mention here subordination of the individual-in-the-female-group because it is the simplest to consider on account of numbers. Other groups have different premises for subordination, with a wide gamut of subordinate groups that come from the cultural-national formation of the group and its dominance and domination, and with a more trying number in proportion

[9] The citation above, which I take from a rich correspondence in June 2024 with Jane Mansbridge, gives me the occasion to thank her again for her thorough criticism of the book, this chapter in particular. Its final form is radically different from the one she read as a reviewer, and I took to task examining her incisive remarks time and again and read some of the political science literature on representation, of which she is probably the leading scholar in the world. In 'Should blacks represent blacks and women represent women? A contingent "yes"', *The Journal of Politics*, 61, 1999, 628–57, she answers with a qualified yes based on efficacy (how far necessary representation improves the subordinated group's interests in effect). The approach is amplified in 'deliberative democracy' works by Anne Philips and Melissa Williams originally drawing on feminist studies: see for a summary of their extensive publications Anne Phillips and Hans Asenbaum, 'The Politics of presence revisited', *Democratic Theory*, 10, 2023, 80–9; and Melissa Williams, 'Représentation de groupe et démocratie délibérative: une alliance malaisée', *Philosophiques*, 29, 2002, 215–49. The focus of my work differs from theirs in two critical ways: in the first place, the important theoretical and empirical work achieved does not seem to have jelled yet into a radically novel theory of democracy. The other difference is my purposeful thinking within a more rigid constitutional framework, which forces the translation of anti-subordination remedies into legal/constitutional rights.

to the population than a fifty-fifty gender divide. I propose next to seek a common substratum for subordination beyond the immense variety of subordinated groups.

Subordination

If the government does not represent the *group* of 'boy scouts', or 'engineers', or 'daily commuters', or 'bingo-players', or 'mass attenders', or 'Phd-holders', in proportion to their numbers in society, there is no reason to be alarmed. In a Prévert-like taxonomy, nuns, bird-watchers, and movie-goers are off the national representation map.[10] They are not perceived as subordinate, nor do they perceive themselves as subordinate to claim their right to be represented in government. 'Pederasts' and 'convicts' have no claim either, because there are reasons aplenty in law and in fact for their criminal status to stand against a claim for their representation in government in the first place. The question does simply not arise. Nor is size important. Regardless of its vast membership, the 'football-attending group' of millions of fans, a sizeable community in several countries, does not qualify. Sport-engaged crowds are not groups in a situation of subordination.[11]

Subordination of the group is key then, and defining subordination requires a more precise consideration. Subordination is never context- or history-free. One must qualify subordination with the elusive and changing verdict of history. Subordination is man-made and must be human-unmade.

[10] For the non-French reader, randomness in groups is charmingly conveyed in Jacques Prévert, 'Tentative de description d'un dîner de têtes à Paris-France' (*Paroles*, 1947), cited here in *Œuvres Complètes*, Gallimard: Pléiade 1992, vol.1, 3–12, with two sets of absurd inventories of groups brought together only in the imagination of the poet: 'Ceux qui pieusement/Ceux qui copieusement/Ceux qui tricolorent ...', at 3–4, and 'ceux qui écaillent le poisson/ceux qui mangent la mauvaise viande/ceux qui fabriquent les épingles à cheveux ...', at 11–12. I take the 'Prévert' random imagery from Robert Fossaert.

[11] Guillaume Tusseau noted that this statement is 'not evident at all. Many small-scale groups lament that their views are simply ignored. See the vegan, bikers, nudists, etc.' I would add that the logic of his remark even poses a problem for larger-scale groups, such as 'bachelors', who suffer fiscally and socially compared to married couples. Yet a first answer is that these groups tend to be represented 'naturally', randomly, in a national government. More importantly, these groups do not vie for representation in order to protect their interests. They operate more as a lobby, an interest group, than as a historically subordinate group which, as we shall see next, bears immutable traits which also prevent an exit from the group, and less compellingly for Democracy, an entry to the group.

It always bears a complex genealogy as a social construct, with *longue durée* attested in some cases, and exceptions which confirm the rule in others.

The intensity of subordination also varies. In the time immemorial subordination of women, the iteration goes from their confinement to private spaces, to their exclusion from the vote, to their slow rise in assuming governmental responsibilities, on to full parity in power, which is for Democracy the inevitable outcome of the end of subordination. The common denominator is the varying historical context of the subordination exercised over them by the ruling male gender group.

Subordination weighs occasionally to disturb the balance on the opposite side. In a country emerging from a long and bloody fight against colonialism or apartheid, the individual-in-the-Black- or -brown-group is likely to emerge as a top-government representative to the exclusion of whites. In Africa, the Middle East and the Indian subcontinent, in Asia generally, the exclusion of Whites from government does not disturb the democratic legitimacy of the freed society so long as exclusion does not last beyond a certain amount of time. A striking example of the importance of context is that of a country defeated after a just war. Its society cannot expect proper democratic inclusion immediately, not only because of a host of complications tied to the war aftermath, but because a limited period of domination justifies actions such as de-Nazification, which also meant in that case a rejection of a white, allegedly blue-blooded physical type, as opposed to Jews or Romas. As the spectre of defeat vanishes, subordination starts withering, in the Nazi case because of the obvious democratic path of Western Germany after the Second World War.

We come now to the harder core of what may be used to define a subordinated group.

A defining trait of the discrete nature of the group qua minority is its fixed nature, its immutability. Immutability means 'no exit'. Fixed traits mean that the individual-in-that-group cannot abandon it. Immutability is also context-sensitive, but subordination trumps immutability. No subordination, no need to ask if the trait is fixed or changeable. The reverse is not true, for immutability of trait does not necessarily undermine Democracy in the absence of subordination. All subordinated groups in society must be represented in government. Not all groups sharing immutable traits must. For all groups, the test of immutability comes second to the test of subordination.

What are the fixed traits that prevent a group from being exited by those who share them? What is a group with no exit? In a random taxonomy, individuals who cannot easily exit their group are, pell-mell, females, males, homosexuals, Iraqi Shiʿis, Chinese Christians, blue-eyed individuals, Blacks, Whites, tall people, French speakers, California-born Americans, Inca descendants, people disabled in one leg, drug addicts, property-owners, slum dwellers, the poor, factory workers, etc. There is a long list under 'etc.'

Is a group which a member cannot *exit* the same as a group where one cannot *enter*? One rarely thinks of this reverse aspect of the exit, because the 'can enter' test is less discriminatory than the 'can exit' trait. The distinction complicates matters, but it is not decisive. In one of the examples below, 'the French-speaker' is a category which can be entered but can hardly be exited.

To further clarify the definition of a subordinate group with no enter and no exit, let me now bring together the random Prévert-like lists above:

> Nuns, birdwatchers, movie-goers, boy scouts, engineers, daily commuters, bingo-players, mass attenders, Phd-holders, females, males, homosexuals, Iraqi Shiʿis, Chinese Christians, blue-eyed individuals, Blacks, Whites, tall people, French speakers, California-born Americans, Inca descendants, one-leg disabled, drug addicts, property-owners, factory workers, slum dwellers, the poor.[12]

Let us arrange this list, also randomly, in alphabetical order, then proceed on its basis to a more systematic theory of Democracy. In the groups below, necessary representation in government on a proportional basis is contingent on Yes in subordination and in immutability, with immutability generally reinforced by both N for 'can exit' and N for 'can enter' sub-characterisations.

There may also be different types of exits, and one should approach the whole matrix with an assessment beyond rare or meaningless singularities in

[12] This list is mine, constructed in a haphazard way, and the reader will easily adjust the country context of some of these groups. Subordination in some cases can easily be gainsaid by scholars with a sharper expertise than mine. I know for instance that members of the Falung religious group are persecuted in China, I am less certain that Chinese Christians (or Christian Chinese) are. Uighurs and Tibetans obviously belong to historically subordinate groups. In contrasting contexts, Blacks remain historically subordinate in the Americas but not in Black Africa, and Chinese Christians are meant as Christians in China not Chinese Christians in the United States. Also, I understand that the use of 'gay' might be preferred to 'homosexuals'.

any one group. Immutability, long considered incontrovertible in gender binary groups, is no longer fully true in crossing the physiological divide. One is entitled to single out one or the other counterexample, but a woman cannot usually be a man and vice-versa. A 'yellow' or 'Black' man cannot be 'white'. Historically, one could change one's gender in twenty-first century clinics or seek to 'pass' for what the colour of her skin is not. 'Passing' is now universally condemned and/or ignored. Changing one's gender remains an unusual exit; it usually moves in the group representation to one or the other side of the gender divide. In both cases, passing and gender-changing remain, for now at least, a rare occurrence.

In Table 13.1, I added asterisks for only six groups that require further comment. Three of them (poor, slumdwellers and factory workers) are groups whose subordination is determined economically. I discuss them in the Critique section below. The other three, convicts, drug-addicts and pederasts, are not entitled to be represented in government for obvious reasons, which add to their entry into their group as a consequence of their actions superseding their inability to exit.

As for a gender-less individual, or the individual in a particular sexual group, a commonsense perspective is also required. The government may not discriminate against those who call themselves 'queer' or 'Q', and discrimination is a negative concept which is acknowledged as part of any basic right. But Democracy is a positive, active expression of power in group representation, so the question is whether the government composition needs to include Qs? If Qs appear as an open object of exclusion, no doubt. Yet the issue cannot rise to a serious problem at the level of national representation so long as the number of queers or hermaphrodites remains infinitesimal, and Qs and hermaphrodites benefit from their being part of the larger historically subordinate and fixed LGBT group. For Qs, representation in government includes him or her (or it or they) in the LGBTQIA2S+ group taken as a whole. Queers, as one component of the ever more extensive acronym, are better seen within a larger group which includes gay men or women whose historical subordination must be remedied by their appropriate representation in government.

For the physically disabled group, though perhaps not for the mentally disabled, members must also be represented in government in rough

Table 13.1 Democracy in Prévert-style random groups

Group	Historically Subordinate	Trait Immutable	Can Exit	Can Enter	Result: is effective representation necessary for Democracy?
Bingo players	N	N	Y	Y	N
Birdwatchers	N	N	Y	Y	N
Blacks	Y	Y	N	N	Y
Blue eyed	N	Y	N	N	N
Boy scouts	N	N	Y	Y	N
California born	N	Y	N	N	N
Chinese Christians	N	Y	N	N	N
Convicts	Y	N	N	Y	N*
Daily commuters	N	N	Y	Y	N
Drug addicts	Y	N	N	Y	N*
Engineers	N	N	Y	Y	N
Factory workers	Y	N	N	Y	N*
Females	Y	Y	N	N	Y
Football fans	N	N	Y	Y	N
French speakers	N	N	N	Y	N
Homosexuals	Y	Y	N	Y	Y
Inca descendants	Y	Y	N	N	Y
Iraqi Shi'is	Y	Y	N	N	Y
Males	N	Y	N	N	N
Mass attenders	N	N	Y	Y	N
Movie-goers	N	N	Y	Y	N
Nuns	N	N	Y	Y	N
One-leg disabled	Y	Y	N	Y	Y
Pederasts	Y	N	N	Y	N*
Phd-holders	N	N	N	Y	N
Poor	Y	N	Y	Y	N*
Property-owners	N	N	Y	Y	N
Slum dwellers	Y	N	N	Y	N*
Queers	Y	Y	N	Y	Y
Tall	N	Y	N	N	N
Whites	N	Y	N	N	N

proportion to their size in the country.[13] This is also the case for 'the one-leg disabled' group. Approximation requires, in the same vein as the discussion

[13] The inclusion of the physically disabled as opposed to the mentally disabled group in representation in government for obvious reasons I leave the reader to consider, although the exercise after Michel Foucault is not as straightforward as one may think. This is also true for the convict category.

of the Queer group, to include them in the larger subset, in this case of the physically disabled. Commonsense also helps dispel such singularities as mixed groups and discrete traits. I discuss this briefly in the section below on intersectionality.

Skin colour and religious membership, more ponderously, come with variations that have suffered in history from massive and cruel subordination. Being a one eighth, half, or third Black or white person, carried different degrees of subordination under legal systems as distinct as those of American and Islamic law. We have also seen that religious group membership includes members who are agnostic or atheist. The agnostic or atheist in the Middle East-type countries can neither enter nor exit his religious group. A Sunni, a Jew or a 'Alawi cannot convert away to the inexistent agnostic or atheist category in communal-religious countries.

It is helpful for the theory to consider the contrastive example of regional identity because it has long been solved in most countries. When a large city or region is persistently missing in adequate government membership, the problem is certain to arise. One cannot have in a Democracy a French government where Paris-originating membership is enduringly overrepresented, and Lyon-originating membership systematically unrepresented. In a federal system, the overrepresentation of smaller states in the upper house should not obscure the reason for this *numerus clausus* stopgap. This regards only the legislative level of representation. On the executive level, over a certain span of time, alarm bells will ring if California or Bavaria residents are not represented in the Washington or Berlin cabinet, and such unDemocratic oddities must be corrected. The reason why the problem does not generally arise – although it did of course for US Southern States long after the Civil War, in contrast for instance to East Germany after reunification – is because the proper proportional representation has been consciously or intuitively incorporated in most countries. And when a national group's necessary national representation is ignored in multi-national countries, there is inevitably a problem. Federalism might dent the subordination, but it cannot resolve the problem at its core.

Consider now the argument of mirroring *ad absurdum*: The list above includes the individual-in-the-blue-eyed-group. As a factual matter, several countries can be divided into citizens who have coloured eyes and citizens who have dark eyes. It makes no sense to check whether their government mirrors the coloured- or blue-eyed citizens. The logic is similar for tall and short people. The case sounds absurd because fixity of traits is trumped by the lack of subordination.

The situation would require closer scrutiny if it turns out that blue-eyed or tall people systematically stand at a significantly higher representation in power than their counterparts. This is an improbable question, because scrutiny will not hold for blue eyes, shoe size, or thickness of eyebrow. Nevertheless, should the situation arise as a persistent trait of skewed representation, brown-eyed or short people would be right to question their government in its failure to represent them under this, defining test of Democracy.

We can see now why Chiha's conception of government as one of associated religious groups provides the basis of a new theory of Democracy. The necessary representation of a subordinated group in government proportionate to its numbers extends beyond religious segmentation or sectarian identity. Necessary representation in Democracy is valid for all subordinated groups in proportion to their numbers. And when that representation endures, the result is the group's historical subordination turning slowly into as much of a non-issue as that of the blue and brown eyed groups.

This universalisation of the theory would no doubt surprise Chiha, who did not see fit to extend it to Western societies, on account of their full equality for the citizen in his pure, naked, Rawlsian-Kantian veil of ignorance individuality. This is because Chiha did not consider the constitutional scene beyond religious sects, the hallmark of Lebanon and the Middle East.

I sought to free the theory from the Lebanese communities' constraint and extend it to other subordinated categories. I propose therefore for my theory of Democracy to be formulated in the shape of a two-level rule: Individuals in a persistently subordinate group are entitled to be present in government commensurately to their numbers in society as a *sine qua non*. At a second level, such representation must not be simply formal; it needs to be effective to lessen and eventually remove the subordination. The levels appear generally in chronological order, but this is not always the case.

This approach adds a further leg to the Lincoln paean, where democracy is government of, by, and for the people: Democracy requires government to look *like* the people by letting in members of the subordinated groups, in an arithmetical *sine qua non* commensurability, together with an intensity and effectiveness to be gauged in a perspective that ends the concerned groups' subordination.

Critique

Let me now consider a set of critical arguments of the theory, divided into topics ranging from the easiest to the hardest.

Subordination, domination, exploitation, hegemony

The concept of 'subordination' which is privileged in my proposed theory of Democracy differs in connotation and nuance from various similar concepts over the past two centuries. Eighteenth-nineteenth century Western societies used domination and exploitation rather than subordination. Domination is associated with the position of the master (*dominus*) in the heyday of slavery and colonialism. In the twentieth century, the concept of hegemony became common in Gramsci-like circles, but the retreat of Marxist theory left the road open to the more benign-sounding 'discrimination'. Discrimination sounds less aggressive and responds to the practice of governments after voting has become universal. Discrimination operates laterally with groups being formally unequal; subordination addresses a vertical order. Domination and discrimination tend to be binary; subordination operates on several levels with varying intensities.

Subordination can also be subsumed under the general canopy of (in)justice and (un)fairness, but it loses its analytical edge when relegated to such generality. Whatever the nuances, it may not be worth parsing too bright a line between hegemony, domination, discrimination, and subordination. All do the job of characterising unDemocratic society.

Within subordination and its sisters, there is a frequent definitional overlap. All these concepts, mostly sociological and historical, then adjusted to political philosophy and constitutional theory, carry with them a rich and perceptive scholarship. There is no gainsaying their convergence on the more abstract level, and their overlap is equally undeniable. The intellectual scene adds sophisticated enquiries of shared and conflicting identities, threshold and descriptive representation in government, as well as government's inclusivity or diversity. There is no need for the overall theory to parse here an immense variety of analytical and empirical nuances.

Nor is there subordination without members-of-a-subordinating group forcing members-of-a-subordinated group's absence from government. Group identity without self-identification is hard to conceive, and a subordinate group usually requires the presence of a competing group in a negative, domineering, subordinating projection. The construction of groups, ergo their contextuality, raises the group members' self-consciousness, in a tradition which goes back at least to Hegel in the *Phenomenology*'s master-slave dialectic.

Giving due attention to all the nuances entailed by each category or concept would require at least a large tome straddling large fields and disciplines. It is not worth the trouble for the purpose of the present argument of Democracy. With slight adjustments, these terms are interchangeable.

Intersectionality

Society is far more complex than the naked individual v. the member of one specific group. Society mixes groups, pays attention to some more than others, and moves on a thousand planes. Groups operate at several levels in their relation to each other and individuals belong to many groups. Intersectionality, which is concerned with a person belonging to several subordinated groups, does not undermine the proposed theory of Democracy, as I will now discuss.

Intersectionality involves a multiplicity of memberships and identities, calling for a complex approach to ending subordination, and a calibrated response. Montesquieu answered the multiplicity in group membership with an elegant *pensée*:

> If I knew something that was useful to me and detrimental to my family, I would put it out of my mind. If I knew something useful to my family, and not to my country, I would seek to forget it. If I knew something useful to my country and detrimental to Europe, or useful to Europe and detrimental to humankind, I would regard it as a crime.[14]

[14] 'Si je savais quelque chose qui me fût utile et qui fût préjudiciable à ma famille, je le rejetterais de mon esprit. Si je savais quelque chose utile à ma famille, et qui ne le fût pas à ma patrie, je chercherais à l'oublier. Si je savais quelque chose utile à ma patrie, et qui fût préjudiciable à l'Europe, ou bien qui fût utile à l'Europe et préjudiciable au Genre humain, je la regarderais comme un crime'. Montesquieu, *Pensées* (posthumous, ca 1750), cited e.g. in Robert Derathé, 'La Philosophie

Montesquieu's tiering remains appealing: humanity, Europe, France, family, individual, even if one might quarrel with the precedence of one or the other identity as history unfolds in the longer *durée*. It is insufficient in two respects.

If one is French in the year 2000, none of the five categories he mentions are in a situation of historical subordination. But in the five categories chosen, there is no mention of the French Breton, and Montesquieu's formula breaks down in the case of the individual-in-the-Breton-group in eighteenth century France, whose subordination as Breton opposes his French- or Europeanness. For members of the historically subordinate group of Basques in twentieth century Spain (and in twentieth century France differently, with less subordination), or Kurds in twenty-first century Turkey and Iraq, Montesquieu's formula does not work. Historical subordination undergirds the legitimacy of Basques and Kurds standing up as Basques or Kurds against being forced into being Spanish or Turkish.

The limits of Montesquieu's 'solution' are not only historical. Montesquieu's *pensée* is for the Enlightenment which flattens citizenry into equal individuals. Democracy as a system arises in the assessment of government in the nation-state context of membership in a subordinate group vis-à-vis membership in the ruling group, not from the *honnête homme* of the eighteenth century who places his manifold allegiances on the mythical plane of humanity as citizenship.

The corresponding answer to the individual standing at an intersection of unequally dominated sub-groups is simple. A gay black woman in most Western countries is entitled in a Democracy to the parity mirror of her gender in government, a less considered mirroring of her skin colour, and a likely lesser mirroring of her homosexuality. A theory of Democracy is not particularly affected by these variations. It just requires some calibration.

Tokenism

Much has been written about tokenism or the lack of active representation of their group by elected members-of-such-subordinated-group. A black

des lumières en France: Raison et modération selon Montesquieu', *Revue Internationale de Philosophie*, 21, 1952, 275–93, at 291; and in Sélim Abou, *Les Libertés*, Beirut: Les Presses de l'Université Saint-Joseph 2003, 30.

congressman might cater, or not, to his black constituency; a male minister may be more attentive to the interests of the female population than a female minister. Again, the easy example is that of gender. The history of political events is replete with several token instances of female leadership, from Hatshepsut to Margaret Thatcher, and of admirable white Americans who stood up in great courage against the racist debasing of their government.

Tokenism does not fundamentally disturb the theory of Democracy for three reasons.

The first is simple enough. Democracy absorbs tokenism by common sense. In the absence of a solid pattern where representation in government is also representation in power, token representation is a persisting anomaly that hides the forest by the trees. The odd-woman as prime minister or pharaoh, the odd-Black-man as president of the United States are just that: oddities. An occasional exception simply confirms the rule. The limited effect of tokenism on the theory of Democracy does not mean that the absence of a woman president in Washington or in Paris is not a persistent failure of French or American democracy over respectively a century- or two centuries-plus.

A more cogent reason, which is related to the tokenisms just described, goes to the heart of the theory of Democracy by combining the concept of *glass-ceiling* with *intendance*. I explain:

With a glass-ceiling, individuals-in-the-subordinated-group are prevented from reaching further up the social rung, defined primarily in my theory by government membership. Democracy responds by breaking multiple glass-ceilings in public office. The glass-ceiling emerges not only at the top tier of governance; it operates also at lower levels such as elected mayorships, governorates, and unelected public office further down in the administration. And public governance glass-ceilings are not the only type. The glass-ceiling in private governance, typically in large corporations as CEOs and on boards, requires a different approach to women or other groups in a situation of structural subordination, even if their subordination is evident. But governing a country is not the same as governing a company, and adjustments are necessary to avoid the fight of tokenism turning into the destruction of merit.

A third answer to tokenism is *intendance*, as in Charles de Gaulle's famous quip, '*L'intendance suit*'. When a general orders his troops forward, food and other logistics follow, so one should not worry too much about their procurement. Islamic law has an analogous rule, *al-tabe' tabe'*, what follows follows.[15] Once the locomotive moves, the wagons do not have the choice to stay immobile. Representation at the top forms a template which reverberates at the lower rungs. Tokenism cannot last when Democracy is consistently active in the higher rungs of government.

Yet tokenism helps lay the groundwork for the expansion of the theory in two directions I have not discussed, and which are the two faces of the same reality.

One face is international. In the present study, Democracy is defined exclusively in the context of a circumscribed nation-state. There is no natural anchor for government representation of individuals-in-a-subordinate-group outside the national context. This does not prevent the theory from being integrated into the so-called 'best international practice' beyond the planet-wide solipsism of the nation-state. The clamor for a female UN Secretary-General has risen inexorably over three quarters of a century of the Organisation's establishment.

More importantly, the application of the theory domestically does not need to be restricted to the public ambit of government. The ideal of equal pay for equal work suffuses the gendered workplace in several countries, no matter whether the work is public or private. Equal pay at work is an evident illustration of Democracy in the private sphere, and various adjustments are needed for the myriad cases of subordination in the immense non-governmental civil society.

Poverty, exploitation, precarity

What of poverty? We left pending the discussion of the poor, slumdwellers and factory workers in Table 13.1 above.

In a Democracy, must a government mirror individuals-in-a-historically-subordinate-group that includes the tired, poor, huddled masses?

[15] De Gaulle denied in a televised interview that he ever said 'L'intendance suit', or even believed in it, during his 1965 presidential campaign. https://www.ina.fr/ina-eclaire-actu/video/i00012580/charles-de-gaulle-petite-phrase-l-intendance-suit. It is unfortunate that such a brilliant phrase remains author-less. The Islamic law rule can be found in the Ottoman Civil Code of 1876, Article 47.

The simple answer is no. The group described as 'poor' passes the test of subordination but fails the test of fixity. Poverty is not immutable. Even the test of subordination does not easily pass, because the category 'rich' is fluid, and because the rich does not necessarily subordinate the poor. A rich person does not sit in government because the poor person sits outside it.

There is a reading to poverty which is less benign. Despite the demise of communism, charitable Christians and scientific materialists (as Marxists were once called) continue to share a common left-leaning view of the great social divide as a duality between rich and poor. 'Let the poor come to me' and 'the need for the (poor) worker to force an end to his exploitation by the (rich) capitalist' encapsulate for Democracy a common presupposition: for both Jesus and Marx there are no poor unless there are rich, and in Marx's case, there is no subordination of a worker unless the owner of capital exploits him in his job.

Marx follows Rousseau here. Rousseau introduced the first well-known challenge to the concept of poverty. In a celebrated passage of his *Discourse on Inequality*, he ascribes inequality to the mythical first person in history who built a fence around a plot of land and made it his exclusive property.[16] The individual on the other side of the fence was no longer poor because he was a free-floating victim of fate; he was poor because he was the victim of the one who shut him out of the plot.

Marx as heir to Rousseau replaced the concept of poverty with the concept of exploitation. Rousseau's inequality between plot owner and the non-owning neighbour is reformulated by Marx as 'the exploitation of man by man'. In the large historical world scene drawn by Marx, the worker is the

16 'The first man who, having enclosed a piece of ground, bethought himself of saying "This is mine," and found people simple enough to believe him, was the real founder of civil society. From how many crimes, wars, and murders, from how many horrors and misfortunes might not any one have saved mankind, by pulling up the stakes, or filling up the ditch, and crying to his fellows: "Beware of listening to this impostor; you are undone if you once forget that the fruits of the earth belong to us all, and the earth itself to nobody".' ('Le premier qui, ayant enclos un terrain, s'avisa de dire: Ceci est à moi, et trouva des gens assez simples pour le croire, fut le vrai fondateur de la société civile. Que de crimes, de guerres, de meurtres, que de misères et d'horreurs n'eût point épargnés au genre humain celui qui, arrachant les pieux ou comblant le fossé, eût crié à ses semblables: Gardez-vous d'écouter cet imposteur; vous êtes perdus, si vous oubliez que les fruits sont à tous, et que la terre n'est à personne'. Rousseau, *Discours sur l'origine et les fondements de l'inégalité parmi les hommes* (1754), Part II, opening paragraph, Cole translation in English, 1913 (Wikisource).

quintessential individual-in-the-subordinate-group excluded from the means of production by the capitalist-in-the-ruling-group who owns these means of production. This is on the macro-level. On the micro-level, the worker is exploited by the capitalist wrenching away from his work a surplus-value on which the whole capitalist system is built.

In this world of inequality with two converging readings, one a charitable but inconsequential Christian view, the other a judgmental one based on capitalist exploitation, it is the author of *Capital* who provides the most accurate analytical tool for poverty to date. In his long and pell-mell disquisitions around *Capital* lies Marx's 'scientific discovery' of surplus value – *Mehrwert*, defined as the robbed portion of the worker's labor by the capitalist, and analysed *ad infinitum* to account for the subordination of man by man as class exploitation.[17] In Marx's analysis of his philosophy of history as 'scientific materialism', the ruling capitalist class exploits the-individual-in-the-subordinated-class, also known as the workers-proletariat. There is no exit for the exploited workforce outside an end of history where classes are abolished in favor of common, communist, property. Applied to our theory, the individual-in-the-economically-exploited-group requires Democracy to abolish that exploitation. Until then, the poor are trapped by a subordinating economic system from which there is exit only in some revolution to come, doing away with the struggle between a ruling class and its subordinated class or classes, and finally abolishing surplus value from the subordinated world of laboring human beings.

This is the key fracture of the reading of injustice, unfairness, and now subordination in the poverty/exploitation category, a reading which has divided political actors on the right-left fracture since the Atlantic Revolution. For the

[17] Of these studies, surplus value is defined in the first volume of Marx's *Capital* (1867) under the basic distinction between its absolute conception (extension of worker's labor time to generate profit for the capitalist) and relative form (increase in intensity and productivity of the worker's labor time) within the basic production process. The treatment of surplus value extends in the second, posthumous volume (1885) to the circulation process; and, in the third volume (1894) to a comprehensive mode of capitalist production that includes the three main forms of surplus value (profit, interest, rent) and its financial expression leading to a theory of crises under the concept of 'the tendency of the rate of profit to decline'. The fourth volume (*Theories of Surplus Value*, in three tomes in the English edition) is a historical critique of surplus value by earlier economists, especially Ricardo, who was the first to mention the concept. It consists, like the *Grundrisse* and the *Critique of Political Economy*, of Marx's research notebooks, many written before 1867. *Capital*, with surplus value in the mode of wealth production as its key discovery, consists of the ensemble of the above large volumes.

conservative, right-leaning democrat, even if subordination of the poor or the worker is admitted, exiting the group is possible. The poor/worker disposes of a reasonable enough exit, described as free, along with public education and corresponding assistance. The sundry social elevator opportunities available throughout a person's life provide the exit; to extirpate the poor, the slumd-weller or the factory worker from the group requires a bit of chance and a lot of hard work. This is facilitated, for the champions of capitalism, by their strong belief that the system delivers economic prosperity and a corresponding sense of happiness shared by the poor. After all, it is in times of economic crises and domestic insecurity that groups turn inwards and identity politics become the exclusive name of the political game.

For the socialist left-leaning democrat, the-individual-in-the-exploited-group stands in the political minority, and a government which keeps the large group of exploited individuals out of power fails the test of Democracy. Against the rosy picture generally associated with the conservative right, skeptics towards the benign nature of capitalism move the analytical needle to define poverty as a result of exploitation of the individual-in-the-slum, ghetto, or dilapidated neighbourhood, to which the twenty-first century adds the subordination of the individual-in-the-migration-group fleeing war and misery.

On balance, the objection of poverty/exploitation to the theory of Democracy does not undermine it. The poor/exploited can exit their group. The chances are slim for individuals in such groups to exit them, but they exist. Taxation is another common way to close the gap for those unable to exit the group. There are other options. I have suggested elsewhere replacing *ownership* as determinant of wealth by *precarity* as determinant of structural economic inequality to provide an arithmetical criterion for poverty.[18]

Trappings of the poor, slum-dwellers and factory workers – as in both being trapped and the dominant group's idiosyncrasies – elicit a second level of Democracy, much in the same way that the 'first generation' of human rights does not include the poor as a legally recognised group. This is the reason why Table 13.1 above adds an asterisk to the categories of poor, slum-dwellers and factory workers: to indicate a historically subordinate group which is provided

[18] Mallat, 'Précarité', in Mallat, *Boussole et Autres Journalismes*, Beirut: Bada2e3 2019, 253–6. (Calculation of precariousness as 'the marginal rate of the last dollar(s)'.)

with forms of exit. When the door is firmly shut and no exit from subordination turns into an iron rule, the result in the last column in Table 13.1 should be changed.

The tyranny of the majority

What if numbers in government correspond to the subordinated groups and change nothing because representation in government keeps subordination in place, since the minority by definition does not command enough votes in all branches of government to oppose the majority's will and interests?

Tyranny may be an excessive word for a majoritarian democracy, where physical violence inflicted by the government on the minority group rarely rises to what the word tyranny denotes. The tyranny of the majority is an oxymoron. But in a persistently subordinating government, which relies on its majoritarian position to stay at the helm and keep the minority groups subordinated, the risk of violence increases with the intensity and length of the deadlock. Tyranny may not be the right word, but it conveys the sense of systematic and enduring frustration by historically subordinate groups.

With this book's lengthy study of Lebanon in mind, I propose for ease of argument to subject the proposed theory of Democracy to a surface test of political and constitutional practice in three (almost) randomly selected countries. Two countries have a long-established democratic tradition, Canada and Switzerland. In the third country chosen, Iraq's struggling political system seeks its way to a stable, democratic, government with great pain. I am testing the theory here at an abstract level and exclude the benefit of federalism, which operates in all three countries to significantly attenuate the dominance of a group in the territories where a national minority may be numerically majoritarian.

Using the subset of the Prévert-like categories in Table 13.1 with a Y in the last column (effective representation in government is necessary to redress subordination), we have Blacks, Female, Homosexuals, Inca descendants, Iraqi Shi'is, One-leg disabled and Queers. Contextuality helps discard Inca descendants and Iraqi Shi'is in Canada and Switzerland.

In Canada, in a rough approximation, Blacks form a small group compared to non-Blacks, Females are at numerical parity with the Male group,

Homosexuals form a small group compared to 'Straight', and Queers an even smaller group, which is better considered together with Homosexuals within the more meaningful group of LGBT+. In Canada, historically subordinated groups include also, noticeably, Native Canadians[19] and French-speakers.[20] A mixture of majoritarian dominance and persistent subordination accompanies their history in Canada through most of the last century. We add therefore to the list Native Canadians and French-speakers, both minority groups number-wise, both of meaningful size and historical salience in Canadian society in terms of subordination.

Democracy means that the Canadian government in all its branches is Democratic only if it generally reflects the corresponding numbers of each historically subordinate group in society. It may not matter that subordination for the Canadian Native is profoundly different from the subordination of the Canadian Québecois French, or of the subordination of the Canadian Female. There will be natural political offsets within the central government, with a distribution of power over different portfolios, and over positions in other branches and within the Canadian administration. While the country continues to operate under majoritarian rule, the political game fractures the system into government and opposition, both adhering to the proportional representation rule as a constitutional requirement. If the arrangement does not work, it will be because the majority exercises its exclusion or subordination power systematically on the basis of its numerical dominance in the voting booth.

Let me now consider Iraq, and the random categories just applied to Canada: Blacks, Females, Homosexuals, Inca descendants, Iraqi Shi'is, One-leg disabled and Queers. Once more, contextuality disposes of Blacks, not a discrete Iraqi group, and Inca descendants. In contrast, Iraqi Shi'is provide a typical example of historical subordination. Iraq has been dominated since the eleventh Buyid century by Sunni rulers, with Shi'is a subordinated group. In the modern state of Iraq following the collapse of Ottoman Sunni rule,

19 According to the 2021 Census on Wikipedia 'Demographics of Canada' entry, the 'Indigenous people' tab puts them at 5 pc of the overall population.

20 2024 statistics at: https://www.canada.ca/en/canadian-heritage/services/official-languages-bilingualism/publications/statistics.html, with 76 per cent English speakers, 22 per cent French speakers, and 18 per cent bilingual. French Canadians are to be considered in the Table with a Y in the last column rather than an N for most other countries in the world, including France.

Shiʿis continued to be treated as a subordinate group under the Monarchy. As the institutions of the new state developed, Iraqi Shiʿis were increasingly brought into the government, while a process of ethnolysis was developing in the society at large. The large *fresque* of Hanna Batatu on Iraq through most of the twentieth century remains the reference work for continued political subordination of the community, its slow but steadily increasing representation in government, and signs of ethnolysis removing the inter-marriage stigma in the 1950s.[21] The next period saw the Monarchy's frail institutions collapse under successive coups, the rise of sectarian subordination to extreme proportions since the mid-1960s, culminating in large-scale massacres in the second half of the twentieth century.

Iraq is composed of salient religious groups, like Lebanon and most of the Middle East, except that it also contemplates another major fracture which is linguistic/ethnic/national. As a rule of thumb estimate on which distribution of power is based, the country is roughly composed of 60 per cent Shiʿis (religion), 20 per cent Sunnis (religion), and 20 per cent Kurdish (language/ethnicity), and includes smaller religious and ethnic communities such as Turkmen (language/ethnicity) or Sabeans (religion). Shiʿis as a linguistic-national group are Arab, and so are the 20 per cent Sunnis. Kurds are predominantly Sunni, but they operate as group mostly on the basis of their distinct language and ethnicity, and, from their perspective, a right to their own national homeland.

When intense subordination of Shiʿis and Kurds came to an abrupt end with the US invasion of the country in 2003, the very first question for the new government was the representation of these groups as a way out of their historical subordination, and the repositioning of all the other communities, including the previously dominant Arab Sunni group. When an interim government was formed in 2003, there was no option but for membership to correspond to the social composition of all Iraqi groups, including the three main

[21] Hanna Batatu, *The Old Social Classes and the Revolutionary Movements of Iraq*, Princeton: Princeton University Press 1978. The figures in next paragraph on population breakdown into religious and national categories are taken from Batatu, but the number of Shiʿis is likely be now much larger in proportion to the other groups in the population at large. When a census was finally carried out twenty years after the end of the old regime, it did not include the religious denomination of the citizens.

ones. We encountered briefly the 'Governing Council' in a previous chapter. During the year or so of its fleeting existence, it was composed of twenty-five members, 13 of whom Shi'i, five Sunni, and five Kurds, with two members representing smaller communities. The Council also included an ingenious mechanism of rotation in the presidency on a monthly basis.

The early Iraqi transitional government was Democratic in so far as the subordination of all religious and ethnic groups was remedied by its composition. However, only three members of the Governing Council were women, and government failed the Democratic test since parity is required to end gender subordination. Similarly, the absence of Iraqi homosexuals or physically handicapped (the latter considering the toll on the population that three successive major wars on previously able-bodied men, making the 'One-leg disabled' group meaningful under a larger physically disabled or handicapped category), was and remains a failure of Democracy.

The Governing Council was soon replaced by a government in the parliamentarian tradition. The fleeting success of Iraqi Democracy at the religious-ethnic level was jettisoned by the inability of elections to produce a government that could consecrate the Governing Council experience. Soon a transitional, then a final constitution were adopted, with two features of relevance to Democracy: a 25 per cent quota for women in Parliament, and a distribution of the top three positions in the State in a rigid system which endures. The prime minister is the head of the executive, going by silent agreement to Shi'is; a presidency of the state who has some residual executive powers, going to Kurds; and a speakership with relative powers over Parliament going to Sunnis. This is a replica of the Lebanese model. Like Lebanon, the top three positions in government are not explicitly assigned to the three Iraqi groups. Not surprisingly, Iraq suffers from structural ungovernability, with persistent deadlocks at every important constitutional turn.

One hurdle for the theory has emerged in full light: electoral laws can hardly be fashioned to serve Democracy. Despite the fact that the law includes the gender quota, the numerical breakdown of the population is such that the large number of Shi'i voters in the country translates into their dominance over the cabinet. Since Parliament needs to be elected on the basis of the one-person, one-vote principle, it inevitably reflects the larger number of Iraqi

Shiʿis. As proven in the Lebanese case over a full century, the electoral law plays havoc with citizens from the perspective of equality. It poses a quandary for Democracy, eluding a satisfactory electoral arrangement.

Let me now turn to the Swiss constitutional system, in large part because of its signal success in accommodating linguistic-ethnic (or linguistic-national) groups over a long period of time.

Switzerland is composed of three main communities divided by language and related ethnicity, German (74 per cent) Italian, French (20 per cent) and Italian (4 per cent), in addition to the Romanches (1 per cent).[22] Religion has acted historically as an important divide that has all but disappeared over time. Ethnicity and language are muted politically for several reasons, mostly because of territorial federalism, which allows compact communities to run their respective cantons without other ethnic/linguistic interference. The dominant number of Germans in the country is checked by the federal arrangements and the multiplicity of speakers of a language other than their mother tongue, but government membership is mostly a function of the consensual/consociational system. In Switzerland, executive power vests mainly in the Federation Council, a seven-member cabinet which is elected by the Federal Assembly, itself composed of two chambers, one national and the other cantonal. Under the Constitution, the composition of the Federation Council must take into account linguistic and regional groups.[23] This is an important recognition which translates well in the key executive institution and constitutionalises a reality prevailing since the mid-1850s without being derailed by electoral laws. In contrast, gender inclusion took a long time to reach parity in the Federation Council, the first time as late as 2010.

This sampling of cases for the adequacy of the theory of Democracy leaves us with a hard conclusion concerning electoral laws. In Canada the numerical superiority of White and English-speaking groups is increasingly adjusted to the interests and demands of numerically smaller subordinate groups; in Iraq only the brief life of the Governing Council allowed all groups a real say in

[22] https://www.about.ch/statistics/index.html

[23] Swiss Constitution, Art. 175.4 (Amendment in 1999): 'Les diverses régions et les communautés linguistiques doivent être équitablement représentées au Conseil fédéral'. Chiha found in the Swiss model a vindication of the Lebanese Constitution, minus the stigma of religion, see Ch. 10, section 'The Swiss example'.

government; and in Switzerland a stable system with a Federation Council is based on the constitution's request for 'equitable' distribution between the various regions and the linguistic communities. In all three cases, elections are not allowed to undermine the system.

Electoral laws constitute the most difficult obstacle to Democracy. They have a rightfully central impact on the distribution of power in the legislative branch but cannot in and by themselves secure adequate representation in the executive branch, in the judiciary, or in the administration. They need to be dampened, bypassed, even ignored, together with the majority they produce, for Democracy to work.

In this trying section for the critique of Democracy, electoral laws need to be set aside to the extent that they do not translate into a government that prevents the majority from perpetuating the historical subordination of one or the other minority group in the country. But ignoring the results of an electoral law is easier said than done, and flies in the face of the basic understanding of any democracy. Here democracy and Democracy are at their greatest odds. I prefer to preserve the latter, for the failure of Democracy means that if its proportional participation in government does not end the subordination of a group, there is little recourse left to its subordinated members but the street.

Government paralysis

Ungovernability is the converse problem of the tyranny of the majority. There is no magic formula to the paralysis of government in communal countries. Once Democracy as a system catering to historically subordinate groups is conceived as a form of separation of powers, a combination of remedies must be constantly sought and reimagined to prevent or lessen the risk of the country becoming ungovernable.

Throughout this book, a central problem of communitarianism has been identified as the paralysis of government. When leaders of a sizeable group choose to block governance, the system facilitates their task. Once a community is recognised constitutionally, it rises in status to become an inescapable partner in government, with the risk that governmental action against the group's interests undermines the government for months on end. The groups' conflicting interests must constantly align to prevent ungovernability, which explains why communalism is also called concordance.

Here also the size of the community matters. When one group is numerically dominant, for instance the English-speaking group in Canada or the German group in Switzerland, a condition for governability is constant attention to the smaller, historically subordinated group in addition to proportional representation in government. In time, forms of compromise may develop. In Switzerland, a balance between the communities was found early. A strong territorial federalism with a large leeway given to a multiplicity of cantons as opposed to a large uniform language-based territory in a federated State, combines with sacrifices in representation by the numerical majority. For instance, in the Federation Council more French and Italian Swiss councilors are appointed than their respective size warrants. In a country where several official languages are spoken, multilingualism helps, although it is never decisive. In Canada, a lasting balance was not found before the end of the twentieth century. In Iraq and Lebanon, the search out of paralysis continues.

One important factor to prevent ungovernability is the multiplication of group representation, in particular of gender and region. Federalism helps, as does the soothing oversight role played by the courts. Even more important is membership in a political group operating nationally to transcend the immutable traits of historically subordinate groups.

Still, nation-wide parties are hemmed in by the electoral system, and they are not always capable of smoothing out the political process because groups are also consciously defending their cohesion on the basis of their immutable traits, which they rightly consider as an enrichment to the rest of society. They often do not wish to see these characteristics melt in the larger national pot.

In countries like Lebanon and Iraq, where a national political substratum has been particularly difficult to construct precisely because of the dominance of the fixed traits of religious groups (Lebanon) and of religious and linguistic groups (Iraq), compromise is more difficult because the political scene continues to be shorn of such national groupings as developed over time in Switzerland and Canada. We have seen that the electoral law in both Lebanon and Iraq encourages groups to cohere in ways that are detrimental to the nation. What makes the compromise harder is when groups change in size, upsetting concordance further. This explains the extreme sensitivity of any new nation-wide census, which exposes changes away from a compromise previously reached on the basis of now-antiquated numbers.

To sum up: Replacing subordination by hegemony, domination, exploitation, marginalisation and other expressions of inequality alters little the theory of Democracy overall. Tokenism does not undermine the principle of necessary representation of historically subordinate groups, it just draws attention to the risk of representation being shorn of effectiveness. Tokenism finds its response in ignoring the glitz of the odd female prime minister and the Black US president as panacea, breaking all glass ceilings, and making sure that the wagons are tied to the locomotive where real power lies.

In the consideration of poverty, or exploitation, and more generally of economic inequality, the misery cage stands short of the necessary representation of the poor in government as members of a historically subordinate group, since subordination is premised on the absence of exit which is belied by the proverbial *ascenseur social*. When upward mobility fails structurally, the group defined by poverty – more accurately by precariousness – needs to be represented in government for Democracy to be achieved. However, proportional representation in government makes no sense for the categories of poor or slum-dwellers, less perhaps for the group of factory workers. In the gamut of subordinated groups, economic exploitation or marginalisation requires its own sophisticated set of remedies.

More importantly, the need to invent an appropriate remedy other than impossible or vacuous proportionate representation of the poor in government underlines the need for a multiplicity of measures to address the specific nature of the historical subordination of any particular group. Ending the subordination of women requires tools that have little in common with ending the subordination of gays or slum-dwellers.

The final two sections of the Critique are dour, but I believe they do not undermine my proposed redefinition of democracy. I have in previous chapters considered several mechanisms to open constitutional windows onto the democratic system.[24] If implemented, they are likely to attenuate the strictures of communalism. In deep communal crises resulting from the tyranny of the majority or government paralysis, they may not be sufficient.

[24] See in particular the section in Ch. 11 on 'Constitutional windows out of communalism'.

Should the tyranny of a majority continue despite the application of a proportional system to secure representation in government, the only way for the subordinated group to find justice must be sought outside the normal institutional process. If the ensuing confrontation is sustainably nonviolent, the tyranny of the majority may be checked. If not, and the expression of nonviolently channeled anger fails, Democracy needs to be redefined again.

Conversely, should governance be systematically paralysed by groups in power refusing to compromise, while recourse to elections maintains and reproduces a stifling status quo, novel mechanisms should be devised, in the courts or elsewhere, to overcome paralysis.

Conclusion

In simple, practical form, a member of a historically subordinate group has the right to be adequately represented in government. Democracy in any country is fulfilled only when individuals in subordinate groups which they cannot exit are included in government representation proportionately to the size of the group. Such representation is a *sine qua non*. It is not sufficient if subordination persists.

In more abstract terms: in a nation-state of historically subordinate groups with no exit, Democracy is achieved only when the individual-in-the-subordinated-x-group(s) is represented in government with sufficient power obtaining from such participation to end the group's subordination.

14

Epilogue

But remember that perfection cannot be attained in a day.[1]

Nothing is more exhilarating than the work on archival material and untapped texts, especially when they deal with the founding social contract of a country. The Chiha archive will no doubt trigger a new *élan* in political, constitutional, and historical scholarship in and around Lebanon. The constitutional material now available will be perused again with new perspectives, other avenues, and fresh minds. It is bound to be enriched by more research in national and international archives and private papers, and by a closer reading of the contemporaneous press.

As the departure point of modern Lebanese history, the notables assembled in Mount Lebanon in 1697 triggered a new era of political consultations which took another hundred and fifty years to begin maturing in formal texts. What happened in Simqaniyya was unusual insofar as a group of notables would dare put forward the leader they wanted, and not simply receive an order from higher-up Ottoman officials to implement Istanbul's choice. This, in turn, calls for a better understanding of the change of dynasties under Ottoman rule in provincial areas, and the distinct Ottoman history of Lebanon in the vast Empire.

The next institutional breakthrough came with the consultative councils established by the founder of modern Egypt in regions which he conquered, the Levant in particular, in the decade starting in 1830. The earthquake occasioned by the French occupation of Egypt, enabling the tempestuous reign of

[1] The Editor, *The Eastern Times*, 9 March 1947. This was the last issue of the daily newspaper in English which Michel Chiha published, and the last editorial.

Muhammad 'Ali, conjures up historical and comparative perspectives across an immense geography between 1805 and 1848, from the Hijaz and Somalia in the South all the way to Greece in the North. Here also, the patchwork created by consultative councils in cities like Tripoli, Damascus and Beirut is merely adumbrated in the present work, and councils established elsewhere deserve to be compared in terms of composition and effectiveness. New vistas are wide open to historians and lawyers.

The whole scene of Middle Eastern constitutionalism must be revisited with the tools of institutional control and relays which the founder of modern Egypt created in the vast territories he conquered, and which he was bent on using had the European forces not interfered militarily, time and again, to defeat his ambitions. In the constitutional history of the Middle East, scholarship had generally marked the Ottoman Tanzimat reforms since 1839, or the Tunisian charter of 1861, as the first regional experiments with modern constitutionalism. Surely this no longer holds, and one can confidently push prequels to governing *shura* councils established in the Levant in the 1830s all the way back to the 1829 Cairo Council. Minutes of the Council of Beirut have been preserved. I have used some of them, but the sources consulted are just the tip of the iceberg.

The period of the Mutasarrifiyya in Lebanon has received closer scholarly attention than other Ottoman-ruled regions in the second half of the nineteenth century. Mount Lebanon, and the regions and cities surrounding it, are the subject of solid scholarship, mostly of a socio-economic nature. We still know too little about the electoral patterns, the work of courts, and the activities of the Mutasarrifiyya's Administrative Council or the cities on the Lebanese Mediterranean shores. This book has tried to better circumscribe them, with renewed work on parallel Ottoman institutional developments in Istanbul and burgeoning elections in the fledgling Empire.

This, again, is the tip of the iceberg. Archives are available locally, regionally and internationally for new institutional questions, as well as wider sociohistorical research. Minutes of meetings, names of notables, voters and elected officials, court decisions, all await more attentive investigations. Research on the late Ottoman legal period has been intense in the last two decades, but it has mostly been the work of historians. Lawyers have a vast agenda ahead of them.

The First World War caused an earthquake across the Middle East region which created a logic of nation-states dominant to date, and the extension of European colonialism to the territories formerly part of the Ottoman Empire. The French Mandate which obtained remains a poor cousin of scholarship on Lebanese history. With the Chiha archives now available, more visibility into the Mandate's significant impact on Lebanese institutions is possible. The study of Lebanese communal constitutionalism can benefit from a fresh start with the availability of Chiha's constitutional drafts, but the world of the French Mandate deserves many more enquiries. This book opens new perspectives on the competition between French-appointed administrators and the local notables around a timid Chamber of Deputies amidst a lively political scene, but it just skirts the surface. More importantly, electoral processes superimposed on time-honoured communalism create a difficult template which merits closer examination.

Democracy redefined

The written legacy of Chiha goes beyond Lebanon. Chiha wrote a constitution for Lebanon which benefits from its allure as dean of the Middle Eastern constitutions, and which endures alongside the dozen or so constitutions in the world that have survived the hundred years mark. Its emergence is enriched by Chiha's legacy as an active member in civil society, columnist, public intellectual, and *éminence grise*; his manifold writings, mostly on history, culture, and entrepreneurship, put the communal constitution he wrote in wider perspective.

What I find remarkable in Chiha's articles and longer essays is how citable his phrases are, in an experience that also strikes me in Tocqueville's writings. Chiha and Tocqueville are comfortable moving back and forth between the larger picture and narrow examples with great ease. This makes them both eminently quotable, and it may be no coincidence that both were liberals in the John Stuart Mill sense. All three paragons of liberalism share a sense of nuance, a reformist zeal, an absence of dogmatism, and a straightforward and simple honesty. It is a rare blessing for a writer to pen sentences which are used repeatedly, cited for their beauty and their always contemporary meaningfulness. The flipside is elasticity and imprecision, but style always trumps substance in my book.

The contributions of the non-official Chiha who resigned all state positions in 1929 provide the ideological shaping of civil society with a rich tapestry: against fanaticism, against theoretical straitjackets, for tolerance, against tutelage, for women's equality with men, for an open society, for a meaningful understanding of history and sociology, for useful and practical economics, for a minimally intrusive state, for an enlightened concern with troubling neighbours, for an understanding of the international setting and for a subtle appreciation of the weight of history. All his forays provide material for further investigation, in context, for themselves and for a better understanding of past and present Lebanon.

Mostly, Chiha is a reluctant theoretician who forces onto less reluctant theoreticians the need to redefine democracy. In the conceptualisation of democracy from the iconic Greek agora where every free citizen participates in government, to citizenry in the American and French revolutions' majoritarian rule by elected delegates, the missing link is the member of a persistently subordinate group.

Chiha's free citizens belong to groups defined religiously, and he manages to elaborate a constitutional system where no one group is left out of representative power, and where members of the subordinated group are elected competitively by the population at large. This comes at a heavy cost for the basic equality of the citizen.

Perhaps the constitutionally religious system of Lebanon was anathema to Chiha, both as a citizen and as the member of a group straitjacketed out of any meaningful position in government. Perhaps Chiha was not ambitious enough to push the small Lebanese sample as a model for the larger world. Whatever the reason, a hundred years after Chiha's constitution was adopted in Lebanon, its historical and theoretical revisitation concludes with a much wider horizon for a theory of government. The ambition of this book is to redefine Democracy by putting at its center the individual-as-member-of-a-structurally-subordinate-group.

Democracy finds its ultimate proof when the representation of subordinate groups in government becomes so normal that no one pays attention to it any longer. The presence and effectiveness of the subordinated citizen in power is then so ingrained in Democratic governance that it joins the coloured-eyed, stoutly-built, or thick eye-browed citizen in political and constitutional insignificance.

General Bibliography

Only the books and journal articles cited are included here. Michel Chiha's books are not cited again. Shorter articles in newspapers and magazines are not included, and some references (for example Rousseau's *Contrat Social*) are classics famous enough for the reader to find on the Internet in original or standard editions.

Reference to constitutions and official documents

For the Lebanese Constitution of 1926 and its amendments, the Arabic and French original versions have been printed under the auspices of the Lebanese Ministry of Justice in 1995 in a bilingual booklet. The French original version, together with other useful institutional documents, have been collected on the site of the University of Perpignan, 'Digithèque MJP', https://mjp.univ-perp.fr/constit/lb.htm. The Arabic and English versions can be found on the site of the Lebanese presidency, www.presidency.gov.lb and on several other sites. I sometimes use my own translation in English.

The 1989 *Wathīqat al-wifāq al-waṭanī* (Document of National Accord, Document d'Entente Nationale, also known as the Ta'ef agreement) can be found in Arabic, French and English on the Lebanese presidency site.

Other current constitutions can be found on the site constituteproject.org.

Older constitutions (for instance the French Third Republic Constitution of 1875 or the Latvian Constitution of 1922) are easily available in a simple internet search.

Middle Eastern constitutions since the 1820s are referenced in the appropriate footnotes.

Newspapers, magazines, official journals

al-Aḥrār al-Muṣawwara
*al-Jarīda al-Rasmiyya (*French *Journal Officiel)*

al-Ma'raḍ
Bulletin Mensuel
Düstūr
The Eastern Times
L'Orient
Le Réveil

Main websites

corpus.quran.com
michelchiha.org
constituteproject.org
arabiclexicon.hawramani.com
lp.gov.lb
presidency.gov.lb

Books and articles cited

'Abd al-Qāder 'Iṣmat, *Dawr al-Nuwwāb al-'arab fi Majlis al-Mab'uthān al-'uthmānī 1908–1914* (The role of the Arab deputies in the Ottoman parliament 1908–1914), Beirut: Al-dār al-'arabiyya lil-mawsu'āt 2006

Abi-Rached Joelle and Diwan Ishac, 'The economic legacy of the French Mandate in Lebanon', *Economic Research Forum*, Cairo, Working Paper 1614, November 2022

____, 'Ce que l'économie du Mandat a légué au Liban', *Revue du Droit Public*, 139, 2023, 60–81

Abi Rached Nadi, 'Les origines historiques du système électoral libanais', *Travaux et Jours*, 93, 2018, 21–45

Abou Selim, *Les Libertés*, Beirut: USJ Press 2003 (English translation, *Freedoms*), Beirut: USJ Press 2005

Aboultaif Eduardo Wassim, *Power Sharing in Lebanon-Consociationalism since 1820*, New York: Routledge 2019

Abu-Husayn Abdul-Rahim, 'The Shihab succession (1697): A reconsideration', in *Essays on Ottoman Civilization, Proceedings of the 12th Congress of the Comité International d'Études Pré-Ottomanes et Ottomanes, Prague 1996*, Prague: Oriental Institute 1998, 9–16

____, *The View from Istanbul: Lebanon and the Druze Emirate in the Ottoman Chancery Documents, 1546–1711*, Oxford: Centre for Lebanese Studies 2004

'Ahd al-Nadwa al-Lubnāniyya-Les Années Cénacle, Beirut: Nahār 1997

Ajami Fouad, *The Arab Predicament: Arab Political Thought and Practice since 1967*, Cambridge: Cambridge University Press 1981

Akarli Engin, 'The Administrative Council', in Nadim Shehadi and Dana Haffar Mills eds, *Lebanon: A History of Conflict and Consensus*, London: I. B. Tauris 1988, 79–100

____, *The Long Peace: Ottoman Lebanon 1861–1920*, Berkeley: California Press 1993

al-Ali Zaid (with Jörg Fedtke). *The Constitution of Iraq: A Contextual Analysis*, Oxford: Hart 2010

Akiba Jun, 'The Local councils as the origin of the parliamentary system in the Ottoman Empire', in Tsugitaka Sato ed., *Development of Parliamentarism in the Modern Islamic World*, Tokyo: The Toyo Bunko 2009, 176–204

Alibert-Fabre Véronique, 'La pensée constitutionnelle du Général de Gaulle à « l'épreuve des circonstances »', *Revue Française de Science Politique*, 40, 1990, 699–713

Amanat Abbas, *Iran: A Modern History*, New Haven: Yale University Press 2017

'Āmel Mahdī, *Madkhal ilā Naqd al-Fikrī al-Tā'ifī: Al-Qadiyya al-Filisṭīniyya fī Idiulujiyyāt al-Burjwāziyya al-Lubnāniyya* (Introduction to the critique of sectarian thought: the Palestinian question in the ideology of the Lebanese bourgeoisie), Beirut: Dār al-Fārābi 1980

Amīn Sāmī, *Taqwīm al-Nīl: wa-Asmā' man Tawallaw Amr Miṣr wa-Muddat Ḥukmihim 'alayhā* (The measuring of the Nile: and the names of those who ruled in Egypt and the duration of their rule), Cairo: al-Maṭba'a al-amīriyya, 3 vols, 1915–33

Ammoun Denise, *Histoire du Liban Contemporain*, vol. 1, *1860–1943*, Paris: Fayard 2014; vol. 2, *1940–1990*, Paris: Fayard 2005

d'Andurain Julie, *Le Général Gouraud- Un Destin hors du Commun, de l'Afrique au Levant*, Paris: Perrin 2022

Aristotle, *The Politics*, Jowett tr., Oxford: Clarendon Press 1885, vol. 1

Arjomand Saïd Amir, *After Khomeini. Iran under his Successors*, New York: Oxford University Press 2009

____, 'The Kingdom of jurists: Constitutionalism in Iran', in Rainer Grote and Tilmann Röder eds, *Constitutionalism in Islamic Countries: Between Upheaval and Continuity*, New York: Oxford University Press 2011, 147–70

Artistarchi Bey (Grégoire) ed., *Législation Ottomane ou Recueil des Lois, Réglements, Ordonnances, Traités, Capitulations et Autres Documents Officiels*, Constantinople: Bureau du Journal Thraky 1874

Aujol Jean-Louis, *Un Avocat dans le Siècle, de Poincaré à Mitterrand*, Paris: Gazette du Palais 1988 (Kindle)

'Awaḍ Walīd, *Bishāra al-Khūrī Fāris al-Mawārina al-'Arab* (Béchara El-Khoury knight of the Arab Maronites), Beirut: Dār al-Afkār 2009

Baer Gabriel, 'The Beginnings of municipal government in Egypt', *Middle Eastern Studies*, 4, 1968, 118–40

Barakāt Dāwūd, *Al-Baṭal al-Fāteḥ Ibrāhīm wa Fatḥuh al-Shām 1832* (The conquering hero Ibrahim and his conquest of Syria 1832), Cairo: Wikālat al-ṣaḥāfa al-'arabiyya 2021 (Original 1931)

Bart Pierre, 'Biographie [de Michel Chiha]', October 1955 (Chiha Archive)

du Bellay Joachim, *Les Regrets* (1558)

Benhabib Seyla, 'Introduction- The Democratic moment and the problem of difference', in Seyla Benhabib ed., *Democracy and Difference*, Princeton: Princeton University Press 1996, 3–10

Beydoun Ahmad (Bayḍūn Aḥmad), *Identité Confessionnelle et Temps Social chez les Historiens Libanais Contemporains*, Beirut: Librairie Orientale 1984

____, *Mughāmarāt al-Mughāyara (Adventures of otherness)*, Beirut: Nahār 2005

____, *La Dégénérescence du Liban*, Paris: Actes sud 2009

Bishāra Azmī, *Al-Ṭā'ifa, al-Ṭā'ifiyya, al-Ṭawā'ef al-Mutakhayyala* (Sect, sectarianism and imagined sects), Beirut: Arab Center for Research and Policy Studies 2018

Brecht, Bertolt, *Kalendergeschichten*, Berlin: Bertelsman n.d. (ca 1948)

al-Bustānī Sulaimān, *'Ibra wa dhikrā aw al-dawla al-'uthmāniyya qabl al-dustūr wa ba'dah* (Lesson and recollection, or the Ottoman state before and after the Constitution), Khāled Ziādeh ed., Beirut: Arab Center for Research and Policy Studies 3d ed 2019

al-Bustānī Fu'ād Efrem and Rustum Asad, *Tārikh Lubnān al-Mūjaz* (Short history of Lebanon), n,p, n.d, 1937

de Caix Robert, 'L'organisation donnée à la Syrie et au Liban de 1920 à 1923 et la crise actuelle', in Gérard Khoury ed., *Une Tutelle Coloniale, Le Mandat Français en Syrie et au Liban- Ecrits Politiques de Robert de Caix*, Paris: Belin 2006, 394–456

Chalabi Tamara, *The Shi'is of Jabal 'Amil and the New Lebanon*, New York: Palgrave-McMillan 2006

Chaoul Melhem (Shāwul Melḥem), *Al-Iftirāq wal-Jam'* (Separation and union), Beirut: Sharq al-Kitāb 1996

Chevallier Dominique, *La Société du Mont Liban à l'Epoque de la Révolution Industrielle en Europe*, Paris: Geuthner 1971

Chiha Michel, 'Économie et Humanisme', *Bulletin de l'Association Guillaume Budé*, 12, 1950, 55–74 (for the collection of Chiha's books, see section above)

Condorcet, *Essai sur l'Application de l'Analyse à la Probabilité des Décisions Rendues à la Pluralité des Voix*, Paris: Imprimerie royale, 1785

____, *Esquisse d'un Tableau Historique des Progrès de l'Esprit Humain*, Paris: Librairie philosophique J. Vrin, 1970 (Original 1793–1794)

Conthenau Georges, *La Civilisation Phénicienne*, Paris: Payot 1928

Corm Georges, *Contribution à l'Etude des Sociétés Multiconfessionnelles*, Paris: Librairie générale de droit et de jurisprudence 1971

____, *Le Liban contemporain. Histoire et Société*, Paris: La Découverte 2003

Ḍāher Mas'ūd, *Al-Judhūr al-Ṭārikhiyya lil-Mas'ala al-Ṭā'ifiyya fī Lubnān 1697–1861* (The historical roots of the communal question in Lebanon 1697–1861), Beirut: Fārābi 2nd ed. 2009 (original 1986)

____ *Tārīkh Lubnān al-Ijtimā'ī al-Mu'āṣir* (Contemporary social history of Lebanon), Beirut: Nahār 2022

Derathé Robert, 'La Philosophie des lumières en France: Raison et modération selon Montesquieu,' *Revue Internationale de Philosophie*, 21, 1952, 275–93

Donohue John, 'Changing the Lebanese Constitution: A Postmodern History', *Cardozo Law Review*, 50, 2008–2009, 2509–34

Doumet-Serhal Claude, *Sceaux et Cylindres Orientaux: la Collection Chiha*, Freiburg, Switzerland: Editions Universitaires 1992

____ and Hélou-Nahas Michèle, *Michel Chiha 1891–1954*, Beirut: Fondation Michel Chiha 2001

Ducruet Jean, *Livre d'Or de la Faculté de Droit, Sciences Politiques et Economiques, 1913–1993*, Beyrouth: Publications de l'Université Saint-Joseph de Beyrouth 1995

Duguit Léon, *Traité de Droit Constitutionnel*, Paris: Boccard then Cujas, 3rd ed. (first edition 1911), 5 vols, 1927– n.d

Dusenbury David Loyd, *I Judge No One: a Political Life of Jesus*, New York: Oxford University Press 2023, 203

al-Dwaihī Isṭifān, *Tārikh al-Ṭā'ifa al-Mārūniyya* (History of the Maronite community), Beirut Catholic Press 1890

Eddé Carla, *Beyrouth, Naissance d'une Capitale (1918–1924)*, Paris: Actes Sud 2009

Edwards Richard, *La Syrie 1840–62*, Paris: Amyot 1962

Ekmekji Arda, 'Confessionalism and Electoral Reform in Lebanon,' Aspen Institute Papers, 2012, 9–12

Ely John Hart, *Democracy and Distrust*, Cambridge, MA: Harvard University Press 1980

Engelhardt Edouard, *La Turquie et le Tanzimat, ou Histoire des Réformes dans l'Empire Ottoman, depuis 1826 jusqu'à nos jours*, Paris: Cotillon 1882

Esmein Adhémar, *Eléments de Droit Constitutionnel Français et Comparé*, Paris: Sirey 7th ed. 1921

Fahmy Khaled, 'Era of Muhammad Ali Pasha', in *The Cambridge History of Egypt*, vol. 2, *Modern Egypt, from 1517 to the End of the Twentieth Century*, M. W. Daly ed., Cambridge: Cambridge University Press 1998, 139–79

Farah Caesar, *The Politics of Interventionism in Ottoman Lebanon, 1830–61*, Oxford: Centre for Lebanese Studies 2000

Farha Mark, *Lebanon- The Rise and Fall of Secular State under Siege*, Cambridge: Cambridge University Press 2019

Fawaz Leila, *An Occasion for War: Civil Conflict in Lebanon and Damascus in 1860*, Berkeley: University of California Press 1994

Fayrūzabādi (or Fīrūzabādi), *Al-Qāmūṣ al-Muḥiṭ*, Cairo: Dār al-ḥadīth 2008

Febvre Lucien, *Le Problème de l'Incroyance au 16ème Siècle- La Religion de Rabelais*, Paris: Albin Michel 1937

Fillon Catherine, 'Le Jésuite, l'universitaire et le politique: stratégies de recrutement du corps enseignant de l'école Française de droit de Beyrouth (1913–1939)', in Jean-Christophe Aven et Frédéric Audren eds, *Les Facultés de Droit de Province aux XIXe et XXe Siècles*, 3 vols, Toulouse: Presses de l'Université Toulouse 1, Vol. 3, 2012, 115–38

Firro Kais, 'Lebanese Nationalism versus Arabism: From Bulus Nujaym to Michel Chiha', *Middle Eastern Studies*, 40, 2004, 1–27

Fisk Robert, *Pity the Nation: Lebanon at War*, Oxford: Oxford University Press 1990

Fiss Owen, 'Groups and the Equal Protection Clause', *Philosophy and Public Affairs*, 5, 1976, 107–77

Flory Maurice et al. eds, *Les Régimes Politiques Arabes*, Paris 1990

Fouchet (or Foulcher) de Chartres, *Historiae Hierosoliemitana* (tr. *Histoire des croisades*), Paris: n.p. 1825

Fournié Pierre, 'Le Mandat à l'épreuve des passions françaises: l'affaire Sarrail (1925)', in Nadine Méouchy ed., *France, Syrie et Liban 1918–1946*, Damascus: IFPO 2002, 125–68

Fournié Pierre and Riccioli Jean-Louis, *La France et le Proche-Orient 1916–1946*, Paris: Casterman 1996

Fossaert Robert, *Le Monde au 21ème Siècle*, Paris 1991

____, *Les Etats*, vol. 5 of *La Société*, 8 vols, Paris: Seuil et al 1978–1996

____, *L'Avenir du Socialisme*, Paris: Stock 1996

Frangieh Samir, *Voyage au bout de la Violence*, Beirut: L'Orient des Livres 2011

'French Mandate for Syria and the Lebanon', *The American Journal of International Law*, 17, Supplement: Official Documents (July 1923), 177–82

Frey Albert, *A Dictionary of Numismatic Names*, New York: The American Numismatic Society 1916

Fromkin David, *A Peace to End all Peace: the Fall of the Ottoman Empire and the Creation of the Modern Middle East 1914–922*, New York: Macmillan 1989.

Gaspard Toufic, *A Political Economy of Lebanon*, Leiden: Brill 2004

Gendzier Irene, *Notes from the Minefield: United States Intervention in Lebanon and the Middle East, 1945–1958*, New York: Columbia University Press 1997

Gerges Fawaz, *Lebanon: A Critical Assessment*, Bonn: Friedrich Ebert Stiftung 2001

Ginsburg Tom and Dixon Rosalind eds, *Comparative Constitutional Law*, Cheltenham: Edward Elgar 2011

Godechot Jacques and Palmer Robert, 'Le problème de l'Atlantique du XVIIIe au XXe siècle', in *Relazioni del X Congresso Internazionale di Scienze Storiche, Roma, 1955, vol. 5. Storia Contemporanea*, Florence: Sansoni, 1955, 175–239

____, *Les Révolutions 1770–1799*, Paris: Presses Universitaires de France 1963

Goitein Samuel, *A Mediterranean Society: the Jewish Communities of the Arab World as Portrayed in the Documents of the Cairo Geniza*, 5 vols, Berkeley: University of California Press 1967–88

Hakim Carol, *The Origins of the Lebanese National Idea 1840–1920*, Berkeley: University of California Press

al-Ḥalabī Anṭūn, *Ḥurūb Ibrāhīm Bāshā al-Miṣrī fī Sūriā wal-Anaḍūl* (The wars of the Egyptian Ibrahim Basha in Syria and Anatolia), Asad Rustum ed., Heliopolis n.d. (ca 1927)

Hallāq Hassān, '*Al-Malāmeh al-'umrāniyya wal-Iqtiṣādiyya wal-Ijtimā'iyya wal-'askariyya fī Bayrūt al-'uthmāniyya* (Urban, economic, social and military aspects in Ottoman Beirut),' *Tārikh al-'Arab wal-'Ālam* (n.d.), 24–39

____, *Al-Tārīkh al-Ijtimā'i wal-Iqtiṣādi wal-Siyāsi fi Bayrūt wal-Wilāyat al-'uthmāniyya fil-Qarn al-Tāse' 'ashar* (Social, economic and political history of Beirut and the Ottoman provinces in the 19th century), Beirut: Al-Dār al-jāmi'iyya 1987

____, *Baladiyyat Bayrūt al-Maḥrūsa (1840–1943)* ('Municipality of Beirut 1840–1943), vol. 1, Beirut: Dār al-nahda al-'arabiyya 2013

Ḥamādeh Sa'īd, *Al-Nizām al-Naqdī wal-Ṣarrāfī fī Sūriā* (The monetary and cambist system in Syria), Beirut: American University of Beirut 1935

Hamdan Kamal, *Le Conflit Libanais: Communautés Religieuses, Classes Sociales et Identité Nationale*, Reading: Garnet 1997

Ḥammād Muḥammad, *Qiṣṣat al-Dustūr al-Maṣrī* (The story of the Egyptian constitution), Cairo: Jazīrat al-ward 2011, digitally at University of Minnesota Human Rights Library, http://hrlibrary.umn.edu/arabic/Egyptian_Constitution/EG-CON.1837.pdf

Hamoudi Haider Ala, Negotiating in Civil Conflict- *Constitutional Construction and Imperfect Bargaining in Iraq*, Chicago: University of Chicago Press 2013

Hanf Theodor, *Coexistence in Wartime: Lebanon*, Oxford: Center for Lebanese Studies 1993

Hanssen Jens-P., *The Effect of Ottoman Rule on Fin de Siècle Beirut, 1888–1914*, St. Antony's College, University of Oxford, Phd 2001

____, *Fin de Siècle Beirut- The Making of an Ottoman Provincial Capital*, Oxford: Oxford University Press 2005

Harik Iliya, *Politics and Change in a Traditional Society, Lebanon 1711–1845*, Princeton: Princeton University Press 1968

Harris William, *Lebanon: A History, 600–2011*, New York: Oxford University Press 2012

Hartman Michelle and Olsaretti Alessandro, ""The First Boat and the First Oar": Inventions of Lebanon in the Writings of Michel Chiha", *Radical History Review*, 86, 2003, 37–65

Haykal Rayan and Hariri Nizar, 'La pensée économique de Michel Chiha: Variations sur le thème de la liberté,' *Travaux et Jours*, 86, 43–72

Hegel G. W. F., *Phenomenology of Spirit* (1807)

Hirst David, *Beware of Small States: Lebanon, Battleground of the Middle East*, London: Faber and Faber 2010

Hitti Philip, *Lebanon in History*, London: St Martin's Press 1957

Hokayem Antoine, *La Genèse de la Constitution Libanaise de 1926*, Antélias: Les Editions Universitaires du Liban 1996

____, *Min Mutaṣarrifiyyat Jabal Lubnān ilā Dawlat Lubnān al-Kabīr 1914–1920* (From Mount Lebanon's mutasarrifiyya to the State of Great Lebanon 1924–1920), Beirut: al-Dār al-lubnāniyya lil-nashr al-jāmiʿī, 2018

____ ed., *Documents Diplomatiques Français Relatifs à l'Histoire du Liban et de la Syrie à l'Epoque du Mandat 1914–1946*, 3 vols, Beirut: Les Editions Universitaires du Liban 2003–2016

Horowitz Donald, *Ethnic Groups in Conflict*, Berkeley: U. of California Press 1985

Hourani Albert, *Syria and Lebanon- A Political Essay*, New York: Oxford University Press 1946

____, 'Political society in Lebanon Massachusetts Institute of Technology: An historical introduction,' Center for International Studies, Cambridge, MA. 1985

ibn Khaldūn, *al-Muqaddima*, Cairo: Maṭba'at al-taqaddum 1904

Jaulin Thibaut, 'Démographie et politique au Liban sous le Mandat', *Histoire et Mesure*, 24, 2009, 189–210

Jisr, Bāsim, *Fu'ād Shihāb Dhālik al-Majhūl* (Fouad Chehab, that unknown), Beirut: Sharikat al-Maṭbū'āt 1988

Jouplain M., *La Question du Liban*, Paris: Rousseau Press 1908.

Kahn Paul, 'Comparative constitutionalism in a new key', *Michigan Law Review* 101, 2003, 2677–705

Kançal Salgur and Thobie Jacque, 'L'impossible homogénéisation du système monétaire ottoman', *Relations Internationales*, 99, 1999, 251–68

Kant, *Critique of Practical Reason* (1788)

Karpat Kemal. *Ottoman Population, 1830–1914*, Madison: University of Wisconsin Press 1985

Kassir Samir, *Histoire de Beyrouth*, Paris: Fayard 2003

Kawtharānī Wajīh, *Al-Ittijāhāt al-Ijtimā'iyya al-Siyāsiyya fi Jabal Lubnān wal-Mashriq al-'arabī 1860–1920* (Social and political trends in Mount Lebanon and the Arab Levant 1860–1920), Beirut: Ma'had al-inmā' al-'arabī 1976

Kayalı Hasan, 'Elections and the Electoral Process in the Ottoman Empire, 1876–1919', *International Journal of Middle East Studies*, 27, 1995, 265–86

____, *Arabs and Young Turks: Ottomanism, Arabism, and Islamism in the Second Constitutional Period of the Ottoman Empire, 1908–1918*, Berkeley: University of California Press 1997

Kansu Aykut, *The Revolution of 1908 in Turkey*, Brill, Leiden 1997

____, *Politics in Post-revolutionary Turkey, 1908–1913*, Brill, Boston 2000

Kedourie Elie, 'The Capture of Damascus, 1 October, 1918', *Middle Eastern Studies*, 1964, 66–83

Khair Antoine, *Le Moutaçarrifat du Mont-Liban*, Beirut: Publications of the Lebanese University 1973

Khairallah Shereen, *Dr Ayyub Tabet (1875–1947)*, Beirut: Dergham 2014

Khalaf Samir, 'Michel Chiha and the Struggle for Palestine', talk at conference on 'The Lebanese system: A critical assessment,' American University of Beirut, 18–19 May 2001 (On file with author)

____, *Civil and Uncivil Violence in Lebanon*, New York: Columbia University Press 2002

Khalīfeh 'Iṣām, *Abḥāth fi tārīkh Lubnān al-Mu'āṣer* (Studies on the history of modern Lebanon), Beirut: Dār al-Jīl 1985

Khalīfeh Nabīl, *Mīshel Shīḥā, Awwal Anbiyā' Lubnān wa Ākher Anbiyā' Falasṭīn* (Michel Chiha, the first Lebanese prophet, and the last prophet of Palestine), Byblos: Markaz biblos lil-dirāsat 2013

Khāṭer Laḥd, *'Ahd al-Mutaṣarrifīn fi Lubnān 1861–1918* (The Rule of the governors in Lebanon 1861–1981), Beirut: Publications of the Lebanese University 1967

al-Khaṭīb Anwar, *Al-Dawla wal-Nuẓum al-Siyāsiyya- Dustūr Lubnān 1* (The State and political norms 1) Beirut: n.p 1970

El-Khoury Béchara (al-Khūri Bishāra), *Haqā'eq Lubnāniyya* (Lebanese truths), Beirut: Awrāq lubnāniyya 1960, Vol. 1

Khoury Gérard, *Une Tutelle Coloniale, Le Mandat Français en Syrie et au Liban-Ecrits Politiques de Robert de Caix*, Paris: Belin 2006

Khoury Philip, *Syria and the French Mandate: The Politics of Arab Nationalism, 1920–1945*, Princeton: Princeton University Press 1987

Khūrī Amīn ed., *Al-Qānūn al-Asāsī* (The Basic Law), Beirut: Ādāb 1908

Khūrī Fu'ād, *Al-Niyāba fil Lubnān min 1860 ilā 1977* (Parliamentary membership in Lebanon from 1860 to 1977), Beirut: n.p. 1980

Koç Yahya, 'Yerel İktidar ve Denetim Bağlaminda i Şihāboğullari ve Cebel-i Şūf Emāreti (1697–1770) (The Shehab dynasty in the Emirate of Mount Lebanon in the perspective of local power and control)' *Tarih Dergisi* (Istanbul), 69, 2019, 51–86

Korany Bahgat, Maurice Flory et al. eds, *Les Régimes Politiques Arabes*, Paris 1990

Lammens Henri, 'Histoire de la nationalité syrienne', *La Revue Phénicienne*, 4, 1919, 193–207

____, *Syrie: Précis Historique*, Beirut: Imprimerie Catholique 1921, Vol. 1

Laurens Henry, *L'Expédition d'Egypte 1798–1810*, Paris: Armand Colin 1989

Lançon Daniel, 'Exil, Terre natale, terre rêvée: Naissance de la Francophonie littéraire libanaise dans et par la Grande Guerre', in Carole Dagher and Myra Prince eds, *De la Grande Guerre au Grand-Liban*, Paris: Geuthner 2015, 151–84

Lauzanne Stéphane, *Les hommes que j'ai Vus*, Paris: A. Fayard et Cie 1920

Leenders Reinoud, *Spoils of Truce: Corruption and State-Building in Postwar Lebanon*, Cornell: Cornell University Press 2012

Lewis Bernard, *The Emergence of Modern Turkey*, Oxford: Oxford University Press 2nd ed. 1968

Lijphart Arend, *Democracy in Plural Societies: A Comparative Exploration*, New Haven: Yale University Press 1977

____, 'Constitutional design for divided societies', *Journal of Democracy*. 15, 2004, 96–109

____, *Patterns of Democracy: Government Forms and Performance in Thirty-Six Countries*, New Haven: Yale University Press 2012

Lohéac Lynne, *Daoud Ammoun et la Création de l'Etat Libanais*, Paris: Klincksieck 1978

Longrigg Stephen, *Syria and Lebanon under French Mandate*, London: Oxford University Press 1958

Lutfi al-Sayyid Afaf, *Egypt in the Reign of Muhammad Ali*, Cambridge: Cambridge University Press 1984

Maila Joseph, *The Document of National Understanding: A Commentary*, Oxford: Centre for Lebanese Studies 1992

al-Mallāḥ 'Abdallāh, *Mutaṣarrifiyyat Jabal Lubnān fī 'ahd Muẓaffar Bāshā* (Mount Lebanon's Mutasarrifiyat under Muzaffar Basha), Beirut: Khalifeh 1985

Makdisi Ussama, *The Culture of Sectarianism. Community, History, and Violence in Nineteenth-Century Ottoman Lebanon,* Berkeley: University of California Press 2000

____, 'Corrupting the Sublime Sultanate: The Revolt of Tanyus Shahin in Nineteenth-Century Ottoman Lebanon,' *Comparative Studies in Society and History*, 42, 2008, 180–208

Mājed Khalīl Mājed, *Al-Intikhābāt al-Niyābiyya 1861–1992* (Parliamentary elections 1861–1992), Beirut: al-Mu'assasa al-jāmi'yya lil-dirāsāt wal-nashr 1992

Mallat Chibli (Mallāṭ Shiblī), '*Fin-naẓariyya ad-dustūriyya al-amīrkiyya al-mu'āṣira: Robert Bork wa John Hart Ely*' (On contemporary American constitutional law: Robert Bork and John Hart Ely), *Proche-Orient Etudes Juridiques* (Beirut), 1987, 9–26

____, *Al-Ri'āsa al-Lubnāniyya Baynal-Ams wal-Ghad* (The Lebanese presidency between yesterday and tomorrow), Beirut: Nahār 1998

____, 'Trouble with the neighbours', *Index on Censorship*, 5, 2000, 158–60

____, *March 2221. Lebanon's Cedar Revolution- An Essay on Justice and Non-violence*, Beirut: [Lir] 2007

____, *Introduction to Middle Eastern law*, Oxford: Oxford University Press 2007

____, *Iraq: Guide to Law and Policy, Austin: Aspen/Kluwer Law* International, 2009

____, *Philosophy of Nonviolence: Revolution, Constitutionalism, and Justice beyond the Middle East*, New York: Oxford University Press 2015

____, *Boussole et Autres Journalismes*, Beirut: Bada2e3 2019

____, 'A Middle Eastern tradition', in Peter Cane et al. eds, *Oxford handbook of comparative administrative law*, Oxford: Oxford University Press 2021, 97–116

____, *The Normalization of Saudi Law*, New York: Oxford University Press 2022

____, and Elham Fakhro, 'Introduction: Three circles and a few promises, in *Promises of constitutionalism in the Gulf States, al-Abhath*, Special issue 70, 2022, 5–27

Mallat Hyam (Mallāṭ Hiyām), *'30 ḥuzairān 1892– Waqfat al-ḥāzimiyya* (30 June 1892– Taking the stand in Hazmiyyeh)', in Tāmer Mallāṭ, *Diwān* (Collection of poetry), Beirut: Badā2e3 2016, 241–52

____, *Le Liban, Emergence de la Liberté et de la Démocratie au Proche-Orient,* Paris: Geuthner 2014

Mallat Tamer (Mallāṭ Tāmer), *Aḥkām* (Judgments), Beirut, Badā'e' 1999

Mallat Wajdi ed., *Chibli Mallat Poet of the Cedars, A School for National Identity*, Beirut: Raidi Press 1999

Malsagne Stéphane, *Fouad Chéhab (1902–1973): Une Figure Oubliée de l'Histoire Libanaise,* Paris: Karthala 2011

Ma'n Ḥusain ibn Fakhreddīn ibn, *Kitab al-tamyīz*, Beirut: Dar al-shurūq 2001

Manigand Christine, *Henry de Jouvenel*, Limoges: Presses Universitaires de Limoges et du Limousin 2000.

Mannheim Karl, 'The Sociological Problem of Generations', in Mannheim, *Essays on the Sociology of Knowledge,* London: Taylor and Francis 1998, 163–94

Mansbridge Jane, *Beyond Adversary Democracy*, Chicago: University of Chicago Press 1980

____, 'Should blacks represent blacks and women represent women? A contingent "yes"', *The Journal of Politics*, 61, 1999, 628–57

____, 'Rethinking representation', *American Political Science Review*, 97, 2003, 515–28

____, 'Clarifying the Concept of Representation', *American Political Science Review,* 105, 2011, 621–30

Marx Karl, *Grundrisse* (1857–8)

____, *A Contribution to the Critique of Political Economy* (1859)

____, *Theories of Surplus Value*, 3 vols (1861–3)

____, *Capital*, 3 vols (1867–94)

Mas'ad Būlos, *Lubnān wal-Dustūr al-'uthmānī* (Lebanon and the Ottoman Constitution), Cairo: Maṭba'at al-Ādāb 1909

al-Mashnūq Muḥammad, *Ḥukūmat Bayrūt* (The Beirut government), Beirut: Masters 1995

Maspéro Gaston, *Histoire Ancienne des Peuples de l'Orient*, Paris: Hachette 1912 (original 1895)

Mathew John, *India's Communal Constitution*, Cambridge: Cambridge University Press 2023

Mawla Seoud (Mawlā Su'ūd), *Fil-Ḥiwār wal-Muwāṭana wal-Dawla al-Madaniyya* (On dialogue, citizenship, and the civil state), Beirut: Manhal 2012

Mazzucotelli Francesco, 'From Ottoman Lebanon to the French Mandate: The End of the "Long Peace"?', in Ahmad Feroz and Yavuz M Hakan eds, *War and Collapse: World War I and the Ottoman State*, Salt Lake City: University of Utah Press 2015, 1134–61

Menassa Béchara, *Dictionnaire de la Constitution Libanaise*, Beirut: Nahar 2010

Ménassa Gabriel, *Les Mandats A et leur Application en Orient: Il Faut Convoquer les Assemblées Constituantes*, Paris: Jouve 1924

____ and Naggear Joseph, *Plan de Reconstruction de l'Economie Libanaise et de Réforme de l'État*, Beirut: Editions de la Société libanaise d'économie politique 1948

Meouchi Nadine and Sluglett Peter eds, *The British and French Mandates in Comparative Perspectives*, Leiden: Brill 2004, 63–100

Messarra, Antoine, *Théorie Générale du Système Politique Libanais*, Paris: Cariscript 1994

Ministry of Justice (Iraq), *Translations of the Ottoman Constitutional Laws, the Wilayet Administrative Law, the Municipal Law and Various Other Laws*, Baghdad: 1924 n.p.

Mirow Matthew, 'Léon Duguit: (1859–1928)', in O. Descamps and R. Domingo eds, *Great Christian Jurists in French History*, Cambridge: Cambridge University Press 2019, 358–71

Mohr Thomas, 'Religious minorities under the constitution of the Irish Free State, 1922–1937', *American Journal of Legal History*, 61, 2021, 235–72

Montesquieu, *De l'Esprit des Lois* (1748)

____, *Pensées* (1750)

Moreau Hugues, *Henry de Jouvenel- Répertoire Numérique*, Tulle: Département de la Corrèze, Archives départementales 2010

Mouawad Youssef, 'La famine occultée et la Grande-Guerre de 1914–1918 au Liban', in Carole Dagher and Myra Prince eds, *De la Grande Guerre au Grand-Liban*, Paris: Geuthner 2015, 37–60

____, 'Jamal Pacha, en une version libanaise', in *Maronites dans l'Histoire*, Beirut: L'Orient des Livres 2017, 143–76

Moynihan Daniel, *Pandemonium*, New York: Oxford University Press 1994

Murād Ghīnā, '*Al-Ḥamla al-Miṣriyya wa Ātharuhā 'alā Wilāyat Ṭrablus* (The Egyptian campaign and its effects on the district of Tripoli), in Khaled Ziadeh and Boutros Labaki (Khāled Ziyādeh and Buṭros Labaki) eds, *Al-Manāteq al-Lubnāniyya Khilāl al-Ḥukm al-Maṣrī 1831–1840* (The Lebanese regions during Egyptian rule 1831–1840), Beirut: Dār Sā'er al-Mashreq 2022, 403–61

Murād Muḥammad, *Al-Intikhābāt al-Niyabiyya fi Lubnān 1920–2009* (Parliamentary elections in Lebanon 1920–2009), Beirut: Publications of the Lebanese University 2013

Naccache Georges, *Un Rêve Libanais (1943–1972)*, Beirut: Fiches du Monde arabe 1983

Najjar Alexandre, *L'Enfant Terrible, Michel Zaccour (1896–1937)*, Beirut: L'Orient-Le Jour 2010

Najm Marie-Claude, *Principes Directeurs de Droit International Privé et Conflit de Civilisations*, Paris: Dalloz 2005

Nassif Nicolas (Nāṣīf Niqūlā), *Jumhūrriyat Fu'ād Shihāb* (The republic of Fouad Chehab), Beirut: Nahār 2008

Nujaym Būlos, '*Lamḥa fī tārikh lubnān* (Note on the history of Lebanon)', in Fuād Efrem al-Bustānī ed., *Mabāḥeth 'ilmiyya wa Ijtimā'iyya* (Lebanon, scientific and social studies), Beirut: Manshūrāt al-jāmi'a al-lubnāniyya 1969 (Originally published by Ismā'il Ḥaqqī bey 1916), vol. 2

Perrier Ferdinand, *La Syrie sous le Gouvernement de Méhémet-Ali jusqu'en 1840*, Paris: Arthus Bertrand 1842

Perthes Volker, *Problems with Peace: Post-war Politics and Parliamentary Elections in Lebanon*, Hamburg: Nah- und Mittelost-Verein 1992

Phillips Anne and Asenbaum Hans, 'The Politics of presence revisited', *Democratic Theory*, 10, 2023, 80–9

Picard Elizabeth, *Liban, Etat de Discorde*, Paris: Flammarion 1993

Pitkin Hanna, *The Concept of Representation*, Berkeley: University of California Press 1967

Polk William, *The Opening of South Lebanon 1788–1840*, Cambridge, MA: Harvard University Press 1963

Platt Charles Malcom, 'A Triad of political conceptions: State, sovereign, government', *Political Science Quarterly*, 1895, 292–323

Porath Yehoshua, 'The Peasant Revolt of 1858–61 in Kisrawan,' *Asian and African Studies*, 2, 1966, 77–158

Postgate Nicholas, *Early Mesopotamia*, London: Routledge 1992

Prévert Jacques, *Paroles*, in *Œuvres Complètes*, Gallimard: Pléiade 1992, vol. 1

Puaux Gabriel, *Deux Années au Levant- Souvenirs de Syrie et du Liban, 1939–1940*, Paris: Hachette 1952 (Kindle)

Qalqashandī, *Subḥ al-A'shā fi Ṣinā'at al-Inshā*, Cairo: Dār al-kutub al-miṣriyya, 14 vols, 1914–22. (Shamela.ws website)

Quilleré-Majzoub Fabienne and Majzoub Tarek, 'Recherche les véritables auteurs de la Constitution libanaise de 1926 désespérément ...', *Revue française de droit constitutionnel*, 131, 2022, 641–60

Rabah Makram, *Conflict on Mount Lebanon: The Druze, the Maronites and Collective Memory*, Edinburgh: Edinburgh University Press 2020

Rabbath Edmond, *La Formation Historique du Liban Constitutionnel*, Beirut: Lebanese University Publications, Beirut 2nd ed. 1986 (original 1973)

____, *La Constitution Libanaise: Origines, Textes et Commentaires*, Beirut: Publications de la Librairie Orientale 1982

al-Rāfi'ī 'Abd al-Rahmān, *'Aṣr Muḥammad 'Alī* (The era of Muhammad 'Ali), Cairo: Ma'āref, 5th ed. (original ed. 1930)

Randal Jonathan, *Going All the Way: Christian Warlords, Israeli Adventurers, and the War in Lebanon*, New York: Viking 1983

Reeves Emery, *Anatomy of Peace*, New York: Harper 1945

Renan Ernest, *Qu'est-ce qu'une Nation?*, Paris: Calmann Lévy 1882 (Wikisource)

Restatement of the Law, Law of American Indians (2022)

Röder Tilman, 'The Separation of powers in Muslim countries', in Rainer Grote and Tilman Röder eds, *Constitutionalism in Islamic Countries*, New York: Oxford University Press 321–72

Rosenfeld Michel and Sajo Andras eds, *Oxford Handbook of Comparative Constitutional Law*, Oxford: Oxford University Press 2012

Rousseau, *Discours sur l'origine et les fondements de l'inégalité parmi les hommes* (1754)

____, *Du Contrat social (1762)*

Rustum Asad ed., *Al-Uṣūl al-'arabiyya fī 'ahd Muḥammad 'Alī Bāshā* (Arabic sources in the reign of Muhammad 'Ali Basha), Beirut: American University of Beirut 1934, Vols 3 and 4, 1934

____, *Lubnān fi 'ahd al-Mutaṣarrifiyya* (Lebanon in the era of the Mutasarrifiyya), Beirut: Nahār 1973

Saint-Pierre Abbé (de), *Projet de Paix Perpétuelle*, 3 vols (1712–13)

Nawaf Salam (Salām, Nawwāf), *La Condition Libanaise*, Beirut: Nahar 1998

____, *Ab'ad min al-Tā'ef* (Further than Ta'ef), Beirut: Jadīd 1998

Salem Jean, *Introduction à la Pensée Politique de Michel Chiha*, Beirut: Samir 1970

Salibi Kamal, *Modern History* of *Lebanon*. London: Weidenfeld & Nicolson 1965

Salim Su'ād and Merhej Su'ād, '*Majāles al-mashūra (al-shūrā) fī Lubnān Ayyām Muḥammad 'Alī* (the Consultative council in Lebanon at the time of Muhammad 'Ali)', in Khāled Ziādeh and Buṭros Labakī eds, *Al-Manāṭeq al-Lubnāniyya*

Khilāl al-Ḥukm al-Maṣrī 1831–1840 (The Lebanese regions during Egyptian rule 1831–1840), Beirut: Dār Sā'er al-Mashreq 2022, 487–99

Sālem Laṭīfa Muḥammad, *Al-Ḥukm al-Maṣrī fil-Shām* (Egyptian rule in Syria), Cairo: Madbūlī 2nd ed. 1990 (1st ed. 1983)

Sassine Farès, 'Chute d'un président ou la révolution de septembre 1952', *Ecrits I*, Beirut: L'Orient des livres 2022, 167–79

Shahrastānī, *Al-Milal wal-Niḥal* (Sects and creeds), Beirut: Dar al-Ma'rifa 1992

Schayegh Cyrus and Arsan Andrew eds, *The Routledge Handbook of the History of the Middle East Mandates*, London: Routledge 2015

Schirazi Asghar, *The Constitution of Iran: Politics and the State in the Islamic Republic*, London: I. B. Tauris 1992

Servais Jean and Mechelynk E. eds, *Code Civil Précédé de la Constitution Belge*, Bruxelles: Bruylant 1923

Sfeir Antoine Charif, *Genèse du Liban Moderne 1711–1864*, Paris: Riveneuve 2013

Shaki Mansur, *Dastur*, in *Encyclopedia Iranica* (online, 2011)

Shehadi Nadim, 'The Idea of Lebanon: Economy and state in the Cénacle Libanais 1946–54', Papers on Lebanon 5, Oxford: Centre for Lebanese Studies 1987

____ and Haffar Mills Dana eds, *Lebanon: A History of Conflict and Consensus*, London: I. B. Tauris 1988

al-Shidiāq Tannūs, *Akhbār al-A'yān fi Jabal Lubnān* (History of notables in Mount Lebanon), Fuād Efrem al-Bustāni ed., Beirut: Manshurāt al-jami'a al-lubnaniyya 1969 (Original 1855)

Shihāb Ḥaydar, *Lubnān fi 'ahd al-Shihābiyyin* (Lebanon during the rule of the Shihabs), Fu'ād Efrem al-Bustāni and Asad Rustum eds, Beirut: Imprimerie Catholique, 1933, vol. 2

Simard Marc, 'Doumergue et la réforme de l'Etat en 1934: La dernière chance de la République', *French Historical Studies*, 16, 1990, 576–96

Simon James, 'The role of the Administrative Council of Mount Lebanon in the creation of Greater Lebanon,' *Journal of Third World Studies*, 1996, 13, 1996, 119–71

Spagnolo John, *France and Ottoman Lebanon 1861–1914*, London: Ithaca Press 1977

Spears Edward, *Fulfilment of a Mission, Syria and Lebanon 1941–1944*, London: Leo Cooper 1977

Spinoza Baruch, *Theological-Political Treatise* (1670)

Tābet, Ayyūb *Mashru' al-Naẓām al-Asāsī li-Dawlat Lubnān* (Draft of a basic law for the State of Lebanon), Beirut: al-Sabāḥ 1926

Takla Youssef, 'Corpus juridique du mandat français', in Nadine Meouchi and Peter Sluglett eds, *The British and French Mandates in Comparative Perspectives*, Leiden: Brill 2004, 63–100

Ṭarabain Aḥmad, *Lubnān Mundhu 'ahd al-Mutaṣarrifiyya ilā Bidāyat al-Intidāb 1861–1920* (Lebanon from the Mutasarrifiyya era to the beginning of the Mandate 1861–1920), Beirut: Ma'had al-būhūth wal-dirāsat al-'arabiyya 1968

Tarazi Philippe (di Ṭarazī Filīp), *Tārikh al-Ṣaḥāfa al-'arabiyya* (History of the Arabic press), Windsor: Hindawi 2023 (rpt of 1913 edition)

Testa Ignaz (Baron de) ed., *Recueil des Traités de la Porte Ottomane*, Paris: Amyot then Bibliothèque Diplomatique, 1864–1911

Thompson Elizabeth, *How the West Stole Democracy from the Arabs: The Syrian Arab Congress of 1920 and the Destruction of Its Historical Liberal-Islamic Alliance*, London: Grove Press UK 2020 (Kindle)

Touma Toufic, *Paysans et Institutions Féodales chez les Druses et les Maronites du Liban du XVIIe siècle à 1914*, 2 Vols, Beirut: Librairie orientale 1971

Toynbee Arnold, *A Study of History*, Vol II: *The Geneses of Civilizations*, part two, Oxford: Oxford University Press 1934

Traboulsi Fawaz (Ṭrabulsī Fawwāz), *Ṣilāt bilā Waṣl: Michel Chiha wal-Idiyūlūjiyya al-Lubnāniyya* (Connections without link: Michel Chiha and the Lebanese ideology), London: Riyad al-Rayyes 1999

____, *A History of Modern Lebanon*, London: Pluto press 2007

Tribe Laurence, *Constitutional Choices*, Cambridge, MA: Harvard University Press 1985, 193

Tueni Ghassan, *Liban, Une Guerre pour les Autres*, Paris: Lattes 1985

____, Sassine Fares, Salam Nawaf (Twainī Ghassān, Sāsīn Fāres, Salām Nawwāf), *Kitāb al-istiqlāl* (The Independence Book), Beirut: Nahār 1998

Tusseau Guillaume, *Droit Constitutionnel et Institutions Politiques*, 4th ed., Paris: Seuil 2022

Van Leeuw Michel, *Émile Eddé (1884–1949): Aux Sources de la République libanaise*, Paris: Geuthner 2018, 2 vols.

Wagstaff J. M., 'a Note on some nineteenth-century population statistics for Lebanon', *Bulletin* of the British Society for Middle Eastern Studies, 13, 1986, 27–35

de Wailly Henry, *Syrie 1941, La Guerre Occultée*, Paris: Perrin 2006

Wansbrough John, *Qur'anic Studies*, Oxford: Oxford University Press 1977

____, *The Sectarian Milieu*, Oxford, Oxford University Press 1978

Williams Melissa, 'Représentation de groupe et démocratie délibérative: une alliance malaisée', *Philosophiques*, *29*, 2002, 215–49

Wills Garry, *Lincoln at Gettysburg: The Words that Remade America,* New York: Simon & Schuster 1992 (Kindle Edition)

Yawmiyyāt Lubnānī fi Ayyām al-Mutaṣarrifiyya (Diary of a Lebanese in the days of the Mutasarrifiyya), Hishshī Selīm ed., Beirut: al-Mudīriyya al-ʻāmma lil-āthār 1973

Young Iris Marion, 'Communication and the Other: Beyond Deliberative Democracy', in Seyla Benhabib ed., *Democracy and Difference,* Princeton: Princeton University Press 1996, 120–37

Young Georges ed., *Corps de Droit Ottoman,* Oxford: Clarendon Press 1905, vol. 1

Young Michael, *The Ghosts of Martyrs Square,* New York: Simon and Schuster 2010

Yūnis Fu'ād, *Naẓariyyat al-Tawāfuqiyya Bayn al-Ta'ṣīl wal-Taṭwīr- Dirāsat Ḥālat Lubnān* (The theory of consociationalism between tradition and development: A study of the Lebanese case), Beirut: Ḥalabī 2024

Zabīdī, *Tāj al-ʻArūs* (maajim.con/dictionary)

Zamir Meir, *The Formation of Modern Lebanon,* Ithaca NY: Cornell University Press 1988

____, *Lebanon's Quest: the Search for a National Identity 1926–39,* London: I. B. Tauris 1997

al-Zein Aḥmad ed., *Maḥāḍer Munāqashāt al-Dustūr al-Lubnānī wa Taʻdīlātuh 1926–90* (Minutes of the discussions about the Lebanese Constitution and its amendments), Beirut: Publications of the Chamber of Deputies 1993

Ziādeh Khāled, *Al-Ṣūra al-Taqlīdiyya lil-Mujtamaʻ al-Madīnī* (the traditional image of urban society), Tripoli: Manshūrāt maʻhad al-ʻulūm al-ijtimiāʻiyya 1983

____ and Labakī Buṭros eds, *Al-Manāṭeq al-Lubnāniyya Khilāl al-Ḥukm al-Maṣrī 1831–1840* (The Lebanese regions during Egyptian rule 1831–1840), Beirut: Dar Sā'er al-Mashreq 2022

Index

Abbasid dynasty, 258
Abdelhamid, Sultan, 57
Abou, Sélim, 224, 346
Administrative Council (Mount Lebanon), 43–55, 68, 75, 141
Al-Ahrar al-Musawwara, 88, 92, 100, 102, 133
Al-Ahwal, 103
Alawite (community), 283–5, 293
'Ali, Muhammad (Egyptian Khedive), 8, 24–9, 33, 35, 37, 42, 53, 65, 130
'Amel Mahdi, 81, 225, 242
Amendments (Constitution), 119, 121, 211–13, 273–83
Antelias revolt, 46–9
archives
  Asad Rustum's American University of Beirut papers (Royal Archives/ National Archives in Cairo), 35, 40
  Chiha Archive (CA), xx, 11, 81, 119, 126, 128, 130, 136, 158, 198, 201, 209, 222–5, 265, 267, 361–3
  Chiha Constitutional Papers (CCP), xii, xiv, xx, 85, 87, 88, 93–8, 100, 107, 119, 127, 131–4, 144, 154
  De Jouvenel Family archives, 95
  Fonds Henry de Jouvenel in Corrèze, xvi, 79, 88, 92, 100, 128
  Sciences Po archives, 128–9
Aristotle, 305–6
Armenian community, 252–3
Arrété 1307, 76, 77, 150–3, 180
Art. 95 (Lebanese Constitution), 107, 123, 154–9, 161–2, 253, 291, 293
'Associated Minorities', 223–47, 251, 253–61, 295
Atlantic Constitution, 110–11
Atlantic Revolution, 4, 304
Aujol, Jean-Louis, 133

Baabda, 70, 85, 328
Baalbeck, 105
Balkans, 247
Bashir, Emir, 41–3, 45, 47, 54, 59, 60, 67, 69, 71
basic law
  qanun-e asasi (1876 Ottoman Constitution), 8–9, 59, 60, 65, 145
  qanun-e asasi-ye mashrute (1906 Persian Constitution), 9, 277, 295
Batroun, 55–6
bay'a (acclamation), 19, 43
Bayhum, 'Umar, 170, 268

Beirut, 5, 7, 13–15, 20–9, 33–5, 39–45, 47, 48, 51–5, 58–70, 73–7, 79–81, 83, 85–9, 91, 93–100, 362
Beirut Consultative Council (1834), 15, 23–41, 42, 49, 58, 363–4
Belgium (Belgian Constitution 1831), 101, 128, 255
bicameralism, 117, 218
Bicephalous Executive, 171–5
Bill of Rights, 8, 295, 308
Biqaʿ (Bekaa) valley, 19, 52, 61, 63
'Black Americans', 320, 324–5
Bonaparte, Napoleon, 8, 24, 25, 130
Braudel, Fernand, 5, 326
Brecht, Bertolt, 324, 334
Briand, Aristide, 78, 106, 107, 109, 130, 132
budget, 48, 175–8, 218, 219–21, 239, 331
Bustani, Butros, 8
Bustani, Suleiman, 9
Byzantines, 233, 279

Cabinet, 19, 78, 154, 196, 210
Cairo, xx, 23, 58, 69, 81–3, 225
Caliph, 17, 26, 41, 282
Canada, 80, 83, 89, 225, 352, 353
Carolene Products, 4, 27, 319, 335
Catholics, 50, 225, 251, 252
Cayla, Léon, 87, 100
Cedar Revolution (2005), 277–80, 285–7
Cénacle, 256
Chamber of Deputies, 11, 16, 18, 34, 49, 54, 61, 75, 83, 89, 91, 110, 117, 120, 121, 130, 137, 139, 147–53, 167, 169, 170, 171, 179, 191, 200, 210, 213, 235, 237, 243, 253–61, 273–83, 289, 294, 296, 306, 307, 316, 326
Charters (Beirut, Damascus Councils), 33, 64, 85, 225, 331, 309
Chéhab, Fouad, 283
Chiha, Michel, 5, 15, 18, 28, 32, 34, 43, 48, 67, 70, 75, 80, 85, 100, 141, 175, 222, 251, 364
  architect of the Lebanese Constitution, 80–5
  writings and worldview, 223–47, 363
Chiha/Trad drafts, 97
China, 78, 231, 255
Chronicles, 39, 85, 95
civil war (Lebanon 1975–90), 73–283
colonialism, 20, 21, 54, 83, 100, 154
Commission Administrative (CA French Mandate), 49, 75–6, 80, 83, 85, 100
Commission du Statut Organique (CSO) 80, 89–90
community, communities (Communal, Communitarian), 1, 2, 15–17, 20, 23, 26, 42, 49, 52, 68, 75, 141, 145, 154, 161, 283–5, 288
concessions, 122
Condorcet, 309–10, 333
Congress, 122, 124, 145, 165, 217, 293
consociationalism, 1, 3–5, 253–61, 273–83, 289
Constitution, 5, 6, 15, 18, 19, 28, 34, 42, 49, 67, 68, 71, 75, 80, 85, 100, 110, 141, 163, 175, 195, 222, 251, 273–83, 307, 330
  Constitution of 1926 (structure,

drafting process, inspiration), 75–120, 141–63
Constitution (Amendments 1929), 211
Council of Ministers (Lebanese), 15, 23, 42, 49, 54, 58, 75, 80, 100, 141, 155, 179
courts, 20, 34, 49, 68, 85, 141
Covenant (League of Nations), 33, 75, 225
Crusades, 232

Damascus, 7, 34, 35, 40, 47, 51–6, 59, 63, 64, 68, 85, 87, 88, 93–5, 101, 103, 110, 115, 116, 159, 160, 195, 287, 311, 362
Dammous, Chebl, 82, 85, 90, 94–100, 108
Dammous questionnaire, 82, 90
Da'uq, 'Umar, 82, 265, 268
Dawud, Basha, 51, 54
De Caix, Robert, 76, 87, 135
De Martel, Damien, 200–3, 208
De Reffye, Verchère, 78
Debbas, Charles, 91, 125, 198, 200, 224, 283–5
Democracy (redefined), 303–61
Democratic, 355, 360, 366, 368, 377, 379
Dentz, Henri, 204
Deutungsbedürftigkeit, 141
'discrete and insular minority', 320–2, 325
Doumergue, Gaston, 165, 211, 212, 250
Druze community, 18–20, 43–50, 253–61
Du Bellay, Joachim, 258
Duguit, Léon, 125, 126, 136, 138–40, 163, 311
al-Dwaihi, Istifan, 18

Eastern Times, 81, 250, 361
Les Ebauches, xx, 222–3
economy, 50, 127, 219, 220, 222, 235–41
Chiha on, 235–41
Eddé, Emile, 184, 198, 202, 209, 224, 283
education, 113, 223, 243, 269
Efendi Chekib (Règlement de), 45–7, 50
Egypt, xx, 8, 10, 24, 25
elections, 52, 58, 64, 83, 178, 197, 233, 280
Ely, John Hart, 317, 319–21, 330
enter (category), 339
Equality Clause, 141–3, 273–83, 309, 312
'Etat-moins', 243, 245
Executive Power, 116, 163–75, 211–13, 273–83
exit (category), 338
exploitation, 344, 348
expropriation, 62, 113, 127

factions, 71, 132, 164
Fakhreddin, Husain, 20
Fakhreddin II, 17, 20, 21, 255
Febvre, Lucien, 278
federalism, 273–83
Federalist Papers, 310
finances *see* budget
First World War, xx, 5, 11, 16, 51, 53, 59, 61, 64, 80, 201, 230, 232, 253, 295, 326, 363

Fiss, Owen, 316–19, 321
Fossaert, Robert, 191, 245, 302
France, French
  Francophone legacy, 223–4, 250
  French archives *see* archive
  French constitutional expertise *see* Souchier, Duguit
  French High Commission, 76–80, 89–93, 95, 102, 104–8, 123, 133–5, 149, 156, 159, 172
  French Mandate, 75–85, 363–4
  French military interventions, 50, 53, 69, 70
  French Revolution, 22–4, 295, 308
  French Third Republic, 101, 126, 137, 165, 169, 171, 175, 211
freedom of expression, 113, 247–9

gender representation, 123, 133–5, 149, 156, 159, 172, 247–9, 361
glass-ceiling, 347
Gouraud, Henri, 70–1, 75–6, 157, 220
Governing Council (Iraq), 352–8
Grand-Liban (Great Lebanon), 75–85, 101
Gülhane edict (1839), 65, 295

Haydar, Subhi, 105, 170
Helleu, Jean, 206
hegemony, 344; *see also* subordination
Hemayun, Khatti, 295
High Commission, 75–85, 283–5
Hourani, Albert, 17, 18, 22, 204, 237
human capital, 243

Ibn Khaldun, 7, 121, 221
Ibrahim Basha, x, 24, 44, 24–6, 42, 62
independence (Lebanon 1943), 15, 59, 225, 277–83, 283–5, 318
Islamic Law, 34, 59, 221, 225
Israel, 277–80, 285–7
Istihama, 280
Istanbul, 9, 20–3, 24, 44, 50–2, 60, 62, 66–8, 145, 171, 362

Jerusalem, 61, 65–7, 69
Le Jour, 81, 88, 149
Jouvenel, Henry de, 90, 97, 101, 104, 106–9, 114, 124, 135, 157, 159, 215, 295
  Damascus speech, 91
  on Senate, 31, 149–53, 215
  United States of Syria declaration, 91–3, 136, 137
judicial review, 153–5, 273–83
judiciary, 100, 119, 154, 255

Kaïmacam, 43, 45, 50
Kant, Immanuel, 313–14
Karameh ʻAbd al-Hamid, 226
Khalaf Samir, 4, 303
Al-Khazen, Youssef, 166–7
El-Khoury, Béchara, 146, 175, 184, 198, 202, 205, 223–47, 273–83
  Chiha and ʻthe Khoury episode', 264–7
King-Crane Commission, 130
Kurds, 105, 223, 291 354

Latvian Constitution (early 1920s), 126, 176, 272
League of Arab States, 227
League of Nations (SDN), 68, 75, 79,

89, 99, 106, 124, 130–6, 144, 202, 206
Lebanese National Pact (1943), 283–5
Legislative Power (L), 49, 64, 119, 198
LEJ(F)ARC, 110, 123, 141, 308, 311
liberty, 35, 75, 104, 138, 308
Lijphart, Arend, 1, 331
Lithuanian Constitution, 126, 176

Al-Ma'rad, 88, 91–2, 100, 103, 105
Majlis al-Mab'uthin (Ottoman parliament), 65, 145
mandate, 21, 154, 226, 275
Mansbridge, Jane, xiv, 331, 336
Maronites, 29, 41, 68, 225
Marx, Karl, 344, 349
Maysalun Khan, 71
Menassa, Gabriel, 88, 98, 104, 123–4, 127–8
Metternich, 44
Midhat Pasha, 8, 65
millet see communities, *ta'ifa*
minority, 3, 253–61, 273–83, 315
Montesquieu, 139–40, 243, 296, 309, 323, 332, 345–6
Mount Lebanon, 43–55, 363–4; *see also* Mutasarref
municipalities, Ottoman law of, 61
Mutasarref, Mutasarrifiyya, 43–55, 72, 363–4
Muzaffar, Basha, 56–7

Naccache, Alfred, 71, 129
Nammour, Moussa, 95, 133, 169
nation/nation states, 5, 24, 84, 145, 330
National Pact, 28, 34, 222, 284

L'Orient, 88, 91–2, 100, 103, 105
Ottoman Empire, 19, 41, 94, 154, 226, 279, 295, 361

Palestine, 48, 92, 152, 246, 298
Parliament, 54, 100, 110, 132, 222, 251
participation, 64, 118, 149, 205
parties, 305
Paul-Boncour Commission, 7, 130
Personal Status Laws, 143–5, 253–61, 273–83
Phoenicia, 231–2
plural vote, 189, 303
poetry
  Arabic, 226
  French, 246–7
political parties, 67, 109, 157, 184
political-theological Middle East, 277–9
Ponsot, Henri, 149, 198, 203, 208–9, 283
poverty, 348
precarity, 348
presidential regimes, 165
Protocol of 1861, 51
Puaux, Gabriel, 203

Qanun al-siyasatnameh (1837), 24
quotas, 154, 220, 225

representation, 34, 48, 154, 222
Le Réveil, 81
revision (of Constitution), 98, 100, 111, 119, 121, 254, 271
La Revue Phénicienne, 223
Romanian Constitution (early 1920s), 126

Rousseau, Jean-Jacques, 310, 323, 332, 349

Sa'd, Habib Basha al-, 60, 70, 201, 202
Saint Joseph's University, 223
Sarrail, Maurice, 77–9, 129, 150
Second World War, 5, 101, 105, 197–8, 203–7, 227, 326
sectarianism, 28, 34, 64, 75, 154; *see also* communalism
Senate, 146, 148, 214, 293
separation of powers, 299, 308; *see also* Montesquieu
Shahin, Tanius, 47
Shahrastani, 3
Al-Shidiaq, Tannus, 19, 77, 132
Shihab Bashir, Emir, 18
Simqaniyya, 17, 19–23, 308
Souchier, Paul, 103, 133, 160, 166–7, 174
Souchier Observations (DOC 9), 94, 132, 134
sovereignty, 29, 104, 225
Spears, Edward, 187, 206
state, 20, 48, 100, 154, 222, 299; *see also* nation
Statut Organique, 79, 80, 86–90, 130–2, 199
subordination, 303–61
surplus value, 350
suspension (of Constitution), 197, 208
Switzerland, 268, 270, 352, 356

Ta'ef agreement (1989), 59, 75, 132, 148, 222, 290, 314, 316, 329, 353, 377
Ta'ifa, 2, 315; *see also* community
Tanzimat (Ottoman reforms), 64, 104, 205, 220, 225
Tripoli, 44, 60, 89, 362
Toynbee, Arnold, 234–5
Trad, Petro, 96, 123–4
trade routes, 231
Treaty of Utrecht (1712–13), 5
Treaty of Versailles (1919), 131
Treaty of Westphalia, 5
Tunisia, 8, 27, 88, 154

United Nations, 100, 152, 244

Velayat Law (1864), 59
violence, 60, 104, 142, 225
von Ranke, Leopold, 88
voting, 64, 100, 154, 198

Wansbrough, John, 3, 141
war, 41, 60, 92, 104, 132, 142, 222
Wasa Basha, 56
Wilson, Woodrow, 68, 130
women, 60, 64, 149, 204, 264, 335

Zabidi, 7
Zaccour, Michel, 102
Zionism, 75, 92, 152, 225
Zouein, Georges, 169